W9-BDC-690

The McCall's Book of America's Favorite
Needlework & Crafts

by The Editors of McCall's Needlework & Crafts Magazine

SIMON and SCHUSTER
THE McCALL PATTERN COMPANY
New York

Published by
Simon and Schuster
A Gulf+Western Company
Rockefeller Center, 630 Fifth Avenue
New York, New York 10020
and
The McCall Pattern Company
230 Park Avenue
New York, New York 10017

Typographic design by Beri Greenwald
Layout design by Dorothy Gordineer
Manufactured in the United States of America
By Rand McNally & Company

1 2 3 4 5 6 7 8 9 10

Library of Congress Cataloging in Publication Data

Main entry under title:

The McCall's book of America's favorite needlework and crafts.

1. Needlework. 2. Handicraft. I. McCall's needlework & crafts.
TT750.M17 746.4 76-4982
ISBN 0-671-22209-0

FOREWORD

With this collectors' edition, the editors of *McCall's Needlework & Crafts Magazine* invite you to enter a wonderful world of creativity. The joy of making something yourself has been discovered and rediscovered by generations of Americans, and the joy is two-fold—the satisfaction and the practicality that come from creating something beautiful!

For more than forty years we have endeavored to fill our pages with the best in needlework and craft ideas; it is from these past issues that we have selected our favorites in all techniques. The scope is wide—from crochet to needlepoint, to embroidery, knitting, rugmaking, pottery and more. They are all part of a rich heritage that is ours to enjoy now and for years to come.

So, join us in celebrating the excitement in handcrafts old and new. Try your hand at macrame, weaving, lacemaking, candlemaking, stenciling, or decoupage. Learn a new art or reacquaint yourself with an old favorite. A creative world is waiting for you!

The Editors of
McCall's Needlework & Crafts

CONTENTS

1

Embroidery

GENERAL DIRECTIONS and TIPS

The appearance of your work is greatly influenced by the material that you choose. You can make a delicate piece of work with fragile fabric and a fine thread, or translate the identical design onto coarser fabric, using a heavier thread. The needle to use with each yarn or floss should have an eye large enough to accommodate the yarn, but not larger than needed. Embroidery needles are rather short and have long, slender eyes. They are readily available in sizes 1 to 10; the higher numbers are finest. Some types of embroidery traditionally use a certain yarn or floss, while others technically require a specific kind. Crewel wool, for example, is a fine, twisted 2-ply wool yarn used in crewel embroidery. Chart below relates threads and needles to type of work.

Materials or Type of Work	Thread	Needle
Fine Fabrics or thin material	Six-strand embroidery thread (split for very fine work) Twisted cotton or fine mercerized thread Rayon, silk, or linen embroidery floss	Embroidery or crewel needle No. 1 to 10
Medium Textures such as linen, piqué, or other cottons; or lightweight sweaters of wool, nylon, or angora	Pearl cotton No. 3, 5, and 8. Six-strand embroidery thread (combining number of strands) Rayon or linen embroidery floss Fine wool yarns or crewel yarn	Crewel No. 1 to 10 Tapestry No. 14 to 24 Darning No. 14 to 18
Heavyweight or Coarse Fabrics such as monk's cloth, burlap, felt, wool suitings, or heavy sweaters	Double-strand pearl cotton Metallic cord and thread Tapestry yarn or Persian yarn Sock and sweater yarn nylon, angora, chenille, Germantown Rug yarn	Crewel No. 1 to 10 Tapestry No. 14 to 24 Chenille No. 18 to 22 Darning No. 14 to 18 Needles for rug yarn

Keep a good selection of needles on hand and protect them by storing them in a needle case. It is also advisable to run your needles through an emery strawberry occasionally to clean and sharpen them.

You will need proper scissors. Embroidery scissors should be small, with narrow, pointed blades and must be sharp. Protect the blade points by keeping them in a sheath.

Embroidery is usually worked in a frame. With the material held tautly and evenly, your stitches are more likely to be neat and accurate than if the fabric were held in the hand while working. Many embroidery hoops and frames are equipped with stands or clamps to hold the embroidery piece and leave both your hands free.

Before you begin work on a piece of embroidery, arrange a system for keeping your threads handy and colors neatly separated. Cut skeins into convenient sewing lengths—18″ or 20″ is usually best, as longer threads may become frayed. Place each strand between the pages of a book. Allow one end to extend beyond the edge of the page. Fold the other end back and forth on the page. Or loosely braid all colors to be used together, then pull the end from the braid as each color is used.

Six-strand embroidery floss can be separated into one, two, or more strands for working in fine stitches. To separate strands after cutting thread length, count the desired number of strands and carefully pull them out, holding the remainder apart to prevent tangling and knotting. Plies of wool yarn can also be separated in the same manner for a finer thread.

To thread yarn or floss through the needle eye, double it over the end of the needle and slip it off, holding it tightly as close as possible to the fold. Push the eye of the needle down over the folded end and pull the yarn through.

To begin a stitch, start with two or three tiny running stitches toward the starting point, then take a tiny backstitch and begin. Knots are not advisable for beginning or ending stitches. Where there is a hem, insert the needle under the edge of the fold, taking up two or three threads of the material and bringing the needle out again so the stitch does not show, making a blind stitch. As you work, watch the tension of your yarn—if worked too tight, the background material will be pulled out of shape. Fasten off the thread when ending each motif, rather than carrying it to another motif. Pass the end of the thread through the last few stitches on the wrong side, or take a few tiny backstitches.

To remove embroidery when a mistake has been made, run a needle, eye first, under the stitches. Pull the embroidery away from the fabric; cut carefully with scissors pressed hard against the needle. Pick out the cut portion of the embroidery. Catch loose ends of the remaining stitches on back by pulling the ends under the stitches with a crochet hook.

TO COMPLETE FABRIC EMBROIDERY: When your needlework is completed, it often needs to be pressed or blocked into shape. Sometimes it is soiled from working and must be laundered. This should always be done with care to preserve as much of the freshness of the fabric and thread as possible. Treat embroidery gently.

To help keep your work neat and clean, keep it in a plastic bag when not embroidering. When your embroidered piece is completed, finish off the back neatly by running ends into the back of the work and clipping off any excess strands. If wool embroidery or needlepoint is not really soiled but needs just a little freshening, simply brushing over the surface with a clean cloth dipped in carbon tetrachloride or other good cleaning fluid may be satisfactory. This will brighten and return colors to their original look.

Better results will be obtained by blocking (directions below) rather than pressing an embroidered piece for a picture or hanging. However, articles that are hemmed, such as tablecloths or runners, should be pressed, as blocking would damage the edge of the fabric. To press your embroidered piece, use a well-padded surface and steam iron, or regular iron and damp cloth. Embroideries that have been worked in a frame will need very little pressing. If the embroidery was done in the hand it will no doubt be quite wrinkled and may need dampening. Sprinkle it to dampen and roll loosely in a clean towel. Embroidery should always be pressed lightly so that the stitching will not be flattened into the fabric. Place the embroidered piece face down on the padded surface and press from the center outward. For embroidery that is raised from the surface of the background, use extra thick, soft padding, such as a thick blanket.

If beads or sequins are added to embroidery, take care not to use too hot an iron, as some of these may melt. These should also be pressed right side down. The padding below protects them from breaking.

Embroideries made of colorfast threads and washable fabrics can be laundered without fear of harming them. Wash with mild soap or detergent and warm water, swishing through the water gently—do not rub. Rinse in clear water without wringing or squeezing. When completely rinsed, lift from the water and lay on a clean towel; lay another towel on top and roll up loosely. When the embroidery is sufficiently dry, press as described above.

After blocking or pressing, an embroidered picture should be mounted right away to prevent creasing. To store other embroidery, place blue tissue paper on front and roll smoothly, face in, onto a cardboard tube. Then wrap outside in tissue.

To Block an Embroidered Picture: With needle and colorfast thread, following the thread of the linen and taking ¼″ stitches, mark guide lines around the entire picture to designate the exact area where the picture will fit into the rabbet of the frame. The border of plain linen extending beyond the embroidery in a framed picture is approximately 1¼″ at sides and top and 1½″ at bottom. In order to have sufficient linen around the embroidered design for blocking and mounting, 3″ or 4″ of linen should be left around the embroidered section. Now, matching corners, obtain the exact centers of the four sides and mark these centers with a few stitches.

If the picture is soiled, it should be washed, but it should be blocked immediately after washing. In preparation, cover a drawing board or soft-wood breadboard with a piece of brown paper held in place with thumbtacks, and draw the exact original size of the linen on the brown paper. Be sure linen is not pulled beyond its original size when the measurements are taken. (Embroidery sometimes pulls linen slightly out of shape.) Check drawn rectangle to make sure corners are square.

Wash embroidery; let drip a minute. Place embroidery right side up on the brown paper inside the guide lines and tack down the four corners. Tack centers of four sides. Continue to stretch the linen to its original size by tacking all around the sides, dividing and subdividing the spaces between the tacks already placed. This procedure is followed until there is a solid border of thumbtacks around the entire edge. In cross-stitch pictures, if stitches were not stamped exactly even on the thread of the linen, it may be necessary to remove some of the tacks and pull part of embroidery into a straight line. Use a ruler as a guide for straightening the lines of stitches. Hammer in the tacks or they will pop out as the linen dries. Allow embroidery to dry thoroughly.

To Mount an Embroidered Picture: Cut a piece of heavy white card-board about ⅛″ smaller all around than the rabbet size of the frame to be used. Stretch the embroidery over the cardboard using the same general procedure as for blocking the piece. Following the thread guide lines, use pins to attach the four corners of the embroidery to the mounting board. Pins are placed at the centers of sides, and embroidery is then gradually stretched into position until there is a border of pins completely around picture, about ¼″ apart. When satisfied that the design is even, drive pins into the cardboard edge with a hammer. If a pin does not go in straight, it should be removed and reinserted. The edges of the linen may be pasted or taped down on the wrong side of the cardboard or the edges may be caught with long zigzag stitches. Embroidered pictures can be framed with glass over them, if desired.

EMBROIDERY STITCH DETAILS

Straight Stitch

Outline Stitch

Chain Stitch

Buttonhole Stitch

Lazy Daisy

Backstitch

Stem Stitch

Fly Stitch

French Knot

Satin Stitch

Satin Stitch Leaf

Split Stitch

Couching

Long and Short Stitch

Laid Stitch

Featherstitch

Cretan Stitch

Seeding Stitch

Coral Stitch

Ermine Filling

Bullion Stitch

Flat Stitch

Blanket Stitch

Herringbone Stitch

Running Stitch

Cross Stitch

Fishbone Stitch

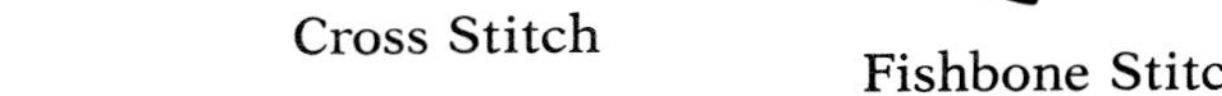

HOW TO CROSS-STITCH: Several different ways to do cross-stitch are described below and illustrated at right. All yield equally good results if care is taken to make sure that the strands of thread or yarn lie smooth and flat. Begin by leaving an end of floss on back and working over it to secure; run end of strand in on back to finish off. Try not to make any knots.

It is important when working cross-stitch to have the crosses of the entire piece worked in the same direction. Work all underneath threads in one direction and all the top threads in the opposite direction. Keep the stitches as even as possible. Be sure to make all crosses touch; do this by putting your needle in the same hole as that used for the adjacent stitch.

An embroidery hoop will help to keep the fabric taut and stitches even. Press finished picture smooth.

Linen or Hardanger Cloth: The threads of an even-weave fabric, such as sampler linen or hardanger cloth, may be counted and each cross-stitch made the same size. For example, in the detail, a three-thread square is counted for each stitch.

Monk's Cloth: The design can easily follow the mesh of a coarse, even flat-weave fabric such as monk's cloth. Here the design may be worked from a chart simply by counting each square of fabric (two horizontal and two vertical threads) for one stitch.

Gingham: A checked material, such as gingham, can be used as a guide for cross-stitch. Crosses are made over checks, following a chart.

Penelope Canvas: Penelope (or cross-stitch) canvas is basted to the fabric on which the design is to be embroidered. First, center canvas over linen, making sure that horizontal and vertical threads of canvas and linen match, then make lines of basting diagonally in both directions and around sides of canvas. The design is then worked by making crosses as shown in detail, taking each stitch diagonally over the double mesh of canvas and through the fabric, being careful not to catch the canvas.

When design is completed, the basting is removed and the horizontal threads of the canvas are carefully drawn out, one strand at a time, then the vertical threads, leaving the finished cross-stitch design on the fabric.

Penelope canvas is available in several size meshes. Choose finer sizes for smaller designs; larger sizes are suitable for coarse work in wool.

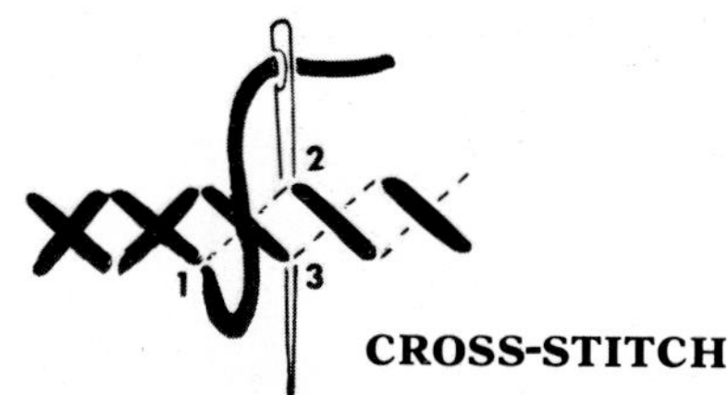

CROSS-STITCH

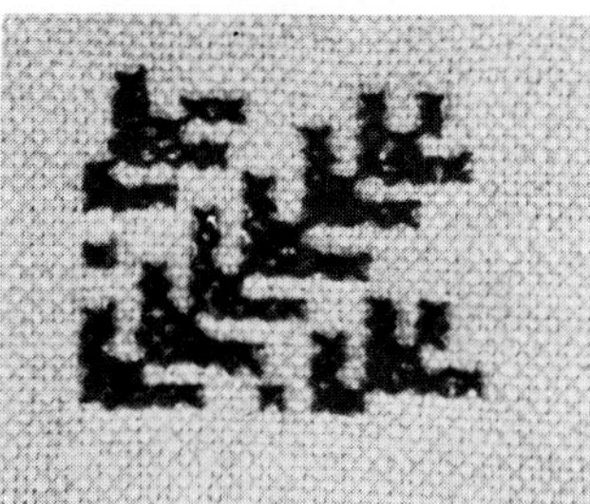
LINEN

MONK'S CLOTH

GINGHAM

PENELOPE CANVAS

Colonial Sampler

This charming sampler first appeared in 1926, on the cover of McCall's Needlework & Crafts *magazine. Effective as ever, it is worked with six-strand cotton.*

SIZE: Design area, 10" x 12¾".

EQUIPMENT: Embroidery scissors. Embroidery needles. Pencil. Ruler. Embroidery hoop (optional). Square. **For Blocking:** Rustproof thumbtacks. Soft wooden board covered with brown wrapping paper.

MATERIALS: White hardanger cloth with 24 threads to the inch, 18" x 22". Six-strand embroidery floss: 1 skein each light coral, red, orange, light yellow, medium blue, brown, magenta, medium yellow-green, black; two skeins emerald green. Stiff white mounting cardboard, 11" x 14". Short straight pins. Masking tape. Wooden frame, 11" x 14" (rabbet size).

DIRECTIONS: Read General Directions and Tips on page 12 and How to Cross-Stitch on page 16. Work all cross-stitch with three strands of six-strand floss in needle. Each cross-stitch is made over three threads of the hardanger cloth. Bring floss to front between two threads of cloth, count up three threads and over three threads and put needle between two threads to back of cloth for half of cross-stitch; count threads in reverse for second half.

Follow illustration as a working chart. In order to determine the number of threads to count between stitches, it may help to draw rule lines on the illustration, vertically and horizontally all the way across, between rows of crosses. Mark accurately over complete illustration. Each resulting square will indicate three threads of the cloth. For initials and date, use chart below.

When embroidery is finished, block and mount picture; see page 14.

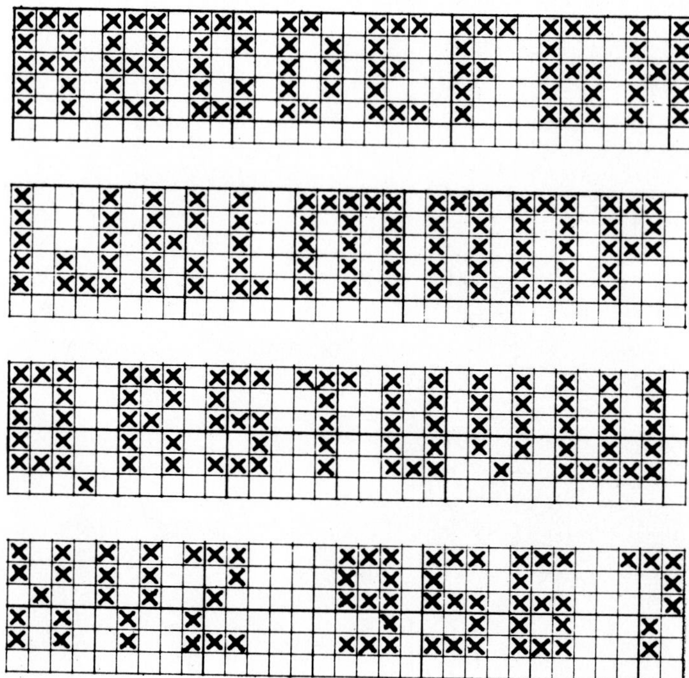

Alphabet and numbers for cross-stitching year and initials on Colonial Sampler

"God Bless Our Home"

Work this gaily colored sampler in cross-stitch, on even-weave fabric, counting an equal number of threads for each stitch.

EQUIPMENT: Scissors. Tape measure. Embroidery needle. Embroidery frame or hoop (optional). Masking tape. **For Blocking:** Rustproof thumbtacks. Soft wooden board covered with brown wrapping paper. Turkish towel.

MATERIALS: Even-weave white or cream-color fabric (see Note below). Six-strand embroidery floss: 1 skein each of medium yellow, gold, light yellow-green, dark emerald green, royal blue, lavender, purple, dark brown, medium gray, and black; 2 skeins each of light scarlet, rose-pink, medium turquoise, and russet brown; 5 skeins of medium green.

NOTE: The fabric to be used must be evenly woven of round threads that can be counted individually. It is important that the count of threads be the same horizontally and vertically. The number of threads to the inch and the number of threads over which you stitch will determine the finished size of your sampler. For example, if the fabric has about 30 threads to the inch and crosses are worked over three threads, the design area will be about 11" x 15". To calculate the size, multiply the number of crosses horizontally (109) and the number vertically (150) by the number of threads over which the crosses will be worked (3, 4, etc.); then divide the total of each side by thread count of fabric to obtain the dimensions. Many fabrics have slightly different numbers of threads to the inch horizontally compared to vertically. Check your fabric for which way you want to work design.

DIRECTIONS: Read General Directions and Tips on page 12 and How to Cross-Stitch on page 16. Cut even weave fabric 3" larger all around than finished design size. To center the embroidery, fold the fabric in half lengthwise, then fold again crosswise; mark the center point with a pin.

To work embroidery, use four or six strands of floss in the needle, depending upon the size of crosses, for all colors except black. Use four strands of black if working the colors with six strands; use three strands of black if working colors with four. Use six strands for larger crosses, four strands or fewer for smaller crosses.

Determine the center point of the chart and

Color Key

- ☑ Light Scarlet
- ⊞ Rose-Pink
- ⊡ Medium Yellow
- ⧅ Gold
- ◩ Light Yellow-Green
- ◪ Dark Emerald Green
- ⊠ Medium Green
- ◫ Medium Turquoise
- ◧ ◨ Royal Blue
- ⊟ Lavender
- ⬓ Purple
- ◩ Russet Brown
- ◙ Dark Brown
- Ⓢ Medium Gray
- ■ Black

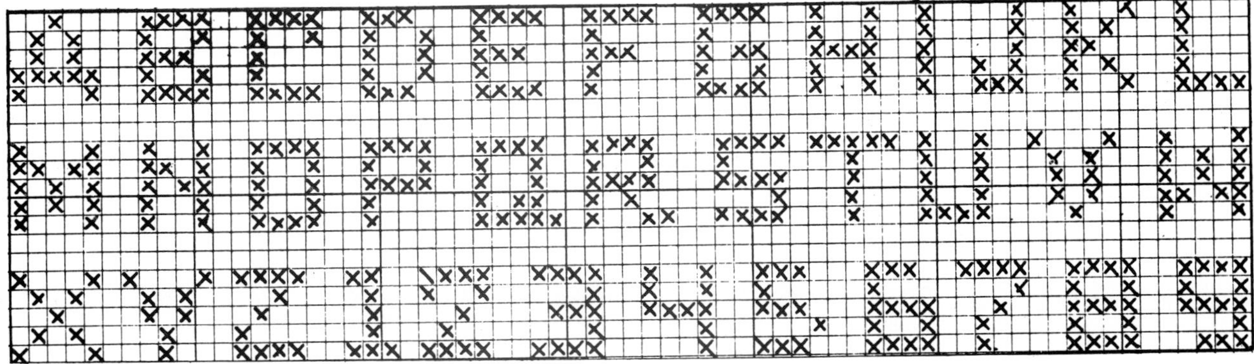

begin working cross-stitch from the center, following the chart for colors and placement of design.

Complete the sampler, if desired, by adding your initials and the date in block letters in positions indicated. Use two strands of black floss in the needle; make smaller crosses than in sampler.

Block and mount (see page 14).

Kindness Sampler

A simple message to ponder as you work it in cross-stitch and turn to for inspiration throughout the year.

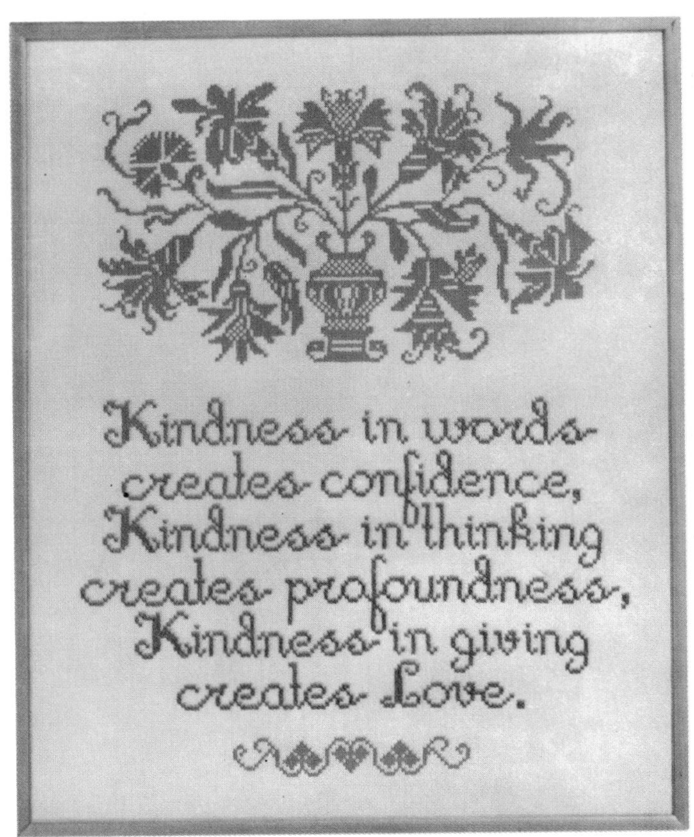

SIZE: Design 16″ x 20⅛″.

EQUIPMENT: Ruler. Pencil. Scissors. Embroidery and sewing needles. Embroidery hoop or wood picture frame (see below). Thumbtacks. Basting and pastel-colored thread. Penelope (cross-stitch) canvas, 10-mesh-to-the-inch, about 19″ x 23″. Felt-tipped pens: pink and green. Tweezers. **For Blocking:** Brown paper. Soft wooden surface. Square. Hammer.

MATERIALS: White or off-white linen fabric, 25″ x 29″. Six-strand embroidery floss (8.7-yd. skeins): pink, 9 skeins; green, 5 skeins. **For Mounting:** Heavy white cardboard. Straight pins. Frame, 19″ x 23″ rabbet size.

DIRECTIONS: Read General Directions and Tips on page 12 and How to Cross-Stitch on page 16, referring to section on Penelope canvas. With pink and green felt-tipped pens, mark design on canvas. Each square of chart represents one mesh of canvas; mark stitch placement in center of mesh. Starting 1½″ from top of canvas, mark flower and heart designs in pink and motto in green. Center canvas on linen and baste in place.

Work crosses over mesh of canvas, using four strands of floss in needle throughout. Work the motto in green and the flower and heart designs in pink. Each X on the chart represents one cross-stitch. When design is completed, remove basting. Cut away excess canvas around edges of design. With tweezers, carefully draw out canvas threads following directions on page 16.

When embroidery is finished, block and mount, following directions on page 14.

Kindness in words
creates confidence,
Kindness in thinking
creates profoundness.
Kindness in giving
creates love.

Two Friendship Samplers

Warm sentiments make a delightful pair of samplers. The stitches are worked with cotton floss on fabric that is trimmed with velvet ribbon. "Wealth," 8" x 10", "Stay," 6½" x 5½".

EQUIPMENT: Pencil. Dry ball-point pen. Heavyweight artist's tracing paper. Dressmaker's tracing (carbon) paper. Embroidery and sewing needles. Embroidery hoop. Thread. Masking tape. Staple gun.

MATERIALS: For "Wealth": Tightly woven medium-weight fabric in a light color (we used beige), 10" x 12". Canvas stretchers, 8" x 10", or a piece of wood, 8" x 10" x ½". Bright blue velvet ribbon, ⅞" wide, 37". Six-strand embroidery floss (8.7-yd. skeins): two skeins of lime green; one skein of each of the following colors: yellow, dark blue, black, dark green, bright blue, bronze, white. **For "Stay":** Tightly woven medium-weight fabric in a light color (we used beige) 8" x 9". Canvas stretchers, 6½" x 5½", or a piece of wood 6½" x 5½" x ½". Dark green velvet ribbon, ⅞" wide, 25". Six-strand embroidery floss: one skein of each of the following colors: dark green, lime green, black, light green, dark yellow.

DIRECTIONS: Read General Directions and Tips on page 12. Trace actual-size patterns. Place dressmaker's tracing paper over right side of fabric to be embroidered. Center traced pattern over dressmaker's carbon. With ball-point pen, lightly trace outlines of pattern to transfer design. Insert fabric in embroidery hoop. For stitch details, see page 15.

ALL THE WEALTH
OF THE WORLD
COULD NOT BUY
YOU A FRIEND
OR PAY YOU FOR
THE LOSS OF ONE
C.D. PRENTICE

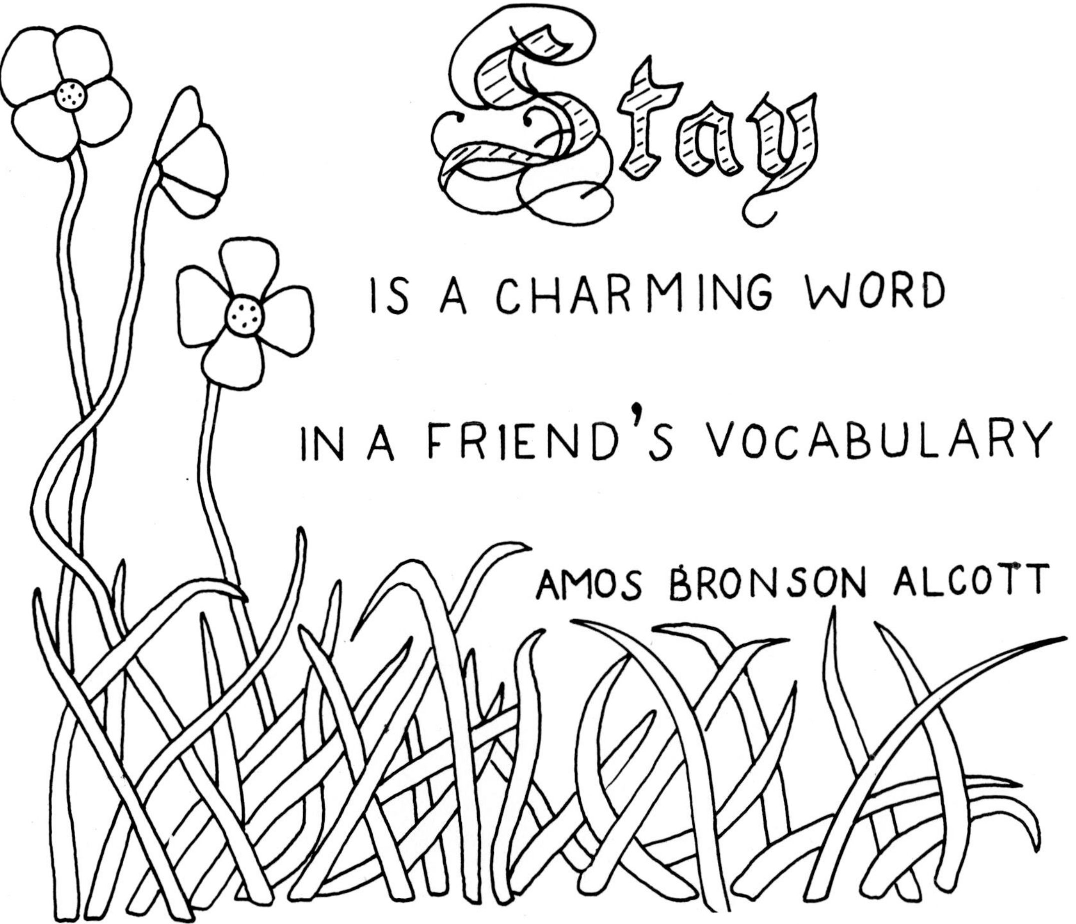

To Block: Place finished embroidery face down on padded ironing board. Steam-press wrinkles and puckers out gently.

To Mount: Press raw edges of fabric under ½". Center fabric, right side up, over canvas stretcher (or wood). With staple gun, staple fabric to sides of canvas stretchers. Stitch two ends of velvet ribbon together on wrong side, taking ½" seams. Trim seam allowance close to stitching. Slip ribbon over sides of stretchers; slip-stitch ribbon in place. Stitch corners of ribbon together on back so they lie flat.

"WEALTH"

Using two strands of bright blue floss, embroider the name "C.D. Prentice" in backstitch. With four strands of bright blue, work remaining words in backstitch. The remaining areas to be embroidered are worked in four strands of embroidery floss. With white, work flower petals in satin stitch; with yellow, work flower centers in French knots. With green, work flower stems in outline stitch. Work berry seeds as follows: With bright blue, make one seeding stitch; with dark blue, make one seeding stitch next to the first stitch. With black, backstitch around outline of berry; then fill in background of berry in seeding stitch. With green, work stems of berries in outline stitch. With bronze, work stems of leaves in outline stitch and center areas of leaves in long and short stitch. With bronze, embroider outline of main stem in outline stitch; then work thorns in satin stitch. Using lime green, fill remainder of stem with several rows of outline stitch. Work all leaves as follows: With dark green, work middle areas in long and short stitch. With lime green, work outer areas in long and short stitch as shown.

"STAY"

Using four strands of black floss, embroider the word "stay" in satin stitch; using two strands of black, work curved lines around the word in backstitch. With two strands of black, embroider the name "Amos Bronson Alcott" in backstitch; with four strands of black, work remaining words in backstitch. Using two strands of light green, embroider stems of flowers in satin stitch. The remaining areas to be embroidered are worked with four strands of floss. With yellow, work center flower in satin stitch. Work petals of other two flowers in satin stitch, and the centers in French knots. Work the grass in split stitch, alternating the colors dark green and bright green for each blade of grass.

Alphabet Sampler

An alphabet sampler with a graceful verse makes a perfect beginner's project: the original has 13 cross-stitches worked to the inch; tightly pulled threads in the first row of letters create a delicate, openwork effect.

SIZE: Original, 12″ x 12½″.

EQUIPMENT: Pencil. Scissors. Masking tape. Embroidery hoop. Embroidery needle. Graph paper, 10-to-the-inch. **For Blocking:** Soft wood board covered with brown paper. Rustproof thumbtacks. Turkish towel.

MATERIALS: Natural color, even-weave linen, 20, 26, or 28 threads to the inch (original is 26-count): ½ yd. of 20-count linen or 2/3 yd. of 26- or 28-count. Brown six-strand embroidery floss, two 7-yd. skeins. Sewing thread to match linen. Stiff corrugated cardboard for backing. Heavy-duty thread. Wooden frame to fit.

NOTE: Chart is given exactly as original sampler was made, with larger crosses worked over two threads and smaller crosses of verse worked over one thread. Chart may be followed this way on any thread count, but the finished size will vary according to fineness or coarseness of the linen used. On 26-count, the finished sampler is 12″ x 12½″, and the larger crosses measure 13 to the inch. On 20-count, the finished sampler will be about 16¼″ square. On 28-count, the finished sampler will be about 11¾″ square.

The chart may also be followed to make crosses

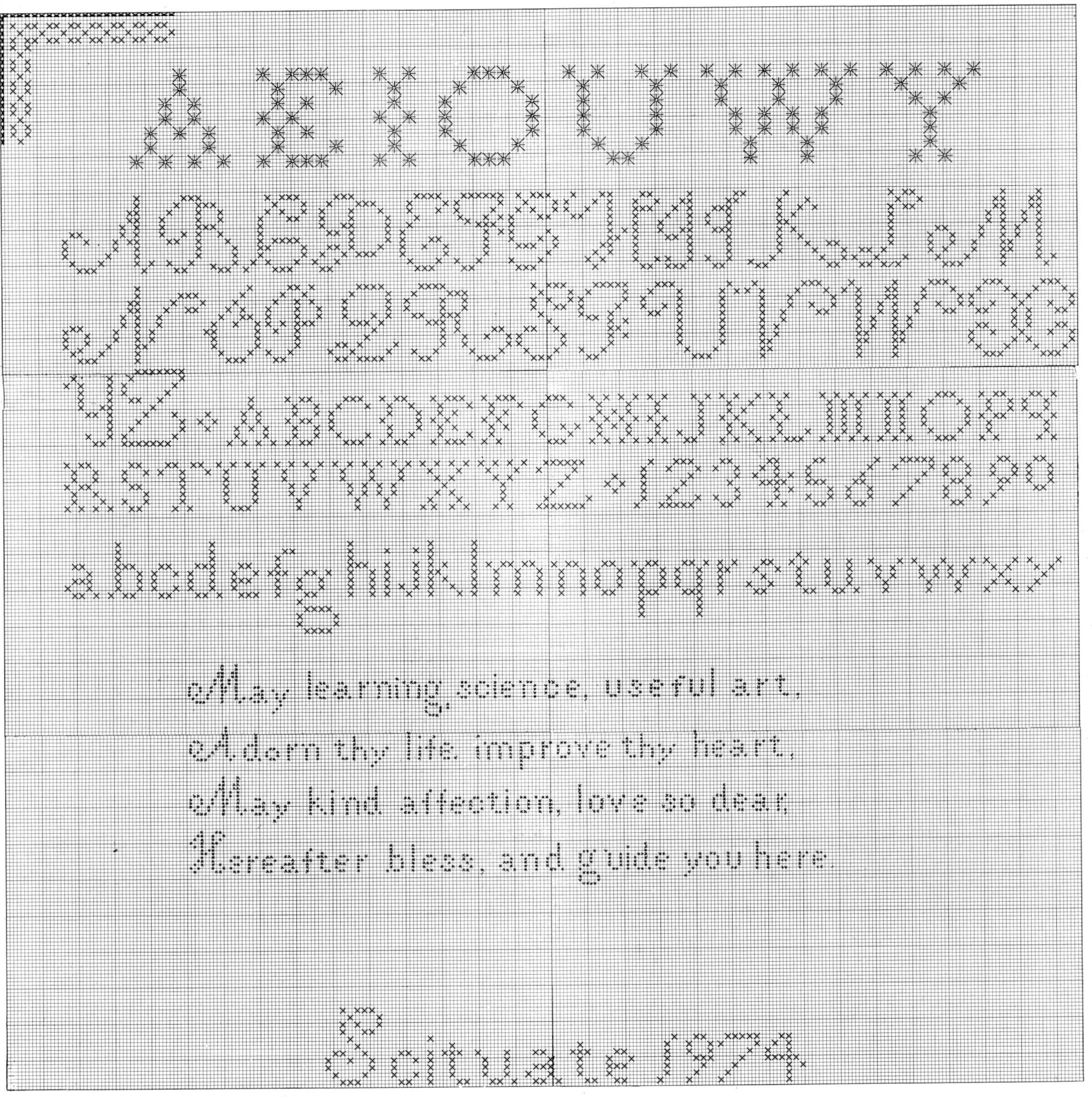

of desired size on any thread count. For instance, crosses may be made over two, three or four threads on a very fine linen. Crosses worked over three or four threads of coarse linen will result in larger crosses and a larger sampler. In working other sizes, be sure to allow threads in multiples of the same amount as used for crosses; each graph line on the chart represents the thread multiple.

DIRECTIONS: Read General Directions and Tips on page 12 and How to Cross-Stitch on page 16. Place linen on a smooth, hard surface. Using pencil, lightly mark on linen the area for actual embroidery: 15¾″ x 16″ for 20-count; 12″ x 12½″ for 26-count; 11¼″ x 11½″ for 28-count. Add ⅝″ for hem around all edges of marked square, and allow at least 3″ for sufficient margin to affix in hoop; cut fabric.

Thread embroidery needle with an 18″ to 20″ single strand of floss. Begin embroidery with first row of eyelet alphabet letters. On the chart, each graph line indicates one thread of linen. Border will be done last, so count threads from corner of embroidery area to bottom left of "A"; begin stitching at this point. Each eyelet is a square consisting of eight overcast stitches. Each stitch is pulled a little in order to exaggerate the center hole of each square.

After the first row, all alphabet and number sets are worked in cross-stitch. Size of stitches is indicated by chart.

To substitute your name, age, and town, use upper-case alphabet from rows 2-4 and lower-case alphabet from row 6. To center these lines, graph them out before embroidering. Complete lettering with current date if desired.

Following border section on chart, continue cross-stitches around all sides; extend right side slightly to allow space between alphabet and border. Do not work outer row of border until sampler is hemmed.

Block sampler, following directions on page 14.

Hemming: Turn all edges under ⅛" and baste around. Fold edges under ¼" and whipstitch around, mitering corners as follows: Fold points ½" toward center. Cut ¼" off points, making sure sides miter well and lie flat when folded.

Complete sampler with final border stitch in hemstitching. Working on charted threads just inside of hem edges at lower left corner, bring needle up between first and second pair of threads; pass over two threads to right before pulling needle to underside; bring needle around backs of same two threads and up through original hole. Crossing in front of same two threads diagonally downward to right, pull needle to underside and catch stitch in hem edge while pulling the two threads tightly together. Bring needle to front in space at right of first stitch, repeat hemstitch over every pair of threads.

Mount sampler, following directions on page 14. Frame as desired.

Pagoda Sampler

A slender pagoda flanked by willow trees suggests a taste for chinoiserie in Miss Linwood's exuberant fantasy! She worked 26 cross-stitches to the inch; create your own Pagoda Sampler in any thread count.

DESIGN SIZE: Original, 12½" x 19".

EQUIPMENT: Tape measure. Scissors. Pencil. Masking tape. Embroidery hoop. Embroidery needle. Optional: Around-the-neck magnifying glass. **For Blocking:** Rustproof thumbtacks. Soft wooden board, at least 14" x 20", covered with brown wrapping paper. Turkish towel.

MATERIALS: White, even-weave linen with 54 vertical and 50 horizontal threads per inch, 36" wide, ⅝ yd. If desired, substitute white or natural color even-weave linen with about 28 threads per inch. Six-strand embroidery floss, 7-yd. skeins:

Color Key

- ⊟ Ecru
- Rose
- Beige
- Ochre
- Gold
- Light Brown
- Medium Brown
- Dark Brown
- Celery Green
- Light Olive Green
- Light Green
- Dark Blue-Green
- Bottle Green
- Pale Yellow
- Ice Blue
- Steel Blue
- Wedgwood Blue
- Gray
- Dark Gray
- Dark Gold
- Medium Green

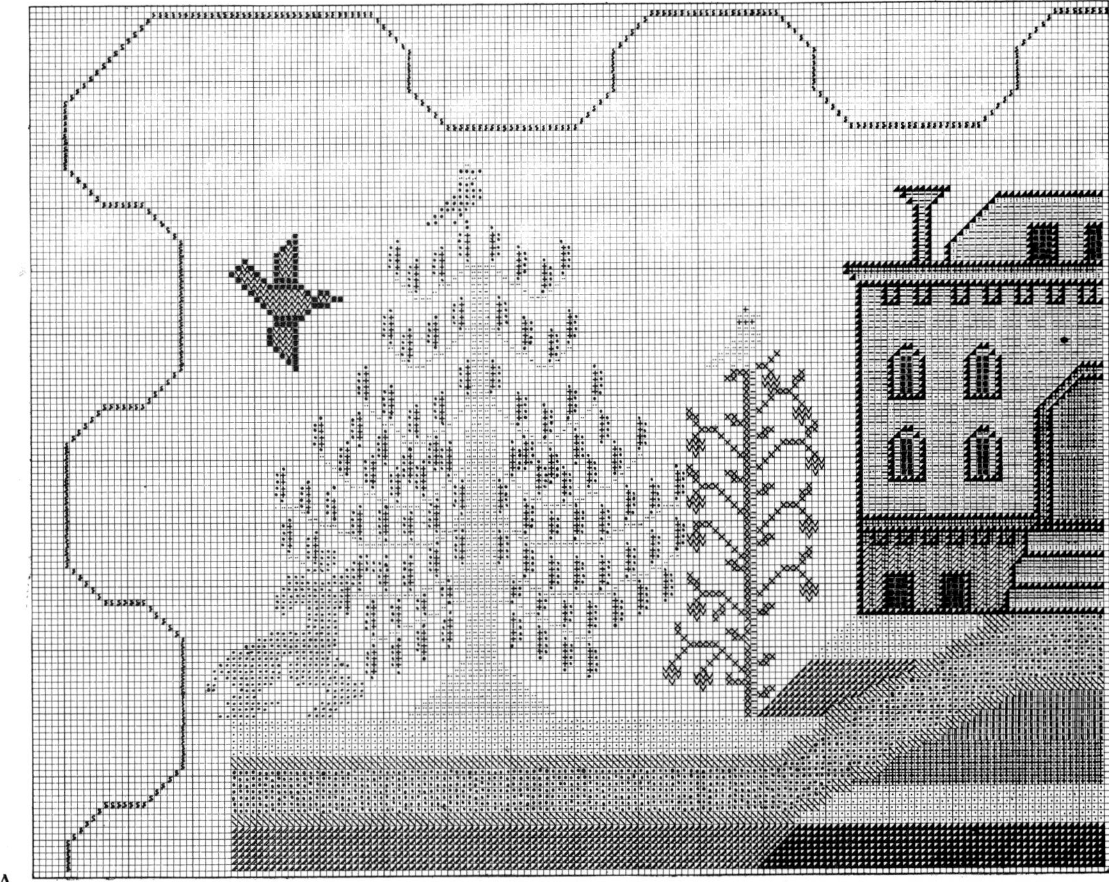

CHART A

ecru, four; rose, four; beige, two; ochre, four; gold, one; light brown, three; medium brown, one; dark brown, one; celery green, four; light olive green, four; dark blue-green, one; bottle green, one; pale yellow, two; ice blue, one; steel blue, one; Wedgwood blue, one; gray, one; dark gray, one; dark gold, one; medium green, one. Sewing thread to match linen. Heavy cardboard cut to size for backing. Masking tape. Wooden frame to fit.

NOTE: Chart has been altered slightly from the original sampler to make both sides the same. Cross-stitches were worked over two threads. Chart can be followed this way on any thread-count linen; the finished size will vary according to fineness or coarseness of the linen used. Original linen for this sampler had 56 vertical and 52 horizontal threads per inch, but this count seems to be unavailable. With 54 x 50-count linen, your sampler will be slightly larger (12⅞" x 19¾") than the original. On 28-count, the finished sampler will be about the same size if crosses are worked over one thread.

The chart may be followed to make crosses over the desired number of threads on any thread count. For instance, if using 28-count linen, crosses can be worked over two threads; the finished sampler will then be twice the size of the original. In working crosses over one, two, or more threads, be sure to allow threads in the unstitched areas in multiples of the same amount as used for crosses.

DIRECTIONS: Read General Directions and Tips on page 12 and How to Cross-Stitch on page 16. Determine the size of actual embroidery area according to the thread count of linen and number of crosses being made per inch. Place linen on smooth, hard surface. Using pencil, lightly mark along linen threads a rectangle for the actual embroidery area: for 50 x 54-thread count, the rectangle will be 12⅞" x 19¾". If using a coarser linen, determine embroidery area and mark these measurements on linen.

Allowing at least 3" on all edges for sufficient margins, cut linen. Place linen tightly but evenly in embroidery hoop.

Thread embroidery needle with a 20"-long double strand of floss. Each graph square on design chart represents a cross-stitch; on 54-thread count, work crosses over two threads; on

CHART B

CHART C

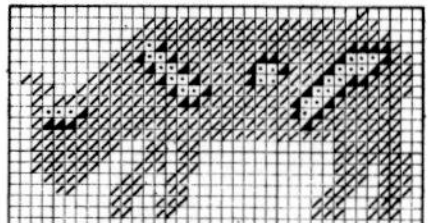

28-thread count, work each cross over one or two threads according to desired size.

Follow color key and design charts to cross-stitch sampler. Design chart A is half-chart of upper embroidery area; to complete, work second half in reverse. Design chart B is half-chart of center and bottom embroidery areas. Except for pagoda, two center birds, and butterfly, reverse chart to work second half of design. Replace deer on left side with cow (chart C) on right side.

When embroidery is complete, block and mount according to directions on page 14.

"Colonial House" Sampler

A cross-stitch sampler in subtle tones is a charming adaptation of one made in 1849 by an eleven-year-old girl! The stitches are worked over 12-to-inch Penelope canvas on white sampler linen.

DESIGN SIZE: About 16" x 21½".

EQUIPMENT: Embroidery needle. Scissors. Sewing thread. Penelope (cross-stitch) canvas, 12-mesh-to-the-inch, about 19" x 25". Embroidery hoop (optional). Tweezers. **For Blocking:** Brown paper. Soft wooden surface. Square. Hammer. Thumbtacks. Turkish towel.

MATERIALS: White or off-white linen, 25" x

Color Key

- Light Old Gold
- Yellow
- Light Green
- Medium Green
- Baby Blue
- Cornflower Blue
- Dark Green
- Dark Old Gold
- Dark Brown
- White

30″. Six-strand embroidery floss: 2 skeins each of light old gold, yellow, light green, medium green; 1 skein each of baby blue, cornflower blue, dark green, dark old gold, dark brown, white. **For Mounting:** Heavy white cardboard 19″ x 25″. Straight pins. Masking tape. Frame, 19″ x 25″ rabbet size.

DIRECTIONS: Read General Directions and Tips on page 12 and How to Cross-Stitch on page 16, referring to section on Penelope canvas. Fold piece of linen in half horizontally, then vertically to find center. Mark point with pin. Carefully center canvas over center point of linen and baste in place to linen.

For embroidery, use two strands of floss throughout, except three strands for white only. Arrows on chart indicate center lines; find center point and begin working cross-stitches from this point, following chart for placement of colors. Each square on chart represents one stitch. Work crosses over mesh of canvas. Solid line on chart indicates backstitch; outline spaces on windows, steps, and awning are satin stitch. To work these after cross-stitch is completed, see "Finishing," below.

Chart is for a little more than one-half of the design with center motifs given complete. Repeat other motifs on second half (see illustration). Border design is slightly more than one-quarter; repeat around all sides, making corners as shown in illustration.

When cross-stitch design is complete, remove basting threads and carefully draw out canvas threads with tweezers following directions on page 16.

FINISHING: With white, work three rows of satin stitch steps; with yellow, work satin stitch windows and awning; with baby blue, work backstitch around steps, and around swan. See stitch details on page 15.

Block and mount finished embroidery following directions on page 14.

Mansion Sampler

A red brick mansion in a berry-vine border is the cheerful work of a very young person! Nine-year-old Miss Hortin counted 27 cross-stitches to an inch; charts and directions for recreating her Mansion Sampler in any desired thread count are given.

SIZE: Original 11″ x 15″.

EQUIPMENT: Tape measure. Scissors. Pencil. Masking tape. Embroidery hoop. Embroidery needle. Optional: Around-the-neck magnifying glass. **For Blocking:** Rustproof thumbtacks. Soft wood board, larger than fabric, covered with brown paper. Turkish towel.

MATERIALS: White, even-weave linen with 54 vertical and 50 horizontal threads per inch, 36″ wide, 2/3 yd. A coarser linen of 25- to 28-thread count may be substituted, but your sampler will be almost twice as large. Six-strand embroidery

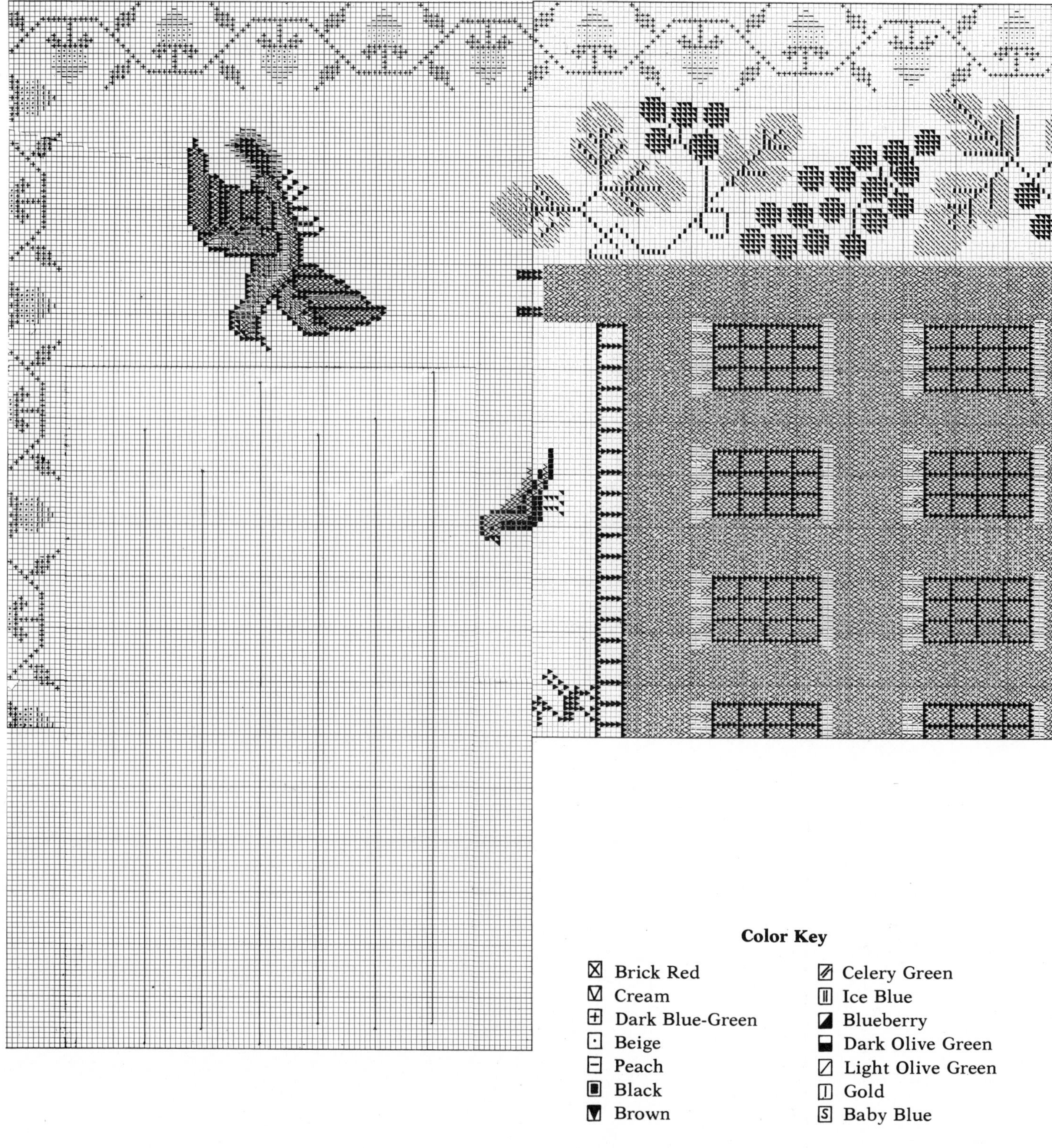

Color Key

☒	Brick Red	▨	Celery Green
☑	Cream	▥	Ice Blue
⊞	Dark Blue-Green	◪	Blueberry
⊡	Beige	⬓	Dark Olive Green
⊟	Peach	◿	Light Olive Green
■	Black	⎕	Gold
▼	Brown	S	Baby Blue

Jesus permit thy gracious Name to stand
As the first Effort of an Infant hand
And while her fingers o'er this Canvas move
Engage her tender heart to seek thy love
With thy Dear Children let her share a part
And write thy Name thyself upon her heart

floss, 7-yd. skeins: one each of beige, peach, black, brown, celery green, ice blue, blueberry, dark olive green, light olive green, gold, baby blue; two each of dark blue-green, cream; three of brick red. Sewing thread to match linen. Wooden frame and corrugated backing to size.

NOTE: Chart is given exactly as original sampler was made—larger crosses worked over two threads, smaller crosses of verse worked over one thread. It can be followed this way on any thread count of linen; the finished size will vary according to fineness or coarseness of the linen used. Original sampler was worked on linen with thread count of 52 vertical threads per inch and 56 horizontal threads per inch.

Turn linen so that selvages are at top and bottom, with the 50-thread count vertical and the 54-thread count horizontal.

The chart may also be followed when making crosses of desired size on any thread count. For instance, crosses may be made over three or four threads if using a fine linen. In working other sizes, be sure to allow threads in the unstitched areas in multiples of the same amount as used for crosses.

DIRECTIONS: Read General Directions and Tips on page 12 and How to Cross-Stitch on page 16. Place linen on a smooth, hard surface; using pencil, lightly mark on 54- x 50-count linen an 11⅜" x 15⅝" rectangle (area for actual embroidery). If using 25- to 28-count linen, your sampler area will vary in measurements—approximately twice the size. Allowing at least 3" on all edges for sufficient margin to affix in hoop, cut linen. Fold linen exactly in half, then in quarters; mark exact center of embroidery area. Place center area of linen evenly but tightly in hoop.

Thread embroidery needle with 18" to 20" double strand of floss. Follow Color Key and design charts to cross-stitch sampler. Each graph square on large chart represents a cross-stitch worked over two threads. Large chart is half-pattern of sampler; work other half in reverse.

Follow separate charts for poem and dog. Horizontal lines at top mark spacing for the poem which is worked in cross-stitch with one strand of black floss worked over one thread. Horizontal line at bottom marks space for dog; reverse dog for opposite side of sampler. Work dog in cross-stitch with two strands of black floss worked over one thread; the tongue, represented by small o's, should be worked in peach floss.

When embroidery is complete, block and mount according to directions on page 14.

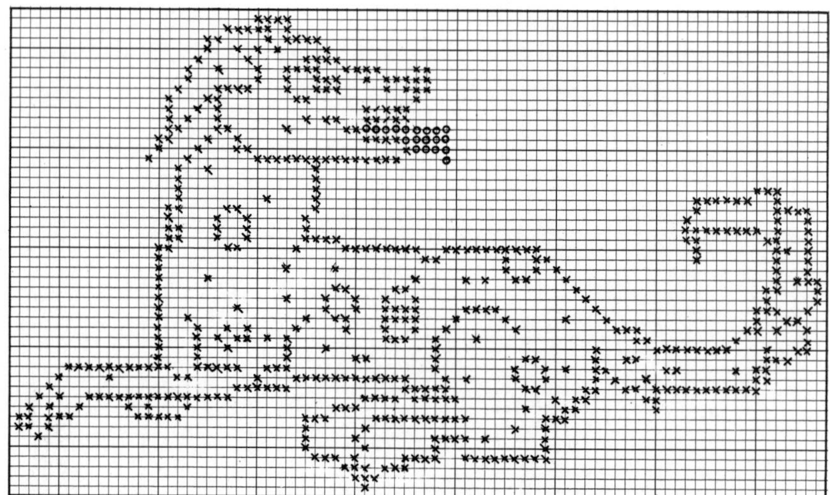

"House," "Squirrel" and "Bird" Crewel Vignettes

Crewelwork, very popular today, was first fashionable in the 17th century when the technique was used for richly embroidered household and personal items. A variety of stitches are worked with crewel wool (thin worsted yarn) on linen. To make these quaint motifs, adapted from an antique petticoat border, trace the ground contours in the actual-size illustrations on page 37, then add details as described in the directions. Transfer designs to linen, using dressmaker's carbon. Work the embroidery in the colors shown, or as desired.

SIZE: Each, 7" x 8".

EQUIPMENT: Long-eyed crewel needle. Tracing paper. Dressmaker's (carbon) tracing paper. Dry ball-point pen. Embroidery hoop.

MATERIALS: Crewel wools in colors illustrated or as desired. Linen fabric, 7" x 8", for each picture. Frames, if desired.

DIRECTIONS: Read General Directions and Tips on page 12. Lay tracing paper over illustrations. Trace entire bird picture; for house and squirrel pictures, trace ground contours and lightly indicate placement of details. Then place the tracings on actual-size patterns and trace details to complete designs. Transfer each design to center of 7" x 8" linen fabric, using dressmaker's carbon and dry ball-point pen.

Embroider in crewel wools in colors illustrated or as desired. Work with one or two strands in the needle. Most of the embroidery may be done in long and short stitch and satin stitch, such as for the house, grounds, bird, squirrel, strawberry, and foliage. Leaves may be done in satin stitch, fishbone stitch, or flat stitch; strawberry leaves are a combination of half satin and half outline and running stitch. Use French knots for strawberry seeds and centers of cherry-branch leaves. Use outline stitch for house details, tree trunks, cherry branch, and strawberry stems. Work lower branches of tree trunks in lazy daisy stitch. Road borders and chimney smoke are chain stitch.

Block and mount, following directions on page 14. Frame as desired.

Robin on a Branch

A jaunty robin is cross-stitched on linen over Penelope canvas—then the canvas threads are drawn out. Other embroidery stitches finish the bird and the branch. Use an oval or rectangular frame.

DESIGN SIZE: About 6½" x 8½".

EQUIPMENT: Ruler. Pencil. Tracing paper. Dressmaker's carbon. Scissors. Sewing needle. Dry ball-point pen. Basting thread. Embroidery needle. Embroidery hoop (optional). Thumbtacks. Penelope or cross-stitch canvas, 7-mesh-to-the-inch.

MATERIALS: White or cream linen, 14" x 18". Six-strand embroidery floss: 2 skeins each of black, dark brown, bright green; 1 skein each of white, medium gray, dark taupe, dark orange, yellow-orange, light yellow-orange, very dark green, green, light yellow-green, very dark blue.

DIRECTIONS: Read General Directions and Tips on page 12 and How to Cross-Stitch on page 16, referring to the section on Penelope canvas. Fold linen in half horizontally, then vertically to find center. Mark point with pin. Cut a piece of canvas 1" larger all around than design size. Carefully center canvas over center point of linen, making sure that horizontal and vertical threads of canvas and linen match. Baste canvas securely to linen, keeping the center point marked.

Cross-stitch is worked with the full six strands of floss in the needle. Find center point of design

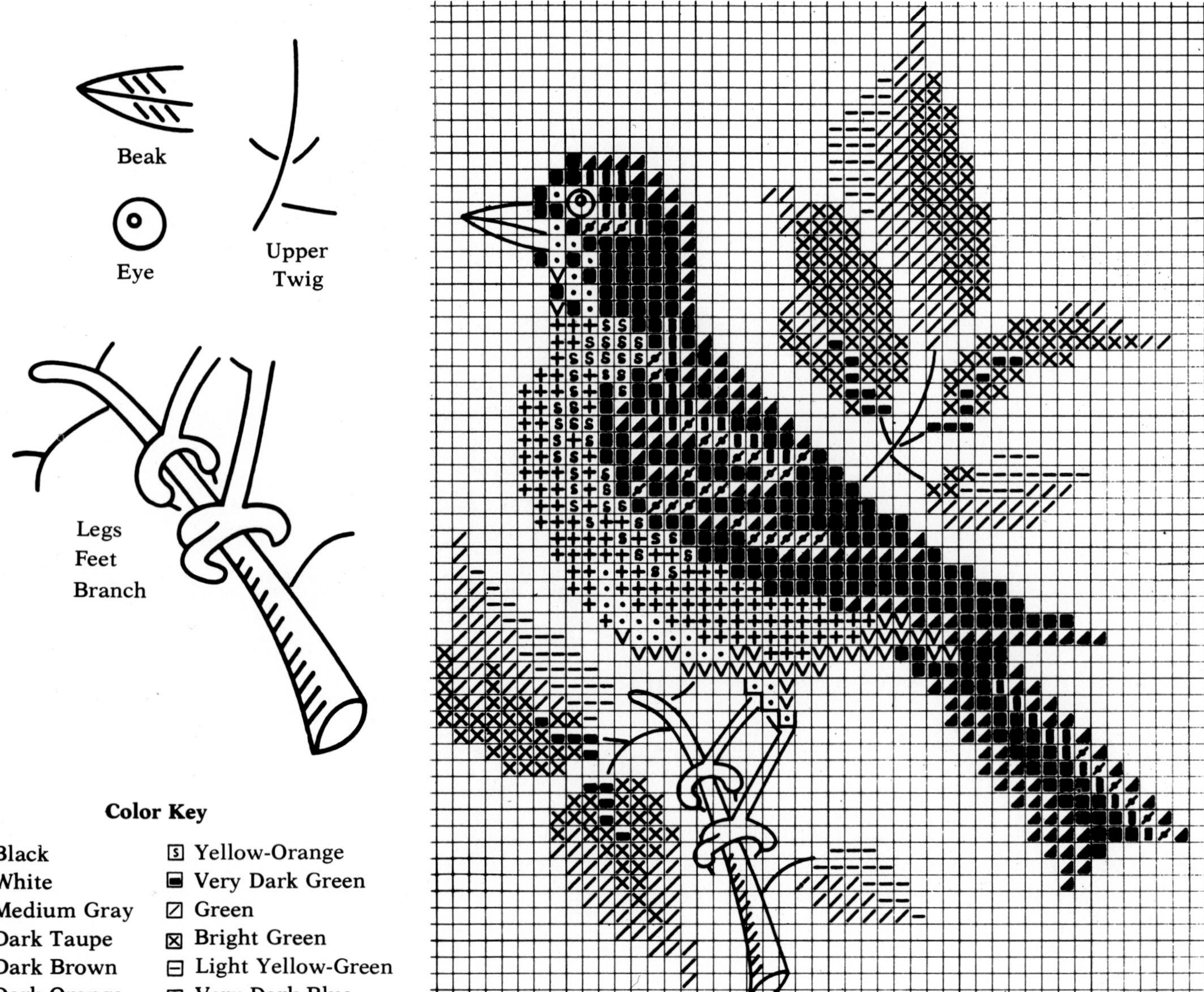

Color Key

- Black
- White
- Medium Gray
- Dark Taupe
- Dark Brown
- Dark Orange
- Yellow-Orange
- Very Dark Green
- Green
- Bright Green
- Light Yellow-Green
- Very Dark Blue

on chart and begin working cross-stitches from center, following chart for placement of colors. Each square of chart represents one stitch. Work crosses over mesh of canvas.

When all the cross-stitch design is complete, remove the basting threads and carefully draw out each canvas thread. Thumbtack cross-stitch embroidery to a firm surface, being sure that all corners are square and background fabric is smooth.

Trace the actual-size patterns for robin's legs, feet, branch and twig, upper twig, beak, and eye. Transfer details to linen, using dressmaker's carbon and dry ball-point pen. Complete embroidery, using four or six strands of floss, as follows: Work eye in black satin stitch with a white French knot center. Embroider beak in satin stitch; upper part is light yellow-orange, lower part is yellow-orange. Legs and feet are black outline stitch. Work branch in outline stitch, using dark taupe for upper side, dark brown for lower side and end; inner lines are dark brown single stitch. Embroider twigs in dark brown outline stitch. Outline the white crosses on leg with backstitch in medium gray, using only two strands of floss in needle.

Block the finished embroidery and frame in an oval, if desired (see page 14).

"Dragonfly" and "Queen Anne's Lace" Pictures

Lacy white and cool green make a perfect combination for a pair of embroideries inspired by flowers of the meadow. Both pictures are worked with various yarns and embroidery floss on linen. The Queen Anne's Lace motif measures 12" by 26"; the Dragonfly is 13¼" square.

EQUIPMENT: Paper for patterns. Pencil. Ruler. Tracing paper. White dressmaker's tracing (carbon) paper. Dry ball-point pen. White coloring pencil. Fine sewing needle. White thread. Large-eyed and regular embroidery needle. Embroidery frame or hoop. Embroidery scissors. Masking tape. **For Blocking:** Soft wooden surface. Brown wrapping paper. Square. Thumbtacks. Tack hammer.

MATERIALS: Green Irish linen (clare weight) for background: 18½" square for Dragonfly; 32" x 18" for Queen Anne's Lace. White yarn: **For Dragonfly:** One skein each of knitting worsted, baby or fingering yarn, and fuzzy orlon bouclé; spool of silver metallic thread mixed with white; and six-strand embroidery floss; **For Queen Anne's Lace:** One skein each of medium-weight acrylic yarn (with sheen), baby or fingering yarn, six-strand embroidery floss; small amount of dark green tapestry wool. Heavy mounting cardboard: 13¼" square for Dragonfly; 26" x 12" for Queen Anne's Lace. Small straight pins.

DIRECTIONS: Read General Directions and Tips on page 12. Enlarge patterns on page 42 by copying on paper ruled in 1" squares. Trace enlarged designs. Center tracing on linen fabric for each with carbon between; tape to hold in place. Transfer all design lines to linen, using dry ball-point pen. With sharp white pencil, go over design lines as necessary. With fine needle and white thread, following threads of the linen and taking small stitches, mark guidelines around the entire design; for Dragonfly, the area is 13¼" square; for Queen Anne's Lace, it is 26" x 12".

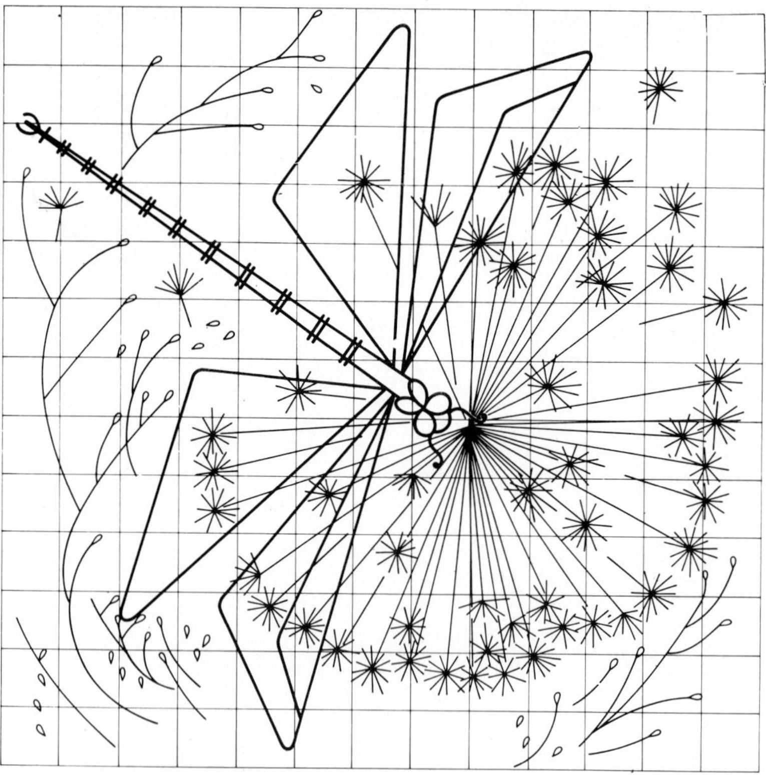

Referring to stitch details on page 15 and individual directions below, work embroidery.

When embroidery is finished, block and mount, following directions on page 14.

DRAGONFLY

For the dandelion puffs use fuzzy bouclé, making straight stitches radiating out from central point. For the stems of the puffs, use silver-and-white thread, couched with double strand of embroidery floss. For the Dragonfly wings, couch knitting worsted with baby or fingering yarn. Work the body, head, and tail in satin stitch with baby or fingering yarn; using knitting worsted, work double stitches across body ten times, dividing body into eleven segments. Embroider the antennae with baby or fingering yarn in outline stitch with a French knot at end of each. The remaining parts of embroidery are done with single strand of embroidery floss: the lines in outline stitch, the loops in lazy daisy stitch.

QUEEN ANNE'S LACE

Use baby or fingering yarn in outline stitch to outline leaves and fill in; make stems with rows of outline stitch. Embroider all the oval areas with French knots (see illustration). Make the smallest French knots around centers with six strands of embroidery floss; use one strand of acrylic yarn for some small knots; two, three, four strands for larger knots, and five strands for largest knots. Work the knots within the oval areas, and add a few extra knots here and there. Make dots at ends of closed flowers with two strands of acrylic yarn. Make the centers of open flowers with one strand of dark green tapestry yarn. Work all remaining lines in outline stitch with embroidery floss; the number of strands for each part is indicated on pattern.

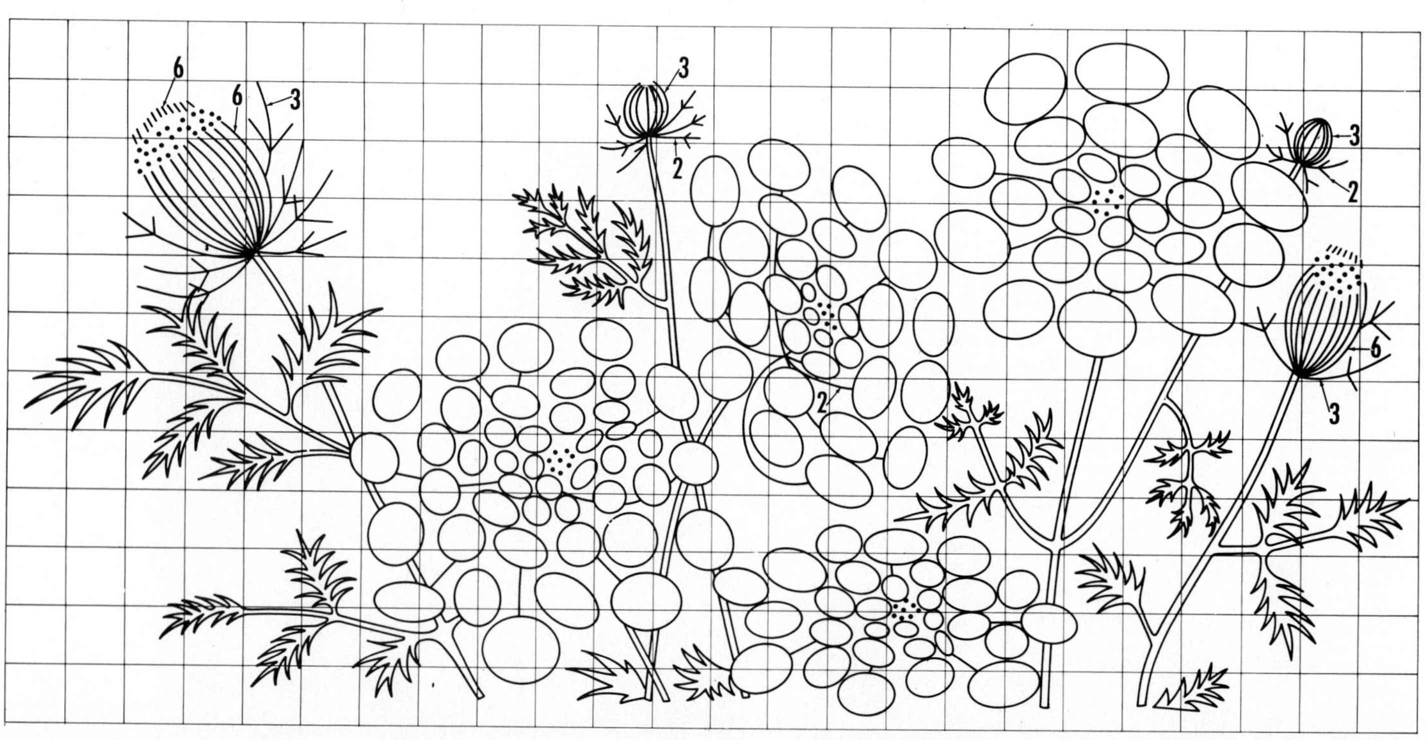

Three Children

Children at their play are charmingly depicted in yarn, and a variety of textures and embroidery stitches are used with interesting dimensional effect.

A girl with a monkey wears a striped dress in bright and heather hues, worked in outline stitch. Hair of strawlike yarn frames her appliquéd face. The 8" x 12" picture is embroidered on gold silk and framed with pine stripping.

A boy with a kite is snugly dressed in a Cretan-stitch pullover with knickers. He stands in a field of straight stitch and French knot flowers, flying a kite that trails a coral-stitch tail. Mohair and knitting worsted are contrasted with white crochet cotton on a hopsacking background. 8" x 10".

A girl holding a garland wears a stylish "crocheted" dress created with blanket stitch. Grass of soft mohair is scattered with straight stitches in a shiny thread for a sunstruck contrast. 10" x 12".

EQUIPMENT: Scissors. Pencil. Ruler. Paper for patterns. Tracing paper. Carbon paper. Large-eyed needle. Stapler. Hammer.

MATERIALS: Fabric with fairly smooth texture (we used silk and hopsacking) for background. Tightly woven cotton fabric for faces. Knitting yarns in various weights and textures (see individual directions). White sewing thread. White crochet cotton. Canvas stretchers or picture frames as indicated in individual directions for working embroidery. Staples. Pine wood stripping ¼" thick, ¾" wide. Cardboard backing for each. Masking tape. Small finishing nails.

DIRECTIONS: Read General Directions and Tips on page 12. Enlarge patterns on page 44 by copying on paper ruled in 1" squares; trace actual-size illustration of Girl with Garland. Cut fabric for background 2½" larger all around than assembled canvas stretchers or frame. Center design on fabric with carbon paper between; pencil over solid lines of design to transfer to fabric (dotted lines show area where embroidery extends). Cut heads of cotton, ⅜" larger than pattern. Turn edges under ⅜" and sew heads in place. Stretch fabric over canvas stretchers or frame, bringing edges to back and stapling. Following individual directions below and illustrations for color, embroider designs on fabric. See stitch details on page 15.

When embroidery is finished, restretch fabric if necessary to make it taut. Staple fabric to sides of stretchers. Cut cardboard slightly smaller than stretchers; tape to back of stretchers. Cut wood stripping into lengths to fit with butt joints, for framing; stain as desired. Nail stripping around stretchers.

GIRL WITH MONKEY

Use canvas stretchers 8" x 12" and gold silk fabric. For eyes, make double cross-stitches with thin yarn. Embroider dress with medium bulky yarns in outline-stitch rows, making wide and narrow bands of various colors. Embroider sleeves in vertical outline stitch: three rows for right sleeve, four rows for left sleeve. Work hands with fine yarn in satin stitch. Work outer rows of each leg in chain stitch, two inner rows in outline stitch. Make hair with wiry strawlike yarn, the top in several layers of long and short stitches; tack many long strands at sides, couching to secure. For Monkey, make eyes with one strand of very fine yarn in cross-stitch. Work arms, legs, and tail with fine yarn in outline stitch. Do hair with same yarn in long and short stitches, shirt and pants in satin stitch with medium yarn.

BOY WITH KITE

Use picture frame 8" x 10" with concave molding; stretch olive hopsacking across front of frame. Make eyes in double cross-stitch with fine yarn. Make sweater and sleeves with knitting worsted in Cretan stitch; work double layer in center. With knitting worsted, make about four layers of Cretan stitch for knickers and three rows of outline stitch for each leg. Make hair with mohair yarn in several layers of long and short stitch. With knitting worsted, make hands in satin stitch with outline stitch around, and make buds in French knots. Make grass of straight stitches in mohair. Make flowers in straight stitch with crochet cotton. Kite is of crochet cotton in straight stitches; make tail in coral stitch. Run cotton from kite under both hands and to ground; secure. Roll cotton into small ball and sew flat near bottom corner.

GIRL WITH GARLAND

Use canvas stretchers 10" x 12" and olive hopsacking. Work entire dress area with medium-weight yarn in buttonhole stitch. Make eye in double cross-stitch with fine yarn. Work inner edges of sleeves with one row each of chain stitch; do rest in buttonhole stitch. Do bangs with soft yarn in long and short stitch; extend braids down sides working in large cross-stitch; work another layer of cross-stitch over braids. Work right hand with crochet cotton in satin stitch. Do legs in crochet cotton in chain stitch. Work stem of garland in medium yarn and outline stitch. Do leaves and some grass blades with medium mohair in straight stitch with same yarn. Do heavier grass blades in thick shiny crochet cotton. Do the spoke flowers in straight stitch with crochet cotton. Work buds with crochet cotton in satin stitch.

Patterns to enlarge for Girl with Monkey and Boy with Kite.

Six Dog Pictures in Cross-Stitch

The Beagle, German Shepherd, Boxer, Boston Terrier, Cocker Spaniel, and Collie are worked in cross-stitch for traditional wall plaques that pay tribute to six of man's best friends.

SIZE: 7″ x 9″ each.

EQUIPMENT: Ruler. Pencil. Scissors. Embroidery and sewing needles. Embroidery hoop (optional). Thumbtacks. Basting thread. Penelope (cross-stitch) canvas, 7-mesh-to-the-inch, about 7″ x 9″ for each picture.

MATERIALS (for each picture): White or cream linen, 10″ x 12″. Six-strand embroidery floss: one skein of each color indicated below (less will be needed, if making all six dogs). Heavy cardboard. Frame, 7″ x 9″, rabbet size.

DIRECTIONS: Read General Directions and Tips on page 12 and How to Cross-Stitch on page 16, referring to section on Penelope canvas. Fold each piece of linen in half horizontally, then vertically to find center. Mark point with pin. Carefully center canvas over center point of linen and baste. Use full six strands of embroidery floss in needle. Follow chart for each picture, working over canvas and through linen. Each square of chart represents one stitch. Find center point of design on chart and begin working cross-stitches from center, following chart for placement of colors.

When design is completed, remove basting threads and draw out canvas threads, leaving the embroidered cross-stitch on linen. Block embroidery as directed on page 14 and frame.

NOTE: The design may also be worked on counted-thread fabric, without using the Penelope canvas.

BOSTON TERRIER

Light, medium and dark green, black, navy, white, very dark brown, medium and dark gray.

BEAGLE

Light, medium, and dark green, white, black, gold and very deep gold, navy, medium and dark gray, medium and dark brown.

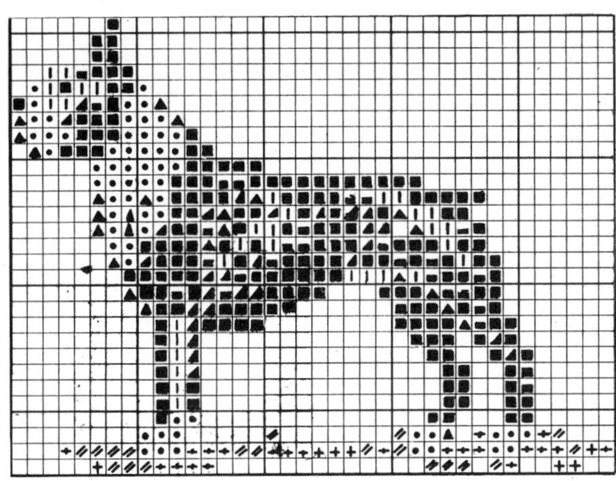

Boston Terrier

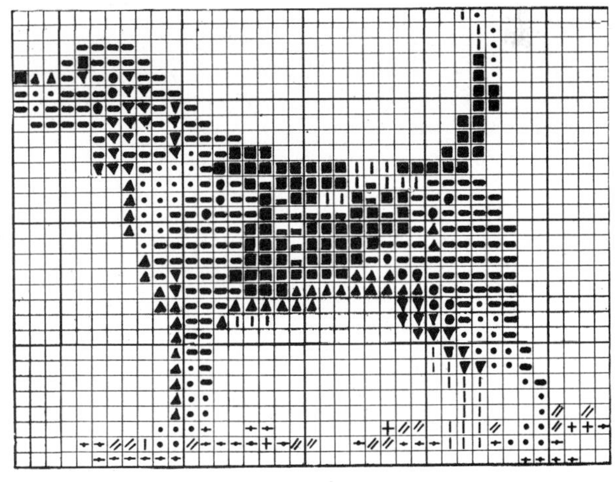

Beagle

Color Key

Black	Medium Brown	Toast	Light Green
Navy	Very Deep Gold	Dark Gray	Dark Beige
Very Dark Brown	Deep Gold	Medium Gray	Light Beige
Dark Brown	Gold	Dark Green	Medium Blue-Gray
Medium Dark Brown	Dark Toast	Medium Green	White

COCKER SPANIEL

Light, medium, and dark green, black, navy, dark gray, medium blue-gray.

COLLIE

Light, medium, and dark green, white, black, very deep gold, medium and very dark brown, toast, medium gray.

GERMAN SHEPHERD

Light, medium, and dark green, black, light and dark beige, deep gold, navy, dark brown, dark toast, dark gray.

BOXER

Light, medium, and dark green, white, deep gold, medium, medium-dark, and very dark brown,

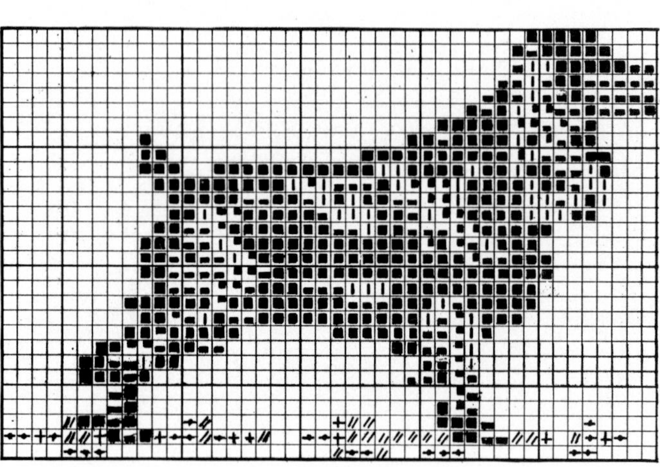

Cocker Spaniel

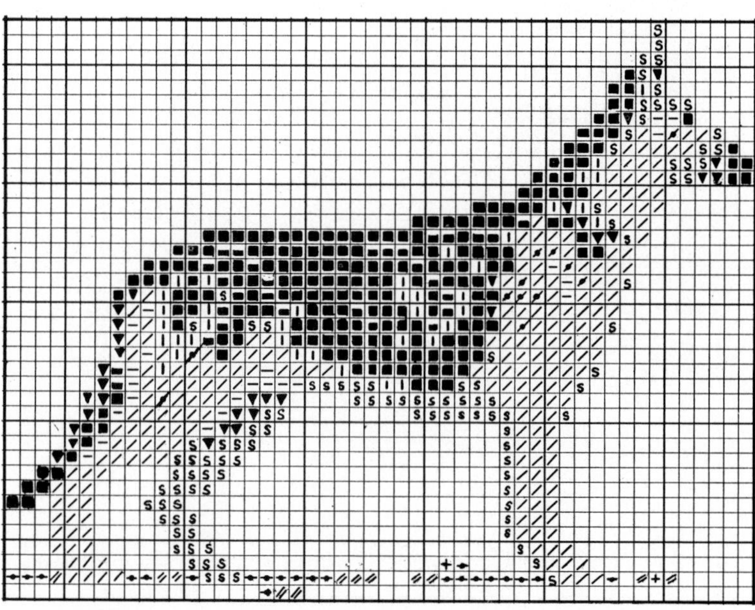

German Shepherd

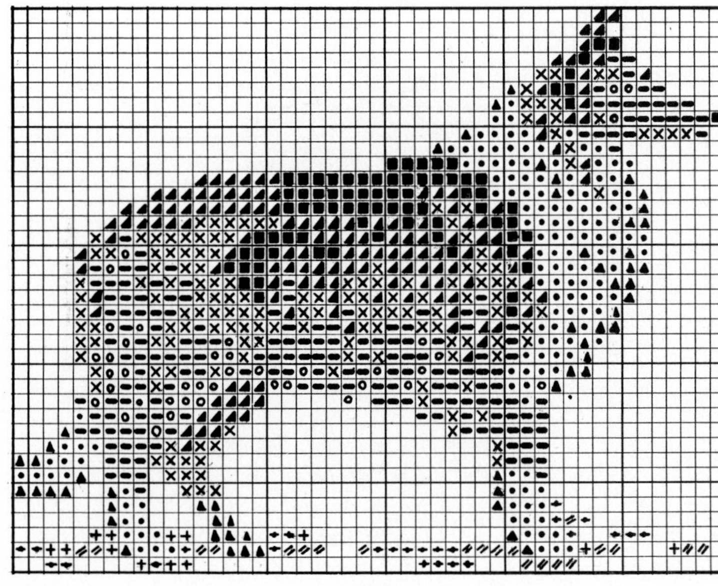

Collie

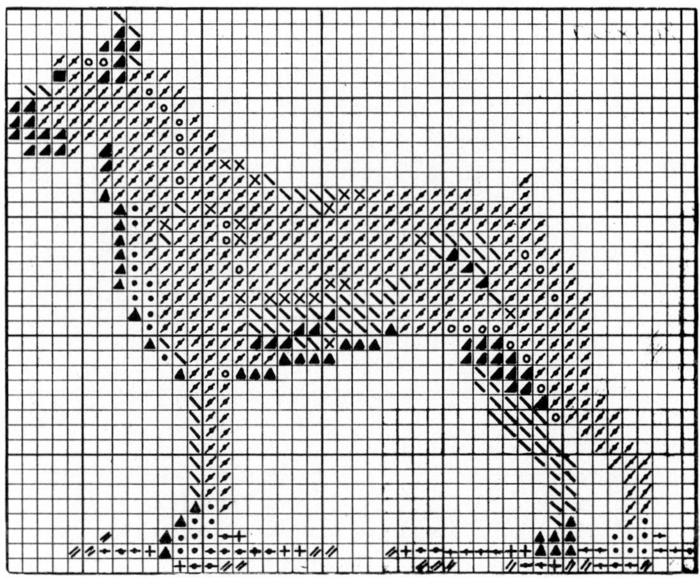

Boxer

Two Victorian Wool Pictures

Wool flowers, puffed and padded, make the unusual embroidery of these Victorian pictures. The technique was a mystery until we were able to examine a third picture in deteriorating condition and saw how the embroidery was made. Petals and leaves are constructed by sewing strands of yarn together, then using resulting yarn piece in various ways as shown, sometimes building extra dimension with padding. The flowers, leaves, and strawberries are sewn on a black fabric background. The stems and smallest flowers are made with embroidery stitches; in one picture, pompons are added. Wreath Design: 16" square. Floral Bouquet 14" x 17".

EQUIPMENT: Paper for patterns. Pencil. White dressmaker's carbon paper. Stiff cardboard. Scissors. Ruler. Sewing needle. Large-eyed embroidery needle. Tack hammer for framing pictures. Dry ball-point pen.

MATERIALS: Black suede cloth or good quality felt, 24" square for Wreath Design; 22" x 26" for Bouquet Design. Tapestry yarn, 8-yard skeins: two skeins of white for each picture, and one skein of colors listed in Color Keys for each, except for Wreath Design which requires two skeins olive green, light olive, deep green, and dark green. Sewing thread to blend with each color group of yarns (see Color Keys). White cotton flannel for stuffing. Carpet thread. **For Wreath Design:** Red pompons from ball fringe, 6. Gold silk or metallic thread. **For Framing:** Heavy mounting cardboard, 20" square for Wreath Design; 18" x 22" for Bouquet Design. Straight pins. Masking tape. Wide shadow-box frame with glass, rabbet size the same as mounting boards. Brown wrapping paper.

DIRECTIONS: The three-dimensional effect of these pictures is achieved by forming separate flowers, petals, and leaves from strands of yarn sewn together and then sewn onto the background fabric. Stems and other flowers are embroidered flat, directly on the background.

Flowers, petals, and leaves made separately are indicated by letters A–H on patterns. Not all leaves and petals are numbered; the unlettered ones should be made the same way as the similar lettered ones in the same area. The letters on each part of the design refer to the Stitch Key; the numbers on patterns indicate color combinations of yarn to use for leaves, flowers, and petals (see Color Keys). Arrange colors of yarn strands from light to dark, so that when strands are folded, either the light or the dark will be at center. Colors and combinations may be changed to suit your own scheme. Try different combinations as you practice making the petals and leaves. To make petal and leaf shapes, follow directions and details.

To prepare yarn for making all separate pieces, cut strands of yarn to length given in individual directions. Work over a small piece of cardboard and sew with thread and a sewing needle (see Fig. 1). Hold strands side by side and tack together with thread in a color that blends with color combination of yarn. Hold strands flat and taut over cardboard as shown in Fig. 1. Carefully sew through each strand from right to left, then from left to right, making each row of stitching about ⅛″ apart. Do not pull thread tight, but have it snug enough to keep strands of yarn close together and flat. Continue stitching through strands along complete length (front and back of cardboard). Form each petal and leaf shape with these stitched strips of yarn.

A—Straight Leaf Strip: Cut number and colors of yarn strands indicated in Color Key, long enough to form complete folded arrangement on pattern for Wreath Design. Sew together as in Fig. 1. Turn under ends of strands and tack. Place strip over pattern, fold and tack to conform with shape on pattern. Tack to black fabric wherever necessary to hold in place.

B—Tulip Shape Stuffed Petals: For each petal, cut number and colors of yarn strands indicated in Color Keys, and sew together, Fig. 1; cut strands twice the length of petals on patterns, plus 2″. Fold strands in half, keeping them flat, and using one finger to hold curve at fold, Fig. 2.

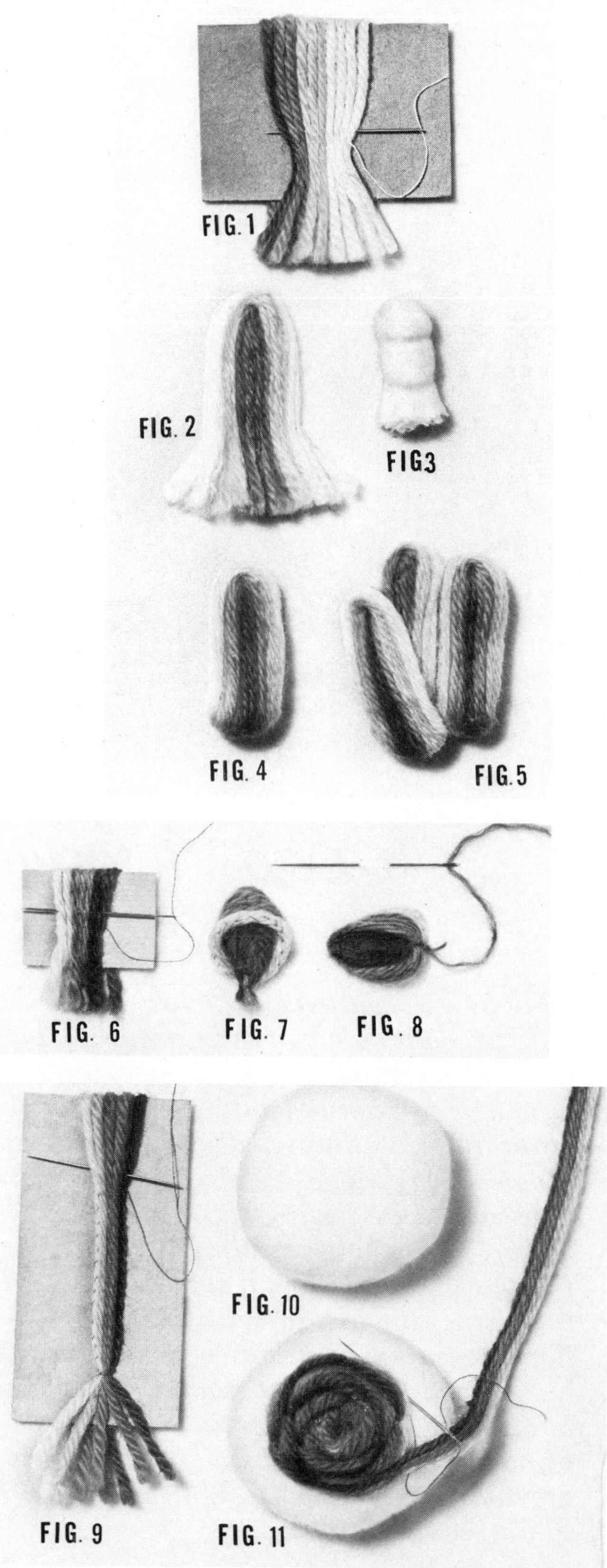

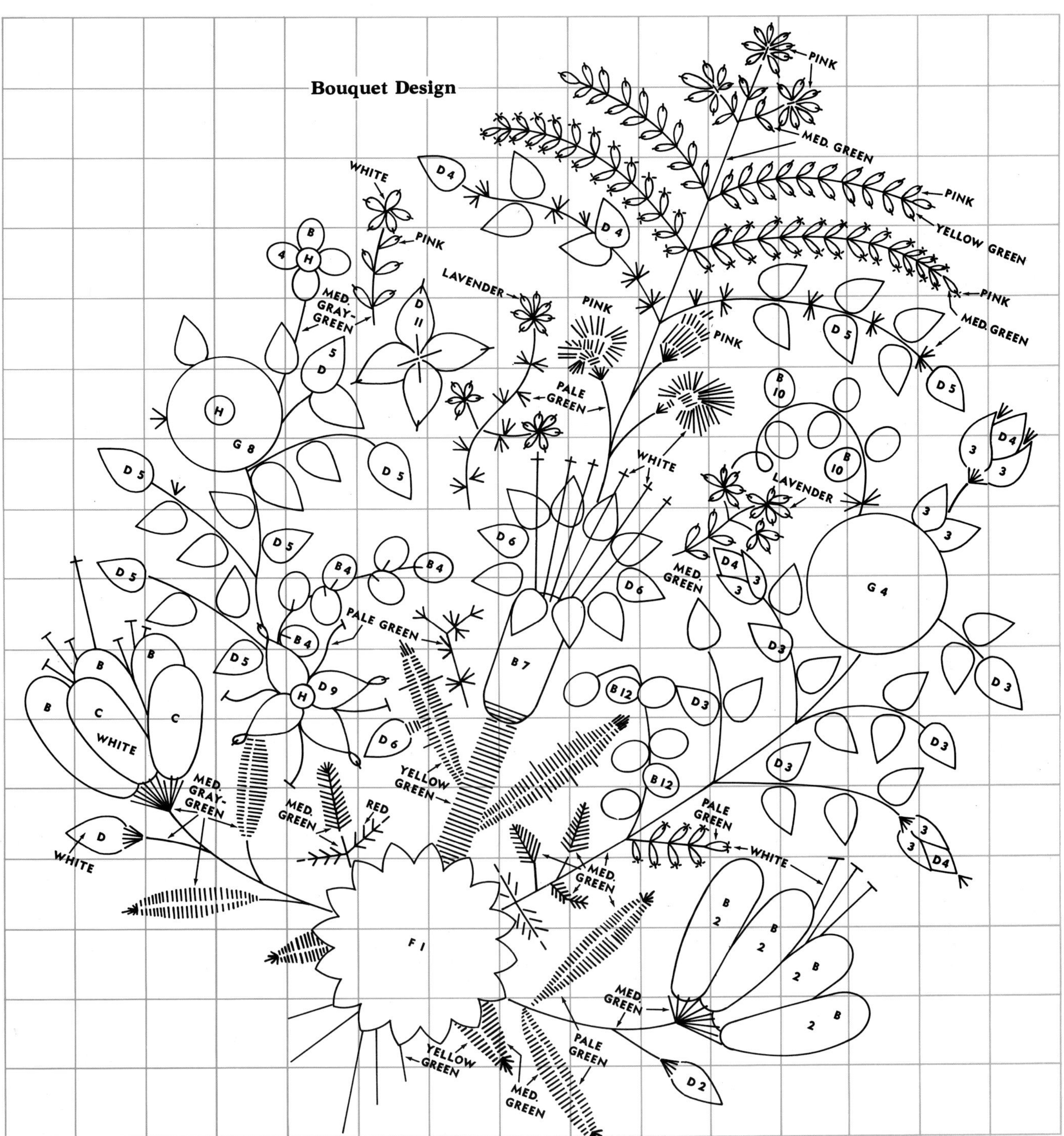

Color Key (Bouquet)

No. 1— 3 Strands Lavender
Flower 2 Strands Medium Purple
2 Strands Plum

No. 2— 1 Strand Coral
Flower 4 Strands Gold
4 Strands Pale Gold

No. 3— 3 Strands Dark Green
Leaves 3 Strands Medium Green
1 Strand Light Olive

No. 4— 1 Strand Medium Rust
Flower 6 Strands Dark Rust

No. 5— 2 Strands Light Gray-Green
Leaves 4 Strands Medium Gray-Green
1 Strand Dark Gray-Green

No. 6— 1 Strand Coral
Flower 2 Strands Salmon
3 Strands Pale Brick Red
1 Strand White

No. 7— Three Groups of
Flower 2 Strands Salmon
2 Strands Pale Brick Red
1 Strand White

No. 8— 3 Strands Pale Brick Red
Flower 3 Strands White

No. 9— 2 Strands Dark Gray-Blue
Flower 2 Strands Medium Gray-Blue
2 Strands Light Gray-Blue
1 Strand White

No. 10—6 Strands Medium Purple
Flower

No. 11—2 Strands White
Flower 2 Strands Pale Gold
3 Strands Gold
1 Strand Coral

No. 12—6 Strands Lavender
Flower

Stitch Key

B Tulip-Shaped Stuffed Petals
C Tulip-Shaped Unstuffed Petals
D Leaves
F Small Petaled Flower
G Padded Rose
H Pompons

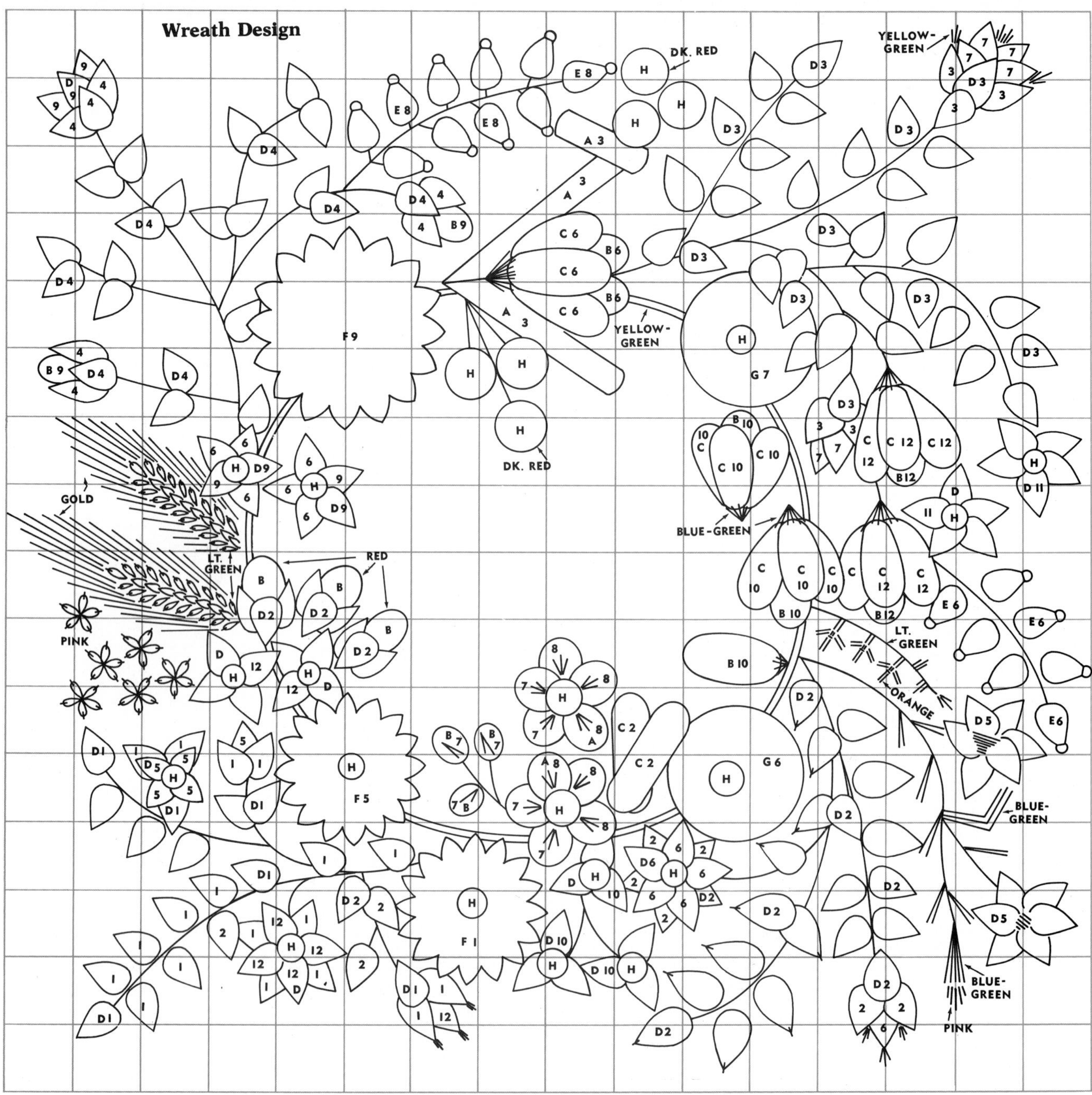

No. 1— 1 Strand #7329 Dark Blue-Green
Leaves 2 Strands #7367 Olive Green
2 Strands #7363 Light Olive
2 Strands #7476 Dark Gold

No. 2— 1 Strand #7329 Dark Blue-Green
Leaves 2 Strands #7387 Dark Green
2 Strands #7386 Medium Green
2 Strands #7361 Pale Olive

No. 3— 2 Strands #7389 Deep Green
Leaves 2 Strands #7367 Olive Green
2 Strands #7363 Light Olive
1 Strand #7402 Pale Green

No. 4— 2 Strands #7389 Deep Green
Leaves 3 Strands #7387 Dark Green
2 Strands #7384 Light Green

No. 5— 1 Strand #7198 Dark Brick Red
Flower 1 Strand #7196 Medium Brick Red
2 Strands #7194 Light Brick Red
1 Strand #7192 Pale Brick Red
1 Strand White

No. 6— 1 Strand #7439 Burnt Orange
Flower 2 Strands #7436 Light Orange
3 Strands #7726 Yellow
3 Strands White

No. 7— 1 Strand #7198 Dark Brick Red
1 Strand #7666 Scarlet
1 Strand #7106 Coral
2 Strands #7104 Salmon
1 Strand #7192 Pale Brick Red

No. 8— 2 Strands White
Flower 4 Strands #7192 Pale Brick Red
1 Strand #7104 Salmon

No. 9— 2 Strands #7219 Maroon
Flower 2 Strands #7211 Pink
3 Strands White

No. 10—1 Strand #7307 Deep Blue
Flower 1 Strand #7318 Royal Blue
1 Strand #7314 Light Blue
3 Strands #7301 Pale Blue

No. 11—1 Strand #7119 Deep Red
Flower 1 Strand #7198 Dark Brick Red
3 Strands #7439 Burnt Orange
1 Strand #7436 Light Orange

No. 12—8 Strands White
Flower 1 Strand #7314 Light Blue

Stitch Key (Wreath)
A Straight Leaf Strip
B Tulip-Shaped Stuffed Petals
C Tulip-Shaped Unstuffed Petals
D Leaves
E Leaves with Stitched Tip
F Flower with Small Petals
G Padded Rose
H Pompon

Sew across strands near ends; sew center strands together.

Form a roll, Fig. 3, by cutting long strips of cotton flannel and rolling tightly to make about ½" diameter. Measure the length of each petal on pattern; cut flannel strips to that width and roll. Wrap white thread around roll and knot thread. Sew across one end for top to make it round. Place sewn strands of yarn over flannel roll, covering top and sides, with folded end of strands over rounded end of roll. Tack in place; turn ends to back and tack, see Fig. 4.

C—Tulip Shape Unstuffed Petals: Make as for stuffed tulip petals, omitting the flannel roll, and turning ends in. Unstuffed petals are placed over stuffed petals to form flower, see Fig. 5.

D—Leaves: Cut number and colors of yarn strands indicated in Color Keys, about 2½" long, and sew together, Fig. 6. Fold in half, keeping all strands flat so a point is formed by strands underneath, Fig. 7. Sew ends together tightly. Turn leaf over and tack to black background at tip and bottom; turn ends under leaf and make a straight stem stitch with yarn, Fig. 8.

E—Leaves with Stitched Tip: Make as for Leaves D. At folded tip, stitch across strands ⅛" from tip, pulling thread tight; knot. Sew to background as for Leaves D.

F—Flower with Small Petals: For each petal, cut number and colors of strands inidcated in Color Keys, 2" long. Make 54 small petals as for Leaves D, but do not tack to background. Cut a cardboard circle slightly smaller than circles F on patterns; pad with a few layers of flannel to make a slight mound. Cover with a larger flannel circle and gather edge of flannel to cover padded mound smoothly. Starting around outside edge, tack a round of petals to mound with points out. Tack another round of petals inside and overlapping last round, with points of petals between those of last round. Make five rounds of petals to center. Sew a small pompon (see below) at center.

G—Padded Rose: Cut long strands of yarn in colors and numbers indicated in Color Keys; sew together, Fig 9. For padding, cut a circle of flannel about 4" in diameter. Gather around circle with small running stitch and stuff circle with pieces of flannel to make a plump mound a little smaller in diameter than pattern circles G. Pull gathers together and knot thread, Fig. 10. Starting at center top, attach end of sewn yarn strands to mound, wind strands around center, tack to flannel mound about every ½"; overlap each round slightly to cover top and sides of mound, Fig. 11. If sewn strands are not long enough to cover mound completely, make another strip the same and add to end of first strip at a tacking place on mound. Sew rose to background around bottom edge. Make a small yarn pompon (see below). Sew pompon to center of rose.

H—Pompons: (Note: Cherries on Wreath Design are pompons from ball fringe.) For all other small pompons, use two colors of yarn. Most of the pompons are white and yellow; some are yellow and brown, or they may be all yellow. Cut two strands of tapestry yarn 36" long. Split each into four single-ply pieces. Cut a strip of cardboard ½" wide. Cut a 6" piece of carpet thread and lay it along one edge of the cardboard. Wind the four split strands of one color yarn around cardboard and thread, and wind two split strands of second color yarn around, on top of first color. Tie all strands together very tightly with the carpet thread; cut strands on opposite side. Fluff out pompon and trim yarn ends to a small pompon ⅜" to ½" in diameter.

To Transfer Designs: Enlarge patterns for Wreath and Bouquet on paper ruled in 1" squares (see page 415). Using white carbon paper on top of black fabric and a dry ball-point pen, go over main outlines of large flowers and stems. Following pattern and Color and Stitch Keys, make each three-dimensional piece. Using pattern as a guide, place pieces on background and tack in place with thread. When all pieces are sewn to background, embroider remaining parts of designs following colors marked on patterns (see Stitch Details on page 15). To do embroidery, split tapestry yarn into four single-ply pieces and use a single ply. Or use other fine yarn. Stems are outline stitch. Loop petals are lazy daisy stitch. Lines close together in an area are satin stitch; remaining lines are straight stitch.

To Frame: Stretch finished picture on mounting board. Insert pins through fabric into edges of mounting board, beginning at center of each side and working to corners. Hammer pins into mounting board. Turn excess fabric to back and tape smoothly in place. Insert and secure picture in shadow-box frame with glass. Seal back by gluing wrapping paper tautly across back of frame to keep picture clean.

Eight Wildflower Prints

The natural beauty of wildflowers is captured with a few simple stitches, chosen to portray the essence of each flower. From top left, the set consists of the violet, bunchberry, wild rose, buttercup, clover, lady's slipper or moccasin flower, and jack-in-the-pulpit. The thistle is shown in closer view on the textured linen background. For all, the stitch tells the story.

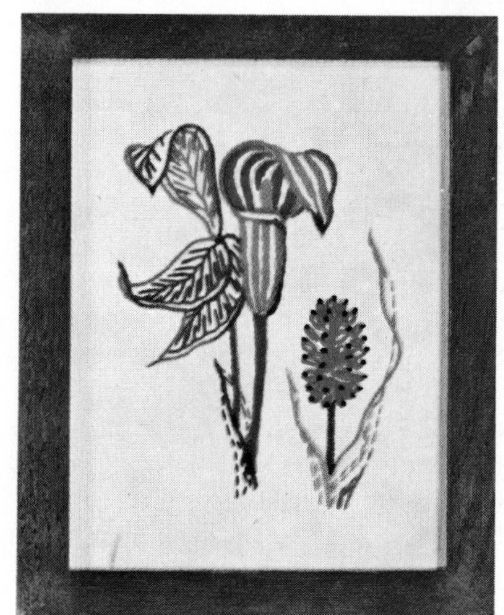

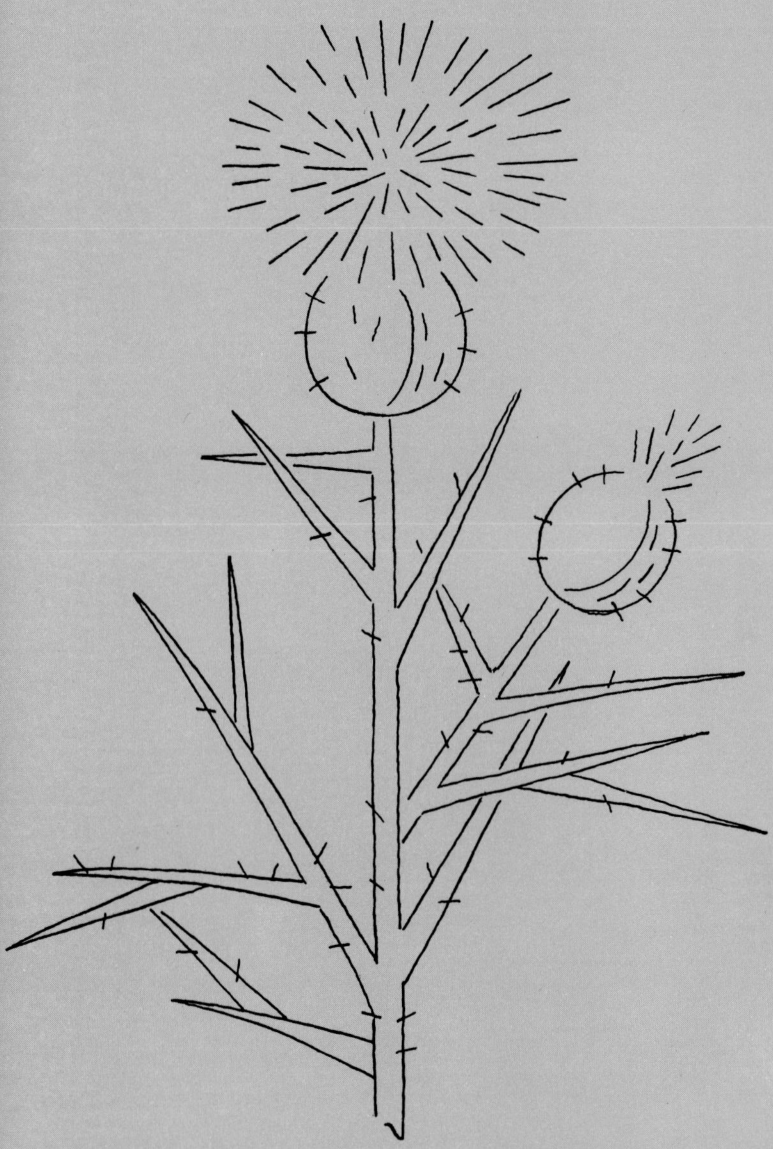

EQUIPMENT: Scissors. Tracing paper. Pencil. Dressmaker's carbon. Embroidery needle. Dry ball-point pen.

MATERIALS: Linen, 9" x 12", for each picture. Six-strand embroidery floss: for stems and leaves, light and dark green; for blossoms, colors as shown.

DIRECTIONS: Read General Directions and Tips on page 12. Trace actual-size patterns on pages 56 through 59. Transfer designs to linen; use dressmaker's carbon and dry ball-point pen.

Using four strands of six-strand embroidery floss in needle, work designs with simple embroidery stitches, such as straight, running, outline, lazy daisy, long and short, satin, backstitch, chain, French knot, blanket, and featherstitch. Work stitches in a loose, free manner, as shown in the close-ups that accompany each pattern.

To block and frame, see page 14.

Strawberry Picture

As fresh as a spring day, this crisp spray of strawberries combines appliquéd felt leaf clusters and hand-embroidered berries, blossoms, and stems.

SIZE: 26″ x 35″ matted.

EQUIPMENT: Paper for pattern. Tracing paper. Dressmaker's tracing (carbon) paper. Soft lead pencil. Ruler. Tape measure. Straight pins. Scissors. Embroidery needle with large eye. Sewing needle. Mat knife. Metal straight edge.

MATERIALS: Heavyweight unbleached muslin fabric, at least 36″ wide, 1 yard. Bright green felt, ½ yard. Pearl cotton size 5, 53-yard balls in the following colors: two red, two brown, one yellow, one green, one white. One spool green cotton sewing thread. **For Mat:** Forest green-and-white dotted cotton fabric, at least 36″ wide, 1¼″ yards. Mat board 30″ x 40″. Foam core 30″ x 40.″ Single- and double-faced masking tape. Red Persian-type (3-ply) yarn, 36 yards or 8½ ounces, for twisted cord. Glue.

DIRECTIONS: Read General Directions and Tips on page 12. Cut muslin to 22½″ x 29″. Enlarge pattern by copying on paper ruled in 1″ squares. Heavy lines on pattern indicate cutting lines; fine lines indicate hand-embroidery lines. Trace design. Using dressmaker's carbon paper, transfer design to muslin. Using pattern and carbon paper, trace each cluster of leaves on green felt where leaves overlap; trace all touching clusters as one piece. Mark outline of strawberries and blossoms on all leaves. These areas will be cut out. Mark lines across leaves where stems cross. Trace vein lines on all leaves. Before cutting out leaves, embroider veins: Using green pearl cotton, embroider center long vein in narrow satin stitch (see stitch details on page 15); embroider other vein lines in outline stitch. Carefully cut out leaf clusters. Cut out berry and blossom areas.

Baste leaf clusters in place on muslin. Cut away strips on leaves along stem lines. With green sewing thread, buttonhole-stitch leaves to muslin around all edges including berry and blossom cut-outs, and along stem edges.

Embroider strawberries with red pearl cotton, working outline stitch around outer edges and filling in with long and short stitch. Embroider strawberry petals with green pearl cotton in satin stitch. Make French knots at each dot with white pearl cotton. Embroider blossoms with white pearl cotton in satin stitch, working outline stitch around outer edges. Work centers with yellow French knots.

Embroider stems last with brown pearl cotton in satin stitch.

Mark foam core to measure 24″ x 31″. Cut out, using mat knife and metal straight edge. Center embroidered work on board, tape. For mat, measure and cut mat board 25½″ x 34½″; for center opening, cut out an area 18″ x 26″. Cut cotton fabric to fit mat board leaving 2″ extra along each edge (including center opening) for folding over edge to back. Cover one surface of mat board with fabric, taping edges to back surface. For center area, clip into corners before turning edges over. Tape foam core to mat board with double-faced tape.

To make twisted cord, divide the yarn into four 9 yard-long strands, then follow instructions for twisting cord on page 416. Glue cord around center opening. Glue ends securely to keep them from raveling.

Frame as desired.

Daisies and Tiger Lilies

An early-morning bird perches beside a vase of daisies and tiger lilies in this easy-to-stitch crewel-embroidered scene.

DESIGN AREA: 11½″ x 18″.

MOUNTED SIZE: 15″ x 22″.

EQUIPMENT: Sewing needle and large-eyed embroidery needle. Ruler. Paper for pattern. Pencil. White dressmaker's carbon (tracing) paper. White pencil. Dry ball-point pen. Masking tape. Embroidery frame or hoop. Embroidery scissors. **For Blocking:** Soft wooden board. Brown wrapping paper. Thumbtacks. Square. Tack hammer.

MATERIALS: Light blue tightly woven cotton or linen fabric for embroidery, 20″ x 27″. White sewing thread. Three-ply Persian yarn (8.8-yard skeins): 1 skein each of pearl gray, yellow, gold, orange, medium yellow-green, pale blue, light gray-blue, medium gray-blue, dark gray-blue, dark blue; two skeins of white. **For Mounting and Framing:** Mounting board ⅜″ thick or three ⅛″-thick pieces of cardboard, 15″ x 22″. Straight pins. Dark blue metal section frame strips (or other desired frame) ready-to-assemble, ¾″ deep with ⅜″ channel for holding picture: one package 15″ and one package 22″ lengths (available at art supply stores). Hangers for metal section frame. Picture hanging wire.

DIRECTIONS: Read General Directions and Tips on page 12. Mark guidelines around picture area as for Poppies and Peonies (see directions on page 65), marking area 15″ x 22″. Also follow Poppies and Peonies directions to enlarge pattern and transfer it to fabric; adjust pattern so that all margins are approximately 1¾″ deep.

Stretch fabric in embroidery frame or hoop. To embroider, use two strands of yarn in needle (however, for stamen, use one strand; see below). Follow Color Key and refer to stitch details on page 15. Refer to illustration for following the directions of the stitches.

Embroider all flowers, stems, bird, pitcher, and window frame in this order:

Lilies: Embroider the yellow and gold sections in split stitch. The fine lines in some petal sections indicate changes in direction of the stitches. The stamens are all worked with one strand of white yarn in straight stitch. Wherever the stamen bends, tack stitch with a small stitch, using the same white yarn. At the tip of each stamen, make a small diagonal straight stitch with orange yarn.

Daisies: Make the center of French knots with gold yarn; make the ring area around center of French knots with white yarn. Using white yarn, make all the petals in satin stitch.

Forget-Me-Nots: Using dark gray-blue yarn, make all the petals in straight stitch with same center point; for center, make one small straight stitch over the center of each.

Bird: Make bird in split stitch unless otherwise indicated. The dark solid areas indicate dark blue yarn in satin stitch. Make the tail section and wing area between the white and dark blue with dark gray-blue in satin stitch. Using gold yarn, make the beak in satin stitch; the fine line indicates the change in direction of stitches. Make eye in satin stitch with dark blue yarn; make small straight stitch in eye area with white yarn where indicated. Make feet in straight stitch with dark blue yarn.

Color Key
1 White
2 Pearl Gray
3 Yellow
4 Gold
5 Orange
6 Medium Yellow-Green
7 Pale Blue
8 Light Gray-Blue
9 Medium Gray-Blue
10 Dark Gray-Blue
11 Dark Blue

Stems: Using medium yellow-green yarn, make stems in straight stitch except for thicker areas, which are worked in satin stitch or long split stitch.

Pitcher: Embroider entirely in long horizontal split stitch with white and pearl gray yarns.

Window Frame: Embroider entirely in 1″ long split stitch in varying shades of blue.

When embroidery is finished, block, mount, and frame picture as indicated for Poppies and Peonies; see page 65.

Poppies and Peonies

Flowers on a sunlit morning capture the essence of summer in this lovely crewel-embroidered wall hanging. A companion piece to "Daisies and Tiger Lilies," shown on page 62.

DESIGN AREA: 13″ x 18″.

MOUNTED SIZE: 16″ x 22″.

EQUIPMENT: Sewing needle and large-eyed embroidery needle. Ruler. Paper for pattern. Pencil. White dressmaker's carbon (tracing) paper. White pencil. Dry ball-point pen. Masking tape. Embroidery frame or hoop. Embroidery scissors. **For Blocking:** Soft wooden board. Brown wrapping paper. Thumbtacks. Square. Tack hammer.

MATERIALS: Green tightly woven cotton or linen fabric for embroidery, 21″ x 27″. White sewing thread. Persian yarn (8.8-yard skeins): 1 skein each of pale yellow, medium orange, deep orange, chartreuse, medium yellow-green, olive green, bottle green, gray-black; two skeins each of white, pale yellow-green, celery green. **For Mounting and Framing:** Mounting board ⅜″ thick or three ⅛″-thick pieces of cardboard, 16″ x 22″. Straight pins. Dark blue metal section frame strips (or other desired frame) ready-to-assemble, ¾″ deep with ⅜″ channel for holding picture; one package 16″ and one package 22″ lengths (available at art supply stores). Hangers for metal section frame. Picture hanging wire.

DIRECTIONS: Read General Directions and Tips on page 12. With sewing needle and white thread, follow thread of fabric and take ¼″ running stitches to mark guidelines around entire picture area, 16″ x 22″. This will designate the exact area which will fit into the rabbet of the frame, allowing for a plain fabric border at top, sides, and bottom. Leave at least 2½″ of fabric all around beyond marked outline. Matching corners, find the exact centers of the four sides and mark these centers with a few stitches.

Enlarge pattern on paper ruled in 1″ squares. Place the enlarged pattern on fabric with dressmaker's carbon paper between. Adjust pattern so that top margin is 1¾″ deep from edge of outline to top of tallest flower, 2¼″ at right side, 1¼″ at left side, and 2¼″ at bottom. Tape pattern and carbon to fabric to hold in place. Using dry ball-point pen, transfer all design lines to fabric. Remove tracing and carbon. To keep lines clear while embroidering, use sharp white pencil to intensify design lines as needed.

Stretch fabric in embroidery frame or hoop. To embroider, use two strands of yarn in needle. Follow Color Key and refer to stitch details on page 15. Refer to illustration for following the directions of the stitches.

Embroider all the flowers and leaves first, then embroider the wooden fence.

Peonies: With white yarn, embroider each completely in satin stitch of irregular length in each section. At base of each petal section only, go over a few stitches with yellow yarn in straight stitch.

Poppies: Embroider all petal sections with medium and deep orange in satin stitch. Fill in the dotted areas with gray-black yarn in French knots. Fill in the remaining irregular inner areas with satin stitch.

Long Leaves at Base of Picture: The center finer line in each leaf indicates the vein, from which point satin stitches are worked on a diagonal in each section.

Smaller Leaves: Using bottle green yarn, make all the remaining leaves in satin stitch leaf; the finer line in each leaf indicates the vein from which all the stitches are worked.

Small Bud: Using bottle green and white yarns, make bud and leaves in satin stitch.

Stems: Work in stem stitch for all stems. Use chartreuse yarn for poppy stems; use bottle green for peony and bud stems.

Ladybug: Using deep orange yarn, make body in satin stitch. Using gray-black yarn, make head in satin stitch and make tiny straight stitches for spots on body.

Wooden Fence: Make the ends only of the crossbars in short satin stitch. Make the rest of the crossbars and posts in long split stitch, making each stitch about 1″ long. Work in individual fine lines, bringing needle out through yarn as shown, thus splitting it.

Color Key

1 Medium Orange	6 Medium Yellow-Green
2 Deep Orange	7 Olive Green
3 Pale Yellow-Green	8 Bottle Green
4 Celery Green	9 Gray-Black
5 Chartreuse	10 White

When embroidery is finished, block and mount picture as indicated on page 14.

To Frame: Following instructions which come with metal strips, assemble frame around mounted fabric. **(Note:** If ⅛″ pieces of cardboard are used, add the two remaining pieces of cardboard.) Attach hangers to back of strips; secure ends of double length of wire to hangers, adjusting length of wire as necessary.

Asters in a Basket

Embroider a basket full of blooms on burlap with just two simple stitches and a variety of yarns. The choice of yarn is important in expressing the character of the flowers and the texture of the basket. Crisp asters are bold, straight stitches worked in a clear yellow and harmonizing colors of knitting worsted and a tweed yarn. Delicate Queen Anne's lace is created by working straight stitches in a loopy mohair. The basket is made with running and straight stitches of heather-tone yarn, and the background shows through the "weave."

SIZE: 18″ x 21¼″.

EQUIPMENT: Paper for planning design. Dressmaker's (carbon) tracing paper. Dry ball-point pen. Pencil. Ruler. Scissors. Large-eyed embroidery and rug needles. Stapler. **For Framing:** Backsaw and miter box. Hammer. Flat paintbrush.

MATERIALS: Dark gold burlap, 23″ x 26¼″. Knitting yarns in various weights and textures, such as mohair, knitting worsted, nubby, looped, and tweed yarns, in yellow and harmonizing colors. Canvas stretchers, 18″ x 21¼″ (available at art supply stores). Pine stripping ¼″ thick, 1″ wide, 7 ft. Small finishing nails. Wood stain in desired color. Heavy paper for backing picture. Glue.

DIRECTIONS: See General Directions and Tips on page 12. Assemble canvas stretchers to make frame 18″ x 21¼″. Stretch burlap over frame, being sure threads are straight; bring excess fabric to back and staple. Plan design on paper to fit the area of picture, using your own ideas for flower effects or following illustration. Sketch a semicircular basket about 7½″ wide and 4″ deep; sketch circles for flowers (about 2½″ in diameter) closely, with some overlapping others. Transfer design to burlap with dressmaker's carbon and dry ball-point pen, placing it slightly below center.

To embroider, use the medium yarns such as knitting worsted and sport yarn double in the needle; finer yarns may be used with three, four, or more strands in the needle. The best effect is achieved if a wide variety of textured yarns is used, in tweed, heather, and solid colors. Embroider flowers in straight stitches fanning out from center, with a long stitch across center. Using a dark heather-tone yarn, outline basket first with long running stitches. Then take running stitches across basket in lines ¾″ apart. Take long diagonal stitches across basket in two opposite directions, then vertical stitches.

When embroidery is finished, restretch burlap if necessary, to make it taut. Fold corners of fabric neatly and staple fabric to back of canvas stretchers. Measure and cut four pieces of pine stripping to fit around sides of picture with mitered corners. Stain; let dry. Fit around picture and nail to canvas stretchers at corners and center of sides with finishing nails. Cut heavy paper slightly smaller than picture frame and glue across back of frame to finish.

A Summer Bouquet

Embroidered summer flowers are artfully arranged in a lace-trimmed felt bowl. The coarse fabric background is mounted on canvas stretchers to hold it taut while embroidering; flowers, leaves are quickly worked with knitting yarn scraps. A frame is made of stained pine stripping.

SIZE: 12″ x 16″.

EQUIPMENT: Pencil. Ruler. Paper. Dressmaker's (carbon) tracing paper. Scissors. Large-eyed embroidery needles. Stapler for framing; small flat paintbrush. Handsaw. Hammer. Dry ball-point pen.

MATERIALS: Light yellow-green homespun-type fabric 17″ x 21″. Canvas stretchers 12″ x 16″ (available at art supply stores). Fine and medium-weight yarns: scraps of purple; lavender; dark, medium, and light mauve; raspberry; coral; pink; white; medium and light violet; plum; medium and bright yellow-green; medium olive green. Bright pink felt 5½″ x 9″. White lace 1¾″ wide, 8″ long. Pine stripping ¼″ thick, 1¼″ wide, 5 feet. Small finishing nails. Green stain.

DIRECTIONS: Enlarge pattern by copying on paper ruled in 1″ squares. With dressmaker's carbon and ball-point pen, mark pattern, centered, on green fabric.

Assemble canvas stretchers to make a frame 12″ x 16″. Stretch fabric over frame, being sure threads are straight; bring excess fabric to back and staple. Cut bowl of pink felt. Glue white lace across bowl 1″ down from top; glue bowl to green background.

Embroider flowers, stems, and leaves with single strand of yarn in needle (see stitch details on page 15). Follow illustration for colors. Embroider solid lines in outline stitch, loops in lazy daisy, straight lines in straight stitch, V's in fly stitch, dots in French knots; fill in large areas of some flowers in satin stitch (see illustration).

When embroidery is finished, restretch fabric if necessary to make it taut. Fold corners of fabric neatly and staple fabric to back of canvas stretchers. Measure and cut four pieces of pine stripping to fit around sides of picture with butt joints. Stain pine pieces green; let dry. Fit around picture and nail to canvas stretchers at corners and center of sides with finishing nails.

EMBROIDERED ITEMS FOR THE HOME

Flower-Ring Tablecloth

A lovely garland of white flowers borders a tablecloth that reverses the "blue onion" color scheme. The repeat pattern is worked in four easy-to-do embroidery stitches with pearl cotton on a 68″ purchased tablecloth.

EQUIPMENT: Paper for patterns. Tracing paper. Ruler. Dressmaker's tracing (carbon) paper (white or yellow). Soft and hard lead pencils. White pencil. Embroidery needle.

MATERIALS: Circular tablecloth of cotton, linen, or similar closely woven fabric (we used cloth 68″ in diameter; to adjust design to any diameter, see directions below). Pearl cotton, size 8, ten 95-yd. spools, white.

DIRECTIONS: Read General Directions and Tips on page 12. Enlarge pattern by copying on paper ruled in ½″ squares. Trace pattern (double motif) from bottom up to dash line. A portion of next motif, which is a repeat of the first, is given above dash line to show how design is continued (refer to illustration).

To make pattern for size of cloth being used, trace outline of one-quarter of the cloth on paper. Place traced double motif near edge of paper quarter-circle, with small ring of dots 1¼″ from hemmed edge (see pattern). Mark area double motif will cover. Continue placing and marking double motif around quarter-circle in same manner to determine how many repeats will be necessary to complete one-quarter of the cloth. If necessary, adjust spacing by leaving more or less space between motifs. Trace all details of each double motif as fitted onto paper quarter-circle. Place pattern on fabric cloth with edges flush and carbon between. Using hard lead pencil, transfer motifs for one quarter to cloth. Position pattern on second quarter of cloth; transfer design as for first. Repeat for third and fourth quarters. Remove pattern and carbon. If necessary, go over lines of design with white pencil to sharpen or correct.

Using one strand of white cotton in needle and referring to numbers on pattern, Stitch Key, and stitch details on page 15, embroider design around cloth as shown in illustration.

Flower-Ring Tablecloth

Stitch Key

1 Outline Stitch	3 French Knot
2 Satin Stitch	4 Star Filling Stitch

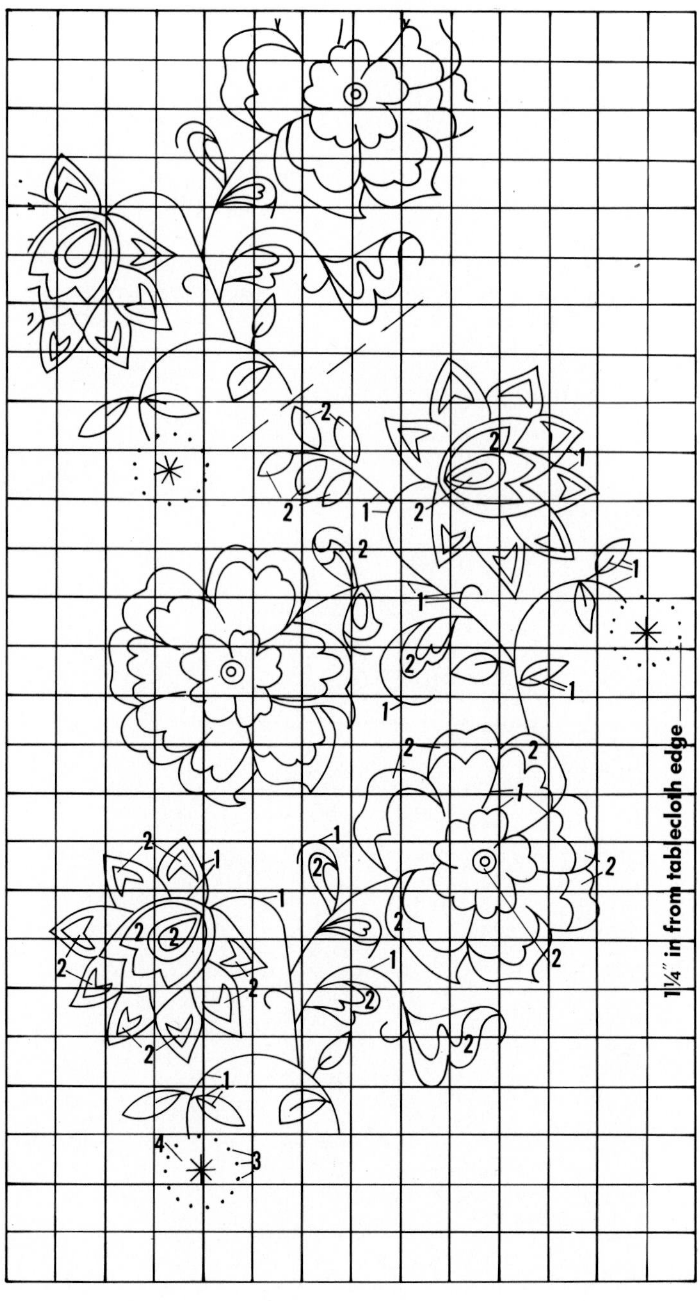

Strawberry Circle Tablecloth

Sweet strawberries, scattered on a field of crisp organdy, are machine appliquéd with a zigzag stitch. Blossoms and stems are embroidered by hand and the finished tablecloth, 60" in diameter, has a scalloped edge.

EQUIPMENT: Pencil. Ruler. Yardstick. Scissors. String. Straight pins. Paper for patterns. Tracing paper. Dressmaker's carbon (tracing) paper. Sewing machine with zigzag attachment. Embroidery hoop, needle, and scissors.

MATERIALS: Organdy (at least 36" wide): 3½ yards white, ½ yard each of green and red. Mercerized cotton sewing thread (not polyester): white, green, and red. Six-strand embroidery floss: white, bright yellow, and medium green.

DIRECTIONS: From white organdy, cut two 36" x 63" pieces. Sew together along 63" edges with ½" seam, using close zigzag stitch. Mark a 60"-diameter circle on fabric (finished size) as follows: Tie a long length of string to a pencil. Find the exact center of fabric and pin other end of string to center, leaving 30" of string between pencil and center. Swing pencil around lightly to mark cloth area. With pencil and yardstick, lightly mark 60"-long center line bisecting center seam line. Mark lines, horizontally and vertically, parallel to two center lines, making them 10" apart (see diagram for one-half of tablecloth; repeat on other half).

Enlarge patterns for strawberries by copying on paper ruled in 1" squares. Heavy lines indicate cutting lines; fine lines indicate hand-embroidery lines. Trace motifs separately. Referring to diagram and using dressmaker's carbon tracing paper, transfer motifs to right side of one half of

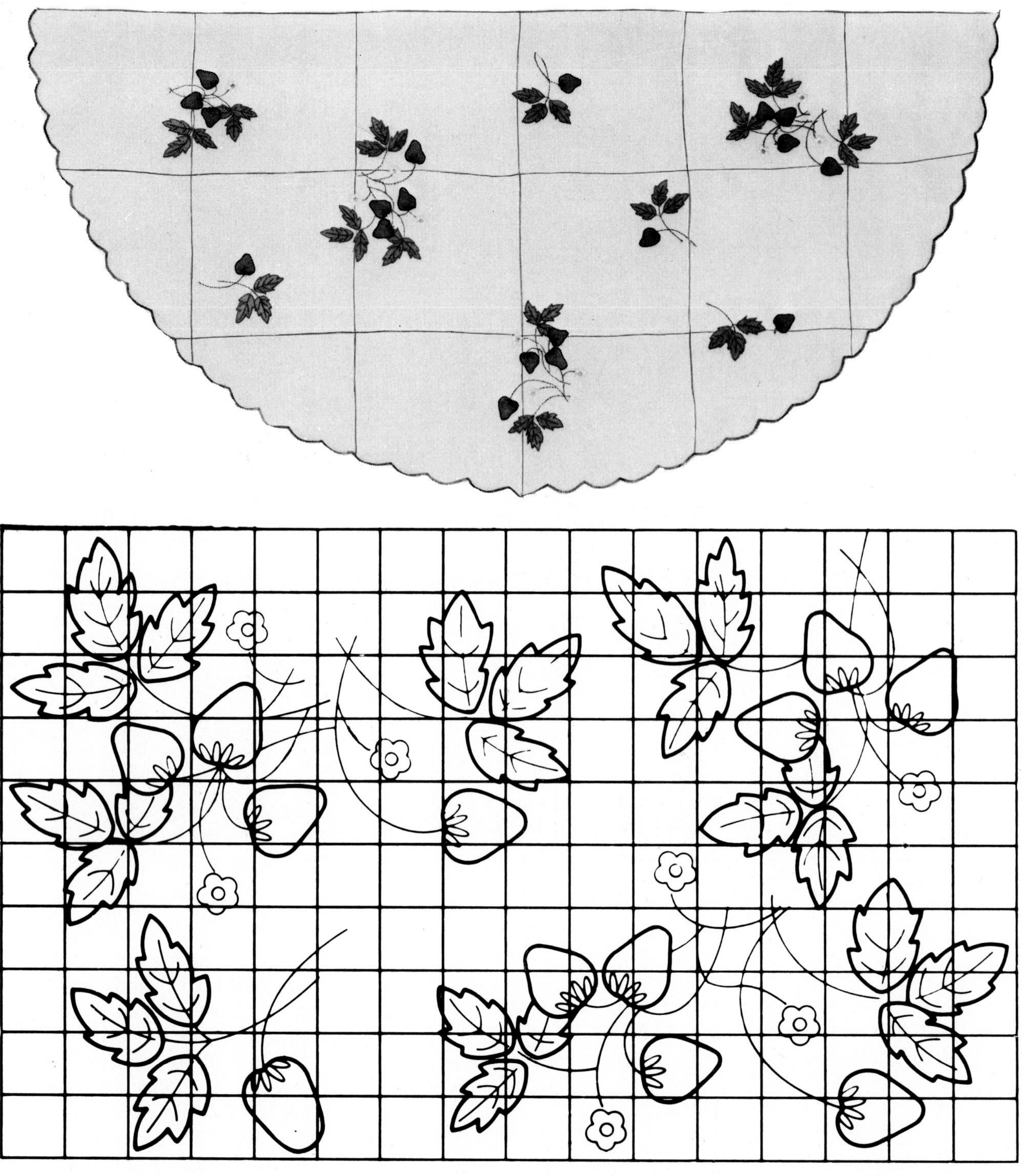

fabric. Reverse arrangement for other half of cloth. Using patterns, trace leaves on green and strawberries on red organdy; cut out each ¼″ larger all around than pattern. Pin leaves and strawberries in place on cloth. With matching thread and close zigzag stitch, sew each piece in place along traced outlines; trim away excess ¼″. If necessary, use a pencil to define embroidery lines.

Refer to stitch details on page 15 and use three strands of floss in needle. With green floss, work stems and leaf veins in outline stitch; work strawberry petals in lazy daisy stitch. In satin stitch, work flower petals in white and flower centers in yellow. When embroidery is finished, use white thread to work close zigzag stitch along horizontal and vertical marked lines. Do not stitch over any motifs. Open out seam allowances of center seam; press. Zigzag stitch over seam; trim seam allowances.

Mark scallops evenly along outer edge of marked circle (see diagram). With green thread, satin stitch (very closely worked zigzag stitch) on machine along scallop outline, making a border 3/16″ wide. Trim fabric beyond stitching. Startch, then press completed tablecloth.

"Blue Onion" Place Mat and Napkin Set

A vine in two blues is embroidered in seven basic stitches on a crisp white linen place mat. The mat's "blue onion" corner motif is repeated on a matching linen napkin for a perfect table-setting pair. Both are worked in cotton floss; the mat measures 14″ by 19½″.

EQUIPMENT: Pencil. Ruler. Tracing paper. Dressmaker's tracing (carbon) paper. Straight pins. Embroidery needle. Embroidery hoop. Sewing needle. Zigzag sewing machine for hemstitched hem.

MATERIALS: White linen or linenlike fabric, 15¾″ x 21¼″ for place mat, 15″ square for napkin. Six-strand embroidery floss, one skein each royal blue and pale aqua. White sewing thread.

DIRECTIONS: Read General Directions and Tips on page 12. Trace actual-size embroidery

"Blue Onion" Set
Stitch Key
1 Chain Stitch
2 Long and Short Stitch
3 Herringbone Stitch
4 Outline Stitch
5 Satin Stitch
6 Buttonhole Stitch
7 Straight Stitch

patterns. For place mat, using dressmaker's carbon, transfer main design to left side of fabric 1¾" in from side and 2½" up from bottom edge. Trace small design in lower right corner 2¼" in from side and 3" up from bottom edge. For napkin, trace small design in one corner of 15" square. Center design about 2½" in from adjacent sides, turning axis of design diagonally across corner (see illustration).

Place fabric in hoop. Using three strands of floss in needle and following stitch details on page 15, embroider design. Use pale aqua to embroider all fine lines and areas outlined in fine lines. Use royal blue for all heavy lines and areas outlined in heavy lines. Numbers on pattern indicate stitches (see Stitch Key). All dots are French knots; use six strands of floss in needle for heavy dots and three strands for small dots. Lines in pointed ends of large leaves indicate direction of satin stitch. Small flowers are filled in with herringbone stitch.

When embroidery is completed, prepare for hemstitching by pulling out two threads of fabric, 1½" from place mat edges and 1¼" from napkin edges. To miter corners, fold fabric ⅞" all around to back for place mat, ¾" for napkin. Pull up fabric at corners so remainder of hem lies flat; flatten and crease mitered fabric to both sides. Stitch adjacent sides of hem together along crease lines at each corner, from tip of corner to outer corners of creases. Refold hem to front; turn under ¼" and baste hem in place. For machine-hemstitched finish, use blind-stitch disk in machine; stitch on top of hem at inner edge, through hem and pulled thread line. Steam-press.

Drawnwork Place Mat

Stitchery stripes define the edges of a handsome burlap mat. The stitches are made in the drawn-thread technique in which open spaces are created by pulling the fabric threads together with satin stitch.

SIZE: 20″ x 14″ (fringe included).

EQUIPMENT: Scissors. Ruler. Tapestry and sewing needles.

MATERIALS: For four mats: Natural colored burlap, 1¼ yds. Mercerized knitting and crochet cotton, 1 ball natural. Basting thread.

DIRECTIONS: On burlap, mark four pieces, each 20″ x 14″, allowing a margin all around each.

All stitching is done between threads. Cut strands of crochet cotton in 20″ lengths and work with single strand.

To start, bring needle to front, leaving 1½″ end of thread on back and work stitching over end; or leave 3″ excess when starting and later, with needle, darn excess through stitches on back so no ends are free; clip ends.

Avoid long jumps across back of mat by ending off, or weave needle through stitches on back to next area to be worked.

Stitching will be worked horizontally across short ends of mat starting at top end. Each graph line is one thread. Follow chart and work from right to left, beginning and ending rows 1″ plus 8 threads in from marked sides. Begin with satin-stitch bars. Refer to embroidery stitch details on page 15. Each satin-stitch bar will cover two threads vertically and will be one thread apart as indicated on chart. Work the two rows across from right to left. Work next line of pyramid stitching as indicated but working as buttonhole stitch on uneven ends of stitches; repeat high and low pyramids across. Work next two rows of stitching in satin-stitch bar. For square eyelet stitch, work in satin stitch but cover threads indicated on chart and always bring needle up through center space. Square eyelets are separated by two rows of satin-stitch bars as indicated on chart; repeat eyelets and bars until you have reached the left (approximately 12 eyelets), allowing 1″ plus 8 threads from edge and making sure to end in two vertical rows of satin-stitch bars. There may be a difference in size due to thickness of burlap threads. To finish band, repeat from star (* on pattern) in reverse.

Thread-trace mat from ends of band along long sides to opposite end of mat with long basting stitches. Work opposite end of mat same as first end. Cut out mat allowing 1″ plus 8 threads beyond embroidery.

Squared Edging: Beginning at right corner on long edge of mat, count four threads from sides of stitching and four threads from last satin-bar stitched row; work from right to left. Following stitching details A through D, repeat across, ending same distance from edge on opposite end. For outer row of squared edging, count up four

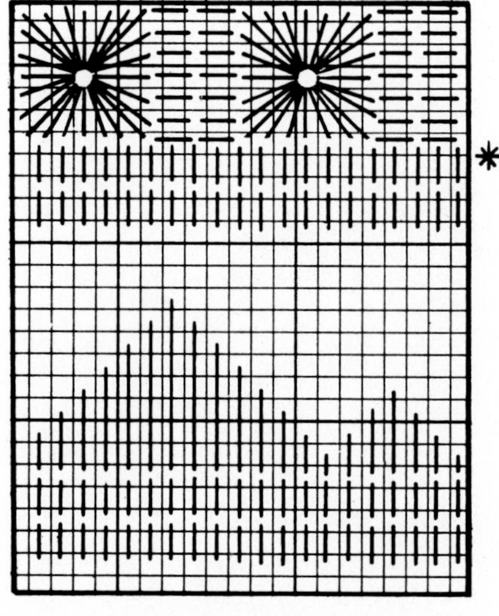

STITCH DESIGN

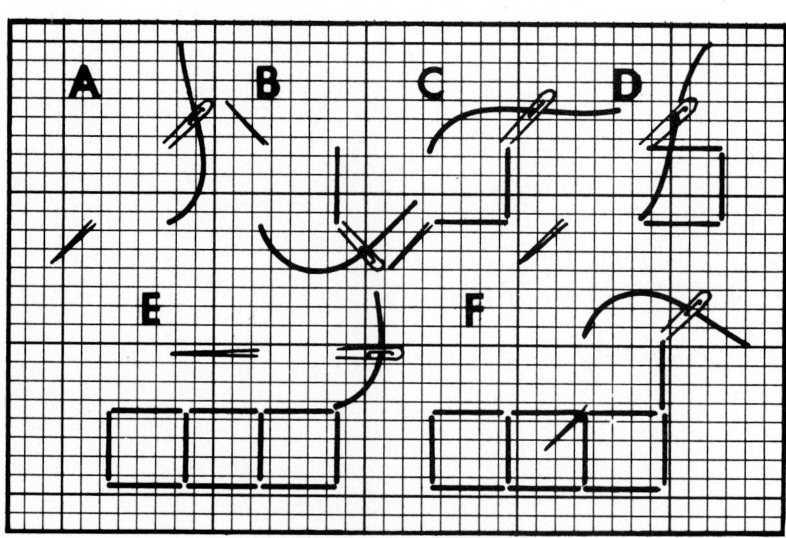

SQUARED EDGING

threads from first row of edging and fray all excess across. Follow diagrams E and F and, working from right to left, repeat across to end of mat making sure step F is pulled more tightly to keep frayed ends bound more tightly. Work edging sequence around entire mat as shown in illustration.

Trim fringe evenly all around. Make four mats.

Turn-of-the-Century Portrait Frames

Turn-of-the-century embroideries, worked with silk floss on linen, are the perfect frames for a cherished photo or a tiny mirror. The embroideries shown were discovered in a New England antique shop.

SIZE: 11⅜" x 13⅜" framed; 10" x 12" mounted.

EQUIPMENT: Paper for patterns. Soft lead pencil. Ruler. Tracing paper. Dressmaker's carbon (tracing) paper. Scissors. Sewing thread. Embroidery and sewing needles. Masking tape. Embroidery hoop or frame. **For Blocking:** Soft wooden surface. Brown wrapping paper. Thumbtacks. Square. Tack hammer. **For Framing:** Single-edged razor blade. Miter box. Backsaw.

MATERIALS: For each: Tightly woven natural-color (dark) embroidery fabric such as linen or Egyptian cotton, 14″ x 14″. Pearl cotton size 5, or six-strand embroidery floss. **For Berry Design:** One skein each of dark red (A), light red (B), light yellow-green (C), dark yellow-green (D). **For Flower Design:** One skein each of pale pink (F), light rose (G), medium rose (H), pale gold (J), dark gold (K). Waterproof felt-tipped ink markers for Berry Design only, dark and medium green. **For Framing:** Thick cardboard 10″ x 12″. Masking tape. Straight pins. Wormy chestnut picture frame molding (rabbeted), 1″ wide, 4½ feet for each (or ready-made frame for 10″ x 12″ picture). Small wire brads or finishing nails. Sobo glue.

DIRECTIONS: Read General Directions and Tips on page 12. Enlarge each pattern by copying on paper ruled in ½″ squares. Trace each enlarged pattern. For flower design, trace top half, swing pattern around, matching center leaves, then complete lower half of design. Place fabric right side up on flat surface; center traced pattern on fabric with carbon between; tape to hold securely. Go over tracing with soft pencil to transfer design to fabric. Remove tracing and carbon. With sharp pencil, go over design lines as necessary. Leave oval area marked, but do not cut out until fabric has been mounted. Mark guidelines with needle and thread 10″ x 12″ around the embroidery area, with design centered; follow threads of the linen and take small running stitches.

To embroider, refer to stitch details on page 15 and follow letters on chart for colors (keyed with colors in "Materials").

For Berry Design: Before working embroidery, color in bow área with medium green ink and leaf center areas with dark green ink. Make all berries in satin stitch; fill in bow knot circles with satin stitch. Make all solid sections of leaves in long and short stitch. Make all fine lines in outline stitch. For bow outline, use pale green; for all leaf stems and veins, use dark green unless otherwise indicated.

For Flower Design: Make all solid sections of leaves and flowers in long and short straight stitches, making the inner edges very irregular. Make all fine lines in outline stitch. For leaf veins, use dark gold and medium rose for lines around flower centers. Using light shade for light flowers and darker shade for dark flowers, make French knot dot in flower centers.

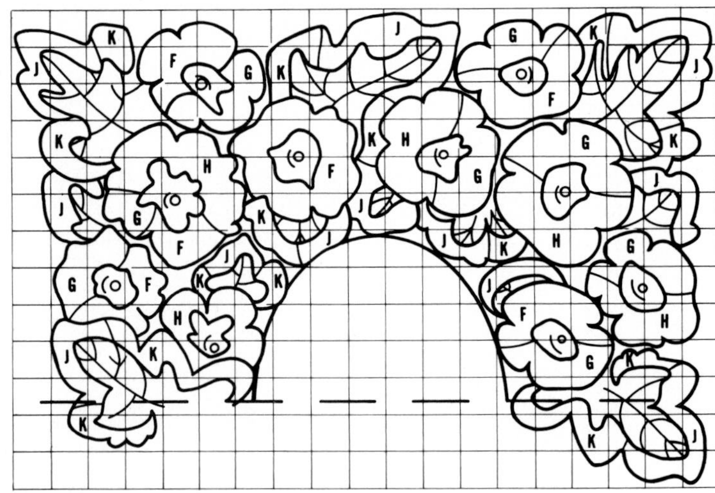

When embroidery is finished, block and mount; see page 14.

Cut oval out of fabric 1″ inside marked lines; clip into edge all around almost to marked line; mark oval area on board; cut out with razor blade. Turn clipped edges over edges of oval to back of board and tape securely all around on back. Tape picture in oval.

To Frame: Measure and mark molding to fit each side of mounted embroidery; cut pieces with mitered corners. Glue frame pieces together, fitting mitered corners well; glue and nail corners.

Fit embroidery in frame; hold in place with brads hammered in on wrong side.

"Sampler" Mirror Frame

A border motif from an Early American sampler is embroidered in cheery reds and greens to frame a mirror. Cross-stitches are worked on an even-weave fabric by counting threads—two threads each way on the fabric, as illustrated in the detail shown. Directions include instructions for framing and for adjusting the design to other-size mirrors.

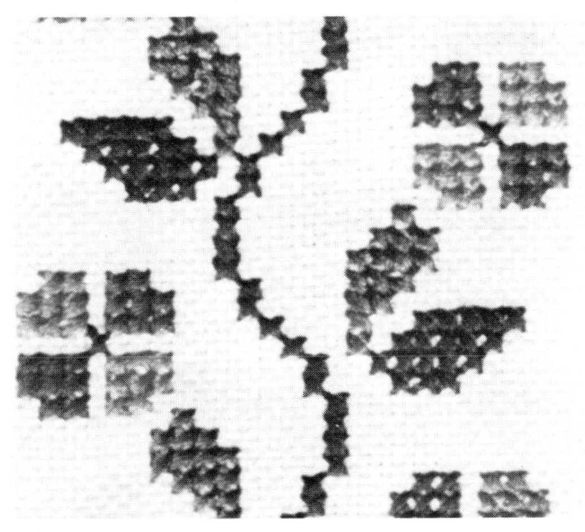

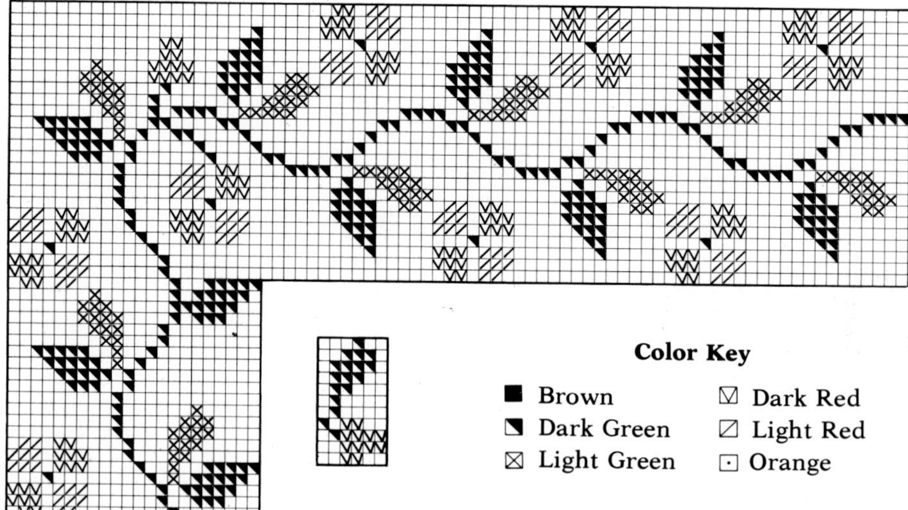

SIZE: 27″ x 30¼″ framed.

EQUIPMENT: Embroidery or tapestry needle. Sewing needle. Scissors. Ruler. **For Framing:** Saw. Miter box. Backsaw. Hammer. Screwdriver. Square. Nail set. Small flat paintbrush. Drill.

MATERIALS: Mirror with wooden frame about 1″ wide and ½″ thick, 22½″ x 19¼″ or desired size. Even-weave fabric (see Note), 33″ x 36″, or size to allow a 6″ border of fabric all around mirror. Six-strand embroidery floss: 3 skeins light red, 3 skeins medium red, 8 skeins dark blue-green, 3 skeins medium yellow-green. Black sewing thread. **For Framing:** Plywood ½″ thick, 26½″ x 29¾″, or size to allow a 3½″ border all around mirror. Half-round molding ½″ wide, 10 ft., or sufficient amount to fit around plywood. Small finishing nails. Eight flat-head wood screws ¾″ long. Small can flat green paint. Walnut varnish-stain. Wood filler. Small screw eyes and wire. Tape.

NOTE: It is important to check carefully the count of the threads both horizontally and vertically before starting work, as sometimes there is a slight variation in the count of the warp and weft threads to the inch. In this case, it is necessary to adjust design area.

DIRECTIONS: Read General Directions and Tips on page 12 and How to Cross-Stitch on page 16. Cut even-weave fabric to a size that will allow a 3½″ border for embroidery and 2½″ for turning back all around mirror frame. To make a guide for embroidery, mark exact outline of mirror frame on the fabric with a line of running stitches, using black sewing thread; measure out 3½″ from this outline and make another line of black running stitches all around. The vine repeat border and corners (see large chart) will fit within this area if you make your crosses 8-to-the-inch and adjust the border design so it will fit a specific length, according to the size of your mirror. Make crosses ⅛″ in size; count the number of threads of fabric in both directions to achieve this size. The full six strands of floss are used in the needle. Each square of chart is one stitch. Start embroidering the vine line only from each corner, working toward center of each side. If the vine does not meet correctly at center, adjust the width of the middle curves, wider or narrower, to fit. Following chart, embroider the flowers and leaves along the vine curves. If an adjustment is made in the middle of a side, in place of the usual flower, embroider a bud or pair of buds on each side and single leaves, following small chart. Near corners, a flower may have to be omitted and a leaf added in its place, or a bud and leaves added on an outer corner curve, to fill an area. Stretch finished embroidery evenly and smoothly over plywood panel. Bring excess fabric to back; tape securely in place.

To frame, measure sides of plywood and with backsaw and miter box, cut half-round molding to fit. Paint molding pieces and mirror frame green. When dry, brush lightly and unevenly with walnut varnish-stain to give an antique look; let dry. Nail molding around plywood; countersink nails and fill holes with wood filler. When dry, touch nail holes with green paint. Center framed mirror on back of plywood and mark outline; remove mirror. Drill two holes at top, bottom, and sides of mirror outline, ¼″ inside line, through plywood. Mark corresponding places on back of mirror frame and drill starting holes in mirror frame. Place mirror on front of embroidered panel and insert screws from back of plywood. Hang with screw eyes, wire.

Silk Desk Set

Green and pink paisleys, embroidered on white silk, make an exquisite five-piece desk set. First, each piece is covered with magenta silk; then the decorative paisley trim is glued in place. The potpourri of embroidery stitches is worked with six-strand cotton floss. The blotter measures 13½" by 22"; the trinket box measures 4¾" by 3⅜".

EQUIPMENT: Tracing paper for patterns. Pencil. Ruler. Scissors. Utility knife (for cutting boards). Steel straight edge. Dressmaker's tracing (carbon) paper and tracing wheel or dry ballpoint pen. Embroidery and sewing needles. Embroidery hoop. Small flat paintbrush for spreading glue.

MATERIALS: Medium and lightweight cardboard. Tightly woven fabric such as medium-weight silk or a fine cotton in a light color and a contrasting dark color (we used silk in off-white and deep pink). Cotton organdy. Six-strand embroidery floss: 6 skeins color A (we used pink); 8 skeins color B (we used green). Glue. **For Padding:** Cotton batting, polyester Fiberfil, or absorbent cotton. Small amount of felt (optional). **For Box:** Octagonal wooden craft box. **For Blotter:** Heavyweight cardboard; blotter paper. **For Pencil Holder:** Cylindrical container, about 4½" high. **For Address Book:** Book measuring about 5¾" x 7¾".

DIRECTIONS: Read General Directions and Tips on page 12. Enlarge paisley patterns by copying on paper ruled in ½" squares. All embroidery is done on the light fabric. Center pattern on right side of the piece of fabric to be embroidered; using dressmaker's carbon tracing paper and tracing wheel, transfer the heavy outlines. Fine lines are guidelines for the height of the longest of the short and long stitches and should be marked by basting. Baste a piece of organdy to wrong side of fabric; insert in embroidery hoop, and embroider following individual directions for color; see stitch details on page 15. Areas marked #1 are worked in featherstitch, #2 is seeding stitch, #3 is French knots, #4 is ermine filling stitch, and #5 is a repeat of six short and long stitches worked as follows: Work one long stitch from marked line to basting. Make three graduated stitches, each one slightly shorter than the last and all starting at marked line. Then make two graduated stitches, each one slightly longer than the last. Repeat the six stitches, beginning with the longest. The innermost heavy line is chain stitch, and the outermost one is outline stitch. Place finished embroidery face down on padded ironing board; steam wrinkles and puckers out gently.

Except for pencil holder, mount embroidered panels as follows: Cut medium-weight cardboard to size indicated in individual directions. Spread and flatten the padding material into a thin layer slightly larger than the cardboard. Dot surface of cardboard with glue near each corner, and place on top of padding; press down lightly. When dry, trim padding to the same size as cardboard. Making sure embroidery remains centered, mark out-

line of cardboard on wrong side of fabric. Cut fabric ½″ outside outline. Place cardboard on wrong side of fabric, padding side down. Pull up fabric margins over to back of cardboard; tape in place temporarily. Check to see that embroidery is centered. Then untape and glue one side at a time, pleating corners as necessary. Let dry.

Cover the object with the dark fabric as directed; let dry. Apply glue to underside of mounted panel, and place on top of object. Weight down with a book, and let dry. Add felt to bottom of box and pencil holder, if desired.

BLOTTER

From heavy cardboard, cut one 13½″ x 22″ piece for main part, two 13½″ x 4″ pieces for the sides. To cover main part, cut 15″ x 23½″ piece of dark fabric; center cardboard on fabric. Turn fabric margins to back and glue in place; let dry. For each side piece, cut 6″ x 15½″ piece of fabric. Center cardboard on top; turn fabric margin to back along one long side only; glue in place. With finished long edge toward center, place side on end of main part; make sure top, bottom, and remaining side edges are even. Turn fabric margins of three sides back to underside of main piece; glue in place. For embroidery, cut two 17″ x 8″ pieces of light fabric. Enlarge and transfer the long pattern as directed above. Transfer the design as given to one fabric piece; embroider areas 1, 2 and 5 of top motif in color A; work the two heavy lines in color B. Reverse the colors for the second motif. Repeat color sequence for the third and fourth motifs. For second side, flop pattern and reverse the entire color sequence of the first side. Cut medium-weight cardboard 3½″ x 13″; finish as directed above and glue to side pieces of blotter. Insert paper cut to fit.

BOX

Cover box top and bottom with dark fabric as follows: Cut two 21½″-long strips, one 6½″ wide for bottom, and one 3½″ wide for top. With brush apply thin layer of glue all around outside of bottom section. Beginning at what will be center back, wrap 6½″-wide strip around outside, with ¾″ of fabric extending beyond bottom edge; fold overlapping end under ½″ at center back. Apply glue to bottom and fold excess fabric under, pleating as necessary for a smooth surface. Apply glue to rim, insides, and ½″ around inside bottom. Press fabric to inside. Cut a 4″ x 5¼″ piece of matching fabric; fold under ¼″ all around. Apply glue to inside bottom of box and place fabric on glue. Repeat with box top, with ¾″ extending at top instead of bottom.

For embroidery, cut light fabric 8½″ x 10″. Enlarge and transfer the pattern as directed above. (**Note:** The dash line on pattern is for cutting cardboard; do not transfer to fabric. The outside heavy line and inner fine line are for short and long straight stitch embroidery.) Work areas 1, 2, and 5 of one motif in color A; work the two heavy lines in color B. Reverse the colors for second motif. Work border in color B. Following dash line of pattern, cut cardboard. Finish as directed.

BOOK

To cover book: Measure height and width of front and back covers together while book is closed (book measures wider when closed, because of flexible binding at center). Mark this size on wrong side of dark fabric. Cut out fabric 1″ larger all around. Place open book on fabric, face up; turn fabric margins along marked outline of short edges to inside covers; glue in place. Close book to make sure you have allowed enough play. Open book, and turn remaining fabric margins to inside covers; if necessary, trim fabric at center binding to fit. Glue in place; let dry. Cut two lightweight cardboard pieces ⅛″ smaller all around than inside cover. Cut a piece of light fabric ½″ larger all around than cardboard; glue to cardboard as before. Glue covered cardboard to inside covers.

For embroidery, cut fabric about 2″ larger all around than outside front cover. Transfer the paisley pattern for box in reverse; omit lines for border, and reverse the colors when embroidering. Work the border to fit the size and shape of the book. Cut medium-weight cardboard ¼″ smaller all around than front cover; finish as directed.

PENCIL CUP

To cover container: Add about 3″ to height of container and 1″ to circumference; cut dark fabric this size. Apply glue to outside of container; wrap fabric around with ½″ extending at bottom; fold the overlapping end under ½″. Apply glue to bottom, and fold excess fabric under. Apply glue to inside of container; neatly fold the excess fabric at top to inside of cup.

Add 4″ to circumference and to height of container; cut fabric to be embroidered this size. Transfer any single motif with areas 3 and 4, and embroider as directed. Add border of short and long straight stitches on long sides. Add ½″ to circumference of container, and subtract ¼″ from container's height; cut lightweight cardboard this size. Center cardboard on wrong side of embroidery, and mark outline. Cut embroidered fabric 2″ longer on two long sides and one short end. Glue, as above, omitting padding. Glue to container, overlapping ends at back. Hold in place with string or rubber band until glue has dried.

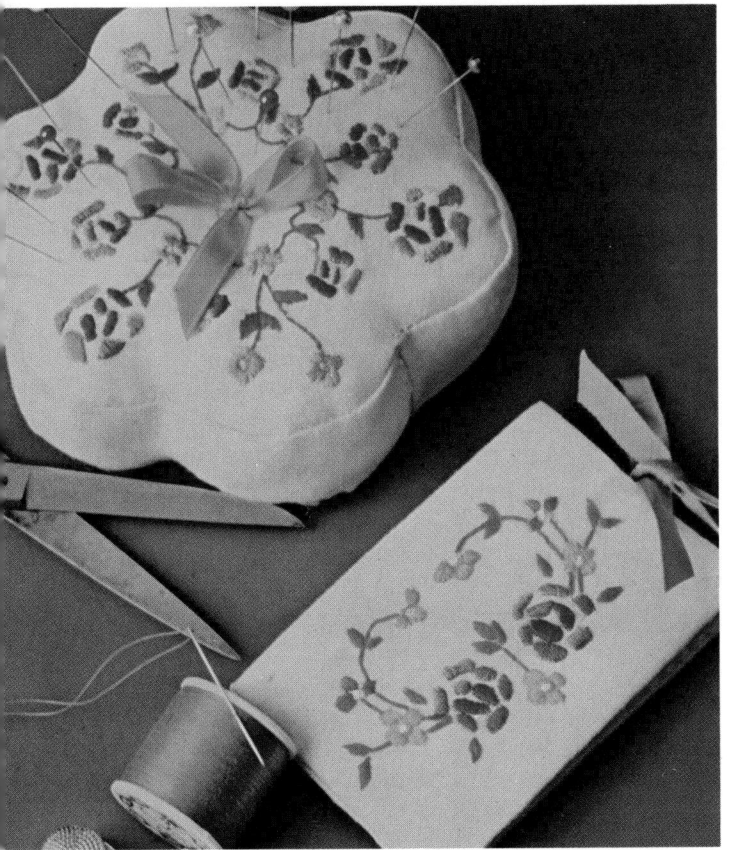

Sprigged Pincushion and Needlebook Set

A charming pair for the embroiderer and a lovely gift idea. The pincushion is worked in embroidery floss on muslin; the needlebook has felt "leaves," and ribbon bows add the final touch.

EQUIPMENT: Tracing paper. Pencil. Blue dressmaker's tracing carbon. Embroidery hoop, needle, and scissors. Regular scissors. Ruler. Pins. Pinking shears.

MATERIALS: Unbleached muslin, 8″ x 18″ for pincushion; 6″ x 8″ for needlebook. Off-white sewing thread. Six-strand embroidery floss: one skein each of the following: yellow, rose pink, green, deep purple, medium purple, lavender, pale blue. Pale green satin ribbon ⅜″ wide, 1 yd. Stiff white cardboard. Small amount of white felt. Glue. Absorbent cotton for stuffing.

DIRECTIONS: Read General Directions and Tips on page 12. Trace patterns for pincushion and needlebook; complete half-pattern for pincushion indicated by dash line. To complete pattern for needlebook, flop pattern (matching center) for right side of design; do not repeat center.

With dressmaker's tracing carbon, transfer design to fabric as indicated in individual directions. Place fabric in embroidery hoop. Referring to stitch details on page 15, work all flowers, flower centers, and leaves in satin stitch with three strands of floss in needle. Work all stems in backstitch with two strands of floss in needle. Use two shades of purple and lavender for sections of larger flowers; use pink and blue for petals of smaller flowers; use yellow for flower centers. Use green for leaves, stems. Finish following individual directions.

PINCUSHION

Using pattern, mark and cut two scalloped pieces of muslin, adding ¼″ all around for seam allowances; cut one scalloped piece of cardboard same size as pattern. Work embroidery design on one piece of muslin.

To assemble, cut strip of muslin 2″ x 17″. With right sides facing and making ¼″ seams, pin one long edge of strip to edges of embroidered piece; sew all around. Repeat with other scalloped muslin piece at remaining long edge of strip, leaving a 6″ opening at point where narrow ends of strip meet. Clip into seam allowances all around. Turn to right side. Insert cardboard, making sure it is flat against bottom piece of muslin. Stuff fully with absorbent cotton. Turn edges of openings in and slip-stitch closed. Cut 10″ length of ribbon. Knot one end of length of full six strands of floss in a needle; insert needle into center bottom of pincushion and out through center top. Catch center of ribbon, and insert needle back into pincushion (just 1/16″ away); bring needle out through bottom; knot. Tie bow.

NEEDLEBOOK

Cut pieces of muslin each 4¾″ x 6¼″. Mark off 1″ margin on each. Transfer and work embroidery on one marked-off area.

To assemble: With right sides facing, place muslin pieces together; sew across one end on marked line 2¾″. Cut two pieces of cardboard 2¾″ x 4¼″. Place each on wrong side of muslin within marked area. Fold 1″ margins, mitering corners, to wrong side and glue to cardboard. Using pinking shears, cut two white felt needle pages 2¼″ x 4½″. Cut two pieces of cardboard 2¼″ x 3¾″. Cut two pieces of ribbon 6″ long. Glue ¾″ of one end of one felt page to one end of cardboard; fold felt over to other side of cardboard. Catching in ½″ of ribbon at center of outside end, glue cardboard side to one wrong side of book with felt page attached at center. Repeat at other side.

Nostalgic Bouquet Album Cover

A bouquet of embroidered flowers—reminiscent of pressed blossoms—covers an album or memory book with sweet nostalgia. Soft pink fabric provides the perfect background for these rainbow-colored flowers embroidered with Persian or tapestry yarns in four basic stitches—chain, outline, lazy daisy, and French knots. The design, 7¾″ across, would make a wonderful framed picture, too!

DESIGN SIZE: 7¾″ x 8″.

EQUIPMENT: Tracing paper. Pencil. Dressmaker's tracing (carbon) paper. Dry ballpoint pen or hard-lead pencil. Ruler. Scissors. Sewing needle. Masking tape. Embroidery hoop. Large-eyed embroidery needle. **For Blocking:** Soft wooden surface. Brown paper. Square. Thumbtacks. Towel.

MATERIALS: Coarsely woven fabric such as heavy linen or rayon, 36″wide, about 1 yard. Sewing thread. Any type of medium-weight yarns such as Persian, tapestry, acrylic, in desired colors (a variety of leftover yarns from other projects would create interesting and different textures and would be very suitable; we used four shades of green; three shades each of orange, red, and mauve; two shades each of pink and light blue; yellow, gold, white, purple, and violet). Two pieces of heavy cardboard each the size of book to be covered (9″ x 11″ for phone book). Two pieces of thin foam the same size as cardboard. Glue.

DIRECTIONS: Read General Directions and Tips on page 12. Design is perfect for phone book cover generally 9″ x 11″ or album 9″ x 12″. Cut piece of fabric the size of book cover, plus about 5″ extra on all sides. Mark outline of design area in center of fabric with pins. With needle and thread, make running stitches along this outline.

Trace complete pattern. Place tracing in center of outline on right side of fabric; place carbon between. Go over design with dry pen or hard pencil to transfer it to fabric. Remove tracing and carbon. Go over any lines, if necessary, with pencil to sharpen lines.

Place fabric in hoop. To work embroidery, refer to embroidery stitch details on page 15 and Stitch Key, and also to color illustration for shading. Embroider the roses (smallest circular flowers) with rows of chain stitch as shown in Fig. 1, using a different shade of yarn in the center area of each but continuing the same circular chain stitch. Work the stems in outline stitch and continue into the leaves, filling leaves solidly in outline stitch as shown in Fig. 2. Embroider the large circular flowers with concentric rows of lazy daisy stitch as shown in Fig. 3. Fill the centers of these flowers with French knots. Work petaled flowers in lazy daisy stitch, remaining solid areas in satin stitch and single lines in straight stitch.

When embroidery is finished, block according to directions on page 14.

To make book cover, glue foam onto one surface of each piece of cardboard: let dry. Place foam surface of one cardboard piece down on wrong side of fabric, centering it over embroidered area. Pull fabric edges over to other side and glue securely. For back cover, repeat with plain fabric, cardboard, and foam the same size as front cover. For inside covers, cut two more pieces of fabric the size of covers; press and glue edges under 1″. Cut a strip of fabric 5″ x 16″; fold raw lengthwise edges to center on one side; press and glue. Make another in same manner. To make loops, cut piece of fabric about 4″ x ¾″. With wrong sides facing, fold in half lengthwise; stitch together along length only, ¼″ in from raw edges. Turn to right side and fold in half; tack ends together. Make three more in same manner for two pairs of back loops. Sew two loops to wrong

Stitch Key
1 Outline Stitch
2 Lazy Daisy Stitch
3 Satin Stitch
4 Straight Stitch
5 Chain Stitch
6 French Knot

side of each inside cover along one side for back edge of book, placing them about 2½″ from top and bottom. Place the 16″ folded strips across right side of inside covers 2½″ in from edges opposite loops. Fold 2″ ends of strips to wrong side of inside covers and stitch across ends to secure. Glue inside covers on center of wrong side of outer covers with ends of each strip and loop ends between. Be sure pieces are glued securely; weight down until dry. Slip book covers through fabric cover strips. Tie back loops together with yarn.

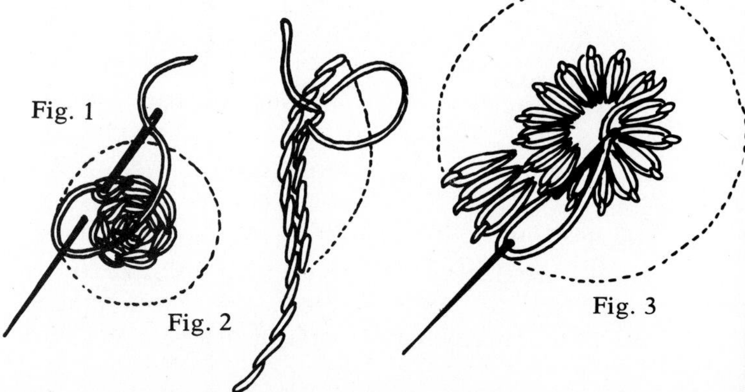

Floral Embroidered Screen

This dramatic folding screen is emblazoned with big, bright floral motifs for on-the-spot elegance. Each motif, 13″ wide, is made with craft yarn couched on fabric, using a conventional sewing machine.

FINISHED SIZE: 45″ x 8″.

EQUIPMENT: Saw. Pencil. Ruler. Hammer. Screwdriver. Yardstick. Scissors. Staple gun and staples. Paper for patterns. Tracing paper. Dressmaker's tracing (carbon) paper. Dry ball-point pen. Straight-stitch (or zigzag) sewing machine. #11 sewing needles. Tweezers.

MATERIALS: Stock lumber for frame: 1″ x 2″, six pieces, each 8′ long; nine pieces, each 11½″ long. Pressed board, three pieces, each 8′ x 15″. Double-action screen hinges with screws, six. 3″ finishing nails. Fabric: tightly woven homespun cotton, three pieces, each 21″ wide x 102″ long. Acrylic rug yarn, 70-yd. skeins, one skein each, in colors indicated on Color Key. Fine nylon thread, size 10-15. Any color sewing thread. Scraps of firm fabric and yarn for practice.

DIRECTIONS: Enlarge pattern by copying on paper ruled in 1″ squares. Trace enlarged design six times lengthwise, spacing motifs approximately 4½″ apart and reversing design for every other one, as pictured. Transfer design to fabric, using dressmaker's carbon and dry ball-point pen.

Remove presser foot from machine; lower feed dog (teeth) or cover with a plate; turn stitch dial to "0" or fine; loosen top tension to 1½-2; use bobbin tension as for regular sewing; thread needle with invisible nylon thread; use any color sewing thread in bobbin. The yarn is laid on the fabric following the design (use tweezers to guide yarn). As the fabric is moved to form the desired stitch, the up-and-down movement of the nylon-threaded needle secures the yarn to the fabric. The top nylon thread cannot be seen and the bobbin thread does not show.

See stitch description and details. When stitching one layer of yarn on top of another, let the threaded needle catch the yarn lightly at several points. If stitched down too heavily, the three-dimensional effect may be lost and the needle may break.

Before working on actual fabric, practice on scraps of fabric.

FOLDING SCREEN: Screen is made of three 8′ x 15″ panels attached with hinges. To make frame for each panel, nail three 11½″ long 1″ x 2″ pieces of lumber between two 96″-long pieces: one flush with top edges, one flush with bottom edges, and one across center. For front, nail a piece of pressed board to each frame.

To attach embroidery to frame, stretch fabric over edges around perimeter of board; staple to frame all around. Attach hinges.

STITCH DESCRIPTION AND DETAILS

A. Outline or Running Stitch: Used for stems, straight lines, or curves. Attach one end of yarn at beginning point of design. Using tweezers to guide yarn, stitch lightly along yarn, following design outline.

Aa. Outline Filling: Continue making rows in same manner as outline stitch, but move inward toward center, following contour.

B. Lazy Daisy Continuous Loops: Used for petals and centers. With a long strand, stitch end of yarn at base of petal (1); loop yarn clockwise to form petal; attach yarn again at base. Make succeeding loops the same way (2). (When yarn is looped the same way for each loop, flower will lie smoothly.) Repeat until you have made a multiple-loop flower; cut off excess yarn.

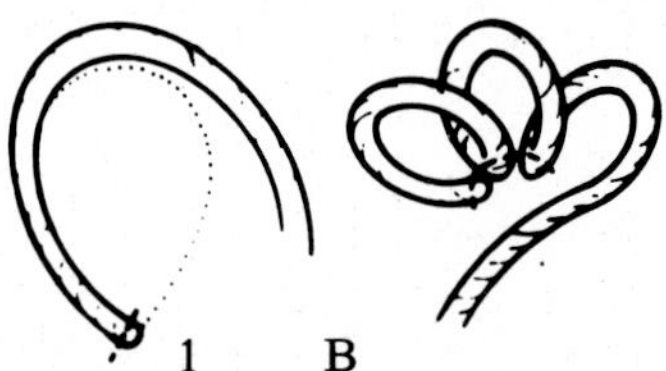

C. Satin Stitch (Filled-In Stitch): Used for leaves. Sew one end of yarn at the left-hand side of the leaf near the base (1); move fabric until the needle is on the opposite side (right) of the leaf. Bring the yarn over to the needle; stitch down. Move fabric again so needle is at left-hand side. Bring yarn back to left-hand side; stitch down. Make sure yarn rows lie close together. Repeat, following design shape (2), until leaf is filled in.

To make a vein on leaf, stitch along center point to base with nylon thread.

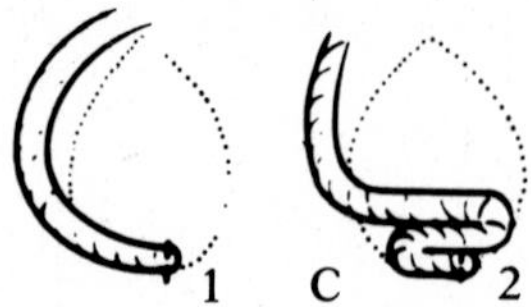

D. Single Lazy Daisies: Used for petals. With tweezers, hold down one end of yarn at the base of one flower petal. Stitch across end to secure (1). With threaded needle only, stitch down center of the petal to point; leave needle in fabric; bring yarn around needle. Holding yarn down with tweezers, stitch across yarn at point of petal (1). With threaded needle only, stitch back to base; bring yarn down to base; stitch across to secure. Without cutting yarn, go to next petal (2); repeat until flower is completed.

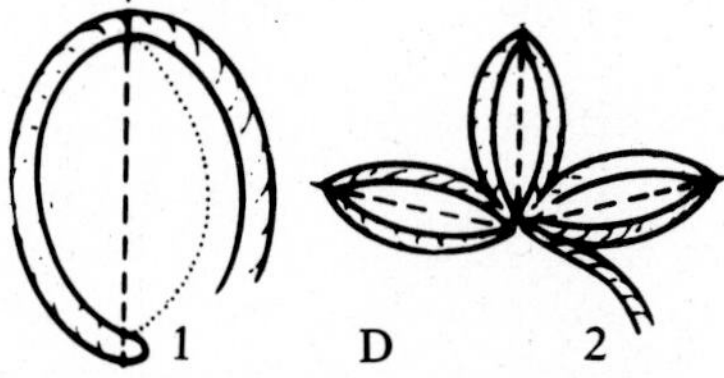

E. French Knot: Used for flower centers and berries, these are actually small loops. With tweezers, hold down one end of yarn; sew across to secure. Use tweezers to hold up a small loop; sew across yarn again. Without cutting yarn, make another loop and stitch again. Repeat until area is filled with small loops placed side by side; cut excess yarn.

Make one French knot for each berry.

Color Key

1 Olive Green
2 Pale Green
3 Royal Blue
4 Navy Blue
5 Light Blue
6 Persimmon
7 Orange
8 Bright Yellow
9 Gold
10 Dark Green

Needlepoint

GENERAL DIRECTIONS

NEEDLEPOINT

"Needlepoint" is the general term for an embroidery stitch used to cover canvas, as well as for the finished embroidered piece. When this stitch is worked on canvas 20-meshes-to-the-inch or smaller, it is called petit point. When worked on 14- to 18-to-the-inch mesh, it is called simply needlepoint. On 8- to 12-to-the-inch mesh, it is called gros point. Larger meshes, 5- and 7-to-the-inch, have been used in the past for making rugs and are sometimes referred to as large gros point. However, we call it quick point.

NEEDLEPOINT STITCH

The basic needlepoint stitch can be worked in three methods: half cross-stitch, continental stitch, and diagonal stitch. Each method makes an identical stitch on the front of the canvas, but the coverage on the back is different, thus affecting the wearing quality of the finished piece. The half cross-stitch covers the least on the back and therefore should be used only on pieces where the wearing quality is not a factor. It uses less yarn than the other two methods. The continental stitch covers the back well, with a padding of longer diagonal stitches, making it durable and practical for pillows. The diagonal stitch makes the best covering on the back, forming a basket weave that reinforces the canvas; this stitch should be used for rugs or chair seats. See details.

HALF CROSS-STITCH

Start at upper left corner of canvas. Bring needle to front of canvas at point that will be the bottom of the first stitch. The needle is in a vertical position when making stitch (see figure). Always work from left to right; turn work around for return row.

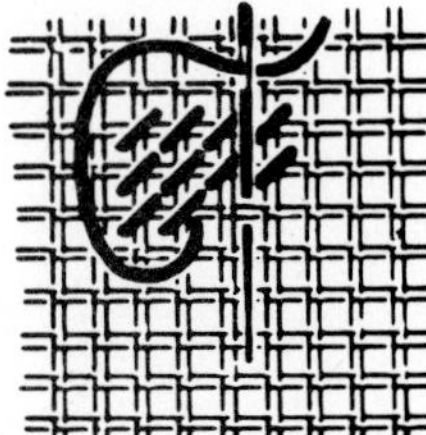

CONTINENTAL STITCH

Start at upper right corner and work across to left. Bring needle out to front of canvas at point that will be bottom of first stitch; needle goes under two meshes of canvas, diagonally, as shown. Details show placement and direction of needle; turn work around for return row. Always work from right to left.

DIAGONAL STITCH

Begin by tying a knot at end of yarn and putting needle through middle of canvas to back, diagonally down from upper right-hand corner of work. Never turn work; hold it in the same position. **Step 1:** Bring needle up at A, down through B and out through C. **Step 2:** Needle in D, out through E. **Step 3:** Needle in F, out through G. **Step 4:** Start next row in at H and out through I.

Step 5: You have now worked four stitches. Stitch No. 5 is your next stitch. It extends from space I to A (see Step 4 detail). Complete the stitches to 10 on diagram in numerical order to finish the diagonal row. Stitch No. 11 starts the next row upward.

After starting row going up, needle is horizontal for each stitch and goes under two meshes of canvas. Needle slants diagonally to begin new row down, as in Step 1. Going down, needle is always vertical, as in Step 2, and goes under two meshes of canvas; and again, when the last stitch is made, the needle slants diagonally to begin next row up, as in Step 3.

Work as far as knot; cut off knot. All other strands of yarn may be started and ended by running through work on back.

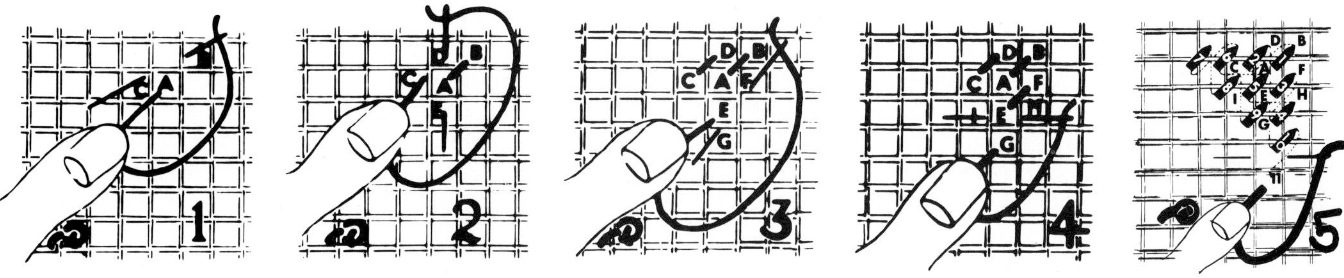

LEFT-HANDED

If you are left-handed, turn the stitch details upside down and start at lower left corner rather than upper right for continental and diagonal methods. Work from left to right. Generally speaking, any canvas stitch can be worked left-handed in this way.

Instructions for other needlepoint stitches are given with individual projects in this chapter.

STARTING YOUR NEEDLEPOINT

When starting a canvas piece, allow at least a 2″ margin of plain canvas all around the background area. Cut canvas in square or rectangular shape, even if working a circle. Before beginning, bind all raw edges of canvas, using masking tape, adhesive tape, or a double-fold bias binding—or turn the raw edges over and whipstitch to keep from raveling. The selvage edges of the canvas are the sides of your piece. It is vital that the work not be turned sideways, so mark top with a colored thread. Mark center of each side of canvas at edge. Cut yarn strands in 18″ lengths (do not break yarn, as this will stretch it). To thread yarn, double it over the end of the needle and slip it off, holding it tightly and as close as possible to the fold. Push the flattened, folded end through the needle eye and pull yarn through. To start, leave 1″ of yarn at back of canvas and cover this as the work proceeds. Work needlepoint in method desired, being careful not to pull yarn too tightly. Hold thumb on yarn near stitch until you have pulled yarn through the canvas, then lift thumb and pull yarn gently into place. To avoid thin places in work, drop yarn now and then and let it untwist. When close to the end of a strand, fasten yarn by weaving through a few stitches on back of work. Immediately clip ends close to avoid tangles. When a mistake is made, pluck out yarn with blunt end of needle, or run needle under stitch and snip yarn with embroidery scissors close to needle. Do not reuse pulled-out yarn. If not using a frame, roll canvas as you work, from the bottom up or the top down, for ease in handling.

CLEANING AND BLOCKING

Try to keep your needlepoint clean; store it in a plastic bag between work sessions. If your piece should need a little freshening, however, simply brush over the surface with a clean cloth dipped in carbon tetrachloride or other cleaning fluid. Colors will brighten and return to their original look.

No matter how badly a piece is out of shape, it may be blocked squarely. Block needlepoint pieces with the bound edges still intact. Do not trim canvas until piece is blocked.

Cover a soft-wood surface with brown paper. Mark canvas outline on this paper for guide, being sure that corners are square. Mark center of each side on canvas. Mark center of each side on guidelines. Place the needlepoint, right side down, over the guide unless piece has been worked with raised stitches; in this case, piece should be blocked right side up. Match center marks of canvas and guide on each side; tack canvas to board at each center mark. Stretch upper right and left corners to match guide; tack. Stretch each lower corner and tack in place. Working from center of each side to corners, fasten canvas to board, placing tacks inside bound edges of canvas and ½″ to ¾″ apart. Be careful to stretch canvas evenly out to guidelines.

If you are not sure the yarn is colorfast, sprinkle salt over needlepoint piece generously. Wet thoroughly with cold water by sponging water completely over needlepoint and canvas. Let needlepoint dry in a horizontal position. If work was badly warped out of shape, it may have to be restretched, wet, and dried again.

YARNS AND CANVAS

In general, you can use one strand of 3-ply Persian wool on canvas 18- to 22-meshes-to-the inch. Use two strands of Persian wool on 14- to 16-mesh canvas. Use one strand of tapestry wool or all three strands of Persian wool on 10- to 12-mesh canvas. For larger mesh canvas, use rug yarn or at least two strands of tapestry wool. Canvas and weights of wool vary, so it is important always to experiment with the wool in relation to the canvas, to be sure the canvas will be covered but not crowded. If possible, use wool and canvas made by the same manufacturer, as they will be coordinated.

NEEDLES

A blunt tapestry needle is always used. Needles range in size from fairly fine to the large rug needles. The needle to use with each yarn should have an eye large enough to accommodate the yarn, but not larger than needed.

ESTIMATING THE AMOUNT OF YARN

Select the type of yarn best suited to the mesh of your canvas. Work a 1″ square and note the amount of yarn used. Figure the number of square inches to be covered by each color in your design, then multiply by the amount used to work the 1″ square. This gives you the approximate yardage for each color. To figure the number of skeins needed, divide the yardage needed by the number of yards in a skein.

HOW TO FOLLOW A CHART

Each square of a graph chart represents one stitch on the blank canvas. A different symbol is used for each color of the design; follow the color key for color represented by each symbol on chart.

To follow a design from a chart, start at top right corner when working in continental or diagonal stitch and work background to beginning of design area. Then work the design area, following chart and filling in the background as you go. Work areas of one color in rows as much as possible. Single or scattered stitches of one color are worked as they come.

HOW TO MOUNT PICTURES

After canvas has been blocked, stretch it over heavy cardboard or plywood cut the same size as worked portion of canvas. Use heavy cardboard for small pictures (12″ or less); for larger pictures and panels, use ¼″ plywood. If cardboard is used, hold canvas in place with pins pushed through canvas into edge of cardboard. If canvas is mounted on plywood, use carpet tacks. Push pins or tacks only partway into edge; check needlepoint to make sure rows of stitches are straight. Carefully hammer in pins or tacks the rest of the way. Using a large-eyed needle and heavy thread, lace loose edges of canvas over back of cardboard or plywood to hold taut; lace across width, then length of picture.

Frame mounted picture as desired.

UPHOLSTERY PIECES

In order to work needlepoint only in the area of the canvas that will show after the piece has been upholstered, it is necessary to make a pattern. It is important in time and money saved and the appearance of the finished upholstery to work only the necessary area of canvas. Remember to allow at least 2″ margin of canvas around pattern for blocking.

To make a muslin pattern, use a piece of muslin a little larger than the area of a seat, for instance of a chair, to be upholstered. Mark a vertical and horizontal line at center. Draw corresponding center lines on chair seat. Place muslin on chair, matching lines. Beginning at center, pin muslin to seat along lines, Fig. 1, spacing pins 3″ apart. Slash muslin to fit around back posts and tuck it down. Pin corners to make miters if necessary for smoothness.

Mark all around lower edge of chair seat; mark around back posts, reaching down into tucked-in area; mark on both sides of the mitered corners; make a line to indicate top area of seat to be used in placing design for needlepoint. Remove muslin from chair and pin down on a board with threads straight. You will find that despite great care, the shape of the muslin is slightly irregular. Make a perfectly symmetrical paper pattern from muslin version, making sure measurements check with chair seat. Mark horizontal and vertical lines and outline of top area. Cut out paper pattern, Fig. 2.

Mark center horizontal and vertical lines on canvas, Fig. 3. Place pattern on canvas, matching lines. Mark pattern outline on canvas. Save paper pattern to use later as a guide in blocking needlepoint piece.

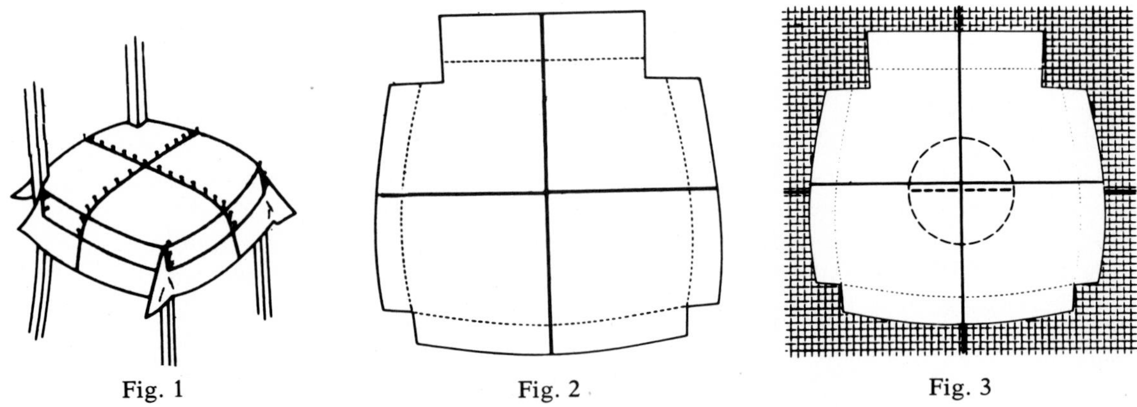

Fig. 1 Fig. 2 Fig. 3

HOW TO MAKE A PILLOW

If foam rubber form is used, the finished needlepoint should be exactly the size of the foam rubber. If a pillow form of kapok, feathers, or similar material is used, the finished needlepoint should be about ¼″ smaller all around.

Trim the canvas around blocked needlepoint piece to 1″. Turn canvas margins to back and whip to back of needlepoint. Cut fabric back with ½″ seam allowance all around. Turn in seam allowance and whip in place. Whip needlepoint top to fabric back around three sides. Insert pillow form and whip third side closed. Slip-stitch a twisted cord (see page 416) over seams.

For a boxed pillow, work boxing strips in needlepoint. Trim canvas edges and turn back as for pillow top. Join boxing pieces to top by whipping together at right angles; whip corners of boxing pieces together, matching rows of needlepoint. Sew fabric back to edges of three sides of boxing; insert pillow form and sew fourth side of boxing to fabric back.

"Patchwork" Flower Sampler

Each petal is worked in a different geometric pattern, using a marvelous variety of vibrant hues and novelty needlepoint stitches. The background is a solid-color stem stitch. The multicolored frame echoes the flower's colors and gives a modern touch to a traditional look. The design measures 9" x 11" and is worked in Persian yarn on 10-mesh-to-the-inch canvas.

SIZE: 13" x 15".

EQUIPMENT: Masking tape. Tapestry needle. Scissors. Pencil. **For Blocking:** Thumbtacks. Soft wooden surface. Brown wrapping paper. Square. Ruler. **For Framing:** Staple gun. Hammer.

MATERIALS: Needlepoint canvas, 10-mesh-to-the-inch, 18" x 20". Persian yarn (8.8-yard skeins): one skein each magenta, fuchsia, yellow, turquoise, light turquoise, pale yellow, yellow-orange, celery green, pale pink, dark blue; two skeins olive green; 15 skeins very light green. Piece of ¼" plywood, 13" x 15". Wooden picture frame with 13" x 15" rabbet. Striped fabric in colors matching yarn (optional). All-purpose glue. Staples. Brads.

DIRECTIONS: Read General Directions on page 90. Mark outline of picture 13" x 15", allowing about a 2½" margin of canvas all around. Following chart, work the design first, then fill in background. Refer to stitch details, page 90–91; work design in continental or diagonal stitch, except as directed below.

Area # 1: Work a single cross-stitch in center of light turquoise squares.

Area # 2: Work center area (yellow-orange and turquoise) in mosaic stitch variation. Use turquoise for long stitches, and yellow-orange for short stitches.

Color Key
- Yellow
- Magenta
- Fuchsia
- Pale Yellow
- Turquoise
- Light Turquoise
- Yellow-Orange
- Olive Green
- Celery Green
- Pale Pink
- Dark Blue

Area #3: Work the magenta stitches that fall on the turquoise lines in cross-stitch.

Area #4: Work padded half-star in each square using pale yellow and yellow-orange.

Area #5: Make French knots, following detail on page 139, with magenta yarn in center of light turquoise squares, twisting yarn around needle twice.

Area #6: Work entire turquoise area in continental stitch, alternating the direction of stitch every vertical row, following chart.

Background: Work entire background in very light green, using the stem stitch. To work stitch, turn canvas so design is sideways.

Block needlepoint (see page 92) and mount over the plywood, using staples to secure excess canvas to back.

Framing: Cut fabric into four strips, large enough to cover front and sides of frame; glue to frame, mitering fabric corners. Let dry. Insert mounted needlepoint in covered frame; secure with small brads driven partially into inside back edges of frame around all four sides.

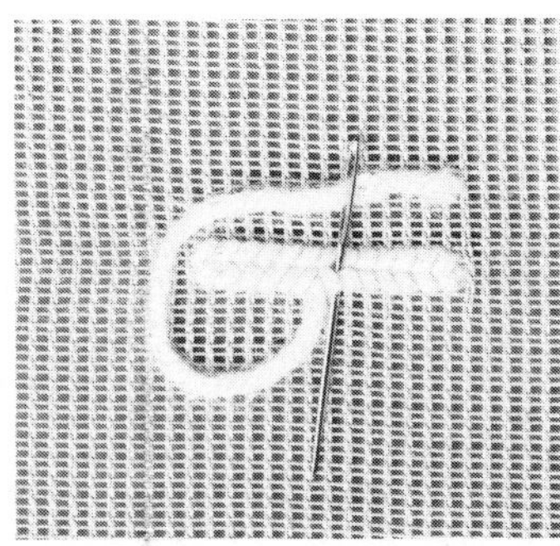

CROSS-STITCH: Work a horizontal row of diagonal stitches over one mesh. Then go back and work diagonal stitches in opposite direction, completing the crosses. When working isolated cross-stitches, complete each cross separately.

MOSAIC STITCH VARIATION (with two colors): Starting at lower right, work diagonal rows of diagonal stitches over one mesh, working upward and to the left. Then work diagonal rows of diagonal stitches between them, going over two meshes.

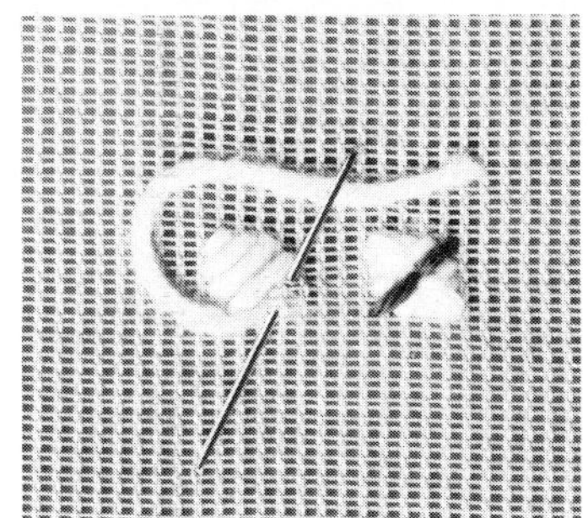

PADDED HALF-STAR: Starting in the upper left corner, work diagonal stitches from left to right over first one mesh, then two meshes, then three meshes, skip the space where four meshes would be worked, work over three meshes, then two, then one. From the center mesh, work two diagonal stitches over two meshes, in opposite direction over first stitches. From center mesh, use contrasting color to work two diagonal stitches over two open meshes in same direction as first stitches.

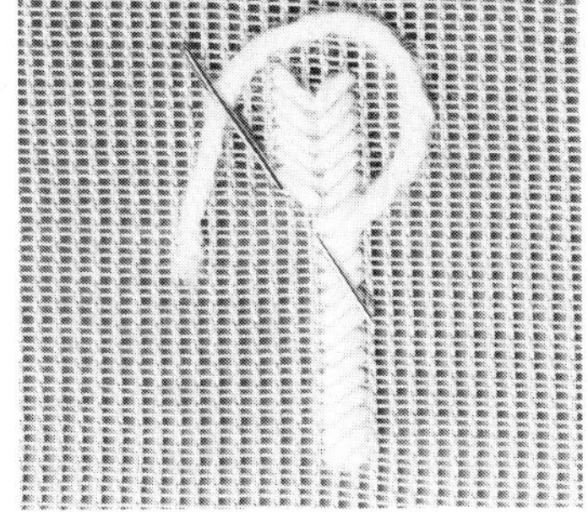

STEM STITCH: Work diagonal stitches from the top to the bottom, over two meshes of canvas each way; make each stitch one mesh below last. Work the second row in diagonal stitches in opposite direction, with lower end of stitches in same meshes as first row. To square off beginning or end of row, work a diagonal stitch over one mesh.

Embroidery Sampler in Needlepoint

Here is a traditional embroidery motif worked in tapestry yarn on 10-mesh-to-the-inch canvas. The picture measures 14" x 18".

EQUIPMENT: Masking tape. Tape. Tapestry needle. Pencil. **For Blocking:** Thumbtacks. Soft wooden surface. Brown wrapping paper. Ruler. Square.

MATERIALS: Needlepoint canvas, 10-mesh-to-the-inch, 19" x 23". Tapestry yarn, 8-yard skeins: 4 skeins coral; 2 skeins pink; 2 skeins fuchsia; 2 skeins purple; 2 skeins red; 2 skeins blue; 2 skeins rust; 1 skein orange; 5 skeins light green; 3 skeins medium green; 1 skein dark olive green; 28 skeins gold. **For Framing:** Heavy mounting cardboard, 14″ x 18″. Straight pins. Frame, 14″ x 18″ rabbet size.

DIRECTIONS: Read General Directions on page 90 for working a needlepoint piece. Mark size of picture, 14″ x 18″, on canvas, leaving 2½″ margins.

Starting at upper right corner of marked area, work picture, using illustration on page opposite as guide.

Block and mount picture, following directions, pages 92–93. Frame as desired.

Alphabet Sampler

This traditional alphabet design is worked in rich contemporary colors, with fruit motifs between the lines and all around. It is worked entirely in the simple needlepoint stitch on 10-mesh-to-the-inch canvas.

SIZE: 17″ x 19″.

EQUIPMENT: Masking tape. Ruler. Pencil. Scissors. Tapestry needle. **For Blocking:** Soft wooden surface. Brown wrapping paper. Square.

MATERIALS: Needlepoint canvas 10-mesh-to-the-inch, 22″ x 24″. Tapestry wool: gray-blue, 35 skeins; bright green, 4 skeins; orange, 4 skeins; watermelon, 2 skeins; fuchsia, 2 skeins; light yellow, 1 skein; gold, 1 skein. **For Mounting:** Plywood, ¼″ thick, 17″ x 19″.

DIRECTIONS: Read General Directions on page 90. Mark outline of sampler 17″ x 19″ on canvas with pencil, allowing 2½″ margin all around. Use either continental or diagonal stitch, with one strand of tapestry yarn in needle. Following chart, work design; fill in background as you go.

Block and mount according to directions on pages 92–93. Frame as desired.

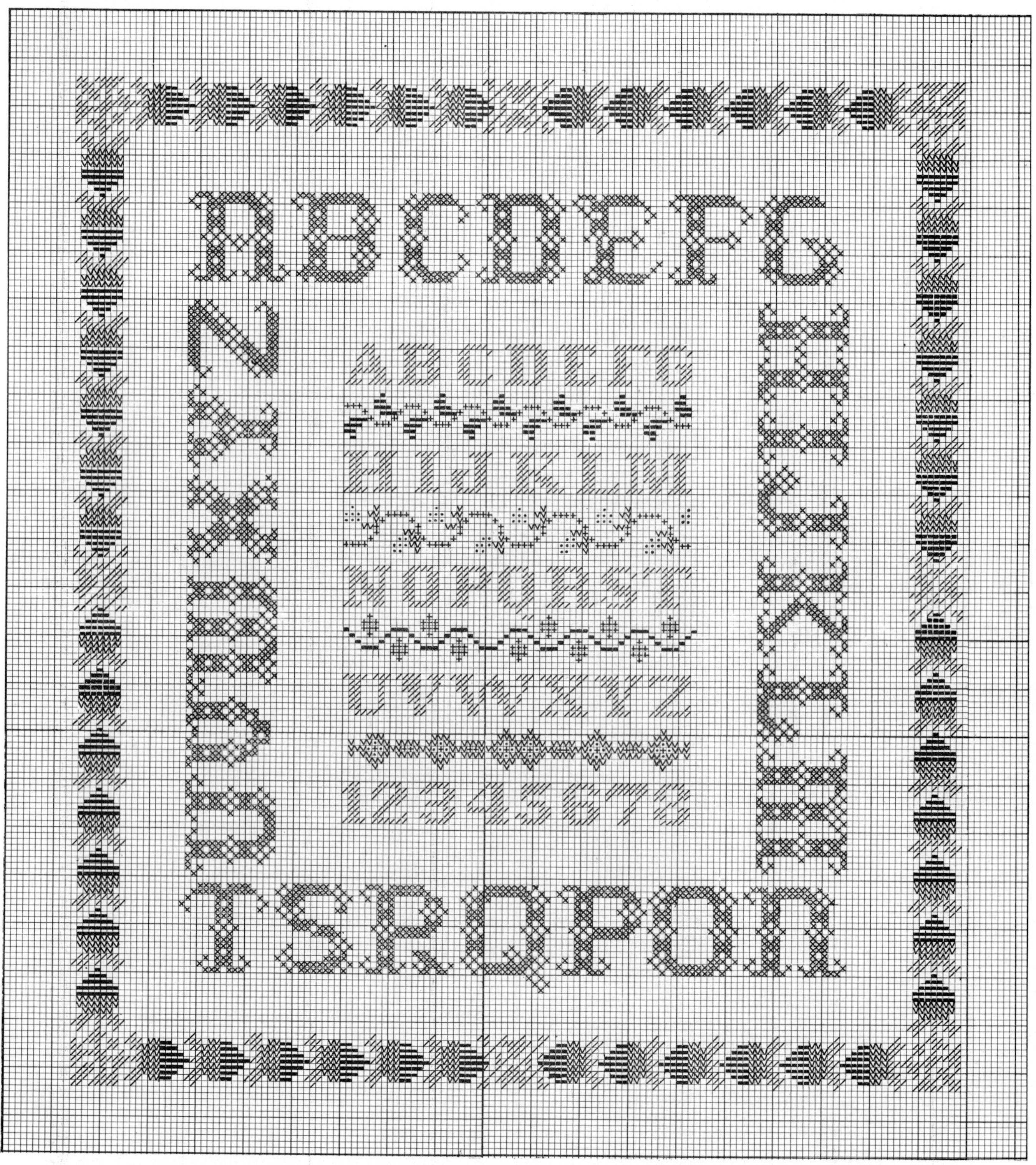

Color Key
- ⬓ Fuchsia
- ☑ Watermelon
- ☒ Orange
- ▨ Bright Green
- ⊞ Gold
- ☐ Gray-Blue
- ⊡ Light Yellow

Memory Sampler

Reminiscent of the classic cross-stitch samplers, this motto is worked in needlepoint. Work this saying, or make a sampler of your own, using the complete alphabet provided. Border chart is easy to adjust.

SIZE: 13⅜" x 15¼".

EQUIPMENT: Scissors. Ruler. Pencil. Masking tape. Tapestry needle. Straight pins. **For Blocking:** Soft wooden surface. Brown wrapping paper. Square. Rustproof thumbtacks. Graph paper.

MATERIALS: Tapestry wool: ecru or ivory, 28 skeins; blue, 3 skeins; green, 4 skeins; purple, 2 skeins; red, 1 skein; orange, 1 skein. Needlepoint canvas, 10-mesh-to-the-inch, 17½" x 19¼". **For Mounting:** Heavy cardboard 13⅜" x 15¼". Straight pins. Picture frame. Small nails.

DIRECTIONS: Read General Directions on page 90. Starting in upper right-hand corner 2" down and 2" in, work 10 rows of needlepoint background in ivory to measure 15¼" across. On next row at right, work 10 stitches in, then follow border chart halfway across top; repeat in reverse to left side. Work border down side to halfway point, following chart; repeat chart in reverse to bottom, omitting last stitch on chart, which is center stitch. Make rest of border to match.

On graph paper, mark outline of area within border; each mesh of canvas is one square on graph. Using the upper- and lower-case alphabets, make a chart for lettering, using motto in sampler shown or one of your own choosing. Include horizontal motifs given in border chart between lines on your chart. Following your chart, work lettering in blue yarn; follow color chart for horizontal motifs. Fill in remainder of background, making 10 rows of needlepoint all around blue line of border.

Block and mount sampler, following directions on pages 92–93. Frame as desired.

Border Chart

Color Key

- ⊠ Green
- ⊡ Orange
- ⧅ Red
- ☑ Blue
- ◪ Purple

Victorian Parrot

This Victorian parrot on a floral crescent was originally embroidered in cross-stitch on black monk's cloth. However, it adapts beautifully to 10-mesh-to-the-inch canvas.

SIZE: 13½″ or 18½″ square (see below).

EQUIPMENT: For Needlepoint: Masking tape. Tapestry needle. Pencil. **For Blocking**: Thumbtacks. Soft wooden surface. Brown wrapping paper. Ruler. Square. **For Cross-Stitch:** Embroidery scissors. Pencil. Ruler. Large-eyed embroidery needle. Penelope (or cross-stitch) canvas, for linen.

MATERIALS: For Needlepoint: Needlepoint canvas, 10-mesh-to-the-inch, 28″ x 29″ (design area about 18½″ square). Tapestry yarn, 8-yard skeins: 2 skeins pale gray-green; 2 skeins medium gray-green; 3 skeins dark gray-green; 1 skein each apple green; medium bright green; deep green; pale yellow-green; light olive green; olive green; deep olive green; pale cocoa; light cocoa; medium cocoa; dark cocoa; light red-brown; medium red-brown; dark red-brown; tan; gold; antique gold; pale mauve; light mauve; medium mauve; dark mauve; lavender; purple; deep purple; light blue; medium blue; dark blue; light coral; medium coral; red; maroon; black for background, 47 skeins. **For Mounting:** Heavy cardboard or ¼″ plywood, 22¾″ x 23½″. **For Cross-Stitch:** Monk's cloth, about 14-squares-to-the-inch, 20½″ x 21½″ (design area about 13½″ square). Or linen, 28″ x 29″, and Penelope (cross-stitch) canvas, 10-mesh-to-the-inch (design area about 18½″ square). Crewel wool or six-strand embroidery floss in colors listed above.

DIRECTIONS: Antique picture was worked on

Color Key

- Pale Gray-Green
- Medium Gray-Green
- Dark Gray-Green
- Apple Green
- Medium Bright Green
- Deep Green
- Pale Yellow-Green
- Light Olive Green
- Olive Green
- Deep Olive Green
- Pale Cocoa
- Light Cocoa
- Medium Cocoa
- Dark Cocoa
- Light Red-Brown
- Medium Red-Brown
- Dark Red-Brown
- Tan
- Gold
- Antique Gold
- Pale Mauve
- Light Mauve
- Medium Mauve
- Dark Mauve
- Lavender
- Purple
- Deep Purple
- Light Blue
- Medium Blue
- Dark Blue
- Light Coral
- Medium Coral
- Red
- Maroon

black monk's cloth with wool. The stitches were counted and worked directly on the monk's cloth, using the even weave of the fabric as a guide; each cross-stitch covers one square of the weave. However, as black monk's cloth is not available, another method will have to be used to obtain a black ground—such as needlepoint, using black yarn to fill in all of background area. If desired, picture can be worked in cross-stitch on linen, working over Penelope canvas.

Needlepoint Picture: Read General Directions on page 90. Mark outline of picture 22¾" x 23½", allowing 2½" margin all around. Following chart, work parrot design, using one strand of tapestry yarn in needle. Find center of chart and center of outlined area of canvas. Work design from center to right side. Continue working design to left, then fill in background to marked outline.

Block and mount picture, following directions on pages 92–93. Frame as desired.

Cross-Stitch Picture: Read How To Cross-Stitch on page 16. On monk's cloth, work cross-stitches over each square of fabric, following chart. Leave background free. On linen, baste Penelope (cross-stitch) canvas over fabric first (see Penelope canvas instructions on page 16). Work cross-stitches over canvas and through linen in same manner as above. When cross-stitching is complete, pull away strands of canvas horizontally and vertically one at a time, leaving the cross-stitches on the linen. Mount cross-stitch picture as for needlepoint.

Turtledoves in a Wreath

Turtledoves, exchanging fond glances, and their perch, a lush wreath of pink and red roses and yellow blossoms, bear out the date of our antique needlepoint picture—1895! Birds and flowers were popular subjects for ladies' needlework around that time, and canvas stitches recorded "sweet sentiment." Our picture was found in an antique shop in Maine. Its colors faded, as you can see, but when we took it out of its frame, the yarn colors on the reverse side were bright and sharp—a vivid coral for the right side's faded pink, etc. In order that your reproduction will have fresh, intense colors, we matched yarn colors on the picture's reverse side with new colors shown at right. The mottled background—different black yarns, faded—when worked in one black yarn, will have a rich, deep effect. The charming old frame is bird's eye maple with gold leaf mat. To work the picture, use 10- or 11-mesh-to-the-inch canvas and tapestry yarn, following colors, chart symbols, and chart.

SIZE: About 15¼" x 18½" on 10-to-inch canvas (13¾" x 17", 11-to-inch canvas).

NOTE: Antique picture was worked on 11-to-the-inch canvas. We are specifying 10-to-the-inch canvas since it is easier to find. For 11-to-the-inch canvas, follow measurements given in parentheses.

EQUIPMENT: Making tape. Pencil. Tapestry needle. Thumbtacks. Soft wooden surface. Ruler and square. Brown paper.

MATERIALS: Needlepoint canvas: 10-to-the-inch, 21" x 24" (19" x 22"). Tapestry yarn, 8-yard skeins: 3 skeins white; 1 skein pink; 1 skein coral; 1 skein rose; 2 skeins dark red; 2 skeins maroon; 12 skeins black; 1 skein gray; 1 skein yellow; 1 skein pale gold; 1 skein pale yellow-green; 1 skein medium green; 1 skein light green; 1 skein emerald green; 1 skein golden brown; 1 skein light brown; 1 skein dark brown; 1 skein dark rust; 1 skein light rust; 14 skeins beige. **For Mounting:** Heavy mounting cardboard 15¼" x 18½" (13¾" x 17"). Straight pins. Black thread. Sewing needle.

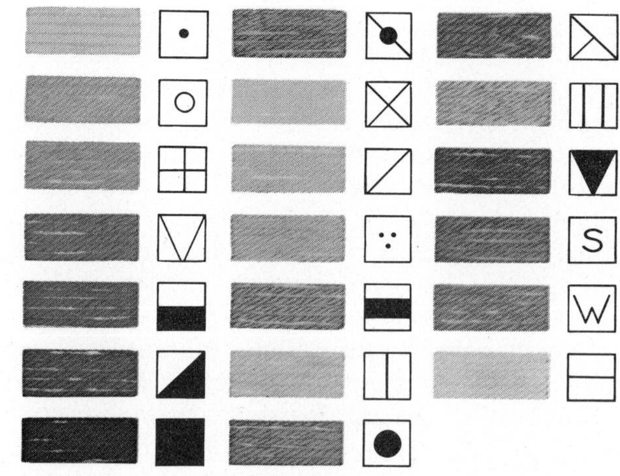

New Colors

DIRECTIONS: Read General Directions on page 90 for working needlepoint. With selvages at the sides, mark outline of picture 15¼" x 18½" (13¾" x 17"), allowing 2½" canvas margins all around. Use either continental or diagonal stitch and work with one strand in needle.

With needle and black thread, run a vertical and horizontal line at center of canvas. Find center of bird chart. Following chart and color key, work design area out from center to right side; complete design. Fill in black background, adding nine rows of black beyond both top and bottom design area; adding eight stitches beyond right design area; adding seven stitches beyond left design area. Now start beige background area as follows: Eight rows across at top and bottom; eight stitches across at left and right sides. Following corner chart, start border design at upper right corner; repeat chart in reverse to left and to bottom. Work remainder of border. Fill in outer beige background by working twelve rows at top and bottom; twelve stitches at left and right sides.

Block and mount; see pages 92–93.

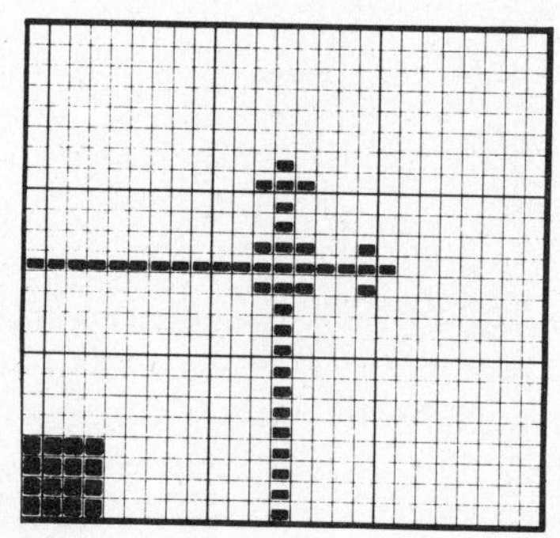
Corner

Center

Center

Dragon of Good Fortune

Here is an Oriental treasure to stitch in tapestry yarn on 16-to-the-inch canvas.

SIZE: Unframed, 23½" x 18".

EQUIPMENT: Paper for pattern. Waterproof marking pen with fine point. Ruler. Masking or adhesive tape. Tapestry needles. Scissors. Soft wooden surface. Rustproof thumbtacks. Artist's canvas stretcher frame, 18" x 20" (old picture frame or needlepoint frame may be used). Optional: Staple gun and staples. Straight pins. **For Blocking:** Brown wrapping paper. Square.

MATERIALS: Needlepoint canvas, mono 16-

mesh-to-inch, 28½" x 23". Tapestry yarn, 8.8-yd. skeins as follows: 18 beige, 10 red-orange, 1 ice blue, 2 pale blue, 6 Wedgwood blue, 7 Delft blue, 6 medium blue, 5 royal blue, and 3 navy blue. **For Finishing:** Mounting board, 23½" x 18". Cardboard backing in same size. Frame to size. Picture-hanging wire and two screw eyes.

DIRECTIONS: Read General Directions on page 90. Keeping all margins equal, mark outline of needlepoint area, 23½" x 18", onto canvas. Enlarge dragon pattern on paper ruled in 1" squares. Tape or tack dragon picture pattern onto wooden surface; tack canvas on top, keeping pattern within marked needlepoint area. Using waterproof marker (test its fastness yourself to be sure), carefully trace complete pattern (without the numbers) onto canvas. Do not try to indicate individual stitches around curves onto the canvas

PLACEMENT OF STITCHES AND COLOR CHANGES

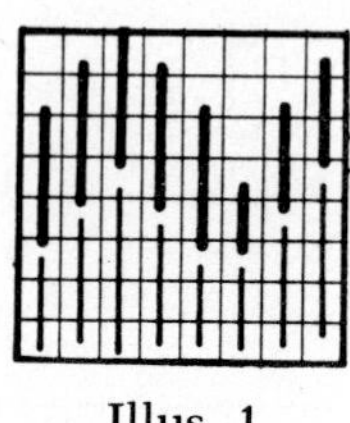
Illus. 1

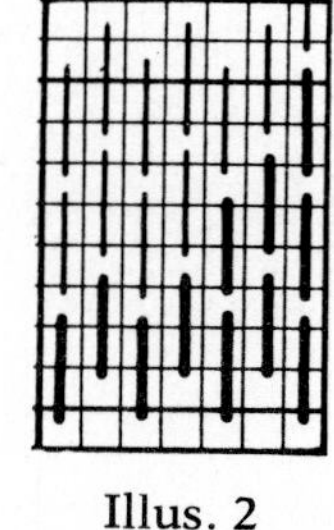
Illus. 2

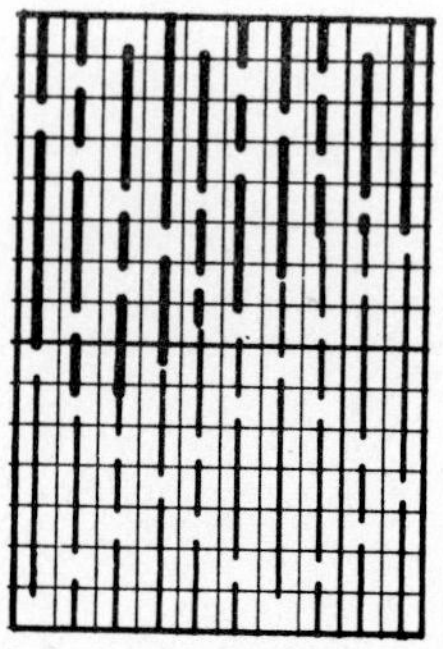

Illus. 3

Illus. 4

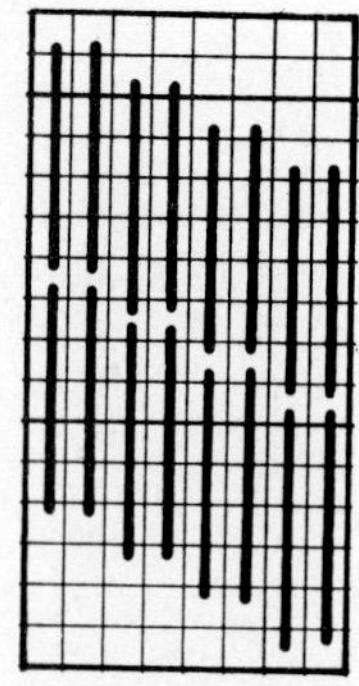
Illus. 5

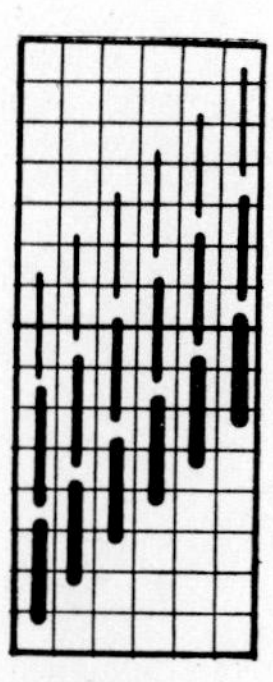
Illus. 6

WORKING STITCH DETAILS

Fig. 1

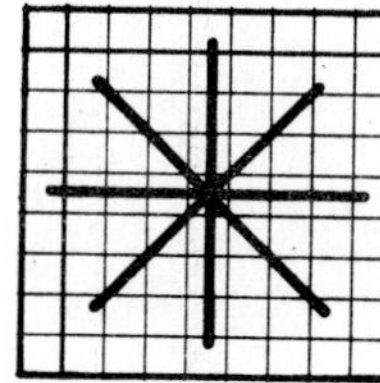
Fig. 2

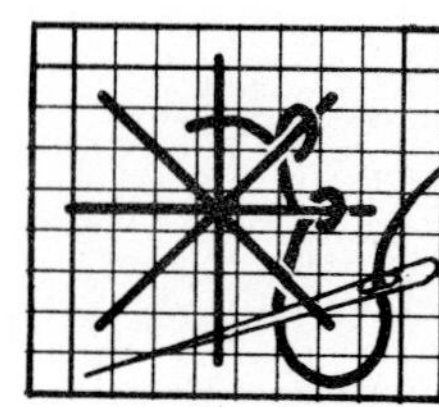
Fig. 2A

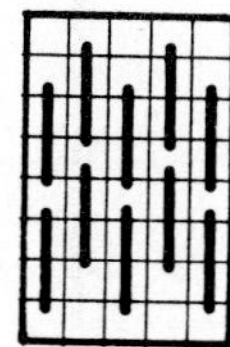
Fig. 3

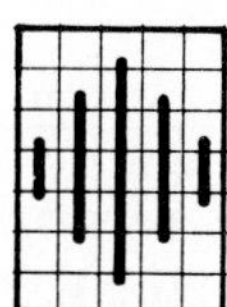
Fig. 4

Color Key

1 Navy Blue
2 Royal Blue
3 Medium Blue
4 Delft Blue
5 Wedgwood Blue
6 Pale Blue
7 Ice Blue
8 Red-Orange
9 Beige

as this will work out in the stitching. It may be necessary to lift canvas occasionally to check pattern underneath in order to follow lines in complicated areas. You may find it helpful to stick straight pins in as guideposts. Let ink dry completely; remove canvas from board.

Keeping canvas meshes straight, staple or tack lower half of canvas onto frame, being sure the needlepoint area lies over the open center. If using needlepoint frame, attach according to instructions.

Use single strand of yarn in needle throughout work. To facilitate changing colors frequently, you may want to keep several needles threaded with different colors. Following numbers on pattern and Color Key, work head of dragon first, then work the pearl; then work body of dragon, clouds, and background. Work entire area within frame opening. As work progresses, move unworked area of canvas onto frame. Except for eyes, all stitches are variations of upright stitch (Fig. 1) over varying numbers of canvas threads. Detailed instructions are below.

Begin areas marked 7 around the eyes. Work upright stitches to completely fill the outline. Eyes, area 1, are Whipped Spider Web stitches (Fig. 2A-B) worked in navy blue. To work Spider Web, start with four crossing foundation stitches (Fig. 2A) within outlined area (to edge of area 7). Working clockwise, bring yarn under two spokes and back over one spoke (Fig. 2B); use your fingers to push stitches toward center. Repeat around spokes several times, continuing to push stitches to center, making a raised mound and covering spokes completely.

Following Color Key, complete dragon head and pearl, using upright stitches within outlined areas on your canvas. For example, in color areas 7 of eyes, ends of stitches meet ends of stitches from area 5 in the same meshes along the outline. Make upright stitches over all canvas threads within an area until you reach the outline; stitch lengths will vary tremendously to accomplish this (Illustration 1). Very fine lines around eyes and on head area indicate stitch outline separations using the color of yarn designated in the large area. Any unnumbered areas outside the dragon outline are background clouds (see below).

Dragon Feet: Claws are worked in upright stitches. Work talons up to dotted lines on dragon legs in brick stitch (Fig. 3), making each stitch over three canvas threads. Begin brick stitches in middle of inner color area outlines. For example, on the lower left talon, begin in wide area where colors 4 and 5 adjoin; work color 4 out to claws, then work color 5 out to claws (Illustration 2 demonstrates color change for brick stitch). Use fill-in stitches where necessary to keep within the outline.

Dragon Body: Spines are worked in upright stitches within each outline. Body is worked in diamond stitch (Fig. 4). Begin stitching on interior area of body in center of a color area. From first diamond, work all others within that color area in same diamond pattern, having ends of adjoining stitches meeting in same meshes. At outside edges, use partial diamonds and fill-in stitches to keep within outline. For color changes, adjust stitching within a diamond to keep within color outlines (Illustration 3). Adjacent stitches of next color are then adjusted to complete each diamond shape. Working one color area at a time is easiest.

Cloud Background: Entire area is worked in varying lengths of upright stitches, whose ends lie along the inner cloud detail lines (Illustration 4). Adjust length of stitches to conform to cloud lines, having ends of stitches meeting in same meshes between adjoining areas.

Red Background: Work pairs of upright stitches, each over six threads, staggered to follow diagonal lines (Illustration 5).

When the lower half is complete, carefully remove canvas from the frame and mount the upper half onto the frame. Work dragon body and foot as you did for lower half. On each body section, be sure to begin with diamond stitches in center of area, then work outward.

Dragon Tail: Starting from dotted line, work in diagonal rows of upright stitches, each over three canvas threads (Illustration 6). Follow the color area outlines (curved lines) to get the color changes within the diagonal lines. Use fill-in stitches where needed to complete outline. Work clouds as for the lower portion. Begin stitching for red background in center where the diagonals meet.

To block needlepoint see General Directions on page 92.

Mounting: Place needlepoint, right side up, over mount board. Turn canvas margins to back side of board; tape around to secure all canvas. Insert into frame; place cardboard backing in frame and secure. Mount hanging wire onto back of frame using two screw eyes.

Independence Hall

Here's a magnificent bicentennial wall plaque to stitch in brilliantly colored yarn. Embroidery and canvas stitches combine in an unusual way to create the richly textured picture. use Persian yarns on 16-to-the-inch canvas.

SIZE: 22″ x 16″, unframed.

EQUIPMENT: Ruler. Masking tape. Tapestry needles. Scissors. **For Transferring Pattern:** Waterproof marking pen with fine point; or tracing nylon, waterproof marking pen and pinless pattern holder (or other spray adhesive). **For Blocking:** Soft wooden surface. Rustproof thumbtacks. Brown wrapping paper. Square.

MATERIALS: Mono needlepoint canvas 16-to-the-inch, 27″ x 21″. Persian yarn (3-ply): 1 oz. each of red, light blue, sky blue, medium blue, royal blue, pale yellow-green, olive green, dark olive green, apple green, medium green; ½ oz. each of pewter gray, charcoal gray, off-white, cream, black; small amounts of silver gray, tan, light brown, white. **For Finishing:** Mounting board 22″ x 16″. Straight pins. Frame as desired.

DIRECTIONS: Read General Directions on page 90. Tape raw edges of canvas to prevent raveling. Keeping all margins equal, mark outline of needlepoint area 22″ x 16″ on canvas. Mark center of each side on canvas margins.

Cut yarn into 18″ lengths. Split 3-ply yarn and

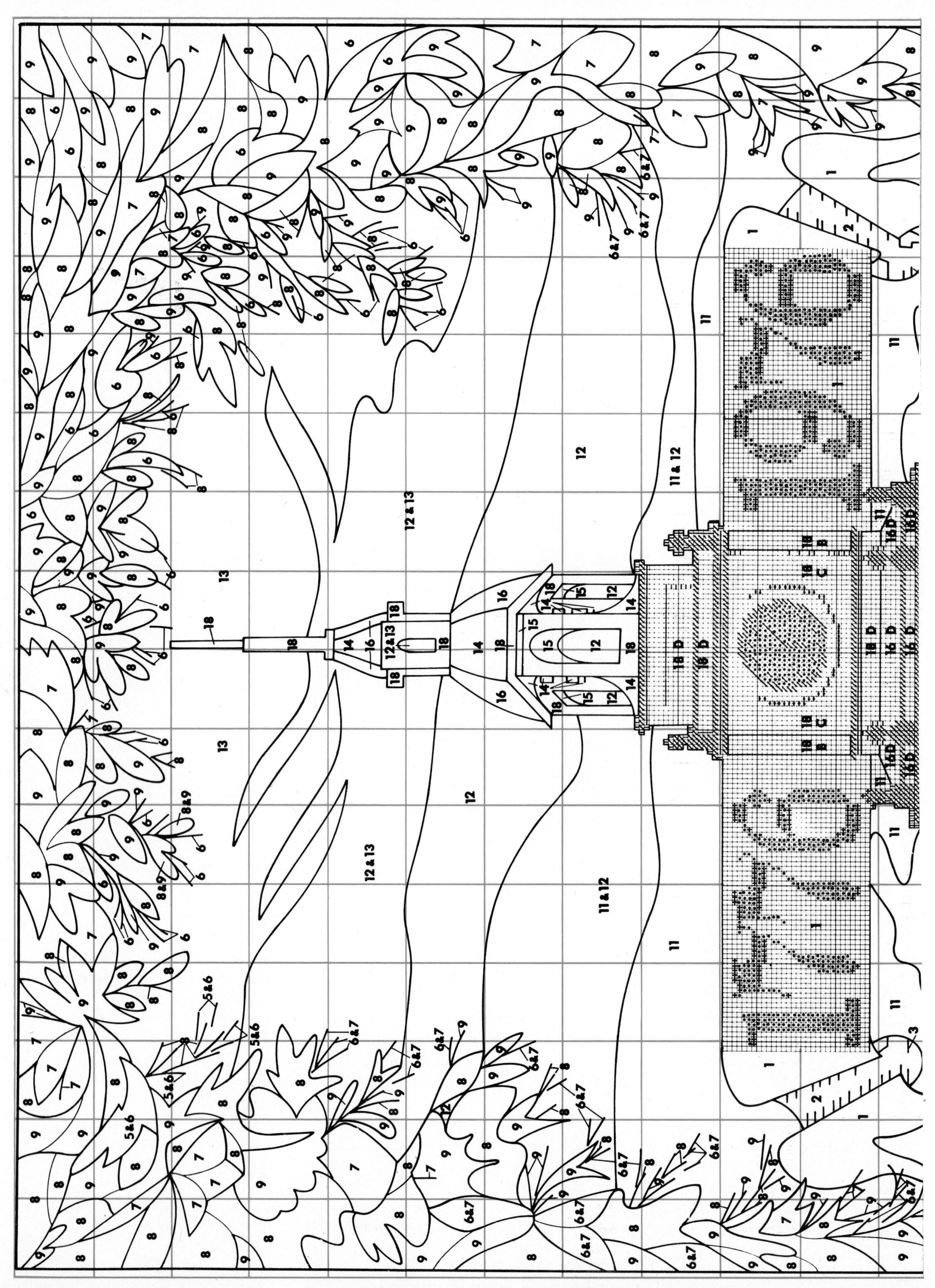

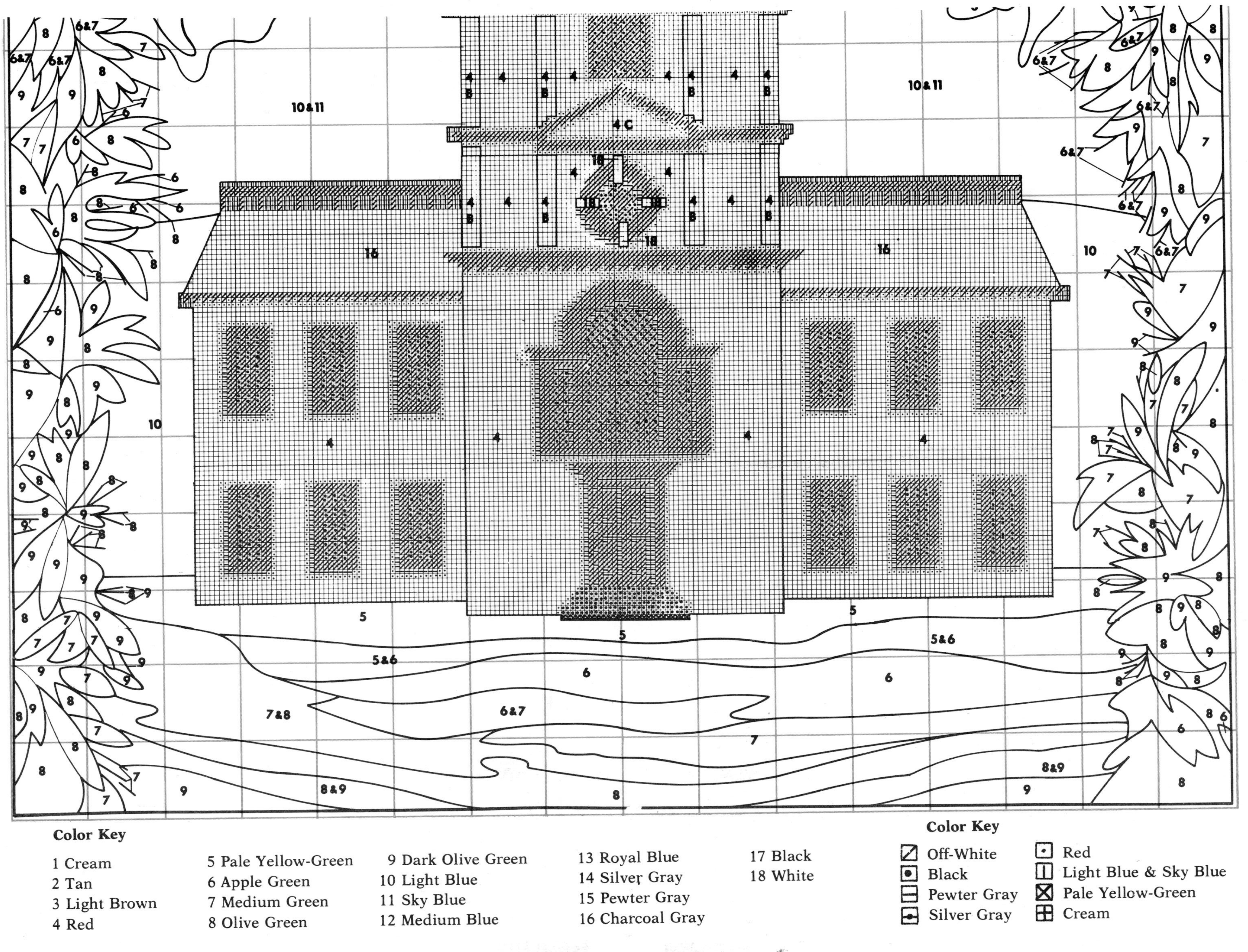

Color Key

1 Cream
2 Tan
3 Light Brown
4 Red
5 Pale Yellow-Green
6 Apple Green
7 Medium Green
8 Olive Green
9 Dark Olive Green
10 Light Blue
11 Sky Blue
12 Medium Blue
13 Royal Blue
14 Silver Gray
15 Pewter Gray
16 Charcoal Gray
17 Black
18 White

Color Key

- Off-White
- Black
- Pewter Gray
- Silver Gray
- Red
- Light Blue & Sky Blue
- Pale Yellow-Green
- Cream

use single strand of yarn throughout unless otherwise specified. To facilitate changing colors, you may want to keep several needles threaded with different colors.

To Transfer Pattern to Canvas: Enlarge outer colored-square area of pattern on paper ruled in 1″ squares. Inner graphed area is a chart and need not be enlarged. **Method One:** Tape or tack enlarged pattern on smooth wooden surface; tack canvas on top, keeping pattern within marked needlepoint area. Lines of pattern will show through canvas meshes. Using waterproof marker (test its fastness yourself to be sure), carefully trace all lines of leaf border, sky, ground, steeple, 1776-1976 banner and clock area; do not trace remainder of graphed pattern (all symbols on graphed pattern are to be worked in needlepoint stitch). Do not try to indicate individual stitches around curves on canvas mesh, as this will work out in the stitching. It may be necessary to lift canvas occasionally to check pattern. You may find it helpful to stick straight pins in as guideposts. Let ink dry completely before removing canvas from pattern.

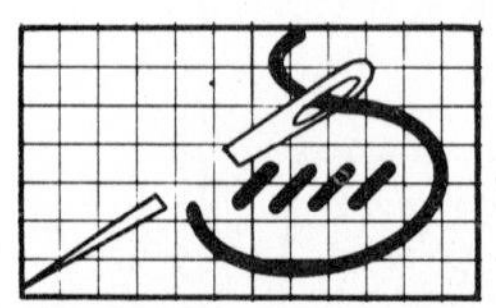

CONTINENTAL STITCH
Detail 1

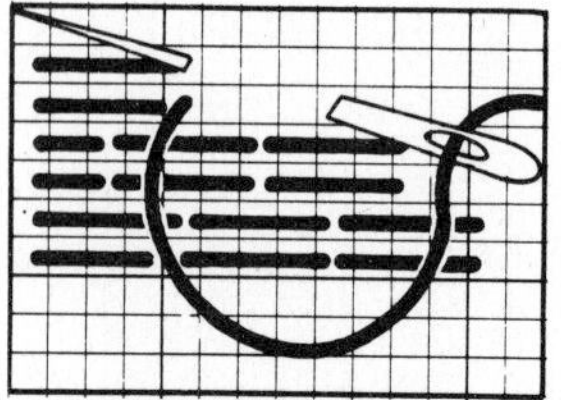

BRICK STITCH
Detail 2

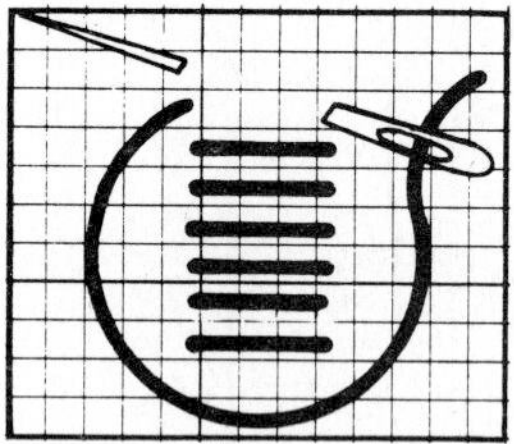

HORIZONTAL STITCH
Detail 3

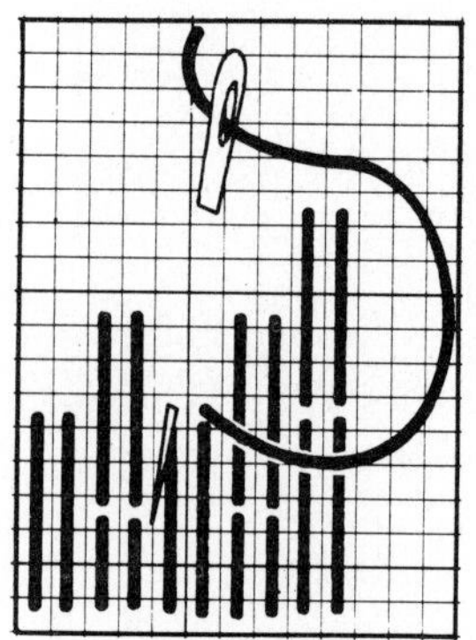

VERTICAL BRICK
Detail 4

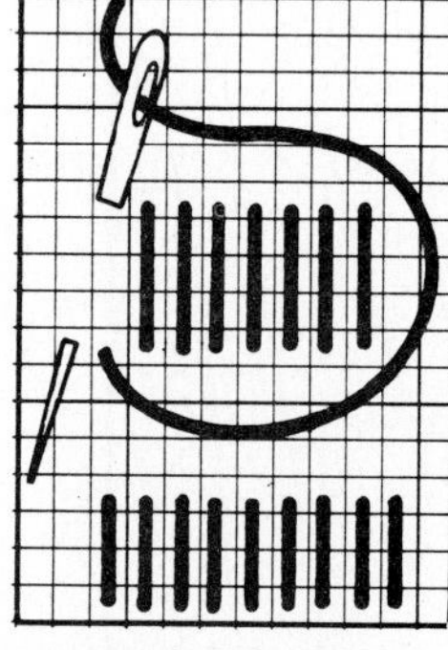

VERTICAL STITCH
Detail 5

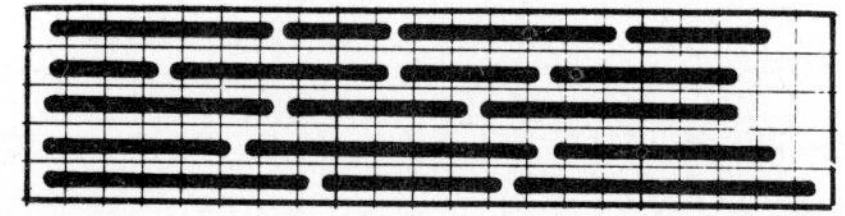

RANDOM HORIZONTAL STITCHES
Detail 6

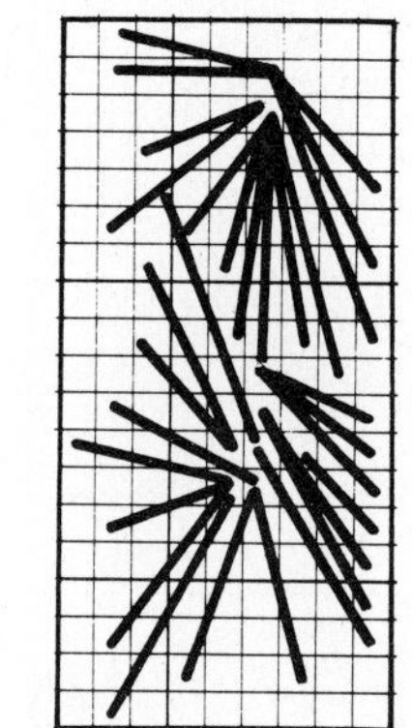

ANGLED STITCHES
Detail 7

Method Two: Use a piece of tracing nylon a little larger than pattern. This is a weblike material that can be purchased by the yard at pattern counters. Although it is not entirely transparent it is clear enough to see plainly a design placed under it.

Lay the design down on a flat, hard surface and cover it with tracing nylon the same size as design. Tape the edges securely together to keep them from slipping. Use waterproof marking pen to trace the outlines of design onto the nylon. Trace all areas indicated for Method One.

Carefully separate the nylon from the design. Save the design for color reference. If it is necessary to retouch any outlines, lay the nylon over a sheet of white paper for better visibility.

Spray the canvas with pinless pattern holder or other adhesive and place the marked nylon web over it, pressing and smoothing it lightly until it adheres; let dry. Baste the nylon web to canvas around all edges outside of design area.

Work needlepoint directly over nylon-covered canvas, through the nylon and canvas meshes. The web material is so thin that it is not difficult to pass the needle through.

To Work Building: Work graphed needlepoint area first following chart and Color Key. Starting at bottom center, work the line of pale green needlepoint below steps at edge of marked area on canvas in continental stitch. (Detail 1); then work steps in black continental stitch. Continue working all areas indicated by symbols on chart in continental stitch. Fill in building with brick stitch (Detail 2) in red; use shorter stitches as necessary for edges of windows, door and sides. Upper red portion is worked in brick stitch also, except areas marked 4B and 4C. Work areas 4B in horizontal stitches all the same length (Detail 3) except where indicated; work area 4C in long horizontal stitches, shortening them to fill space as you work up to point.

Work roof (area 16) in a vertical variation of brick stitch (Detail 4). Shorten stitches at sides, top, and bottom as necessary to conform to shape. Work areas 11 in horizontal stitches of varying lengths. Work areas 16D and 18D in vertical stitches (Detail 5) to fill, following Color Key. Work symbols in clock and around it in needlepoint stitch; fill area outside of clock marked 18C with long horizontal stitches; remainder marked 18B is horizontal stitches worked to fill areas.

On banner, work numbers first in black continental stitch. Fill banner with horizontal stitches to fit between numbers; fill with single needlepoint stitches as necessary to cover canvas. On banner ends, work areas 2 in horizontal stitches, using darker shade to work just the stitches indicated by fine lines. Fill pointed ends with horizontal stitches. Continue working up steeple in horizontal stitches following Color Key.

For Ground and Sky: Use two strands of yarn in needle for most of work. Work in random horizontal stitches (Detail 6) following colors indicated for marked areas. Continue horizontal stitches at sides far enough into leaf border design to be sure no canvas will show. Gradually shade next color into first using a single strand, then continue color with two strands. Work sky in same random horizontal stitch, blending two shades in areas where two numbers are given. Continue up to top gradually blending into darkest blue.

For Greenery Border: Work long straight stitches, at various angles and different lengths (Detail 7), using two strands of yarn in needle for most of work; add single-strand stitches for leafy appearance. To keep a light, open look, do not fill each shape solidly toward inner edges of border. If necessary, fill openings with background color. Blend shades as they come together by making stitches in different lengths.

Blocking: To block needlepoint see General Directions on page 92.

Mounting: Mark center of each side of mounting board. Place needlepoint, right side up, on mounting board. Match center marks on sides of board and canvas. Push pins through canvas and into sides of board at center of each side. Stretch corners of needlepoint to corners of board and insert pins into sides at corners. Continue stretching canvas evenly, inserting pins into board all around every ¼″. Smooth excess canvas to back and tape in place. Frame picture as desired.

Three Cat Portraits

Here are three delightful pets to needlepoint: a Persian, a tabby, and a Siamese. All are worked on 10-mesh-to-the-inch double-thread canvas in tapestry yarn. The eyes are petit point; the canvas is split for finer detail.

SIZES (finished needlepoint area): **Tabby:** 8½″ diameter. **Persian:** 13¼″ x 13½″. **Siamese:** 10½″ square.

EQUIPMENT: Waterproof marking pen with fine point. Ruler. Masking or adhesive tape. Scissors. Tapestry needles. Compass for Tabby. **For Blocking:** Soft wooden surface. Brown wrapping paper. Pencil. Square. Rustproof thumbtacks.

MATERIALS: Double-mesh (Penelope) needlepoint canvas, 10-mesh-per-inch, as follows: Tabby, 13½″ square; Persian, 18¼″ x 18½″; Siamese, 19″ square. Tapestry wool, 8.8-yd. skeins, in colors listed; see Color Key. One skein of each color unless otherwise noted in parentheses. Six-strand embroidery floss, 7-yd. skeins, one of each color listed in Color Key. **Note:** If doing more than one cat needlepoint, you will need fewer skeins of the sparsely used colors. For example, one skein of rust, which is used in the Tabby and the Persian, will be sufficient for both. For the floss, one skein of black will do for all three cats. **For Finishing:** Mounting board, cardboard backing and frame to size. If desired, mat board and fabric covering may be used. Picture-hanging wire and two screw eyes.

DIRECTIONS: Read General Directions on page 90 to begin needlepoint. Keeping margins equal, mark outline of finished needlepoint area (see sizes) onto canvas: For circular outline of Tabby, use compass to mark area; do not cut away canvas. For Siamese, see individual directions below. Mark center of each side on canvas margins.

NOTE: We would suggest that you attach the appropriate symbol used in the Color Key to the skein of yarn for easy identification. Use single strand of yarn in needle throughout work, except for eyes. To facilitate changing colors frequently, you may want to keep several needles threaded with different colors.

Following head chart and Color Key (directions for eyes are below), work design in tent (continental) stitch (Details 1 and 2) and reversed tent stitch (Details 3, 4, 5). Work each stitch over double thread of canvas; each square on graph represents one stitch on canvas. Begin at upper right corner, working tent stitch and reversed tent stitch from right to left to end of row. For clarity, right and left sides of charts have been separated where you change from tent stitch to reversed tent stitch. See individual directions for Siamese. At the end of each row, turn work upside down to return; always work from right to left.

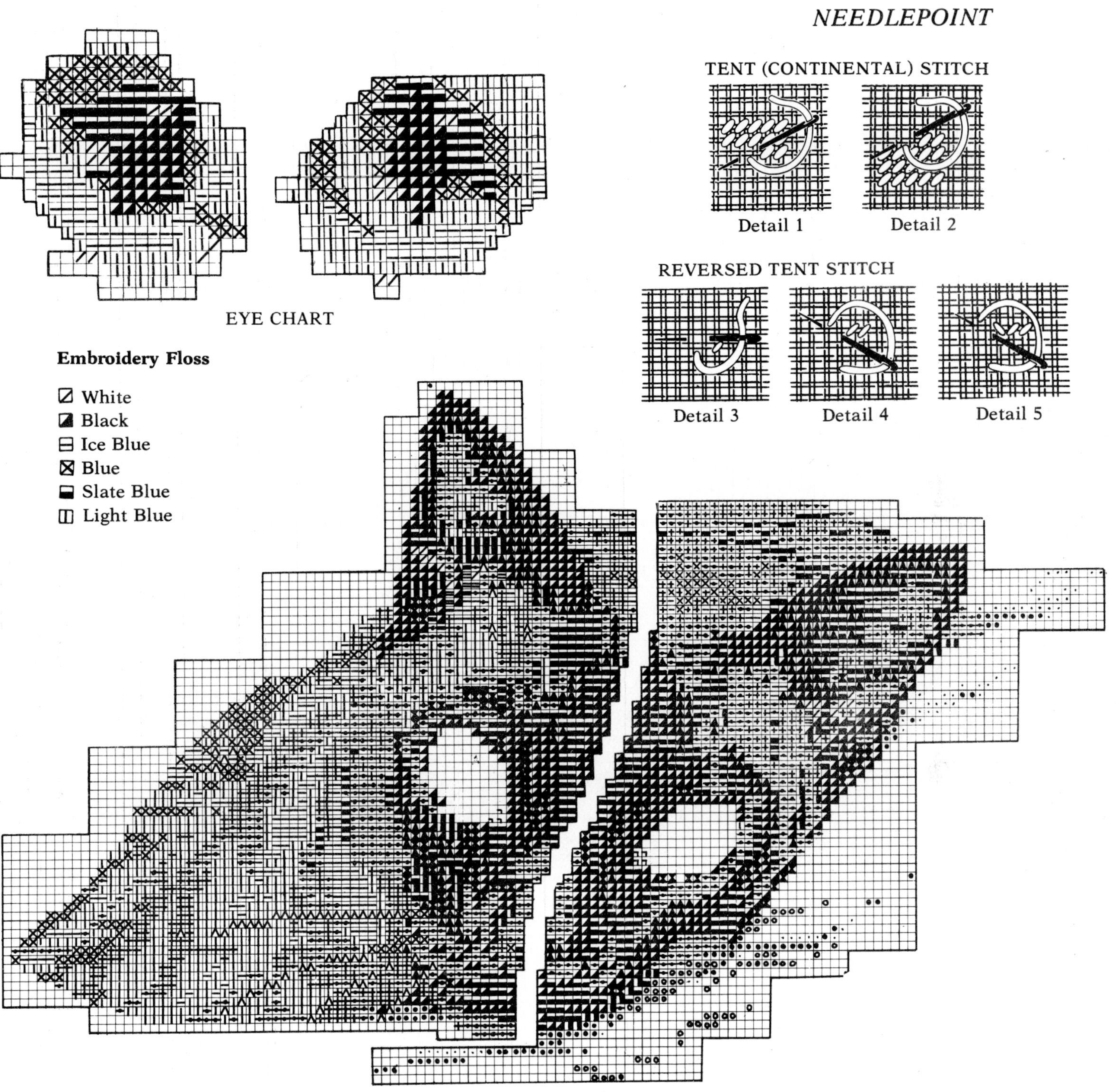

Color Key (Siamese) Tapestry Wool

- Brown-Black
- Cream-Beige
- Umber
- Tan
- Burgundy
- Russet
- Brown
- Camel
- Chocolate
- Medium Camel
- Ivory
- Gray-Beige
- Medium Brown
- Light Red-Brown
- Background: Light Blue (7)
- Medium Blue
- Blue-Gray
- Green-Gray
- Taupe

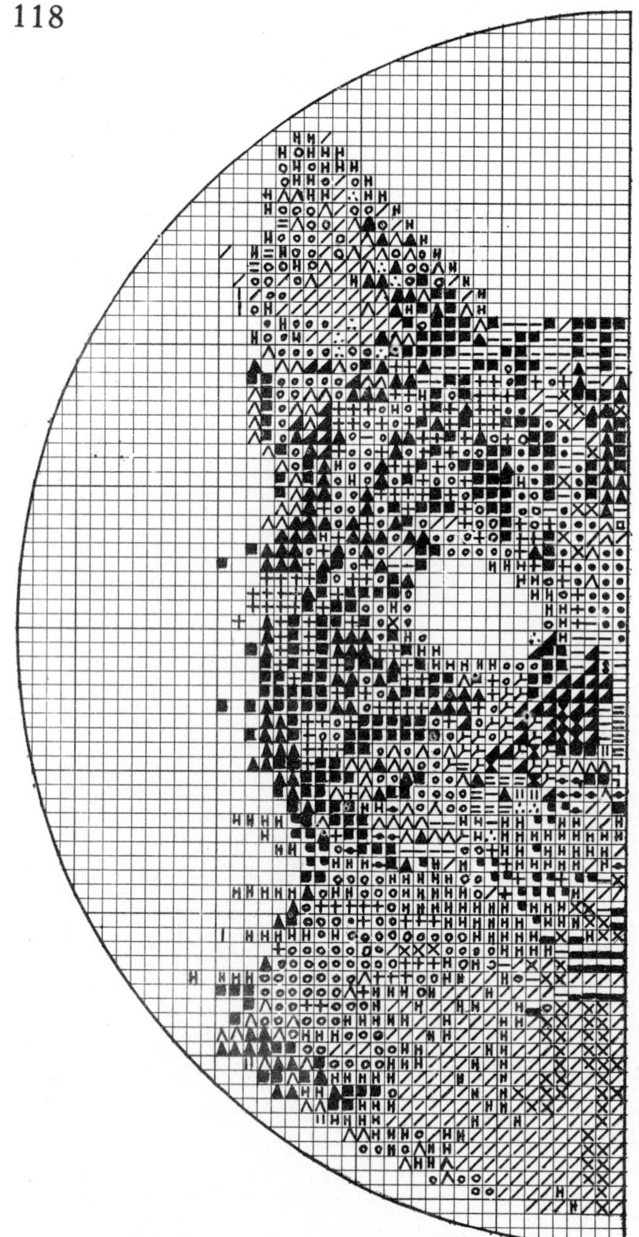
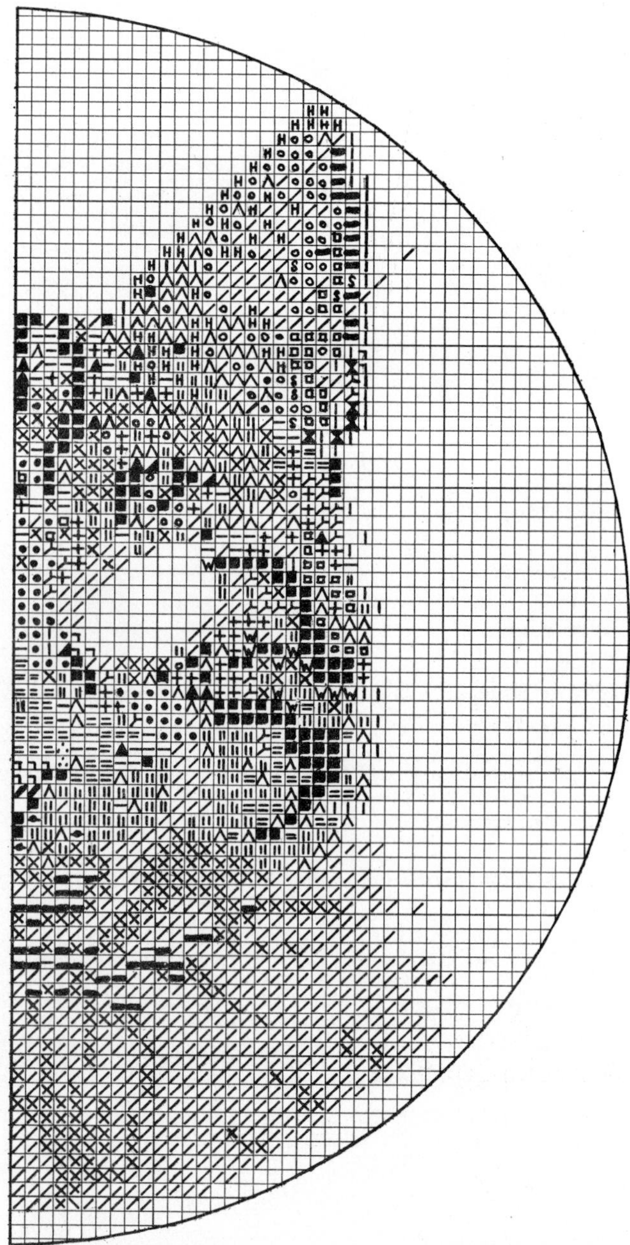

Color Key (Tabby)
Taspestry Wool

- Background; Brown-Gold (4)
- White (2)
- Black
- Brown-Gold
- Mustard
- Ginger
- Pale Yellow
- Olive Green
- Pale Olive Green
- Gray
- Cream-Beige
- Sand
- Cream-Tan
- Tan
- Light Taupe
- Pale Brown
- Light Gold-Brown
- Bronze
- Rust
- Dusty Rose
- Gold-Beige
- Khaki
- Beige
- Light Camel
- Ocher
- Dark Brown
- Green-Beige

EYE CHART

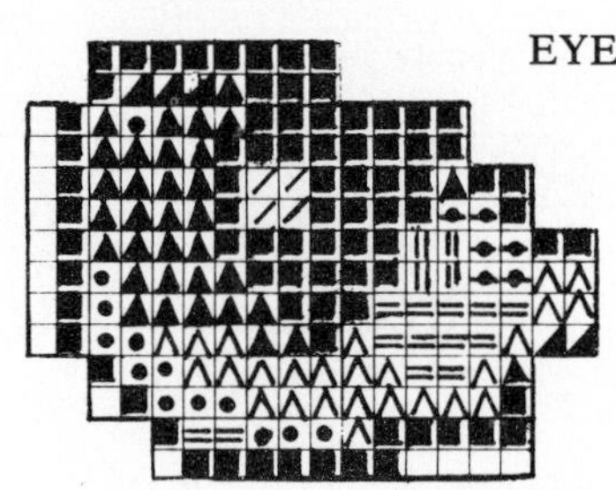
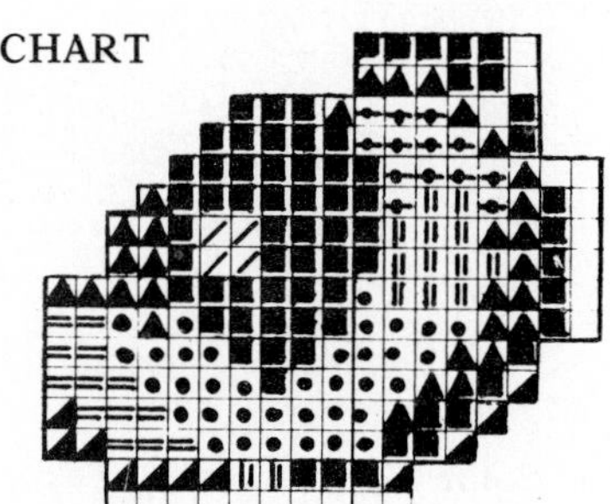

Embroidery Floss

- White
- Black
- Cream
- Mustard
- Gold
- Celery Green
- Light Olive Green
- Olive Green
- Brown

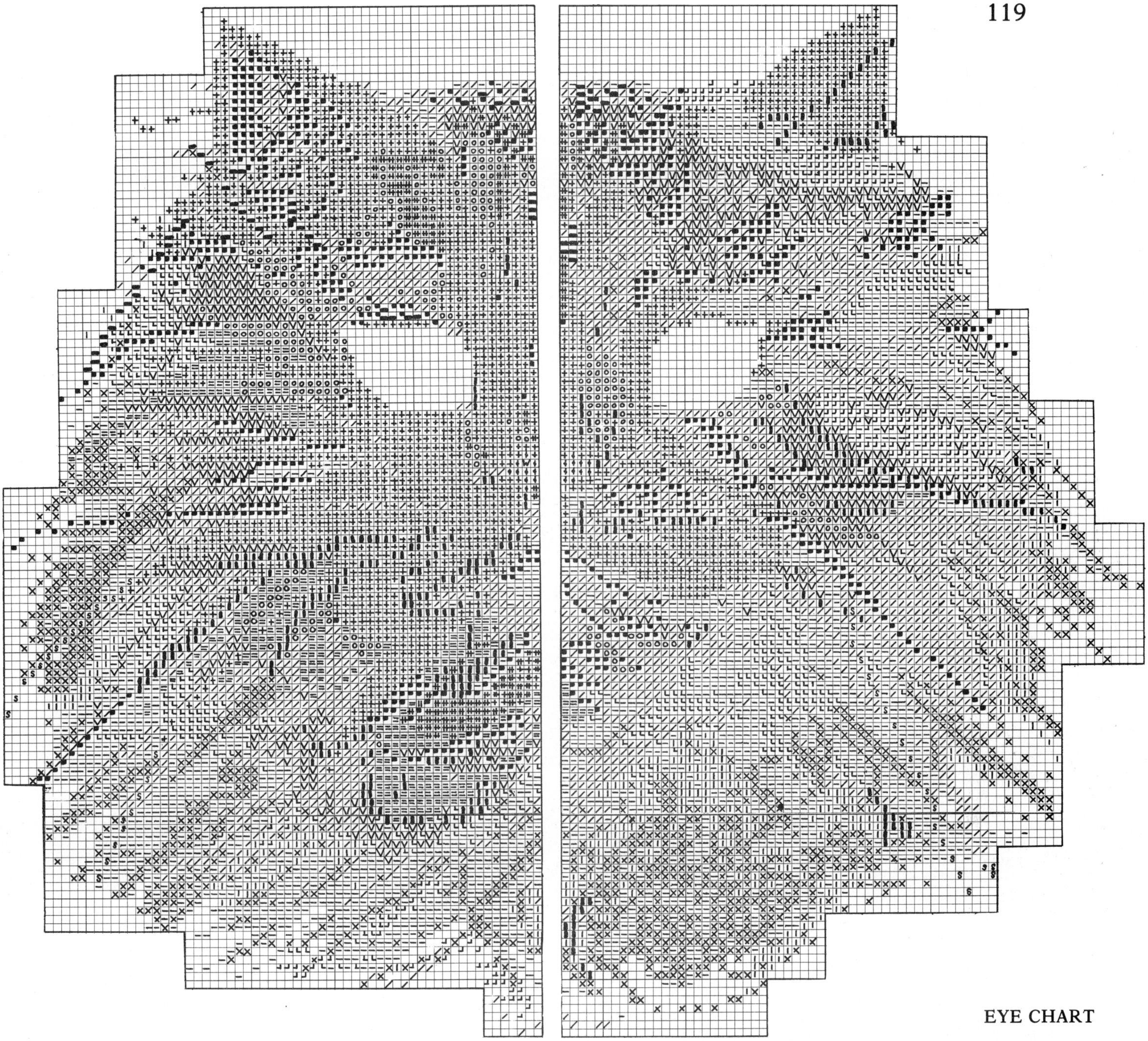

EYE CHART

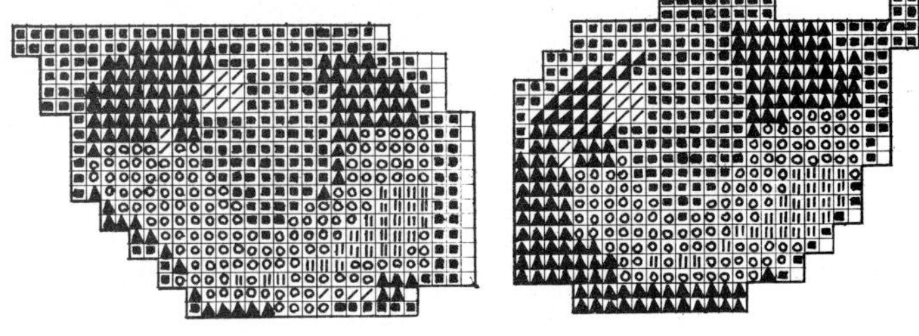

Color Key (Persian)
Tapestry Wool

- White
- Black (2)
- Background: Turquoise (5)
- Yellow-Green
- Rust
- Taupe
- Ocher (2)
- Dark Camel
- Light Brown
- Nutmeg Brown
- Coffee Brown
- Fawn Brown
- Soft Brown
- Seal Brown
- Gold
- Medium Camel
- Burnt Umber
- Brown-Black
- Dark Charcoal

Embroidery Floss

- White
- Black
- Cream
- Celery Green
- Olive Green
- Brown

Work complete head before filling in eyes.

To work the eyes, the double threads of canvas are split and petit point is worked using the full six strands of embroidery floss. To split the double threads in the eye area, run the pointed end of your needle between the double vertical and horizontal threads of the canvas to separate them. The petit point stitch is the tent stitch worked over each single thread, making twice as many stitches per inch as you have been working. Follow the eye chart and Color Key: each graph square represents one petit point stitch. Where there are blank spaces, omit the petit point stitch; these abut the head stitches and would distort the eye shape if filled in.

Complete Persian cat following above direcions; follow individual directions for Tabby and Siamese. Block and finish as directed on pages 92–93.

Mounting: Place needlepoint, right side up, over mounting board. Turn canvas margins to back side of board; tape around to secure all canvas. Insert into frame. (If using a mat, insert it into frame first.) Place cardboard backing in frame and secure. Mount hanging wire onto back of frame using two screw eyes.

Tabby: In the head chart there is one blank center space: leave it blank as it helps define the tip of the nose. After needlepoint is completed, separate one yarn strand of white into its four plies; thread needle with one ply. Stitch whiskers in long straight stitches as shown in photograph.

Siamese: This piece is centered at a slight diagonal on the canvas square. Mark outline of needlepoint area on canvas as follows: Mark a vertical line 2¼″ in from right edge of canvas; mark a horizontal line 2¼″ below top edge. Mark a point on vertical line 7″ from top edge; mark a point on horizontal line 11⅝″ from right edge. Draw a line between two points 10½″ long, for top edge of needlepoint area. Using square, draw three more lines to complete 10½″ square area.

Begin at upper corner of marked square and work 30 rows of background in tent stitch. Then, following chart, begin ear tip in reversed tent stitch. Chart is separated where stitches change direction in head area only; background is worked entirely in tent stitch.

Red Pony Portrait

This beautiful wall hanging is a needlepoint adaptation of an antique cross-stitched doily. The modern version has a plain needlepoint background; the horse and border are worked in cross-stitch.

SIZE: 19″ x 20¼″.

EQUIPMENT: Masking tape. Pencil. Tapestry needle. Stapler. Hammer. **For Blocking:** Thumbtacks. Soft wooden surface. Brown wrapping paper. Ruler. Square.

MATERIALS: Needlepoint canvas, 10-to-the-inch, 24″ x 25″. Tapestry yarn, 8-yard skeins: 14 red, 32 ecru. Heavy cardboard or ⅛″ plywood for mounting, 19″ x 20¼″. Plywood ½″ thick for frame, 26½″ x 27¾″. Red felt 36″ wide, 1 yard. Staples. Beige sewing thread. Four small finishing nails.

DIRECTIONS: Read General Directions on page 90 for working a needlepoint piece. Mark outline of picture 19″ x 20¼″, allowing about 2½″ margin of canvas all around. Inside outline, mark off border area, 18 meshes wide. Using illustration as chart, work border in cross-stitch with red

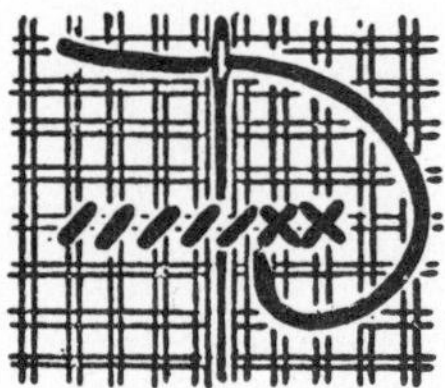

Cross-Stitch on Canvas

and ecru yarn. See detail of cross-stitch on canvas. Work the crosses over two threads of canvas instead of one as shown in detail (there will be five crosses to the inch). Starting at upper right inside border, with ecru yarn, work needlepoint background, in diagonal or continental method, to horse. Work horse and foliage below in cross-stitch with red yarn. Work horse shadings in cross-stitch with ecru yarn. Fill in remainder of background and horse's eye in needlepoint with ecru.

Block and mount picture, following directions on pages 92–93. Make a twisted cord with two strands of ecru yarn, following directions on page 416. Sew cord around edge of picture, overlapping ends of cord at a corner and sewing under cord.

To frame, smooth felt over one side of ½" plywood; bring excess felt neatly over edges and staple to back. Center picture on felt-covered plywood; secure in place by nailing at each corner of picture into frame; hide nailheads by lifting up canvas with needle to cover.

Noble Eagle

This dynamic eagle is worked on 10-to-the-inch canvas. It can also be embroidered on linen, using six strand embroidery floss in colors that match the photograph shown.

SIZE: 20" square.

EQUIPMENT: Masking tape. Tapestry needle. Pencil. **For Blocking:** Thumbtacks. Soft wooden surface. Brown wrapping paper. Ruler. Square.

MATERIALS: Needlepoint canvas, 10-to-the-inch, 24" square. Tapestry yarn, 15-yard skeins, in amounts and colors given with Color Key (six-strand embroidery floss or crewel wools may be substituted for hard-to-find yarn colors). Tapestry yarn in 40-yard skeins, 19 skeins beige for background. **For Framing:** Frame 20" square, rabbet size. Heavy cardboard at least ⅛" thick, 19¾" square. Straight pins. Finishing nails.

DIRECTIONS: Read General Directions on page 90 for working a needlepoint piece. Mark size of picture, 20" square, on canvas. Mark hori-

Color Key

- 1 Pale Silver (ribbon)
- 1 Lemon Yellow (leaves)
- 2 Gold-Yellow (flag, sword, ribbon)
- 2 Champagne (flag, eagle, eye)
- 1 Rose (flag)
- 1 Pale Gray-Green (flag)
- 2 Bright Yellow-Green (leaves)
- 1 Medium Green (leaves)
- 2 Dark Green (leaves)
- 1 Off-White (flag)
- 1 Beige (eagle)
- 5 Deep Beige (eagle, flag)
- 10 Taupe (eagle, flag)
- 6 Dark Gray (eagle)
- 4 Black (eagle, sword, flag, spear)
- 1 Light Slate Gray (sword, spear)
- 1 Dark Slate Gray (sword, spear)
- 1 Gold (beak, claws)
- 1 Burnt Orange (beak, claws, spear)
- 1 Rust (beak, claws, spear, flagpole)
- 1 Orange (flag, sword)
- 2 Bright Red (flag)
- 1 Medium Red (flag)
- 1 Dark Red (flag)
- 2 Medium Blue (flag)
- 1 Dark Blue (flag)
- 1 Light Violet (ribbon)
- 1 Dark Violet (ribbon)

zontal and vertical center lines as guide for placing eagle in center. Following chart, work eagle design first; then fill in background with beige yarn to marked outline. Work in regular needlepoint stitch, using one strand of tapestry yarn in needle.

An interesting effect may be obtained by using six-strand embroidery floss for some parts. For instance, in this antique eagle picture, embroidery floss was used for the champagne color and rose color in the flag stripes, and for the gold-yellow in stars and ribbon. When working with embroidery floss, use full six strands in needle and work in cross-stitch (see page 122). Crewel wool may be substituted for tapestry yarn colors you are unable to find easily. If using crewel wools, use two or more strands in needle to cover canvas.

Block and mount picture, following directions on pages 92–93. Frame as desired.

Weather Vanes in Gros Point

Old weather vanes inspired these four silhouettes, effective in black and white or in light and dark shades of green. You can make 10⅜"-square pictures, using 10-to-the-inch mesh, or plump quick point cushions, 20" square, on 5-to-the-inch mesh.

Color Key

☐ Light Green
☒ Bottle Green

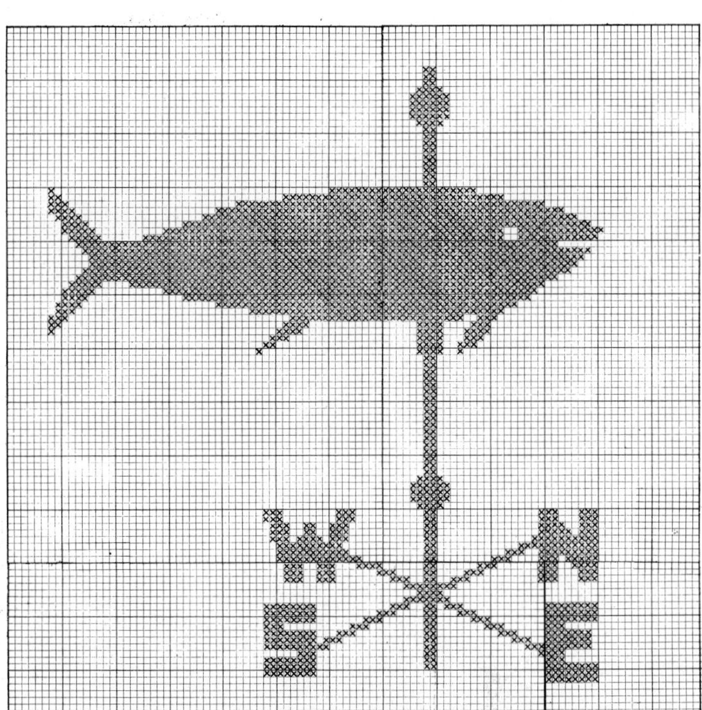

SIZE: 10⅜″ square.

EQUIPMENT: Tapestry needle. Masking tape. Scissors. Pencil. Ruler.

MATERIALS (for each picture): Tapestry yarn, 40-yard skeins: 2½ skeins for background, 1 skein contrasting color for design. Needlepoint canvas, 10-mesh-to-the-inch, 16½″ square.

DIRECTIONS: Read General Directions on page 90 for working a needlepoint piece. Cut a piece of canvas for each picture, 16½″ square. Allow about a 3″ margin of canvas around picture area. Start at top right corner and follow chart. Work needlepoint in continental or diagonal stitch, using single strand of yarn.

Block and mount, following directions on pages 92–93.

Nature's Kingdom

Do this handsome wall hanging or rug in quick point on 5-mesh-to-the-inch rug canvas with rug yarn. The majestic lion, in the foreground, is pictured with twelve other subjects of the animal kingdom in lush jungle colors.

SIZE: 30″ x 59″.

EQUIPMENT: Masking tape. Pencil. Ruler. Extra-large-eyed tapestry needle. Scissors. **For Blocking:** Soft wooden surface. Brown wrapping paper. Square. Rustproof thumbtacks. **For Mounting:** Power saw. Hammer. Screwdriver. Staple gun.

MATERIALS: Rug canvas, 5-mesh-to-the-inch, 40″ wide, 1⅞ yards. Rug yarn: ½ pound each of hunter green, dark olive green, celery green, gray-blue green, chartreuse green, bottle green, gold; ¼ pound each of pale pink, shrimp pink, russet brown, dark greenish brown, dark brown, medium brown, gray-beige, purple, pale blue, medium blue, white. **For Mounting:** Two pieces of 1″ x 3″ pine, each 54″ long. Beaver board 30″ x 59″. Straight pins. Four large right-angle irons. Screws. Finishing nails. Felt ¼ yard, 36″ wide. All-purpose glue.

DIRECTIONS: Read General Directions for needlepoint on page 90. With pencil, mark outline of area to be worked, 30″ x 59″.

Use either the continental or diagonal method of working needlepoint. Cut working strands about one yard long and use one strand in needle. Starting in upper right-hand corner, follow chart to work design. Large areas of one color have been blocked off and numbered according to the chart number listed in Color Key. Smaller areas of these colors are designated by symbols as shown under chart symbols on the Color Key.

When needlepoint is finished, block as directed on page 92.

Mounting: For mounting flat on wall, stretch canvas over board 30″ x 59″, keeping lines of

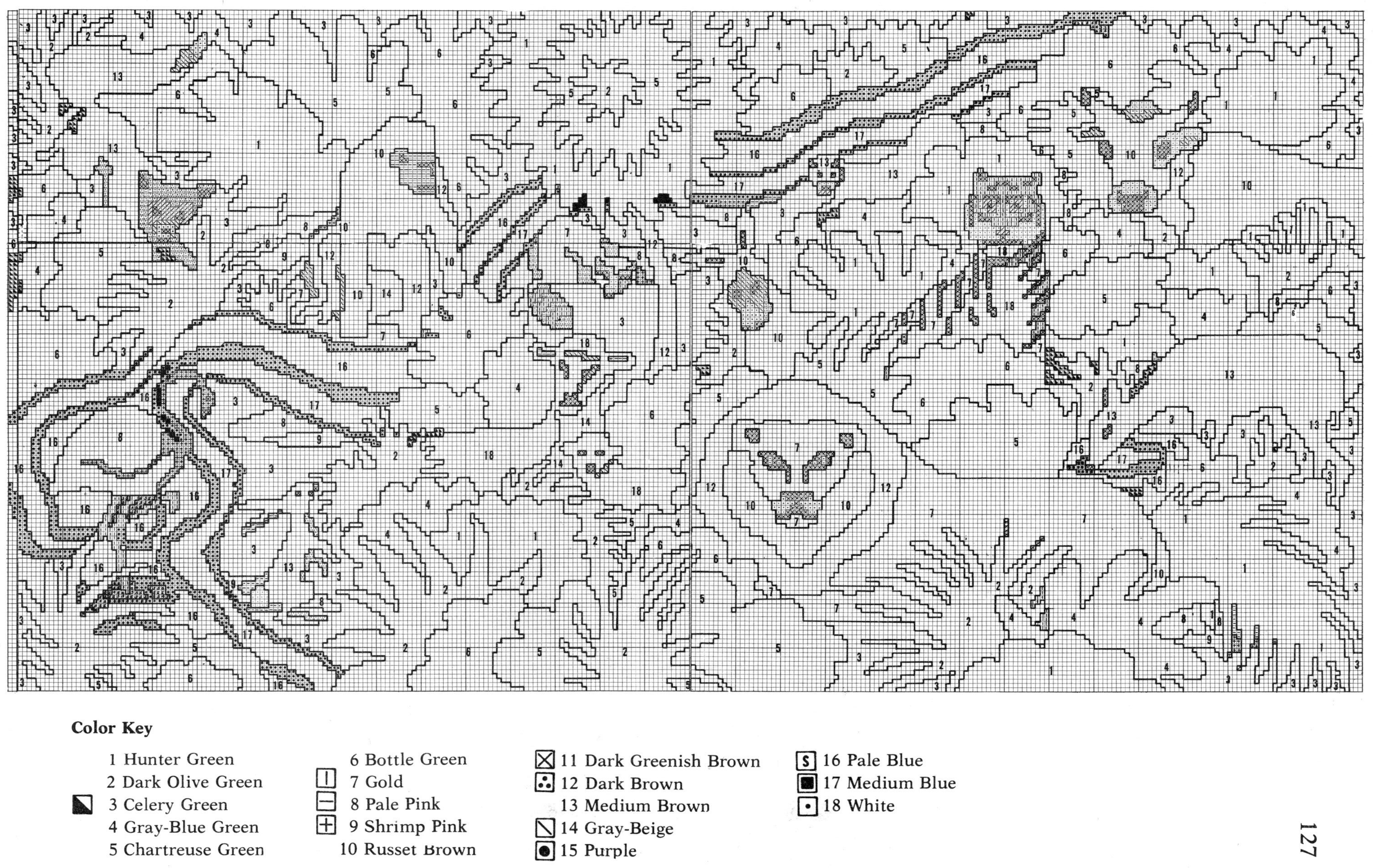

Color Key

	1 Hunter Green
	2 Dark Olive Green
◣	3 Celery Green
	4 Gray-Blue Green
	5 Chartreuse Green
	6 Bottle Green
⏐	7 Gold
−	8 Pale Pink
+	9 Shrimp Pink
	10 Russet Brown
☒	11 Dark Greenish Brown
⁘	12 Dark Brown
	13 Medium Brown
⧅	14 Gray-Beige
●	15 Purple
S	16 Pale Blue
■	17 Medium Blue
·	18 White

stitches straight. Fasten canvas with straight pins pushed into edges of board. Begin pinning at center of each side and at corners; continue, placing pins ¼″ apart. Tape excess canvas to back.

For curved mounting, use two pieces of 1″ x 3″ pine, each 54″ long. Following Diagram 1, make

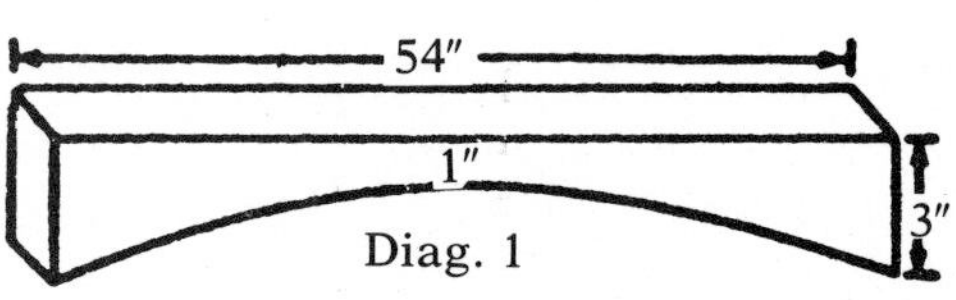

Diag. 1

cutting line first with pencil on one 3″ surface of each. Using saw, cut curve out of each piece. Use one piece 3″ up from bottom and one 3″ down from top. Plan placement of strips on wall and attach angle irons to wall at points where they will support pine strips at each end at top and at each end at bottom. Stretch needlepoint over beaver board; staple on back to secure. Cut felt to cover back of beaver board at side edges only; glue. Bend beaver board to fit curve and attach to curved part of pine strips by nailing between stitches on front. Attach pine strips to angle irons.

Folk Art Hanging

This cheerful wall hanging was adapted from the primitive motifs of flowers, animals, and playing children that often appear in Middle Eastern rugs. Glowing colors were used to work design, 29" x 53", on 4-mesh-to-the-inch canvas. Multicolor tassels add authentic touch.

SIZE: 29½" x 57".

EQUIPMENT: Masking tape. Large-eyed rug needle. Scissors. **For Blocking:** Thumbtacks. Large soft wooden surface. Brown wrapping paper. Ruler. Square. Pencil. Sewing needle.

MATERIALS: Rug canvas 4-mesh-to-the-inch, 36" wide, 1¾ yards. Rug yarn, 1-ounce skeins: 12 skeins lime green; 5 skeins fir green; 2 skeins emerald; 2 skeins white; 2 skeins amber; 2 skeins teal blue; 2 skeins scarlet; 2 skeins walnut; 2 skeins medium orange; 2 skeins royal blue; 2 skeins salmon. Fiberboard 29½" x 57". Large straight pins. Sewing thread.

DIRECTIONS: See General Directions on page 90 for working a needlepoint piece. Mark outline of hanging 29½" x 57" on canvas, leaving about 3" margins all around. Use either continental or diagonal method. Start at upper right-hand corner of marked area on canvas. Follow illustration for design and colors. Work border for a short distance on top and side; work motifs; then fill in background and finish the border.

Block and mount on fiberboard, following directions on pages 92–93.

Finishing: Make 10 tassels 3½" long, using all colors of yarn in each; see page 416 for method.

Make a twisted cord to fit around edges of panel, using three strands of lime green, each 14 yards long (or make two cords, using yarn strands half this length); see page 416. Tie ends with thread. Sew twisted cord around panel edges through canvas. Tie tassels onto cord with top ends of tassel yarn; tape tie ends on back.

Four Contour Needlepoint Projects

The fabulous Shell, worked in classic proportions, rests in a frame of receding bargello waves. Pictured here as a footstool cover, it would also make a wonderful pillow.

Flame-Stitch Fireworks spark from a center worked in more conventional needlepoint to make an exciting pillow. It is worked here in Persian yarn on 14-to-the-inch canvas.

Poppies bloom in swirling cadences of bright bargello bands. The center motifs are worked with two plies of three-ply Persian yarn. The bargello bands are worked in three-ply. This footstool cover is worked on 14-to-the inch canvas.

Anemones are the central design here. The border is an innovative contour-designed bargello. The pillow is worked in eight colors of Persian yarn on a 14-to-the-inch canvas.

EQUIPMENT: Masking tape. Pencil. Ruler. Scissors. Tapestry needle. **For Blocking:** Thumbtacks. Soft wooden surface. Brown paper. Square.

MATERIALS: Persian yarn, 3-ply. (**Note:** Amounts given take regrouping of plies into consideration.) Mono needlepoint canvas, 14-mesh-to-the-inch.

DIRECTIONS: Read General Directions on page 90 for working a needlepoint piece. Referring to individual directions, mark outline of area to be worked on canvas, allowing about 2½" margins all around. Mark exact center of canvas; mark center of each side on marked outline of area. Use 2 plies of 3-ply yarn for center motif and center background. Use full 3-ply for bargello. Following chart and color key for each design, first work center motif in continental stitch. Start at exact center of motif (center side and bottom rows of design are marked by *'s; exact center of canvas is point at which the two starred rows intersect). Chart for each design includes one-quarter of bargello border and also indicates outline for background of center motif. Mark this outline all around center motif. After completing motif, work background of center area in continental stitch. Begin bargello border at left side of chart and work to the right. After completing first quarter, continue design for second quarter by repeating design in reverse, omitting those stitches which are worked over center mesh. Repeat in reverse for second half of border.

Block needlepoint, following instructions on page 92. See pages 93 and 94 for instructions on making a pillow and upholstering.

FIREWORKS PILLOW

Size: 12" x 12¼".

Materials: Canvas 17" x 17¼". Persian yarn (given in yds.): dark orange, 22; medium orange, 15; light orange, 22; bright pink, 38; yellow, 52.

Repeat chart in reverse for remaining quarters, omitting center lines for repeats. Include center motifs in each area (it is given only once). Add 10 rows of pink in continental all around for border.

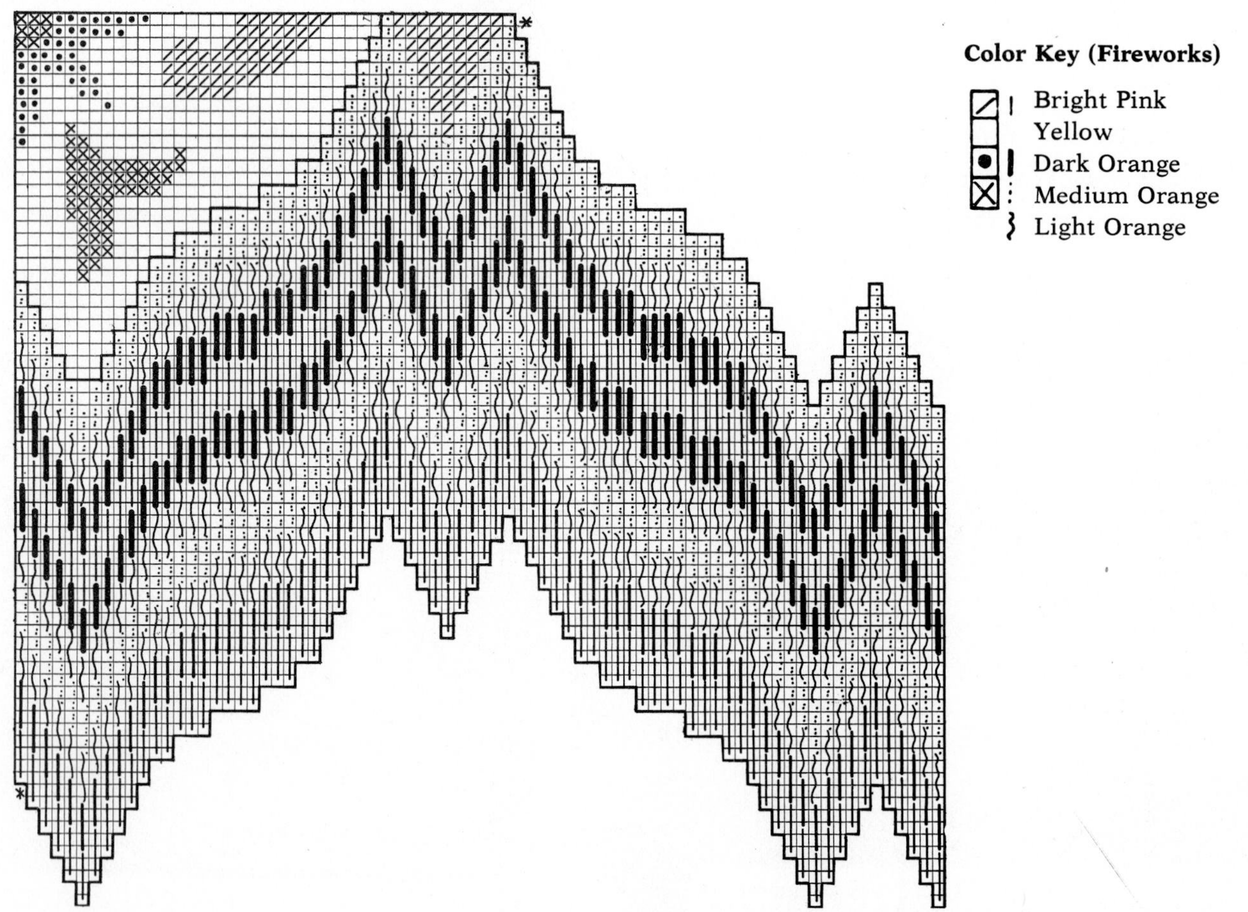

SEASHELL FOOTSTOOL

Size: 14¾″ x 12½″.

Materials: Canvas, 19¾″ x 17½″. Persian yarn (given in yds.): dark blue, 47; medium blue, 84; light blue, 127 (center background included); very light blue, 40; white, 3.

Color Key (Seashell)

- ■ | Dark Blue
- ⁄ ⌇ Medium Blue
- • Light Blue
- ⊞ White
- ⋮ Very Light Blue

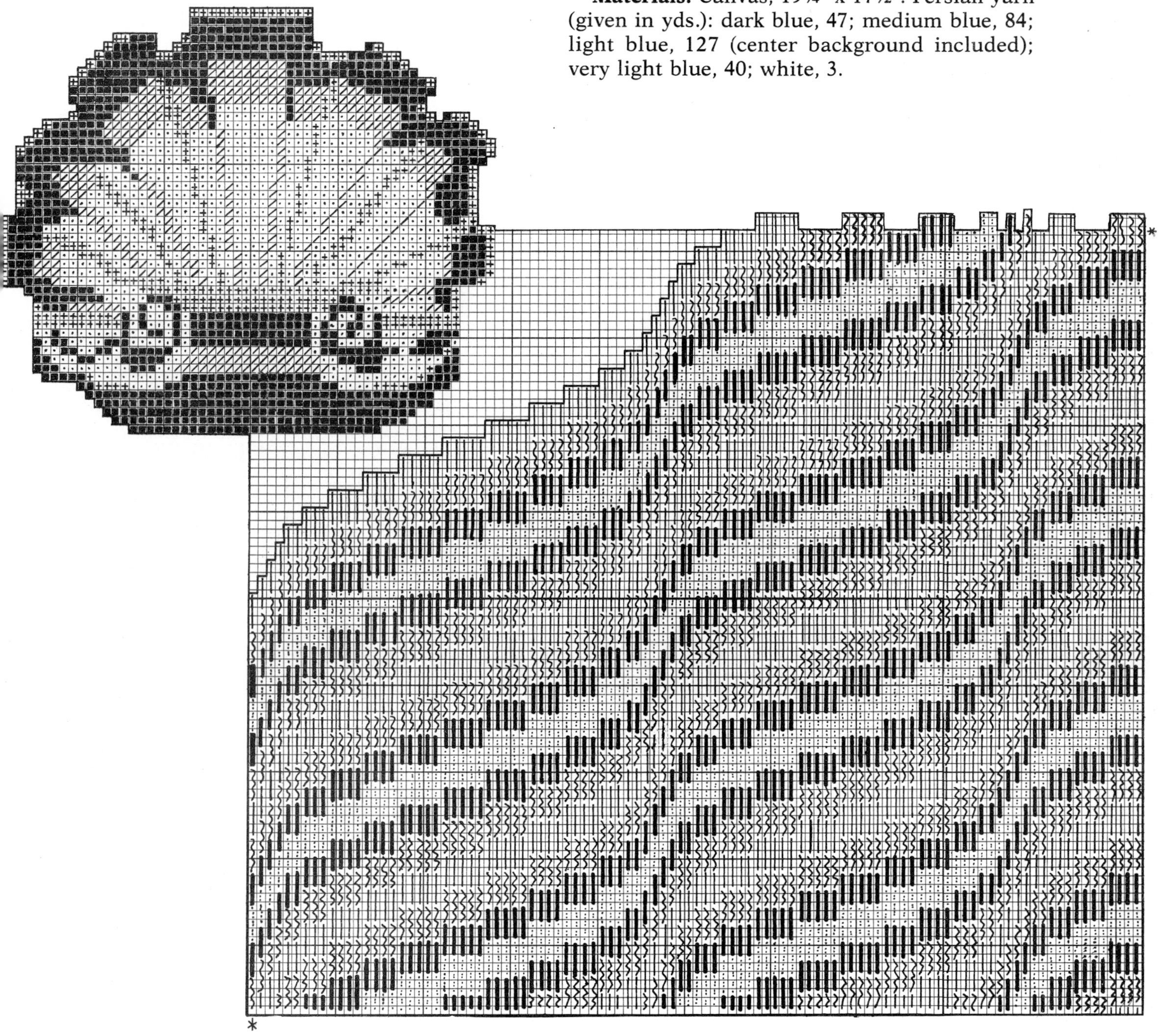

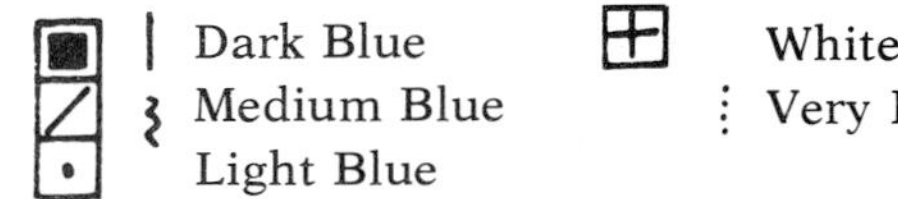

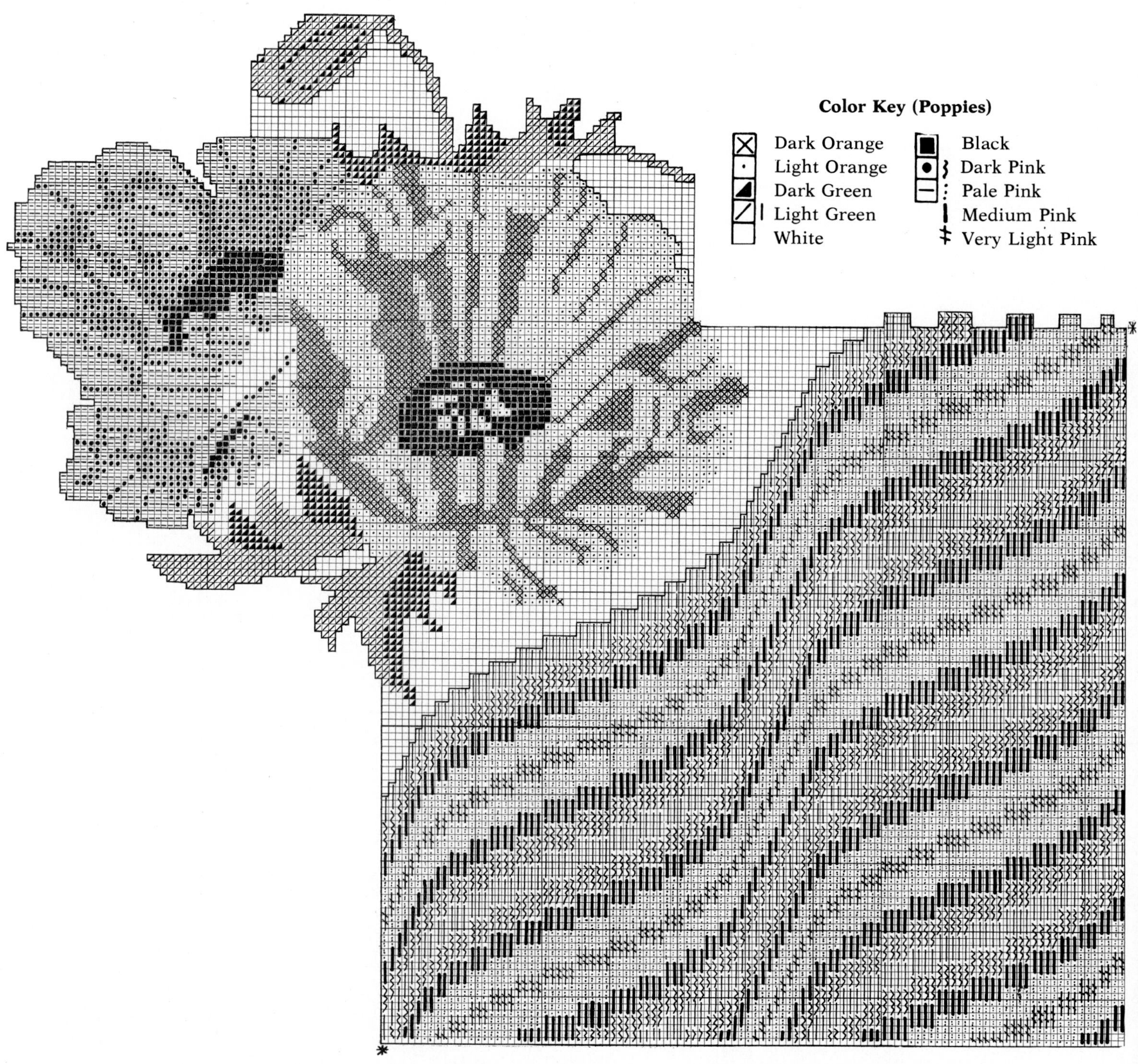

POPPIES FOOTSTOOL

Sizes: 15¾" x 15¼".

Materials: Canvas, 20¾" x 20¼". Persian yarn (given in yds.): dark orange, 15; light orange, 20; dark pink, 67; medium pink, 64; pale pink, 78; very light pink, 24; dark green, 7; light green, 39; black, 4; white (center background), 94.

ANEMONES PILLOW

SIZE: 17½″ x 15½″.

MATERIALS: Canvas 22½″ x 20½″. Persian yarn (given in yds.): dark purple, 45; medium purple, 54; lavender, 44; pale lavender, 156; dark green, 6; light yellow-green, 28; black, 3; white, 94 (center).

To complete second bargello stripe, repeat chart once in reverse (omitting pale lavender row) and once again, as shown, to pale lavender row. Continue bargello pattern out to corners with pale lavender.

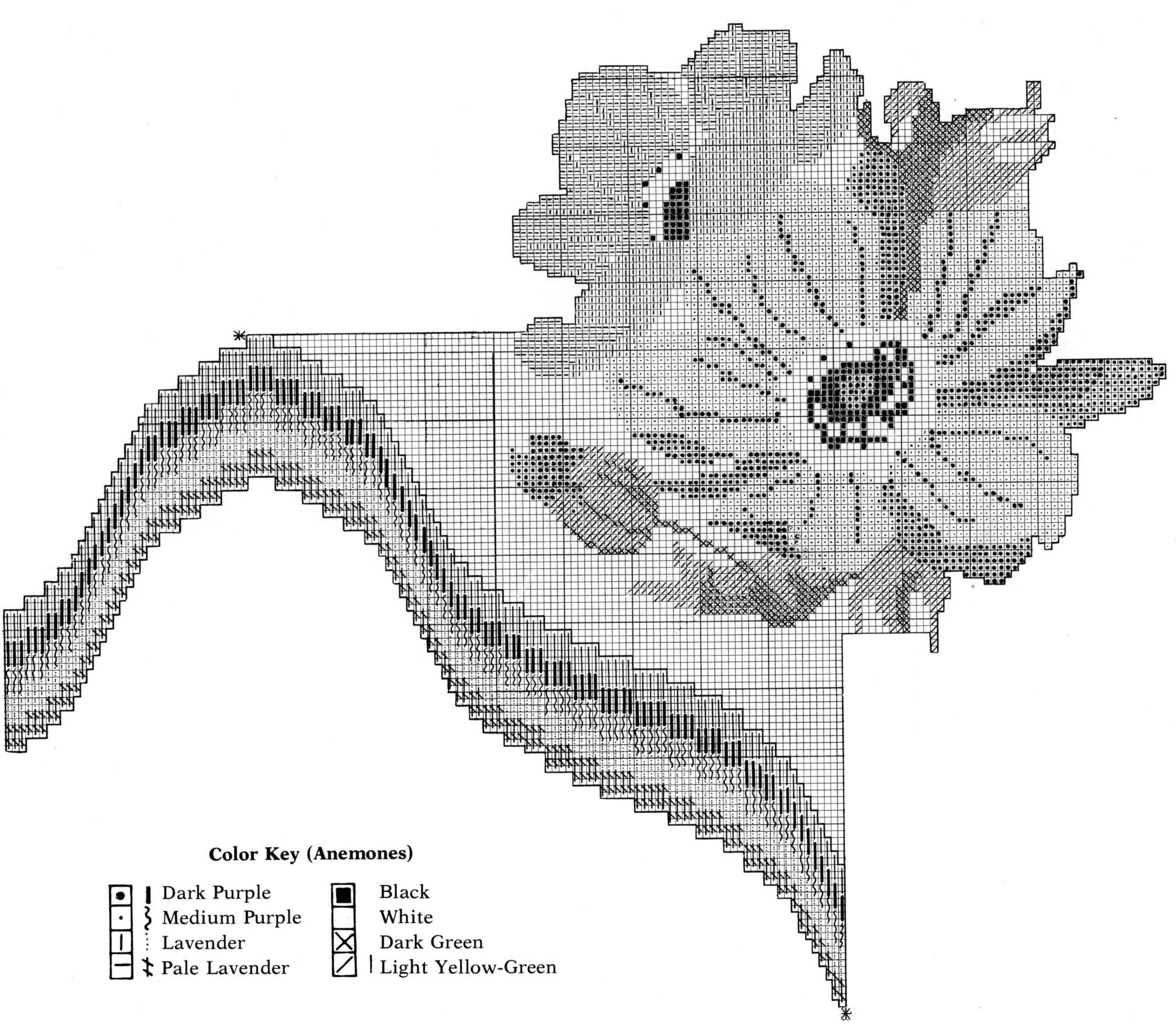

Three Needlepoint Mirror Frames

Golden ripples frame a small mirror in beautiful four-way bargello. The inner and outer edges and corners of the design are worked in plain needlepoint. This is mounted to folded cardboard for extra dimension.

The red mirror frame has a garland of white star flowers centered with French knots. Other novelty stitches are worked into the plain background. The piece measures 15" x 19" before framing.

The blue bargello design is repeated on all four sides, joining at the corners for a mitered effect. The inner and outer edges are finished with twisted cords. The framed mirror measures 11½" x 12".

GOLD MIRROR FRAME

SIZE: Approx. 9¾" x 11".

EQUIPMENT: Masking tape. Ruler. Scissors. Pencil. Tapestry needle. Straight pins. **For Blocking:** Soft wooden surface. Brown wrapping paper. Pencil. Square. Rustproof thumbtacks. **For Frame:** Utility knife. Triangle with 45° angle. Staple gun.

MATERIALS: Mono needlepoint canvas, 12-mesh-to-the-inch, 17" x 18". Persian yarn: pale yellow, 10 yards; light yellow, 10½ yards; gold, 12 yards; mustard, 12½ yards; brown, 92 yards; blue, 3½ yards plus 5½ yards for twisted cord. Stiff illustration board. All-purpose glue. Mirror 4¼" x 5¾" (see note below). Staples for staple gun.

DIRECTIONS: Read General Directions on page 90 for working a needlepoint piece. Mark a 4¾" x 6¼" rectangle at center of canvas. (This size is approximate, since needlepoint canvas may vary slightly in the number of meshes per inch

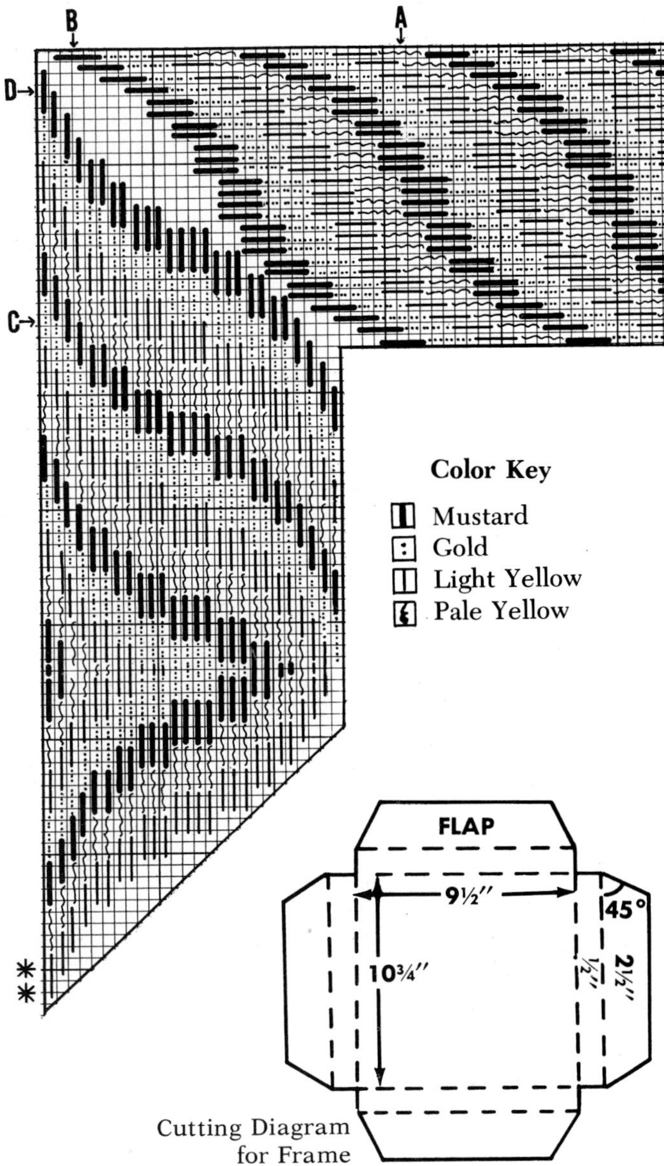

Cutting Diagram for Frame

vertically and horizontally.) Follow chart and color key for two sides and corner of frame. The rectangle you have marked at center of canvas is the guideline for inner edge of bargello portion of frame. The horizontal graph lines on the chart represent the horizontal threads of canvas, and the vertical lines represent vertical threads. Using full 3-ply strand, work bargello stitches vertically over 4 threads (stitch length is modified at center of sides to maintain pattern). Work succeeding rows below with the top of the stitches in the same mesh as bottom of previous row.

Turn chart so letters D and B are in upper right corner. Work row B (mustard) from left to right to establish position and pattern. Continue working chart downward to starred row. Then work the eight rows from A to B as in first half (in reverse to keep the pattern). Turn canvas and chart to work other side (D and B are at upper left). Work side as shown in chart, up to double starred row. Then work the six rows from C to D as for A to B above. Work remaining two sides in same manner. Blank squares on chart indicate plain needlepoint to be filled in after completing bargello. Split the yarn, and use only 2-ply strand for all plain needlepoint areas. With brown, fill in the corners and the two rows that form the inner border. (**Note:** If mirror in size needed is unavailable, use slightly smaller mirror and work a few more rows of plain needlepoint around inside rectangle to compensate; or, cut down a larger mirror with glass cutter.)

Work plain needlepoint (page 90) around outside edges as follows: Work two rows brown all around, then one row blue, and one row brown all around. Mark off a 1″ square in each corner at edge of needlepoint. Still using brown, work an additional 1″ plain needlepoint on all sides, leaving the corner squares blank. (This reduces bulk when folding needlepoint onto frame.) When finished, block needlepoint as directed on page 92.

To make frame, cut corrugated cardboard as shown in diagram. The dimensions of the rectangle (9½″ x 10¾″) should correspond to the dimensions of the needlepoint marked by the row of blue; if they do not, alter size of cardboard accordingly. Use the triangle to get the 45° angle of flaps. Cut out on solid lines of diagram. Using straight edge and utility knife, score on dash lines. Bend frame area around center upward. Fold flaps down and under so angled corners meet. This forms beveled frame, ½″ deep at outside. Glue flaps in this position; let dry thoroughly. Stretch needlepoint over frame, pinning blank center rectangle to recessed center of frame temporarily. Tape canvas margins to back of frame. Staple two opposite sides to back of cardboard, near last row of needlepoint. Remove tape from these two sides; trim excess canvas. Repeat with two remaining sides. Coat blank canvas rectangle with glue; place mirror on top. Weight down with books or other heavy object until dry.

Following twisted-cord directions on page 416 and using three strands of blue yarn, make cord to go around mirror edge. Glue cord around mirror, concealing any canvas which may be visible. Use pins to hold in place until dry, and overlap the ends slightly.

Finish the back by gluing or taping a piece of thin cardboard to cover the cut canvas edges.

RED MIRROR FRAME

SIZE: 15″ x 19″ unframed.

EQUIPMENT: Masking tape. Tapestry needle. Scissors. Ruler. **For Blocking:** Rustproof thumbtacks. Soft wooden surface. Square. Brown wrapping paper. Pencil. **For Framing:** Staple gun.

MATERIALS: Needlepoint canvas 10-mesh-to-the-inch, 19″ x 23″. Persian yarn (2 ply, 3 strands): bright red, 4½ ounces; dark red, about 9 yards; off-white, about 25 yards (sold in 30″ strands). Wood-framed mirror exactly 9″ x 12″ (outside measurements). Picture frame to match mirror frame in color and style, rabbet size 15″ x 19″. Heavy- and light-weight cardboard for mounting and finishing. Staples. (**Note:** If frames in these exact sizes are unavailable, get mirror frame slightly smaller and picture frame with slightly larger rabbet; adjust needlepoint by adding the required number of rows of needlepoint at center and outside edges.)

DIRECTIONS: Read General Directions for working needlepoint on page 90. With pencil, mark a 15″ x 19″ rectangle on canvas, leaving equal margins all around. Then mark a 9″ x 12½″ rectangle in exact center of first. Refer to stitch details for working the novelty stitches. Chart shows placement of stitches at corners; horizontal lines represent horizontal threads of canvas, and vertical lines represent vertical threads. Unless otherwise specified, use full three strands of yarn in needle.

Turn canvas with long sides at top and bottom. With bright red yarn, work a row of crossed Scotch stitch all around outside of inner rectangle, leaving center unworked. Using off-white, work star flower stitch all around; begin the stitches that are closest to center of canvas one mesh away from Scotch stitch; adjacent star flowers meeting in same mesh. Using bright red yarn, make four French knots in centers, one at each corner. Using dark red, work one French knot in the very center. Beginning one mesh away from outermost stitch of star flowers, work a row of Smyrna cross with bright red yarn. Fill in background areas with plain needlepoint stitch (page 90); work 4 or 5 rows within the inner rectangle to make sure that no canvas shows around mirror frame. Using two strands of dark red, work one row of backstitch between needlepoint stitch areas and Smyrna cross and Scotch stitch areas. Using off-white, work three-stitch cross variation over needlepoint where star flowers meet.

Block needlepoint as directed on page 92. Cut heavy cardboard ⅛″ smaller than rabbet of picture frame. Center cardboard on wrong side of needlepoint, and stretch the canvas margins over the cardboard. Hold canvas in place by pushing pins through canvas into cardboard edge. Center mirror at inner rectangle of needlepoint; secure by stapling through the cardboard into the frame. Insert needlepoint in picture frame. Tape cardboard on back of frame to finish.

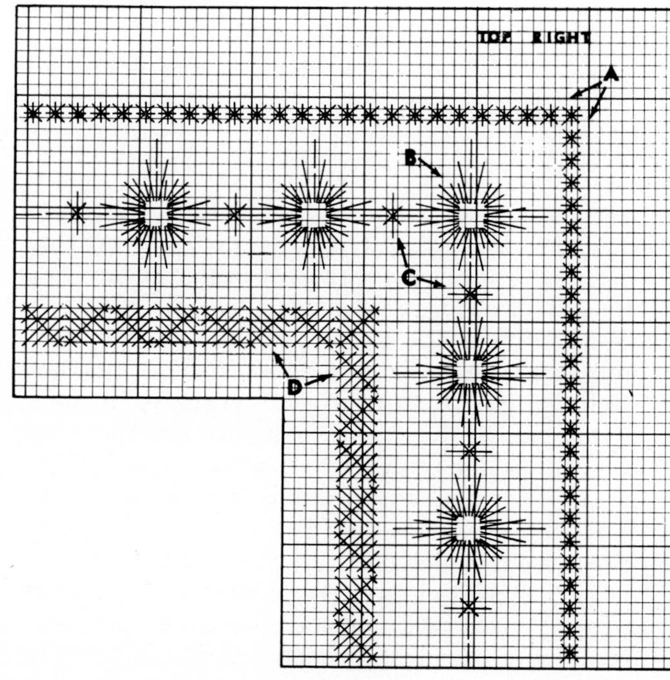

Crossed Scotch Stitch Variation

CROSSED SCOTCH STITCH VARIATION: Starting in the upper left corner, work diagonal stitches from left to right over first one mesh, then two, then three, then four, then three, then two, then one mesh. Cross these stitches with a diagonal stitch in opposite direction, going into open meshes at corners. Repeat for next stitch, working in same spaces as previous stitch, but start in lower left corner, and make the diagonal stitches in the opposite direction.

Three-Stitch Cross Variation

THREE-STITCH CROSS VARIATION: Make a horizontal stitch over four meshes where center of cross will be. Bring needle out at lower left, and make a diagonal stitch to the right over two meshes. Make second half of cross in opposite direction over two meshes.

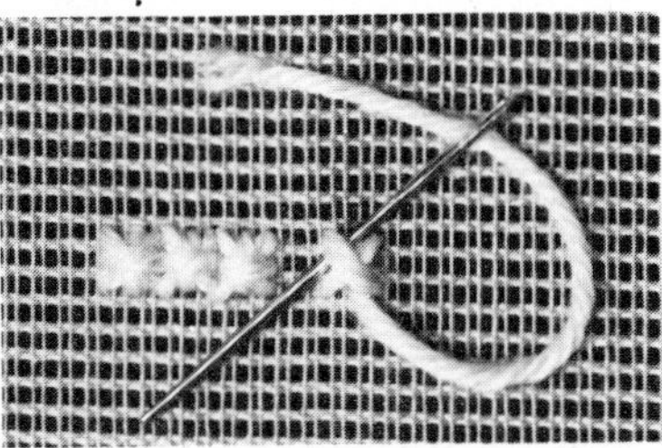
Smyrna Cross

SMYRNA CROSS: Starting at lower left, make a diagonal stitch to the right over two meshes. Then make a diagonal stitch to the left over two meshes, forming an X. Make a vertical stitch over two meshes, and then a horizontal stitch over two meshes.

Backstitch

BACKSTITCH: Bring yarn up to front of canvas. Insert needle one mesh to right, and bring up two meshes to the left. Working from right to left, continue in this manner, making stitches touch so they form one continuous line.

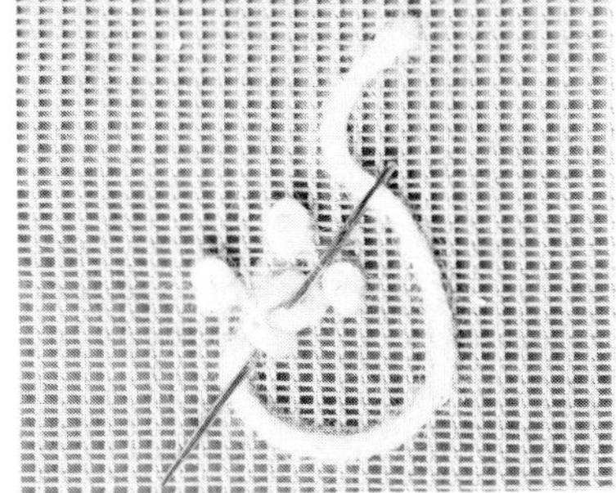
French Knots

FRENCH KNOTS: Bring yarn up to front of canvas. Hold needle with right hand; with left hand, wrap the yarn over and around the needle (the number of times yarn is wrapped determines the size of knot). Pull the yarn fairly taut on the needle and insert needle in same mesh; pull yarn through to tighten.

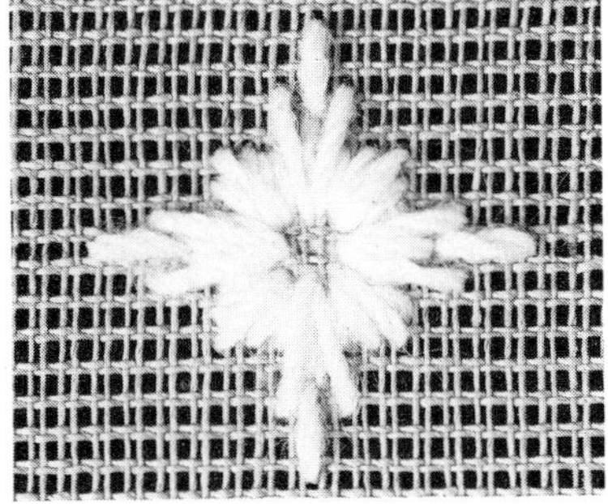
Star Flower Stitch

STAR FLOWER STITCH: Leave center mesh unworked until later, for French knots. Begin stitches in the eight meshes that form a square around center mesh. Each of the four long points consists of four stitches. Take three stitches at base of point, starting in center mesh on one side of square: one vertical straight stitch over three meshes and a slightly diagonal stitch one mesh over at each side and four meshes up; make fourth (straight) stitch starting in same mesh as center stitch, over three meshes. Make a long point at each side of center mesh.

For short points, work five stitches starting in mesh between long points, over two meshes each, forming a square corner. Make one square corner between each long point.

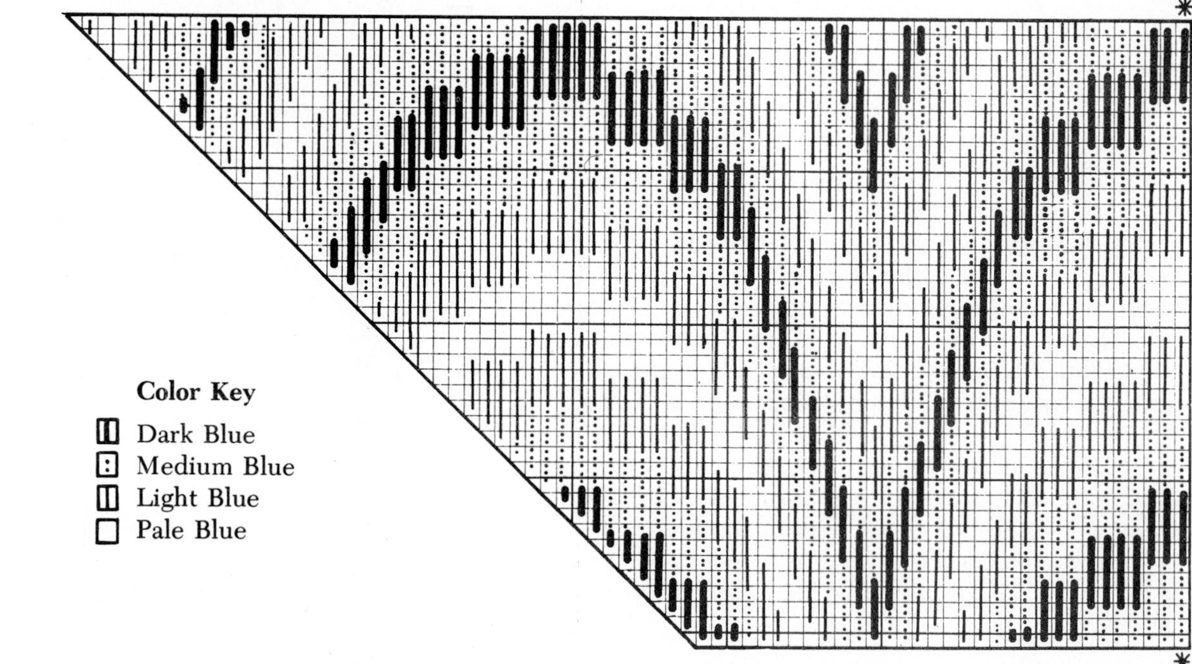

BLUE MIRROR FRAME

SIZE: Approx. 11½" x 12".

EQUIPMENT: Scissors. Ruler. Pencil. Masking tape. Tapestry needle. Straight pins. **For Blocking:** Soft wooden surface. Brown wrapping paper. Square. Rustproof thumbtacks. **For Frame:** Utility knife. Staple gun.

MATERIALS: Mono needlepoint canvas, 12-mesh-to-the-inch, 18¼" x 18¾". Persian yarn: pale blue, 14 yards; light blue, 28 yards; medium blue, 34 yards, plus about 29 yards for twisted cords; dark blue, 54 yards. Mirror, about 4½" x 4¾" (see Note below). Corrugated cardboard or ½" plywood. All-purpose glue. Staples for staple gun.

DIRECTIONS: Read General Directions on page 90 for working needlepoint. At center of canvas, mark 4½" x 4¾" rectangle; since the mirror will be glued over it, this area will remain blank. (This size is approximate since needlepoint canvas may vary slightly in the number of meshes per inch vertically and horizontally.)

Follow chart and Color Key to work bargello design. The horizontal graph lines of the chart represent the horizontal threads of the canvas, and the vertical lines represent the vertical threads. Work chart as shown (chart gives one half of one side [top] and shows how to miter corners). Work stitches so top of chart starts on marked rectangle. Using full 3-ply strand throughout, work over five threads except around edges as shown. Work one row of one color from right to left. Work top of stitches of succeeding rows in same mesh as bottom stitches of preceding rows. Complete the second half of this side in reverse, omitting the starred row (there are five stitches at center). Turn canvas and work the three remaining sides the same as the first, with mitered corners of adjacent sides meeting in same mesh.

Split the dark blue yarn and use 2-ply strand to work two rows of plain needlepoint (see page 90) all around outside of bargello. Mark off a ½" square in each corner next to needlepoint. Work an additional ½" plain needlepoint on all sides, leaving marked squares blank (this reduces bulk and makes folding easier). **Note:** If mirror in size required is unavailable, use slightly smaller mirror and work a few rows of plain needlepoint around inside rectangle to compensate. Block needlepoint as directed on page 92.

Cut plywood exact size of outside of bargello portion. If using cardboard, cut a few pieces this size so that when they are glued together in layers, they measure ½" thick. Stretch needlepoint over wood or cardboard; tape canvas margins temporarily to back. Staple two opposite sides to board near last row of needlepoint. Remove tape; trim excess canvas. Repeat with two remaining sides. Coat blank canvas rectangle with glue; place mirror on top. Weight down with books or other heavy object until dry.

Using five strands of yarn, make two twisted cords of the medium blue yarn—one for mirror edge and one to go around edge of frame (see directions on page 416). Glue cords around the appropriate edges, using pins to hold in place until dry; overlap the ends of cord slightly.

Finish the back by gluing or taping a piece of thin cardboard to cover the cut canvas edges.

A Pillow and Panel in the Classic Rose Design

A French mise-en-carte (literal translation: "placed on card") design, used originally in the eighteenth century by silk weavers in the looming of their exquisite fabrics, is reinterpreted for a pillow and headboard worked in quick point. The original design shown here dates from 1775. The single rose and bud motif, adapted from the traditional French fabric pattern, makes a charming little pillow. Worked with double strands of needlepoint wool on rug canvas, the pillow is 12" in diameter. The quick-point rose panel is 12½" x 31½" and can decorate a single-bed headboard or a bench top. Worked in rug yarns on rug canvas.

WHITE ROSE PILLOW

SIZE: 12″ in diameter.

EQUIPMENT: Masking tape. Tapestry and sewing needles. Scissors. **For Blocking:** Thumbtacks. Soft wooden surface. Brown wrapping paper. Pencil.

MATERIALS: Rug canvas, 5-mesh-to-the-inch: one piece 16″ square, one piece 5″ wide and 40″ long. Tapestry yarn (40-yd. skeins): 1 each white, yellow, pink, light green, jade, forest green, gold, dark red; 4 lime. Light yellow felt, one piece 12½″ square. Round foam rubber box pillow 12″ in diameter. White carpet thread. Lime sewing thread.

DIRECTIONS: Read General Directions on page 90 for working a needlepoint piece. Use wool double in needle throughout. Round corners of the 16″ square canvas; this allows a 2″ margin of unworked canvas all around needlepoint. Following chart on opposite page, work design in diagonal or continental stitch. Fill in background on chart to make circle.

Boxing: On 5″ x 40″ canvas strip, work 9 rows of needlepoint 37″ long across length of strip, leaving about 1½″ of unworked canvas all around.

Block; see directions on page 92.

Finishing: Trim unworked canvas on pillow top to 1″. Clip this 1″ of canvas about every 2″ all around edge of needlepoint. Turn unworked canvas neatly to wrong side all around edges of needlepoint and baste in position, overlapping clipped edges to make it flat.

Trim away unworked canvas around boxing strip to ½″. Clip this one-half inch of canvas about every 2″ all around edge of needlepoint. Turn to wrong side of work and baste. Whip ends together with carpet thread. Pin edge of boxing to edge of

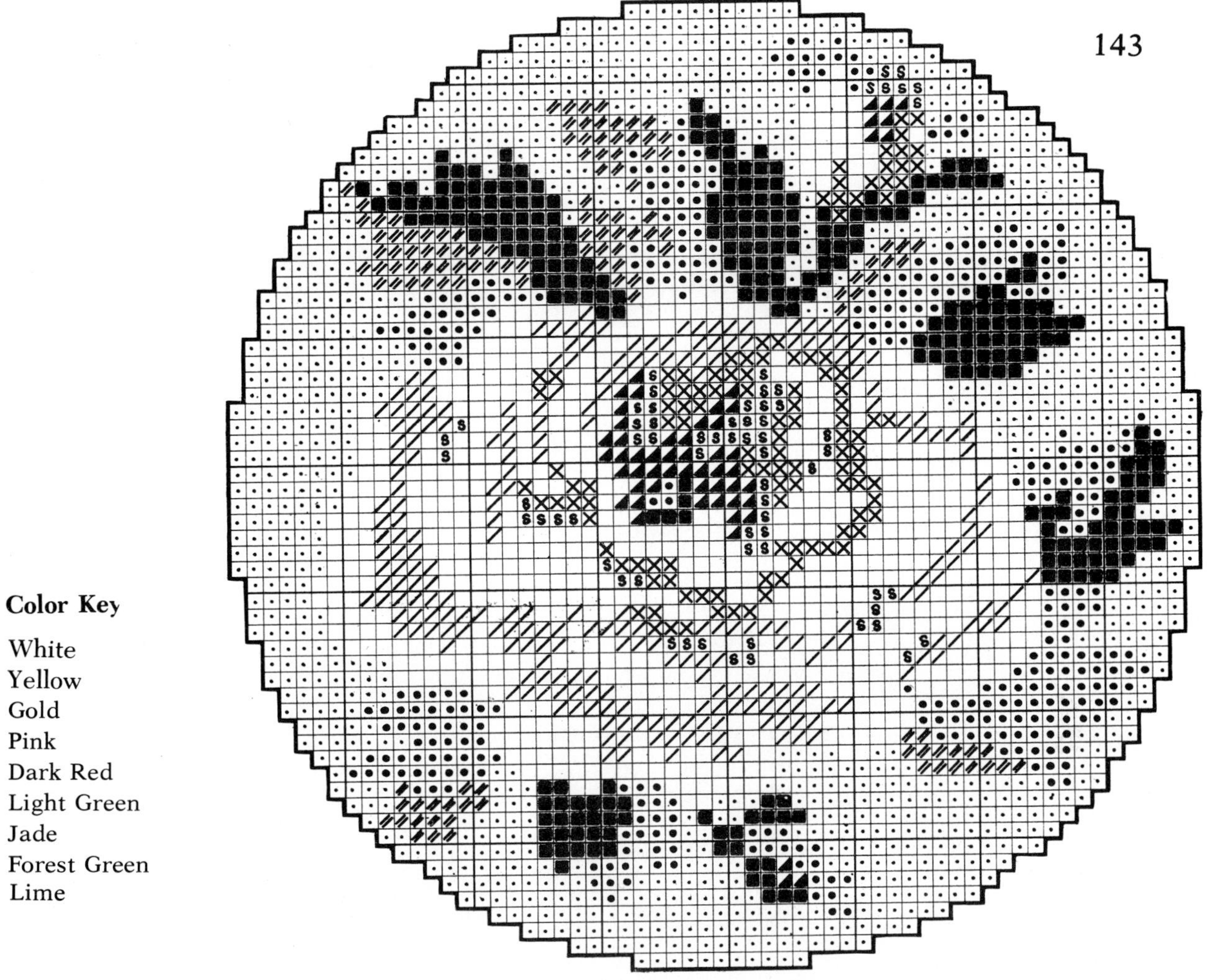

pillow top and whip together. Insert foam rubber pillow. Cut felt into a circle 12¼" in diameter for bottom of pillow. Turn in ⅛" all around edge of felt and baste. Place on pillow, pin edge of felt to free edge of boxing and whip together all around with carpet thread. Finish top and bottom joinings with a twisted cord (see page 416) of lime yarn, sewn on with lime thread.

WHITE ROSE PANEL

SIZE: 12½" x 31½", with stripping.

EQUIPMENT: Masking tape. Rug needle. Scissors. Backsaw. Miter box. Tack hammer. **For Blocking:** Thumbtacks. Soft wooden surface. Brown wrapping paper. Pencil.

MATERIALS: Rug canvas, 5-mesh-to-the-inch, one piece 18" x 37". Rug yarn (approx. 21-yd. skeins): 1 each dark gold, medium gold, light rust, dark rust; 2 each dark green, medium green, light green, and white; 4 yellow-green. Carpet tacks. Plywood for mounting panel, ½" x 12" x 31". Lattice stripping, 3/16" thick and ⅝" wide, 8 ft. Wire brads, ½" long. Six 1" flathead wood screws.

DIRECTIONS: Read General Directions on page 90 for working a needlepoint piece. Starting 2¾" in from top right corner of canvas, work corner of background to start of design, following chart above. Work in continental or diagonal method. Work design, then fill in rest of background.

Block; see page 92.

To Mount Panel: Place needlepoint on plywood mounting panel, right side up. Fold unworked canvas over edge and onto back of panel. Fasten canvas around edge of panel with carpet tacks; before tacks are hammered in, check to make sure rows of stitches are straight and piece is completely smooth. Tack loose edges of canvas to back of mounting panel.

Fit lattice stripping along one side of panel; mark and miter corners, using backsaw and miter box. Fit and cut other three sides of lattice in same way. Finish lattice stripping, including ends, to match your headboard. With wire brads 3" apart, nail lattice strips to edges of panel, covering canvas. Cover up nail heads to match finish of stripping. Attach panel to headboard with flathead wood screws.

Color Key

☐ Yellow-Green	☒ Dark Gold	⧄ Light Green
⊡ White	S Light Rust	● Medium Green
⧄ Medium Gold	◪ Dark Rust	■ Dark Green

Pomegranate Motif Upholstered Chair

Plump pomegranates on a mustard gold background make a stunning pattern for upholstery. The center motif is repeated on the armrests, and the same design can be used for a handsome accompanying pillow. This is worked on 10-mesh-to-the-inch canvas with tapestry yarn.

EQUIPMENT: Masking tape. Ruler. Pencil. Scissors. Tapestry needle. Muslin and paper for patterns. **For Blocking:** Soft wooden surface. Brown wrapping paper. Square.

MATERIALS: Needlepoint canvas 10-mesh-to-the-inch; see directions below for figuring amount. Tapestry yarn; black, light gold, dark gold, orange; see directions below for figuring amounts.

DIRECTIONS: Read General Directions on page 90 for working a needlepoint piece. To figure amount of canvas required, measure each part of chair to be upholstered, including curved sides. Allow 2½" extra all around, outside widest part. On 10-mesh-to-the-inch canvas, one yard of tapestry yarn will work approximately one square inch of needlepoint.

Make muslin and paper patterns for each upholstery piece and mark on canvas, following directions for Upholstery Pieces on page 93.

Mark horizontal and vertical lines on canvas at center. With vertical center line of a pomegran-

ate motif on vertical marked line of canvas, plan the placement of the horizontal rows of motifs to fit the area in most pleasing manner. One pomegranate motif, actual size, measures 3⅜" x 5½". Large chart gives repeat of motifs. Work in continental or diagonal stitch. The small chart is for the arm piece shown in our chair illustration. This small repeat pattern can also be used to make a matching pillow.

When needlepoint is complete, block pieces following directions on page 92; use paper pattern.

We recommend having the chair upholstered by a professional, using your needlepoint pieces, unless you are doing a simple chair seat.

Color Key

- □ Light Gold
- ▨ Dark Gold
- ☒ Orange
- ■ Black

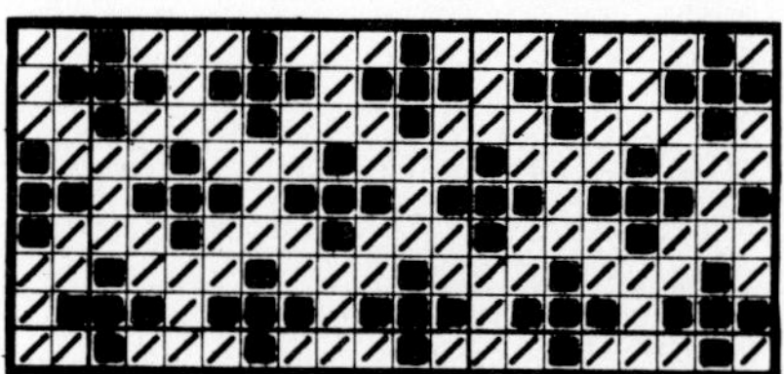

Tulip Motif Upholstered Chair

Here graceful tulips are set in stripes to make an easy repeat pattern that is beautifully suited to a chair and footstool, but which could be adapted as well to a bench, small sofa or pillow. It is worked in Persian or tapestry wool on 10-to-the-inch canvas.

EQUIPMENT: Scissors. Pencil. Ruler. Masking tape. Tapestry needle. Muslin and paper for pattern. **For Blocking:** Soft wooden surface. Brown wrapping paper. Square.

MATERIALS: Needlepoint canvas 10-mesh-to-the-inch; directions below for figuring amount. Tapestry or Persian yarn (approximate yardage given for one repeat only; work out

Color Key

- ■ Black
- ◪ Brown
- ◪ Dark Green
- □ Beige
- ⊠ Medium Green
- ◪ Gold
- ◪ Marigold
- ⊡ Yellow

amount needed according to number of repeats): 14 yards beige, 6 yards greenish brown, ½ yard antique gold, 2 yards marigold, 2 yards yellow, 4 yards medium green, 2½ yards dark green, 4 yards black.

DIRECTIONS: Read General Directions on page 90 for working a needlepoint piece. To figure amount of canvas required, measure chair seat or stool to be upholstered, allowing sufficient amount to cover thickness of seat filling. Allow 2½" extra all around, outside widest part.

Make muslin and paper patterns for each piece to be upholstered and mark on canvas, following directions for Upholstery Pieces on page 93.

Work needlepoint design within marked area, using continental or diagonal method. Start at top right of canvas and follow chart, repeating motif for first vertical row. Begin second vertical row at heavy black lines in center of chart, and then repeat whole chart as before for remainder of second row, thus staggering flowers and leaves in adjacent rows. Repeat first and second vertical rows until marked area of canvas is completely filled. Fill in the background with beige yarn as you complete design.

Block piece, following directions on page 92; use paper pattern.

"Slipcover" Lamp Bases

Slipcover a lamp base with needlepoint! The blue scroll design is easily adapted to any size and the five-color paisley pattern can be adjusted by widening the background. Both designs are worked on 10-to-the-inch canvas with tapestry yarn.

EQUIPMENT: Masking tape. Tape measure. Tapestry and sewing needles. Scissors. Pencil. **To Block:** Thumbtacks. Soft wooden surface. Brown wrapping paper. Square.

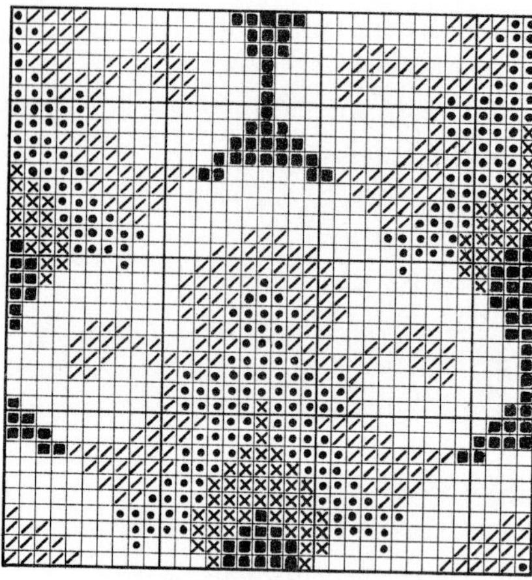

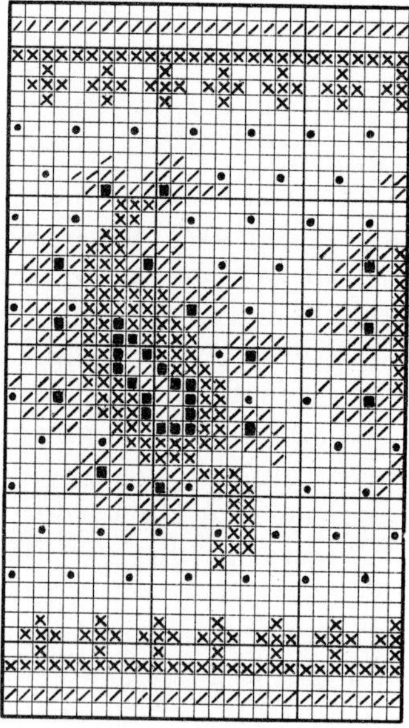

**Color Key
(Scroll Lamp Base)**

- ☐ Pale Turquoise
- ⧄ Bright Turquoise
- ⊡ Light Blue
- ☒ Deep Blue
- ■ Navy Blue

**Color Key
(Paisley Lamp Base)**

- ☐ Brown
- ☒ Apricot
- ⧄ Blue
- ■ Bright Orange
- ⊡ Pale Orange

MATERIALS: Needlepoint canvas, 10-mesh-to-the-inch (large enough to fit around lamp base plus 2½″ margin all around). Amounts of yarn will depend upon size of piece. For Paisley Design: 3-ply Persian yarn: 5 skeins brown; 2 skeins blue; 3 skeins apricot; 1 skein bright orange; 1 skein pale orange. For Scroll Design: Tapestry yarn: 7 skeins pale turquoise; 5 skeins bright turquoise; 5 skeins light blue; 2 skeins deep blue; 3 skeins navy blue. Sewing thread. Lamp bases: Large drum, base 6″ in diameter x 12″ tall; small drum, base 4½″ in diameter x 9″ tall.

DIRECTIONS: Read General Directions on page 90 for working needlepoint. Mark off outline of design on canvas. If using lamps shown, outline for paisley design (yellow lamp) is 4⅝″ x 12¼″; for scroll design (blue lamp) outline is 6¼″ x 16½″. If using other lamps, measure depth and circumference for design size.

Hold canvas with selvage edges at sides and work needlepoint in either diagonal or continental stitch (see directions on page 90.) Follow charts for designs; each square of chart represents one needlepoint stitch. Repeat designs for length and width of marked area of canvas.

Block finished canvas following directions on page 92. Cut canvas margins to 1″; turn under and sew to back of needlepoint. If desired, make twisted cord, using one color of yarn to go around top and bottom edges (see page 416). Tack cord to edges. Wrap needlepoint in place around lamp base; with sewing thread, whip edges neatly together at back of lamp base with matching color sewing thread.

Navajo Pillows

Traditional Navajo blankets are transformed into a pair of brilliantly colored pillows. Each is worked in an easy bargello stitch variant that covers from 2 to 10 canvas meshes at a time. Use tapestry yarn on 16-mesh-to-the-inch canvas.

RED DIAMONDS PILLOW

EQUIPMENT: Pencil. Ruler. Masking tape. Scissors. Tapestry needle. Sewing needle. **For Blocking:** Brown wrapping paper. Soft wooden surface. Square. Rustproof thumbtacks.

MATERIALS: Mono needlepoint canvas, 16-mesh-to-the-inch, 16½" x 22". Tapestry yarn, 8.8-yd. skeins: 12 skeins blue; 6 skeins red; 5 skeins beige; 2 skeins each of orange and yellow; 1 skein gold. Piece of red upholstery fabric for backing at least 36" wide, ½ yard. Cable cord ¼" thick, 1¾ yards. Red sewing thread. Muslin for inner pillow, ½ yard. Dacron fiberfill for stuffing.

DIRECTIONS: Read General Directions on page 90 to begin needlepoint. On canvas, mark outline of finished pillow size 11¼" x 16¾", leaving equal margins on all edges.

Using single strand of yarn in needle, work design following chart and Color Key.

Chart for pillow is one-quarter of the design, except for longer stitches which are worked across the center. The exact horizontal and vertical center lines of design are indicated by arrows. Mark these lines on canvas. Work straight stitches over number of meshes indicated on chart, changing direction of stitches as indicated. Be sure ends of all stitches are in same mesh of canvas as ends of next stitches. Work center diamond first, then work upper left hand quarter as shown on chart; repeat chart in reverse for the remaining quarters, omitting center row A for left side of pillow.

When bargello is complete, block, following

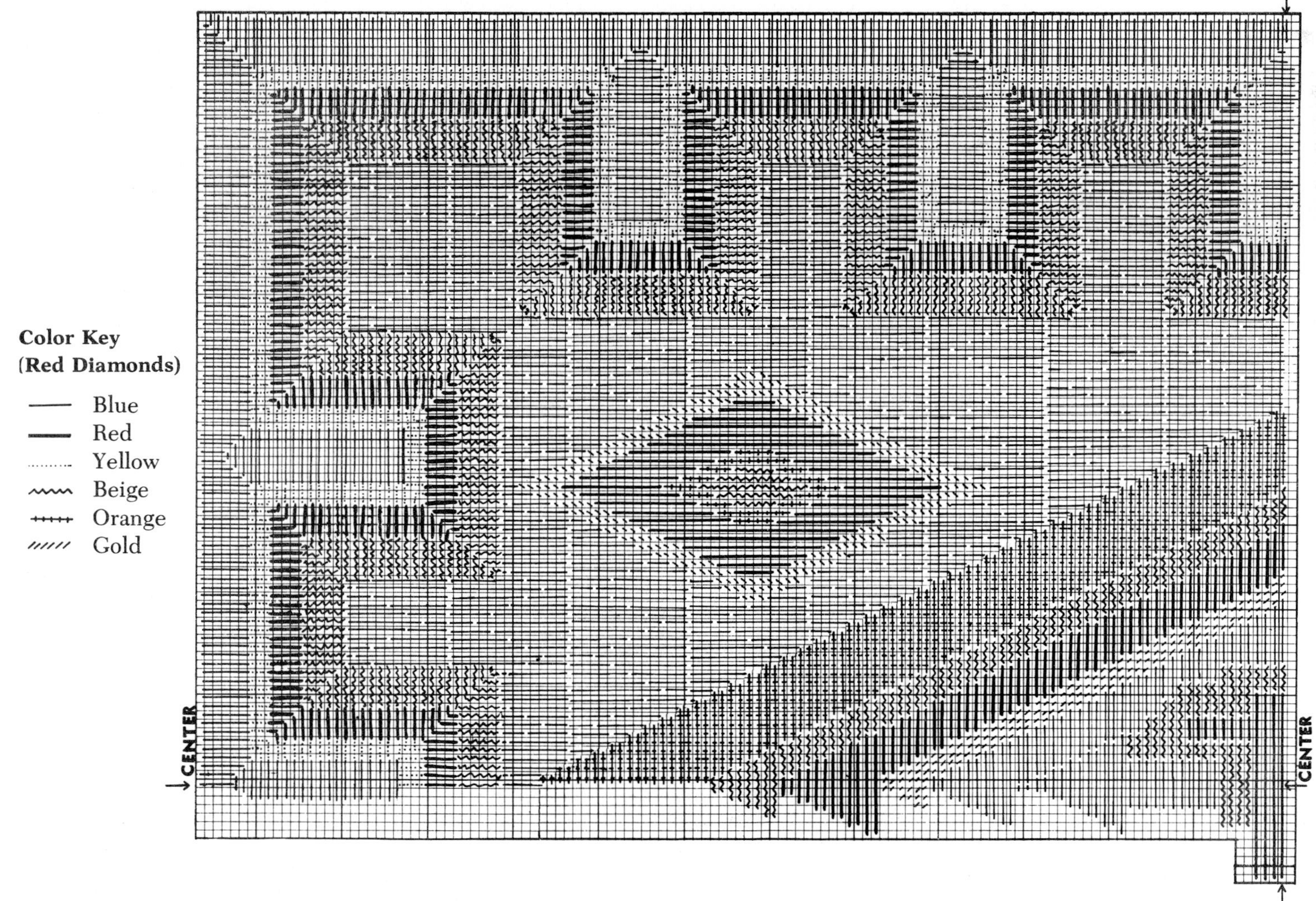

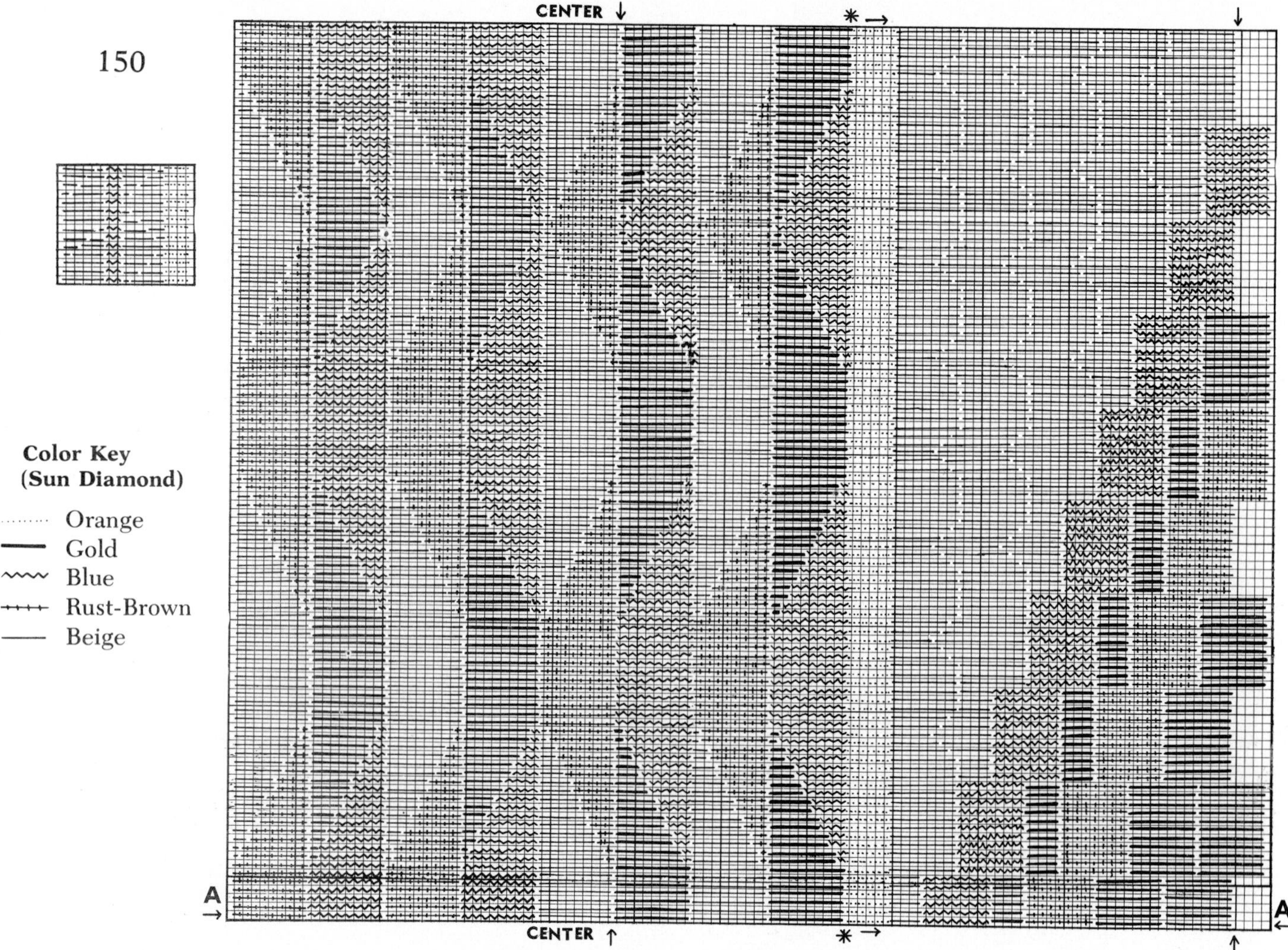

directions on page 92. On brown paper, mark horizontal and vertical center lines of drawn rectangle. Lay canvas on paper as directed matching center markings on canvas with center markings on paper; tack. Trim margins to 1″.

Cut backing fabric same size as canvas. For piping, cut 1½″-wide bias strips from remaining fabric; join to make strip long enough to fit perimeter of pillow with ½″ overlap. Lay cable cord along center length of strip on wrong side of fabric; fold strip over cord and stitch along length of strip close to cord.

With raw edges even, baste piping to right side of finished canvas along four sides. To finish ends of piping neatly, cut cord off about ½″ inside each fabric end; turn raw edges of one end inside and insert other end of piping in this end; sew ends securely and neatly together. With right sides of canvas and fabric facing, and piping between, pin pieces together. Stitch together, making 1″ seam and leaving 10″ opening in center of one long edge. Trim seams and cut into corners of canvas. Turn to right side.

Make inner pillow of muslin. Cut two pieces of muslin each 13¼″ x 18¾″. With right sides facing, sew edges together with ½″ seams, leaving 6″ opening in center of one long edge. Turn to right side. Stuff inner pillow fully. Turn edges of opening in and sew closed. Insert inner pillow into outer pillow. Add stuffing in corners if necessary. Turn raw edges of fabric in and slip-stitch closed.

SUN DIAMOND PILLOW

EQUIPMENT: Same as for Red Diamonds Pillow.

MATERIALS: Mono needlepoint canvas, 16-mesh-to-the-inch, 18″ x 21½″. Tapestry yarn, 8.8-yd. skeins: 10 skeins beige; 6 skeins rust-brown; 5 skeins each of gold and blue; 1 skein orange. Red upholstery fabric for backing, at least 36″ wide, ½ yd. Red sewing thread. Cable cord ¼″ thick, 1¾ yds. Muslin for inner pillow, ½ yd. Dacron fiberfill for stuffing.

DIRECTIONS: Read General Directions on page 90 to begin needlepoint. On canvas, mark outline of finished pillow size 13″ x 16½″, leaving equal margins on all edges.

Using single strand of yarn in needle, work bargello design following charts and Color Key.

Work straight stitches over number of meshes indicated on chart. Be sure ends of all stitches are in same mesh of canvas as ends of next stitches.

Large chart for pillow is one-quarter of each section of design, except chart for diamond section includes those stitches worked across center line of section. Begin by working upper right quarter of design as follows: Start at center line (arrow on chart) at top of 21½" edge. Work to the right; work quarter diamond as shown, then repeat quarter diamond in reverse. For second half of diamond section below top half, repeat design in reverse, omitting center Row A. For next section of design (from center arrow to left) work stripes as shown on chart. For bottom half of this section, follow chart in reverse, omitting Row A. To complete design, repeat striped portion from starred row to left edge of chart. Follow small chart for last four stripes of color at left. Follow, repeating and reversing procedure as above for working bottom half of stripes, and for reversing zigzag pattern in last four stripes at left.

Block, following directions on page 92 and referring to directions for Red Diamonds Pillow. Trim canvas margins to 1".

Make backing, piping, inner pillow (cutting muslin pieces 15" x 18½"), and assemble, following instructions for Red Diamonds Pillow.

African Kuba Cushions

These dazzling geometrics are drawn from an African textile. They are quick to make, using 5-mesh-to-the-inch canvas, for lavish floor pillows!

EQUIPMENT: Masking tape. Pencil. Ruler. Scissors. Sewing needle. Large, blunt rug needle. **For Blocking:** Brown wrapping paper. Soft wooden surface. Square. Rustproof thumbtacks.

MATERIALS (for each): Rug canvas, 5-mesh-to-the-inch, 40" wide, 1 yard. Acrylic rug yarn (1¾-ounce skeins), colors and amounts given

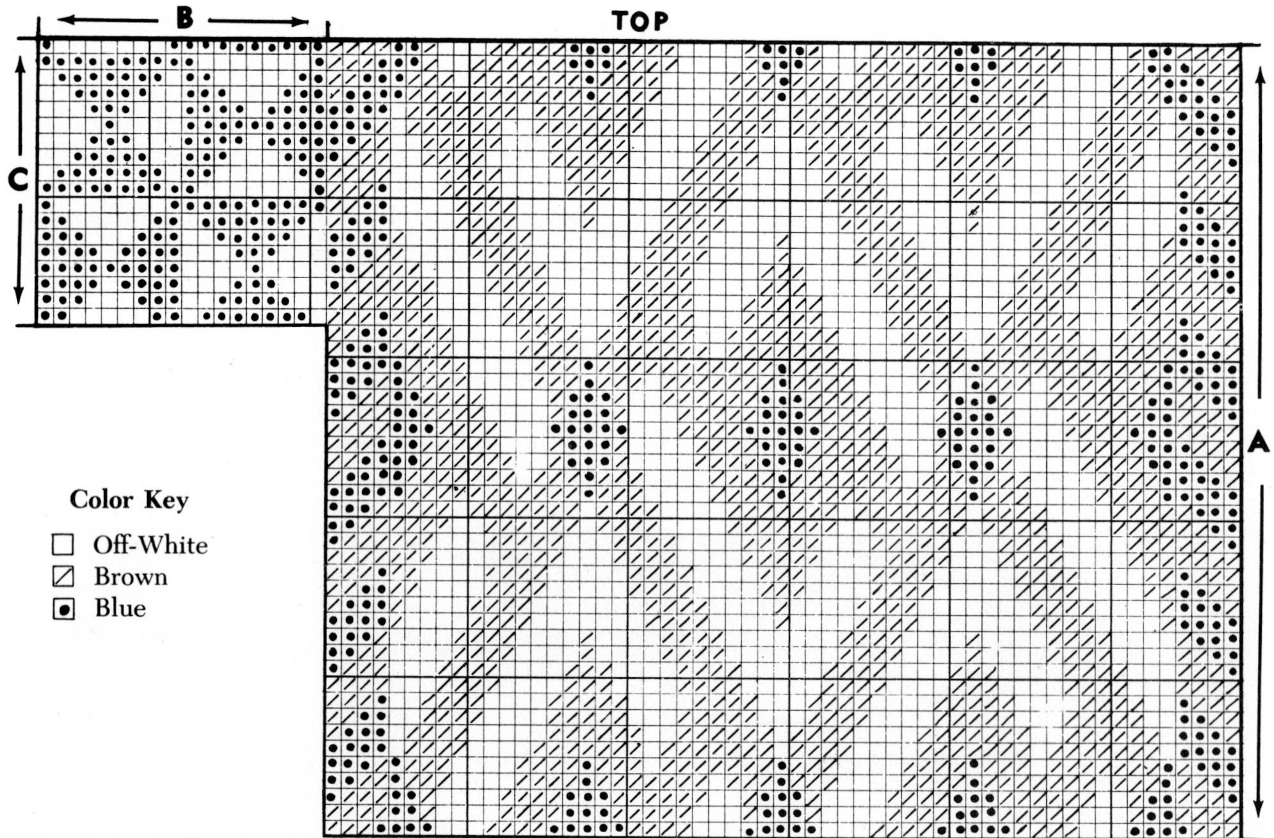

below. Felt or closely woven cotton fabric for backing, 36″ wide, ¾ yard. Inexpensive fabric such as muslin for inner pillow, 1½ yards. Dacron fiberfill for stuffing, about two 1-lb. bags, depending upon the desired degree of firmness. Sewing thread to match backing.

DIRECTIONS: Read General Directions on page 90 before starting. Prepare canvas as directed; refer to individual directions below for method of working repeats. Following chart and Color Key for design, work in continental stitch throughout. Thread needle with single strand of yarn; length of yarn should be about 30″ long for this project in order to eliminate too many yarn ends on back. However, in order to avoid tangles, do not make strands any longer.

When needlepoint is completed, block, following directions on page 92. Trim canvas margins to about 1″. Cut backing fabric same size as canvas. With right sides facing, stitch backing and needlepoint together, making 1″ seam. Leave about a 15″ opening at center of one side. Trim corners and whip canvas margins to back of needlepoint; turn right side out.

To make inner cushion, cut two pieces of muslin 1″ larger all around than finished cushion top. Stitch muslin pieces together, making ½″ seams; leave 6″ opening in center of one side. Turn right side out; stuff fully. Turn raw edges of opening in ½″; slip-stitch opening closed. Insert inner cushion in needlepoint cushion. Turn raw edges of opening in, and slip-stitch opening closed.

TWO-PANEL CUSHION

Mark needlepoint area 26″ x 27″ (finished size) on canvas, leaving margins all around. For this cushion you will need yarn in the following amounts: off-white, 4 skeins; blue, 5 skeins; brown, 3 skeins.

Following the chart and Color Key, repeat sections indicated to marked outline as follows: Begin at upper right, and work the broken diamond panel (A); repeat downward to 26″; repeat the portion of the small triangle panel marked B to the left to 27″, and the portion marked C downward to 26″. Finish cushion, following directions above.

THREE-PANEL CUSHION

Mark needlepoint area 23½" x 29½" (finished size) on canvas, leaving margins all around. You will need yarn in the following amounts: off-white, 7 skeins; blue, 4 skeins; brown, 2 skeins.

Follow chart and Color Key as follows: Begin at upper right, and work design to the left. Reverse design for left side, and begin with single starred row. This gives you the top half of the design. For bottom, begin with double starred row, and work downward, reversing the entire top half. Finish cushion, following directions above.

Victorian Beaded Pincushions

Crystal-clear beads add a rich frosting to our needlepoint pincushions, reflecting the Victorians' fondness for fancywork. The beads are sewn onto the canvas with a needlepoint stitch to make the motif or central design. The background can be worked in double cross-stitch. These projects are finished with beaded loops or fluffy cotton fringes. They measure from 7" to 9" square and are worked on 10- to 13-mesh-to-the-inch canvas.

The pincushions as shown were worked on canvas 12- or 13-mesh-to-the-inch. Following the charts, designs may be worked on a coarser mesh, such as 10-to-the-inch. The beads will not cover the canvas if a coarser than 10-to-the-inch mesh is used. Designs may be worked with a plain needlepoint background or in a double cross-stitch (see lower row, canvas detail). Work needlepoint in continental stitch and sew beads on in same manner (see top row, canvas detail). Designs may be worked entirely in needlepoint, eliminating the beading if desired. Work needlepoint on 10-to-the-inch canvas in tapestry yarn with a medium tapestry needle; on 12- or 13-to-the-inch, use crewel wool doubled and a fine tapestry nee-

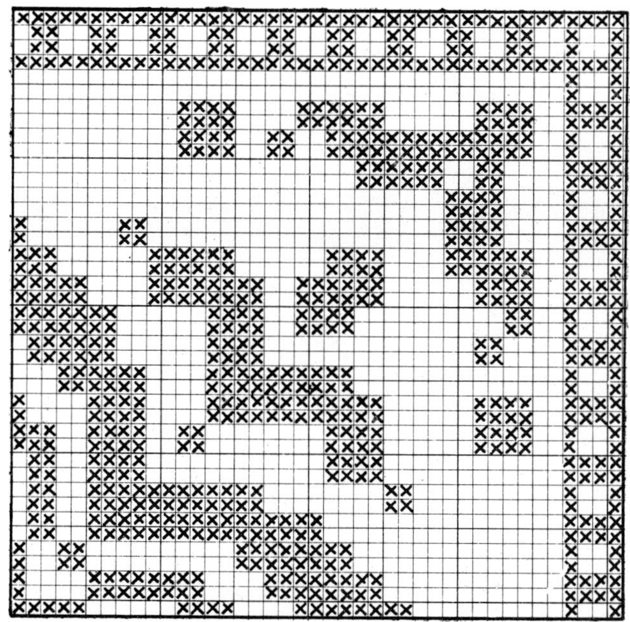

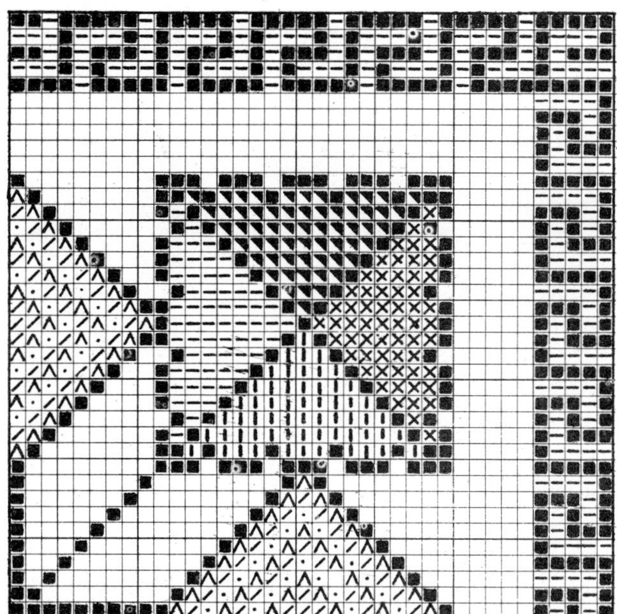

Color Key

■ Black	◪ Brown	Ⅰ Purple
⊡ Beige	⋀ Dark Brown	◥ Green
	☒ Red	▯ Peach

dle. For the beading, use beading thread or nylon thread, a beading or fine needle.

Pincushion sizes will be governed by the canvas count (number of meshes to the inch). To figure the size, count number of squares in the design chart (two charts are quarter-patterns; two are complete) and count the same number of meshes on canvas being used. Mark design area on canvas. Add desired width of border all around and mark outline on canvas.

Read General Directions for needlepoint on page 90. Start at upper right corner of chart and work design, following color key and symbols on charts; X's on charts indicate beads. When designs are complete, fill in the background.

Tan pincushion was worked entirely in needlepoint. Chart is a quarter of design; left and bottom lines of chart are center lines; repeat remainder of chart in reverse to left and to bottom to complete design.

Small red pincushion was worked with beads for design indicated by X's, and background in double cross-stitch over two meshes of canvas.

Aqua pincushion was worked in needlepoint for leaf design and outer background, with seed beads filling center area.

Large red pincushion was worked with seed beads for wreath design (X's on chart) and needlepoint background.

When needlepoint is finished, block piece, following directions on page 92. Block all needlepoint pieces right side down; block pieces with beading right side up.

To make pincushion, make a plump pillow of muslin or other fabric. The pillow top should be slightly larger than needlepoint, when stuffed firmly. Trim canvas margin to 1″, slash into corners of canvas, and turn margin to back. Slipstitch canvas in place, cutting away corners of canvas as necessary to make a neat turning. Sew needlepoint to pillow top along seam.

Trim edges with a cotton fringe or make beaded fringe. To make beaded fringe, attach thread to edge of canvas and string on number of beads to make loop of desired length. Take a back stitch from right of bead strand to left, pull thread taut, forming loop. Repeat all around. For a fancy fringe, string on all but last three beads for loop desired; bring needle again through third bead from beginning; string on last three beads. Take small stitch in canvas edge ¼″ to left. String on all but three beads again, bring needle through last loop; finish as for first loop. Take a stitch ¼″ to left. Repeat loops all around.

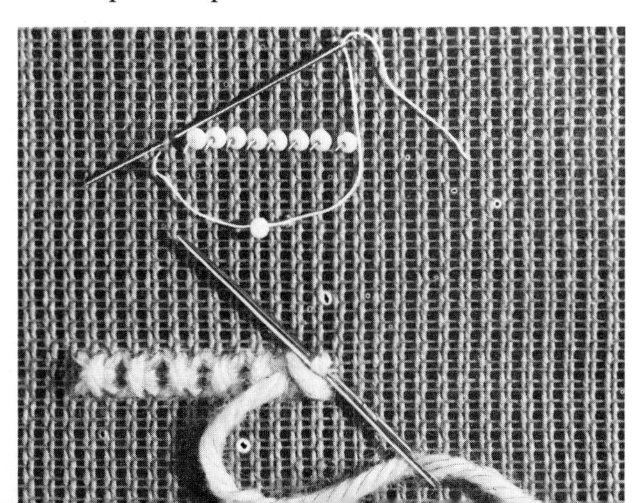

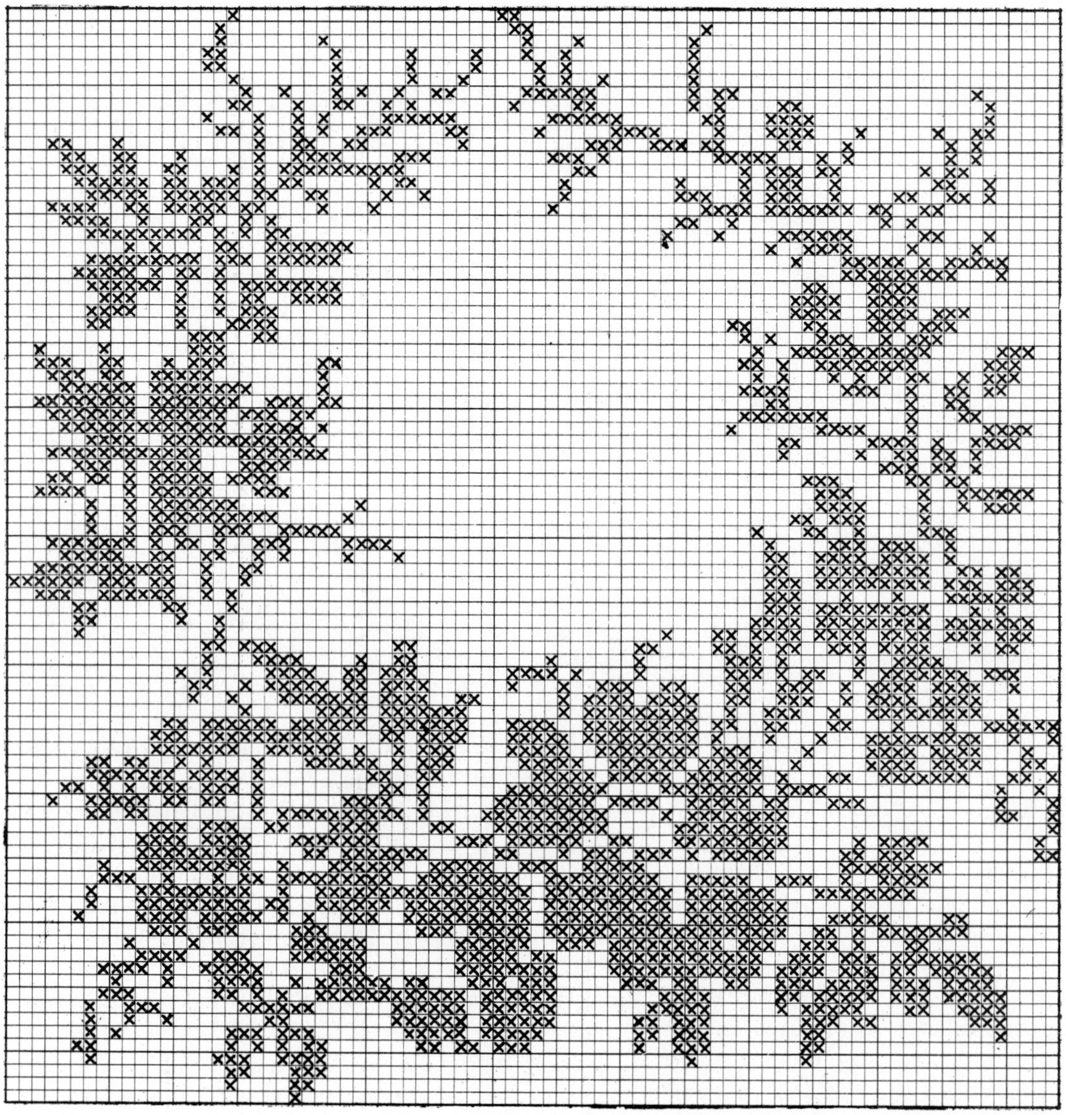

Color Key

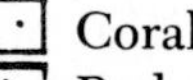

- Coral
- Red
- Maroon
- Gold
- Deep Gold
- Brown
- Dark Brown
- Chartreuse
- Medium Green
- Dark Green

Quilting, Patchwork and Appliqué

GENERAL DIRECTIONS FOR MAKING QUILTS

MAKING THE QUILT TOP

Patterns and Patches: Following individual directions for each quilt, make patterns for patches or appliqués. If making patterns that will be used repeatedly, as for a patchwork quilt, trace master pattern on thin cardboard and cut out with sharp scissors. Because pattern edges become frayed from marking, cut several of each piece. Discard frayed patterns as necessary.

Press all fabric smooth. To determine the straight of the fabric, pull a thread. Place each pattern piece on wrong side of fabric, making sure each piece is placed in correct relationship to the straight of fabric.

Squares and oblongs must be placed with the weave of the fabric parallel to edges. Diamond-shaped patches need two sides on straight of the fabric. Right-angle triangles may be cut with two sides on the straight of the goods. For tumbler shapes, the half-pattern should be cut with the fold on the straight of the fabric.

Using light-colored pencil on dark fabric and dark-colored pencil on a light fabric, trace around each pattern. When tracing a number of pieces on one fabric, leave space between patterns for seam allowances. For patches and appliqué pieces, you will need ¼" seam allowance all around.

Note: Yardage requirements in this book are based on careful placement of pattern on fabric. Unless otherwise indicated, patterns should be placed leaving ½" between two—this will give you the full ¼" seam allowance that is necessary for each.

After cutting a large number of varied patches, separate pieces according to shape and color. String each group together by running a single thread, knotted at one end, through the centers. This will keep pieces easily available; simply lift off each as needed.

Piecing: Hold patches firmly in place, right sides facing. Using sewing thread, carefully take tiny running stitches along marked outlines to join. Begin with making a small knot; end with a few backstitches. To avoid bunching of fabric, excess thickness at seams may be trimmed as pieces are assembled. If two bias edges come together, keep thread just taut enough to prevent seams from stretching.

Unless otherwise indicated, press pieced sections with seams to one side; open seams weaken construction. Compare finished units to make sure all are the same size.

When sewing blocks together, make sure all strips are even with one another.

The size of an all-over geometric quilt is easily controlled, for piecing may stop anywhere without the danger of throwing the design out of balance.

PREPARING TO QUILT

The quilting design is usually marked on the quilt top after the top is completed but before it is joined to the batting and lining. Select your quilting design carefully to suit the quilt. The designs shown here are some of the more popular and some of the easiest to do. They should be enlarged to three or four times the size shown. Border designs are to be traced around the outside, with all-over quilting in the center.

There are two simple methods for transferring the quilting design. The first is to mark the fabric using dressmaker's carbon and a dressmaker's tracing wheel or dry ball-point pen. The second method is to make perforated patterns. Trace the pattern on wrapping paper and, with needle unthreaded, machine-stitch along lines of the design. The design is marked by laying the perforated pattern on the quilt top, rough side down, and rubbing stamping powder or paste through the perforations. Straight lines can be marked with a ruler and tailor's chalk. For very simple quilting that follows the lines of patchwork, appliqué, or print of, fabric, it is not necessary to mark the fabric.

After quilting design has been marked on the quilt top, assemble top, batting, and lining. Cut or piece lining fabric to equal size of quilt top. Place lining, wrong side up, on large flat surface. Place one layer of cotton or Dacron batting on top of lining, smoothing out any bumps or wrinkles. If quilt is planned for warmth, interlining may be thicker. Remember, the thinner the layer of padding, the easier and finer the quilting will be. Before adding quilt top, baste batting to lining by taking two long stitches in a cross.

Place quilt top on top of batting, right side up. Pin all layers together to hold temporarily. Baste generously through all thicknesses. To prevent shifting, first baste on the lengthwise and crosswise grain of the fabric. Then baste diagonally across in two directions and around sides, top, and bottom. **Note:** If quilting is to be done using a quilting hoop, extra care must be taken to keep basting stitches close, so they will hold in place as you change the position of the hoop.

QUILTING

Quilting may be done by hand or on the sewing machine.

When quilting by hand, the quilt may be stretched on a frame or in a quilting hoop (more easily handled and movable). If neither frame nor hoop is

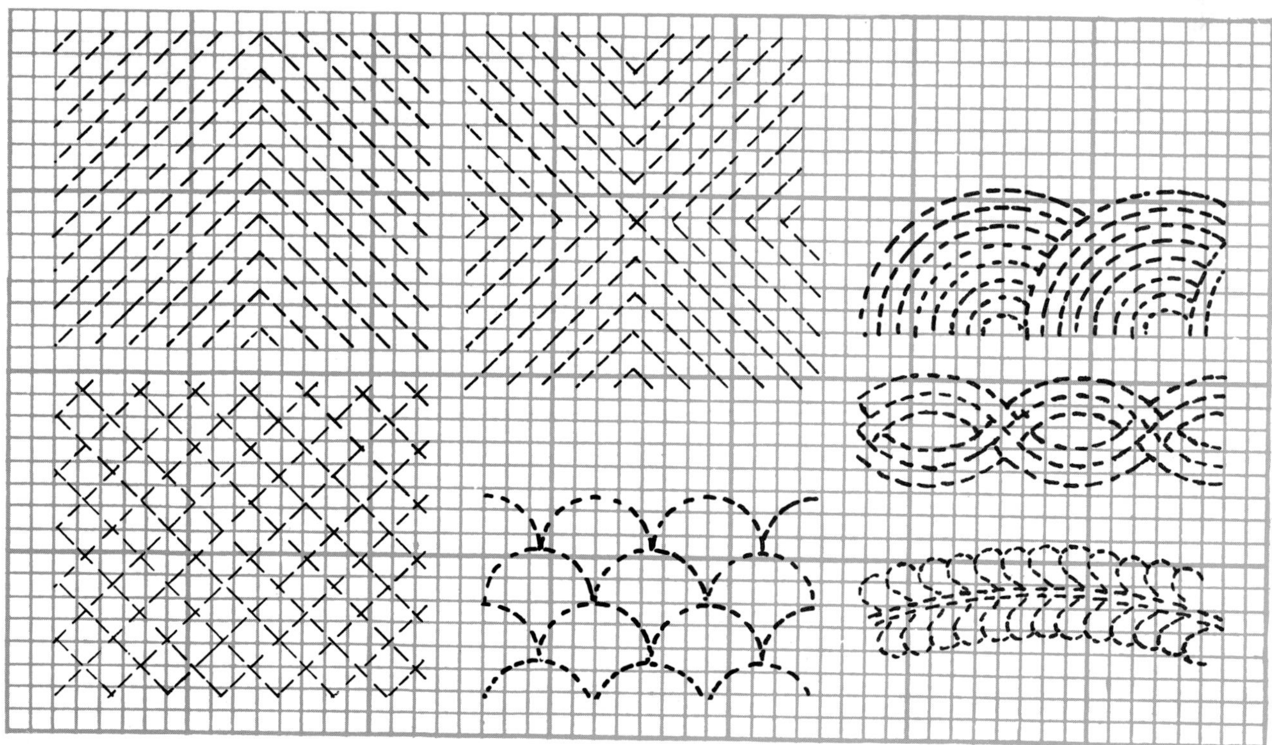

used, quilting may be done in the lap over small areas at a time. The first method for making quilting stitches (see below) is best in lap quilting.

Quilting on a frame: If a frame is used, sew top and bottom edges of lining to the fabric strips which are attached to the long parallel bars of your quilting frame. Using strong thread so that quilt will not pull away from frame when stretched taut, sew securely with several rows of stitches. After quilt is secured in frame, start quilting midway between the long parallel bars of frame and sew toward you.

Quilting with a quilting hoop: The quilting is started at the center of the quilt, then worked toward outer edges. Pull quilt taut in hoop and move any extra fullness toward the edges. If necessary, cut basting thread as work progresses. As your quilting comes closer to the edge, smaller embroidery hoops may be substituted for the larger quilting hoop, thereby assuring that fabric will remain taut.

The quilting stitch is a short, even running stitch. There are two methods of making this stitch. One is done in two separate motions—first pushing the needle down through the three thicknesses, then pushing it up again close to the first stitch. One hand is always under the quilt to guide the stitch; stitches should be of equal length on both sides of the quilt.

The second method is to take two or three little stitches before pulling the needle through, holding quilt down at quilting line with the thumb of one hand. (Tape this thumb to prevent soreness.) Make from five to nine stitches per inch, depending on thickness of the fabrics.

If you are a beginner, practice quilting a small piece in an embroidery hoop to find the easiest and best way for you to work.

The usual quilting needle is a short, sharp needle—No. 8 or 9—although some experienced quilters may prefer a longer one. Strong white sewing thread between Nos. 30 and 50 is best. To begin, knot end of thread. Bring needle up through quilt and pull knot through lining so it is imbedded in interlining. To end off, make a simple backstitch and run thread through interlining.

Quilting on a machine can be done with or without a quilting foot. When working on a sewing machine, the best quilting patterns to use are sewn on the diagonal or on the bias. Fabric gives a little when on the bias, making it easier to keep the area you are working on flat. Cotton batting should be quilted closely (quilting lines running no more than 2″ apart); Dacron lining may be quilted with the lines no more than 3″ apart.

As a rule, machine quilting is done with a straight stitch. Stitch-length control should be set from 6 to 12 per inch. Pressure should be adjusted so that it is slightly heavier than for medium-weight fabrics.

If you are using a scroll or floral design, it is best to use the short open toe of the quilting foot, so you can follow the curved lines with accuracy and ease.

TUFTING

If you wish to tuft rather than quilt, use several layers of padding between the top and the lining. Mark evenly spaced points on the top surface with tailor tacks or pins. Thread a candlewick needle with candlewick yarn, or use a large-eyed needle with heavy Germantown yarn or knitting worsted. Using thread double, push needle from top through layers to back, leaving thread end on top. Push needle back up again to surface, about ¼″ away. Tie yarn in firm double knot. Clip ends to desired length (at least ½″).

QUILT CARE

Dry-clean all fine quilts. If a quilt is washable, you may put it in the automatic washer on a short-wash cycle. Be sure to use only a mild soap or detergent. Do not wring or spin dry. Let quilt drip dry, and do not iron.

GENERAL DIRECTIONS FOR APPLIQUÉ

HOW TO APPLIQUÉ

Choose a fabric that is closely woven and firm enough so a clean edge results when the pieces are cut. Cut a pattern piece for each shape out of thin, stiff cardboard, and mark the right side of each piece. Press fabric smooth. Place cardboard pattern, wrong side up, on wrong side of fabric. Using sharp, hard pencils (light-colored pencil on dark fabric and dark pencil on light fabric), mark the outline on the fabric. When marking several pieces on the same fabric, leave at least ½" between pieces. Mark a second outline ¼" outside the design outline. Using matching thread and small stitches, machine-stitch all around design outline, as shown in Fig. 1. This makes edge easier to turn and neater in appearance. Cut out the appliqué on the outside line, as in Fig. 2. For a smooth edge, clip into seam allowance at curved edges and corners. Then turn seam allowance to back, just inside stitching as shown in Fig. 3, and press. Pin and baste the appliqué on the background, and slip-stitch in place with tiny stitches, as shown in Fig. 4.

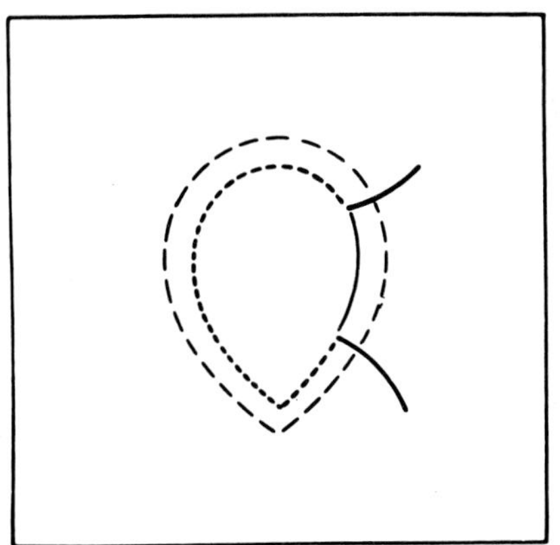

Fig. 1

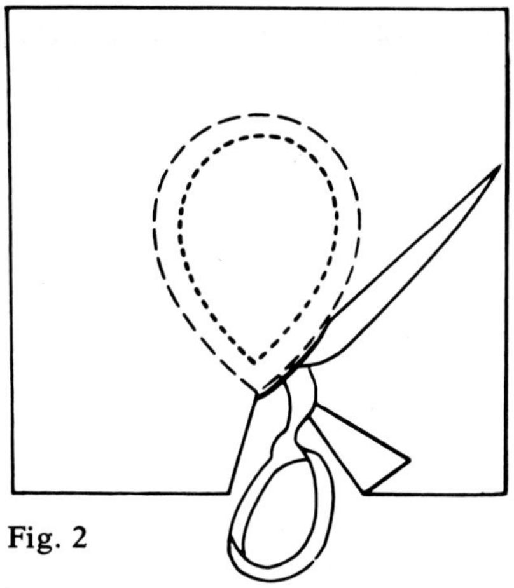

Fig. 2

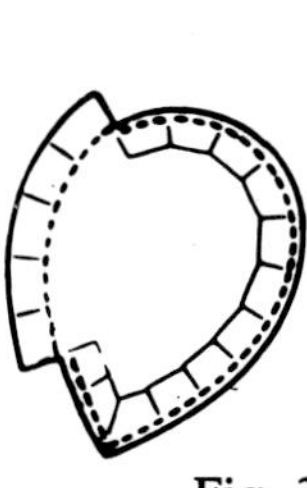

Fig. 3

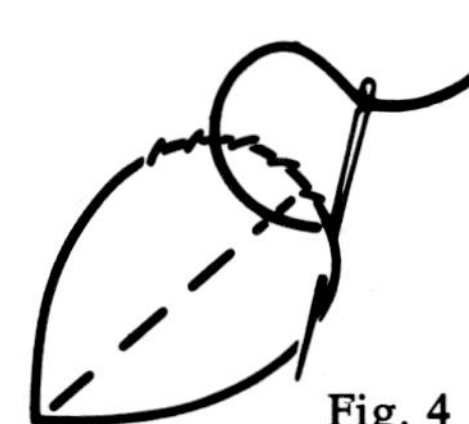

Fig. 4

DESIGNING APPLIQUÉS

It's easy to design your own appliqué pattern with paper and scissors. First, fold a square of paper into quarters or eighths, then cut away the center point and the edges in a design as simple or elaborate as you like. Continue cutting out paper designs until you find the pattern or patterns that please you most.

PATCHWORK AND APPLIQUÉ QUILTS

Album Quilt

A pink and navy harvest sun makes a splendid center for a quilt of many patterns, including Dutch Star, Courthouse Square, Wild Goose Chase, and Log Cabin. Although the quilt blocks vary in size, they are pieced with borders where necessary to make a quilt 71" x 88".

EQUIPMENT: Ruler. Pencil. Paper for patterns. Stiff cardboard. Scissors. Straight pins. Quilting needle. Quilting frame (optional).

MATERIALS: Cotton percale fabric in various colors and prints. Unbleached muslin for plain patches. Print fabric for lining 45" wide, 4 yards. Cotton batting. Sewing and quilting thread.

DIRECTIONS: Read General Directions on page 158. Quilt may be assembled using all the different patterns or by repeating a few patterns for the whole quilt. Some patterns are repeated with different colors. Plan colors of each block of patch pieces. Patterns are given on squares; shaded areas on patterns indicate darker colors, plain areas are muslin or light colors. To enlarge the squared patterns, rule paper into ½", ⅜", or ¼" squares as indicated under each pattern. A few of the patterns indicate two sizes of squares, which may be used to make the block large or small. Rule the same number of squares as given on the graph, and copy the heavy outlines of pattern on the larger squares. Make a separate cardboard pattern for each different size patch piece. Cut out patches, marking patterns on wrong side of fabric and adding ¼" seam allowance all around. To piece together star-pattern blocks, read directions, "Joining Diamonds" on page 166.

Following graph patterns, assemble blocks. For appliqué block, enlarge pattern on 1" squares, completing half-pattern indicated by dash lines. Cut muslin for block 10" square. Cut appliqué from print fabric, adding ⅛" seam allowance all around. Cut out oval shapes ⅛" in from their outlines; clip into ⅛" seam allowances around curves; turn allowance in and press. Pin appliqué to center of muslin square and slip-stitch around outside and around edges of ovals to secure.

To plan quilt, lay out all pieced blocks on a large flat surface, using large star block as center. Add strips of dark-color fabric between and around blocks, in width required to make them fit together (remember to add ¼" seam allowance around each strip). Use the small blocks as borders, repeating them in various colors. Quilt shown has wide borders along sides and narrower borders across top and bottom. Join strips and blocks in same manner as for joining patches. Sew small blocks together for borders, and add the borders to sides, top, and bottom.

Make lining 1" larger all around than quilt top. Cut batting same size as quilt top.

Quilting: With ruler and tailor's chalk, mark quilting lines 1¼" apart in a zigzag pattern down length of quilt. Center quilt top and batting over lining and pin and baste together; start with the lengthwise and crosswise grain of fabric, then baste diagonally across in two directions and around sides, top, and bottom. Starting in center of quilt and working outward, quilt on marked zigzag lines.

To finish quilt, turn excess lining to front, turn in edges ¼", and slip-stitch to quilt top.

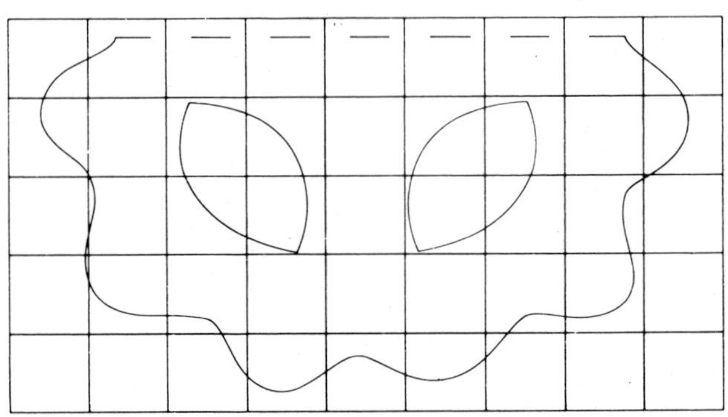

Appliqué Pattern

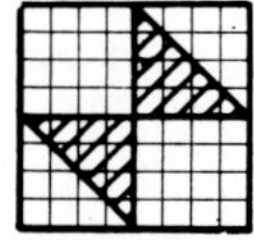
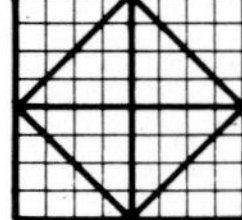
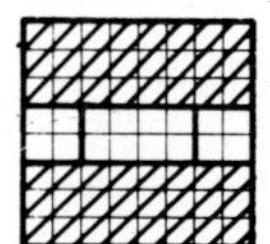
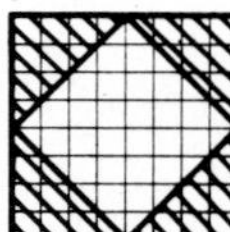

Each Square = ½"

Border Blocks

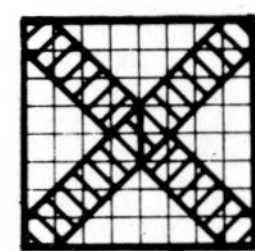
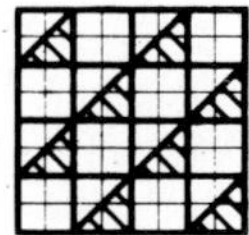

Each Square = 1"

Each Square = ½″

Each Square = ¾″ or 1″

Each Square = ½″

Each Square = ¾″

Each Square = ½″

Each Square = ½″

Each Square = ½″

Each Square = ½″ or ¾″

Each Square = ½″

Each Square = ½″ or ¾″

Each Square = ½″

Each Square = ½″

Each Square = ½″

Each Square = ½″

Each Square = ½″

Each Square = ½″

Each Square = ½″

Each Square = ½″

Each Square = ½″

Each Square = ½″

Each Square = ½″

Each Square = ½″

Broken Star Quilt

Here, in flaming gold, is a magnificent variation of the star theme. The quilt is entirely pieced—with diamonds for inner and outer stars, squares and triangles for the background, and stripes for the border. From Missouri, circa 1930.

SIZE: About 92″ square.

EQUIPMENT: Ruler. Scissors. Pencil. Thin, stiff cardboard. Tracing paper. Paper for pattern. Dressmaker's carbon (tracing) paper. Tracing wheel or dry ball-point pen. Sewing and quilting needles. Quilting frame (optional).

MATERIALS: Closely woven cotton fabric 45″ wide: 2⅝* yds. each of dark orange (A), light yellow (B), gold (C), light orange (D), and medium orange (E); 3 yds. white. Fabric for lining 50″ wide, 5¼ yds. (***Note:** Less fabric will be required if you wish to piece border strips.) Dacron polyester or cotton batting. White sewing thread.

DIRECTIONS: Read General Directions on page 158. Quilt is made up of a "broken" star pieced from diamond patches and set in a white background, bordered with stripes.

Diamond Patches: Trace actual-size pattern; complete quarter-pattern indicated by dash lines for diamond shape. Cut several diamond patterns from cardboard, replacing when edges begin to fray. (**Note:** Before cutting fabric patches, test accuracy of pattern by drawing around it eight times, to create an eight-pointed star; there should be no gaps or overlapping of diamond segments.)

Marking patterns on wrong side of fabric and adding ¼″ seam allowance all around, cut diamond patches as follows: Cut 256 diamonds from dark orange (A), 128 from light yellow (B), 192 from gold (C), 256 from light orange (D), and 320 from medium orange (E).

Joining Diamonds: Center star of quilt is made up of eight identical pieced diamond-shaped sections meeting at center point; each section is made up of six rows of six diamond patches each. See Piecing Diagram for one section. Outer portion of large star is made up of 24 more of the same diamond-shaped sections, joined for a circular design. Make 32 diamond-shaped sections as follows.

To make one section, stitch together six rows, following Piecing Diagram and color key; start first row with a dark orange patch (A), second row with light yellow (B), etc. Use one of the two methods for joining diamonds described in the following paragraph. When joining diamonds to form a row, stitch patches together along sides cut on straight of goods. Stitch from the wide-angled corner towards the pointed ends. Trim seam at points as you piece. Matching corners carefully, join the six rows together to make a diamond-shaped section. When joining rows together, you will be stitching along the bias edges; keep thread just taut enough to prevent seams from stretching. Press pieced sections with seams to one side; open seams tend to weaken construction.

There are two methods for joining the diamonds. **First method:** Hold patches together, right sides facing; seam together with small running stitches on pencil lines. If the problem of sharp points and true meeting of seams proves difficult with this method, prepare each patch as follows: **Second method:** Cut firm paper patterns the exact size and shape of cardboard pattern. Fit paper pattern within pencil outline on wrong side of patch; hold patch with paper pattern uppermost. Fold seam allowance over each side, and tack to the paper with one stitch on each side, allowing the thread to cross the corners. Finish by taking an extra stitch into the first side; cut the thread, leaving about ¼″. To make removal of tacking easier, do not knot thread or make any backstitches. Hold prepared patches right sides together, matching the edges to be seamed exactly. Whip together with fine, even stitches (about 16 to the inch), avoiding the paper as much as possible. The paper patterns may remain in place until the star shape is completed. To remove the papers, snip tacking thread once on each patch and withdraw thread; lift papers out.

Assembling: For center star, join four sections for each half, with dark orange (A) points meeting in center; join halves for star. Each point of star should measure 12″ (plus outside seam allowance) along side edges.

For background blócks, cut cardboard pattern 12″ square. Marking pattern on wrong side of fabric and adding ¼″ seam allowance all around, cut 20 blocks from white fabric. Cut cardboard pattern in half diagonally for triangle pattern and cut eight triangles from white fabric in same manner.

Sew eight square background blocks to the center star, fitting two sides of a block between two points of star. Sew remaining diamond-shaped pieced sections together in eight groups of three sections each, as if assembling three points of a star. Sew three-pointed sections in the wide angle formed by the square background blocks; sew adjacent sections to each other. Sew remaining 12 square blocks into four corner sections of three blocks each. Sew corner sections and triangle background blocks to star; see illustration. Piece should measure 82″ square, plus outside seam allowance.

Border: Cut four strips 1″ x 84″ from light yellow fabric, adding ¼″ seam allowance all around. Sew a strip to each side of quilt top, with an equal amount extending at each end. Miter corners, following directions on page 177 for Cornucopia Quilt. Cut four 1″-wide strips from remaining colors as follows, adding ¼″ seam allowance all around and sewing on in same manner: gold 86″, light orange 88″, medium orange 90″, and dark orange 92″. Quilt top should measure 92½″ square, including outside seam allowance.

Lining: Cut two pieces 47″ x 93″. Sew together on long sides with ½″ seams; press seams open. Lining measures 93″ square. Cut batting 92″ square.

Quilting: With ruler and tailor's chalk, mark lines ¼″ and ¾″ in from seams around square blocks, two sides of triangle blocks. Enlarge Feather Quilting Pattern on a paper ruled in 1″

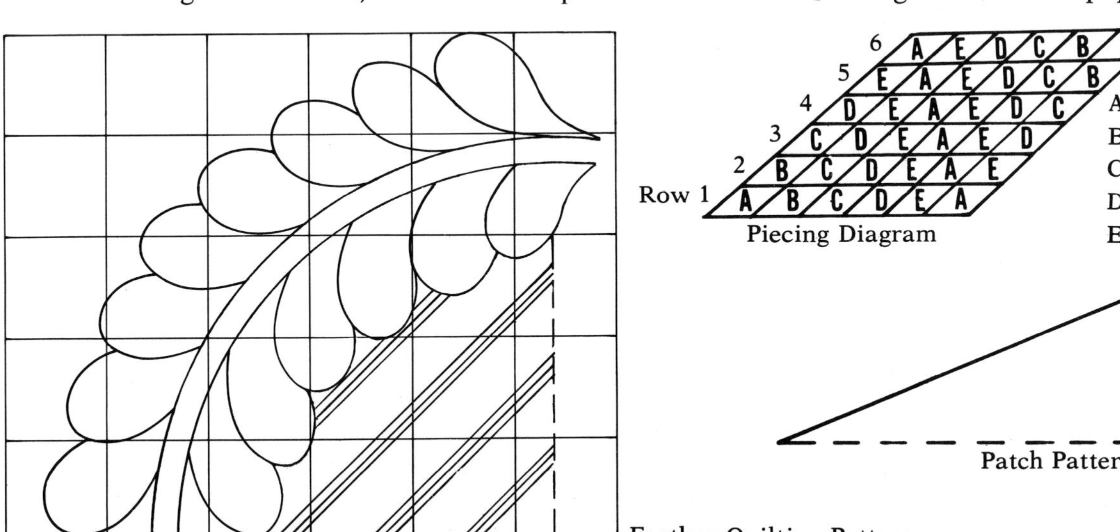

Feather Quilting Pattern

Piecing Diagram

Color Key
A Dark Orange
B Gold
C Light Orange
D Medium Orange
E Light Yellow

Patch Pattern

squares; complete quarter-pattern. Using carbon and a tracing wheel (or dry ball-point pen), transfer pattern to center of square background blocks. Transfer half of pattern to triangle blocks, with half-line of pattern on seam.

Following General Directions, pin and baste quilt top, batting, and lining together, centering layers. Lining extends ½″ all around beyond batting, and quilt top extends ¼″. Starting in center and working around and outward, quilt on all marked lines and ¼″ in from all seams of diamond patches and border strips.

Edges: Turn excess ½″ of lining over edge of batting and baste in place. Turn in ¼″ seam allowance of quilt top. Slip-stitch folded edges of lining and quilt top together. Press edges.

Rob Peter, Pay Paul Quilt

Quilt Courtesy of The Pink House Antiques, New Hope, Pennsylvania

This personal, possibly unique version of the "lend and borrow" theme is made of triangles and hexagons that seem to change places in a swirl of images. It was made in New Jersey, around 1880.

SIZE: 80⅜" x 86⅜".

EQUIPMENT: Pencil. Ruler. Scissors. Thin, stiff cardboard. Tailor's chalk. Straight pins. Sewing needles.

MATERIALS: Closely woven cotton fabric: red print 36" wide, 5 yds.; solid yellow 45" wide, 4 yds. Fabric for lining 45" wide, 5 yds. Dacron polyester or cotton batting. White sewing thread.

DIRECTIONS: Read General Directions on page 158. Quilt is made up of 156 pieced blocks, plus a pieced border. See Piecing Diagram for one block; each block is made up of four patches, and each patch has three patch pieces. (Dotted lines indicate quilting pattern.)

Patterns: To make patterns for patch pieces, draw a 3" square on cardboard. Mark a point on one side, 1¼" from a corner; mark another point on adjacent side, 1¼" from same corner; draw a line between points. Mark off corner diagonally opposite in same manner. See 3" square patch indicated by heavy lines on Piecing Diagram. Cut on marked lines, making one hexagon pattern and two identical triangle patterns.

Patches: Marking patterns on wrong side of fabric and adding ¼" seam allowance all around, cut 624 triangles and 312 hexagons each from red and yellow fabrics. Sew two yellow triangles to one red hexagon for a 3" patch (see Piecing Diagram); sew two red triangles to one yellow hexagon for an alternate patch. Assemble all patch pieces in same manner, to make 624 3" patches.

Blocks: Assemble four patches to make one 6" block, alternating two red-hexagon patches with two yellow-hexagon patches; see Piecing Diagram. Make 155 more blocks in same manner.

Assembling: Sew completed blocks into 13 rows of 12 blocks each, keeping all blocks in same position within a row, so that colors alternate throughout. Sew rows together, again keeping all blocks in same position. Piece should measure 72" x 78", plus outside seam allowance.

Border: Draw a 4" square on cardboard; connect two opposite corners with a diagonal line. Cut on marked lines for large triangle patterns. Cut 78 large triangles each from red and yellow fabrics, marking pattern on wrong side of fabric and adding ¼" seam allowance all around. Assemble triangles into 78 4" squares, joining a red and a yellow triangle on their long sides for each square. Join squares into two strips of 20 squares each and two strips of 19 each, alternating colors and with red triangles always on one side of strip and yellow triangles on the other side. Cut four 1½" x 4½" pieces from red fabric. Sew one red piece to each end of the 19-square strips with ¼" seam allowance. Sew 19-square strips to longer sides of quilt, then 20-square strips to shorter sides, keeping red triangles on outside of quilt. Quilt top should measure 80½" x 86½".

Lining: Cut two pieces 40¾" x 86½". Sew together on long sides with ½" seams; press seams open. Cut batting same size as lining and quilt top.

Quilting: With ruler and tailor's chalk, mark quilting lines on hexagon patch pieces; see dotted-line pattern on Piecing Diagram. On border, mark off square patches in halves, then quarters, and then eighths (with two corner-to-corner diagonal lines). Following General Directions, pin and baste quilt top, batting, and lining together. Starting in center and working around and outward, quilt along seam lines and on all marked lines.

Edges: Cut four 1¼"-wide strips from yellow fabric, two 81" long and two 87" long. Sew strips to front of quilt, right sides together and with ¼" seams. Fold strips to back of quilt, making a ⅜"-wide binding on front and back; turn in edges ¼" and slip-stitch to lining. Press all edges.

Piecing Diagram

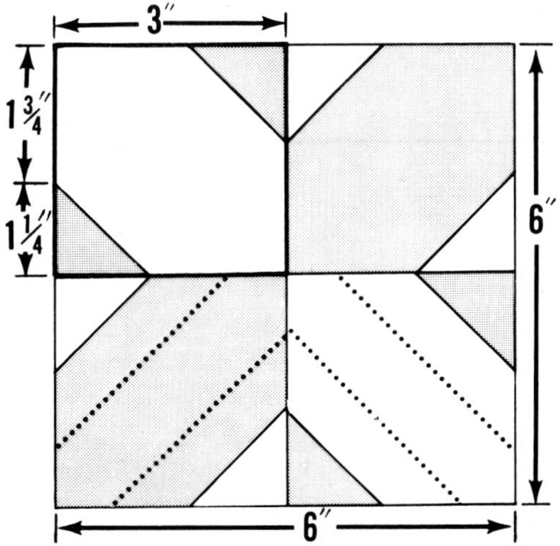

Amish Bars Quilt

This characteristically bold and simple quilt needs only a few geometric shapes to create its effect. Typical Amish notes are the offbeat colors (for 1890, that is, when this quilt was made), the use of strong corner blocks, and the elaborate quilting. The inner beige border is quilted with a cable pattern, and a beautiful, wide, feathered scroll covers the outer red border. The quilt was made in Lancaster County, Pa.

SIZE: 74" x 82½".

EQUIPMENT: Ruler. Scissors. Pencil. Tailor's chalk. Dressmaker's (carbon) tracing paper. Tracing wheel or dry ball-point pen. Paper for patterns. Tracing paper. Pins. Sewing and quilting needles. Quilting frame (optional).

MATERIALS: Closely woven cotton fabric 45" wide: 2¼ yds. dark red, ¼ yd. pink, 1⅓ yds. blue, 1⅓ yds. beige (or 2⅓ yds; see "Edges" below). Fabric for lining 45" wide, 4⅛ yds. Dark blue sewing thread. Dacron polyester or cotton batting.

DIRECTIONS: Read General Directions on page 158. Following the dimensions in the Piecing Diagram, mark strips and squares on fabric (omit outside beige border). Cut out pieces, adding ¼" all around for seam allowance.

Assembling: Join pieces, following Piecing Diagram and beginning with vertical strips in center section (beige, blue, pink, blue, dark red, etc.). Join small blue squares to ends of remaining beige strips and sew to top and bottom of center section. Join long dark red strips to sides of center section. Sew large blue squares to ends of remaining dark red strips and sew to top and bottom of piece made. Quilt top should now measure 71½" x 80", including outside seam allowance.

Lining: Cut two pieces 41¾" x 74". Sew together on long sides with ½" seams; press seam open. Cut batting same size as lining.

Quilting: With ruler and tailor's chalk, mark diagonal lines 1" apart in both directions over center strips (blue, pink, dark red only) of quilt

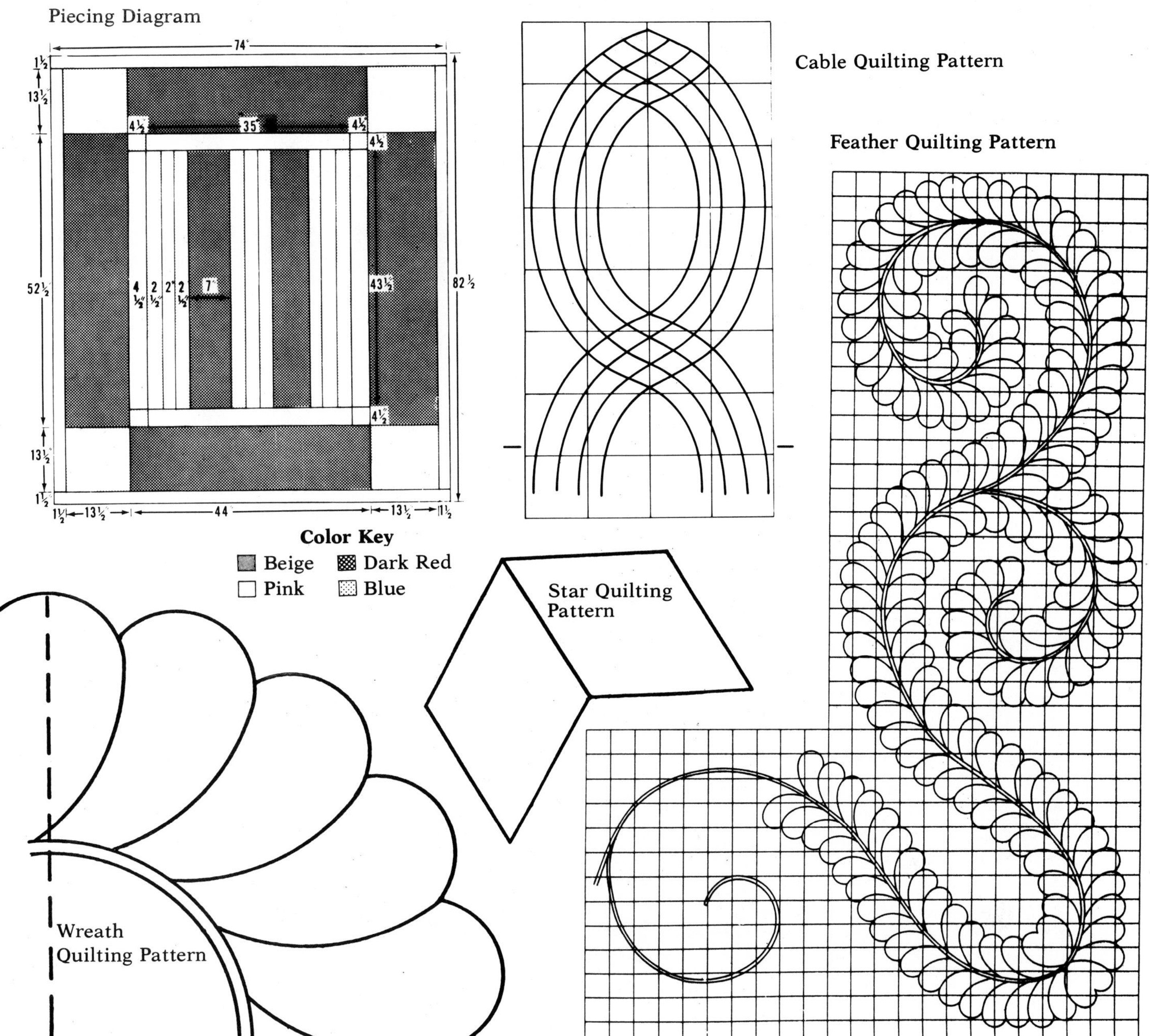

top. Trace actual-size quilting patterns for Wreath and Star and enlarge Cable and Feather patterns on paper ruled in 1" squares. Complete quarter-pattern of wreath, indicated by dash lines. Pattern for feather border shows only one side completed. Transfer patterns to quilt top, using dressmaker's carbon and tracing wheel (or dry ball-point pen). Place cable pattern on beige strips, starting at one end of each strip at cross-lines of pattern and repeating cable across to other end. Star pattern is one-third of six-pointed star. Place a star in center of each small blue square, rotating pattern and retracing it three times around center point. Place feather border pattern four times around quilt top, positioning pattern in each large blue square of corners and continuing pattern out from corners on both sides, ½" from beige strips. On top and bottom dark red strips, patterns should just meet at center of strip. On each side strip, fill in spaces between patterns with two wreaths placed side by side.

Following General Directions, center quilt top over batting and lining; pin and baste layers together. Starting in center and working around and outward, quilt on all marked lines.

Edges: From beige fabric, cut four 3½"-wide strips, two 83" long and two 74½" long, piecing to get lengths (if you prefer not to piece edges, buy 2⅓ yds. fabric). Sew strips to front of quilt, right sides together and with ¼" seams. Fold strips in half and turn to back of quilt; turn in edges ¼" and slip-stitch to lining. There will be a 1½" binding on both front and back.

Flower Mosaic Quilt

Seventeen hundred hexagonal patches are joined to create a "field of flowers." Made of taffeta, this mid-nineteenth-century quilt was obviously meant for show rather than utility. It is worked from the center out in progressively larger circles, and the final design is determined by the placement of the first pieces.

Quilt from the Brooklyn Museum

SIZE: About 82½" x 95".

EQUIPMENT: Scissors. Ruler. Thin, stiff cardboard. Light- and dark-colored pencils. Tracing paper. Sewing and quilting needles. Quilting frame (optional).

MATERIALS: Quilt top: closely woven taffeta fabric 45" wide: pink, 4½ yds.; a variety of colors in prints or plains totaling about 5½ yds. Lining: cotton fabric 45" wide, 5⅓ yds. Pink sewing thread. Dacron polyester or cotton batting.

DIRECTIONS: Read General Directions on page 158. Quilt is constructed of about 1,742 hexagonal patches. Trace actual-size pattern for hexagons; complete half-pattern indicated by dash lines. Make several cardboard patterns and replace when edges begin to fray. Marking pattern on wrong side of fabric and adding ¼" seam allowance all around, cut hexagons as follows, placing pattern so that two sides are on straight of fabric. For flower petals, cut six of the same color for each of 127 flowers, making a total of 762 hexagons. Cut 127 hexagons for flower centers from a variety of colors. Cut 764 pink hexagons.

Make 127 flowers, sewing six hexagons of one color around a seventh hexagon of a contrasting color for each flower. Choose a flower for center of quilt and sew 18 pink hexagons around it. (This quilt was apparently worked from the center out, but quilt may also be pieced in vertical rows if desired; see illustration). Place a second flower directly above piece made, with one straight edge of second flower parallel to a straight edge of first flower's center; then shift second flower one step down to the right, so it is slightly off-center, and sew to pink hexagons on the three adjacent sides.* Sew two pink hexagons together. Continuing around first circle in clockwise direction, join the two pink hexagons to second flower and to next pink hexagons in circle. Add five more flowers around with a two-hexagon piece between them to complete larger circle, making a pattern of alternating colors in circle of flowers if desired (see illustration). Add a row of pink hexagons around flowers. Add a row of 12 flowers in same manner as before. Continue until center flower is encircled by five rows of flowers and six rows of pink hexagons.

Position pieced hexagon shape with a point at top and bottom and two long edges vertical. To make hexagon shape into a rectangle, add rows of flowers and pink hexagons to each of the four diagonal edges at top and bottom, a row of five flowers first, then three, then one, with a row of pink hexagons between.

To complete edges of quilt top, cut 89 hexagons in flower colors, to make 21 strips of three hexagons each and 13 strips of two hexagons each, using same colors in each strip. Fill in edges around quilt top with the strips as needed, adding pink hexagons to corners. Trim edges of quilt top as shown in illustration or as desired, allowing ⅜" extra all around edges for binding. Piece should measure approximately 82½" x 95". Measure your quilt top before proceeding with the lining.

*(**Note:** To make quilt with a crenellated edge, set second flower in quilt with adjacent edge directly opposite an edge of first flower's center. Finish quilt as directed above; however, edges of quilt will have a more regular pattern and need not be filled in.)

For lining, cut two pieces 41¾" x 95". Right sides together, join on long sides with ½" seams; press seams open. Cut batting same size as lining and quilt top.

Quilting: Following General Directions, pin and baste lining, batting, and quilt top together. Starting in center and working around and outward, quilt on each hexagon patch, ¼" in from seam line; quilt a second line ¼" in from first.

To bind edges, cut four strips 1¼" wide from pink fabric, two 83" long and two 95½" long. Right sides together, sew strips to front of quilt ⅜" from edges with ¼" seams; fold strips to back; turn in edges ¼" and slip-stitch to lining. Press edges.

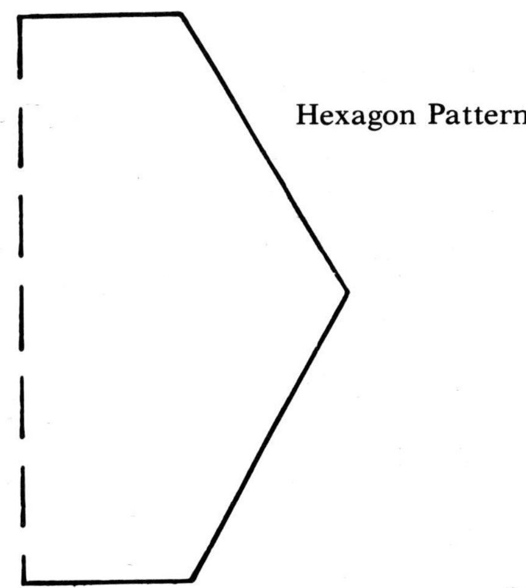
Hexagon Pattern

Crazy Quilt

This crazy quilt from Victorian times shows the gay haphazardness of design that was characteristic of this popular coverlet—although our spread is not actually quilted, in the strict sense. Lavish embroidery decorates scraps of fabric and joins the seams; some of the most commonly used stitches are shown here. Quilt-makers searched for unusual and luxurious bits of material—ribbons, satin, grosgrain, velvet, painted motifs on silk, as well as special scraps printed with appealing pictures. To add variety, patches were cut in different shapes, then fitted together to form a quilt of desired size. The handsome sateen ruffle and backing in a maroon shade complete this elegant quilt.

This type of quilt traditionally utilizes luxurious fabric scraps in rich colors. Scraps are cut in squares, rectangles, triangles, and other shapes to fit together to form the desired quilt size.

Lay out the scraps of fabric on a large, flat surface, cutting the pieces where necessary to fit together. Care should be taken in choosing the adjoining colors for a pleasing effect. Overlap the pieces about ½" and turn in raw edges of top piece (finished ribbon edges do not have to be turned under). Baste the pieces together. To join the pieces, use decorative embroidery stitches in silk, rayon, pearl cotton, or embroidery floss. The illustration at right shows some of the stitches used in our quilt. You may, of course, use any embroidery stitches you like. For drawings of embroidery stitches, see page 15. Combine stitches as desired over seams and also in centers of some patch pieces, if desired. One or more colors may be used to embroider the bands for a decorative effect, but the main object is to have the embroidery hold the pieces of fabric together. As shown in the details, at least part of the stitching goes over the seam. Choose colors of floss that complement the colors of the adjoining patches.

The stitch detail at top of page is two rows of buttonhole stitch in groups of three. The first row joins the fabrics, the second has the groups alternating with the first row. To make buttonhole stitch, loop thread to left, take stitch from top to bottom with loop under needle; pull up thread to tighten.

The second detail is herringbone stitch with vertical crosses between. Work herringbone from left to right, taking a short backstitch first at top, then at bottom.

The third detail is two rows of herringbone. Work the second row on top of first, making the short backstitches between stitches of first row.

The fourth detail is featherstitch with clusters of straight stitches between. This is straight featherstitching. Work from right to left; loop thread first above seam and take a small stitch with needle over loop, then loop thread below and take a small stitch.

Fifth detail is lazy daisy stitch in three alternating rows. Bring thread around in a loop, take a stitch the length of lazy daisy desired, with needle over loop. Anchor loop with a short stitch over end.

Sixth detail is lazy daisy clusters with French knots between. To make French knots, bring thread to front, wrap thread over and under needle, crossing beginning thread. Insert needle in fabric close to where it came up and pull to tighten knot.

Seventh detail is clusters of straight stitches alternating up and down across seam, with French knots at tips.

Eighth detail is vertical crosses topped with diagonal crosses to form stars.

Ninth detail is herringbone stitch, couched over top and bottom and at middle of each strand with straight stitches.

It is not necessary to interline this type of quilt, but it does need a lining. Trim off edges of patch pieces on all sides to make straight edges. Cut a piece of lining fabric, such as sateen, the same size as patched top. For ruffle, cut strips of same fabric 9″ wide (to make a 4″ ruffle) on the bias, or partial bias; join strips diagonally to make a length twice the perimeter of the quilt. Fold strip in half lengthwise and gather slightly. Sew gathered edge around quilt top with sides together and raw edges out. Turn ruffle out and press seam allowance toward center. Turn in edges of lining and slip-stitch to back of quilt over seam line, covering raw edges of the ruffle and quilt top. Ruffle may be omitted, and the edges of quilt can be bound with 1½″-wide bias strips of fabric in a dark, solid color.

Quilt from Margaret Pennington

Cornucopia Quilt

This beautifully executed quilt won a first prize at the Indiana State Fair in the late 1920s. The background quilting features princess feathers in undulating rows against a pattern of converging lines.

SIZE: About 83½" square.

EQUIPMENT: Ruler. Scissors. Pencil. Paper for patterns. Tracing paper. Thin, stiff cardboard. Dressmaker's (carbon) tracing paper. Tracing wheel. Straight pins. Sewing and quilting needles. Quilting frame (optional).

MATERIALS: Closely woven cotton fabric 44"-45" wide: white, 8½ yds. (includes lining); red, 1 yd.; green, 2½ yds.; blue, ½ yd.; pink, ½ yd.; tan, ¼ yd.; peach, ¼ yd. Dacron polyester or cotton batting (Taylor Bedding). Matching sewing thread.

DIRECTIONS: Read General Directions on page 158 and appliqué instructions on page 161. Quilt is made up of nine appliquéd blocks set with white joining strips and border. Enlarge appliqué patterns on page 178 by copying on paper ruled in 1" squares; complete quarter- and half-patterns indicated by dash lines. For blocks, cut nine pieces from white fabric 14½" square, adding ¼" seam allowance all around. Using dressmaker's carbon and tracing wheel, transfer pattern for cornucopia appliqué to eight of the blocks; transfer pattern for center appliqué to the ninth block; center the designs so that there is an equal margin on opposite sides. For cornucopia blocks, make cardboard patterns for appliqués, making a pattern for each separate part of the six flower designs and the cornucopia design; make one leaf pattern; make a pattern for each of the stem pieces. Following directions in appliqué instructions, cut and prepare appliqué pieces for each block, following colors in illustration. Pin, baste, and slip-stitch pieces in place, inserting stems into opening of cornucopia; sew overlapped pieces first, such as stems, buds, and leaves. For center block, use flower and leaf pattern from cornucopia appliqué for cutting appliqué pieces; cut new patterns for stems. Pin, baste, and slip-stitch pieces as for cornucopia blocks.

For joining strips, cut eight 5"-wide pieces from white fabric: two 53½" long and six 14½" long, adding ¼" seam allowance all around. Arrange the nine appliquéd blocks in three rows of three blocks each; see illustration for placement of blocks (note that cornucopias point up in bottom row, down in top row, and alternate in middle row around the center block). Place the shorter joining strips between blocks to make three vertical rows; sew together with ¼" seams. Place the two longer joining strips between the vertical rows and join in same manner, to make center of quilt top. Piece should measure 53½" square, plus outside seam allowance.

For borders, cut four pieces from white fabric 15¼" x 83½" (measurements include ¼" seam allowance). Transfer pattern for border appliqués to each border piece, centering on both width and length. Use patterns from cornucopia appliqué for the large leaf and three flower designs; make new cardboard patterns for the whole bud design, small leaf, and short stems. For long curving stems, cut ¾"-wide strips on the bias; turn in each long edge of strips 3/16" to make ⅜"-wide strips. Pin, baste, and slip-stitch appliqué pieces in place on all four border pieces.

To assemble quilt top, sew a border strip to each side of center piece, with an equal amount of border extending beyond center at each end. **To miter corners:** lay piece flat, right side down. Hold adjacent ends at corners together with right sides facing. Keeping border flat, lift up inner corners and pin together diagonally from inner corners to outer corners; baste, then stitch on basting line. Cut off excess fabric, leaving ¼" seam; press seam open.

For lining, cut two pieces from white fabric 42¼" x 83½". Sew together on long sides with ½" seams. Cut batting same size as lining and quilt top.

Quilting: Trace actual-size quilting pattern on page 179. Using dressmaker's carbon and tracing wheel, transfer pattern to joining strips as shown in quilting diagram on page 179, starting at junction of four blocks and continuing out to sides of quilt-top center. For corner motif, use sections of same pattern to make two curving lines, each about 11½" long, 13½" from corners. Use ruler and tailor's chalk to mark straight quilting lines ½" apart over remainder of quilt top, skipping over quilting patterns already marked and the appliqués. See quilting diagram for pattern of straight lines; in each appliquéd block, lines converge in center from the four corners.

Pin and baste quilt top, batting, and lining to-

Center Appliqué

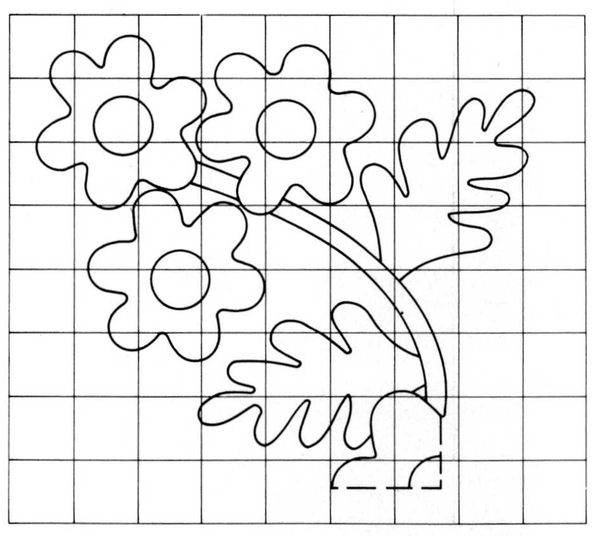

Border Appliqué

Cornucopia Appliqué

gether, following General Directions. Starting in the center and working outward and around, quilt on all marked lines.

To bind edges, cut four 1″-wide strips from green fabric, each 84″ long, piecing to get lengths. Right sides together, sew strips to top of quilt with ¼″ seams. Turn strips to back of quilt, turn in raw edges ¼″, and slip-stitch to lining.

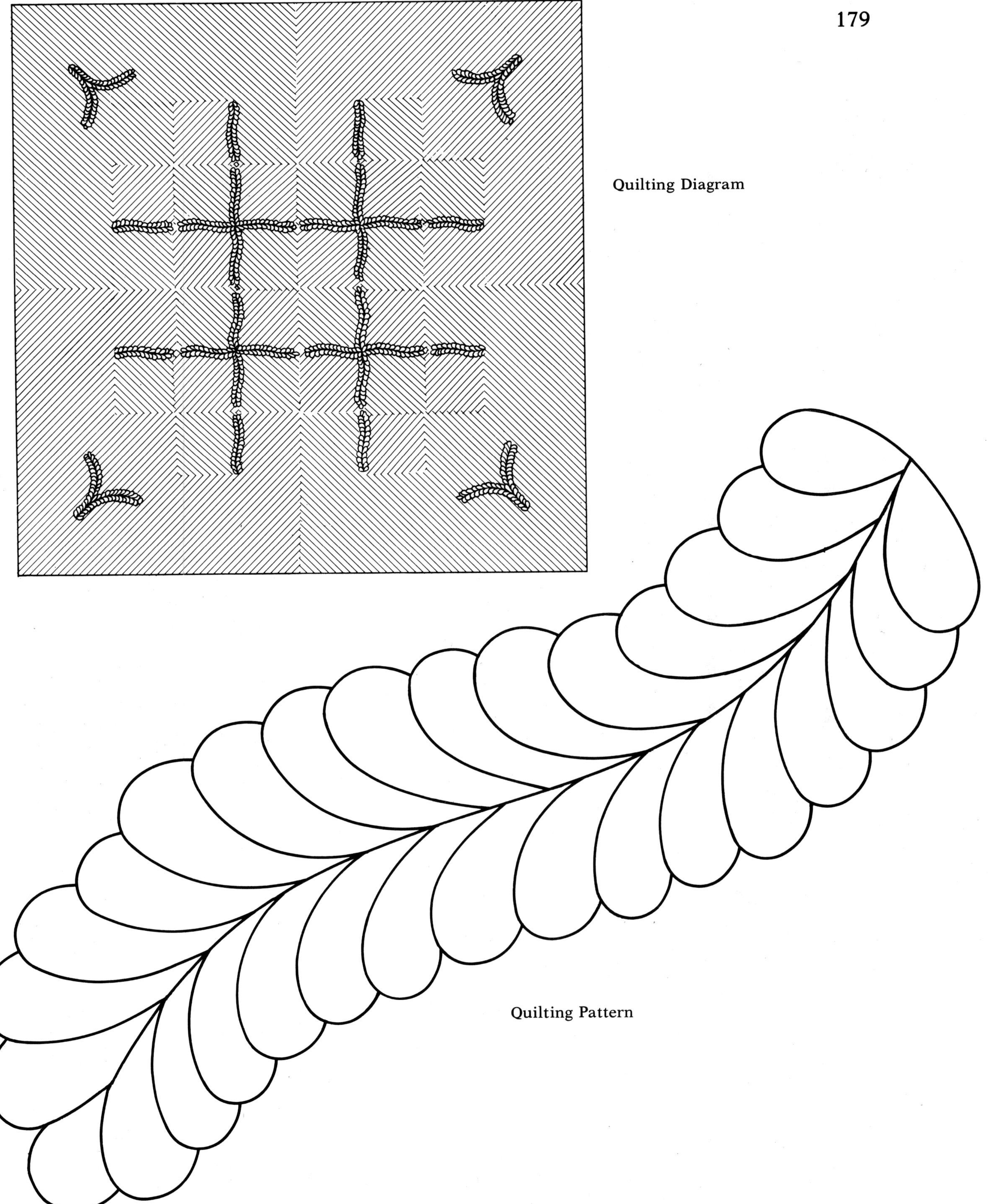

Quilting Diagram

Quilting Pattern

Plume Quilt

Pennsylvania Dutch in design, this quilt was made in the 1880s. Four squares of blue are joined for the main part of the quilt, and each is appliquéd with a plume-and-star motif; a medallion flower in the center and tulips along the borders complete the design.

SIZE: 85″ square.

EQUIPMENT: Tracing paper. Pencil. Stiff cardboard. Scissors. Sewing needle. Quilting needle. Tape measure. Straight pins.

MATERIALS: Closely woven cotton fabric, 36″ wide: dark blue, 6 yards; small plaid (for lining), 6 yards; orange, 2 yards; red, 2½ yards. Sewing thread to match fabrics. Cotton batting.

DIRECTIONS: Read General Directions on page 158 and appliqué instructions on page 161. Enlarge patterns for appliqués on 1″ squares. **Note:** Enlarge only one diamond piece of Border Flower: complete half- and quarter-patterns indicated by long dash lines. From cardboard, cut out each pattern.

Following directions for appliqué, cut and prepare appliqué pieces. From orange fabric, cut 16 plumes, 10 scallops, 32 diamonds, and piece 1 of center flower. From red fabric, cut 10 scallops, 16 plumes, 4 stars, piece 2 of center flower, 40 diamonds, 16 stems, and piece 1 of border flower.

For background of quilt top, cut four pieces of blue fabric each 35″ square; cut two pieces 9″ wide and 86″ long; cut two pieces 9″ wide and 69″ long.

Pin a red star at center of each blue fabric square. Place plumes around star, radiating out from center and alternating red and orange fabric. Space evenly and pin in place. Baste appliqués to blue fabric. With matching thread, slip-stitch each appliqué in place.

Stitch the four blue squares together with right sides facing, taking ½″ seams. Over center joining of the four squares, appliqué the orange and red flower pieces as shown. Along opposite sides of the joined squares, stitch a 69″-long piece with ½″ seams, for borders. Along remaining opposite sides, stitch the 86″ border pieces with equal ends extending. Stitch ends of shorter border pieces to side edges of longer border ends. Place five orange and red scallop pieces along the edge of the four sides of border, alternating colors and spacing evenly; pin in place. For border flowers, sew together four diamonds as shown on pattern, with ⅛″ seams, placing red diamonds on outside and orange in middle. Sew two red diamonds together along one side for each corner of border.

Between each border scallop, pin a stem and flower as shown. Pin two joined red diamonds between tops of corner scallops. Baste all in place; slip-stitch appliqués to background.

For quilt lining, cut two pieces of plaid fabric 36″ x 86″ and one piece 16″ x 86″. Stitch the long edges of the 26″pieces along each long edge of 16″ piece, taking ½″ seams. Press seams open.

Quilting: Following General Directions, pin and baste quilt top, batting, and lining together. Make quilting lines ⅛″ inside each appliqué piece, following outline, then about ½″ apart along length of scallops and plumes and within center flower; on stars, quilt star shapes following border flower diamond pattern. On quilt background, make lines of quilting around appliqué pieces ½″ away and then ½″ apart to fill areas. (**Note:** If desired, quilting lines may be marked with pencil or chalk before basting the three layers together.)

After quilting is completed, remove the basting stitches. Turn margin of plaid lining over edges of quilt to front for edging. Turn in about ¼″ of margin and slip-stitch plaid edging to front of quilt for a neat finish.

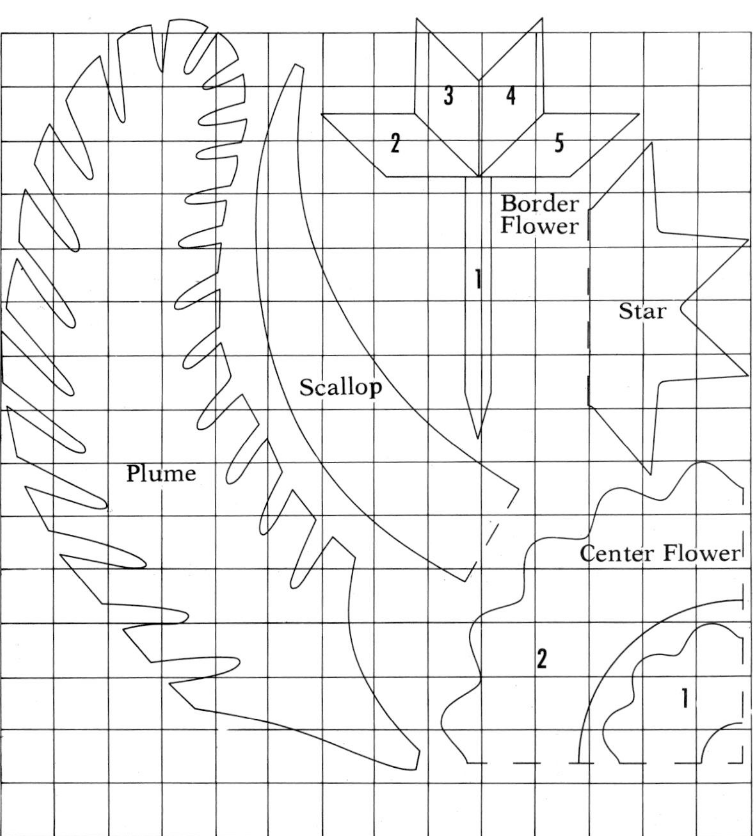

Missouri Beauty

This quilt hangs dramatically from a high railing to give almost full display to its strong symmetry of design. Small appliquéd blocks are joined to the four sides of the pieced blocks for an interweaving pattern of sharp and soft elements. From Missouri around 1880. Pattern: Whigs' Defeat.

SIZE: 83″ square.

EQUIPMENT: Pencil. Ruler. Scissors. Thin, stiff cardboard. Paper for patterns. Tracing paper. Dressmaker's (carbon) tracing paper. Tracing wheel or dry ball-point pen. Tailor's chalk. Sewing and quilting needles. Compass. Quilting frame (optional).

MATERIALS: Closely woven cotton fabric 45″ wide: red, 1⅔ yds.; dark blue-green, 2½ yds.; white, 5¼ yds. Fabric for lining 45″ wide, 4⅔ yds. Dacron polyester or cotton batting. White sewing thread.

Quilt Courtesy of Bryce and Donna Hamilton, Tipton, Iowa

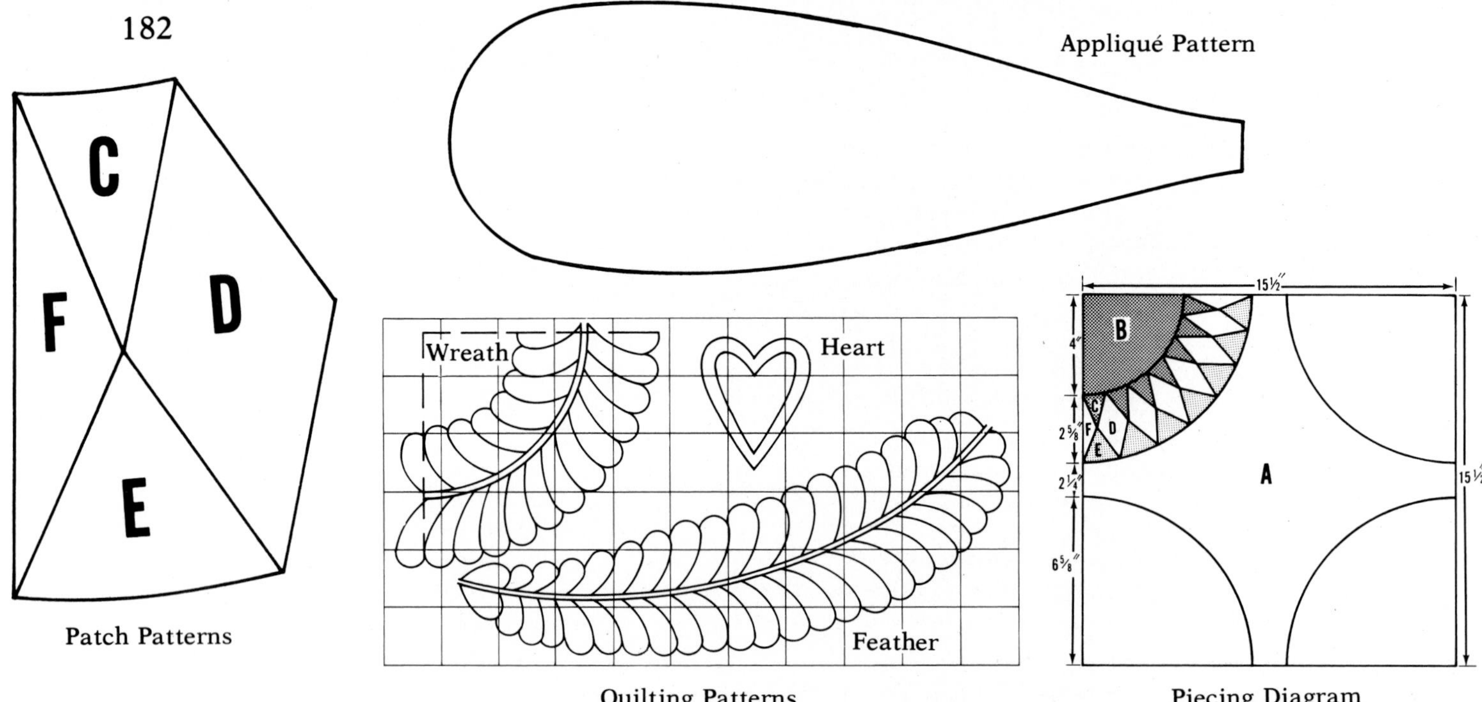

Patch Patterns

Quilting Patterns

Piecing Diagram

DIRECTIONS: Read General Directions on page 158. Quilt is constructed of nine pieced blocks set with appliquéd blocks and panels.

Pieced Blocks: See Piecing Diagram for one block. To make patterns for patch pieces, draw a 15½″ square on cardboard. Set compass for 4″ spread; place point of compass in one corner of square drawn, and draw an arc for piece B. Set compass for 6⅝″ and draw a second arc in same corner. To complete piece A, draw a 6⅝″ arc around the other three corners. Cut along marked lines for patterns. Trace actual-size patterns for pieces C, D, E, and F, and make a cardboard pattern for each.

Marking patterns on wrong side of fabric and adding ¼″ seam allowance all around, cut patch pieces as follows: From green fabric, cut 36 B pieces and 252 C pieces. From red fabric, cut 252 E pieces. From white fabric, cut nine A pieces, 216 D pieces, and 72 F pieces.

To make one block, assemble pieces as shown in Piecing Diagram. Join seven C pieces, seven E pieces, six D pieces, and two F pieces into a curving strip, then join strip to a B piece for corner section. Make three more corner sections and join the four to an A piece, for a block measuring 15½″ square, plus outside seam allowance. Make eight more blocks in same manner.

Appliquéd Blocks: Trace actual-size appliqué pattern. Following General Directions for appliqué (see page 161), cut and prepare 148 appliqués from red fabric and 100 from green.

For background of blocks, make cardboard pattern 6″ x 15½″. Marking pattern on wrong side of fabric and adding ¼″ seam allowance all around, cut 18 blocks from white fabric. On one long side of each block, mark off a center section 2¼″ wide (6⅝″ from each end). Place five appliqués in a fan cluster on each block (two green flanking three red), with base of appliqués within marked center section; pin, baste, and slip-stitch in place.

Sew two appliquéd blocks to opposite sides of each pieced block, matching appliquéd edges to white space (piece A) of larger block.

Join the sections made into three rows of three sections each, matching white edges of appliquéd blocks. Rows should measure 15½″ x 82½″, plus outside seam allowance.

Appliquéd Panels: For inner panels, cut two pieces 12″ x 82½″ from white fabric, adding ¼″ seam allowance all around. At both ends of each piece, appliqué a cluster in same pattern as before.

From raw edge of each end, measure in 27¾″ and mark center points. Appliqué three green and three red appliqué pieces in alternating fashion around each point, for circular flower design; see illustration.

Join the three block rows and the two appliquéd panels together on their long sides, in alternating fashion.

For outer panels, cut two pieces 6″ x 82½″ from white fabric, adding ¼″ seam allowance all around. On one long side of each, mark a point 27¾″ from raw edge of each end. Appliqué a fan cluster at each point. On opposite long side of each piece, mark a point 14″ from raw edge of each end and a third point in center of same long side. Appliqué a fan cluster at each point.

Join appliquéd panels to both sides of quilt top, matching the three clusters to white sections of pieced blocks. Quilt top should now measure 83″ square.

Lining: Cut two pieces 42″ x 83″. Sew together on their long sides with ½″ seams; press seam open. Cut batting same size as lining and quilt top.

Quilting: Enlarge wreath, feather, and heart quilting patterns on paper ruled in 1″ squares; complete quarter- and half-patterns indicated by dash lines. Using dressmaker's carbon and tracing wheel (or dry ball-point pen), transfer patterns to quilt top. Place a wreath in center of each white A piece. Place a heart in each side section of A pieces. Place feather four times around each appliquéd circular flower, making an oval shape. Place feather twice for a half-oval around the eight clusters that edge quilt top. Place a heart inside pointed ends of ovals and half-ovals. Fill in remaining white areas of quilt top with hearts, arranging them in groups of two or four with pointed ends meeting.

Mark concentric circular lines on corner sections of pieced blocks; mark lines ¼″ apart in groups of three, making groups ½″ apart.

Following General Directions, pin and baste quilt top, batting, and lining together. Starting in center and working around and outward, quilt on all marked lines and around appliqués; within appliqués, quilt two lines ⅛″ apart.

Edges: Trim corners of quilt slightly for rounded shape. From green fabric, cut bias strips 1″ wide; sew together for a total of about 9⅓ yds. for binding. Right sides together and with ¼″ seams, sew binding to front of quilt. Turn binding to back of quilt, turn in edges ¼″, and slip-stitch to lining. Press edges of quilt.

Hawaiian Quilt

The breadfruit tree was the natural inspiration for this spectacular design. Two giant appliqués, cut "snowflake" fashion from a colored sheet, are sewn to a white sheet. The distinctive "wave" quilting is also typically Hawaiian, with the stitches following the lines of the appliqués.

SIZE: 101″ square.

EQUIPMENT: Ruler. Pencil. Soft pencil. Brown wrapping paper 50½″ square for pattern. Regular and embroidery scissors. Straight pins. Sewing and quilting needles. Quilting frame (optional).

MATERIALS: For quilt top and lining: two white king-size flat percale and muslin sheets (preshrunk) 104″ x 115″. For appliqué design: one king-size sheet (preshrunk) in contrasting color, or closely woven cotton fabric (preshrunk) 36″ wide, 8½ yds. Basting thread, matching thread, and strong thread for quilting. Dacron polyester or cotton batting 101″ square. White bias binding tape ½″ wide, 11½ yds.

DIRECTIONS: Read General Directions on page 158.

Patterns: Fold the brown paper square in half diagonally to form a triangle. Enlarge the pattern by copying on brown triangle ruled in 2″ squares, with diagonal along fold. Shaded areas indicate those areas to be cut away. Cut out paper design, in two pieces.

Appliqué: Cut colored sheet for appliqué design into 101″ square. If using fabric, cut three 101″ lengths, each 34″ wide. With right sides facing, sew the three strips side by side, with ¼″ seams, making 101″ square. Fold square carefully into eighths. Lay the folded paper patterns on folded fabric, matching center point of one pat-

tern (indicated by dot) with center point of fabric, and outer edge of border pattern with edge of fabric. Pin patterns to cloth securely at many points so they will not slip when cutting. Beginning at center fold and working outward, cut through all eight layers of fabric at one time, ⅛" outside all edges of pattern outlines, for turning under when appliquéing. Unfold fabric and you have the complete appliqué design.

Cut white sheet for quilt top to 101" square. Lay sheet on flat surface and place appliqué pieces on it, being careful to place them accurately in center and on edges. Pin, then baste securely in place all around motifs about ¼" in from edges. To appliqué, use matching thread. Starting from the center, slip-stitch entire outline of appliqué to sheet with tiny, barely visible stitches, turning raw edges under ⅛" as you sew.

Lining: Cut remaining white sheet or fabric to 101" square. Cut batting same size.

Quilting: Following General Direction on page 158, pin and baste quilt top, batting, and lining together. Mark over-all quilting pattern with a soft pencil, following pattern of appliqués in concentric rows about ½" apart. Mark entire quilt top, white and colored. Starting in center and working around and outward, quilt on all marked lines (see General Directions).

Edges: Trim edges of quilt evenly. Insert edges of quilt into fold of bias tape and stitch in place.

Gingham Dog and Calico Cat

Two favorite nursery pals are multiplied by three for six go-to-sleep friends. Appliqué each dog or cat with bright scraps of calico or gingham, add winsome faces with simple embroidery, and frame them in cheerful yellow calico. An interesting square-in-square quilting design sculpts the border.

SIZES: 33¾" x 44¼".

EQUIPMENT: Scissors. Ruler. Pencils. Thin, stiff cardboard. Tailor's chalk. Paper for patterns. Dressmaker's (carbon) tracing paper. Tracing wheel or dry ball-point pen. Sewing and quilting needles. Quilting frame (optional).

MATERIALS: (All fabrics should be washable cotton or cotton blends.) Yellow and red calico 36" wide 2½ yds. (includes lining). Small amounts (about 6" x 9") of three ginghams and three calicos; scraps of fabric in red and contrasting solid colors. Red gingham for binding, ¼ yd. White fabric 36" wide, ⅝ yd. White and matching sewing threads. One skein black cotton embroidery floss. Dacron polyester or cotton batting.

DIRECTIONS: Read General Directions on page 158 and appliqué instructions on page 161. Quilt is constructed of six appliquéd blocks set with calico background.

Appliqués: Enlarge dog and cat patterns on paper ruled in 1″ squares. Make a separate cardboard pattern for each appliqué piece (heavy lines on patterns): for dog—body, hind legs, head, two ears, tongue, five parts of bow; for cat—body, hind legs, tail, head, five parts of bow. Following appliqué directions, cut and prepare appliqué pieces, using a different gingham for each of three dogs and a different calico for each of three cats; cut bow pieces in a contrasting solid color for each. Cut three dog's tongues from red.

Blocks: From white fabric, cut six pieces 9-3/16″ x 9½″, adding ¼″ seam allowance all around. Using dressmaker's carbon and tracing wheel (or dry ball-point pen), transfer main outlines of dog to center of three white blocks and cat to remaining three blocks, placing 9-3/16″ edges of blocks at sides.

Pin, baste, and slip-stitch appliqués in place, starting with pieces that will be overlapped by others.

Embroidery: See stitch details on page 15. Transfer embroidery pattern (light lines on pattern and noses, eyes and pupils) to appliquéd dogs and cats. Using full six strands of black embroidery floss, embroider eyelashes in straight stitch and remaining lines in outline stitch; embroider eye pupils and noses in satin stitch.

Background and Assembling: From yellow calico, cut four strips 2″ x 9½″ and one strip 2″ x 31½″, adding ¼″ seam allowance all around. Sew appliquéd blocks into two vertical rows of three blocks each, with a short joining strip between blocks; make one row dog, cat, dog, and other row cat, dog, cat. Join rows, with long strip between. Piece should measure 21″ x 31½″, plus outside seam allowance.

For borders, cut two pieces from yellow calico 6″ x 21″ and two pieces 6″ x 43½″, adding ¼″ seam allowance all around. Sew shorter pieces to top and bottom of quilt top, then longer pieces to sides. Quilt top should measure 33½″ x 44″, including outside seam allowance.

Lining: Cut lining 33½″ x 44″. Cut batting same size.

Quilting: With ruler and tailor's chalk, mark quilting lines as follows: On white background, mark diagonal lines 1⅜″ apart, alternating direction of lines from block to block as shown in illustration. Mark a square around each block, ¼″ away from seams. In each row of blocks, mark lines to connect squares drawn. Mark two X's in center of long joining strip, connecting corners of blocks as shown.

For border quilting design, cut a piece of cardboard 3¾″ square. Starting at upper left area of border, place square as a diamond with two opposite corners of pattern centered on seam joining top and side borders; draw around with tailor's chalk. Continuing to the right, draw around diamond four more times with adjacent points touching; corners of fifth diamond will be on seam joining top and right borders. Repeat pattern on bottom border. Fill in side borders with same pattern, making seven diamonds on each side border; start by placing one side of pattern against side of first diamond drawn. Extend lines to corners of quilt top to complete pattern.

Make another cardboard pattern 1¾″ square. Place pattern in center of all squares drawn and mark around with tailor's chalk. Cut pattern in half diagonally for a triangle pattern. Place triangle inside larger triangles (with 1″ margins) all around both outer and inner edges of border, and mark around.

Following General Directions, pin and baste quilt top, batting, and lining together. Quilt around each separate appliqué piece and around embroidery defining front legs, noses, eyes, cats' mouths, and dogs' tongues; quilt on all marked lines.

Edges: From red gingham, cut bias strips 1¼″ wide; sew together to make strip about 158″ long for binding. With right sides together, and with ¼″ seams, sew strips to front of quilt. Turn strip to back of quilt, turn in raw edge ¼″, and slip-stitch to lining, making ⅜″-wide binding on front and back. Press edges.

DECORATING WITH PATCHWORK AND APPLIQUÉ

House and Tree Pillows

Here are country scenes to patch and embroider. Pretty fabrics give these pieces a look of primitive realism. Each pillow is bordered by rich dark velveteen and embellished with embroidered flowers.

SIZES: House Pillow 19″ x 17″; Tree Pillow 15½″ square.

EQUIPMENT: Paper for patterns. Pencil. Ruler. Cardboard. Scissors. Straight pins. Sewing and embroidery needles. Iron.

MATERIALS: House Pillow: Velveteen, dark blue-green, 45″ wide, ¼ yard; small amounts of red for chimneys and door (D); small amount of turquoise for roof piece (E); scrap of light blue for window (F). Small amounts of three different floral prints: white background for house (B); blue background for sky (C); and tan background for ground (A). Dark print, ½ yard for back. Sewing thread to match fabric. Six-strand embroidery floss, less than one skein of green, light blue, red, pink. Dacron polyester for stuffing. Batting for interlining. **Tree Pillow:** Dark blue-green velveteen, 45″ wide, ¼ yard. Small amounts of three different floral prints: blue background for sky (B); dark red background for tree (C); and off-white background for foreground (A). Dark print, ½ yard, for back. Sewing thread to match fabrics. Six-strand embroidery floss, less than one skein of dark green, chartreuse, red, light blue, pink, yellow. Dacron polyester for stuffing. Batting for interlining.

DIRECTIONS: To Make Patterns: Enlarge patterns by copying on paper ruled in 1″ squares. Cut each individual shape out of cardboard. Cut several of each of the shapes used repeatedly so you can discard patterns as they become frayed.

To Cut Fabric: Refer to letters given in materials and on patterns for fabrics to be used for specific patch pieces. Press fabric smooth. Place cardboard pattern on wrong side of fabric, mak-

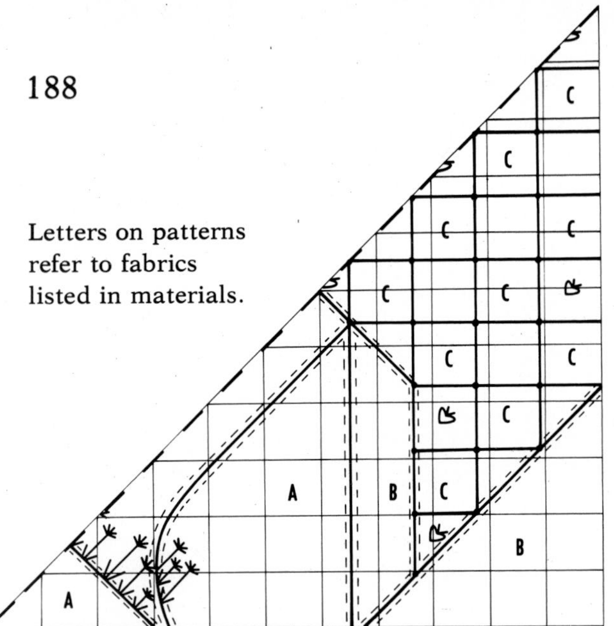

Letters on patterns refer to fabrics listed in materials.

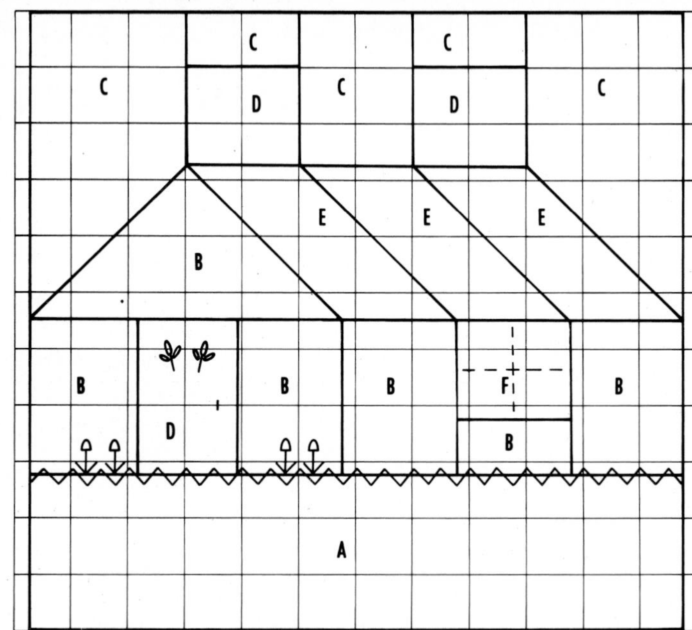

ing sure one straight side of each piece is placed on the straight of the fabric. With pencil, mark around each pattern; this outline will be seam-line. Cut each piece out of fabric, adding ¼″ all around each for seam allowance.

To Patch: With right sides facing, pin patch pieces together, then sew until entire block design area is complete. Design block of House Pillow is 11½″ x 11″ plus seam allowance; Tree Pillow is 11″ square, plus seam allowance.

To Embroider: Refer to Stitch Details on page 15 and to individual directions. Use two strands of floss in needle throughout.

To Quilt: Cut batting the size of design block area and baste to back of block. With tiny running stitches and two strands of floss in needle, quilt along both sides of seamlines, just inside each piece.

To Assemble: Cut four border strips out of dark blue-green velveteen for each (see sizes in individual directions). With right sides facing, pin, then sew the two shorter strips to each side of design block, making ¼″ seams. Do the same with longer pieces at top and bottom. Make medium-length running stitches along border strips ⅛″ from seam, with contrasting color floss.

Cut the fabric for back the same size as finished front. With right sides facing, pin the front and back together; sew, making ½″ seams and leaving a 6″ opening in center of one side. Turn to right side; push out corners. Stuff pillow fully. Turn edges of opening in and slip-stitch closed.

HOUSE PILLOW

To Embroider: Make the flower stems and leaves on each side of door in green chain stitch. Make these flowers in red satin stitch. Make stems of flowers on door in blue chain stitch; make leaves of these flowers in blue satin stitch; make flowers in pink satin stitch. Make door knob in green satin stitch. Make line across top edge of ground where indicated by zigzag line with green floss in straight featherstitch. Make lines of green running stitch on window where indicated by short dash lines.

To Quilt: Use green floss for chimneys, door, and window; red for house pieces; pink for sky pieces; light blue for roof pieces.

For Border Strips: Cut two pieces of velveteen 4½″ x 11½″, and two pieces 3¾″ x 20″.

TREE PILLOW

All non-lettered pattern pieces are to be cut of dark blue-green velveteen, with ¼″ added all around for seam allowance.

To Embroider: Embroider apples in red satin stitch, leaves on apples in chartreuse lazy daisy stitch. Make all the leaves and flower stems in chartreuse chain stitch. Make all flowers in radiating straight stitch in red, blue, pink, and yellow.

To Quilt: Quilt only where indicated by dash lines on pattern: use green floss along blue-green edges on tree, and light blue floss along white and blue edges. At each dot on pattern, make tufts by tacking through the two thicknesses as follows: with full six strands of dark green floss, insert needle through dot and bring out at point very close to dot; make a double knot, and clip yarn leaving ¼″ ends.

For Border Strips: Cut two pieces of velveteen, 16½″ x 3″, and two pieces 11½″ x 3″.

Scented Ribbon Pillows

These elegant balsam pillows to scent closets and drawers make a perfect "little gift." They're easy to make by combining and sewing together the prettiest ribbons you can find. The heart, about 8" wide, is made by creating a ribbon "fabric" and then cutting out the shape. A ribbon ruffle finishes the edge. The box-tied pillow, about 10" square, is made of fabric trimmed with ribbon stripes.

EQUIPMENT: Paper for patterns. Tissue paper. Pencil. Ruler. Scissors. Straight pins. Sewing needle. Sewing machine with zigzag and ruffler attachments. Glass jars. Screen. Props to keep screen elevated in horizontal position.

MATERIALS: Balsam needles, 8-10 cups. Salt, 2 tablespoons per each cup of needles. Optional: Cedar bark. One tablespoon cedar bark and one teaspoon oil of pine per jar. Tan sateen, 44" wide, ⅓ yd. Ribbons: Red and white flowered, 1" wide, 4⅔ yds.; 1⅜" wide, 13". Blue velvet ribbon, ⅝" wide, 3 yds. Cable cord, ¼" diameter, 1¼ yds. Blue, tan, and white sewing threads.

DIRECTIONS: Read General Directions on page 158. If a balsam tree is not accessible, use any fragrant pine needle. Selecting new growth of needles at branch tips, strip needles from branches. Prop screen horizontally so that air circulates above and below: spread needles on screen to dry. Leave one week or longer, until thoroughly dry. Put into jars, adding two tablespoons of salt for every cup of needles. Allow to "fix" for three weeks, turning and shaking jar occasionally. If desired, add one tablespoon cedar bark and one teaspoon oil of pine to each jar.

To make pillows, enlarge patterns by copying on paper ruled in 1" squares; complete half-patterns indicated by long dash lines. Copy markings of ribbon positions onto patterns. Assemble pillows according to individual directions. When zigzag stitching ribbons together, align ribbon edges, leaving no seam allowances.

SQUARE PILLOW

From tan fabric, cut two 10½" squares. On the bias, cut enough lengths of 1"-wide strips of tan fabric to measure 41". From ⅝"-wide blue velvet ribbon, cut four 6" pieces and one 22" piece. From red and white flowered ribbon, 1" wide, cut four 8½" pieces and four 13" pieces.

On right side of one tan fabric square, zigzag stitch a 6" length of blue ribbon diagonally across each corner, having outer long edge of ribbon 2¼" from corner point of fabric. Straight-stitch an 8½" piece of flowered ribbon ¼" in from blue ribbon (ends will cross each other slightly at center of each side). Mitering corners, baste 22" length of blue ribbon in diamond shape ¼" in from flowered ribbons. Zigzag-stitch in place.

Join bias lengths of tan fabric to make strip 41" long. Place cording along lengthwise center on wrong side of bias strip. Fold strip in half; stitch along strip close to cording. With raw edges even, baste piping on right side of pillow front along four sides. Join ends of piping by cutting off cord

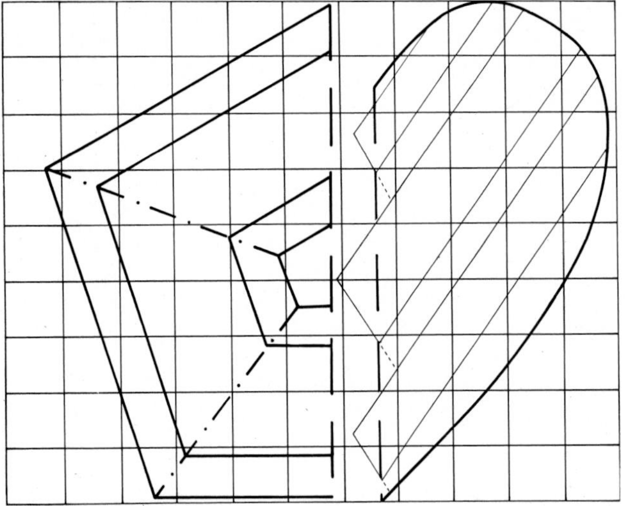

about ½″ inside one end and inserting the other end. Sew ends together neatly. Stitch piping to pillow front ¼″ from edges. With right sides facing, place pillow front and back together; stitch around, leaving 4″ opening in center of one side. Turn to right side. Tie a bow from each 13″ piece of flowered ribbon. Tack bow to pillow at center of each side edge. Fill pillow loosely with balsam needles: whipstitch opening closed.

HEART-SHAPED PILLOW

Using pattern and adding ¼″ seam allowance, cut one heart shape from tan fabric. From blue velvet ribbon cut two 2″ pieces, two 5¼″, two 7″, two 6½″, and one 16″. From 1⅜″-wide red and white flowered ribbon, cut two 6½″ pieces. From 1″-wide flowered ribbon, cut two 4¼″ pieces, two 7½″, two 4″, and one 48″.

From tissue paper, cut one heart pattern with ¼″ seam allowance. Trace onto tissue the solid lines indicating ribbon positions. Pin ribbons onto tissue heart, leaving ¼″ seam allowance at outer ends; do not overlap lengthwise edges of ribbons. Pin ribbons from top of heart to bottom as follows: Blue velvet 2″, 1″ flowered 4¼″, blue velvet 5¼″, 1⅜″ flowered 6½″, blue velvet 7″, 1″ flowered 7½″, blue velvet 6½″, 1″ flowered 4″. At center junction, blue ribbons have left ends overlapping right ends; flowered ribbons have right ends overlapping left. Using zigzag stitch and blue thread, stitch ribbon pieces together. Straight-stitch around heart outline. Carefully remove tissue paper from fabric heart.

With right sides facing, place front and back of heart together. Stitch around edges, leaving opening at indentation at top of heart. Stuff pillow loosely and whipstitch opening closed. Using ruffler attachment with adjusting lever set on spacing #1 and stitch length on #6, insert 48″ length of flowered ribbon into separator guide and pleat entire length. Adjust ruffle to fit around heart. With right sides together, seam ruffle ends. With ruffle ends at top of heart, whipstitch back of ruffle on stitching line to seam around heart. From 16″ blue ribbon, make bow; tack on as shown.

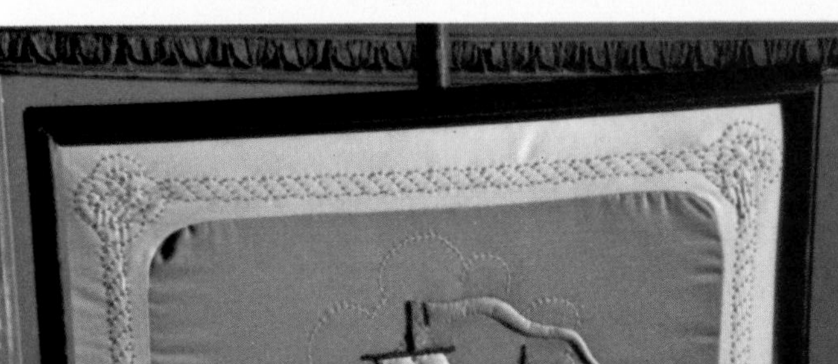

Lofty Schooner Fire Screen

Fire screen can be displayed on a stand or on the wall. The sails and ship are separate pieces, which are hand-appliquéd over padding. The detailing is done in satin stitch and quilting.

SIZE: 23″x 20″ unframed.

EQUIPMENT: Paper for pattern. Tracing paper. Hard- and soft-lead pencils. Ruler. Scissors. White dressmaker's tracing (carbon) paper. Tracing wheel. Sewing and embroidery needles. Straight pins. Staple gun. Iron.

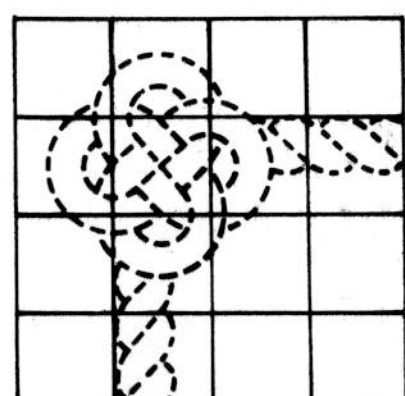

MATERIALS: Closely woven polished cotton fabric, 36″ wide: light tan ¾ yard; medium tan ¼ yard; medium light blue ½ yard; royal blue ⅛ yard; small pieces of red, orange, dark tan, and ecru. Sewing thread to match all fabrics. Six-strand embroidery floss, one skein each of dark brown, medium brown, dark tan, ecru, yellow-gold, red, light blue, royal blue, and black. Piece of Dacron batting 23″ x 20″, plus scraps. Wooden canvas stretcher 23″ x 20″. Staples.

DIRECTIONS: Read General Directions on page 158. Design is made up of appliqué, embroidery, and quilting. Read instructions for appliqué on page 161, and refer to embroidery stitch details on page 15. Use sewing thread to match fabric when appliquéing or sewing pieces together.

To Make Patterns: Enlarge patterns by copying on paper ruled in 1″ squares. Make a tracing of each pattern. On ship pattern, heavy solid lines on pattern indicate pieces to be appliquéd. Fine lines on pattern indicate lines and areas to be embroidered. Dash lines indicate lines to be quilted.

To Prepare Background: Cut light blue fabric for sky 16″ x 16¼″; cut royal blue fabric for sea 3½″ x 16¼″. With right sides facing sew together along 16¼″ edges, making ¼″ seam. With dressmaker's carbon and tracing wheel, transfer complete pattern to background fabric, omitting quilting and embroidery lines on appliqué pieces only.

To Appliqué: On tracing paper, retrace all the ship appliqué pieces separately, including all fine and dash lines on these pieces; complete pieces where they overlap (see illustration and pattern). Pin patterns onto appropriate fabrics: banner and rear of ship on red; top flag on orange; each sail on medium tan; upper portion of ship hull on ecru, lower portion of ship hull on dark tan. With carbon and tracing wheel or hard-lead pencil, transfer all quilting and embroidery lines to appliqué fabrics. Adding ¼″ for seam allowance all around each piece except rear piece, cut appliqués out of fabric. Turn under ¼″ edges around all appliqués, except rear piece, and press. Pin appliqué pieces in place, except rear. Refer to illustration for overlapping pieces. Place small amounts of batting under sails, flag, and banner. Appliqué all pieces in place.

To Embroider: Pin ship rear piece in place. Stitch rear piece in place by working satin stitch all around edges with four strands of yellow-gold floss. Do the same along the two cross lines. Fill small square windows and letters on banner in satin stitch with four strands of light blue floss. With one strand of light blue floss, make small running stitches on banner. With four strands of red floss, work vertical satin stitch along top and bottom edges of ecru ship hull. With four strands of black floss, make all cannons in vertical satin stitch; with four strands of royal blue floss, make the rectangular cannon openings in horizontal satin stitch. With one strand of dark tan floss, make running stitches along curved lines on each sail. Do not embroider the diagonal lines across sails or sky; these are quilting lines. Embroider all the masts in horizontal or vertical satin stitch with four strands of dark brown floss.

To Make Border: Using outer solid line of ship pattern, transfer rectangular outline with rounded corners to center area of light tan fabric. Cut opening in center of fabric ¼″ inside marked line. With right sides facing, center and pin border fabric to appliquéd ship fabric. Sew together all around ¼″ from edges. Turn fabric to right side and press.

To Quilt: With tracing carbon and hard-lead pencil, transfer rope knot motif to each corner of border ½″ in from seam line. Continue rope design between knot motifs to complete border. If any quilting lines on background fabric have faded, retransfer design.

Center and pin 23″ x 20″ piece of batting to wrong side of background. Baste through all thicknesses, lengthwise and crosswise; then baste diagonally across in two directions and around sides, top, and bottom.

Quilt through all thicknesses by hand with short running stitches using two strands of floss in needle. Use ecru floss for waves and clouds; use medium brown for lines across sails and sky lines; use dark tan floss for rope border.

To Mount: Assemble canvas stretchers to 23″ x 20″ rectangle. Place design over canvas stretcher; pull fabric evenly to back and staple in back making fabric taut. Trim excess fabric. Frame as fire screen or as desired.

Hearth and Farm Primitive "Paintings"

An old-fashioned hearth and a fanciful farm make delightful pictures. The print and polka-dot backgrounds are quilted and the details are appliquéd with running stitches, embroidered with floss—or both! The mat size of the hearth is 23″ x 17½″; the farm scene measures 19½″ x 23½″.

EQUIPMENT: Paper for patterns. Tracing paper. Pencil. Ruler. Dressmaker's tracing (carbon) paper. Scissors. Tailor's chalk. Hard-lead pencil. Straight pins. Sewing and embroidery needles. **For Mat:** Mat knife, metal edge.

MATERIALS: Unbleached muslin 36″ wide, 1 yard for each. Batting (see individual directions). Pieces of cotton print fabrics for backgrounds (amounts given in individual directions). Large and small pieces of print and plain fabrics as illustrated or as desired which are suitable for the appliqués. Six-strand embroidery floss (colors given in individual directions). Sewing thread to match fabrics. Print fabric for each mat, 36″ wide, ⅝ yard. Mounting cardboard and mat board (same size as matted size given above). Rubber cement. Double- and single-faced masking tape.

DIRECTIONS: Read General Directions on

page 158 and the directions for appliquéing on page 161. Instead of slip-stitching appliqués, sew pieces together and in place with tiny running stitches ¼″ apart, using double strand of matching sewing thread. When working embroidery, refer to embroidery stitch details on page 15.

To Make Patterns; Enlarge complete patterns by copying on paper ruled in 1″ squares. The heavier lines on pattern indicate pieces to be cut out and appliquéd. The dash lines indicate pieces that are to be tucked (see directions for Farm Scene). The finer lines indicate what is to be embroidered. Trace pattern for each appliqué piece.

To Make Background: Cut the background fabrics as indicated in individual directions. Cut batting and muslin for backing the same size: 11½″ x 17½″ for Hearth; 13½″ x 18″ for Farm Scene. Place the muslin on back of batting; place background fabrics on top of batting, overlapping the lower piece of background on upper piece ½″. Turn top edge of lower fabric under ¼″ and, with running stitch and double strand of thread, sew together through all layers where they overlap.

Quilt background with double strand of matching sewing thread and tiny running stitches. Use a random pattern for quilting or select a pattern appropriate to the design (note stitching pattern on sky in Farm Scene suggests cloud formations).

To Make Appliqués: Place separate patterns on the particular fabric for a specific part of the scene with carbon between; transfer the outline with hard-lead pencil to the fabric. Cut the individual pieces out of fabric, adding ¼″ all around each piece. Fold under ¼″ along each edge of each piece; press, then appliqué each piece in place on background with tiny running stitches spaced ¼″ apart, using double strand of matching sewing thread. Embroider parts as indicated in individual directions.

To Embroider: Embroidery is done in satin stitch with all six strands of floss in needle unless otherwise indicated. Embroider through top background layer of fabric only; do not work through all layers.

To Make Border: Cut four strips of print fabric each 3″ wide: two the width of design plus 2″ and two the length of design plus 2″. Fold each strip in half lengthwise and turn in ¼″ on each long edge; press. Insert ¼″ along each side of picture between turned-in edges of border strips. With two strands of sewing thread and tiny running stitches, sew border strips to each side 1/16″ in

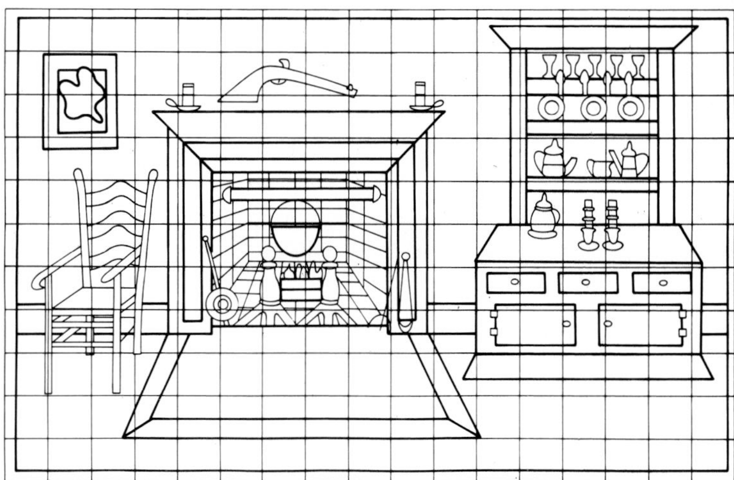

from fold. Repeat with remaining two strips at top and bottom of picture.

To Make Mat: Cut opening in center of mat board using mat knife and straight edge: 15″ x 19½″ for Farm Scene; 13″ x 19″ for Hearth. Spread rubber cement over one surface of mat and cover with fabric; pull excess fabric over outer edge to other side and cement in back to secure. Clip into center of fabric and cut out 1½″ away from inner edges of mat. Clip into corners to mat; fold fabric over to back and cement. Tape finished fabric scene to center of mounting cardboard. Place double-faced masking tape around edge of mounting cardboard; place mat over picture and cardboard and press to secure. Frame as desired.

FARM SCENE

Using separate patterns, cut fabric background pieces for sky and ground adding ¼″ to top, side, and bottom edges. Assemble, following General Directions.

Cut out all individual pieces for appliqués as indicated on pattern. Cut cow and lady out of muslin; cut skirt of fabric and appliqué to muslin lady. Sew to background. Cut horizontal strips of fence; sew these down first, then cut and sew vertical strips on top.

For farmhouse and barn roofs, use pieces of muslin twice the height of appliqué patterns; do the same with printed fabric for farmhouse roof; do not cut shape out of fabric yet. Make ¼" horizontal tucks across pieces to resemble clapboards (see illustration). Cut the separate pieces, adding ¼" so that tucks will be angled correctly for perspective when lines meet. Sew the two house pieces together; sew roof to house. Sew barn pieces together; sew roof to barn. Then sew each structure in place on background. Assemble parts of the well and sew to background.

Embroider the trees, working satin stitch in opposite directions on each side of center to suggest branches. Embroider the spots, hoofs, and features of cow in satin stitch. The flowers are all satin stitch: do the centers in pink first, then do the petals. Embroider stems and leaves in straight stitches. Work chickens in satin stitch; do the legs and feet in outline stitch. Fill in the windows and doors of barn in white satin stitch. Work weather vanes in straight stitches, with satin stitch top. Make the lines in windows and on doors of both structures in outline stitch. Fill in the lady's hair and blouse in satin stitch over muslin.

HEARTH SCENE

Cut and join the wall and floor as for Farm Scene background. Cut a strip of muslin the width of scene for molding; sew in place. On floor fabric, use ruler and tailor's chalk to mark diagonal quilting lines ½" apart to imitate floor boards. Appliqué hearth to floor and add muslin border. Quilt background (including hearth) following General Directions. Cut the pieces for cupboard and sew them all together as appliqués before sewing complete cupboard to background.

Assemble and sew the individual parts of fireplace together before appliquéing to background: first cut out piece for interior, then add muslin frame. Embroider all the lines on interior of fireplace, the fireplace tools and pot handle in outline stitch. Use satin stitch for the remaining details.

Boat Wall Hanging

This boat scene is a perfect picture for a child's wall, or it can be stuffed and made into a giant pillow. Use cheerful colors in many prints; stitch and quilt on the machine.

SIZE: About 25" x 33".

EQUIPMENT: Ruler. Pencil. Brown wrapping paper. Dressmaker's tracing (carbon) paper. Tracing wheel. Straight pins. Sewing needle. Zigzag sewing machine.

MATERIALS: Closely woven medium-weight cotton fabrics, in several prints: blue for ocean, ⅓ yd.; yellow for boat bottom, ¼ yd.; blue and green scraps for remaining appliqués. For background, ¾ yd. solid light blue fabric. For edging, ⅓ yd. solid yellow-green fabric (or 3¼ yds. bias binding tape, ¾" wide). For lining, ¾ yd. lightweight fabric. Dacron batting, one piece approximately 25" x 33". Sewing thread in dark blue, green, and yellow-green.

DIRECTIONS: Read General Directions on page 158 and appliqué instructions on page 161. Enlarge pattern by copying on paper ruled in 2″ squares. Cut blue background fabric and lining, each 25″ x 33″. Transfer pattern to background fabric, marking on right side with dressmaker's carbon and tracing wheel. Transfer outlines of water and boat pieces to desired printed fabric pieces. Mark position of overlapping portholes and windows on main boat appliqué pieces.

Cut pieces from fabric. Place background fabric on top of lining fabric with batting in between. Baste all three layers together, making vertical and horizontal basting lines along center, diagonally from corner to corner, and around perimeter 1″ in from edges. Pin appliqués in place and baste carefully, about ¼″ in from raw edges. Set machine to fine-stitch length and #3 width. Stitch all around appliqués, encasing raw edges with stitching. Stitch line for flagpole. Trim edges of appliquéd piece, batting, and backing. Cut 1¼″-wide bias strips from edging fabric (or use bias tape). Piece together to form two 25½″ strips and two 33½″ strips. Right sides facing, stitch each of the longer strips to top and bottom of hanging, making ¼″ seams. Turn raw edges under ¼″, fold over to back, and slip-stitch to back of hanging. Repeat on sides with remaining strips.

Egg Basket Picture

This basket of eggs and milk pitcher is a homey scene to create with a combination of techniques.

SIZE: 18¾″ x 15″, without frame.

EQUIPMENT: Paper for patterns. Pencil. Iron. Ruler. Scissors. Straight pins. Sewing needle. Dressmaker's carbon.

MATERIALS: Organdy, ½ yard. Scraps of cotton or linen fabric (follow illustration for colors of fabrics, or use colors desired): Wall, 17″ x 22¾″; table, 6½″ x 22¾″; pitcher, 7″ x 11½″; eggs (various shades of off-white and beige and one turquoise), about 3″ x 4″ for each; basket, 9″ x 11½″. Sewing thread in colors to match fabrics. Cotton batting for padding. Heavy cardboard, 18¾″ x 15″. Fusible web. Feather. All-purpose glue.

DIRECTIONS: Read General Directions on page 158 and appliqué instructions on page 161. Steam-press all fabric pieces. Enlarge pattern by copying on paper ruled in 1″ squares. Make a separate pattern for each piece. Dash lines indicate where pieces overlap; fine lines on basket indicate quilting.

Using pattern piece as rough guide, mark wall background piece on fabric; cut fabric, leaving about a 2″ margin all around. Following manufacturer's directions, fuse a piece of organdy to

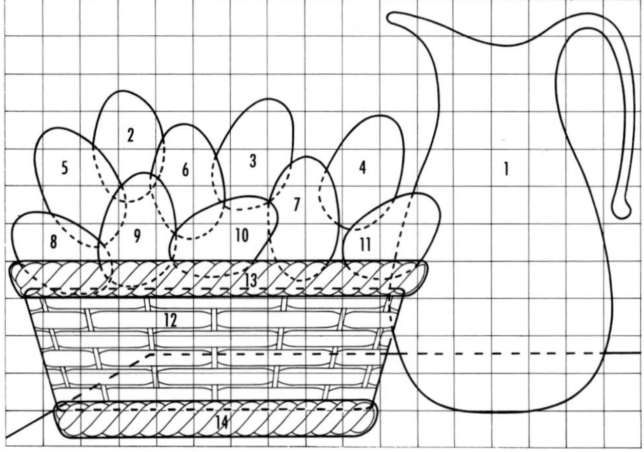

back of fabric piece. Then cut off bottom of fabric on solid and lower dash lines, leaving the 2″ margin at sides and top. Cut table fabric piece, using pattern, with a 2″ margin at sides and bottom. Fuse the wall piece on the table piece along seam allowance (overlap indicated by dash lines on pattern).

Place remainder of pattern pieces on wrong side of fabric with carbon paper in between; go over entire outline with pencil to transfer shape to fabric. When transferring more than one piece to same fabric (eggs, basket pieces), leave at least ½″ spaces between for seam allowance. Cut each fabric piece ¼″ outside marked line. Stitch around each piece on solid marked line. Cut a piece of batting for each fabric piece, cutting on solid line of pattern. Cut a piece of organdy for each part of basket using solid pattern line.

Baste batting to the wrong side of corresponding fabric pieces. On basket pieces, use fabric and organdy pieces, with batting in between. Before appliquéing basket pieces, quilt along fine lines, using running stitches and single strand brown thread. Turn under seam allowance and clip into seams at corners and around curves. Referring to pattern, pin and baste appliqués in proper position on background fabric in numerical order (piece #1 goes down first, #2 next, etc.). Slipstitch each piece all around. When stitching pitcher down, move handle in toward body of pitcher, as in illustration.

When all pieces have been appliquéd, glue work to cardboard, leaving 2″ fabric margin all around. Turn over and glue margins to back of cardboard. Tuck feather in behind basket top as shown. Frame as desired.

Wall Phone and Calico Coffee Mill Appliqué Pictures

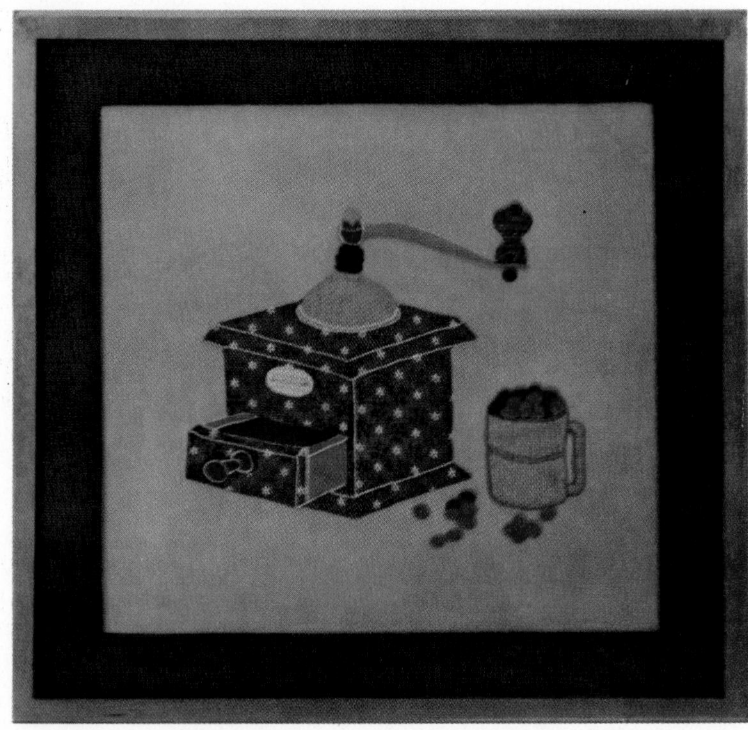

Here's a wall phone from the turn of the century, with twin bells and separate ear and mouth pieces to appliqué. Cotton and felt are the materials used here, and the detailing is done with French knots and chain and straight stitches. The picture measures 17" x 11¾" with the frame.

The colorful coffee mill is made of scraps of fabric and felt appliquéd and embroidered with outline stitch and French knots. The finished piece, including the frame, measures 16" x 16½".

EQUIPMENT: Scissors. Tracing paper. Pencil. Ruler. Single-edged razor blade. Square. Embroidery and fine needles. Backsaw. Miter box. Hammer. Nail set. Sandpaper. Paintbrush.

MATERIALS: Cardboard: two pieces 15¼" x 15¾" for Coffee Mill; one piece 11" x 16¼" for Telephone. Tightly woven lightweight cotton fabric: for backgrounds, gold and gray each 15¼" x 15¾" for Coffee Mill, and blue 11" x 16¼" for Telephone; large and small scraps of fabric in solid colors and small designs such as paisley, calico, gingham checks, polka dots, and stripes (see illustrations and follow individual directions for colors and patterns used). Scraps of felt: blue, yellow for Telephone; pale and olive green, tan, rust, and dark brown for Coffee Mill. Six-strand embroidery floss: black, green, tan, white. White sewing thread. For Telephone: gold metallic thread; gold cord 17" long. All-purpose glue. **For Frames:** Picture molding with 3/16" rabbet: 5½' for Coffee Mill; 5' for Telephone. Wood filler. White and gold paint. Small brads.

DIRECTIONS: Read General Directions on page 158. Enlarge patterns for Coffee Mill and Telephone on paper ruled in 1" squares; make separate pattern for each piece. Short dash lines on patterns indicate where pieces are overlapped. Following individual directions and using patterns, cut each piece of fabric, adding ¼" seam allowance on all fabric edges. Clip curved edges; turn all seam allowances under and press flat. Cut pieces of felt as indicated in individual directions, with no seam allowances.

Pin appliqué pieces to background, placing pieces that are underneath down first. Slip-stitch in place with tiny stitches as illustrated in General Directions for Appliqué on page 161.

For embroidery, use three strands of floss in needle. Make outline stitches along all long dash lines; outline those pieces indicated in individual directions in outline stitch. Solid black dots indicate French knots. Shaded areas indicate satin stitches. Tiny dash lines indicate backstitches. Dot-dash lines indicate chain stitches. See stitch details on page 15.

Embroider some felt pieces before appliquéing as indicated in individual directions.

Steam-press picture on back with moist cloth. Spread glue all along edges of cardboard and secure picture smoothly to appropriate-sized cardboard. Make mat for Coffee Mill as indicated in individual directions.

To Frame: Using miter box and backsaw, cut picture molding to fit sides of picture; sand smooth. Glue and nail frame pieces together. Countersink nails and fill holes with wood filler. Paint frame with two coats of white paint; let dry. Paint front edges gold. Put picture inside frame; secure picture in place with brads.

COFFEE MILL

Cut A and B of green calico. Cut C and D of pale green stripe. Cut E and F of rust. Cut G of white with tan check. Cut H and I of brown paisley. Cut J and M of tan felt. Cut K of dark brown felt. Cut L of olive green felt. Cut N of gold felt. Cut O of pale green felt. Cut coffee beans of dark brown and tan felt. Embroider and outline J and M with white floss before appliquéing. Appliqué all pieces except coffee beans, as indicated in General Directions. Embroider lines on A and B, D, E, and G with white floss. Outline bottom of D; outline E, F, G, and K with white floss. Embroider lines on and outline C with medium green floss. Make French knots on G with tan floss. Tack coffee beans in place as shown, overlapping edges of some.

To make mat, measure 1½" from edges on all sides of second 15¼" x 15¾" piece of cardboard and mark, using square. Cut out center with razor blade and discard; remaining piece of cardboard is mat. Cut out piece of gray fabric the same shape as mat, with ½" on all sides for turning. Center mat over gray fabric. Clip fabric diagonally at inner corners. Turn excess fabric on all edges to back of mat and glue smoothly. Glue mat to picture front.

TELEPHONE

Cut A of brown striped paisley. Cut B of white with gray flower pattern. Cut C and D of solid gray. Cut E and F of yellow and white tiny gingham check. Cut G of black with white polka dots. Cut H of tiny black and white check. Cut I of rust. Cut J of blue felt. Cut K, L, M, and N of yellow felt. Work backstitch with black floss on K and L as indicated. Appliqué as indicated in General Directions, tacking on gold cord for telephone wire as shown. Embroider A with white floss. Then outline A and D with white floss. Embroider line and dots on D, and embroider lines on F with black floss. Outline F and I with black floss. With gold thread, make pencil chain and satin stitches on N for pencil eraser. Blacken tip of N in pencil.

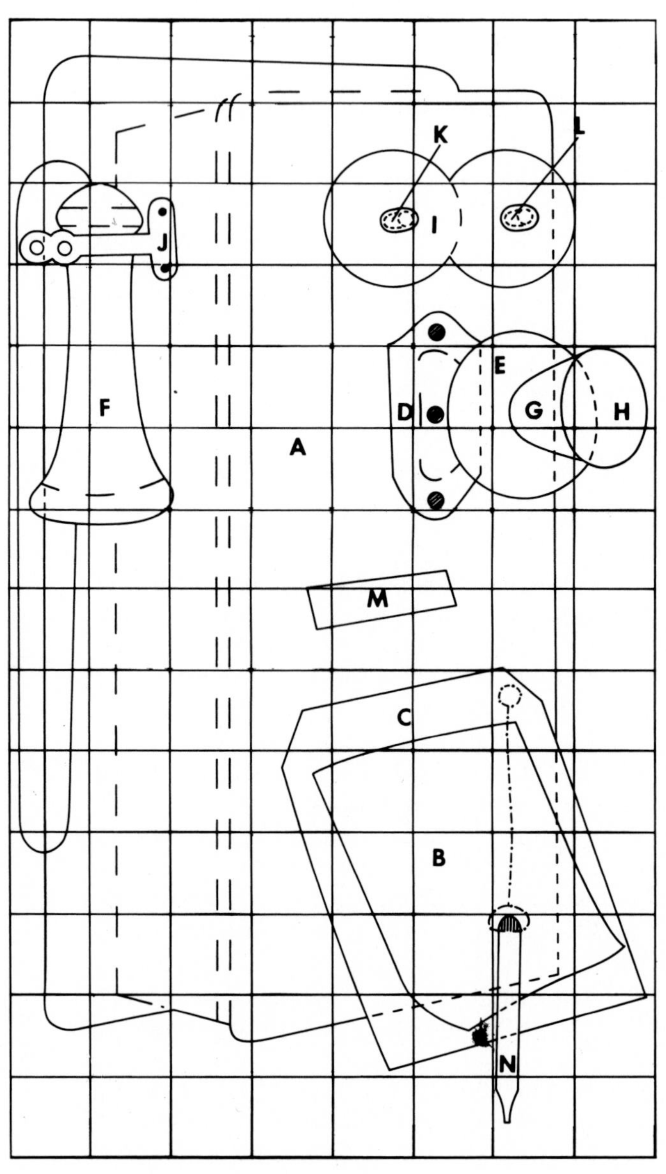

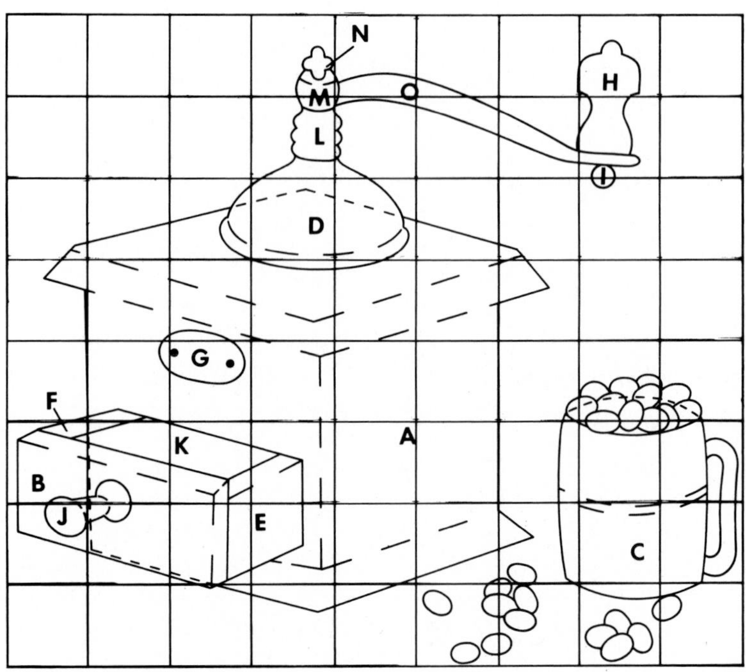

Eight Vegetable Banners

Hang a garden on your wall. These colorful vegetable flags have bright calico borders and backgrounds to offset the machine-appliquéd vegetables. The onion and pepper are cut from solid fabrics; the others are tie-dyed for natural effects. The banners are 14¾" x 16" and hang from wooden dowels.

EQUIPMENT: Flat pan. Two spring clothespins. Wooden stick or spoon. Stove or hot plate. Iron. Newspaper. Facilities for rinsing with cold water. Measuring spoons. Paper for patterns. Tracing paper. Pencil. Ruler. Scissors. Dressmaker's tracing (carbon) paper. Tracing wheel. Zigzag sewing machine,

MATERIALS: Fabrics for each banner: One rectangle of calico or desired cotton fabric measuring 12¼" x 13½" for background; one 16" square of contrasting calico or desired fabric for border; unbleached muslin or white cotton for dyed pieces. For leaves, ¼ yard 36"-wide medium green cotton and small piece of light green cotton. Small amounts of other fabrics (see individual instructions for types and colors). Wooden dowel for each, 17" long, 5/16" diameter. Small amount of polyester fiberfill. Sewing threads to match fabrics. Fabric dyes, one package each of the following colors: yellow, tangerine, purple, wine, forest green, fuchsia, olive green (see individual directions for dyeing).

DIRECTIONS FOR DYEING: Read directions on dye package and relate to the following procedure. Prewash fabric to be dyed; iron. Wet fabric to be dyed; gather and clip with clothespin for mottled effect, as directed in individual instructions. Fill flat pan with water approximately 1″ deep (unless otherwise specified) and boil. Add dye according to individual directions; stir thoroughly. Place fabric in simmering dyebath for 10 minutes. Remove clothespins. Rinse in cool running water until water runs clear; roll fabric in newspaper and squeeze out excess moisture. Hang or lay on newspaper to dry. If second color is to be dyed, repeat the dyeing process with second color.

Beet: Add one teaspoon of purple and one tablespoon of wine dye to water. Gather wet 9″ square of muslin in random folds and clip. Gathering should be totally haphazard so as to produce a mottled, uneven effect with varying shades of purple. Place fabric in dye so that part of fabric is out of dye. Simmer, rinse, dry, and iron.

Eggplant: Same as for Beet using two tablespoons of purple dye.

Asparagus: First, dye wet 13″ x 10″ muslin in mixture of one tablespoon each of olive green and yellow dye. Rinse. Gather four points of fabric and secure with clothespin. Place in dyebath of two tablespoons of purple dye so that only the points are submerged. Again, a mottled effect with predominantly purple shades along the edges and green shades in the center of the cloth will result. Simmer, rinse, dry, and iron.

Artichoke: Repeat as for Asparagus with 9″ square of muslin.

Cucumber: Dye entire wet 11″ x 4″ piece of muslin in one tablespoon yellow dye dissolved in one cup of water. Rinse. Gather fabric in lengthwise folds to create an uneven stripe effect; hold with two clothespins. Place in dyebath of one tablespoon forest green dye dissolved in one cup of water so that part of fabric held by clothespins is out of water. Simmer, rinse, dry, and iron.

Radish: Randomly gather wet 9″ square of muslin to produce uneven mottled effect; hold together with clothespin. Dissolve two tablespoons fuchsia dye in one cup of water. Place fabric in dyebath so that pinched fabric is out of dye. Simmer, rinse, dry, and iron.

Leaves and Stems: Dissolve one-half package yellow and one tablespoon olive green dye in pan. Place wet fabric in dye and push to one side so that part of fabric is out of water. Simmer. Before removing fabric from dye, spread fabric out in pan so that entire piece is in dye; simmer two minutes more. Rinse, dry, and iron.

TO MAKE BANNERS: Enlarge patterns by copying on paper ruled in 1″ squares. On pattern, solid lines represent cutting lines; dotted lines represent detail stitching lines. Pattern indicates where pieces overlap (short dash lines). All appliqué is done with machine-appliqué satin stitch in 2 widths: wide (machine-stitch width setting 1 approx.) and narrow (machine-stitch width 0-1 setting).

Center design on background fabric; using carbon paper and tracing wheel, carefully transfer outline of each design to right side of background fabric to indicate placement of appliqué pieces. Make patterns for each vegetable, stem and leaf as indicated: add all inner detail lines.

Using pattern and following arrows showing straight grain of fabric, cut pieces as directed in individual directions. Trace inner detail lines to right side of fabric. Following directions below, make banners.

Borders: Cut four 4″-wide strips from contrasting calico or desired fabric: two strips 14″ long, two strips 15¼″ long. Turn in ½″ to wrong side of long edges on 14″ strip; fold in half lengthwise with wrong sides together. Pin strips in place on sides of background fabric, overlapping folded edges of strips ½″ on background piece and having ¼″ at top and bottom. Topstitch ¼″ from inner edge of strip on border through all thicknesses with matching thread. Turn in ½″ along long edges and ends of 15¼″ strips. Topstitch ¼″ in across ends. Fold in half lengthwise with wrong sides together. Pin and stitch strip across top and bottom of background same as for sides.

Insert dowels through opening of upper border to hang.

BEET

Cut beet from area of dyed fabric with light and dark shadings; cut three leaves from green dyed fabric. Sew leaves in place on background fabric with wide satin stitch and dark green thread (except dotted line indicated by P); stitch on dotted line of center leaf along line G. Sew beet on background fabric using wide satin stitch and purple thread, leaving a 3″ opening; stuff lightly with polyester fiberfill; complete sewing around beet. With purple thread and wide satin stitch, sew stems, inner detail lines of leaves, and line P.

EGGPLANT

Cut eggplant from area on dyed fabric with var-

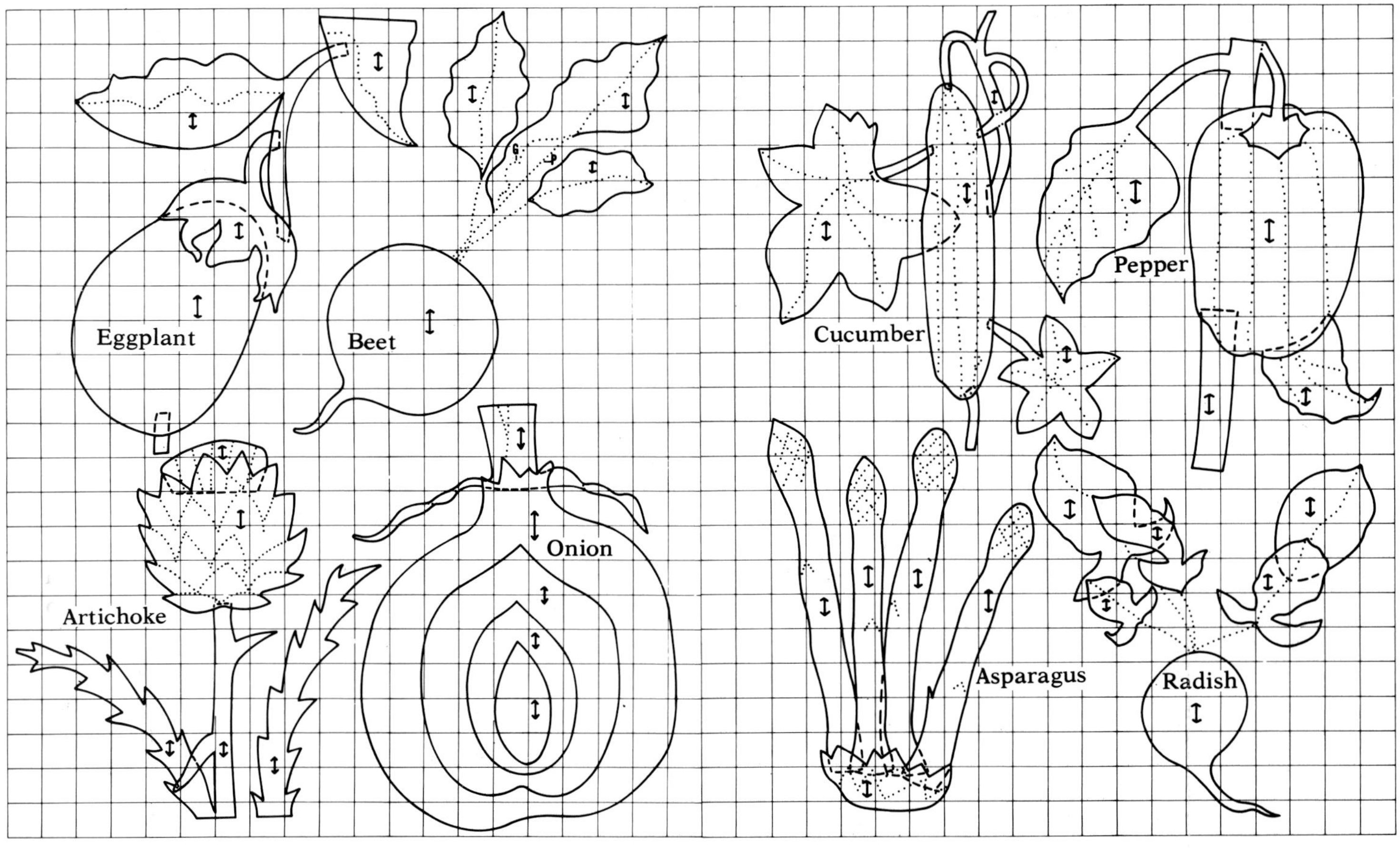

iegated shadings; cut leaves and stems from green dyed fabric. Sew edges of bottom stem in place first, with wide stitch and medium green thread. Sew eggplant on background, overlapping stem where indicated, using wide stitch and purple thread; leave top open; stuff lightly; complete stitching. Place stems and leaves at top on background fabric, overlapping where indicated; stitch edges same as for bottom stem.

ASPARAGUS

Cut four stalks from dyed fabric having tips on purple areas; cut separate base on variegated area. Sew stalks in place with wide stitch and light green thread; sew around one side and tips of the two back stalks (first and third from left); stuff lightly; complete stitching. Repeat with remaining stalks, overlapping fabric and stitching where indicated. Place base on background, overlapping stalks; stitch edges using wide stitch and purple thread. Stitch along all inner detail lines using narrow stitch and purple thread.

ARTICHOKE

Cut leaves from green cotton fabric, stem from green dyed fabric, artichoke from area of dyed fabric with some purple but predominantly green, and top purple shade from dyed fabric. Fray upper curved edge of purple shape by pulling out several rows of horizontal threads. Sew in place as follows: leaves with wide stitch and light green thread; purple shape on sides and detail lines with wide stitch and purple thread; stem with wide stitch and light green thread; artichoke with wide stitch and light green thread. Sew inner lines of artichoke with wide stitch and dark green thread.

CUCUMBER

Cut leaves and stems from green cotton and cucumber from dyed fabric with vertical light and dark areas. Sew leaves and stems in place on background with wide stitch and medium green thread. Place cucumber on background, stitching around one side and two ends with wide stitch and light green thread; stuff lightly; complete stitching. With medium green thread and narrow stitch, sew cucumber detail lines. With gold thread and narrow stitch, sew inner detail lines on leaves.

RADISH

Cut two larger leaves from dark green cotton, three smaller leaves from dark green cotton, and radish from area of dyed fabric so that root is light and round part is mostly red. Sew dark green leaves in place, and second and fourth stem lines with wide stitch and medium green thread. Sew inner detail lines with narrow stitch and same thread. Sew light green leaves in place, and first, third and fifth stem lines with wide stitch and light green thread; sew inner detail lines with narrow stitch and same thread. Sew radish in place around upper three-quarters of piece with wide stitch and red thread; stuff lightly; complete stitching with wide stitch and white thread.

PEPPER

Cut leaves and stems from green dyed fabric, pepper from 6″ x 8″ piece of red-orange cotton. Place all leaves and stems in place; sew around all edges, except stem that overlaps pepper, with wide stitch and medium green thread. With dark green thread and narrow stitch, sew inner detail lines on leaves. Sew pepper in place with red thread and wide stitch, leaving a 3″ opening; stuff lightly; complete stitching edges and detail lines. Sew around edges of stem that overlaps pepper with wide stitch and medium green thread.

ONION

Cut stem and leaves from green dyed fabric, onion pieces from rust, dark gold and light gold corduroy, yellow cotton, in order of diminishing size. Sew stem and leaves in place with wide stitch and medium green thread. Sew largest corduroy piece in place and remainder in diminishing order with wide stitch and matching thread. Sew yellow center with wide stitch and matching thread, leaving a small opening; stuff lightly; complete stitching.

Patchwork Tableskirt and Chair Cushion

The tableskirt is made of seven prints and plain gold, pieced together in a harmony of patchwork pattern. The skirt is sewn on the machine to make a series of diamonds that radiate from a square center.

The chair cushion is a simplified version of the tableskirt pattern, using several of the same fabrics.

SIZE: 90″ in diameter.

EQUIPMENT: Brown paper 4′ x 4′. Pencil. Yardstick. String, 4′. Scissors. Straight pins. Cardboard.

MATERIALS: Cotton fabric, 35″ or 44″ wide (all fabrics must be of same weight): Fabric A, 1¾ yd.; B, 1½ yd.; C, ¾ yd.; D, 1½ yd.; E, 1 yd.; F, 1½ yd.; G, ¾ yd. (**Note:** Allowance made for matching stripes and designs.) Sewing thread in colors to match fabrics. Seam binding in predominant color of fabrics.

DIRECTIONS: Use fabrics in colors desired; we used brown with white design (A), beige with black stripes (B), white with brown design (C), solid gold (D), black with gold dots (E), gold with brown design (F), gold with brown-beige-pink design (G). It is suggested you use at least one solid color. All strips are cut crosswise.

On brown paper 4′ x 4′ (if necessary, piece to make this size), make a pattern as follows: **Diagram A:** Draw diagonal from corner to corner. Make a mark, point A, on this line near upper right corner (this will be center of circle). Make a compass by attaching pencil, close to point, to one end of string. Measure 45″ from pencil along string. Hold string at 45″ mark on point A; hold pencil, perpendicular to paper, in other hand with string taut. Mark a partial circle with 45″ radius. Point where diagonal meets arc is point B. Mark two points C 17½″ each side of point B. Draw straight lines connecting points C and A. You now have the outer dimensions of a one-eighth pattern (shaded area of diagram).

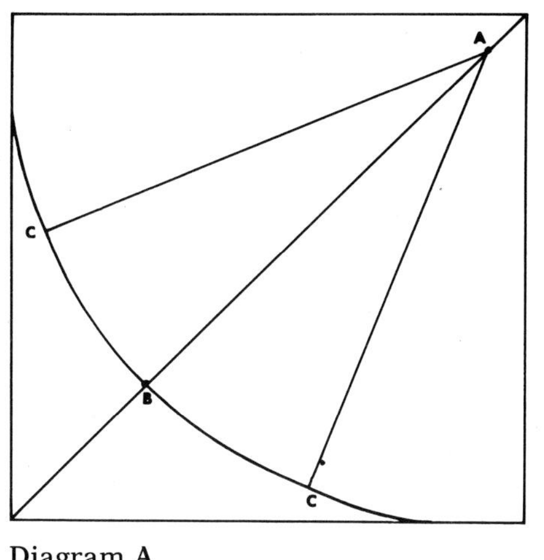

Diagram A

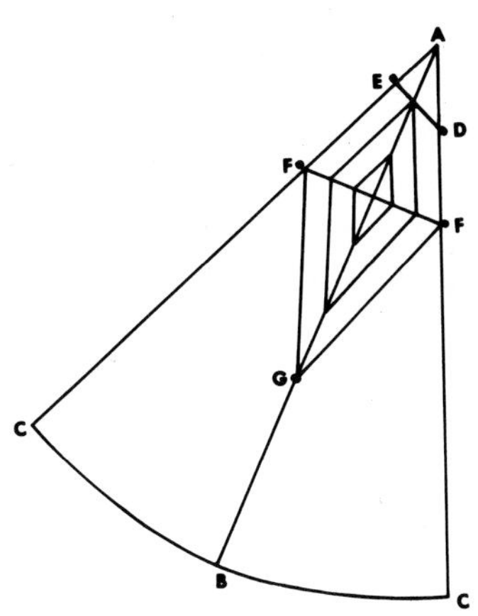

Diagram B

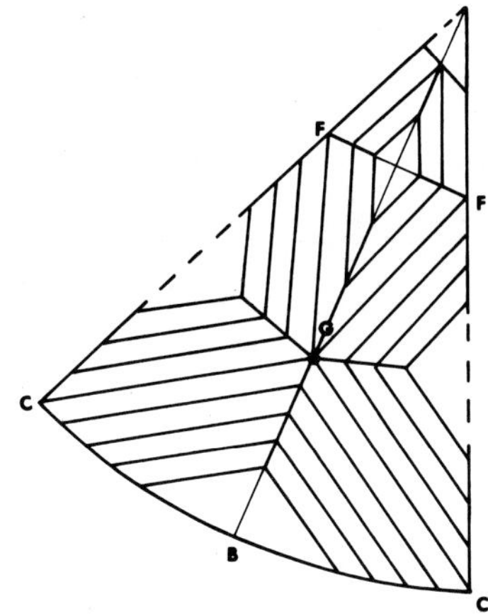

Diagram C

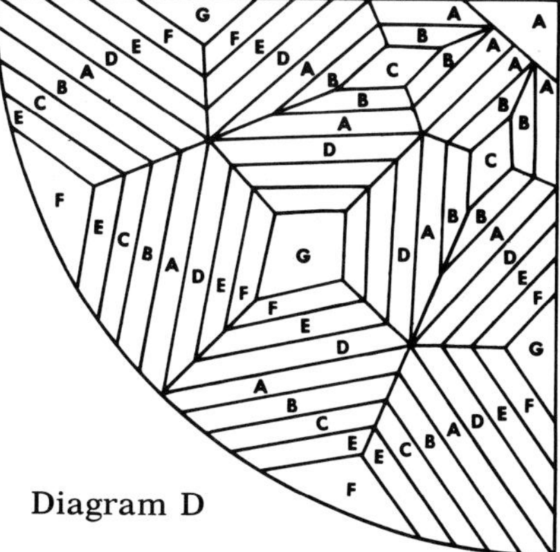
Diagram D

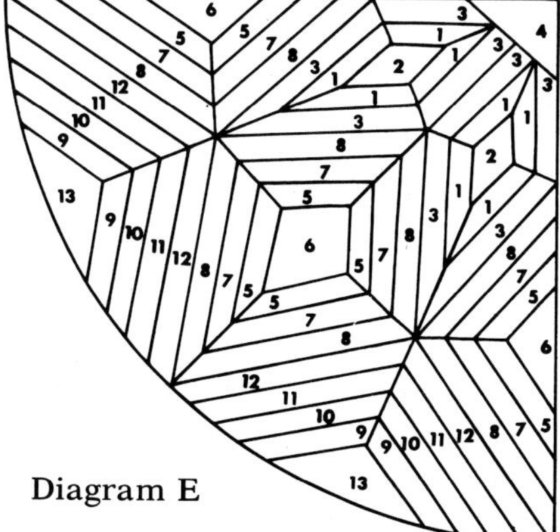
Diagram E

G
E
C
B
A

Color Diagram for Patchwork Cushion

Diagram B: Mark point D 7¼″ from A; mark E 5″ from A; connect points D and E. Mark two points F 15″ from A; connect them. Mark point G 30″ from A. Connect points F and G. Draw 2″-wide strips as shown, parallel to lines FE, FG, and DF.

Diagram C: Connect point C to G. Draw 2″-wide strips as shown, parallel to lines FG and CG. Draw a line from G to sides, through points where 2″ strips meet. Erase guidelines through center, at top, diamond shape, and bottom triangle shape (finer lines on diagram). Dash lines indicate half of diamonds (left and right sides of diagram) and one-eighth pattern for center square; complete these shapes and cut out as complete patterns.

Using paper pattern, cut a cardboard pattern for each section. Using Diagram D as a guide (letters indicate fabrics), place cardboard pattern on wrong side of fabric and mark required number of each cardboard outline with pencil or tailor's chalk. When transferring more than one pattern to same fabric, leave 1″ between pieces for seam allowance; leave 1″ allowance for hem on bottom edge of pieces that border the outside. Cut pieces ½″ outside marked line (except border ends); use solid line as stitching line.

Assembling: All seams are ½″; finish by overcasting edges, if desired. Press seams open as you work. Begin with diamond sections closest to center; make eight. Following Diagram E, sew the four #1 pieces in each section together in diamond shape. Sew #2 piece in place at center of #1 pieces. Then sew the four #3 pieces around the #1 pieces, and to each other. Join the eight sections by sewing the #3 pieces of adjacent sections together. Sew center square (#4) in place.

Repeat procedure for middle diamond sections: sew four inner strips of each section together, then sew center diamond in place; add surrounding strips. Sew a middle diamond section in between the center diamond sections, as shown.

For third (partial) diamond sections (at border), begin by sewing a #9 to appropriate #10 piece; then sew #11 to #10, and so on. Then, matching strips, sew these together in a V-shape. Sew piece #13 in place. Sew a completed section between middle sections, as shown.

Finishing: Trim lower edge if necessary. Stitch seam binding all around on right side. Turn under a 1″ hem.

CUSHION

EQUIPMENT: Brown paper for pattern. Pencil. Ruler. Scissors. Straight pins.

MATERIALS: Small amounts of cotton fabrics in six different patterns, all of the same weight. For cushion bottom and boxing, one fabric piece the size of chair seat, plus ½″ all around for seam allowances, and a strip for boxing 2½″ wide and as long as the perimeter of chair seat, plus 1″ for seam allowance. Sewing thread to match fabrics. Kapok, cotton, or Dacron batting for stuffing.

DIRECTIONS: Use fabrics in desired colors, or see tableskirt directions for color scheme. Match letters of diagram on page 203 to those in tableskirt directions. We used F for cushion bottom and boxing.

On brown paper, make pattern exact size and shape of chair seat. Make notches in back to accommodate chair back, if desired. Cut seat shape from desired fabric, adding ½″ all around for seam allowances. Cut boxing strip 2½″ wide, long enough to fit around your cushion. Cut center piece G (see diagram) 2½″ square; set aside until later.

Mark exact center on paper pattern. With pencil and ruler, make vertical and horizontal lines to divide into four quarters. Mark point 4″ from center on one horizontal line and adjacent vertical line; draw line connecting these points. Measure 2″ out from this diagonal line and draw parallel diagonal line across quarter, marking off 2″-wide area; repeat 2″ out from this line. Repeat on other three quarter-sections. Cut these pieces out. Referring to color diagram, pin each pattern piece crosswise on four layers of same fabric. Adding ½″ to all edges for seam allowances, cut all four thicknesses. With right sides facing and making ½″ seams throughout, sew four parts of one quarter together, then sew two quarters together, and then sew two halves together. At center, cut away a diamond-shaped area 1½″ square. Pin center (piece G) in place; sew.

With right sides facing, pin and sew boxing around patchwork top; sew ends of boxing together. Pin boxing to bottom with right sides facing; leaving a 6″ opening at side, sew pieces together. Turn cushion to right side. Stuff softly. Turn edges of opening in and sew closed.

HOUSEHOLD ITEMS OF PATCHWORK AND APPLIQUÉ

Tea Cozies and a Plate Mat

Here are three delightful creations that will charm your friends and keep the teapot warm as well. The snug little cottage and the napping tabby are appliquéd and embroidered; the clamshell tea cozy is made entirely in patchwork. The Dresden Plate Mat is as simple to make as it is pretty and useful. The top is patched from four different prints, and decorated with rickrack. The finished piece measures 14½" in diameter.

COTTAGE TEA COZY

EQUIPMENT: Paper for pattern. Pencil. Ruler. Scissors. Straight pins. Dressmaker's tracing (carbon) paper. Tracing wheel. Sewing and quilting needles. Tailor's chalk.

MATERIALS: Closely woven cotton fabric: yellow, 36" wide, ¾ yard; gray, 6" x 14"; scraps of red, green, white, and calico for appliqués. Soft fabric for interlining, ⅜ yard. Matching sewing thread. Dacron batting. Pearl cotton, size 5: one ball each of black, green, yellow, and blue. Small amounts of embroidery floss: gold, red, white, and blue.

DIRECTIONS: Enlarge house pattern by copying on paper ruled in 1" squares; add 1" to bottom of pattern for hem. Dash lines indicate quilting lines. Using dressmaker's carbon and tracing wheel, mark outline only of house four times on wrong side of yellow fabric, leaving at least ½" between pieces. Cut out each of the house pieces, adding ¼" for seam allowance.

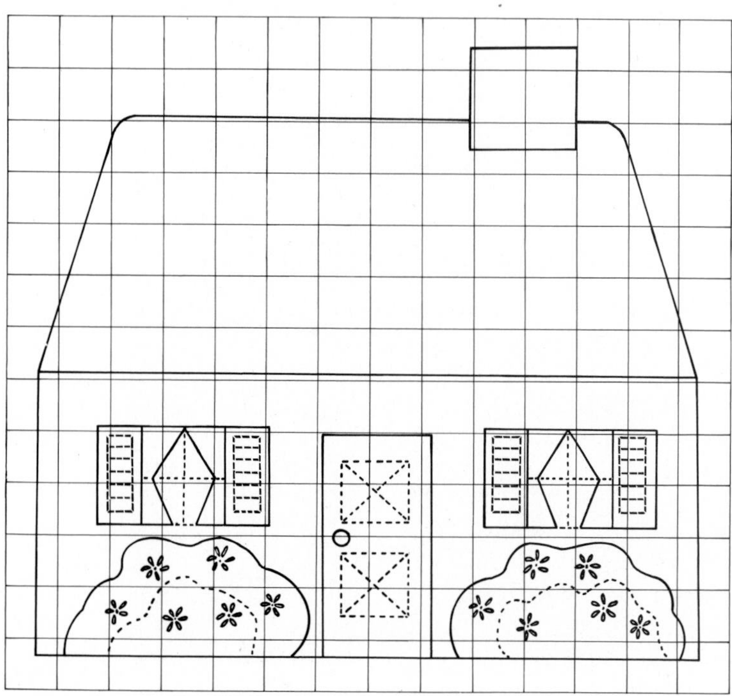

To Appliqué Motif and Quilt Front: Mark position of appliqués on right side of one house. Cut out appliqués for roof, door, shutters, curtains, and bushes in colors shown, adding ¼" to turn under. Slip-stitch appliqués in place on marked house piece. Embroider flowers in embroidery floss with lazy daisy stitch petals and French knot centers; work doorknob in satin stitch. See Stitch Details on page 15. Mark the horizontal quilting lines on house and roof ½" apart, using ruler and tailor's chalk. Mark vertical shingle lines on roof 1" apart, alternating placement on every other row. Transfer quilting lines of pattern to shutters, windows, door and bushes, using dressmaker's carbon and tracing wheel. Using house pattern, cut batting and interlining. Pin and baste house, batting and interlining together.

Quilt roof shingles with blue pearl cotton; house siding with yellow; shutters with green; around and inside bushes with green; window panes, outlines of door and paneling with black. With right sides facing, stitch quilted house and one unquilted house together on all sides except bottom. Leave wrong side out.

To Make Lining: Cut house shape from interlining fabric and from batting, adding ¼" seam allowance; add 1" hem on interlining. Mark 2" grid on interlining piece, using ruler and tailor's chalk. Pin and baste interlining piece and another yellow house piece together, with batting in between. Machine-stitch along grid lines. Stitch quilted interlining to third yellow house piece along three sides, with right sides of yellow fabric together; leave wrong side out. Assemble lining and outer piece as for Tabby Tea Cozy.

To Make Chimney: Mark pattern on right side of red fabric (front chimney); mark chimney shape again directly above to double pattern (back chimney). With ruler and tailor's chalk, mark quilting lines on front chimney only: four horizontal lines ½" apart; two vertical lines in first and third rows, one vertical line in second and fourth row. Cut out batting and interlining in double-chimney-shaped pattern. Pin and baste batting and interlining beneath red fabric; quilt on marked lines with yellow pearl cotton. Mark parallel lines 1″ beyond both sides of chimney for added width. Cut out entire red piece, adding ¼″ all around for seam allowance. Fold in half lengthwise, right sides facing. Stitch lengthwise seam. Turn right side out and press so that seam is in center of back. Finish both ends by turning in raw edges and slip-stitching closed. Fold in half crosswise with ends of chimney overlapping front and back of roof; slip-stitch in place.

TABBY TEA COZY

EQUIPMENT: Paper for patterns. Pencil. Ruler. Scissors. Straight pins. Sewing and quilting needles. Dressmaker's tracing (carbon) paper. Tracing wheel.

MATERIALS: Lightweight cotton fabric such as broadcloth, 36″ wide, ⅔ yard beige, scraps of royal blue. Soft fabric for interlining, ⅜ yard. Dacron batting. Pearl cotton size 5: one ball each light orange, yellow, navy, maroon, gold. Beige sewing thread.

DIRECTIONS: Enlarge patterns for cat body and separate head by copying on paper ruled in 1″ squares; on head, complete half-pattern details indicated by dash lines.

For Front: Transfer patterns onto beige fabric, marking on right side of fabric with dressmaker's carbon and tracing wheel; transfer dash-line quilting design. Leave at least 1″ between the two patterns and 1″ along bottom of cat body for hem; do not cut out. Cut two inner ears of blue fabric allowing ¼″ all around to turn under; slip-stitch appliqués to head.

To Quilt Front: Pin and baste marked beige fabric, batting, and interlining together. Quilt along dash lines with pearl cotton, making stitches about ⅛″-¼″ long. Make tiger-stripe lines yellow and orange, following illustration; outline ears in orange; make whiskers, mouth, paws, outline of tail and leg, and inside of ears maroon; make eyes navy. Embroider yellow French knots under nose; embroider nose in satin stitch with gold. See Stitch Details on page 15. Cut out the cat head and body, adding ¼″ all around for seam allowance, plus 1″ hem at bottom of body.

To Complete Outside: Cut one more head piece and one more body from beige fabric, marking on wrong side of fabric and adding ¼″ seam allowance all around, plus 1″ hem on body. With right sides facing, stitch quilted and unquilted head pieces together, leaving 2″ unstitched. Turn head right side out; slip-stitch closed.

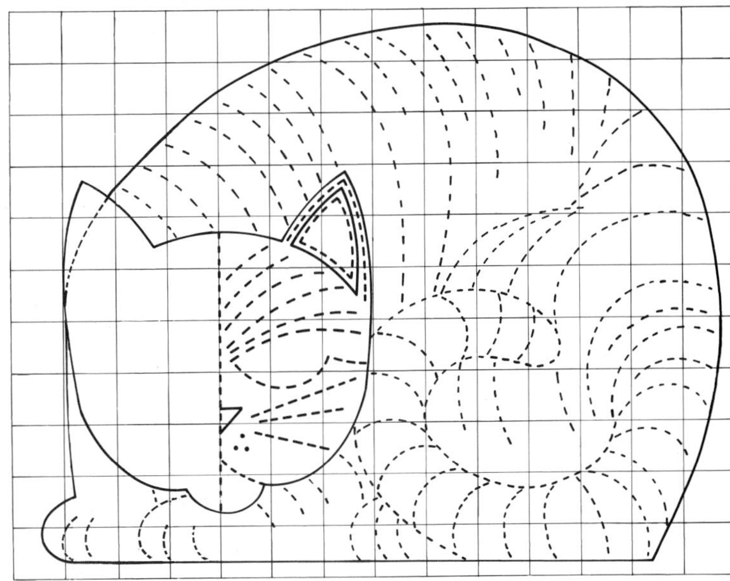

Sew quilted cat body to unquilted body along curve, right sides together; leave open all along bottom and leave piece wrong side out.

To Make Lining: Cut one cat body from interlining fabric and from batting, and two from beige fabric, adding ¼″ seam allowance and 1″ hem. Mark 2″ grid on the interlining piece, using ruler and tailor's chalk. Pin and baste interlining piece and a beige body piece together, with batting in between. Machine-stitch along grid lines. Stitch quilted interlining to another cat body along curved edge, with right sides of beige fabric together; leave wrong side out.

To Assemble: Place lining and outer piece together so that unquilted side of outer piece faces quilted side of lining; pin and baste along curved edge, leaving last 2″ free at beginning and end of curve; stitch. Turn outer piece over lining, so that wrong sides of both pieces are on the inside of tea cozy. Turn up both lining and outer piece separately for 1″ at bottom, so that hems are hidden inside tea cozy; slip-stitch closed along bottom edge. Position cat's head and slip-stitch in place.

CLAMSHELL TEA COZY

EQUIPMENT: Paper for patterns. Pencil. Ruler. Scissors. Straight pins. Sewing and quilting needles. Thin, stiff cardboard.

MATERIALS: Fabric for patches in five different small-print cottons 36″ wide: four ⅛-yard pieces; one ¼-yard piece to include ruffle. Lining fabric, 36″ wide, ⅜ yard. Soft fabric for interlining, ⅜ yard. Dacron batting. White thread.

DIRECTIONS: Enlarge pattern by copying on paper ruled in 1″ squares; complete half-pattern indicated by dash lines. Make seven separate cardboard patch patterns, one for shell A and one each for partial shells B through G. Mark an X on

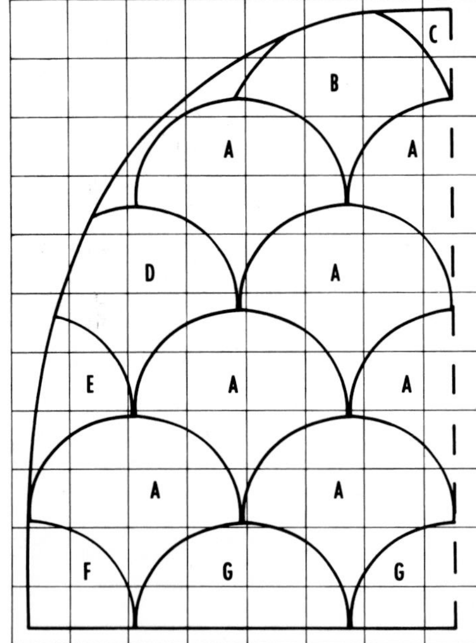

right side of patterns B, D, E, and F (to reverse for other half of tea cozy). Mark patterns on wrong side of fabric with X's face down. Add ¼″ seam allowance all around patches A-E; for patches F and G, add ¼″ on sides, 1″ on bottom. Cut patches as follows: 24 of A; two of B; two of C; two of D; two of E; two of F; six of G. Reverse patterns B, D, E, and F with X's face up and cut two more of each.

To Patch Front and Back: Sew patches together by hand with small running stitch, holding them with right sides together and stitching on marked seam line; fit one-half of top curve of one shell into curved point of another shell. Begin at bottom, following pattern, with one F, three G, one F in Row 1; four A in Row 2; one E, three A, one E in Row 3; one D, two A, one D in Row 4; and three A in Row 5. In Row 6, use one B, one C and one B. Make front and back pieces the same. Clip curves and trim corners; press seams open. Lay patched piece flat, right side up. Place complete tea cozy pattern over patched piece, positioning symmetrically. Fill in remaining areas at both sides of Rows 5 and 6 with scraps of fabric, adding ¼″ seam allowance.

To Quilt: Cut batting and interlining same size as patched front. Pin and baste piece for front, batting and interlining together. Quilt around each patch, ⅛″ from seams on either side by taking small, even running stitches. Quilt back the same. Trim off edges of batting ¼″ around curve and 1″ at bottom.

To Assemble: For ruffle, cut bias strips 4″ wide, and piece to make strip 58″ long. Fold strip in half lengthwise and gather long raw edges. Baste ruffle to curved edge of quilted front piece, right sides together with raw edges out, and stitch with ¼″ seam. With right sides facing and ruffle inside, stitch front and back quilted pieces together ¼″ from edge (leave bottom open). Leave wrong side out.

For Lining: Cut two pieces of lining fabric, using tea cozy pattern, adding ¼″ for seam allowance around curve and 1″ at bottom for hem. Stitch pieces together along curve, right sides facing. Leave wrong side out. Place outer tea cozy and lining together; stitch through all thicknesses, ¼″ from edges along curve, leaving last 2″ free at beginning and end of curve. Turn outer piece over lining, so that wrong sides of both pieces are on inside of tea cozy. Turn up both lining and outer piece separately for 1″ at bottom, so that hems are hidden inside tea cozy; slipstitch closed along bottom edge.

DRESDEN PLATE MAT

SIZE: 14¾″ diameter.

EQUIPMENT: Paper for pattern. Pencil. Ruler. Compass. Scissors. Thin, stiff cardboard. Straight pins. Sewing needle. Iron.

MATERIALS: Fabric for patched top: four different prints each with a different background color (we used white, red, yellow, and blue), 36″ wide, ¼ yard each. For lining and interlining: tightly woven lightweight fabric 36″ wide, ½ yard. Cotton batting, one 14½″ circle. Rickrack, 2 yards. Sewing thread to match fabrics.

DIRECTIONS: To Cut Wedge-Shaped Patches: Enlarge wedge pattern by copying on paper ruled in ½″ squares; complete half pattern indicated by dash line. Cut several patterns out of cardboard and replace each as it becomes frayed.

For patches, place cardboard pattern on wrong side of printed fabric; with pencil, trace around pattern outline. Cut out patch, adding ¼″ seam allowance beyond marked outline at side edges only. The marked lines on fabric will be seam lines. Cut four patches of each color.

To Make Patched Top: For interlining, cut out 15″ circle; cut 5″ circle from center. Patches are to be sewn on interlining, alternating the four colors. Place first patch on interlining with right side up and edges even. Pin and sew along one long side seam line. Place second patch on top of first patch, right sides together, matching stitched side seam line. Stitch through all thicknesses on matching seam line. Flop second patch over to right side; press. *With right sides facing, place next patch on top of previous patch, matching unstitched side seam line. Stitch through all thicknesses along matching seam line. Flop this patch over to right side; press.* Repeat from * to * until all patches are used. At end, cut into interlining along raw edge of first patch. Pull side edges of first and last patches out through cut in interlining with right sides facing; sew these edges together. Insert back through opening. Stitch all around ¼″ in from outer edges to mark seam line.

To Assemble: Cut a 15″ circle for lining. Center and baste filling circle to lining. Baste rickrack around right side of patched top, with center of rickrack on seam line. With right sides facing, baste patched top to lining. Stitch together all

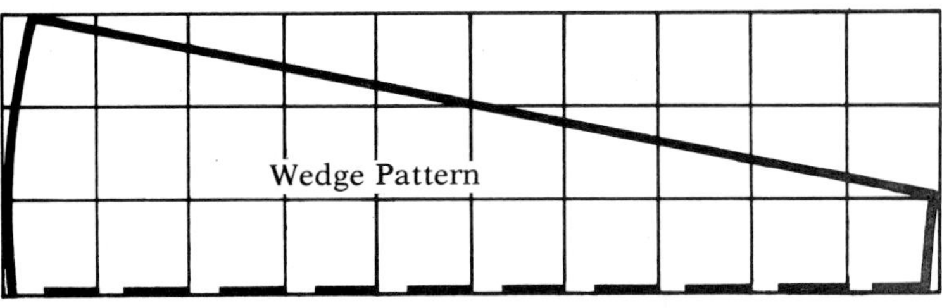

around outer edge, making ¼″ seam. Turn right side out through center opening; press. To keep work flat, topstitch around center opening ⅜″ in from raw edge through all thicknesses.

Cut 6¼″ circle from one remaining piece of print fabric; stitch ⅜″ seam line all around. Stitch rickrack to 6¼″ circle, with center of rickrack along seam line. Turn edge of circle under ⅜″ all around, leaving only tips of rickrack exposed; press. Baste circle over opening of patched top. Topstitch over rickrack, as close to edge of circle as possible, stitching through all layers. To quilt, stitch along seam line on right side between each patch, stitching through all layers.

Patchwork and Applique Potholders

These little potholders will brighten up any kitchen. Six are patched; the gingerbread cookie potholders are appliquéd.

PATCHWORK POTHOLDERS

EQUIPMENT: Paper for patterns. Pencil. Ruler. Scissors. Thin, stiff cardboard. Sewing needle. Straight pins.

MATERIALS: Preshrunk pieces of tightly woven cotton fabric in solid colors and small prints as shown or as desired. White and matching sewing thread. Outing flannel for padding. White plastic ring 1″ diameter for each.

DIRECTIONS: Read General Directions on page 158. Enlarge patterns for designs by copying on paper ruled in 1″ squares; complete quarter-patterns indicated by long dash lines. The fine dash lines indicate quilting lines. Make a separate cardboard pattern for each part of design. Cut patches according to General Directions, marking on wrong side of fabric and adding ¼″ seam allowance all around.

Following patterns, sew all the pieces together to complete potholder tops. For back, cut one complete potholder shape of matching or contrasting solid-color fabric, adding ¼″ all around for seam allowance. For each potholder, cut two thicknesses of flannel the shape of potholder but ⅜″ smaller all around. Baste both layers of flannel to top to hold in place. Place the top and back together with right sides facing; sew together along edges, making ¼″ seams and leaving an opening large enough to turn. Turn to right side; turn edges of opening in ¼″; sew closed.

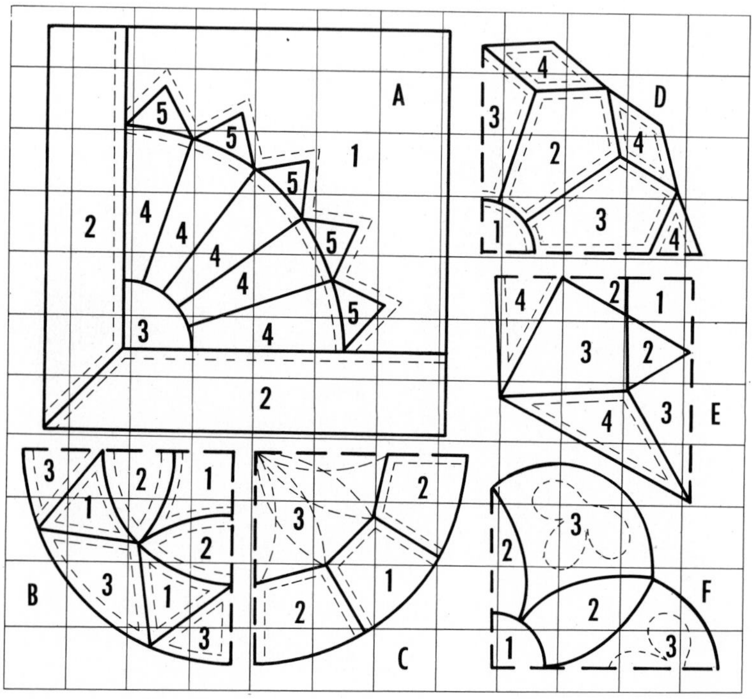

Each potholder is quilted through all thicknesses with white sewing thread. Quilt along all fine dash lines (see pattern) and along some seams. Remove basting stitches. Sew ring to back near edge of potholder.

Pattern A: Cut 5¼″ square for piece 1 of white; cut pieces 2 of white; cut piece 3 of orange; cut pieces 4 of five different printed fabrics; cut pieces 5 of gold color. Sew the pieces of the fan shape together; pin in place on piece 1; turn under edges of points and sew in place. Sew pieces 2 in place. Cut ¾″-wide bias strips of solid-color fabric and sew together with ¼″ seams to make one strip long enough to fit all around potholder. With right sides facing and making ⅛″ seam, sew one edge all around potholder top. Turn binding to back. Turn raw edge under ⅛″ and slip-stitch to fabric, mitering corners.

Pattern B: Cut pieces 1 of orange; cut pieces 2 of yellow; cut pieces 3 of white. For ruffled edge, cut a strip of orange on the bias about 45″ long, 1½″ wide. With right sides facing, sew ends together, making ¼″ seam. Turn to right side. Fold in half lengthwise; press. Gather raw edge to fit circumference of potholder. Before sewing top and back together, baste ruffle around top with right sides facing and raw edges out. When sewing top and back together, make sure ruffle is on inside.

Pattern C: Cut pieces 1 of red; cut pieces 2 of red-and-white checked gingham; cut piece 3 of white. Sew together and quilt by machine, using red thread for center design, white for other quilting. Make ruffled edge as for Pattern B.

Pattern D: Cut piece 1 of bright pink; cut pieces 2 of dark green; cut pieces 3 of pink print; cut pieces 4 of white.

Pattern E: Cut piece 1 of blue; cut pieces 2 of orange; cut pieces 3 of blue-yellow print; cut pieces 4 of yellow.

Pattern F: Cut piece 1 of orange; cut pieces 2 of yellow; cut pieces 3 of aqua. Quilt through all thicknesses only along seams. Stitch along short dash lines through top fabric only and draw thread up tightly for puckered effect.

COOKIE POTHOLDERS

EQUIPMENT: Paper. Ruler. Pencil. Sewing machine with zigzag and other pattern attachments. Straight pins. Sewing needle. Compass.

MATERIALS: Cotton fabric: 8″ x 15″ background color for each; scrap of contrasting color for appliqué. Sewing thread: matching background, contrasting colors. Dacron batting for padding, 7¼″ x 7¼″ each. Double-fold bias binding tape in color to contrast with background.

DIRECTIONS: Enlarge designs by copying on paper ruled in 1″ squares. Using patterns, cut designs for appliqués in colors shown.

Mark circle 7½″ in diameter on fabric for potholder background; cut two pieces. Pin and baste appliqué to center of one circle. Using thread to match appliqué, machine-stitch appliqué to background with narrow satin stitch all around edge of appliqué. Following fine lines on patterns, machine-embroider fancy borders and designs on appliqué, using contrasting colors shown or as desired.

Place appliquéd and plain fabric circles together with a 7¼″ circle of batting between. Baste all three thicknesses together around the edge, and diagonally, horizontally and vertically across. With sewing machine, stitch quilting lines through all thicknesses as shown in illustration.

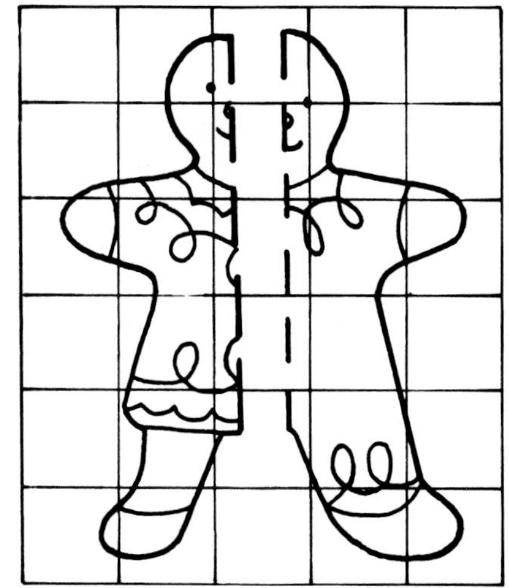

Starting at center top of holder, baste binding tape over edges all around; bring tape over beginning end, and leave 3″ of excess tape to form hanging loop. Stitch tape all around and continue stitching tape edges together to end of excess. Form end into a loop; turn under ¼″ of end and sew to back of each potholder.

Three Leaf Potholders

These pretty potholders have machine-embroidered veins for a quilted look. The leaf with the ladybug is about 8″ wide.

EQUIPMENT: Paper for pattern. Tracing paper. Dressmaker's tracing (carbon) paper. Tissue paper. Pencil. Ruler. Scissors. Straight pins. Sewing and embroidery needles. Zigzag sewing machine (for Maple Leaf only). One knitting needle or similar long, thin object.

MATERIALS: Tightly woven cotton fabric: bright or light green, 36″ wide, ¼ yard for each; brown 7″ square for Maple Leaf; contrasting shade of green 6″ x 9″ for Dragonfly Leaf. Dark olive green sewing thread. Small amounts of six-strand embroidery floss: orange, black, yellow for Beetle; gray, black, white, magenta, medium and pale orchid for Dragonfly. Thin layer of cotton or Dacron batting, same size as each leaf.

DIRECTIONS: Enlarge leaf patterns by copying on paper ruled in 1″ squares. Solid lines indicate cutting lines. Short dash lines indicate stitching lines. Make a separate pattern for inner leaf of Maple Leaf design and flap of Dragonfly Leaf.

From green fabric, cut one complete leaf shape (outer lines) for each, adding ¼″ all around for seam allowance; reverse pattern for each and cut second leaf shape. Using pattern, cut one piece of batting, omitting seam allowance and stems, which will be hanging loops. Using carbon paper, transfer stitching lines to right side of one leaf shape. Trace beetle and dragonfly patterns; complete dragonfly by adding wings on other side of body. With carbon paper, transfer beetle and dragonfly to leaves as shown. Using two strands of floss in needle, embroider beetle and dragonfly following individual directions; refer to Stitch Details on page 15.

Baste batting in place on wrong side of one leaf piece; pin tissue paper over batting. Place two leaf shapes together with right sides facing. Stitch together all around ¼″ from edge; continue stitching along edges of stem on Beetle and Dragonfly leaves. Leave a 3″ opening along one side. If necessary, trim batting to stitching line and remove tissue. Clip into seam at curves. Turn to right side (use a knitting needle or similar object to turn stems). Fold edges of opening in ¼″; slip-stitch closed.

To quilt, machine-stitch along marked lines through all thicknesses, using long stitch setting; stitch over vein lines twice to make them more prominent. To make loop, fold stem to back of leaf and stitch securely in place.

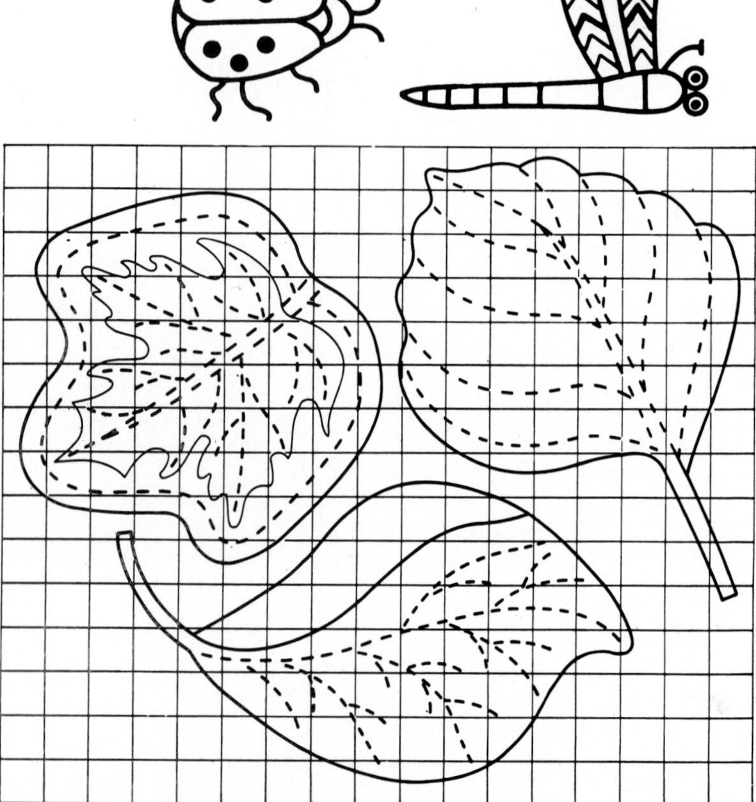

LEAF WITH BEETLE

Embroider each side of body in satin stitch with orange floss. Using black floss, make French knots at dots on body, work satin stitch for head and back end of body, work outline stitch for legs and antennae. Work small section between head and body in satin stitch with yellow floss.

LEAF WITH DRAGONFLY

Using gray floss, work body and head in satin stitch. For tail, couch 12 strands of gray with black floss. Using gray floss, work two legs in outline stitch. For eyes, make French knots with white floss. With magenta floss, work outline stitch around each wing. Using magenta and medium pale orchid floss, fill in wing sections in satin stitch worked diagonally as indicated on pattern.

To make leaf flap, cut two pieces of contrasting shade of green fabric, adding ¼″ all around each for seam allowance. With right sides facing, sew together ¼″ from inner edge only. Clip into seam at curves. Turn to right side. Place on front leaf shape with raw edges even. Sew only bottom layer of flap to leaf ¼″ in from inner seam. Cut piece of batting the shape of flap and insert. Assemble potholder following Directions.

MAPLE LEAF

Cut inner leaf of tan fabric. On machine, zigzag-stitch the edges of tan leaf to front leaf shape. Assemble potholder following Directions. When quilting, stitch around outline of inner leaf also. For loop, cut bias strip of tan fabric 1″ wide and 5″ long. With right sides facing, fold in half lengthwise; sew long edges together ¼″ from edge. Turn to right side. Turn ends in; slip-stitch closed. Fold strip in half to form loop. Sew ends securely to front and back at broad end (bottom) of leaf.

4

Knitting and Crochet

GENERAL DIRECTIONS

KNITTING NEEDLES															
U. S.	0	1	2	3	4	5	6	7	8	9	10	10½	11	13	15
English	13	12	11	10	9	8	7	6	5	4	3	2	1	00	000
Continental — mm.	2¼	2½	3	3¼	3½	4	4½	5	5½	6	6½	7	7½	8½	9

CROCHET HOOKS (ALUMINUM OR PLASTIC)										
U. S.	1/B	2/C	3/D	4/E	5/F	6/G	8/H	9/I	10/J	10½/K
English	12	11	10	9	8	7	6	5	4	2
Continental — mm.	2½	3		3½	4	4½	5	5½	6	7

Abbreviations

k—knit
p—purl
st(s)—stitch(es)
yo—yarn over
rnd—round
sl—slip
inc—increase
dec—decrease
tog—together
beg—beginning
dp—double-pointed
psso—pass slip stitch over
sk—skip
pat—pattern
lp—loop
sp—space
ch—chain
sl st—slip stitch
sc—single crochet
dc—double crochet
hdc—half double crochet
tr—treble crochet
dtr—double treble
tr tr—triple treble

STITCHES AND SYMBOLS

Yo When Knitting—Bring yarn under right-hand needle to front, then over needle to back, ready to knit next stitch.

Yo When Purling—Wind yarn around right-hand needle once. Yarn is in position to purl next stitch.

Pick Up and Knit Stitches on Edge—From right side, insert needle into edge of work, put yarn around needle, finish as a k stitch. When picking up on bound-off or cast-on edge, pick up and k 1 st in each st (going through 2 lps at top of each edge st); pick up and k 1 st in each knot formed on edge of each row on front or side edges.

To Slip a Stitch—Insert needle in st as if to knit st (unless directions read "as if to p") and sl st from one needle to the other without knitting or purling it.

Psso (pass slip stitch over)—When directions read "sl 1, k 1, psso," insert left-hand needle from left to right under slipped stitch on right-hand needle, bring it over the knit stitch and off needle.

Single Crochet—Start with a loop on hook, insert hook in work, draw yarn through, yarn over hook and draw through both loops.

Double Crochet—Start with a loop on hook, put yarn over hook, insert hook in work, draw yarn through, yarn over hook and through two loops, yarn over hook again and through two remaining loops on hook.

Half Double Crochet—Start with loop on hook, put yarn over hook, insert hook in work, draw yarn through, yarn over hook and through all three loops on hook.

Treble Crochet—This is made the same way as double crochet, with the yarn wrapped around the hook twice instead of once and then worked off —yarn over and through two loops, yarn over and through two loops, yarn over and through two loops. For a **Double Treble,** yarn over hook three times; for a **Triple Treble**, yarn over hook four times, working off two loops at a time as in treble.

Slip Stitch—Insert hook through stitch, catch yarn and, with one motion, draw through both stitch and loop on hook.

* **(asterisk)**—Repeat directions following * as many extra times as directed. "* 2 dc in next st, dc in next st, repeat from * 4 times," means to work directions after first * until second * is reached, then go back to first * 4 times more. Work 5 times in all.

( ) **(parentheses)**—When parentheses are used to show repetition, work directions in parentheses as many times as specified.

Multiple—In pattern stitches, multiple means number of stitches required for 1 pattern. Number of sts to be worked should be evenly divisible by the multiple. If pattern is a multiple of 6 sts, number of sts to be worked might be 120, 126, 132, etc. If directions say "multiple of 6 sts plus 2," 2 extra sts are needed: 122, 128, 134, etc.

Work Even—Work same stitch without increasing or decreasing.

Gauge—Before starting knitted or crocheted article, be sure you can work to the exact gauge specified in the directions. To test your knit gauge, cast on 20 to 30 stitches, using needles suggested in "Materials." Work 3″ in pattern stitch. Smooth out swatch, pin down. Measure across 2″ counting number of stitches; measure 2″ down counting number of rows. If you have **more** stitches and rows to the inch than directions specify, you are working too tightly. Use larger needles. If you have **fewer** stitches and rows to the inch, you are working too loosely. Use smaller needles. Knit new swatches until gauge is correct. Test crochet in same way.

HOW TO KNIT

TO CAST ON: 1. Make a slip loop on needle. 2. Loop yarn around left thumb. 3. Insert needle. 4. Remove thumb. 5. Pull yarn to tighten stitch. Repeat Figures 2-5 for desired number of stitches.

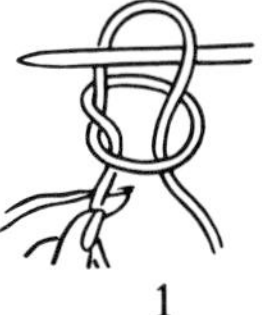
1

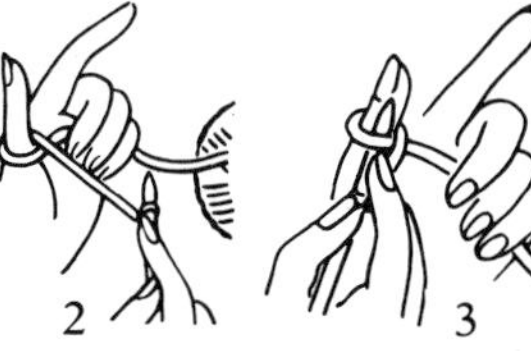
2

3

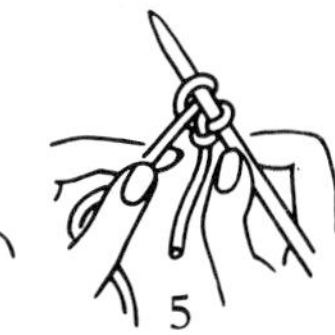
4 5

TO KNIT: 1. Hold needle with cast-on stitches in left hand. Weave yarn over index finger of right hand, under middle finger, over third finger and under little finger. Hold second needle in right hand like a pencil. With yarn in back of work, insert right needle in the front of first stitch toward back. 2. Put yarn around needle. 3. Pull loop of yarn through the stitch. 4. Slip stitch off left needle.

1
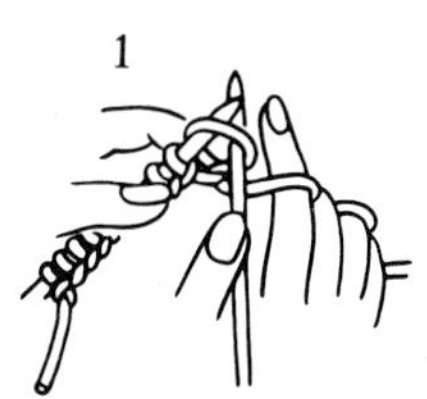

2
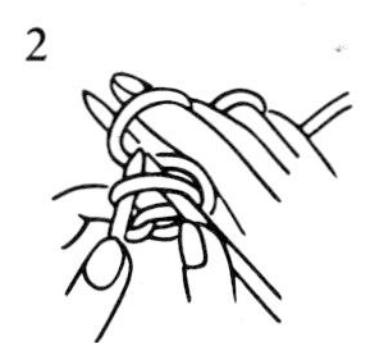

3
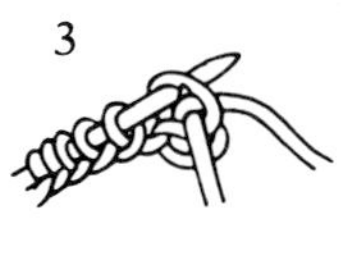

4

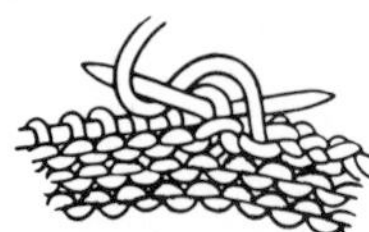

TO PURL: With yarn in front of work, insert needle from right to left in first stitch, put yarn around needle, pull loop through stitch. Slip stitch off needle.

SEED STITCH: Cast on an uneven number of stitches. * Knit 1, purl 1, repeat from * across, end with knit 1. Repeat this row for seed stitch pattern.

TO BIND OFF: Knit 2 stitches. * With left needle, bring first stitch on right needle over second stitch and off needle. Knit next stitch and repeat from *.

HOW TO CROCHET

CHAIN STITCH (ch st): Make loop on hook. 1. Pass hook under yarn to catch yarn with hook. 2. Draw yarn through first loop. 3. Repeat to make required number of chains.

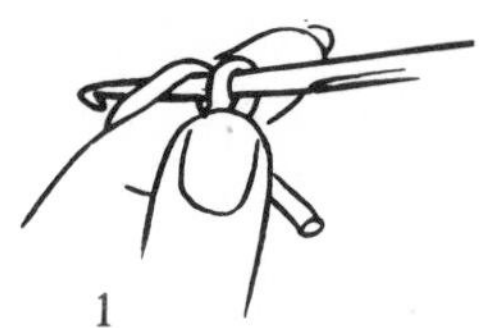

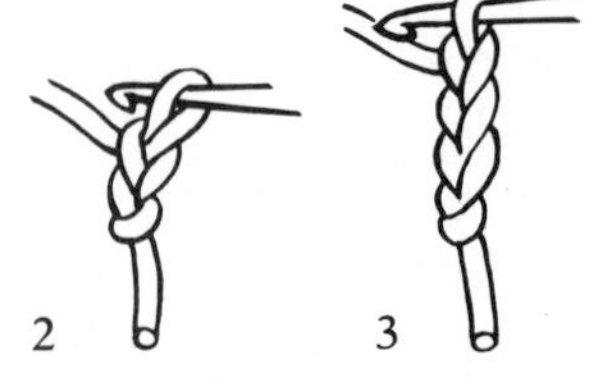

SINGLE CROCHET (sc): 1. Insert hook under top 2 threads of 2nd chain from hook. 2. Catch yarn with hook. 3. Draw through chain. 4. Yarn over hook. 5. Draw yarn through 2 loops on hook—1 sc made. 6. Insert hook in next chain and repeat. At end of row, chain 1, turn work so reverse side is facing you. Work first single crochet of next row under top 2 threads of first stitch.

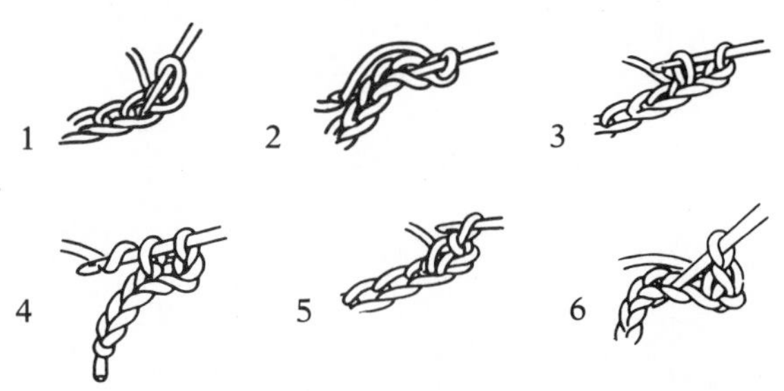

DOUBLE CROCHET (dc): 1. Yarn over hook, insert hook under top 2 threads of 4th chain from hook. 2. Catch yarn with hook. 3. Draw yarn through chain. 4. Yarn over hook. 5. Draw through 2 loops on hook. 6. Yarn over hook. 7. Draw through remaining 2 loops on hook—1 dc made. 8. Yarn over hook, insert hook in next chain and repeat from 2. At end of row, chain 3 to turn. Turn work so reverse side is facing you. Turning chain is counted as first double crochet of next row. Work 2nd double crochet under top 2 threads of next double crochet of first row.

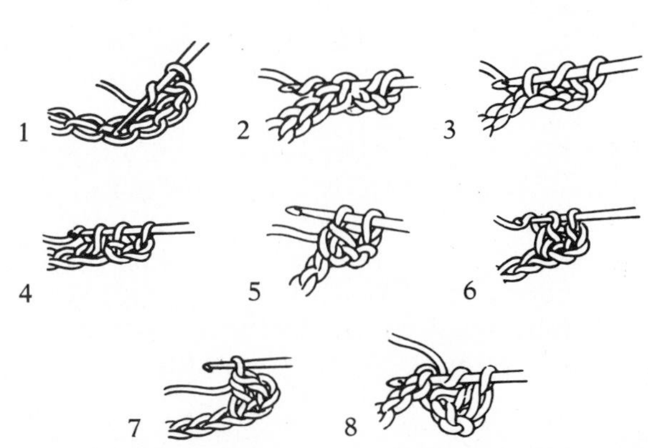

Victorian Carriage Robe

This nineteenth-century carriage robe was embroidered in a glorious Victorian style by a New Englander, perhaps for her parson. The basic robe is worked in afghan crochet—a separate section for the center and eight sections for the border. Each section is then embroidered in cross-stitch, then joined to the others. If you prefer, substitute another dog's head for the religious symbol in the lower left corner, and put a new date in the corner opposite.

SIZE: 58″ x 71″, plus fringe.

MATERIALS: Knitting worsted, 16 4-oz. skeins black for background; 1 skein each of the following colors for embroidery (or use tapestry wool, crewel wool, or leftover yarns):

Four reds: pale red, light red, medium red, cardinal.

Three purples: lavender, light purple, dark purple.

Three old-rose tones: light old rose, medium old rose, dark old rose.

Four greens: pale almond green, light almond green, medium almond green, dark almond green.

Four beige tones (white rose): oyster white, natural heather, celery, camel.

Five tans (horse and dogs): parchment, pale russet brown, light russet brown, medium russet brown, dark russet brown.

Four yellow-browns: tobacco gold, copper, wood brown, dark wood brown.

Two rusts: dark apricot, rust.

Yellow.

14″ aluminum afghan hook size 9 or J. Tapestry needles No. 17. Large-eyed rug needle.

GAUGE: 7 sts = 2″; 7 rows = 2″.

AFGHAN ST: Make a chain with same number of ch as desired number of sts.

Row 1: Pull up a lp in 2nd ch from hook and in each ch across, keeping all lps on hook.

To Work Lps Off: Yo hook, pull through first lp, * yo hook, pull through next 2 lps, repeat from * across until 1 lp remains. Lp that remains on hook always counts as first st of next row.

Row 2: Keeping all lps on hook, pull up a lp under 2nd vertical bar and under each vertical bar across. Work lps off as before. Repeat row 2 for desired number of rows.

CENTER SECTION: Ch 155. Work in afghan st on 155 sts for 112 rows. Piece should measure 44¼″ wide, 32″ long.

Next Row: Sl st loosely under 2nd vertical bar and in each vertical bar across. End off.

Mark between 17th and 18th sts from right edge for right edge of cross-stitch design. Mark between 11th and 12th rows from bottom for bot-

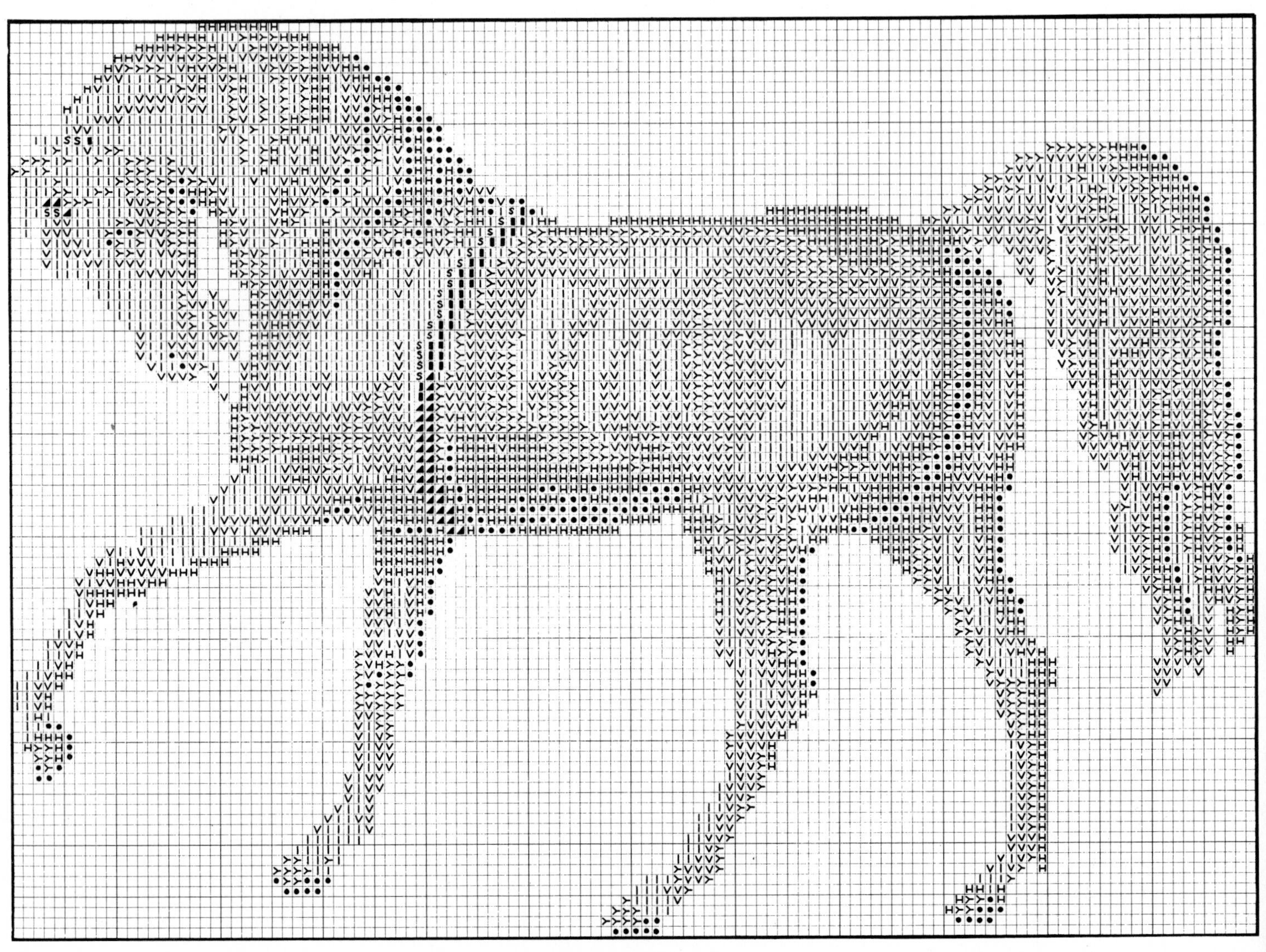

Color Key

- Pale Red
- Light Red
- Medium Red
- Cardinal
- Lavender
- Light Purple
- Dark Purple
- Light Old Rose
- Medium Old Rose
- Dark Old Rose
- Pale Almond Green
- Light Almond Green
- Medium Almond Green
- Dark Almond Green
- Oyster White
- Natural Heather
- Celery
- Camel
- Tobacco Gold
- Copper
- Wood Brown
- Dark Wood Brown
- Dark Apricot
- Rust
- Yellow
- Parchment
- Pale Russet Brown
- Light Russet Brown
- Medium Russet Brown
- Dark Russet Brown

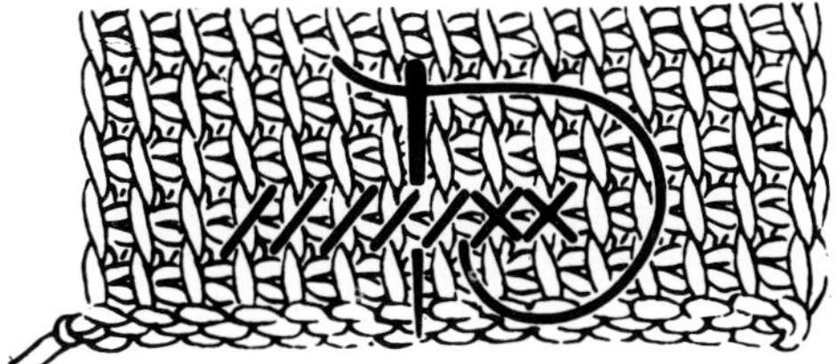

Cross-Stitch on Afghan Stitch

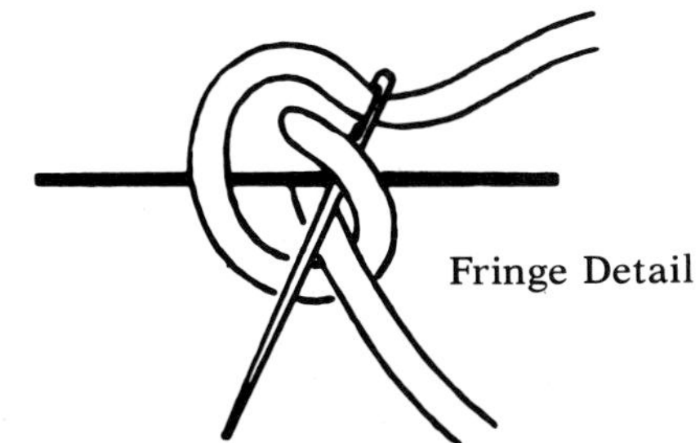

Fringe Detail

Chart 1

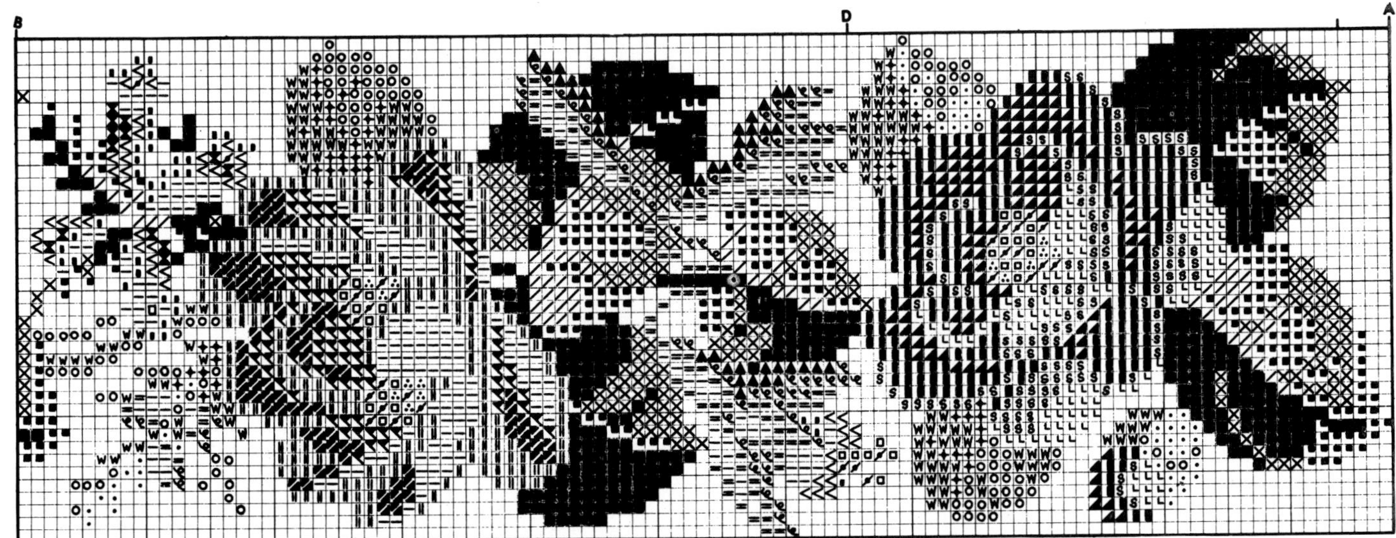

Chart 2

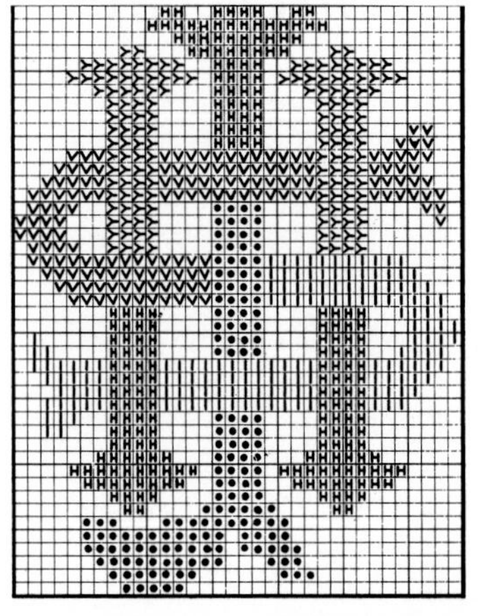

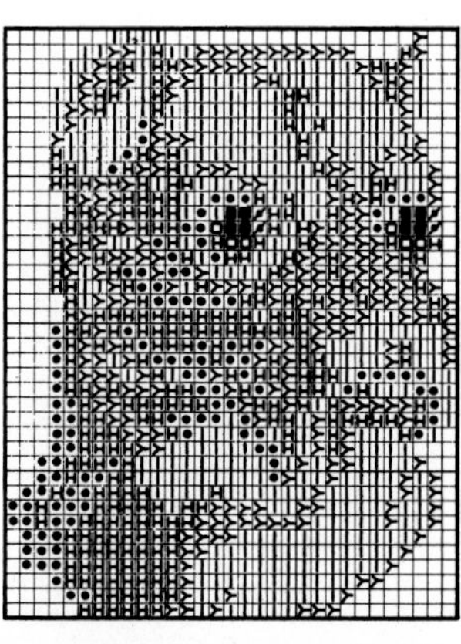

Color Key

Parchment	Dark Russet Brown
Pale Russet Brown	Dark Almond Green
Light Russet Brown	Dark Apricot
Medium Russet Brown	Yellow

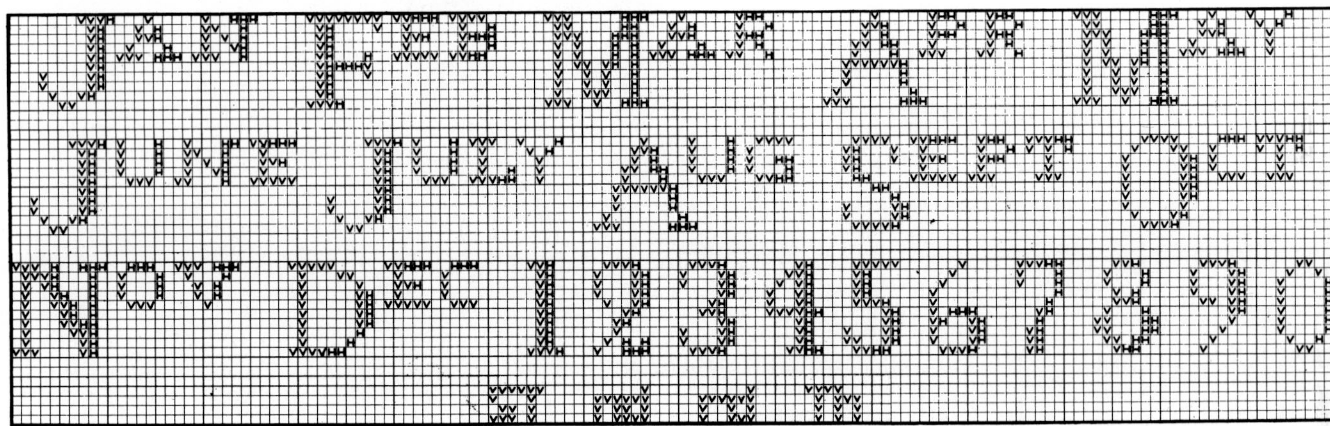

tom edge of design. Following chart, embroider horse in cross-stitch.

SIDE ROSE BORDERS (make 2): Ch 112. Work in afghan st on 112 sts for 46 rows. Piece should measure 32″ wide, 13″ deep.

Next Row: Sl st loosely under 2nd vertical bar and in each bar across. End off.

Mark between 3rd and 4th sts from right edge for right edge of design. Mark between 3rd and 4th rows for bottom of design. Following Chart 1, page 220, embroider rose border.

TOP AND BOTTOM ROSE BORDERS (make 2): Ch 155. Work in afghan st on 155 sts for 46 rows. Piece should measure 44¼″ wide, 13″ deep.

Next Row: Sl st loosely under 2nd vertical bar and in each bar across. End off.

Mark between 4th and 5th sts from right edge for right edge of design. Mark between 3rd and 4th rows for bottom of design. Following Chart 2, **page 219**, embroider rose border from A to B, then repeat end rose only from C to D.

CORNERS (make 4): Ch 46. Work in afghan st on 46 sts for 46 rows. Piece should be 13″ square.

Next Row: Sl st loosely under 2nd vertical bar and in each bar across. End off.

Dog Heads: Mark between 8th and 9th sts from right edge for right edge of design. Starting in 4th row, following chart, page 221, embroider head in cross-stitch. For second corner (top right), follow first corner, reversing design.

Monogram of Jesus: Mark between 6th and 7th sts from right edge for right edge of design. Starting in first row, following chart, embroider monogram in cross-stitch.

Date: Using illustration of afghan as guide, plan date to fit space. Use graph paper, if necessary, to work out most pleasing arrangement of letters and numbers.

FINISHING: Weave in yarn ends on wrong side. Pin out pieces to correct measurements; steam-press. When pieces are dry, sew them together with black yarn. Cover joinings with cross-stitch in palest tone of horse. With same tone, work 1 row of sc around edge, making sc in each st or row, 3 sc in each corner. Join in first sc; end off.

FRINGE: Row 1: Use 4 strands of black yarn, cut 24″ long, in large-eyed rug needle. Hold afghan right side up with edge of afghan toward you. Bring needle up from wrong side through a st on edge. Pull yarn through leaving 2″ end in back. Hold this 2″ end in left hand.

Put needle from right to left under end in left hand, bring it up forming loop at right. Insert needle from top to bottom through loop; pull tight, forming knot on edge. Drop 2″ end. * Skip 3 sc to left on edge, bring needle up from wrong side through next st on edge. Pull yarn through forming scallop of yarn on edge. Insert needle from front to back through scallop. Pull yarn through forming loop. Insert needle from top to bottom through loop (see Fringe Detail); pull tight, forming knot on edge. Repeat from * around edge. Weave in ends on wrong side.

Row 2: Thread 4 strands of black yarn in large-eyed needle. Tie yarn in center of any scallop, leaving 3″ end. Working from right to left as before, * bring yarn up through next scallop and down through scallop just formed, forming a loop. Insert needle from top to bottom through loop; pull tight, forming knot. Repeat from * around, alternating one deep scallop with one scallop straight across. Finish off strands by tying knot and leaving 3″ of yarn hanging. Start new strands with a knot on next scallop, leaving 3″ of yarn hanging. Tie these ends together in a deep scallop and cut ends close.

Finish each deep scallop with a tassel of yarn tied to center of scallop. To make tassel, wind several strands of yarn of different colors around a 3″ piece of cardboard 4 or 5 times. Slide a strand of yarn under one edge and knot it as tightly as possible to hold strands together. Cut through yarn on opposite edge. Wrap and tie a strand of yarn around tassel 1″ from top. Tie tassel to scallop by inserting threaded needle up through tassel, over scallop, then back through tassel. Knot yarn close to wound part of tassel, clip even with bottom of tassel.

Victorian Floral Afghan

Crocheted in warm autumn colors and richly embroidered with floral repeats, this stunning afghan alternates five afghan-stitch panels with four knitted cable-stitch stripes. The floral motifs are worked in half cross-stitch embroidery with tapestry yarn.

SIZE: 60″ wide x 57″ long, plus fringe.

MATERIALS: 4-ply sport yarn, 10 2-oz. skeins gold, 10 skeins scarlet, 5 skeins ivy green, 2 skeins orange-rust, 1 skein yellow. Afghan hook size F or 3. Crochet hook size F or 3. Set of double-pointed needles No. 1 For embroidery: tapestry wool, crewel wool, knitting worsted, or sport yarn used double, in the following colors: peach, pale red, medium rose red, dark rose red, burgundy, pale yellow, light gold, medium gold, taupe, black, bronze, light olive, medium olive, dark olive, light blue-green, medium blue-green, dark blue-green, very dark blue-green, grass green, slate blue, tan. Tapestry needles.

GAUGE: 6 sts = 1″; 6 rows = 1″.

AFGHAN: First Panel (make 2): With gold and afghan hook, ch 60.

Row 1: Pull up a lp in 2nd ch from hook and in each ch across—60 lps on hook. Work lps off as follows: yo hook, pull through first lp, * yo hook, pull through next 2 lps, repeat from * across—60 sts; 1 lp remains on hook and counts as first st of next row.

Row 2: Sk first vertical bar, pull up a lp in each vertical bar across—60 lps on hook. Work lps off: yo hook, pull through first lp, * yo hook, pull through next 2 lps, repeat from * across—60 sts; 1 lp remains on hook. Check gauge; piece should measure 10″ wide. Repeat Row 2 until there are 342 rows. Piece should be about 57″ long. End off.

Second Panel (make 2): With scarlet, work as for First Panel.

Center Panel: With ivy green, work as for First Panel.

EMBROIDERY: Embroider panels before joining them. Work flower centers on gold panels in cross-stitch; work all other embroidery in half cross-stitch (page 90), working each stitch diagonally over one vertical bar of afghan stitch.

Gold Panels: In afghan shown on page 221, gold panels were embroidered with ombré yarn in shaded reds. Use shaded reds if available; if not, use peach, pale red, medium rose red, dark rose red and burgundy, using colors in shaded fashion

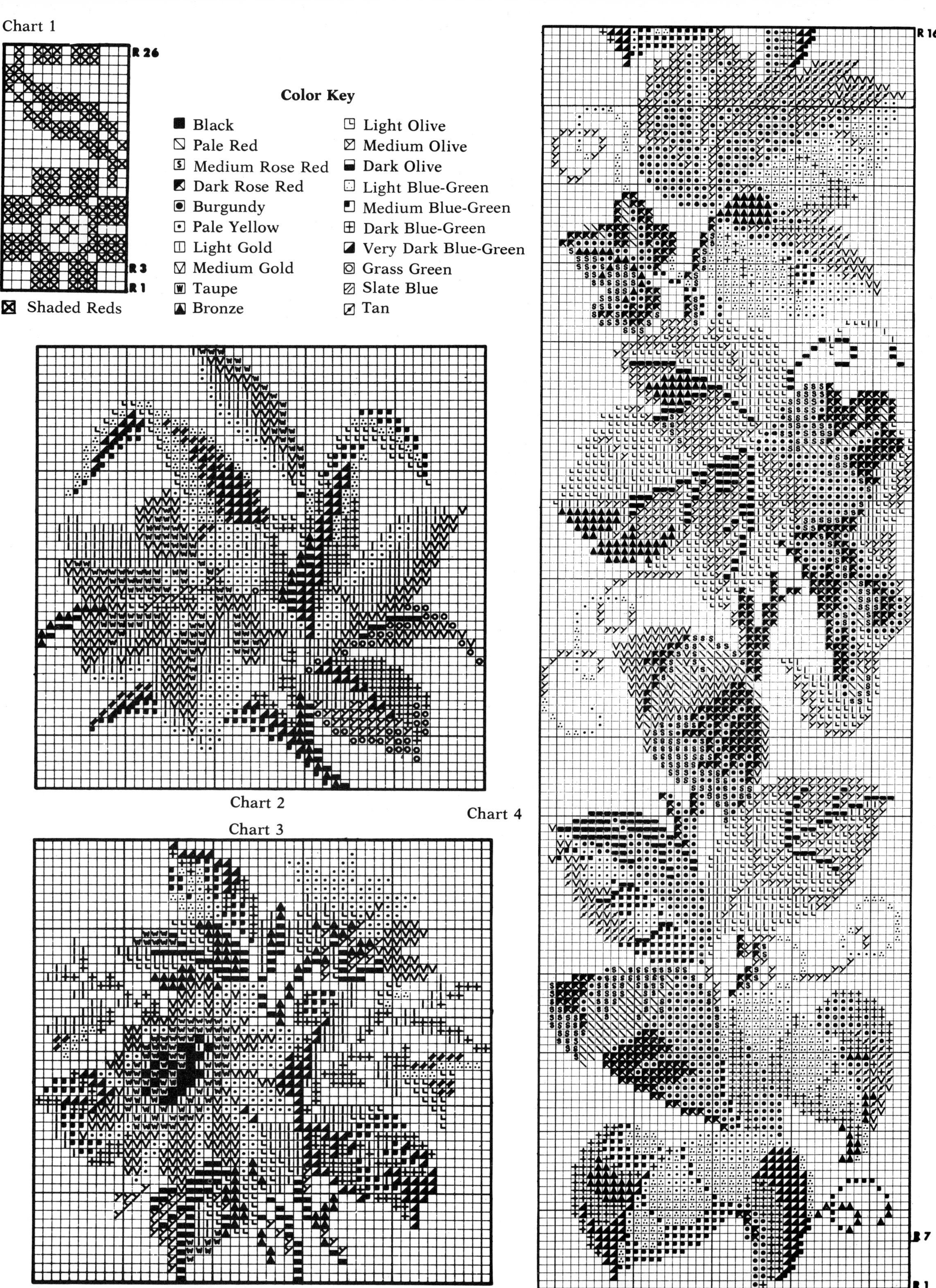
Chart 1
R 26
R 3
R 1
Shaded Reds
Color Key
Black
Pale Red
Medium Rose Red
Dark Rose Red
Burgundy
Pale Yellow
Light Gold
Medium Gold
Taupe
Bronze
Light Olive
Medium Olive
Dark Olive
Light Blue-Green
Medium Blue-Green
Dark Blue-Green
Very Dark Blue-Green
Grass Green
Slate Blue
Tan
Chart 2
Chart 3
Chart 4
R 160
R 7
R 1

as shown, page 222. One gold panel has four cross-stitches at center of each flower as shown on chart; other gold panel has a single cross-stitch at center of each flower. Use either or both styles, as desired. Beginning at lower edge of panel on 9th row from bottom, embroider design on center 13 sts of panel (there will be 24 plain sts on one side, 23 plain sts on other side). Start at Row 1 of Chart 1, work to Row 26, then repeat from Row 3 to Row 26 12 times, then work last 11 rows of flower, omitting 2 sts at right top corner of flower.

Scarlet Panels: Mark lower edge of design on panel with pins or basting thread between 20th and 21st rows of panel. Mark right-hand edge of design between 5th and 6th sts. Markings indicate placement of first flower. Embroider one panel following Chart 2 and one panel following Chart 3. Leave 13 rows free between flowers.

Green Panel: Mark right-hand edge of design on panel with pins or basting thread between 6th and 7th sts. Marking indicates right-hand edge of Chart 4. Beginning in 3rd row from bottom of panel, embroider panel following Chart 4 from Row 1 to Row 160, then repeat from Row 7 to Row 160. Repeat from Row 7 to top of panel, leaving one or two rows free at top.

CABLE STRIPS: (make 4): With orange-rust and double-pointed needles No. 1, cast on 14 sts. K 1 row.

Row 1 (right side): K 5, turn; (p 4, turn; k 4, turn) twice, p 4, turn; k 4, sl next 4 sts to another dp needle, hold in back of work, k last 5 sts.

Row 2: P 9, p 4 from dp needle, p last st.

Row 3: K across—14 sts.

Row 4: P 5, turn; (k 4, turn; p 4, turn) twice, k 4, turn; p 4, sl next 4 sts to dp needle, hold in front of work, p last 5 sts.

Row 5: K 9, k 4 sts from dp needle, k last st.

Row 6: P across—14 sts. Repeat Rows 1-6 until strip measures same as crocheted panels. Bind off.

FINISHING: Steam-press pieces.

Joining Edge: With yellow and crochet hook, from right side, work 1 row of sc along side edges of scarlet and green panels, working 1 sc in each end st—342 sc each edge. Repeat on inside edge only of each gold panel. With ivy green, work 1 row of sc along side edges of all cable strips, working 342 sc on each edge—about 6 sc to 1″. Join crocheted panels to knitted strips as follows: Hold knitted strip behind crocheted panel, wrong sides tog, edges even. With ivy green, make lp on hook. Sc edges tog for 4 sts; begin 5th sc, drop green, pull lp of yellow through 2 lps on hook. * Working over green strand, work 5 sc in yellow, changing to green on 5th st; working over yellow strand, work 5 sc in green, changing to yellow on 5th st; repeat from *, joining edges.

Side Edging: From right side, work along outer edge of each gold panel as follows: With gold, make lp on hook, sc in end st of first row, * ch 3, sk 3 rows, sc in end st of next row, repeat from * across. With scarlet, make lp on hook; join with sl st in first ch-3 lp; ch 3, dc in first ch-3 lp, ch 2, sc in top of dc for picot, (dc in same ch-3 lp, ch 2, sc in top of last dc made, for picot) 3 times, sk next ch-3 lp, sc over sc between lps into end st of panel, * sk next ch-3 lp; in next ch-3 lp, work shell of 8 dc with 8 picots, sk next ch-3 lp, sc over sc between lps into end st of panel, repeat from * across, end with half-shell of 4 dc with 4 picots in last ch-3 lp, ch 3, sl st in last lp. End off.

Top and Bottom Edging: From right side, work along top edge of afghan as follows: With gold, make lp on hook, sc in first st of gold panel, * ch 3, sk 2 sts, sc in next st, repeat from * across gold panel; end off. Join orange-rust in same st as last gold st, work 5 ch-3 lps across joining edges and knitted strip, end in first st of scarlet panel. Join scarlet in same st as last orange-rust st, work ch-3 lps across scarlet panel as for gold panel. Continue across top, working ch-3 lps to match panels. Repeat on bottom edge.

FRINGE: Cut strands 20″ long to match panels (wind yarn around 10″ cardboard, cut through strands at one edge).

First Row of Knots: Hold 5 strands tog, fold strands in half, pull folded end through matching ch-3 lp, pull 10 ends through loop; tighten knot. Knot a fringe in each ch-3 lp across top and bottom edges.

Second Row of Knots: Separate first fringe into 2 groups of 5 strands. Repeat with second fringe. With 5 strands of first fringe and 5 strands of second fringe tog, make a knot ¾″ below first row of knots. With remaining 5 strands of second fringe and 5 strands of third fringe tog, make a knot ¾″ below row of knots. Repeat across, knotting pairs of strand groups.

Third Row of Knots: Separate second fringe into 2 groups of 5 strands. With 5 strands of first fringe and 5 strands of second fringe tog, make a knot ¾″ below second row of knots. Continue across, knotting pairs of strand groups.

Irish Afghan

The rich textures of Irish knits are borrowed for this beautiful afghan, all in crochet and worked in one piece.

SIZE: About 45″ x 61″, plus fringe.

MATERIALS: Knitting worsted, 17 4-oz. skeins. Aluminum crochet hooks sizes I and J.

GAUGE: 19 sc = 5″; 1 panel = 4″; 24 rows = 5″ (size I hook).

STITCH PATTERNS: Note: Do not work in stitch directly behind raised dc or double raised dc, or in eye of a cluster.

CLUSTER: (Yo hook, draw up a lp in st) 4 times, yo and draw through all 9 lps on hook. Ch 1 tightly to form eye. (Cluster is worked from wrong side but appears on right side.)

RAISED DC: Dc around upright bar of dc 1 row below, inserting hook behind dc from front to back to front, for ridge on right side.

DOUBLE RAISED DC: Holding back last lp of each dc on hook, make 2 dc around upright bar of st 1 row below, yo and through all 3 lps on hook.

POPCORN: 4 dc in st, drop lp off hook, insert hook in top of first dc, pick up dropped lp and pull through.

NOTE: This afghan is difficult to start. Once you have completed row 3 and "set" your stitches correctly, the work becomes relatively easy. Before starting afghan, make a swatch of one pattern to familiarize yourself with the stitches. Ch 28 and work Row 1—27 sc.

Row 2: Sc in each of first 5 sts, cluster in next st, sc in each of next 15 sts, cluster in next st, sc in each of last 5 sts.

Row 3: Sc in each of first 3 sc, count off 3 sts on row 1 and work dc around next post, sk the sc on row 2 behind the dc just made and make 1 sc in each of next 3 sts (be sure to work in the cluster st only once; do not work in the eye of the cluster), sk 3 sc on row 1 from last raised dc and work a raised dc around next st, sk the sc on row 2 behind the dc just made, sc in each of next 4 sc; sk 4 sc on row 1 from last raised dc and make double raised dc around next sc, sk the sc behind it and work 1 sc, sk 1 sc on row 1 and make another double raised dc, sk the sc behind it and work 4 sc; sk 4 sc on row 1 and work a raised dc around the next sc, sk the sc behind it, work 3 sc (the cluster st is the center st of these 3 sc), sk 3 sc on row 1 and work another raised dc around the next sc, sk the sc behind it, work sc in each of last 3 sts.

Beginning with row 4 of the afghan, work pattern without repeats on 27 sts. On all right-side rows from row 3 on, the raised dc's are worked around the previous raised dc's and the double raised dc's are worked around the double raised dc's.

AFGHAN: With I hook, ch 172 loosely.

Row 1: Sc in 2nd ch from hook and in each ch across—171 sc. Ch 1, turn each row.

Row 2 (wrong side): Sc in each of first 5 sts, (cluster in next st, sc in each of next 15 sts) 10 times; end cluster in next st, sc in each of last 5 sts.

Row 3 (right side): Sc in each of first 3 sc, * work dc around post of next sc 1 row below (row 1), sk next sc on row 2 (see Stitch Patterns: Note), sc in each of next 3 sts, dc around post of next sc 1 row below, sk next sc on row 2, sc in each of next 4 sc; holding back last lp of each dc on hook, make 2 dc around next sc 1 row below, yo and through 3 lps on hook, sk next sc on row 2, sc in next sc, sk 1 sc on row 1, make 2 dc around next sc as before, sk next sc on row 2, sc in each of next 4 sc, repeat from * across, end dc around post of next sc 1 row below, sc in each of next 3 sts, dc around post of next sc 1 row below, sc in each of last 3 sc.

Row 4: Sc in each of first 4 sts, (cluster in next sc, sc in next sc, cluster in next sc, sc in each of next 13 sts) 10 times, end cluster in next sc, sc in next sc, cluster in next sc, sc in each of last 4 sts.

Row 5: Sc in each of first 3 sc, * (raised dc in raised dc, sc in each of next 3 sts) twice, (double raised dc in double raised dc, sc in each of next 3 sc) twice, repeat from * across, end (raised dc in raised dc, sc in each of next 3 sts) twice.

Row 6: Repeat row 2.

Row 7: Sc in each of first 3 sc, * raised dc in raised dc, sc in each of next 3 sts, raised dc in raised dc, sc in each of next 2 sc, double raised dc in double raised dc, sc in each of next 5 sc, double raised dc in double raised dc, sc in each of next 2 sc, repeat from * across, end raised dc in raised dc, sc in each of next 3 sts, raised dc in raised dc, sc in each of last 3 sc.

Row 8: Repeat row 4.

Row 9: Sc in each of first 3 sc, * raised dc in raised dc, sc in each of next 3 sts, raised dc in raised dc, sc in next sc, double raised dc in double raised dc, sc in each of next 3 sc, popcorn in next sc, sc in each of next 3 sc, double raised dc in double raised dc, sc in next sc, repeat from * across, end raised dc in raised dc, sc in each of next 3 sts, raised dc in raised dc, sc in each of last 3 sc.

Row 10: Repeat row 2.

Row 11: Repeat row 7.

Row 12: Repeat row 4.

Row 13: Repeat row 5.

Row 14: Repeat row 2.

Row 15: Sc in each of first 3 sc, * raised dc in raised dc, sc in next 3 sts, raised dc in raised dc, sc in each of next 4 sc, double raised dc in double raised dc, sc in next sc, double raised dc in double raised dc, sc in each of next 4 sc, repeat from * across, end (raised dc in raised dc, sc in next 3 sts) twice.

Repeat rows 4-15 until 24 diamond patterns have been completed. End off. From right side, work 1 row sc across last row, end 2 sc in last st. Do not end off.

Edging: Rnd 1: Working down side of afghan, from right side, * sc in end st of next 2 rows, sk 1 row, repeat from * to corner, 3 sc in corner st, sc in each st across end to corner, 3 sc in corner; working up side, repeat from first * to beg of rnd, sl st in first sc.

Rnd 2: Join another strand of yarn. Using double strand and J hook, working from left to right, work sc in every other sc, inc at corners to keep work flat. Join; end off.

Fringe: Cut strands 14″ long. Hold 10 strands tog, fold in half. With hook, pull fold through edge of afghan, pull ends through loop; tighten knot. Knot a fringe in center of each diamond and cluster panel at each end and in each corner. Trim fringe.

Quick-Knit Afghan

Easy to knit, this textured afghan is worked in two yarns: two strands of knitting worsted for the main color, one strand of bulky for contrast. Center panel and borders are knitted in one piece; side borders are picked up, knitted in garter stitch.

SIZE: About 48″ x 60″, plus fringe.

MATERIALS: Wool or orlon of knitting-worsted weight, 11 4-oz. skeins main color (MC). Bulky wool or orlon yarn, 9 2-oz. skeins contrasting color (CC). Two pairs of 18″ "jumper" knitting needles or 36″ circular needle No. 13. Aluminum crochet hook size K.

GAUGE: 3 sts = 1″; 11 rows = 2″ (pat).

NOTES: Use double strand of knitting worsted (MC) and single strand of bulky yarn (CC) throughout afghan. If sts are too crowded on one 18″ needle, keep sts on two needles, knit with third and fourth needles. If circular needle is used, work back and forth on needle.

PATTERN (multiple of 2 sts): sl all sl sts as if to purl. **Row 1** (right side): With CC, * k 1, yarn in back, sl 1, repeat from * across.

Row 2: With CC, * yarn in front, sl 1, yarn to back, k 1, repeat from * across.

Rows 3 and 4: With MC, knit.

Row 5: With CC, * yarn in back, sl 1, k 1, repeat from * across.

Row 6: With CC, * k 1, yarn in front, sl 1, yarn to back, repeat from * across.

Rows 7 and 8: With MC, knit. Repeat these 8 rows for patterns.

AFGHAN: With double strand MC, cast on 120 sts. Work in garter st (k each row) for 24 rows (12 ridges). Join single strand CC, work in pat until piece measures 56″ from start, end with row 2 of pat. Break off CC. With MC, work garter st for 24 rows (12 ridges). Bind off.

Side Border: From right side, with double strand MC, pick up and k 180 sts (about 3 sts to the inch) on one long side edge of afghan. Work in garter st for 24 rows (12 ridges). Bind off. Work border on other long side in same way.

FRINGE: Wind MC around 12″ cardboard; cut on one end. Hold 3 strands tog; fold in half. With crochet hook, draw folded lp through first st on side at lower edge of afghan, pull strands through lp and tighten. Knot fringe in st at other end of same row, then knot fringe in every other st between. Fringe top edge in same way. Trim evenly.

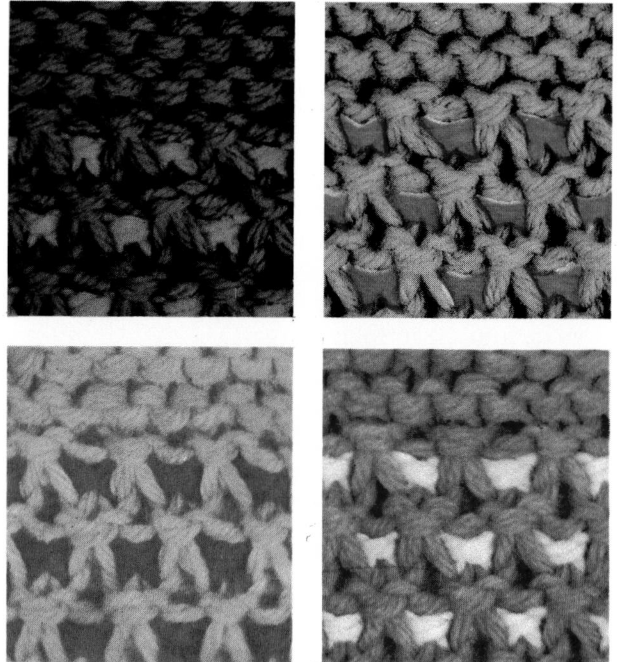

Suggested Color Combinations

Jewel-Tone Afghan

Dazzling jewel tones color this glorious afghan made with granny-type squares in four different sizes. The squares are joined with glowing striped borders that heighten the effect.

SIZE: About 54″ x 80″, plus fringe.

MATERIALS: Yarn of knitting-worsted weight, 4-oz. skeins: 2 skeins each of cerise, scarlet, dark purple, royal blue, and black; 1 skein each of magenta, light purple, teal blue, dark orange, light orange, light turquoise, dark turquoise, light violet, and dark yellow. Crochet hook size K.

GAUGE: 3 dc shell = 1″.

NOTES: Join each rnd with a sl st in top of ch 3. Cut yarn, pull end through lp on hook. Join new color with sl st. Work over ends of previous color and new color to hide them.

AFGHAN: CENTER MOTIF: With cerise, ch 4, sl st in first ch to form ring.

Rnd 1: Ch 3 (counts as 1 dc), 11 dc in ring. Join; end off (see Notes).

Rnd 2: Join scarlet in sp between any 2 dc, ch 3, 2 dc in same sp, ch 1, 3 dc in same sp, * sk 3 dc, 3 dc, ch 1, 3 dc in next sp, repeat from * twice; join; end off.

Rnd 3: Join magenta in ch-1 corner sp, ch 3, 2 dc in same sp, 3 dc in next sp between shells of 3 dc, * 3 dc, ch 1, 3 dc in next corner ch-1 sp, 3 dc in next sp between shells, repeat from * twice, 3 dc in first corner sp, ch 1; join; end off.

Rnd 4: Join light purple in ch-1 corner sp, ch 3, 2 dc in same sp, (3 dc in next sp) twice, * 3 dc, ch 1, 3 dc in next corner ch-1 sp, (3 dc in next sp) twice, repeat from * twice, 3 dc in first corner sp, ch 1; join; end off.

Rnds 5-12: Work as for rnd 4, using dark purple, royal blue, teal blue, black, dark orange, light orange, cerise, and scarlet in order, having 1 extra shell on each side each rnd.

SMALL MOTIF: With dark turquoise, royal blue, dark purple, and cerise, work rnds 1-4 of center motif. Make 8 small motifs the same.

With light purple, dark turquoise, black, and dark purple, work 8 small motifs the same.

Joining: Place small motifs around center motif, alternating colors, having cerise-edged motifs at corners. With loose sc, from wrong side, join small motifs tog, and join small motifs to center motif, using colors to match one edge to be joined.

STRIPED BORDER: Rnd 1: Join black in any corner sp of large block just made. Ch 3, 2 dc in same sp, * dc in next sp between dc's, repeat from * around, making 3 dc in each corner; join to top of ch 3; end off.

Rnd 2: Join light turquoise in sp between any 2 dc, ch 3, * dc in next sp, repeat from * around, making 2 dc in each of 2 sps at corners; join; end off.

Rnd 3: Join royal blue in sp between any 2 dc, ch 3, * dc in next sp, repeat from * around, making 3 dc in each corner; join; end off.

Rnd 4: With light violet, repeat rnd 2.

Rnd 5: With light purple, repeat rnd 3.

MEDIUM MOTIF: With dark yellow, dark orange, light orange, cerise, and scarlet, work rnds 1-5 of center motif. Make 12 medium motifs the same.

With cerise, scarlet, magenta, light purple, and dark purple, work 12 medium motifs the same.

Joining: Place medium motifs around striped border, alternating colors, having scarlet-edged motifs at corners. Join motifs tog and join motifs to striped border with sc.

STRIPED BORDER: Rnd 1: Join black in any sp between 2 dc. Ch 3, * dc in next sp, repeat from * to sp before first corner shell, sk first corner shell, make 3 dc, ch 1, 3 dc in corner, sk 2nd corner shell, repeat from first * around. Join; end.

Rnds 2-5: Repeat rnd 1 with scarlet, dark purple, royal blue, and teal blue.

END MOTIF: With black, teal blue, dark purple, light turquoise, royal blue, and light violet, work rnds 1-6 of center motif. Make 8 motifs the same.

With light turquoise, teal blue, dark turquoise, dark purple, black, and royal blue, make 6 motifs the same.

Joining: Place 7 motifs across each end of afghan, alternating colors. Join motifs tog and to striped border with sc.

END BORDER: Row 1: From right side, join dark purple in corner sp at top edge of afghan; ch 3, dc in each sp between dc's across top edge. End off.

Row 2: Join scarlet in sp between ch 3 and first dc of row 1, ch 3, dc in each sp between dc's across. End off.

Row 3: With cerise, work as for row 2.

Make same border at bottom of afghan.

FINISHING: Join black in any sp between 2 dc on edge. Ch 3, * dc in next sp, repeat from * around, working 3 dc in each corner of afghan. Run in all yarn ends. Steam-press afghan lightly.

Fringe: Wind yarns of all colors around cardboard or book 9″ long. Cut at one end. Using 3 strands tog, fold strands in half, pull folded ends through sp at one end of afghan, pull 6 ends through loop; tighten knot. Knot 6 ends tog below first knot. Knot fringe in every other sp along top and bottom of afghan.

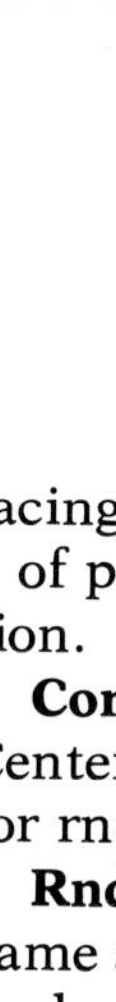

Baby Afghan

A bright baby afghan is formed from fifteen blocks in five different arrangements of white, red and shades of blue. Each block is made of granny squares at the center and solid sections at the corners. The border has scallop shell edges.

SIZE: 34″ x 54″.

MATERIALS: Yarn of knitting-worsted weight, 4 ply, 3 4-oz. skeins each of red and white; 2 skeins dark blue; 1 skein each of medium blue and light blue; about 24 yards of aqua. Crochet hook size H.

GAUGE: 4 sc = 1″; 4 sc rows = 1″. Each square is 10″ square.

NOTE: Afghan is made of separate squares joined together. Squares are all worked in same manner, using different color arrangements.

SQUARE NO. 1 (make 4): **Center:** Beg at center with white, ch 4. Sl st in first ch to form ring.

Rnd 1 (right side): Ch 3, 2 dc in ring, ch 3, (3 dc in ring, ch 3) 3 times. Join with sl st to top of ch 3 at beg of rnd. End off.

Rnd 2: Join medium blue in any ch-3 sp, ch 3, 2 dc, ch 3, 3 dc in same sp, (ch 1, 3 dc, ch 3, 3 dc in next sp) 3 times, ch 1, sl st in top of ch 3. End off.

First Sc Section: Row 1: Join red in any ch-3 sp, ch 1, sc in same sp, sc in each of next 3 dc, sc in next ch-1 sp, sc in each of next 3 dc, sc in next sp—9 sc. Ch 1, turn.

Row 2: Sc in each sc across. Ch 1, turn. Repeat row 2, 11 more times. End off.

2nd, 3rd and 4th Sc Sections: With right side facing, join red in same ch-3 sp with last sc of row 1 of previous sc section, work as for first sc section.

Corner Motif (make 4): With red, work as for Center through rnd 1. With medium blue, work as for rnd 2.

Rnd 3: Join white in any ch-3 sp, ch 3, 2 dc in same sp, ch 3, 3 dc in same sp, * sk next dc, dc in each of next 2 dc, dc in ch-1 sp, dc in each of next 2 dc, sk next dc, 3 dc, ch 3, 3 dc in next ch-3 sp, repeat from * twice, sk next dc, dc in next 2 dc, dc in ch-1 sp, dc in next 2 dc. Sl st in top of ch 3. End off.

Join Corner Motifs: Place corner motifs in corner spaces of square. Baste 2 sides of each motif loosely to side edges of sc rows. Join dark blue to end of basting seam, ch 1. Working through both thicknesses, from right side, sl st in same place where yarn was joined, * ch 1, sl st loosely through next st on both pieces, repeat from * along basted edges, matching inner corner of motif with corner sp of center. End off. Join other 3 motifs in same way.

Edging: From right side, join same color used for joining to any corner sp of square, ch 1, 3 sc in same sp, sc in each st and in each joining around, making 3 sc in each corner sp. End off.

SQUARE NO. 2 (make 4): Work as for Square No. 1, using colors as follows:

Rnd 1: White.
Rnd 2: Aqua.
Sc Sections: Red.
Corner Motifs: Rnd 1: Light blue.
Rnd 2: Red.
Rnd 3: White.
Joining and Edging: Dark blue.

SQUARE NO. 3 (make 4): Work as for Square No. 1 using colors as follows:

Rnd 1: Red.
Rnd 2: Light blue.
Sc Sections: White.
Corner Motifs: Rnd 1: Medium blue.
Rnd 2: Red.
Rnd 3: Light blue.
Joining and Edging: Dark blue.

SQUARE NO. 4 (make 2): Work as for Square No. 1, using colors as follows:

Rnd 1: Aqua.
Rnd 2: Red.
Sc Sections: White.
Corner Motifs: Rnd 1: White.
Rnd 2: Light blue.

1	3	2	3	1
4	2	5	2	4
1	3	2	3	1

Rnd 3: Red.

Joining and Edging: Dark blue.

SQUARE NO. 5 (make 1): Work as for Square No. 1, using colors as follows:

Rnd 1: Red.

Rnd 2: White.

Sc Sections: Light blue.

Corner Motifs: Rnd 1: Dark blue.

Rnd 2: Light blue.

Rnd 3: Red.

Joining and Edging: Dark blue.

Pin squares to measurement on a padded surface; cover with a damp cloth and allow to dry. Do not press.

TO JOIN SQUARES: Following chart for placement of squares, baste squares tog, matching sts and corners. Join 2 top rows tog with dark blue, working through both thicknesses as before, making sl st and ch 1 in each st across. Join bottom row to center row in same way. Join motifs across short rows in same way.

BORDER: Rnd 1: From right side, join dark blue in center sc of any corner 3-sc group, ch 1, 3 sc in same st, * sc evenly across squares, making 35 sc in each square, to next corner, 3 sc in corner st, repeat from * twice, sc evenly across last side. Sl st in first sc. Ch 1, turn.

Rnd 2: Sc in each sc around, 3 sc in each corner st. Sl st in first sc. End off. Turn.

Rnd 3: Join white to same sc as joining, ch 1, repeat rnd 2. Ch 1, turn.

Rnd 4: Repeat rnd 2. End off. Turn.

Rnd 5: Join red to same sc as joining, ch 1, repeat rnd 2. Ch 1, turn.

Rnd 6: Repeat rnd 2. End off. Turn.

Rnd 7: From right side, join red in center sc of any corner 3-sc group, ch 3, make 5 dc in same sc (shell), sk 2 sc, sc in next sc, * sk 2 sc, 6 dc in next sc (shell), sk 2 sc, sc in next sc, repeat from * around, skipping as necessary at corners to have a shell in each corner. Sl st in top of ch 3. End off.

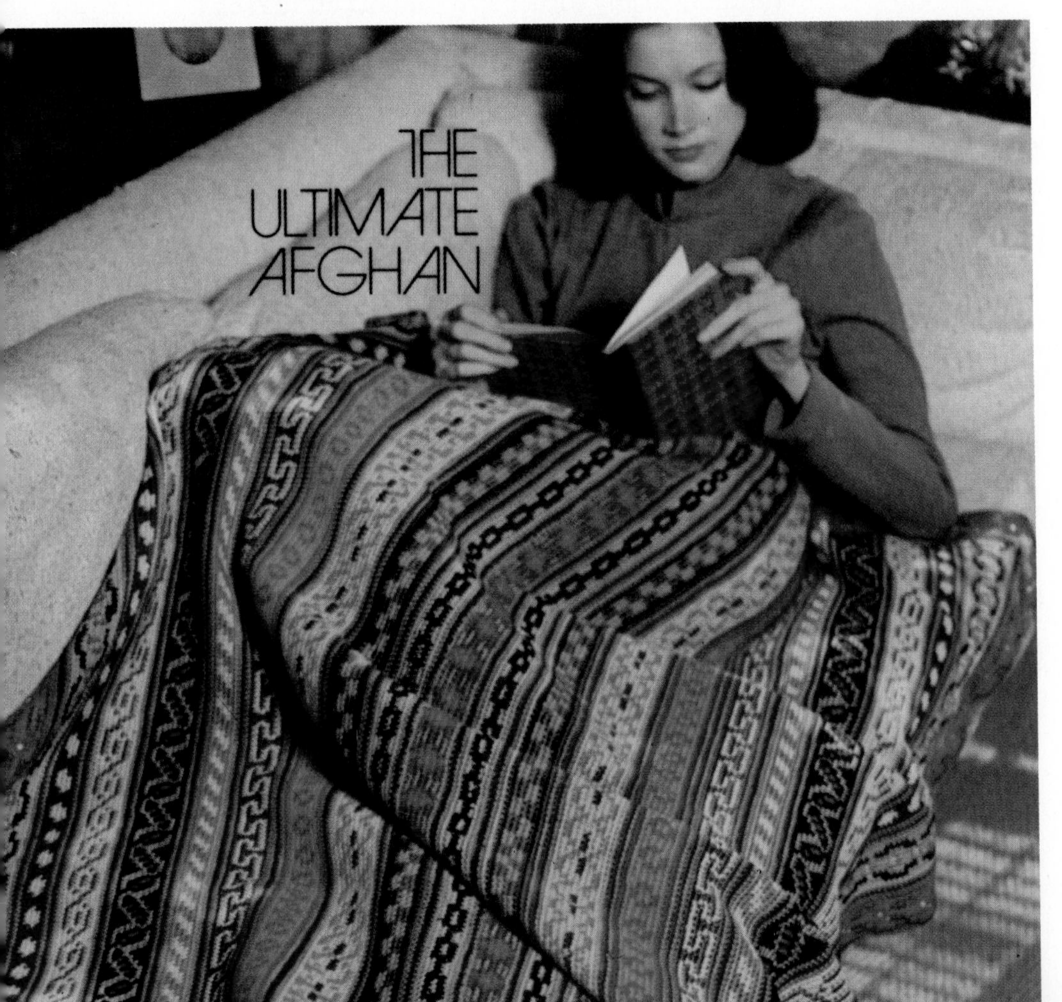

Pattern-Bands Afghan

A glorious array of patterned bands adds up to a tour de force *in crochet! The patterns are worked from a chart in single and reverse single crochet, and the over-all size can be enlarged simply by repeating the designs.*

SIZE: 44" x 64".

MATERIALS: Knitting worsted or orlon yarn of same weight, 60 to 70 ozs. in a variety of colors. The following approximate amounts are needed for afghan as shown: 10 ozs. tan; 8 ozs. brown; 6 ozs. beige; 4 ozs. each of red, black, medium blue, green, yellow; 3 ozs. each of gray, purple, maroon; 2 ozs. each of peach, rose, dark yellow, dark blue, light blue, dark red, aqua; 1 oz. dark green. Steel crochet hook No. 00.

GAUGE: 5 sc = 1"; 5 rows = 1".

Note 1: Afghan is worked vertically from center pattern stripe out to last pattern stripe on side; second half is worked from center pattern stripe out to opposite side using same patterns and colors as first half. A border is then worked around entire afghan.

Note 2: Colors used in afghan are given in directions. Any desired colors may be used. Cut and join colors as needed.

Note 3: Work right side of afghan in sc; work wrong side in reverse sc. Or, work entire afghan in sc from right side.

Note 4: On any row with 2 or more colors, begin row with all colors used on row. Work over colors not being used (lay unused colors along top of row, work sc as usual; unused colors will be hidden inside sts). When changing colors, work last sc or reverse sc of one color until there are 2 lps on hook, drop yarn to wrong side of work, finish st with new color. Continue in pattern, being sure to work over dropped color.

Reverse Sc: With yarn in front of hook, insert hook from back to front in st, catch yarn with hook, draw lp through to back of work, yo hook and through 2 lps on hook.

AFGHAN: FIRST HALF: With tan, ch 301.

Row 1 (right side) Sc in 2nd ch from hook and in each ch across—300 sc. Cut tan. Do not turn.

Row 2 (right side): With green, make lp on hook. Working over maroon and red, and beg in first sc at beg of row 1, work 1 green sc in each of first 3 sts, change to maroon (see Note 4); * work 3 maroon sc, change to red; work 1 red sc, change to maroon; work 1 maroon sc, change to green; work 3 green sc, change to maroon. Repeat from * across; end 1 maroon sc. See Chart 1; row just worked is first row of chart, repeating from A to B across and ending from B to C once. Ch 1, turn.

Row 3 (wrong side): Working in reverse sc and working from chart, work from C to B once, then repeat from B to A across. Cut green. Ch 1, turn.

Row 4: Join yellow. Working in sc and working from chart, repeat from A to B across, ending from B to C once. Cut yellow. Ch 1, turn.

Row 5: Join green; repeat row 3. Ch 1, turn.

Row 6: Working in sc and working from chart, repeat from A to B across, ending from B to C once. Cut all colors. Do not turn.

Row 7 (right side): With tan, make lp on hook. Beg in first sc at beg of last row, work sc in each sc across; drop tan. Do not turn.

Row 8 (right side): With brown make lp on hook. Beg in first sc at beg of last row, work sc in each sc across. Cut brown. Pick up tan; ch 1, turn.

Row 9 (wrong side): With tan, reverse sc in each sc across. Cut tan.

Following charts and working rows 7-9 between charts, work to top of Chart 11. Cut colors. Do not work rows 7-9.

SECOND HALF: From right side, working on opposite side of starting ch, with brown, work sc in each ch across—300 sc. Cut brown. Do not turn.

With tan, work sc in each sc across. Cut tan. Do not turn. Beg with Chart 2, work as for first half of afghan.

FINISHING: Weave in yarn ends. Block afghan.

BORDER: Rnd 1: With tan, make lp on hook. From right side, sc in each sc and in end of each row around afghan, working 3 sc in each corner. Sl st in first sc. End off.

Rnd 2: With brown, sc in each sc around, 3 sc in sc at each corner. Sl st in first sc. End off.

Rnd 3: With tan, repeat rnd 2.

Rnd 4: With green, repeat rnd 2. Do not end off. Working from Chart 12, repeat from A to B around, increasing as necessary at corners to keep work flat and working added sts into pattern. When top of chart is reached, cut all colors but green, work 1 rnd green sc.

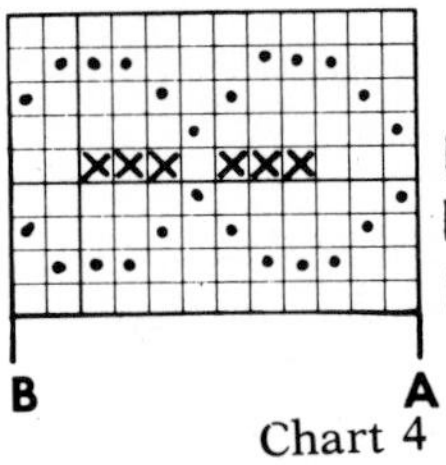

B A

Chart 4

Color Key
- ☒ Brown
- ⊡ Dark Yellow
- ☐ Beige

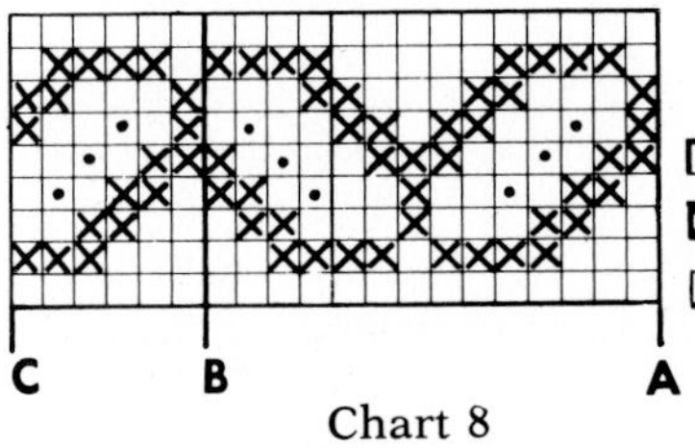

C B A

Chart 8

Color Key
- ⊡ Red
- ☒ Gray
- ☐ Black

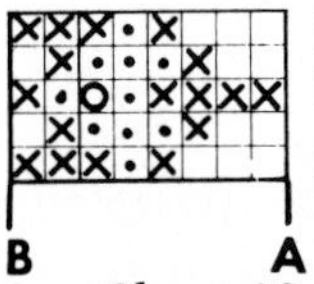

B A

Chart 12

Color Key
- ◘ Yellow
- ⊡ Dark Red
- ☒ Red
- ☐ Green

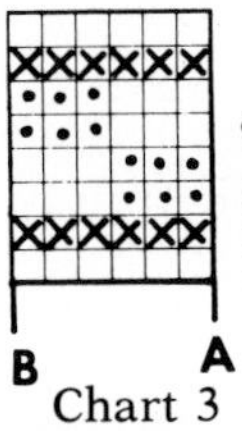

B A

Chart 3

Color Key
- ⊡ Medium Blue
- ☒ Dark Blue
- ☐ Light Blue

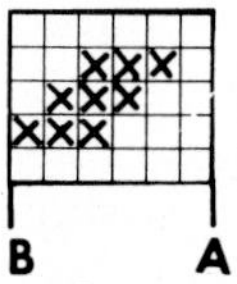

B A

Chart 7

Color Key
- ☒ Peach
- ☐ Blue

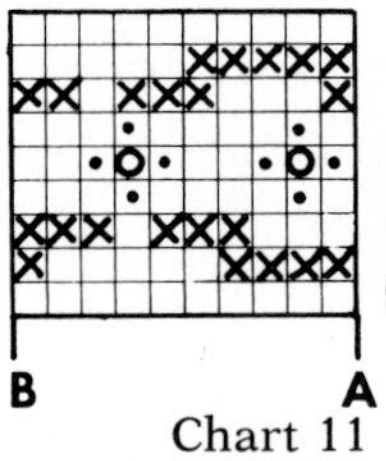

B A

Chart 11

Color Key
- ◘ Yellow
- ⊡ Dark Yellow
- ☒ Dark Green
- ☐ Aqua

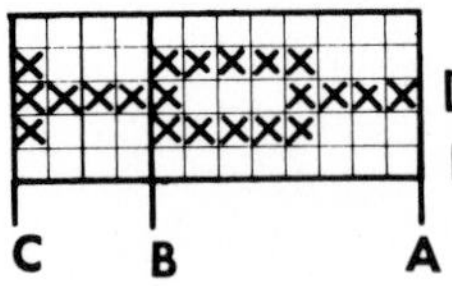

C B A

Chart 2

Color Key
- ☒ Black Gray
- ☐ Gray

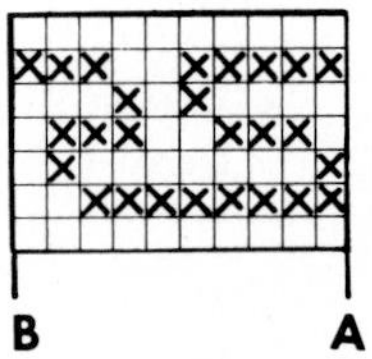

B A

Chart 6

Color Key
- ☒ Yellow
- ☐ Purple

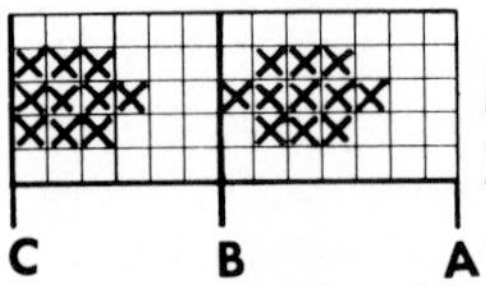

C B A

Chart10

Color Key
- ☒ Beige
- ☐ Brown

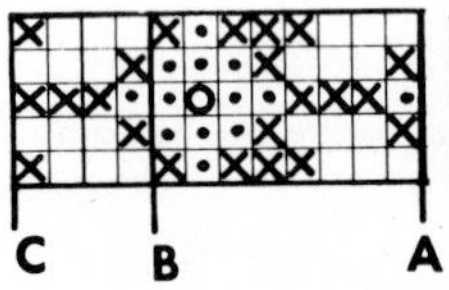

C B A

Chart 1

Color Key
- ◘ Yellow
- ⊡ Red
- ☒ Maroon
- ☐ Green

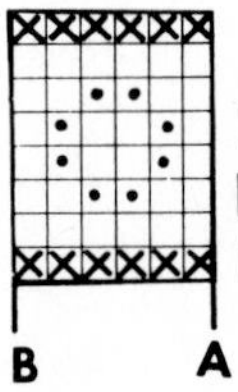

B A

Chart 5

Color Key
- ⊡ Red
- ☒ Maroon
- ☐ Rose

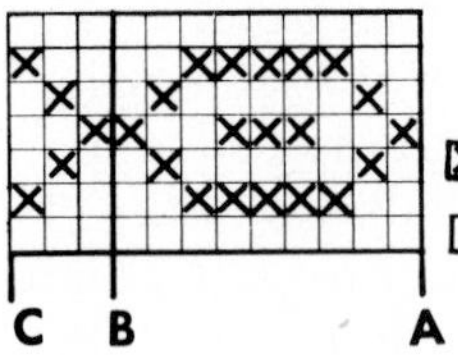

C B A

Chart 9

Color Key
- ☒ Purple
- ☐ Beige

Navajo Afghan

A great tradition—the woven Navajo blanket—inspired this beautiful knitted afghan. Worked entirely in the stockinette stitch, the afghan can be knitted on circular or long knitting needles.

SIZE: 40″ x 56″, plus fringe.

MATERIALS: Knitting worsted, 5 4-oz. skeins royal blue (A); 4 skeins beige (B); 2 ozs. each of light gold (C), medium gold (D), dark gold (E), orange (F) and scarlet (G). 29″ circular knitting needle, or "jumper" needles, No. 8. Crochet hook size G. Twenty-four bobbins.

GAUGE: 5 sts = 1″; 13 rows = 2″.

NOTES: Use a separate bobbin for each color change. Always change colors on wrong side, picking up new strand from under dropped strand. Cut and join colors as necessary. Wind 5 bobbins A, 3 bobbins B; 4 bobbins each of C, D and E; 2 bobbins each of F and G.

AFGHAN: With A, cast on 200 sts. K 2 rows.

PATTERN: Row 1 (right side): P 1, k 1, p 1, * following chart, k from A to B, repeat from * once, end p 1, k 1, p 1.

Row 2: P 1, k 1, p 1, * p from A to B, repeat from * once, end p 1, k 1, p 1. Repeat rows 1 and 2 to top of chart (90 rows), then repeat chart 3 times more, repeat row 1. With A, k 1 row. Bind off in k same tension as sts.

FINISHING: Run in yarn ends on wrong side. Steam-press lightly.

FRINGE: Cut A into 16″ lengths. Hold 2 strands tog; fold in half. With crochet hook draw folded lp through first st on end of afghan, pull strands through lp and tighten. Knot a fringe in each st on each end of afghan. Trim evenly.

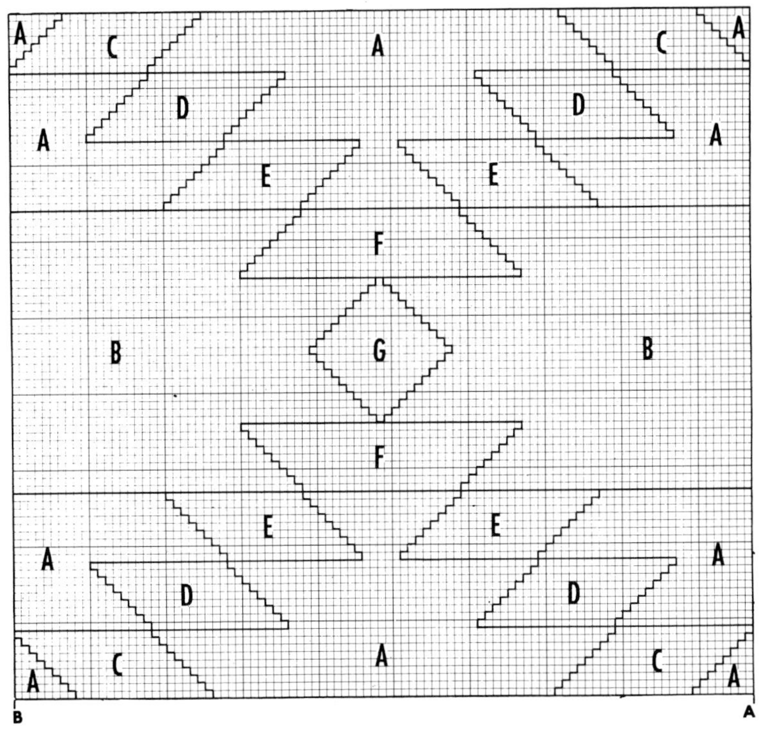

Flag Afghan

Double knitting worsted, worked in stockinette stitch on circular or long needles, gives quick results in creating this inspiring Continental flag. The crocheted edge is fringed; the felt stars are sewn in place.

SIZE: 42″ x 76″.

MATERIALS: Knitting worsted, 6 4-oz. skeins each of red and white, 4 skeins blue, 1 skein gold; 1 oz. black. Circular needle or long knitting needles size 13. Knitting needles size 10. Crochet hook size J. White felt, 72″ wide, ⅛ yd. White sewing thread.

GAUGE: 5 sts = 2″; 4 rows = 1″ (double strand of yarn); 4 sts = 1″ (single strand, size 10 needles).

NOTE: Flag is worked with double strand throughout.

FLAG: Beg a lower edge, with double strand of red, and circular needle size 13, cast on 180 sts. Work even in stockinette st (k 1 row, p 1 row) for 13 rows. * Change to white, work 13 rows. Change to red, work 13 rows. Repeat from * once, then change to white, work 13 rows; end p row.

Next Row: Change to red, k 90. Drop red. With blue, k 90.

Next Row: With blue, p 90; drop blue; pick up red from under blue strand to prevent hole, p 90. Continue with stripes of red and white at right half of flag, solid blue at left half, until 12 rows of 7th stripe have been completed. Bind off in red and blue on next row.

FINISHING: Steam-press.

Band: With white and No. 10 needles, cast on 172 sts.

Row 1: P across.

Row 2: K 40. Join black. Working from row 1 of chart, k sts for letters in black, finish row with white.

Row 3: P 61 with white; reading from left to

Chart for Flag Afghan

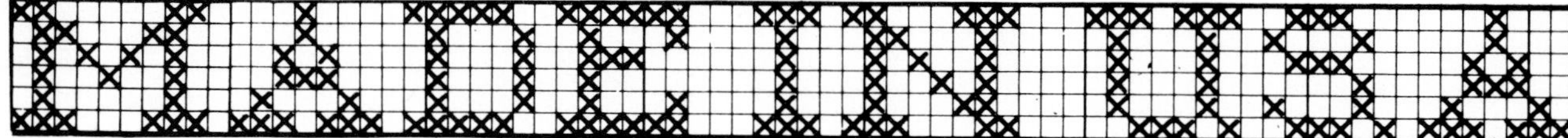

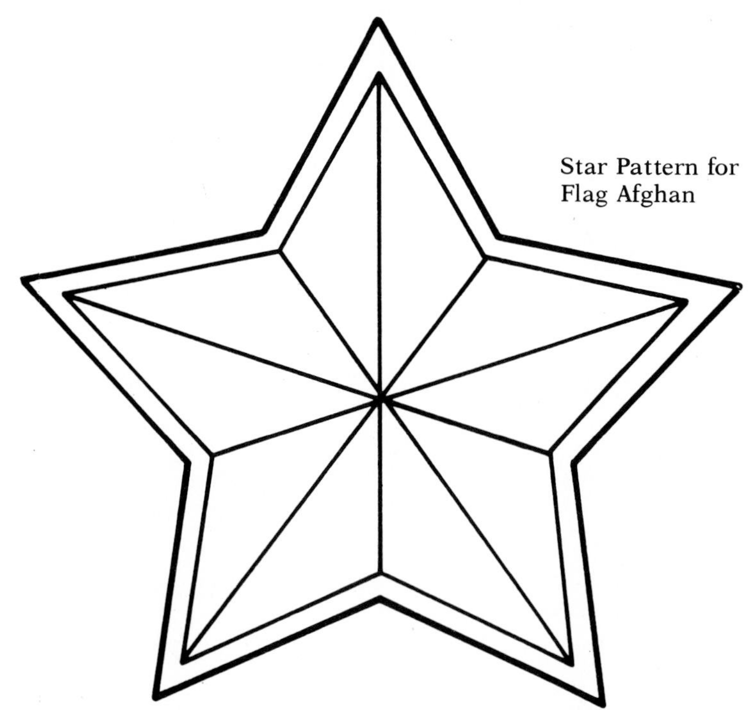

Star Pattern for Flag Afghan

right on row 2 of chart, work next 71 sts from chart, p 40 white. Continue in this manner until top of chart is reached. Break off black. K 3 rows white (center k row forms ridge for folding band). Work even in stockinette st for 7 rows. Bind off. Steam-press band. Fold in half on ridge row. Sew ends closed. Place over left end of flag; sew in place.

With gold and crochet hook, work 1 row sc around bottom, right edge and top of flag, working 1 sc in each st at bottom and top, 1 sc in every other row at side edge and 3 sc in st at each corner. End off.

Cut gold in 6″ lengths. Holding 2 strands tog, knot a fringe in every sc around.

STARS: Using pattern for star, cut 13 stars from white felt. Machine-stitch each star as shown by lines on pattern. From paper, cut a circle 13″ in diameter. Pin to blue section of flag. Place stars around outer edge of circle, 2 points of each star touching circle; arrange stars as shown in illustration. Sew to flag with white thread.

Rosette Bedspread

A rare old bedspread found at an auction is used here with stunning effect—its warm ecru tone enhanced by a very contemporary bright orange. Raised rosettes and "leaf" borders are worked in half double crochet, with filet mesh completing square motifs. For a single bed, omit two rows of the 9" squares.

SIZE: 72" x 81", plus fringe.

MATERIALS: Mercerized crochet cotton No. 10, 138 200-yard balls ecru. Steel crochet hook No. 11.

GAUGE: 2 hdc = 1"; 6 rows = 1". Motif is 9" square.

MOTIF: Ch 6, sl st in first ch to form ring.

Rnd 1: 12 sc in ring. Sl st in first sc.

Rnd 2: Ch 3 (counts as 1 dc, ch 1), * dc in next sc, ch 1, repeat from * around, end ch 1, sl st in 2nd ch of ch 3—12 dc.

Rnd 3: Sl st in next ch-1 sp, ch 2 (counts as 1 dc), dc in same sp, ch 2, 2 dc in same ch-1 sp, * 2 dc, ch 2, 2 dc in next sp, repeat from * around. Join to top of first dc.

Rnd 4: Ch 2 for first hdc, hdc in back lp of next dc, * 2 dc, ch 2, 2 dc in next sp, hdc in back lp of each of next 4 dc, repeat from * around, end hdc in back lp of each of last 2 dc; join.

Rnd 5: Ch 2, * hdc in back lp of each st to next ch-2 sp, 2 dc, ch 2, 2 dc in sp, repeat from * around, end hdc in back lp of each st to last st; join.

Rnds 6-13: Repeat rnd 5. At end of rnd 13, there are 2 dc, 40 hdc, 2 dc each side.

Rnd 14: Ch 2, * hdc in back lp of each st to 4 sts before ch-2 sp, ch 4, sl st in 4th ch from hook for picot (p), sk 2 sts, hdc in back lp of each of next 2 dc, p, dc in ch-2 sp, p, dc in same sp, p, hdc in back lp of each of next 2 dc, p, sk 2 sts, repeat from * around, end hdc in back lp of each st to ch 2; join; end off. There are 36 hdc each side between corner pats.

Rnd 15: Fold one side of motif through center, right sides tog, matching corner pats. With lp on hook, sk 9 hdc after corner on both edges, sc next 9 hdc on both edges tog on wrong side to fold, * ch 3, fold next side as before, sk 9 hdc after corner on both edges, sc next 9 hdc on both edges tog to fold, repeat from * around, end ch 3, sl st in first sc.

Rnd 16: Ch 2 for first hdc, hdc in each of next 8 sc, hdc in each of 3 ch, * ch 2 (corner), (hdc in each of next 9 sc, hdc in each of 3 ch) 3 times, repeat from * twice, ch 2, (hdc in each of next 9 sc, hdc in each of 3 ch) twice, sl st in first hdc—36 hdc each side.

Rnd 17: Ch 2 for first hdc, * hdc in back lp of each st to corner, 2 dc, ch 2, 2 dc in corner, repeat from * 3 times, hdc in back lp of each st to first hdc; join—40 sts each side.

Rnds 18-23: Repeat rnd 17—64 sts each side at end of rnd 23.

Rnd 24: Ch 2 for first hdc, * hdc in back lp of each hdc to corner, 3 dc, ch 3, 3 dc in corner, repeat from * 3 times, hdc in back lp of each hdc to first hdc; join—70 sts each side.

Rnd 25: Ch 4, sk 2 sts, hdc in back lp of next st, (ch 2, sk 2 sts, hdc in back lp of next st) 8 times, * ch 2, sk end st, work dc, ch 3, dc in center ch at corner, (ch 2, sk 2 sts, hdc in back lp of next st) 23 times, repeat from * twice, ch 2, sk end st, work dc, ch 3, dc in center ch of 4th corner, (ch 2, sk 2 sts, hdc in back lp of next st) 13 times, ch 2, sl st in 2nd ch of ch 4—24 ch-2 sps each side.

Rnd 26: Ch 4, hdc in next hdc, (ch 2, hdc in next hdc) 8 times, * ch 2, hdc in dc at corner, ch 2, work dc, ch 3, dc in center ch at corner, ch 2, hdc in next dc, (ch 2, hdc in next hdc) 23 times, repeat from * twice, ch 2, hdc in dc at corner, ch 2, work dc, ch 3, dc in center ch at corner, ch 2, hdc in next dc, (ch 2, hdc in next hdc) 13 times, ch 2, sl st in 2nd ch of ch 4—26 ch-2 sps each side.

Rnd 27: Sl st in next sp, ch 2, 2 hdc in same sp, 3 hdc in next sp; * in next sp, make 3 hdc, ch 2, 2 hdc, (3 hdc in next sp) twice, repeat from * twice; † in corner sp make 2 dc, ch 3, 2 dc; ** (3 hdc in next sp) twice, 3 hdc, ch 2, 2 hdc in next sp, repeat from ** 7 times, (3 hdc in next sp) twice, repeat from † around, ending 3 hdc, ch 2, 2 hdc in last sp; join.

Rnd 28: Working in back lps only, make hdc in each hdc and dc around, working 2 dc, ch 2, 2 dc in each ch-2 sp and 2 dc, ch 3, 2 dc in each ch-3 sp at corners. Join.

Rnds 29 and 30: Repeat rnd 28. End off.

Rnd 31: Make lp on hook. ** Place a corner point and next point tog, right sides tog; * sk 5 sts from chs at points on both edges, sc edges tog on wrong side with 6 sc to fold, ch 3; fold next 2 points tog, repeat from * 7 times; sk 7 sts from points on both edges, sc next st on both edges tog;

fold corner point to right side; from right side, sc next 3 sts tog on all 3 edges, picking up back lp only of top st, sc in back lp of next 4 sts, sc, ch 3, sc in corner sp, sc in back lp of each of next 5 sts, repeat from ** around, join in first sc of rnd.

Rnd 32: Working in back lps only, make hdc in each sc and ch around; at corners, make 2 dc, ch 3, 2 dc in ch-3 sp—91 sts each side. Join.

Rnd 33: Working in back lps only, make hdc in each hdc and dc around, 2 dc, ch 3, 2 dc in each corner sp—95 sts each side. Join.

Rnd 34: Sl st in next st. Ch 4, sk 2 sts, hdc in back lp of next st, (ch 2, sk 2 sts, hdc in back lp of next st) 26 times, * ch 2, sk last 2 sts on side, work dc, ch 3, dc in center ch at corner, (ch 2, sk 2 sts, hdc in back lp of next st) 31 times, repeat from * twice, ch 2, sk last 2 sts on 4th side, work dc, ch 3, dc in center ch at corner, (ch 2, sk 2 sts, hdc in back lp of next st) 3 times, ch 2, join in 2nd ch of ch 4 at beg of rnd—32 sps each side.

Rnd 35: Ch 4, hdc in next hdc, * ch 2, hdc in next hdc, repeat from * around, working dc, ch 3, dc in center ch at each corner. At end of rnd, ch 2, join in 2nd ch of ch 4. End off.

Make 70 motifs for bedspread, 72″ x 81″.

FINISHING: Block each motif 9″ square. Crochet motifs tog on wrong side with sc, working in top lp of each st around. Join 8 rows of 8 motifs, then join 1 row of 6 motifs to center 6 motifs on one edge for bottom of bedspread.

For fringe, cut strands 14″ long. Take 15 strands, double strands to form loop. Insert hook in mesh on edge, draw loop through. Draw ends through loop; pull up tightly to form a knot. Make a fringe in every other mesh on sides and bottom. Trim ends evenly.

Sunburst and Flower Pillows

The crocheted Sunburst Pillow has a popcorn-stitch center with fluted rays in sunny yellows, oranges and browns. The Flower Pillow is worked in double crochet clusters and spaces on one side, with a rose motif on the other.

FLOWER PILLOW

SIZE: 12″ in diameter.

MATERIALS: Knitting worsted, 4 ply, 1 2-oz. skein each of white (A), green (B), yellow (C), orange (D) and light brown (E). Plastic crochet hook size H. Foam rubber pillow, 12″ in diameter, 2½″ or 3″ thick, ½ yard white fabric. Matching sewing thread. Tapestry needle.

GAUGE: 5 dc = 1″.

PILLOW TOP: Beg at center with A, ch 7. Join with sl st in first ch to form ring.

Rnd 1: Ch 3 (counts as 1 dc), 19 dc in ring. Do not join.

Rnd 2: * Ch 7, sk 4 dc, sl st in back of work around bar of next dc, repeat from * twice, end ch 7, sl st in first ch of ch-7 lp at beg of rnd—4 lps.

Rnd 3: Work sc, hdc, 8 dc, hdc, sc in each ch-7 lp, end sl st in first sc—4 petals.

Rnd 4: * Ch 5, sl st in back of work around bar of 4th dc of same petal, ch 5, sl st in first sc of next petal, repeat from * 3 times, end sl st in first ch of rnd—8 ch-5 lps.

Rnd 5: Work sc, hdc, 7 dc, hdc, sc in each ch-5 lp, end sl st in first sc—8 petals.

Rnd 6: Ch 3, * sl st in back of work around bar of 4th dc of next petal, ch 7, repeat from * 7 times, end sl st in first sl st—8 ch-7 lps.

Rnd 7: Work sc, hdc, 10 dc, hdc, sc in each ch-7 lp, end sl st in first sc—8 petals.

Rnd 8: * Ch 5, sl st in back of work around bar of 5th dc of same petal, ch 5, sl st in first sc of next petal, repeat from * 7 times—16 ch-5 lps.

Rnd 9: Work sl st, ch 2, 7 dc, ch 2, sl st in each ch-5 lp, end with sl st in first st—16 petals. End off.

Rnd 10: Join B with a sl st in 4th dc of next petal, work ch 3, 2 dc in same dc, ch 3, work tr between sl sts at end of petal, * ch 3, work 3 dc in 4th dc in next petal, ch 3, tr between sl sts at end of petal, repeat from * around, end ch 3, sl st in top of ch 3.

Rnd 11: Sl st in next dc, ch 5, * (dc in next ch-3 sp) twice, ch 2, dc in center of dc of 3-dc group, ch

Front of Flower Pillow

2, repeat from * around, end ch 2, sl st in 3rd ch of ch 5. End off.

Rnd 12: Join C with a sl st in center of 2-dc group, ch 5, * (dc in next ch-2 sp) twice, ch 2, dc between 2 dc of next 2-dc group, ch 2, repeat from * around, end ch 2, sl st in 3rd ch of ch 5. End off.

Rnd 13: Join D in ch-2 sp after 2 dc, ch 3, 2 dc in same ch-2 sp, * ch 1, 3 dc in next ch-2 sp, ch 1, dc between 2 dc, ch 1, 3 dc in next ch-2 sp, repeat from * around, end ch 1, dc between next 2 dc, ch 1, sl st in 3rd ch of starting ch. End off.

Rnd 14: Join C in next ch-1 sp between 3-dc groups, ch 5, * 2 dc in next ch-1 sp, 2 dc in next ch-1 sp, ch 2, dc in next ch-1 sp, ch 2, repeat from * around, end last repeat ch 2, sl st in 3rd ch of starting ch. End off.

Rnd 15: Join A in last ch-2 sp made before sl st, ch 2, 2 hdc in same sp, * ch 1, 3 hdc in next ch-2 sp, ch 1, sk 2 dc, work 2 hdc between 2-dc groups, ch 1, sk 2 dc, work 3 hdc in next ch-2 sp, repeat from * around, end last repeat ch 1, sl st in top of starting ch.

Rnd 16: Ch 5, 2 hdc in next ch-1 sp, * ch 3, 2 hdc in next sp, ch 2, 2 hdc in next sp, ch 3, 2 hdc in next sp, repeat from * around, end last repeat ch 2, hdc in last sp, sl st in 2nd ch of starting ch. End off.

Rnd 17: Join E with sl st in next sp, ch 3, 2 dc in same sp, * ch 1, 3 dc in next sp, repeat from * around, end ch 1, sl st in top of starting ch.

Rnd 18: Sl st in next 2 dc, sl st in ch-1 sp, ch 3, dc in same sp, * ch 1, 2 dc in next sp, repeat from * around, end ch 1, sl st in top of ch 3. End off.

Rnd 19: Join A with sl st in any sp, ch 2, hdc in same sp, * ch 1, 2 hdc in next sp, repeat from * around, end ch 1, sl st in top of ch 2.

Rnd 20: Sl st in next hdc, sl st in ch-1 sp, ch 2, hdc in same sp, * ch 1, 2 hdc in next sp, repeat from * around, end ch 1, sl st in top of ch 2. End off.

Rnd 21: Join E with sl st in any sp, ch 3, dc in same sp, * ch 1, 2 dc in next sp, repeat from * around, end ch 1, sl st in top of ch 3.

Rnd 22: Sl st in dc, sl st in ch-1 sp, ch 3, dc in same sp, * ch 1, 2 dc in next sp, repeat from * around, end ch 1, sl st in top of ch 3. End off.

PILLOW BACK: Beg at center with A, ch 7. Sl st in first ch to form ring.

Rnd 1: Ch 3, 21 dc in ring. Join with a sl st in top of ch 3.

Rnd 2: Ch 5, sk next dc, * dc in next dc, ch 2, sk next dc, repeat from * around, end ch 2, sl st in 3rd ch of starting ch 5—11 sps.

Rnd 3: Sl st in sp, ch 3, 2 dc in same sp, * ch 2, 3 dc in next sp, repeat from * around, end ch 2, sl st in top of ch 3. End off.

Rnd 4: Join A in next ch-2 sp, ch 3, 3 dc in same sp, * ch 2, 4 dc in next sp, repeat from * around, end ch 2, sl st in top of ch 3. End off.

Rnd 5: Join C in 3rd dc of 4-dc group, ch 5, * 3 dc in next ch-2 sp, ch 2, dc in 3rd dc of next 4-dc group, ch 2, repeat from * around, end ch 2, sl st in 3rd ch of starting ch. End off.

Rnd 6: Join D in center dc of 3-dc group, ch 5, * 2 dc in next sp, ch 1, 2 dc in next sp, ch 2, dc in center dc of 3-dc group, ch 2, repeat from * around, end last repeat ch 2, sl st in 3rd ch of starting ch. End off.

Rnd 7: Join C in ch-2 sp after 2-dc group, work ch 3, 2 dc in same sp, * ch 1, 3 dc in next ch-2 sp, ch 1, dc in next ch-1 sp, ch 1, 3 dc in next ch-2 sp, repeat from * around, end last repeat ch 1, sl st in top of starting ch. End off.

Rnd 8: Join A in ch-1 sp between 3-dc groups, ch 6, * 2 dc in next sp, ch 1, 2 dc in next sp, ch 3, dc in next sp, ch 3, repeat from * around, end last repeat ch 3, sl st in 3rd ch of starting ch. End off.

Rnd 9: Join E in next ch-1 sp, ch 5, * 4 dc in ch-3 sp, ch 1, 4 dc in next sp, ch 2, dc in next sp, ch 2, repeat from * around, end last repeat ch 2, sl st in 3rd ch of starting ch.

Rnd 10: Ch 3, 2 dc in sp, ch 1, * dc in 3rd dc of 4-dc group, ch 1, dc in ch-1 sp, ch 1, dc in 3rd dc of next 4-dc group, ch 1, 3 dc in ch-2 sp, ch 1, 3 dc in next ch-2 sp, ch 1, repeat from * around, end last repeat ch 1, sl st in top of starting ch. End off.

FINISHING: Run in all yarn ends on wrong side. Cover pillow form tightly with fabric. With A, sc edges of pillow top and back tog over pillow.

SUNBURST PILLOW

SIZE: 12″ in diameter.

MATERIALS: Knitting worsted, 1 ounce each of yellow (A), light orange (B), medium orange (C), dark orange (D), beige (E), light brown (F), medium brown (G), dark brown (H). Steel crochet hook No. 0; plastic crochet hook size 5. Foam rubber pillow, 12″ in diameter, 2½″ thick. Tapestry needle.

GAUGE: 5 sc = 1″ (crochet hook size 5).

PILLOW TOP: Beg at center with A and No. 0 hook, ch 4. Sl st in first ch to form ring.

Rnd 1: 10 sc in ring, sl st in first sc.

Rnd 2: Ch 4 (counts as 1 dc), 3 dc in first sc, drop lp off hook, insert hook from front to back in first dc, draw lp through (popcorn made), ch 1, * 4 dc in next sc, drop lp off hook, insert hook from front to back in first dc, draw lp through (popcorn made), ch 1, repeat from * around—10 popcorns. Join with a sl st in first popcorn.

Rnd 3: Work a popcorn, ch 1, in each st around—20 popcorns. Join in first popcorn.

Rnd 4: Ch 1, (sc in each of next 3 sts, 2 sc in next st) 10 times—50 sc. Join in first sc.

Rnd 5: * Ch 7, sc in 2nd ch from hook and in each of next 5 ch, sl st in next sc, sc in next sc, repeat from * 24 times—25 points. Join in next st. Turn. Work with size 5 hook hereafter.

Row 6: * Sk sc and sl st; sc in back lp of each of next 6 sc; work sc, ch 1, sc in top of point, work 6 sc on side of ch, repeat from * around, end sl st in joining sl st. Turn.

Row 7: Sk first sc; * sc in back lp of each of 6 sc; work sc, ch 2, sc in ch 1, sc in back lp of each of 6 sc, sk next 2 sc, repeat from * around, end last repeat sk next sc, sl st in sl st. Cut A; join B. Turn.

Rows 8-10: With B, sk first sc, * sc in back lp of each of 6 sc; work sc, ch 2, sc in ch-2 sp, sc in back lp of each of 6 sc, sk next 2 sc, repeat from * around, end last repeat sk next sc, sl st in sl st. Turn. Repeat row 8 for pat.

Rows 11-36: Work 4 rows C, 4 rows D, 2 rows H, 2 rows G, 2 rows F, 2 rows E, 2 rows A, 2 rows B, 2 rows C, 2 rows D, 2 rows H. End off.

BACK: Work as for pillow top, working rows 1–7 with E, then 3 rows F, 4 rows G, 2 rows H. End off; leave end for sewing.

FINISHING: Run in all yarn ends on wrong side. Working through back lps, with H, weave edges of pillow top and back tog over pillow.

Victorian Dog Cushion

A delightfully pensive dog in softly muted colors is worked in cross-stitches over an afghan crochet background. The original antique piece was the center of a child's Victorian afghan or carriage robe. The motif makes a lovely box cushion, edged with twisted cord and tassel accents.

SIZE: 10½" x 13".

EQUIPMENT: Afghan hook size H. Large-eyed tapestry needle. Sewing needle. Tape measure. Scissors. Cardboard, 2¾" wide.

MATERIALS: Knitting worsted, 2-oz. skeins: one off-white; one medium gold. Tapestry yarn, small skeins: one each black, white, beige, tan, medium brown, dark brown, light rust, dark copper, dark green, medium green, light green, light yellow-green, deep red, bright red, deep blue, medium blue, light blue, deep yellow, light yellow, magenta, lilac, pale pink. Heavy cotton fabric 48" wide, off-white, ½ yard. Sheet foam rubber 1" x 10½" x 13".

DIRECTIONS: For afghan-stitch background the gauge is: 4 sts = 1"; 7 rows = 2". Using off-white knitting worsted and afghan hook, crochet background for cushion top in afghan stitch as follows: Make a ch 13¼" long. **Row 1:** Skip first ch from hook (loop on hook is first stitch); keeping all loops on hook, insert hook in next ch, yo and pull up a loop; repeat in each ch across. **To Work Off Loops:** Yo, pull through first loop, * yo, pull through next 2 loops, repeat from * across, until one loop remains. Loop that remains on hook always counts as first st of next row. **Row 2:** Keeping all loops on hook, sk first vertical bar, insert hook through next vertical bar, yo and pull up a loop; repeat on each vertical bar across. Work loops off as before. Repeat Row 2 for 10¼".

Work design in cross-stitch, following chart and color key below. On each square of afghan-stitch backbackground, work four cross-stitches (see actual- size detail on page 240 and diagram on page 220); two stitches cover vertical bar and two stitches are worked over horizontal portion of each square. Mark exact center of chart and find center of afghan-stitch background. Work first row of cross-stitch on background from center to left, following chart; complete row from center to right. Finish design following each row of chart.

To cover foam cushion, cut two pieces of fabric

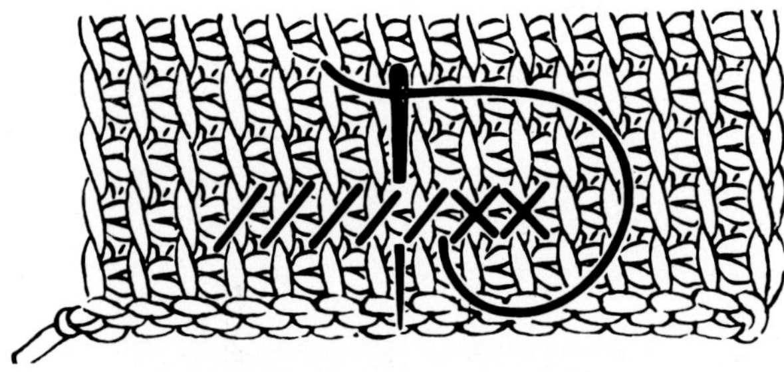

detail of cross-stitch

11″ x 13½″, and a boxing strip 1½″ x 48″. With right sides together, sew boxing strip around edge of one 11″ x 13½″ piece with ¼″ seams, starting at center of one long side; join ends of boxing strip. Sew second piece of fabric to other edge of boxing strip, leaving one end open. Turn right side out; insert foam cushion. Turn in remaining edges and slip-stitch closed. Place embroidered afghan-stitch piece on top of cushion and pin all around edges along top seam line of cushion; turn in edges of afghan-stitch background if necessary to make it fit smoothly. Slip-stitch piece in place.

Make a twisted cord to fit around cushion using four thicknesses of gold knitting worsted, following directions on page 416. Sew cord around top seam of cushion. Make another cord the same and sew around bottom seam. Make four tassels of gold yarn as follows: Wrap yarn 16 times around a 2¾″ piece of cardboard. Tie strands together at one edge of cardboard. Cut strands at opposite edge. Wrap another piece of yarn several times around all strands tightly ½″ below tie. Sew a tassel to each corner just below the top cord.

Color Key

- Dark Green
- Medium Green
- Light Green
- Light Yellow-Green
- Bright Red
- Black
- White
- Pale Pink
- Deep Yellow
- Light Yellow
- Tan
- Medium Blue
- Deep Blue
- Light Blue
- Magenta
- Lilac
- Beige
- Dark Brown
- Medium Brown
- Dark Copper
- Light Rust
- Dark Red

Three Heirloom "Lace" Pillows

Delicate motifs grace the Pinwheel Squares and Rose Wheels pillows, prettily trimmed with picot shells. A big, beautiful rose blossoms on a field of filet mesh for the Rose Pillow.

PINWHEEL SQUARES

SIZE: 18″ square, plus edging.

MATERIALS: Mercerized crochet cotton, size 30, 3 400-yard balls. Steel crochet hook No. 10.

GAUGE: Each motif is 4¼″ square.

FIRST MOTIF: Ch 6, sl st in first ch to form ring.

Rnd 1: Ch 1, 16 sc in ring. Sl st in first sc.

Rnd 2: Ch 1, sc in first sc, (ch 3, sk 1 sc, sc in next sc) 7 times, ch 3, sl st in first sc.

Rnd 3: (3 sc in next lp, ch 3) 8 times.

Rnd 4: (Sk next sc, sc in each of 2 sc, 2 sc in next lp, ch 3) 8 times.

Rnd 5: (Sk next sc, sc in each of 3 sc, 2 sc in next lp, ch 3) 8 times.

Rnd 6: (Sk next sc, sc in each of 4 sc, 2 sc in next lp, ch 3) 8 times.

Rnd 7: (Sk next sc, sc in each of 5 sc, 2 sc in next lp, ch 3) 8 times.

Rnd 8: (Sk next sc, sc in each of 6 sc, 2 sc in next lp, ch 3) 8 times.

Rnd 9: (Sk next sc, sc in each of 6 sc, ch 3, sc in next lp, ch 3) 8 times.

Rnd 10: (Sk next sc, sc in each of 4 sc, ch 3, sc in next lp, ch 3, sc in next lp, ch 3) 8 times.

Rnd 11: (Sk next sc, sc in each of 2 sc, ch 3, sc in next lp, ch 3, sc in next lp, ch 3, sc in next lp, ch 3) 8 times.

Rnd 12: (Sc in next lp, ch 4) 32 times.

Rnd 13: * Dc in next lp, ch 4, dc in same lp, (ch 4, sc in next lp) 7 times, ch 4, repeat from * 3 times. Mark first dc of rnd.

Rnd 14: * Dc, ch 4, dc in next (corner) lp, (ch 4, sc in next lp) 8 times, ch 4, repeat from * around.

Rnd 15: * Dc, ch 4, dc in corner lp, (ch 4, sc in next lp) 9 times, ch 4, repeat from * around.

Rnds 16-19: Work as for rnd 15, having 1 more lp each side each rnd.

Rnd 20: Work as for rnd 15 but work ch-5 lps instead of ch-4 lps—15 ch-5 lps each side, plus ch-5 lp in each corner. End last rnd with ch 5, sl st in corner lp.

SECOND MOTIF: Work as for first motif through rnd 19, end ch 4 before corner.

Joining Rnd 20: Dc in corner lp, ch 2, sl st in corner lp of previous motif, ch 2, dc in corner lp of new motif, (ch 2, sl st in next lp of previous motif, ch 2, sc in next lp of new motif) 14 times, ch 2, sl st in last side lp of previous motif, ch 2, dc in corner lp of new motif, ch 2, sl st in corner lp of previous motif, ch 2, dc in corner lp of new motif, finish motif as for previous motif.

Join 9 motifs tog, 3 x 3, in this way. At corners where 4 motifs meet, join in same joining st.

Border: Rnd 1: Join thread in corner lp of pillow, ch 3, 2 dc, ch 3, 3 dc in corner lp, * ch 1, 3 dc in center ch of next ch-5 lp, repeat from * to next corner, ch 1, 3 dc, ch 3, 3 dc in corner lp, repeat from first * around, end ch 1, sl st in top of ch 3.

Rnd 2: Sl st to corner lp, ch 3, 2 dc, ch 3, 3 dc in corner lp, * ch 1, dc in center dc of next 3 dc, ch 1, dc in next ch-1 sp, repeat from * to next corner, ch 1, dc in center dc of 3 dc at corner, ch 1, 3 dc, ch 3, 3 dc in corner lp, repeat from first * around, end ch 1, sl st in top of ch 3.

Rnd 3: Sl st to corner lp, ch 3, 2 dc, ch 3, 3 dc in corner lp, * ch 1, dc in next ch-1 sp, repeat from * to next corner, ch 1, 3 dc, ch 3, 3 dc in corner lp, repeat from first * around, end ch 1, sl st in top of ch 3.

Rnd 4: Sl st to corner lp, ch 3, 2 dc, ch 3, 3 dc in corner lp, * ch 1, dc in center dc of next 3 dc, ** ch 1, dc in next ch-1 sp, repeat from ** across to next corner, ch 1, dc in center dc of 3 dc at corner, ch 1, 3 dc, ch 3, 3 dc in corner lp, repeat from * around, end ch 1, sl st in top of ch 3.

Rnd 5: Sl st to corner lp, ch 3; holding back on hook last lp of each dc, 2 dc in corner lp, yo and through 3 lps on hook (cluster), ch 5, cluster of 3 dc in corner lp, ch 5; * holding back on hook last lp of each dc, 2 dc in next ch-1 sp, 1 dc in next ch-1 sp, yo and through 4 lps on hook, ch 5, sk 1 sp, repeat from * across to next corner, ch 5, cluster, ch 5, cluster in corner lp, ch 5, repeat from first * around, end ch 5, sc in top of first cluster.

Rnd 6: Work hdc, 7 dc, hdc in corner lp, sc in next cluster, * hdc, 7 dc, hdc in next lp, sc in cluster, repeat from * around, end sl st in first sc.

Rnd 7: Sl st to center of corner scallop, ch 5, dc in center dc of scallop, (ch 2, dc in same place) twice, * ch 4, dc, ch 2, dc in center dc of next scallop, repeat from * across to next corner, ch 4, dc in center dc of corner scallop, (ch 2, dc) 3 times in same st, repeat from first * around, end sl st in 3rd ch of ch 5.

Rnd 8: Sl st in next ch-2 sp, ch 5, dc in same sp, ch 2, sc in next sp, (ch 2, dc) twice in next sp, * ch 2, sc in next ch-4 lp, (ch 2, dc) twice in next ch-2 sp, repeat from * to next corner, (ch 2, dc) twice in first corner sp, ch 2, sc in next sp, (ch 2, dc) twice in next sp, repeat from first * around, end sl st in 3rd ch of ch 5.

Rnd 9: Sl st in next ch-2 sp, ch 5, dc in same sp, ch 2, sc in next sp, ch 4, sc in next sp, (ch 2, dc) twice in next sp, * ch 2, sc in next sc, sk next ch-2 sp, (ch 2, dc) twice in next ch-2 sp, repeat from * across to next corner, sk first ch-2 at corner, (ch 2, dc) twice in next ch-2 sp, ch 2, sc in next sp, ch 4, sc in next sp, (ch 2, dc) twice in next sp, repeat from first * around, end sl st in 3rd ch of ch 5.

Rnd 10: Sl st in next ch-2 sp, ch 1, sc in sp, (ch 5, tr) twice in ch-4 lp at corner, * ch 5, sc in center ch-2 sp of next "scallop," repeat from * to next corner, (ch 5, tr) twice in ch-4 lp at corner, repeat from first * around, end sl st in first sc.

Rnd 11: Work hdc, 7 dc, hdc in next lp, sc in tr, hdc, 3 dc, ch 2, 3 dc, hdc in corner lp, sc in tr, * hdc, 7 dc, hdc in next lp, sc in sc, repeat from * to next corner lp, hdc, 3 dc, ch 2, 3 dc, hdc in corner lp, sc in tr, repeat from first * around, end sl st in first hdc.

Rnd 12: Sl st to center of first scallop, ch 3, 2 dc in center dc of scallop, ch 3, 3 dc in 2nd dc of corner scallop, ch 3, 3 dc, ch 3, 3 dc in corner ch-2 sp, ch 3, sk 1 dc, 3 dc in next dc, * ch 3, 3 dc in center of next scallop, repeat from * to next corner, ch 3, 3 dc in 2nd dc of corner scallop, (ch 3, 3 dc) twice in corner ch-2 sp, ch 3, sk 1 dc, 3 dc in next dc, repeat from first * around, end ch 3, sl st in top of ch 3.

Rnd 13: Ch 4, sk next dc, dc in next dc, ch 1, dc in next sp, ch 1, dc in next dc, ch 1, sk next dc, dc in next dc, ch 1, dc in next sp, ch 1, ** 3 dc, ch 3, 3 dc in corner sp, * ch 1, dc in next sp, ch 1, dc in next dc, ch 1, sk next dc, dc in next dc, repeat from * across to next corner, repeat from ** around, end sl st in 3rd ch of ch 4.

Rnd 14: Sl st in ch-1 sp, ch 4, * dc in next sp, ch 1, repeat from * to corner, 3 dc, ch 3, 3 dc in corner sp, ch 1, repeat from first * around, end ch 1, sl st in 3rd ch of ch 4.

Rnd 15: Work as for rnd 14, but add 1 ch-1 sp each side of corner by working dc in center dc of 3 dc at corner.

Rnds 16 and 17: Repeat rnd 14.

Rnd 18: Sl st in ch-1 sp, ch 3, holding back on

hook last lp of each dc, dc in same sp, dc in next sp, yo and through 3 lps on hook, (ch 3, holding back on hook last lp of each dc, 2 dc in next sp, dc in next sp, yo and through 4 lps on hook) twice (3 clusters made), ** ch 3, 3-dc cluster in sp before corner, ch 3, cluster, ch 5, cluster in corner lp, ch 3, cluster in next ch-1 sp, * ch 3, holding back on hook last lp of each dc, 2 dc in next sp, dc in next sp, yo and through 4 lps on hook, repeat from * across to sp before corner, repeat from ** around, end ch 3, sl st in top of first cluster—64 clusters each side.

Scalloped Edge: Rnd 1: 2 sc, ch 2, 2 sc in next sp, ch 2, 2 sc in next sp, ch 2, 2 sc, ch 2, 2 sc in next sp, ch 2, sc in next sp, (sp before corner); ** in corner lp, work 13 dc, sc in next sp, * (ch 2, 2 sc, ch 2, 2 sc in next sp, ch 2, 2 sc in next sp) twice, ch 2, 2 sc, ch 2, 2 sc in next sp, ch 2, sc in next sp, 7 dc in next sp, sc in next sp, repeat from * 6 times, (ch 2, 2 sc, ch 2, 2 sc in next sp, ch 2, 2 sc in next sp) twice, ch 2, 2 sc, ch 2, 2 sc in next sp, ch 2, sc in next sp (sp before corner), repeat from ** around, end 7 dc in next sp, sc in next sp, ch 2, 2 sc, ch 2, 2 sc in next sp, ch 2, 2 sc in last sp, ch 2, sl st in first sc.

Rnd 2: Sl st to first ch-2 sp, ch 1, 2 sc in sp, (ch 2, 2 sc in next ch-2 sp) 3 times, ** ch 2, sk sp before corner, dc in first dc, (ch 2, sk 1 dc, dc in next dc) 6 times, * ch 2, sk next ch-2 sp, 2 sc in next ch-2 sp, (ch 2, 2 sc in next sp) 6 times, ch 2, sk next ch-2 sp, dc in first dc, (ch 2, sk 1 dc, dc in next dc) 3 times, repeat from * across to corner, repeat from ** around, end 2 sc in last sp, ch 2, sl st in first sc.

Rnd 3: Sl st across to next ch-2 sp, ch 1, 2 sc in sp, (ch 2, 2 sc in next sp) twice, ** ch 2, dc, ch 2, dc in first dc at corner, (ch 2, sc in next sp, ch 2, dc, ch 2, dc in next dc) 6 times, * ch 2, sk next sp, 2 sc in next sp, (ch 2, 2 sc in next sp) 5 times, ch 2, sk next sp, dc, ch 2, dc in next dc, (ch 2, sc in next sp, ch 2, dc, ch 2, dc in next dc) 3 times, repeat from * across to corner, repeat from ** around, end 2 sc in last sp, ch 2, sl st in first sc.

Rnd 4: Sl st across to next ch-2 sp, ch 1, 2 sc in sp, ch 2, 2 sc in next sp, ** (ch 2, dc in next dc, ch 2, sc in next sp, ch 2, dc in next dc) 7 times, * ch 2, sk next sp, 2 sc in next sp, (ch 2, 2 sc in next sp) 4 times, (ch 2, dc in next dc, ch 2, sc in next sp, ch 2, dc in next dc) 4 times, repeat from * across to corner, repeat from ** around, end ch 2, sk next sp, 2 sc in next sp, (ch 2, 2 sc in next sp) twice, ch 2, sl st in first sc.

Rnd 5: Sl st across to next ch-2 sp, ch 1, 2 sc in sp, ** ch 2; working in corner scallop, dc in first dc, (ch 3, dc in next dc, ch 2, sc in next sp, ch 2, dc in next dc) 6 times, ch 3, dc in last dc, * ch 2, sk next sp, 2 sc in next sp, (ch 2, 2 sc in next sp) 3 times, ch 2, dc in next dc, (ch 3, dc in next dc, ch 2, sc in next sp, ch 2, dc in next dc) 3 times, ch 3, dc in last dc of scallop, repeat from * across to corner, repeat from ** around, end ch 2, sk next sp, 2 sc in next sp, (ch 2, 2 sc in next sp) twice, ch 2, sl st in first sc.

Rnd 6: Sl st to first dc of corner scallop, ch 1, ** sc in dc, (hdc, 3 dc, hdc in next ch-3 lp, sc in next dc, ch 3, sc in next dc) 6 times, hdc, 3 dc, hdc in next ch-3 lp, sc in next dc, ch 3, sk next sp, 2 sc in next sp, (ch 2, 2 sc in next sp) twice, * ch 2, sc in next dc, (hdc, 3 dc, hdc in next ch-3 lp, sc in next dc, ch 3, sc in next dc) 3 times, hdc, 3 dc, hdc in next ch-3 lp, sc in next dc, sk next sp, (ch 2, 2 sc in next sp) 3 times, repeat from * across to corner, ch 2, repeat from ** around, end ch 2, sl st in first sc.

Rnd 7: Ch 1, ** (sc in sc, ch 3, sc in next sc, hdc, 3 dc, hdc in next lp) 6 times, sc in sc, * ch 2, sk next sp, (2 sc in next sp, ch 2) twice, sk next sp, (sc in next sc, ch 3, sc in next sc, hdc, 3 dc, hdc in next lp) 3 times, sc in next sc, ch 3, sc in next sc, repeat from * across to corner, ch 2, sk sp before corner, repeat from ** around, end ch 2, sl st in first sc.

Rnd 8: Sl st in first lp, ch 5, sc in 3rd ch from hook for picot, (dc in same lp, ch 2, sc in dc) twice, dc in same lp, * ch 2, sc in center dc of next scallop, ch 2, dc in next lp, (ch 2, sc in dc, dc in same lp) 3 times, repeat from * around corner scallop, (7 picot shells), ** ch 2, sk next sp, 2 sc in next ch-2 sp, ch 2, sk next ch-2 sp, work 4 picot shells in next side scallop, repeat from ** 6 times, ch 2, sk next sp, 2 sc in next ch-2 sp, ch 2, work 7 picot shells around corner scallop, repeat from first ** around, end ch 2, sl st in 3rd ch of ch 5 at beg of rnd. End off.

FINISHING: Block crocheted piece, starching lightly, if desired. Sew to covered pillow inside scalloped edge.

ROSE PILLOW

SIZE: 16″ square.

MATERIALS: Mercerized knitting and crochet cotton, 1 250-yard ball white. Steel crochet hook No. 6. Material for pillow cover, ½ yard. Pillow form, 16″ square.

GAUGE: 4 bls or sps = 1″; 4 rows = 1″.

To Make 1 Space (sp): Dc in st, ch 2, sk 2 sts, dc

in next st (1 space); ch 2, sk 2 sts, dc in next st for each additional space.

To Make 1 Block (bl): Dc in each of 4 sts (1 block); dc in each of next 3 sts for each additional block.

Chart Notes: Spaces are shown on chart as open squares, blocks as dotted squares.

PILLOW TOP: Beg at bottom edge, ch 200. (Always ch more than directions call for; extra ch can be cut off later.)

Row 1: Dc in 8th ch from hook (1 sp), (ch 2, sk 2 ch, dc in next ch) 25 times, dc in each of next 3 ch (1 bl), ch 2, sk 2 ch, dc in next ch (1 sp), dc in each of next 3 ch (1 bl), (ch 2, sk 2 ch, dc in next ch) 36 times. Ch 5, turn each row.

Row 2: Sk first dc, dc in next dc, (ch 2, sk 2 ch, dc in next dc) 35 times, dc in each of next 3 dc (bl over bl), ch 2, dc in next dc (sp over sp), dc in each of next 3 dc (bl over bl), (ch 2, dc in next dc) 25 times, ch 2, sk 2 ch, dc in next ch.

Beg with row 3 of chart, following chart from right to left on right-side rows (odd rows) and from left to right on wrong-side rows (even rows), work to top of chart. Work 5 more rows of spaces at top or as many as needed to make piece square. End off.

FINISHING: Wash piece if necessary; block. Cut 2 pieces of fabric same size as pillow top. Baste pillow top, right side up to right side of one fabric square. Place fabric squares right sides together, and stitch together around three sides, taking ¼″ seams. Turn pillow cover to right side. Insert pillow form. Close opening.

ROSE WHEELS

SIZE: 18″ square, plus edging.

MATERIALS: Mercerized crochet cotton, size 30, 3 400-yard balls. Steel crochet hook No. 10.

GAUGE: One motif = 3¼″.

FIRST MOTIF: Ch 6. Sl st in first ch to form ring.

Rnd 1: Ch 3 (counts as 1 dc), 23 dc in ring. Sl st in top of ch 3.

Rnd 2: Ch 3, sk next dc, dc in next dc, ch 6, dc in top of dc just made (cross-stitch made), * ch 3, yo hook 3 times, draw up a lp in next dc, yo and through 2 lps, yo hook, sk next dc, draw up a lp in next dc, yo and through 2 lps, yo and through 3 lps, (yo and through 2 lps) twice, ch 3, dc in center lps of long st just made (cross-stitch made), repeat from * around, end ch 3, sl st in 3rd ch of ch 6—8 cross-sts.

Rnd 3: Ch 1, * 4 sc in next ch-3 sp, repeat from * around—64 sc. Sl st in first sc.

Rnd 4: Ch 3, dc in same sc as sl st, dc in each of next 3 sc, * 2 dc in next sc, dc in each of next 3 sc, repeat from * around, sl st in top of ch 3—80 dc.

Rnd 5: Ch 6, dc in 4th ch from hook, 3 dc next to dc just made over remaining 2 ch, * sk 3 dc of last rnd, dc in next dc, ch 3, 4 dc over bar of dc just made, repeat from * around, end sl st in same ch with first dc of rnd—20 pats.

Rnd 6: Sl st in each of 3 ch to top of first pat, sc in sp between ch and first dc, * ch 6, sc in top of next pat between ch 3 and first dc, repeat from * around, end ch 6, sl st in first sc.

Rnd 7: * In next lp make sc, 4 hdc, ch 6, sc in last hdc made (picot), 4 hdc, sc; sl st in next sc, repeat from * around. End off.

SECOND MOTIF: Work 2nd motif same as first motif through rnd 6.

Rnd 7: * In next lp make sc, 4 hdc, ch 3, drop lp from hook; insert hook in a picot of previous motif, pick up dropped lp, and pull up through picot, ch 3, sc in last hdc made, 4 hdc, sc in same lp of 2nd motif, sl st in next sc, repeat from * twice (3 picots joined to 3 picots of previous motif), finish 2nd motif as for first motif.

Make and join 16 motifs in this manner, forming a square, 4 motifs by 4 motifs. Leave 2 picots free on each motif at "corners" between joinings of 3 picots on "sides." At the four corners of the square, there will be 12 picots free on each corner motif. On the sides of the square each motif has 7 picots free.

FILL-IN MOTIF (make 9): Ch 5. Sl st in first ch to form ring.

Rnd 1: Ch 3, 15 dc in ring. Sl st in top of ch 3.

Rnd 2: Ch 3, dc in next dc, * ch 4; holding back last lp of each dc, dc in each of next 2 dc, yo and through 3 lps on hook, repeat from * around, end ch 4, sl st in top of ch 3.

Rnd 3: * Sc, 3 hdc in next lp, ch 2, drop lp from hook; insert hook in free picot between four joined motifs, pick up dropped lp and pull through picot, ch 2, sc in last hdc made, 3 hdc, sc in same lp of fill-in motif, sl st in next sc, repeat from * 7 times.

HALF-MOTIFS (make 12): Ch 5. Sl st in first ch to form ring.

Row 1: Ch 3, 9 dc in ring. Ch 3, turn.

Row 2: Dc in next dc, * ch 4; holding back last lp of each dc, dc in each of next 2 dc, yo and through 3 lps on hook repeat from * 3 times, working last dc in top of ch 3. Ch 1, turn.

Row 3: Work as for rnd 3 of fill-in motif, joining 2 picots of half-motif to 2 free picots of a large motif on edge of square and next 2 picots of half-motif to 2 free picots of adjoining large motif on edge of square.

BORDER: Rnd 1: Join thread in 4th free picot (there are 8 free picots) of a corner motif; ch 4, tr in 5th free picot of motif; ch 9, tr in top of ch 4 (corner lp); working along side of pillow, * ch 5, tr in 5th picot of corner motif, ** (ch 5, sc in next free picot) 3 times, ch 5, tr in side of next scallop of just before joined picot, ch 5, sc in next sp of half-motif, ch 5, sc in center ring of half-motif, ch 5, sc in last sp of half-motif, ch 5, tr in side of next scallop just after joined picot, repeat from ** twice, (ch 5, sc in next free picot of corner motif) 3 times, ch 5, tr in next (4th) free picot, ch 5, yo hook 4 times, pull up a lp in 4th picot, (yo and through 2 lps) twice, yo hook twice, pull up a lp in 5th picot, (yo and through 2 lps) 6 times, ch 5, tr in center of long st just made (to complete cross-stitch), repeat from * around, end tr in 4th picot of corner motif, ch 5, sl st in 4th ch of ch 9 at beg of rnd.

Rnd 2: Sl st in corner ch-5 sp, ch 3, 2 dc in same sp, ch 2, 3 dc in same sp, * ch 1, 3 dc in 3rd ch of next lp, ** ch 1, 3 dc in next tr, (ch 1, 3 dc in 3rd ch of next lp) twice, ch 1, 3 dc in next sc, (ch 1, 3 dc in 3rd ch of next lp) twice, ch 1, 3 dc in next tr, (ch 1, 3 dc in 3rd ch of next lp) 4 times, repeat from ** twice, ch 1, 3 dc in next tr, (ch 1, 3 dc in 3rd ch of next lp) twice, ch 1, 3 dc in next sc, (ch 1, 3 dc in 3rd ch of next lp) twice, ch 1, 3 dc in next tr, ch 1, 3 dc in 3rd ch of next lp, ch 1; in corner ch-5 sp work 3 dc, ch 2, 3 dc, repeat from * around, end ch 1, sl st in top of ch 3 at beg of rnd.

Rnd 3: Sl st across next 2 dc, sl st in corner ch-2 sp; ch 3, 2 dc, ch 2, 3 dc in corner sp, * ch 1, dc in next ch-1 sp, ch 1, dc in center dc of next 3 dc group, repeat from * across side, ending dc in ch-1 sp before corner, ch 1, 3 dc, ch 2, 3 dc in corner sp, repeat from first * around, end sl st in top of ch 3 at bet of rnd.

Rnd 4: Sl st across next 2 dc, sl st in corner ch-2 sp; ch 3, 2 dc, ch 2, 3 dc in corner sp, * ch 1, dc in next ch-1 sp, repeat from * to next corner, ch 1, 3 dc, ch 2, 3 dc in corner sp, repeat from first * around, end sl st in top of ch 3 at beg of rnd.

Rnd 5: Repeat rnd 4.

Rnd 6: Sl st across next 2 dc, sl st in corner ch-2 sp; ch 3, 2 dc, ch 2, 3 dc in corner sp, * ch 4; holding back on hook last lp of each dc, dc in each of next 2 sps, yo hook and through 3 lps on hook, repeat from * to next corner, ch 4, 3 dc, ch 2, 3 dc in corner sp, repeat from first * around, end sl st in top of ch 3 at beg of rnd.

Rnd 7: Sl st across next 2 dc, sl st in corner ch-2 sp; ch 6, dc in 4th ch from hook, 3 dc next to dc just made over remaining 2 ch, dc in corner sp, ch 3, 4 dc over bar of dc just made, * dc in next sp, ch 3, 4 dc over bar of dc just made, repeat from * across to corner, (dc in corner sp, ch 3, 4 dc over bar of dc just made) 3 times, repeat from first * around, end dc in corner sp, ch 3, 4 dc over bar of dc just made, sl st in same ch with first dc of rnd.

Rnd 8: Sl st up along 3 ch to top of first pat, ch 3, 2 dc in next dc, ch 2, 3 dc in next dc, * ch 5, sc in first dc of next pat, repeat from * to corner, ch 5, 3 dc in first dc of center pat at corner, ch 2, 3 dc in next dc, repeat from first * around, end ch 5, sl st in top of ch 3 at beg of rnd.

Rnd 9: Sl st across next 2 dc, sl st in corner ch-2 sp; ch 3, 2 dc, ch 2, 3 dc in corner sp, * ch 5, sc in next lp, repeat from * to corner, ch 5, 3 dc, ch 2, 3 dc in corner sp, repeat from first * around, end ch 5, sl st in top of ch 3.

Rnd 10: Sl st across next 2 dc, sl st in corner ch-2 sp; ch 3, 2 dc, ch 2, 3 dc in corner sp, * (ch 5, sc in next lp) 6 times, ** 4 dc, ch 2, 4 dc in next lp, sc in next lp, (ch 5, sc in next lp) 7 times, repeat from ** 3 times, 4 dc, ch 2, 4 dc in next lp, sc in next lp, (ch 5, sc in next lp) 5 times, ch 5, 3 dc, ch 2, 3 dc in corner sp, repeat from * around, end ch 5, sl st in top of ch 3.

Rnd 11: Sl st across next 2 dc, sl st in corner ch-2 sp; ch 3, dc in corner sp, ch 3, sc in corner sp, ch 3, dc in corner sp, ch 3, sc in corner sp, ch 3; holding back on hook last lp of each dc, 2 dc in corner sp, yo and through 3 lps on hook (2-dc cluster), * (ch 5, sc in next lp) 6 times, ** ch 5; in ch-2 sp make 2-dc cluster, ch 3, sc, ch 3, dc, ch 3, sc, ch 3, 2-dc cluster, (ch 5, sc in next lp) 7 times, repeat from ** 3 times, ch 5; in ch-2 sp make 2-dc cluster, ch 3, sc, ch 3, dc, ch 3, sc, ch 3, 2-dc cluster, (ch 5, sc in next lp) 6 times, ch 5; in corner sp make 2-dc cluster, ch 3, sc, ch 3, dc, ch 3, sc, ch 3, 2-dc cluster, repeat from * around, end ch 5, sl st in top of ch 3.

Rnd 12: Sl st to top of ch-3 after sc in corner sp, ch 5, dc in ch-3 lp after dc, * (ch 5, sc in next ch-5 lp) 7 times, ** ch 5, sc in center dc of next pat, (ch 5, sc in next ch-5 lp) 8 times, repeat from ** 3 times, ch 5, sc in center dc of next pat, (ch 5, sc in next ch-5 lp) 7 times, ch 5, dc in ch-3 lp before center dc of corner pat, ch 2, dc in ch-3 lp after center dc, repeat from * around, end ch 5, sl st in 3rd ch of ch 5 at beg of rnd.

Rnd 13: Beg with sl st in corner ch-2 sp, repeat rnd 7.

Rnd 14: Sl st up along 3 ch to top of first pat, ch 3, 2 dc in next dc, ch 2, 3 dc in next dc, * ch 1, dc in first dc of next pat, ch 1, dc in next dc of same pat, repeat from * across side, ch 1, 3 dc in first dc of center pat at corner, ch 2, 3 dc in next dc, repeat from first * around, end ch 1, sl st in top of ch 3.

Rnds 15-18: Repeat rnd 4.

Rnd 19: Repeat rnd 6.

Edging: Corner Scallop: Row 1: (Ch 4, dc in corner sp) twice, ch 4, sc in last dc of corner pat, turn.

Row 2: * Ch 2, yo hook 3 times, draw up a lp in center lp at corner, yo and through 2 lps, yo hook, draw up a lp in same corner lp, yo and through 2 lps, yo and through 3 lps, (yo and through 2 lps) twice, ch 2, dc in center of long st just made (to complete cross-st), repeat from * 3 times, ch 2, sc in next ch-4 lp at corner, ch 3, sc in next lp, turn.

Row 3: (3 dc in next sp, dc in next st) 8 times, 3 dc in next sp, sc in next sp on border, ch 3, sc in next sp on border, turn.

Row 4: Ch 3, 4 dc in last ch-3 sp made, (sk 2 dc on row 3, dc in next dc, ch 3, 4 dc over bar of last dc) 10 times, sc in same lp on border as last sc of row 2, ch 3, sc in next sp on border, turn.

Row 5: (Ch 3, sc under ch 3 of next pat) 11 times, ch 3, sc in same sp on border as sc at end of row 3.

Next Scallop: Row 1: (Ch 5, sc in next lp on border) 6 times, ch 3, sc in next lp, turn.

Row 2: Ch 2, yo hook 3 times, draw up a lp in next ch-5 lp, * yo and through 2 lps, yo hook, draw up a lp in same ch-5 lp, yo and through 2 lps, yo and through 3 lps, (yo and through 2 lps) twice, ch 2, dc in center of long st just made (to complete cross-st), ch 2, yo hook 3 times, draw up a lp in same ch-5 lp, repeat from * until 3 cross-sts are completed, ch 2, sc in next lp, ch 3, sc in next lp; turn.

Row 3: (3 dc in next sp, dc in next st) 6 times, 3 dc in next sp, sc in next sp on border, ch 3, sc in next sp on border, turn.

Row 4: Ch 3, 4 dc in last ch-3 sp made, (sk 2 dc on row 3, dc in next dc, ch 3, 4 dc over bar of last dc) 8 times, sc in same lp on border as last sc of row 2, ch 3, sc in next lp on border, turn.

Row 5: (Ch 3, sc under ch 3 of next pat) 9 times, ch 3, sc in same lp on border as sc at end of row 3.

Repeat Next Scallop 5 times across side (6 scallops on side). Ch 5, sc in next lp on border to lp before corner. Repeat from Corner Scallop around. After last side scallop of last side has been made, (ch 5, sc in next lp) twice. This should bring you to lp before corner scallop.

Rnd 6: Working in corner scallop, (4 dc in next sp, dc in sc) 11 times, 4 dc in next sp, sc in next lp between scallops, ch 5, sc in next lp; * working in side scallop, (4 dc in next sp, dc in sc) 9 times, 4 dc in next sp, sc in next lp between scallops, ch 5, sc in next lp; repeat from * across side, repeat from beg of rnd, end in lp before first corner scallop.

Rnd 7: * Ch 3, sk 3 dc, dc in next dc, ch 4, sc in top of last dc made (picot), (dc in same dc, ch-4 picot) twice, ch 2, sk 3 dc, sc in next dc, repeat from * around scallop, end ch 2, sc in next ch-5 lp, repeat from first * around. End off.

FINISHING: Block crocheted piece, starching lightly, if desired. Sew to covered pillow inside scalloped edge.

Cupid Panel

An appealing cupid makes a delightful motif for a framed filet panel, but it would be equally effective as a coverlet or a curtain.

SIZE: About 45″ x 55″ (double strand of cotton). About 38″ x 46″ (single strand of cotton or baby yarn).

MATERIALS: For panel 45″ x 55″: Mercerized knitting and crochet cotton, 21 250-yard balls white or ecru; steel crochet hook No. 1. **For panel 38″ x 46″**: Mercerized knitting and crochet cotton, 10 250-yard balls; steel crochet hook No. 6. **For baby coverlet 38″ x 46″**: 12 1-oz. balls baby yarn; steel crochet hook No. 3.

GAUGE: 5 sps or bls (spaces or blocks) = 2″; 5 rows = 2″ (double strand of cotton). 3 sps or bls (spaces or blocks) = 1″; 3 rows = 1″ (single strand of cotton or baby yarn).

PANEL: Center: Base Row: With double strand of cotton, or single strand of cotton or baby

yarn, ch 3. Dc in 3rd ch from hook; * ch 3, dc in sp formed by last ch 3 and dc, repeat from * until there are 79 sps. Ch 5.

Row 1: Working over the dc's of last row, dc in first sp, * ch 2, dc in next sp, repeat from * across, end ch 2, sk last sp, dc in end ch—79 sps. Ch 5, turn. Mark 40th sp for center.

Row 2: Dc in next dc (1 sp), * 2 dc in next sp, dc in next dc, repeat from * across to last sp (77 bls), ch 2, dc in 3rd ch of ch 5 (1 sp). Ch 5, turn.

Row 3: Dc in next dc (1 sp), dc in each of next 27 dc (9 bls), (ch 2, sk 2 dc, dc in next dc) 59 times, dc in each of next 27 dc (9 bls), ch 2, dc in 3rd ch of ch 5 (1 sp). Ch 5, turn. Working from center section of chart, beg with row 4, work to top of chart. Each open square on chart is 1 sp; each X square is 1 bl. Read chart from right to left on odd rows, from left to right on even rows.

When top of chart is reached, ch 3, turn; sk first sp, * sc in next sp, ch 3, repeat from * across top of panel, end ch 3, sc in corner sp, (ch 3, sc in same sp) twice.

Side: Row 1: Working down side of panel, * ch 3, sc in next sp, repeat from * to row 2, ch 3, sk row 1, sc in starting ch st, ch 3, dc in same ch, ch 3, turn.

Row 2: Dc in first ch-3 lp, * ch 2, dc in next lp, repeat from * to top, end dc in first corner lp, dc in next sc (center sc of 3 sc at corner). Ch 3, turn.

Row 3: Dc in next dc, * ch 2, dc in next dc, repeat from * across, end ch 2, dc in last dc, dc in last lp. Ch 3, turn.

Rows 4 and 5: Repeat row 3. At end of row 5, ch 3, turn.

Row 6: Sc in next ch-2 sp, * ch 3, sc in next sp, repeat from * across, end ch 3, sc in last dc. End off.

Join yarn with sc in corner sp at opposite side of panel, * ch 3, sc in next sp, repeat from * to lower edge, end ch 3, dc in sp of base row. Ch 3, turn.

Next Row: Dc in first ch-3 lp, * ch 2, dc in next lp, repeat from * to top, end dc in corner lp, dc in corner sc. Ch 3, turn.

Beg with row 3, work 2nd side same as first side. Do not end off at end of row 6.

Border: Row 1: Ch 5, dc in same dc with sc (corner lp made), * ch 2, dc in next sp, repeat from * to next corner, ch 2, dc in corner st, ch 2, dc in same corner st (corner lp made), repeat from first * around, end ch 2, sl st in 3rd ch of ch 5. Sl st to center of corner sp, ch 5, turn.

Row 2: Dc in corner sp, ch 2, dc in next dc; working from border chart, beg with row 2 (row 1 of sps has already been worked), complete 11 rows of border, working dc, ch 2, dc in each corner sp. Join each row as for row 1 of border.

FINISHING: Panel can be framed with colored background behind it, or it can be stretched on an open frame and laced to the frame. Rings can be sewed to the top and panel can be hung as a curtain. If baby's coverlet is made of yarn, line it with colored fabric.

Tea Cloth

Dainty lace crochet, combined with fabric, creates a charming tea cloth that can be made larger simply by increasing the number of square motifs.

SIZE: 41″ Square.

MATERIALS: Daisy Mercerized Crochet, Art. 65, size 30, 8 skeins white. Steel crochet hook No. 13. White sewing thread. ⅞ yard colored linen.

GAUGE: Block = 5½″ square.

Note: Work tightly for best results.

CENTER MOTIF: Beg at center, ch 8, join with sl st to form ring.

Rnd 1: Ch 1, 12 sc in ring. Join with sl st in first sc.

Rnd 2: Ch 8, tr in same sc as sl st, * ch 10, sk 2 sc, (tr, ch 3, tr) in next sc, repeat from * twice, ch 5, join with tr in 5th ch of ch 8—4 ch-3 sps and 4 ch—10 lps.

Rnd 3: * 3 tr in next ch-3 sp, ch 4, sl st in last tr (p made); in ch-3 sp last worked in make (4 tr, p) twice and 3 tr, sc in next ch-10 lp, repeat from * twice, join with sl st in first tr of rnd—4 petals.

Rnd 4: * Ch 7, (tr, ch 5, dtr) in 3rd tr after next p, ch 7, (dtr, ch 5, tr) in 2nd tr after next p, ch 7, sc in sc between petals, repeat from * 3 times, end rnd with sl st.

Rnd 5: Ch 3; holding back on hook last lp of each dc, make 2 dc in next sp, yo and draw tightly through 3 lps on hook (½-cl made), * 4 dc in balance of sp, dc in next tr, 5 dc in next sp, dc in next dtr, 3 dc in next sp, (2 dc, p, 2 dc) in center ch of same sp (corner), 3 dc in balance of same sp, dc in next dtr, 5 dc in next sp, dc in next tr, 4 dc in next sp; holding back on hook last lp of each dc, make tight cl of (2 dc in same sp, dc in sc between petals and 2 dc in next sp, yo and draw tightly through 6 lps on hook), repeat from * 3 times, ending last repeat with first 2 dc of cl, insert hook in first ½-cl of rnd, yo and draw tightly through cl and 3 lps on hook. End off.

BLOCK: Border: Beg with inner 4 sides of block, (ch 6, dc in 6th ch from hook) 48 times. Join with sl st in starting st of border, forming a ring with ch-lps on inside edge and straight dc-sps on outside edge of border.

First Corner Section: Ch 3, 2 dc in same place as sl st, ** (3 dc in next dc-sp, dc in st between dc-sps) 6 times, 2 dc in next dc-sp, ch 7, turn. Sk 4 dc, sl st in next dc, ch 1, turn. 9 sc in lp just made, sl st in top side of last dc, dc in balance of sp on border, dc between dc-sps 3 dc in next dc-sp, dc between dc-sps, 2 dc in next dc-sp; ch 5, turn. Tr in 2nd sc over lp, ch 5, sk 2 sc, (3 tr, ch 5, 3 tr) in next (center) sc, ch 5, sk 2 sc, tr in next sc, ch 5, sk 7 dc over border, sl st in next dc, ch 1, turn, (3 sc, p, 3 sc) in first sp, sc in next tr, (3 sc, p, 3 sc) in next sp, sc in each of 3 tr, 5 sc in next sp, sc in each of 3 tr, (3 sc, p, 3 sc) in next sp, sc in next tr, (3 sc, p, 3 sc) in end sp, sl st in top side of last dc, dc in balance of dc-sp on border, dc between dc-sps, 3 dc in next dc-sp, dc between dc-sps, 2 dc in next dc-sp, ch 5, turn. Sk 7 dc, dtr in next dc, (ch 5, tr in sc over next tr) twice, ch 5, (3 tr, ch 5, 3 tr) in center sc over next sp between 3-tr groups (center sp), ch 5, sk 4 sc, tr in next sc, ch 5, tr in sc over next tr, ch 5, dtr in same dc at base of last row, ch 5, sk 7 dc on border, sl st in next dc, ch 1, turn. (3 sc, p, 3 sc) in each of next 4 sps, sc in each of next 3 tr, 5 sc in next sp (center sp), sc in each of next 3 tr, (3 sc, p, 3 sc) in each of last 4 sps, sl st in top side of last dc on border, dc in balance of dc-sp, dc in st between dc-sps, 3 dc in next dc-sp, 3 dc in st between dc-sps (first half-corner made), ch 5, turn. Sk 7 dc, tr in next dc, (ch 5, dc in center sc between next 2 p) 3 times, ch 5, tr in sc over next tr, ch 5, (3 dtr, ch 7, 3 dtr) in center sc over next sp, ch 5, sk 4 sc, tr in next sc, (ch 5, dc in center sc between next 2 p) 3 times, ch 5, tr in same dc at base of last row, ch 5, sk 7 dc over border, sl st in top of ch 3, ch 1, turn. (3 sc, p, 3 sc in next sp, sc in next st) 6 times, sc in each of 3 dtr, in next sp (center sp) make (sc, a ch-4 p, 4 sc, a ch-7 p, 4 sc, a ch-4 p, sc), sc in each of 3 dtr, (3 sc, p, 3 sc in next sp, sc in next st) 6 times, sl st in top side of last dc of corner 3-dc group made over border, make 3 more dc at base of same corner 3-dc group (2nd half-corner made) **. Make 3 more corner sections, working from first ** to 2nd **, omitting 2nd half-corner at end of last repeat, join with sl st to top of ch 3 at beg of first section. End off.

Stretch the 4 inner sides of dc border of block to form a true square. Cut a square of linen 1/16″ larger all around than outside edge of dc border that forms inner square of block. Pin or baste dc borders around edge of linen. Hem down inner edge of dc border and tack down center of each ch-5 lp. Working on back of work, turn edge of linen under against back of dc border and hem down.

Stretch and pin center motif right side down on ironing board. Steam through a doubled wet cloth, then press motif dry through a doubled dry cloth. Pin motif in center of linen and hem down around outside edge. On back of work, cut out linen ¼″ inside stitching; turn this ¼″ edge under against dc border and hem down.

Make 49 blocks. Join blocks 7 x 7 as follows:

Joining-Edge First Block: Join thread with sc in 3rd sc to right of a corner p on first bl (block), * (4 dc, ch 7, 4 dc) in corner p, sk 2 sc, sc in next sc, (ch 10, sc midway between next 2 p) 13 times, ch 10, sc in 2nd sc to left of next p, repeat from * around, joining final ch-10 with sl st to first sc. End off.

Joining-Edge 2nd Block: Join thread with sc in 3rd sc to right of a corner p on 2nd bl, 4 dc in corner p, ch 3, join with sl st in 1 lp of center st of a corner ch-7 lp on first bl, ch 3, 4 dc back in same corner p on 2nd bl, sk 2 sc, sc in next sc, (ch 5, join with sl st under next ch 10 of first bl, ch 5, sc back midway between next 2 p on 2nd bl) 13 times, ch 5, sl st in next ch-10 lp on first bl, ch 5, sc back in

2nd sc to left of next p on 2nd bl, 4 dc in next corner p, ch 3, join with sl st in 1 lp of center ch of next corner lp on first bl, ch 3, 4 dc back in same p on 2nd bl, sk 2 sc, sc in next sc. Complete edge as for first bl. Forming square, join 3rd bl to 2nd bl, then join a 4th bl to first and 3rd bls in same way. **Note:** Where 4 corners meet, always join to same st where first 2 corners were joined. Continue in this way until all bls are joined.

EDGE: Rnd 1: Join thread with sc in right-hand end of ch-7 lp at one corner of cloth, ** ch 13, sc in left end of same lp, (ch 10, sc in next ch-10 lp) 14 times, * ch 10, sk 4 dc, sc in right end of next joined corner sp, ch 10, sc in left end of next joined corner sp, (ch 10, sc in next ch-10) 14 times *, repeat from first * to 2nd * across side, ch 10, sc in right end of corner ch-7 lp, repeat from ** around. Omit last ch-10 lp, make ch 5 and join with tr in first sc of rnd.

Rnd 2: ** Ch 4, 3 dtr in 5th ch of corner ch-13 lp, (ch 5, sk next ch of same lp, 3 dtr in next ch) twice, ch 4, sc in next ch-10 lp, * (ch 4, 3 dtr in 5th ch of next ch-10 lp, ch 5, 3 dtr in next ch of same lp, ch 4, sc in next lp) *, repeat from first * to 2nd * across side, repeat from ** around, end with sl st instead of sc.

Rnd 3: Sl st in each of 4 sts of next ch, sl st in next 3 dtr, sl st in next sp, ch 7, (2 dtr, ch 5, 3 dtr) in same sp, ** ch 5, sk next dtr, 3 dtr in next dtr, (ch 5, 3 dtr) twice in next sp, * in center sp of next shell make (3 dtr, ch 5, 3 dtr, ch 5, 3 dtr) *, repeat from first * to 2nd * across side, sk first 3 dtr at corner, (3 dtr, ch 5, 3 dtr) in next sp, repeat from ** to end of rnd, end rnd at 2nd *, join with sl st in top of ch 7 at beg of rnd.

Rnd 4: Sc in each of next 2 dtr, 5 sc in next sp, * sc in each of next 2 dtr, make ch-4 p, sc in next dtr, 2 sc in next sp, ch 10 lp, turn, sk p, sl st in 2nd sc over next sp, ch 1, turn, (6 sc, p, 6 sc, 1 sl st) in ch-10 lp just made, ch 1, 3 sc in balance of ch-5 sp, repeat from * twice, sc in each of next 2 dtr, sk 2 dtr, (1 each side of angle), ** sc in each of next 2 dtr, 5 sc in next sp, sc in each next 2 dtr, make p, sc in next dtr, 2 sc in next sp, ch 10 lp, turn, sk p, sl st in 2nd sc over next sp, ch 1, turn, (6 sc, p, 6 sc, sl st) in ch-10 lp just made, ch 1, 3 sc in balance of ch-5 sp, sc in each of next 2 dtr, sk next 2 dtr (1 each side of angle), repeat from ** across side, repeat from beg of rnd, join with sl st in first sc. End off edge.

Placing a rustproof pin in each scallop around edge, pin tea cloth right side down on a large padded board, stretching cloth several inches each way so that it will measure 41″ x 41″.

Steam through a wet cloth, then press dry through a doubled dry cloth. Do not remove pins until cloth is completely dry.

Mimosa Doily

Here is a doily of gossamer lace to challenge the experienced knitter!

SIZE: 16″ in diameter.

MATERIALS: Mercerized crochet cotton, size 70, about 375 yards. Set of double-pointed needles No. 2. Steel crochet hook No. 14.

DOILY: Cast on 8 sts. Divide sts among 3 needles. Join and k around.

Note: On rnds 1, 51, 53, 55, 57, 59, and 61, repeats start and end with yo. On these rnds, there will be 2 yo's together. Be sure to make both yo's between repeats.

Rnd 1: * Yo, k into back of next st, yo. Repeat from * 7 more times.

Rnd 2: * K 2, p 1. Repeat from * 7 more times.

Rnd 3: * K 1, yo, k into back of next st, yo, k 1. Repeat from * 7 more times.

Rnd 4 and All Even Rnds: K around.

Rnd 5: * K 2, yo, k into back of next st, yo, k 2. Repeat from * 7 more times.

Rnd 7: * K 3, yo, k into back of next st, yo, k 3. Repeat from * 7 more times.

Rnd 9: * K 4, yo, k into back of next st, yo, k 4. Repeat from * 7 more times.

Rnd 11: * K 5, yo, K into back of next st, yo, k 5. Repeat from * 7 more times.

Rnd 13: * Sl 1, k 1, psso, k 3, yo, k 1, yo, k into back of next st, yo, k 1, yo, k 3, k 2 tog. Repeat from * 7 more times.

Rnd 15: * Sl 1, k 1, psso, k 3, yo, k 2, yo, k into back of next st, yo, k 2, yo, k 3, k 2 tog, yo. Repeat from * 7 more times.

Rnd. 17: * Sl 1, k 1, psso, k 3, yo, k 7, yo, k 3, k 2 tog, yo, k into back of next st, yo. Repeat from * 7 more times.

Rnd 19: *Sl 1, k 1, psso, k 3, yo, sl 1, k 1, psso, k 3, k 2 tog, yo, k 3, k 2 tog, k 1, yo, k into back of next st, yo, k 1. Repeat from * 7 more times.

Rnd 21: * Sl 1, k 1, psso, k 3, yo, sl 1, k 1, psso, k 1, k 2 tog, yo, k 3, k 2 tog, k 2, yo, k into back of next st, yo, k 2. Repeat from * 7 more times.

Rnd 23: * Sl 1, k 1, psso, k 3, yo, sl 1, k 2 tog, psso, yo, k 3, k 2 tog, k 3, yo, k into back of next st, yo, k 3. Repeat from * 7 more times.

Rnd 25: * Sl 1, k 1, psso, k 7, k 2 tog, k 4, yo, k into back of next st, yo, k 4. Repeat from * 7 more times.

Rnd 27: * Sl 1, k 1, psso, k 5, k 2 tog, k 4, yo, k 1, yo, k into back of next st, yo, k 1, yo, k 4. Repeat from * 7 more times.

Rnd 29: * Sl 1, k 1, psso, k 3, k 2 tog, k 5, yo, k 2, yo, k into back of next st, yo, k 2, yo, k 5. Repeat from * 7 more times.

Rnd 31: * Sl 1, k 1, psso, k 1, k 2 tog, k 6, yo, k 3, yo, k into back of next st, yo, k 3, yo, k 6. Repeat from * 7 more times.

Rnd 33: * Yo, sl 1, k 2 tog, psso, yo, sl 1, k 1, psso, k 5, yo, k 4, yo, k into back of next st, yo, k 4, yo, k 5, k 2 tog. Repeat from * 7 more times.

Rnd 35: * Yo, k 3, yo, sl 1, k 1, psso, (k 5, yo) twice; k into back of next st, (yo, k 5) twice; k 2 tog. Repeat from * 7 more times.

Rnd 37: * Yo, k 2 tog, yo, k 1, (yo, sl 1, k 1, psso) twice, k 5, yo, sl 1, k 1, psso, k 9, k 2 tog, yo, k 5, k 2 tog. Repeat from * 7 more times.

Rnd 39: * Yo, k 2 tog, yo, k 3, (yo, sl 1, k 1, psso) twice; k 5, yo, sl 1, k 1, psso, k 7, k 2 tog, yo, k 5, k 2 tog. Repeat from * 7 more times.

Rnd 41: * Yo, k 2 tog, yo, k 5, (yo, sl 1, k 1, psso) twice; k 5, yo, sl 1, k 1, psso, k 5, k 2 tog, yo, k 5, k 2 tog. Repeat from * 7 more times.

Rnd 43: * Yo, k 2 tog, yo, k 7, (yo, sl 1, k 1, psso) twice; k 5, yo, sl 1, k 1, psso, k 3, k 2 tog, yo, k 5, k 2 tog. Repeat from * 7 more times.

Rnd 45: * Yo, k 2, yo, k 9, yo, k 2, yo, sl 1, k 1, psso, k 5, yo, sl 1, k 1, psso, k 1, k 2 tog, yo, k 5, k 2 tog. Repeat from * 7 more times.

Rnd 47: * Yo, k 3, yo, k 11, yo, k 3, yo, sl 1, k 1, psso, k 5, yo, sl 1, k 2 tog, psso, yo, k 5, k 2 tog. Repeat from * 7 more times.

Rnd 49: * Yo, k 4, yo, k 13, yo, k 4, yo, sl 1, k 1, psso, k 11, k 2 tog. Repeat from * 7 more times.

Rnd 51: * Yo, k 5, (yo, k 2 tog, yo) 3 times; (yo, k into back of next st, yo) 3 times; (yo, sl 1, k 1, psso, yo) 3 times; k 5, yo, sl 1, k 1, psso, k 9, k 2 tog. Repeat from * 7 more times.

Rnd 52: * K 8, (p 1, k 2) 7 times; p 1, k 20. Repeat from * 7 more times.

Rnd 53: * Yo, k 6, (yo, sl 1, k 2 tog, psso, yo) 9 times; k 6, yo, sl 1, k 1, psso, k 7, k 2 tog. Repeat from * 7 more times.

Rnd 54: * K 9, (p 1, k 2) 7 times; p 1, k 19. Repeat from * 7 more times.

Rnd 55: * Yo, k 7, (yo, sl 1, k 2 tog, psso, yo) 9 times; k 7, yo, sl 1, k 1, psso, k 5, k 2 tog. Repeat from * 7 more times.

Rnd 56: * K 10, (p 1, k 2) 7 times; p 1, k 18. Repeat from * 7 more times.

Rnd 57: * Yo, k 8, (yo, sl 1, k 2 tog, psso, yo) 9 times; k 8, yo, sl 1, k 1, psso, k 3, k 2 tog. Repeat from * 7 more times.

Rnd 58: * K 11, (p 1, k 2) 7 times; p 1, k 17. Repeat from * 7 more times.

Rnd 59: * Yo, k 9, (yo, sl 1, k 2 tog, psso, yo) 9 times; k 9, yo, sl 1, k 1, psso, k 1, k 2 tog. Repeat from * 7 more times.

Rnd 60: * K 12, (p 1, k 2) 7 times; p 1, k 16. Repeat from * 7 more times.

Rnd 61: * Yo, k 10, (yo, sl 1, k 2 tog, psso, yo) 9 times; k 10, yo, sl 1, k 2 tog, psso. Repeat from * 7 more times.

Rnd 62: * K 13, (p 1, k 2) 7 times; p 1, k 15. Repeat from * 7 more times.

Next Rnd: K 1. With crochet hook * ch 4, yo, insert hook into next 4 sts and complete as a dc, (ch 8, yo, insert hook into next 3 sts and complete as a dc) twice; (ch 12, yo, insert hook into next 3 sts and complete as a dc) 10 times; ch 8, yo, insert hook into next 3 sts and complete as a dc, ch 8, yo, insert hook into next 4 sts and complete as a dc, ch 4, yo, insert hook into next 3 sts and complete as a dc. Repeat from * 7 more times, sl st into next st. Break off. Soak and wash the finished work in warm lather of soap flakes. Rinse thoroughly and starch lightly. Stretch and pin out to dry.

Three Kings Lace Assemblage

The Three Kings are depicted here in an imaginative arrangement of old laces sewed to a black fabric background. Six kinds of lace were used to make this fanciful assemblage. As shown, a 100-year-old knitted doily of ultra-fine thread makes the star of Bethlehem. In the directions, we substitute a doily of same size knit of heavier cotton. The kings' robes are Irish-crochet edging, lace-trimmed net, a filet crochet camisole top. Embroidered lace motifs and a narrow filet edging form the heads, crowned with gold cord and rick-rack.

SIZE: 16¼″ x 19¾″.

MATERIALS: White lace doily, 12″–14″ in diameter. Old white laces and crocheted edgings. Two 3″ white embroidered lace motifs. Wide gold rickrack, 6″. Narrow gold cord, 10″. Metallic gold sewing thread. White sewing thread. Fine black linen or cotton fabric, ⅝ yard. Thick cardboard, 16″ x 19½″. Two yards gold cord trimming. Black sewing thread. All-purpose glue.

PICTURE: Cut black fabric piece, 18″ x 22″. Mark area, 16″ x 19½″, for picture. Place doily on fabric, covering top right section as shown. (Directions for knitted doily shown are given, page 256.) Sew doily in place around edge with white sewing thread. With gold sewing thread, take long stitches from center of doily to edge at each scallop or point formed by pattern repeat. Take a shorter stitch between long "rays." Arrange laces for robes of three kings and sew in place. In picture illustratd, a filet crochet camisole top was used for king at right. About one yard of lace 2½″-2¾″ wide is required. (Directions for making filet crochet lace shown are given, page 256.) Head is an embroidered lace motif. Crown is made of gold rickrack and narrow gold cord.

King at left has robe of Irish-crochet shamrock edging. (Directions for edging are given, page 254.) Use about 23″ of edging, fold and arrange as shown in illustration, sew in place along straight edge. Fill in "robes" with white catch-stitches. Head is an embroidered motif. Crown is narrow gold cord, folded into four loops. Two separate shamrocks, cut from edging, are sewn on each side of neck for collar.

Center figure is made of lace-trimmed net. Two pieces of narrow filet crochet edging were used for head. (Directions for making edging shown are given below. Gather straight edge of 7″ piece, sew gathered edge to background to simulate head; hide ends under net at neck edge. Sew another 7″ piece behind first piece, hiding ends under first piece at sides. Sew on gold rickrack for crown.

FINISHING: Stretch piece over cardboard, insert pins into cardboard around edge to hold in place. Line back of picture with fabric. Remove pins. Glue gold cord trimming around edge.

SHAMROCK EDGING

SIZE: ¾″ wide.

MATERIALS: Tatting or crochet cotton, size 70. Steel crochet hook No. 13.

EDGING: Beg at narrow end, ch 6.

Row 1: 2 dc in 6th ch from hook, ch 2, 2 dc in same ch. Ch 2, turn.

Row 2: 2 dc in ch-2 sp, ch 2, 2 dc in same sp, dc under ch-6 turning sp. Ch 2, turn.

Row 3: 2 dc in ch-2 sp, ch 2, 2 dc in same sp, ch 8, tr in 3rd ch from hook, (ch 3, tr in 3rd ch from hook) twice, sl st in base of first tr to form ring. Ch 1, turn. Working around ring over tr, make 1 sc, 1 hdc, 3 dc over first tr; remove hook; insert hook under ch-2 turning ch at edge 1 row below, pull dropped lp through; work 3 dc, 1 hdc, 1 sc over same tr (1 leaf completed). (Working over next tr, make 1 sc, 1 hdc, 6 dc, 1 hdc, 1 sc) twice (shamrock completed), 6 sc over ch 5 (stem), ch 1. Do not turn.

Row 4: 2 dc, ch 2, 2 dc in ch-2 sp, dc under turning ch. Ch 2, turn.

Row 5: 2 dc, ch 2, 2 dc in ch-2 sp. Ch 2, turn.

Row 6: 2 dc, ch 2, 2 dc in ch-2 sp, dc under turning ch. Ch 2, turn.

Row 7: 2 dc, ch 2, 2 dc in ch-2 sp, ch 8, tr in 3rd ch from hook, (ch 3, tr in 3rd ch from hook) twice, sl st in base of first tr to form ring. Ch 1, turn. Working over tr around ring, make 1 sc, 1 hdc, 3 dc over first tr; remove hook; insert hook under ch 2 at edge 1 row below, pull dropped lp through; work 3 dc, 1 hdc, 1 sc over same tr. Work 1 sc, 1 hdc, 3 dc over next tr, join as before to center of last leaf of shamrock below, complete leaf, work 3rd leaf, 6 sc over ch 5, ch 1. Do not turn.

Repeat rows 4-7 for edging.

Steam-press edging lightly.

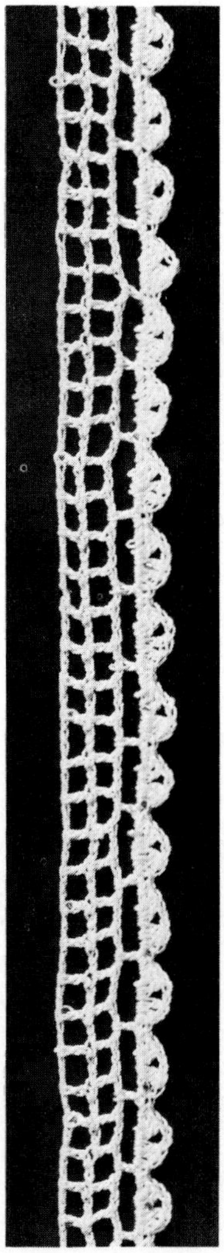

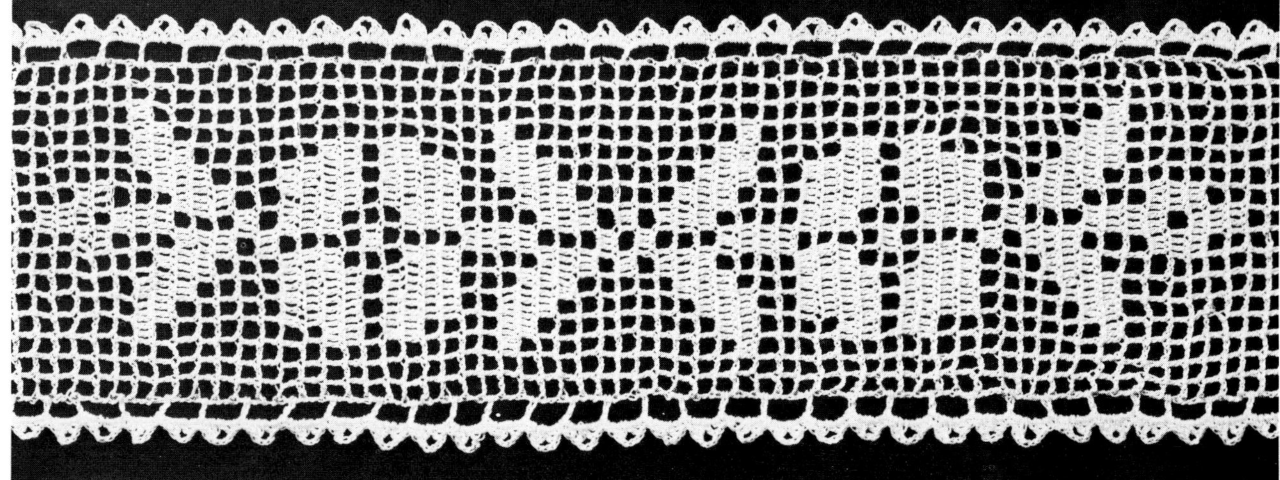

KNITTED DOILY

SIZE: 13″ in diameter.

MATERIALS: Mercerized knitting and crochet cotton, 1 250-yard ball. Set of dp needles No. 2. Steel crochet hook No. 7.

DOILY: Note: On rnds 31, 37, 43, 49, 55 and 59 there will be 2 yo's together. On next rnd, k first yo, p 2nd yo.

Beg at center, cast on 8 sts. Divide sts among 3 dp needles. Join; mark end of rnd.

Rnds 1 and 2: K around.

Rnd 3: * Yo, k 1, repeat from * around.

Rnd 4 and All Even Rnds: K around.

Rnd 5: * Yo, k 2, repeat from * around.

Rnd 7: * Yo, k 3, repeat from * around.

Rnd 9: * Yo, k 4, repeat from * around.

Rnd 11: * Yo, k 5, repeat from * around.

Rnd 13: * Yo, k 6, repeat from * around.

Rnd 15: * Yo, k 7, repeat from * around.

Rnd 17: * Yo, k 2 tog, k 6, repeat from * around.

Rnd 19: * Yo, k 1, yo, k 2 tog, k 5, repeat from * around.

Rnd 21: * Yo, k 2 tog, yo, k 1, yo, k 2 tog, k 4, repeat from * around.

Rnd 23: * (Yo, k 2 tog) twice, yo, k 1, yo, k 2 tog, k 3, repeat from * around.

Rnd 25: * (Yo, k 2 tog) 3 times, yo, k 1, yo, k 2 tog, k 2, repeat from * around.

Rnd 27: * (Yo, k 2 tog) 4 times, yo, k 1, yo, k 2 tog, k 1, repeat from * around.

Rnd 29: * (Yo, k 2 tog) 5 times, yo, k 1, yo, k 2 tog, (yo, k 2 tog) 5 times, yo, k 1, k 2 tog, repeat from * around.

Rnd 31: * Yo twice, k 3, sl 1, k 2 tog, psso, k 3, repeat from * around. See Note, above.

Rnd 33: * (Yo, k 2) twice, sl 1, k 2 tog, psso, k 2, repeat from * around.

Rnd 35: * Yo, k 4, yo, k 1, sl 1, k 2 tog, psso, k 1, repeat from * around.

Rnd 37: * Yo, k 3, yo twice, k 3, yo, sl 1, k 2 tog, psso, repeat from * around.

Rnd 39: * K 2, k 2 tog, yo, k 2, yo, k 2 tog, k 3, repeat from * around.

Rnd 41: * K 1, k 2 tog, yo, k 4, yo, k 2 tog, k 2, repeat from * around.

Rnd 43: * K 2 tog, yo, k 3, yo twice, k 3, yo, k 2 tog, k 1, repeat from * around.

Rnd 45: * Yo, k 2, k 2 tog, yo, k 2, yo, k 2 tog, k 2, yo, sl 1, k 2 tog, psso, repeat from * around.

Rnd 47: * K 2, k 2 tog, yo, k 4, yo, k 2 tog, k 3, repeat from * around.

Rnd 49: * K1, k 2 tog, yo, k 3, yo twice, k 3, yo, k 2 tog, k 2, repeat from * around.

Rnd 51: * K 2 tog, yo, k 2, k 2 tog, yo, k 2, yo, k 2 tog, k 2, yo, k 2 tog, k 1, repeat from * around.

Rnd 53: K 1: move marker to mark end of rnd, * yo, k 2, k 2 tog, yo, k 4, yo, k 2 tog, k 2, yo, sl 1, k 2 tog, psso, repeat from * around.

Rnd 55: * K 2, k 2 tog, yo, k 3, yo twice, k 3, yo, k 2 tog, k 3, repeat from * around.

Rnd. 57: * K 1, k 2 tog, yo, k 3, yo twice, k 4, yo twice, k 3, yo, k 2 tog, k 2, repeat from * around.

Rnd 59: * K 2 tog, yo, k 8, yo twice, k 8, yo, k 2 tog, k 1, repeat from * around.

Rnd 61: K 1; move marker to mark end of rnd, * yo, k 20, yo, sl 1, k 2 tog, psso, repeat from * around. Bind off; do not end off. Sl crochet hook in last st. With crochet hook, * ch 7, sk next st, sc in next st, repeat from * around. End off.

Soak and wash the finished work in warm lather of soap flakes. Rinse thoroughly and starch lightly. Stretch, pin out to dry.

NARROW FILET EDGING

SIZE: ⅝″ wide.

MATERIALS: Tatting or crochet cotton, size 70. Steel crochet hook No. 13.

EDGING: Make a ch a little longer than desired length of edging.

Row 1: Dc in 8th ch from hook (1 sp), * ch 2, sk 2 ch, dc in next ch, repeat from * across until piece is desired length. Ch 5, turn.

Row 2: Sk first dc, dc in next dc (1 sp), * ch 2, dc in next dc, repeat from * across to last sp, ch 2, sk 2 ch of turning ch, dc in next ch. Ch 1, turn.

Row 3: Sc in first sp, ch 8, sk next sp, dc in next sp, * ch 5, sk next sp, dc in next sp, repeat from * across. Ch 1, turn.

Row 4: In each sp across work 1 sc, 2 dc, ch 2, 2 dc, 1 sc. End off.

Steam-press edging lightly.

Shawls

Spider Web Crocheted Shawl

Wrap-up shawl in a lacy spider web pattern, at left, is worked from the bottom point of the design up to the wide top of the triangle. Fringe adds a romantic note.

SIZE: 56″ wide; 28″ deep at center back, plus fringe.

MATERIALS: About 1,200 yards of mercerized knitting and crochet cotton. Steel crochet hook No. 1.

GAUGE: 3 meshes (ch 2, dc) = 1″.

SHAWL: Beg at lower center back, ch 10; join with a sl st to form ring.

Row 1: Ch 5, dc in ring, (ch 2, dc in ring) 9 times. Ch 5, turn each row.

Row 2: (Dc, ch 2, dc) in first ch-2 sp,* (ch 2, dc in next ch-2 sp) 3 times, (ch 2, dc) twice in next ch-2 sp, repeat from * once—12 dc, plus turning ch.

Row 3: (Dc, ch 2, dc) in first ch-2 sp, ch 2, dc in next ch-2 sp, (ch 2, dc) twice in next ch-2 sp, ch 2, dc in next ch-2 sp, ch 2, 3 dc in next ch-2 sp, ch 3, dc in next ch-2 sp, ch 3, 3 dc in next ch-2 sp, ch 2, dc in next ch-2 sp, (ch 2, dc) twice in next ch-2 sp, ch 2, dc in next ch-2 sp, (ch 2, dc) twice in next ch-2 sp.

Row 4:* (Dc, ch 2, dc) in first ch-2 sp, (ch 2, dc in next ch-2 sp) 4 times, ch 2, 2 dc in next ch-2 sp, dc in dc* ch 3, sc in next ch-2 sp, sc in dc, sc in next ch-2 sp, ch 3, sk next 2 dc, # dc in next dc, 2 dc in ch-2 sp, (ch 2, dc in next ch-2 sp) 4 times, (ch 2, dc) twice in next ch-2 sp #.

Row 5: Work from first * to 2nd * on row 4, ch 3, sc in next ch-3 sp, sc in each of next 3 sc, sc in next ch-3 sp, ch 3, sk next 2 dc, work from first # to 2nd # on row 4.

Row 6: Work from first * to 2nd * on row 4, ch 2, sk next dc, dc in next dc, 2 dc in next sp, ch 3, sk next sc, sc in each of next 3 sc, ch 3, 2 dc in next sp, dc in next dc, ch 2, sk next dc, work from first # to 2nd # on row 4.

Row 7: Work from first * to 2nd * on row 4, ch 3, dc in next ch-2 sp, ch 3, sk next 2 dc, dc in next dc, 2 dc in next ch-3 sp, ch 3, sk next sc, dc in next sc, ch 3, 2 dc in next ch-3 sp, dc in next dc, ch 3, dc in next ch-2 sp, ch 2, sk next 2 dc, work from first # to 2nd # on row 4.

Row 8: Work from first * to 2nd * on row 4, ch 3, sc in next sp, sc in dc, sc in next sp, ch 3, sk next 2 dc, dc in next dc, 2 dc in next sp, ch 2, 2 dc in next sp, dc in first dc, ch 3, sc in next sp, sc in dc, sc in next sp, ch 3, sk next 2 dc, work from first # to 2nd # on row 4.

Row 9: Work from first * to 2nd * on row 4, ch 3, sc in next sp, sc in each of next 3 sc, sc in next sp, ch 3, sk next 2 dc, dc in next dc, dc in sp, dc in next dc, ch 3, sc in next sp, sc in each of next 3 sc, sc in next sp, ch 3, sk next 2 dc, work from first # to 2nd # on row 4.

Row 10: Work from first * to 2nd * on row 4, (ch 3, sk next dc, dc in next dc, 2 dc in sp, ch 3, sk next sc, sc in each of next 3 sc, ch 3, 2 dc in next sp, dc in first dc) twice, ch 2, sk next dc, work from first # to 2nd # on row 4.

Row 11: Work from first * to 2nd * on row 4, (ch

3, dc in next sp, ch 3, sk next 2 dc, dc in next dc, 2 dc in sp, ch 3, sk next sc, dc in next sc, ch 3, 2 dc in next sp, dc in next dc) twice, ch 3, dc in next sp, ch 3, sk next 2 dc, work from first # to 2nd # on row 4.

Row 12: Work from first * to 2nd * on row 4, (ch 3, sc in next sp, sc in next dc, sc in next sp, ch 3, sk next 2 dc, dc in next dc, 2 dc in next sp, ch 2, 2 dc in next sp, dc in next dc) twice, ch 3, sc in next sp, sc in next dc, sc in next sp, ch 3, sk next 2 dc, work from first # to 2nd # on row 4.

Row 13: Work from first * to 2nd * on row 4, (ch 3, sc in next sp, sc in each of next 3 sc, sc in next sp, ch 3, sk next 2 dc, dc in next dc, dc in next sp, dc in next dc) twice, ch 3, sc in next sp, sc in each of next 3 sc, sc in next sp, ch 3, sk next 2 dc, work from first # to 2nd # on row 4.

Row 14: Work from first * to 2nd * on row 4, (ch 2, sk next dc, dc in next dc, 2 dc in next sp, ch 3, sk next sc, sc in each of next 3 sc, ch 3, 2 dc in next sp, dc in next dc) 3 times, ch 2, sk next dc, work from first # to 2nd # on row 4.

Row 15: Work from first * to 2nd * on row 4, (ch 3, dc in next sp, ch 3, sk next 2 dc, dc in next dc, 2 dc in sp, ch 3, sk next sc, dc in next sc, ch 3, 2 dc in next sp, dc in next dc) 3 times, ch 3, dc in next sp, ch 3, sk next 2 dc, work from first # to 2nd # on row 4—3 pats.

Rows 16-101: Repeat rows 12-15, having 1 more pat every 4 rows—25 pats. Ch 1, turn at end of last row.

Row 102: Sc in each st across. End off.

FINISHING: Steam lightly.

FRINGE: Wind yarn around 9″ cardboard. Cut one end. With 7 strands tog, fold strands in half, pull loop through ch-5 turning ch, pull end through loop; tighten knot. Knot a fringe in each turning ch on sides of shawl. Trim ends evenly.

Fan-Pattern Crocheted Shawl

The delicate fans and mesh borders of this graceful openwork shawl, opposite at right, are created in double crochet and chain stitch, and a generous fringe is added.

SIZE: 56″ wide; 33″ deep at center back, plus fringe.

MATERIALS: About 1,400 yards of mercerized knitting and crochet cotton. Steel crochet hook No. 1.

GAUGE: 3 meshes (ch 2, dc) = 1″.

SHAWL: Beg at lower center back, ch 19.

Row 1: Dc in 7th ch from hook, (ch 2, sk next 2 ch, dc in next ch) 4 times. Ch 5, turn each row.

Row 2: (Dc, ch 2, dc) in first ch-2 sp, (ch 2, dc in next ch-2 sp) 3 times, ch 2, (dc, ch 2, dc) in last sp—7 dc.

Row 3:(Dc, ch2, dc) in first ch-2 sp, * ch 2, dc in next ch 2-sp, repeat from * across, end ch 2, (dc, ch 2, dc) in last ch-2 sp (do not work in turning ch) —8 dc.

Rows 4-9: Repeat row 3—14 dc.

Row 10:* (Dc, ch 2, dc) in first ch-2 sp, (ch 2, dc in next ch-2 sp) 5 times, ch 2,* 5 dc in next ch-2 sp, ch 2, # (dc in next ch-2 sp, ch 2) 5 times, (dc, ch 2, dc) in last ch-2 sp #.

Row 11: Work from first * to 2nd * on row 10, dc in next ch-2 sp, dc in each of next 5 dc, dc in next ch-2 sp, ch 2, work from first # to 2nd # on row 10.

Row 12: Work from first * to 2nd * on row 10, dc in next ch-2 sp, dc in each of next 7 dc, dc in next ch-2 sp, ch 2, work from first # to 2nd # on row 10.

Row 13: Work from first * to 2nd * on row 10, 5 dc in next sp, ch 4, sk next 3 dc, sc in next dc, ch 4, sk next dc, sc in next dc, ch 4, 5 dc in next sp, ch 2, work from first # to 2nd # on row 10.

Row 14: Work from first * to 2nd * on row 10, dc in next sp, dc in each of next 5 dc, dc in next sp, ch 4, sc in next sp, ch 4, dc in next sp, dc in each of next 5 dc, dc in next sp, ch 2, work from first # to 2nd # on row 10.

Row 15: Work from first * to 2nd * on row 10, (dc in next sp, dc in each of next 7 dc, dc in next sp, ch 2) twice, work from first # to 2nd # on row 10.

Row 16: Work from first * to 2nd * on row 10, (5 dc in next sp, ch 4, sk next 3 dc, sc in next dc, ch 4, sk next dc, sc in next dc, ch 4) twice, 5 dc in next sp, ch 2, work from first # to 2nd # on row 10.

Row 17: Work from first * to 2nd * on row 10, (dc in next sp, dc in each of next 5 dc, dc in next sp, ch 4, sc in next sp, ch 4) twice, dc in next sp, dc in each of next 5 dc, dc in next sp, ch 2, work from first # to 2nd # on row 10.

Row 18: Work from first * to 2nd * on row 10, (dc in next sp, dc in each of next 7 dc, dc in next sp, ch 2) 3 times, work from first # to 2nd # on row 10—3 pats.

Rows 19-99: Repeat rows 16-18, having 1 more pat every 3 rows. Ch 1, turn at end of last row.

Row 100: Sc in each st across. End off.

FINISHING: Steam lightly.

FRINGE: Wind yarn around 8″ cardboard. Cut one end. With 8 strands tog, fold strands in half, pull loop through ch-5 turning ch, pull end through loop; tighten knot. Knot a fringe in each turning ch on sides of shawl. Trim ends evenly.

Diamond Shawl

Soft diamonds, joined at their points, create a lovely latticework effect. The triangular shawl, worked in one piece from the bottom corner, combines double crochet for the diamonds and chain stitch for the filet mesh border.

SIZE: 68″ wide; 32″ deep at center back, plus fringe.

MATERIALS: Sport yarn, 5 2-oz. skeins. Crochet hook size G.

GAUGE: 5 meshes (ch 2, dc) = 3″.

SHAWL: Beg at lower center back, ch 8; join with a sl st to form ring.

Row 1: Ch 5, dc in ring, (ch 2, dc in ring) twice. Ch 5, turn each row.

Row 2: Dc in first dc, (ch 2, dc in next dc) twice, (ch 2, dc in turning ch-5 sp) twice—5 dc plus turning ch.

Row 3: Dc in first dc, (ch 2, dc in next dc) 4 times, (ch 2, dc in turning ch-5 sp) twice—7 dc plus turning ch.

Row 4: Dc in first dc, (ch 2, dc in next dc) 6 times, (ch 2, dc in turning ch-5 sp) twice.

Row 5: Dc in first dc, (ch 2, dc in next dc) 8 times, (ch 2, dc in turning ch-5 sp) twice.

Row 6: Dc in first dc, (ch 2, dc in next dc) 10 times, (ch 2, dc in turning ch-5 sp) twice.

Row 7: Dc in first dc, (ch 2, dc in next dc) 12 times, (ch 2, dc in turning ch-5 sp) twice.

Row 8: Dc in first dc, (ch 2, dc in next dc) 7 times, 2 dc in ch-2 sp, dc in dc, (ch 2, dc in next dc) 6 times, (ch 2, dc in turning ch-5 sp) twice.

Row 9:* Dc in first dc, (ch 2, dc in next dc) 7 times, 2 dc in ch-2 sp, dc in dc, ch 2, sk next 2 dc, dc in next dc*, 2 dc in ch-2 sp, dc in dc, (ch 2, dc in next dc) 6 times, (ch 2, dc in turning ch-5 sp) twice.

Row 10: Work from first * to 2nd * on row 9, ch 2, dc in next dc, # ch 2, sk next 2 dc, dc in next dc, 2 dc in ch-2 sp, dc in dc, (ch 2, dc in next dc) 6 times, (ch 2, dc in turning ch-5 sp) twice #.

Row 11: Work from first * to 2nd * on row 9, (ch 2, dc in next dc) 3 times, work from first # to 2nd # on row 10.

Row 12: Work from first * to 2nd * on row 9, (ch 2, dc in next dc) 5 times, work from first # to 2nd # on row 10.

Row 13: Work from first * to 2nd * on row 9, (ch 2, dc in next dc) 7 times, work from first # to 2nd # on row 10.

Row 14: Work from first * to 2nd * on row 9, (ch 2, dc in next dc) 3 times, ch 2, sk next ch-2 sp, shell of (2 dc, ch 2, 2 dc) in next ch-2 sp, sk next ch-2 sp, (ch 2, dc in next dc) 4 times, work from first # to 2nd # on row 10—1 shell.

Row 15: Work from first * to 2nd * on row 9, (ch 2, dc in next dc) 4 times, ch 2, shell of (2 dc, ch 2, 2 dc) in center ch-2 sp of shell, ch 2, sk next ch-2 sp, dc in dc, (ch 2, dc in next dc) 4 times, work from first # to 2nd # on row 10—1 shell.

Row 16: Work from first * to 2nd * on row 9, (ch 2, dc in next dc) 5 times, ch 2, shell of (2 dc, ch 2, 2 dc) in center ch-2 sp of shell, ch 2, sk next ch-2 sp, dc in dc, (ch 2, dc in next dc) 5 times, work from first # to 2nd # on row 10—1 shell.

Row 17: Work from first * to 2nd * on row 9, (ch 2, dc in next dc) 3 times, ch 2, sk next ch-2 sp, shell of (2 dc, ch 2, 2 dc) in next ch-2 sp, ch 3, shell in center ch-2 sp of shell, ch 3, sk next 2 ch-2 sps, shell in next ch-2 sp, ch 2, sk next ch-2 sp, dc in dc, (ch 2, dc in next dc) 3 times, work from first # to 2nd # on row 10—3 shells.

Row 18: Work from first * to 2nd * on row 9, (ch 2, dc in next dc) 4 times, ch 2, (shell in center ch-2 sp of next shell, ch 3) twice, shell in center ch-2 sp of next shell, ch 2, sk next ch-2 sp, dc in next dc, (ch 2, dc in next dc) 4 times, work from first # to 2nd # on row 10—3 shells.

Row 19: Work from first * to 2nd * on row 9, (ch 2, dc in next dc) 5 times, ch 2, shell in center ch-2 sp of next shell, (ch 2; working over ch-3 sps of last 2 rows, make 1 sc, ch 2, shell in center ch-2 sp of next shell) twice, ch 2, sk next ch-2 sp, dc in next dc, (ch 2, dc in next dc) 5 times, work from first # to 2nd # on row 10—3 shells.

Row 20: Work from first * to 2nd * on row 9, (ch 2, dc in next dc) 3 times, ch 2, sk next ch-2 sp, shell of (2 dc, ch 2, 2 dc) in next ch-2 sp, (ch 3, shell in center ch-2 sp of next shell) 3 times, ch 3, sk next 2 ch-2 sps, shell in next ch-2 sp, ch 2, sk next ch-2 sp, dc in dc, (ch 2, dc in next dc) 3 times, work from first # to 2nd # on row 10—5 shells.

Row 21: Repeat row 18, having 5 shells in center.

Row 22: Repeat row 19, catching 4 groups of ch-3 between shells with a sc.

Rows 23-58: Continue to repeat rows 20-22, having 2 shells more every 3 rows—29 shells. Ch 1, turn at end of last row.

Row 59:* (2 sc in ch-2 sp) 7 times, sk next dc, sc in each of next 2 dc, sk next dc, (sc in ch-2 sp) 7 times* , (sc in center ch-2 sp of next shell, ch 6) 28 times, sc in center of last shell, repeat from first * to 2nd *, end 2 sc in turning ch-5 sp. End off.

FINISHING: Steam lightly.

FRINGE: Wind yarn around 7″ cardboard. Cut one end. With 3 strands tog, fold strands in half, pull loop through sp, pull ends through loop; tighten knot. Knot a fringe in each sp on sides of shawl. Trim.

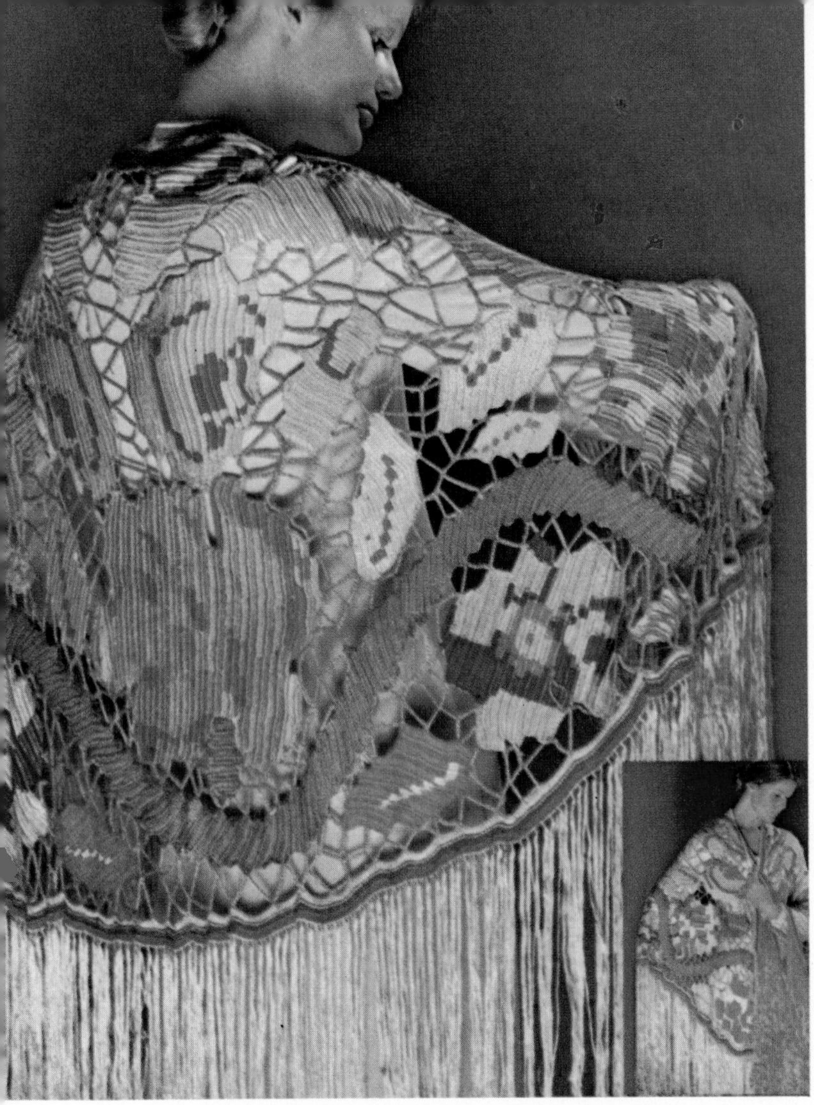

Antique Shawl

A delicate silk shawl, crocheted decades ago, is worked in a yarn that is no longer available; however, we have selected a thread (D.M.C. Pearl Cotton) that will make it possible for you to make a similar shawl in the same technique. Use rose and other flowers you crochet to make your shawl your own creation.

The directions below are given for the technique used in making this shawl. It is not possible to give explicit directions for the shawl photographed. In the first place, the silk yarn used is not available. No other yarn gives exactly the same appearance, works to the same gauge, or is dyed in the same colors. In the second place, stitch-by-stitch directions for the shawl as shown would take many pages of directions and would be so complicated as to discourage the crocheter. The technique, however, can be used to make a shawl of the same size or any other size.

SIZE: 80″ across top, 30″ deep at center, plus fringe.

MATERIALS: Pearl cotton #5 in 10-gram balls (53 yards) was used to make the rose and leaves. For the rose, 4 shades were used: pale pink (P), light rose (LR), bright rose (BR), and dark rose (DR). For the 3 leaves, green was used with brown, gold and cream for veins. One ball each of 4 shades will make 2 roses; 1 ball of green will make 3 leaves of different sizes. Use steel crochet hook No. 6 or 7.

GAUGE: 10 dc = 1″; 4 rows = 1″.

DIRECTIONS: Flowers, leaves, vine, and border are worked in dc.

When adding a new color, finish last 2 lps of dc with new color; work over end of new color and the strand of first color. When changing back to first color, finish last 2 lps of dc with first color, drop new color. Do not work over new color. When picking up new color on next row, work last 2 lps of dc with new color and work over strand of new color that comes up from last row, to hide it.

If a dropped color will be used again in same row, work over it; if it will not be used until the next row, drop it and pick it up on next row. If it will not be used in the next row, cut it and work over the cut end.

To inc at beg of rows: Ch 4 for 2 extra dc, 1 ch more for each additional dc. Dc in 4th ch from hook (counts as 2 dc), dc in each additional ch.

To inc at end of rows: Only 1 extra dc can be made at end of rows by working 2 dc in last st.

To dec at beg of rows: Sl st across number of sts to be decreased.

To dec at end of rows: Leave sts unworked.

To make rounded edges at top of motifs: Work sc at edge, then hdc, then dc, then hdc, then sc at other edge.

To make rounded edges at bottom of motifs: Turn motif upside down, join yarn in starting ch and work extensions as desired, ending with a rounded edge as for top of motif.

ROSE (made like rose about 1/3 in from either side at top of shawl; see photograph and rose motif, opposite): Beg at lower edge, with BR, ch 32.

Row 1: Dc in 4th ch from hook (counts as 2 dc), dc in each ch across—30 dc. Ch 6, turn.

Row 2: Dc in 4th ch from hook (counts as 2 dc),

dc in each of next 2 ch (4 dc added at beg of row), dc in each dc across, 2 dc in top of turning ch—1 dc added at end of row. Ch 3, turn.

Row 3: Sk first dc (ch 3 counts as first dc), dc in each dc across, dc in top of turning ch—35 dc. Ch 4, turn.

Row 4: Dc in 4th ch from hook, dc in each dc across—37 dc. Ch 11, turn.

Row 5: Dc in 4th ch from hook and in each of next 7 ch, dc in each of 11 dc, change to P in last dc, work in P across. Ch 10, turn.

Row 6: Dc in 4th ch from hook and in each of next 6 ch (8 P sts increased), dc in each of next 33 dc, change to BR, dc in each dc across. Ch 9, turn.

Row 7: Dc in 4th ch from hook and in each of 5 ch, 10 BR dc, 3 P dc, 26 LR dc, finish row with P dc. Ch 3, turn.

Row 8: Dc in first dc (an inc), 9 P dc, 9 LR dc, 25 DR dc, 4 LR dc, finish row with BR. Ch 10, turn.

Row 9: Dc in 4th ch from hook and in each of 6 ch, 9 BR dc, 4 LR dc, 8 DR dc, 21 BR dc, 9 DR dc, 5 LR dc, finish row with P. Ch 3, turn.

Row 10: Dc in first dc (an inc), 3 P dc, 4 LR dc, 5 DR dc, 36 BR dc, 4 DR dc, 4 LR dc, finish row with BR. Ch 3, turn.

Row 11: Sk first dc, 8 BR dc, 4 LR dc, 5 DR dc, 39 BR dc, 5 DR dc, 4 LR dc, finish row with P. Ch 3, turn.

Row 12: Dc in first dc (an inc), 4 P dc, 5 LR dc, 6 DR dc, work BR dc in each BR dc, DR dc in each DR dc, LR dc in each LR dc, 4 P dc, finish row with BR. Ch 5, turn.

Row 13: Dc in 4th ch from hook and in next ch, 5 BR dc, 5 P dc, 5 DR dc, 22 BR dc, 12 DR dc, 3 P dc, 6 DR dc, 6 LR dc, 4 P dc. Ch 3, turn.

Row 14: Sk first dc, P dc in each of next 3 dc, 6 LR dc, 3 DR dc, 6 P dc, 15 DR dc, 19 BR dc, 5 DR dc, 3 LR dc, 4 P dc, finish row with BR. Ch 1, turn.

Row 15: Sl st in next st, ch 3, dc in each of next 3 dc, 5 P dc, 3 LR dc, 21 BR dc, 17 DR dc, 3 P dc, 4 DR dc, 5 P dc, 5 LR dc, finish row with P, inc 1 st in last st. Ch 1, turn.

Row 16: Sc in each of first 5 sts; hdc in each of next 4 sts, 5 LR dc, 4 DR dc, 12 P dc, 7 DR dc, 22 BR dc, 3 LR dc, 5 P dc, 2 BR dc. Ch 1, turn.

Row 17: Sl st in each of first 2 sts; with P, ch 3, dc in each of next 5 dc, 4 LR dc, 16 BR dc, 6 DR dc, 14 P dc, 4 DR dc, 10 P dc. Ch 1, turn.

Row 18: Sl st in first 2 sts, sc in each of next 4 sts, hdc in each of next 2 sts, dc in each of next 6 dc, 15 DR dc, 5 P dc, 4 DR dc, 10 BR dc, 5 DR dc, 4 P dc. Ch 1, turn.

Row 19: Sl st in first st, sc in next st, hdc in next st, dc in each of next 5 sts, 4 DR dc, 7 BR dc, 10 DR dc, 16 BR dc. Ch 1, turn.

Row 20: Sc in each BR dc; with P, ch 3, 4 P dc, 8 BR dc, 6 DR dc, 6 P dc, 2 P dc in next dc. Ch 1, turn.

Row 21: Sk first st, sc in each of next 2 sts, hdc in next st, dc in each of next 16 sts. Ch 1, turn.

Row 22: Sk first st, sc in each of next 2 sts, hdc in next st, dc in each of next 3 sts, hdc in each of next 2 sts, dc in each of next 2 sts, hdc in next st, sc in each of next 2 sts, sl st in next st. End off.

SHAWL: Except for largest motif at center bottom and small leaf at center top, all motifs are made twice and reversed for second half of shawl.

Vine: With green, ch 22.

Row 1: Dc in 4th ch from hook (counts as 2 dc), dc in each ch across—20 dc. Ch 3, turn.

Motifs from Antiqe Shawl were crocheted in pearl cotton. Rose is 7½" wide.

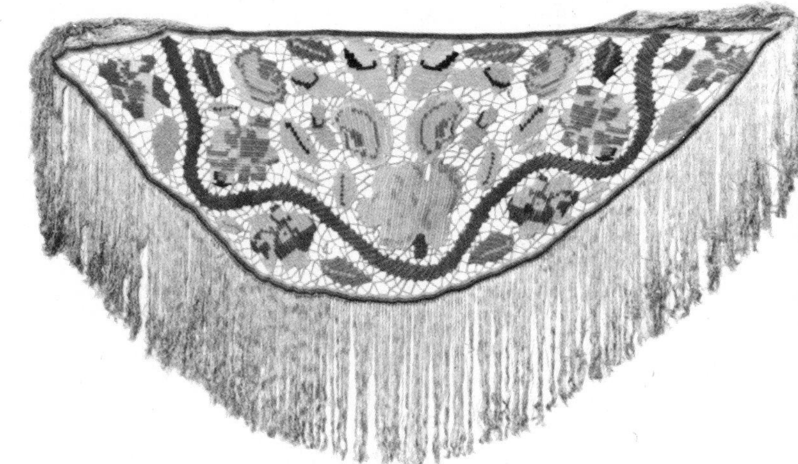

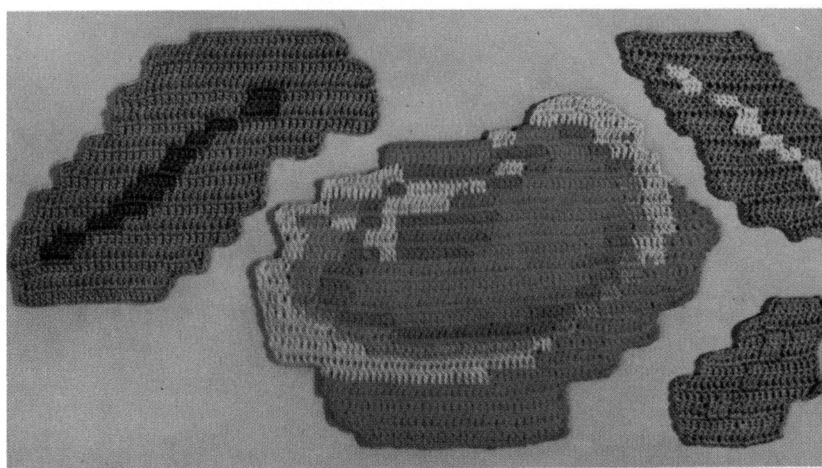

Row 2: Sk first dc, dc in each dc across. Ch 6, turn.

Row 3: Dc in 4th ch from hook and in each of 2 ch, dc in each of next 16 dc—20 dc. Ch 3, turn. Repeat rows 2 and 3 for desired length.

Border: Work one strip of 3 rows of dc, 1 row of sc (outer edge) in desired length for top border; work one strip in same way, but much longer, for side and bottom border. Sew ends of border strips tog.

FINISHING: Pin border out to finished shape on paper, sheet, or other material. Arrange and pin motifs in place. Tack tog any motifs which touch with matching thread. Join all motifs to each other and to border with chains. Join chains to edges of motifs and to each other with a sl st.

Fringe: For 18″ fringe, cut strands 1 yard long. Hold 3 strands tog, fold in half. Insert hook in sp between 2 dc's on last dc row of border, pull folded lp of strands through, pull ends through lp; tighten knot. Sk next sp, knot another fringe in next sp. Tie a knot in 6 ends of each fringe close to first knot.

Lace and Ribbon Shawl

Descending layer on layer, lace and ribbon in a variety of patterns form a triangle of feminine grace. The strips are sewn to chiffon and bordered with double lace ruffles.

SIZE: 62″ across at widest point.

EQUIPMENT: Pencil. Large piece of paper for pattern. Square. Yardstick. Scissors. Straight pins. Sewing machine with ruffler attachment.

MATERIALS: Off-white, soft, sheer fabric (such as chiffon), 36″ or 45″ wide, 1¾ yards. Lace edgings in shades of white, off-white, and tan in 1″, 2″, 2½″ widths (see directions for amounts). Ribbons: velvet and picot-edged taffeta (not satin or grosgrain) in shades of ecru, tan, light brown in ¼″, ½″, ¾″, and 1½″ widths (see directions for amounts). Off-white and tan sewing threads.

DIRECTIONS: To Make Pattern: Using square and yardstick in the center of the lengthwise edge of a large piece of paper, draw a right triangle with the two equal sides each 31″ and the hypotenuse 44″. Fold paper in half along vertical 31″ line and cut out. Open pattern up fully so you have triangular pattern with the lengthwise edge 62″ and each side edge 44″.

To Figure Amounts: The amounts of lace and ribbon for the shawl depend upon the widths and various combinations. You need enough widths to cover the 31″ depth of the shawl; the lengths vary from 62″ long at the top edge to 4″ long at the lowest point. Once you have the widths combined, you can estimate the total yardage needed.

Be sure to account for ribbon trim on top of laces and ribbon accents underneath some laces, as well as the overlap of some edges. For a rough estimate, our shawl required about eight 2-yard and three 1-yard lengths of lace, and about six 2-yard and three 1-yard lengths of ribbon. In addition, you need 9½ yards of one lace trimming for the edging and ruffles. The total yardage depends on the widths and various combinations used.

To Assemble: Trim off one lengthwise selvage of the sheer lining fabric. Lay lengthwise edge of pattern along trimmed fabric edge. Mark and cut out fabric following pattern lines. Stay-stitch fabric on all edges.

Combine laces and ribbons as desired by arranging them on top of the paper pattern. Do not include outer edging lace as it will be sewn on last. Remember that lengthwise edges of each row must overlap slightly or abut. Use narrow ribbons on top of the wider laces; use some ribbons underneath laces as accents. When you have a suitable arrangement, you are ready to sew.

To Sew: Beginning at the long top edge, stitch lace and ribbons onto fabric, one length at a time. If you have combined both ribbon and lace for one length, it is usually easier to sew the two together first and then treat them as one. Stitch along lengthwise edges as necessary; laces used as accents over ribbon do not have to be stitched on the lower lengthwise edge. Abut or overlap edges of the lengths so that the fabric does not show. Trim ends of lengths even with triangular side edges.

When fabric lining is covered by lengths of ribbon and lace, cut a 64″ length of edging lace. Pin one edge of the 64″ length of edging lace along the lengthwise edge, lapping it slightly over first length of ribbon or lace on the shawl and being sure ends extend equally at each side. Stitch in place; trim both ends following triangular shape.

Cut another length of edging lace to measure 90″. Pin to front along both diagonal edges, about ¼″ in from edge, turning 1″ excess at each end over the lengthwise edging lace to the underside. Stitch along one side, turning at the point, then along the other side. Ruffle the remaining edging lace to measure 90″. Turn each end under 1″. Pin onto side edges, placing ruffled lace on top of first layer of edging lace, about ¼″ above first layer so it will show at the outer edges. Stitch in place.

Deep-Fringed Shawl

Worked on a soft wool gabardine with pearl cotton, satin stitch embroidery gives an elegant touch to this double triangle shawl. Flowing knotted braid trim adds a rich, fashionable touch.

SIZE: 38″ deep at center.

EQUIPMENT: Ruler. Yardstick. Pencil. Large piece of paper for pattern. Scissors. Straight pins. Tracing wheel. Blue dressmaker's tracing (carbon) paper. Blue pencil. Darning needle (not yarn darner). Small yarn needle. Sewing needle. Standing or lap embroidery hoop. Steam iron. Pressing cloth. Strip of cardboard at least 3″ long.

MATERIALS: Ecru wool gabardine, 60″ wide, 1⅔ yards. Matching sewing thread. Pearl cotton,

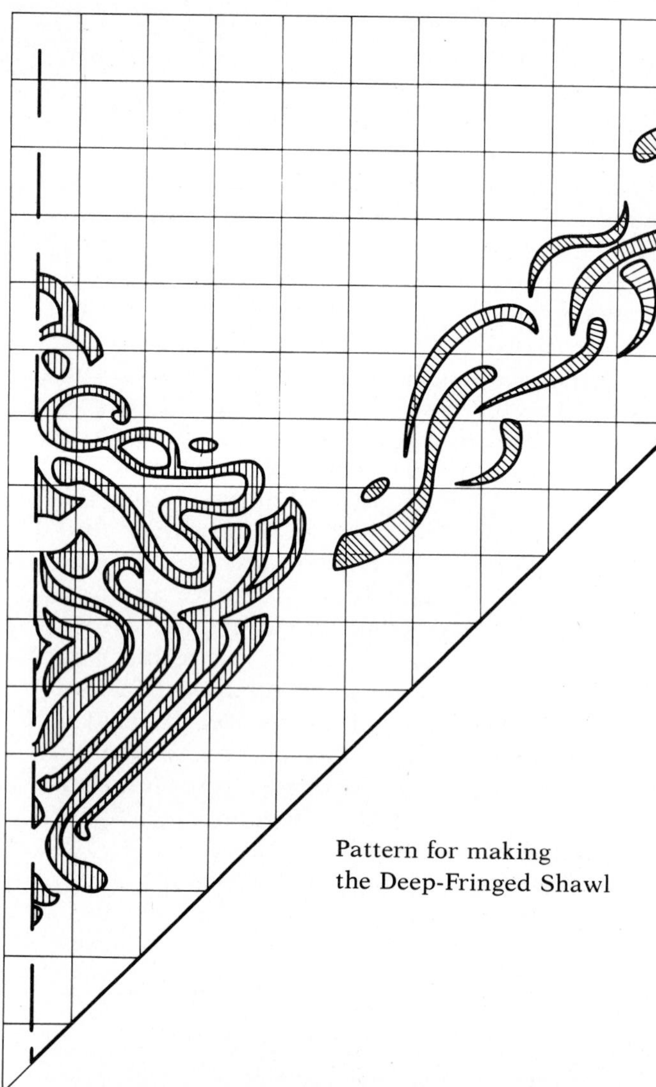

Pattern for making
the Deep-Fringed Shawl

size 5, seven 27.3-yard skeins ecru. Rayon middy braid, ¼″ wide, 480 yards ecru (for fringe).

DIRECTIONS: To Mark Pattern: Enlarge pattern by copying on paper ruled in 2″ squares. Complete half-pattern indicated by dash line, including diagonal guideline. Stay-stitch across each crosswise edge of fabric. On right side of fabric, use blue pencil to mark a straight line for one seamline, 1″ above stitching on lower crosswise edge. Mark a straight line for the other seamline, 1″ to the right of the left selvage along the lengthwise grain. Use the corner of a table to square your lines. Measure 54″ from corner point along each seamline; make small mark. Place lower point of pattern in lower left corner, having both pattern guidelines lie 7″ in from each seamline. Using dressmaker's tracing carbon and wheel, trace design onto right side of fabric (do not trace guidelines).

To Embroider: Begin the embroidery at the lower point of the shawl. Place fabric firmly, without distorting it, in the embroidery hoop so that the twill grain of the gabardine runs vertically; follow this grain for the embroidery stitches (see fine lines on pattern). Thread darning needle with one-yard length of pearl cotton. Work design in satin stitch (see Stitch Detail on page 15). To begin, hold end of pearl cotton on underside until you have worked several stitches to cover it. Begin and end successive strands by catching the ends under previous stitches. Move fabric in hoop as needed to work design. Some stitches will be very long; be careful not to pull these. When finished, the weight of the shawl will keep them taut.

After completing the point design, work the side designs. Work in satin stitch, but do not follow the vertical twill grain. Work stitches mostly at right angle to twill, but radiate them around curves (see fine lines on pattern).

To Assemble: When embroidery is completed, remove from hoop. Fold the plain half of fabric diagonally over the front of the embroidery, being sure bias fold lies across two end marks of seamlines. Pin both thicknesses together along edges. Trim margins to within 1″ of seamlines. Stitch together on both sides leaving an 8″ opening in center of one side. Trim seam allowance, one layer to ¼″ and one layer to ⅜″; trim corners. Carefully turn right side out. Use pressing cloth to press over embroidered area. Press along both stitched edges, but do not press along bias fold.

To Fringe: Cut 360 48-inch lengths of braid. Place shawl right side up. Cut a strip of cardboard 3″ long. To mark points for attaching each fringe, mark ten equally spaced dots along one long edge about 5/16″ apart. Hold cardboard from corner on one stitched edge of shawl; using blue pencil, make ten equally spaced marks. Thread doubled length of braid, loop end first, through yarn needle. Insert needle at first blue mark about ¼″ in from the edge. Bring needle through to underside and remove it from the braid. Pull two braid ends through braid loop; pull tightly. Continue fringing in marked 3″ area; then continue marking and fringing until both side edges are complete.

Press if necessary.

Quilted Shawl

A crisp ruffle accents the edge of this cozy quilted muslin shawl—a flattering creation influenced by Old Mexico. Swirly bands of quilted motifs stitch up fast with pearl cotton in a contrasting color.

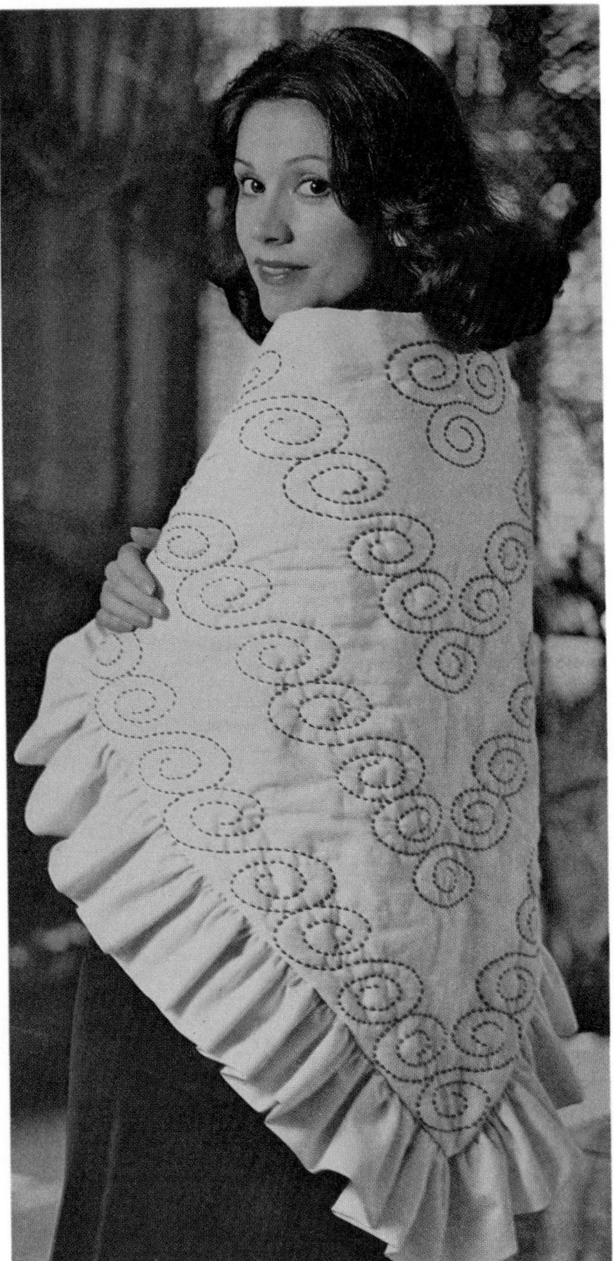

SIZE: 55″ wide at the top, plus ruffle.

EQUIPMENT: Hard and soft lead pencils. Yardstick. Tracing paper (pieced to size 30″ x 58″). Paper for pattern. Red or blue dressmaker's tracing (carbon) paper. Scissors. Straight pins. Regular sewing needle and large-eyed embroidery needle. Sewing machine with ruffler attachment.

MATERIALS: Unbleached muslin, 44″/45″ wide, 4¼ yds. Lightweight Dacron batting, single thickness, 30″ x 58″. Yellow basting thread. Pearl cotton size 3, wine red, two skeins.

DIRECTIONS: Wash muslin to preshrink it and to completely remove sizing. Press well with pressing cloth while damp.

Place fabric on smooth, flat surface. Referring to Cutting Diagram, p. 268 (Diag. 1), and using soft lead pencil, measure and mark on fabric three triangles, each with a 58″ base and a 30″ perpendicular (see Diag. 1); then mark four bias strips, each 8½″ wide. Cut out each piece.

Set aside one triangle for backing and bias strips for ruffle until quilting is finished. Piece tracing paper to size 30″ x 58″ for quilting design pattern. On tracing paper, mark triangular outline of finished shawl with a 56″ base, and a perpendicular 28″ high. Mark line down exact center of triangle. Starting from each side of triangle and referring to Diag. 2 (p. 268), mark off four diagonal areas 3″ wide with 2″-wide areas between, forming seven triangles within outline. The 3″-wide areas are for design. Enlarge quilting pattern (p. 268) by copying on paper ruled in 1″ squares. Referring to Diag. 2, place quilting pattern under marked tracing paper, centering design in triangle points of 3″ areas. With soft lead pencil, trace entire pattern. Working from center point toward base (top edge) of triangle, repeat RIGHT SIDE "S" of design along right side of each 3″ area; then repeat LEFT SIDE "S" in same manner along left side of each 3″ area.

Place muslin triangle for shawl front on flat surface. With pin, mark center of base; using soft pencil, mark finished size of shawl on muslin (56″ base, with a 28″ perpendicular). Center and pin traced quilting pattern to muslin, matching outlines and center points. With carbon paper and hard lead pencil, transfer complete traced design to muslin (do not transfer triangular area guidelines). Remove pattern. Baste along outline of finished shawl on muslin.

For interlining, cut batting same size as muslin. If batting seems too thick, thin it by carefully pulling layer apart and using only half the thickness.

With marked side facing up, place shawl front on muslin lining triangle with batting between. Pin all layers together. Baste diagonally through all thicknesses along inner and outer edges of each design area.

To quilt design, thread large-eyed needle with single strand of pearl cotton. Make small knot at end of thread and insert needle from lining to front. Take two or three little running stitches through all thicknesses on front (See Stitch Details, page 15). Pull thread up tightly to pucker fabric slightly. Do not pull needle through to lining side except to end thread. Make stitches about 3/16″ long with ⅛″ space between each stitch. After a few stitches, you should be able to gauge your stitches evenly. End all threads on lining side with a small knot. Quilt entire design, working from center (right angle) of each 3″ area to outer edge.

When quilting is finished, remove basting threads and trim edges to ½″ for seam allowance. Trim third muslin triangle for backing to same size as quilted triangle.

To make ruffle, sew the four bias strips together to form one strip. Strip should be about 2½ times as long as measurement along one side,

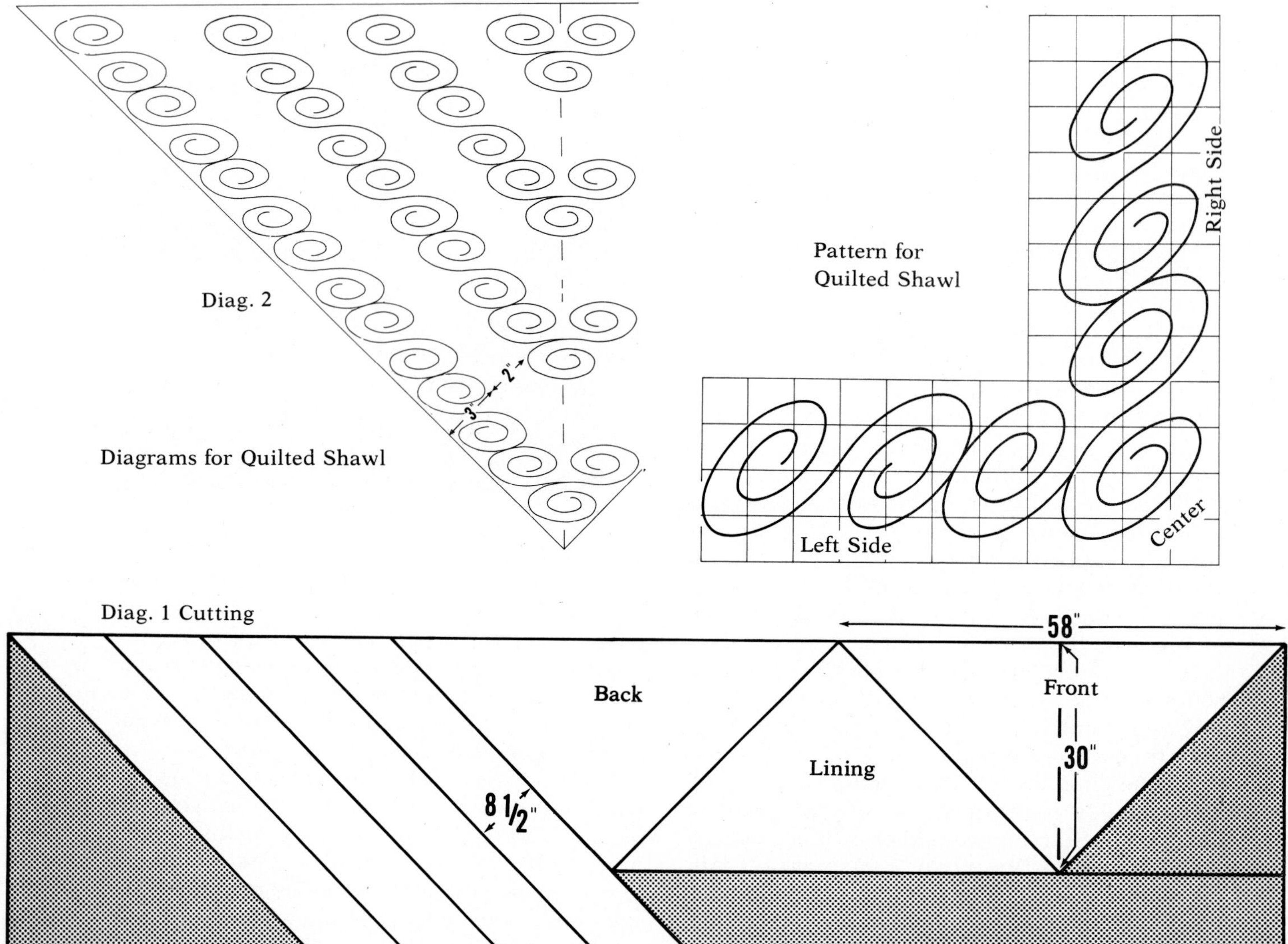

Diagrams for Quilted Shawl

around point, and along other side of triangle, plus about 10″ extra. (Base is not ruffled.) Fold strip in half lengthwise. Sew across one end of strip ⅝″ from raw edges; repeat at other end. Trim corners and turn strip to other side. Pull out corners. Following instructions that come with ruffler attachment, set ruffler on sewing machine to gather strip to required length. (**Note:** Test on scrap fabric first to determine setting: mark 5″ length on scrap; pass through ruffler and measure length. Ruffled scrap should measure about 2″ when setting is correct.)

Ruffle entire length of strip, through both thicknesses, ¼″ from raw edges. Place ruffle on lining with all raw edges flush; make sure ruffle is eased enough at point of triangle to fit. Baste ruffle and edges of shawl together. With ruffle between, pin, then baste remaining triangle for backing. Sew all around through all thicknesses ½″ from raw edges, leaving a 3″ opening at center of long straight edge. Remove basting threads. Clip corners and turn shawl to right side. Turn edges of opening in ½″ and slip-stitch closed. Press only on back of shawl.

Patchwork Shawl

Crisp corners flare when patchwork triangles join in a sumptuous fabric shawl! Broad bands are corduroy; narrow stripes and patchwork insets are of cotton in five go-together prints. Shawl measures a comfy 64″ along its top edge, has a simple cotton lining.

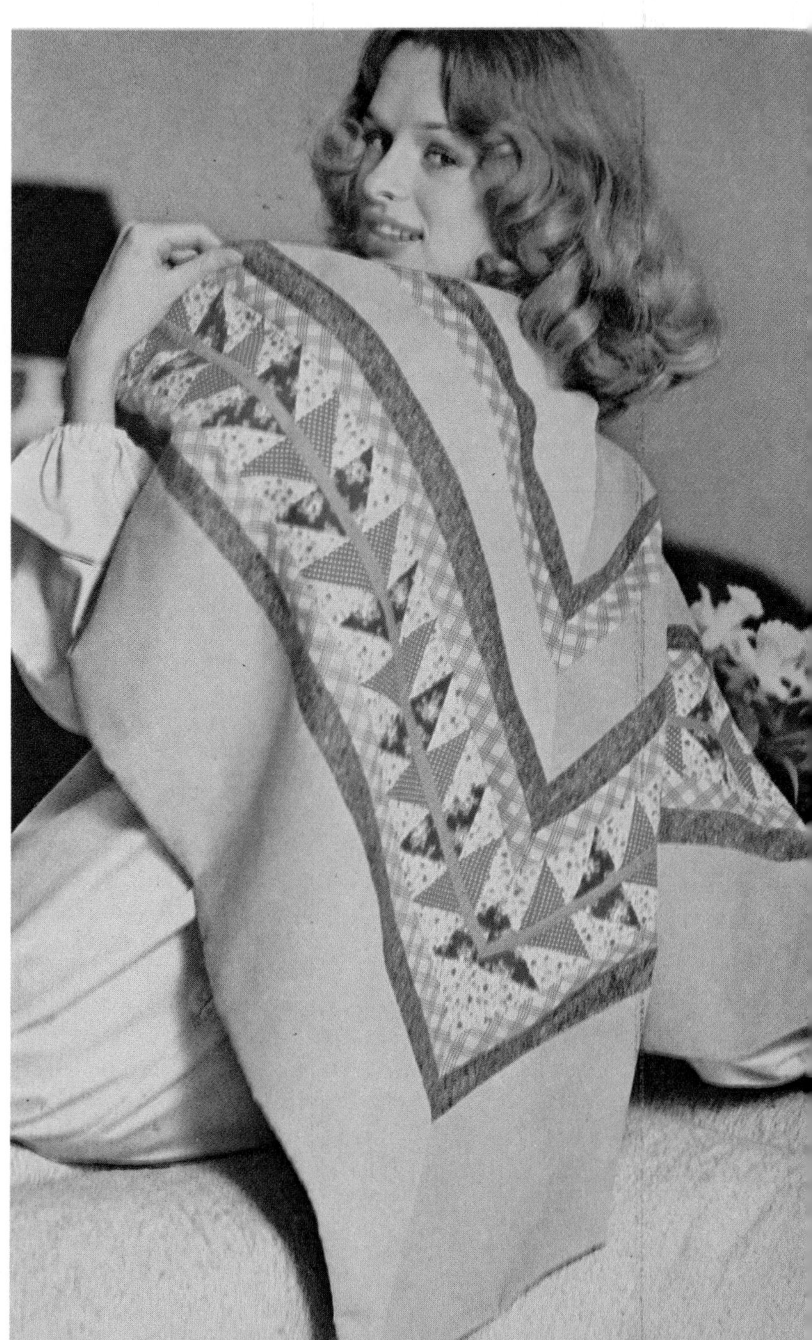

EQUIPMENT: Pencil. Ruler. Scissors. Cardboard. Paper for pattern (about 34″ square). Tracing paper. Square.

MATERIALS: Taupe corduroy, 44″ wide, 1⅓ yds. Cotton fabric, 36″ wide: ¼ yd. each of five cotton print fabrics (we used 2 dark brown, 1 maroon, and 2 beige); ¼ yd. solid light brown cotton. **For Lining:** Dark brown broadcloth, 36″ wide, 2 yds. Off-white sewing thread.

DIRECTIONS: Joining Diagram, page 270, is for right-hand half of shawl. When stitching pieces together, place right sides together and make ¼″ seams.

Following Joining Diagram and using square and ruler, draw actual-size half-pattern on paper. First draw horizontal and vertical lines A and B; connect points A and B with a diagonal line. Measure this line and note it on the Placement Diagram. Line B is center back. Starting from diagonal line and following measurements on diagram, measure and mark lines for all strips. To ensure cutting even fabric strips, cut actual-size

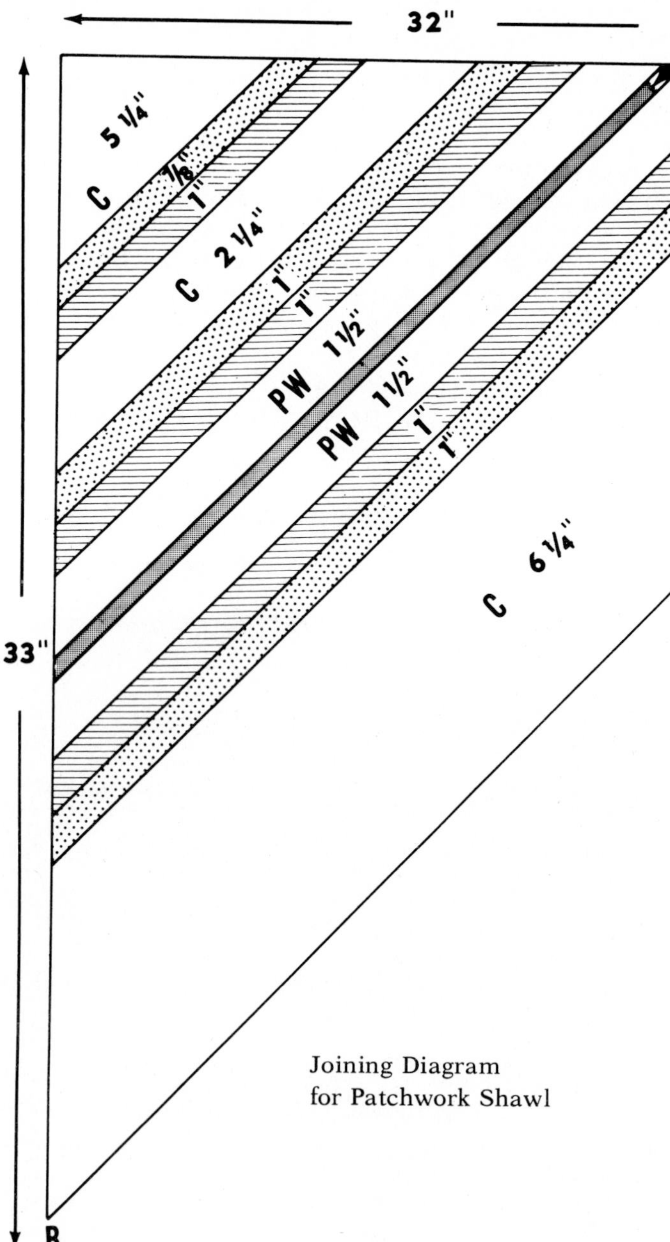

Joining Diagram
for Patchwork Shawl

pattern into individual strips. Allowing ¼″ for seam allowance on all edges, place patterns on fabrics as indicated and trace. Cut out strips.

Place patterns for corduroy strips (C) on lengthwise grain of fabric. Place patterns for cotton fabrics on crosswise grain, except for patchwork strips (PW). Cut two each of the corduroy and cotton strips to make both halves of shawl.

Each half of shawl has two patchwork strips made up of right triangles stitched together to form squares. We used two combinations of fabrics for the squares: light beige floral print is combined with maroon polka-dot, or with a brown floral print. The squares are stitched together to form strips with the two color combinations alternating. These strips are connected by a narrow strip of plain fabric (already cut).

To make patchwork strips, cut 2″-wide bias strips of each of the fabrics to be used. Stitch two strips of each combination together along true bias. Trim; press seam to one side.

Cut a 2¼″ cardboard square for pattern. This includes ¼″ seam allowance. Draw a diagonal line across square from corner to corner. Place pattern on one joined bias strip with diagonal line along seam line of fabric. Trace pattern and cut out square. In same manner make 28 each of the beige-maroon and 30 of the beige-brown combinations. Stitch squares together to make two strips 14 squares long, and two strips 15 squares long. When joining squares for second strip on each half of shawl, check constantly to be sure seams will match seams of first strip. For each half of shawl, stitch one long and one short patchwork strip to each side of tan fabric strip, matching squares at one end. Stitch strips together. Place patterns for patchwork strips on joined pieces and add triangles to each end in colors required. Trim away ends of joined strips to conform to patterns.

Following diagram for half of shawl, stitch cotton strips together. Stitch these strips to corduroy pieces. When stitching, place lightweight cotton on the bottom and corduroy on top to avoid stretching fabric.

Stitch the two halves of shawl together along center back. Following dimensions of half-pattern (see measurement on Placement Diagram) and adding ¼″ seam allowance all around, cut two lining pieces. Stitch together along center back, leaving a 3″ opening in center for turning. With right sides of lining and patchwork together, stitch around all sides, making ¼″ seams. Cut notches in seam allowance at each corner; turn to right side. Turn in edges of opening and slip-stitch; press.

6

Rugmaking

GENERAL DIRECTIONS FOR HAND HOOKING

MATERIALS AND EQUIPMENT: The hand hook for rugmaking resembles a large steel crochet needle embedded in a wooden handle. Firmly woven burlap about 40″ wide is the usual foundation fabric. There are also cotton and linen foundation fabrics called warp cloth that are woven with a somewhat open mesh, allowing the needle to slip in easily. If foundation fabric is not large enough, it can be pieced by lapping one piece of fabric over the other about two inches and running a line of catch-stitching down both edges. Designs must be shown on the top (right) side of the fabric, since work is done from the top. Although you may be able to hook with the fabric in your lap, most rug hookers find it easier to stretch it on a rug hoop or frame.

Hand-hooked rugs are usually made from fabric strips cut from old clothing or blankets, although new fabric may be used to supplement it, or even to make entire rug. Try to use fabric of the same weight, thickness, and fiber content for the whole rug so that it will wear evenly.

If you wish to make your rug washable, it is important that the material be absolutely colorfast. New or old, all material should be washed in hot water and borax to loosen and remove any excess dye. Wash each color separately, then rinse until no more dye comes out. (If the material is soiled, use naphtha soap.) Do not wring; hang in the sun to dry. The colors will not seem faded when hooked, because color is relative and depends upon placement of adjacent colors for the over-all effect.

To obtain the desired colors, you can dye your fabrics yourself. Lovely color effects can be obtained by shading areas. A group of shaded colors for making a motif is known as a "swatch" and is made up of five or six 3″ x 12″ pieces of fabric, which shade from light to dark in the same hue. Swatches may be purchased at art needlework departments, from rug designers, or be prepared at home. Interesting effects are also achieved by mixing materials to include tweeds, herringbone weaves, flannels, and twills. The shadings add variety of tone and make the rug more practical—a slightly variegated background shows less soil. Mingling of color is called "wiggling in."

Estimating Amount of Material: Use the general rule that ½ lb. of fabric will cover 1 sq. ft. of backing; or 1½ to 2 sq. yds. of wool or 2 sq. yds. of cotton will hook about 1 sq. ft.

CUTTING INTO STRIPS: The width of strips varies according to the thickness of the material. Strips of the same fabric should be cut in uniform widths, although strips to be used for fine detail in a small section may be cut narrower. A machine that cuts strips evenly is sold in needlework departments and by mail. Most strips are cut on the straight of the goods, but some prefer them cut slightly on the bias for more give. Fabric should be cut as finely as the weave allows. Closely woven fabric such as flannel is cut in strips as narrow as 1/16″ to 1/8″ wide; more loosely woven fabric is cut from 3/16″ to 5/16″. Cotton strips should be ¼″ to ½″.

FINISHING EDGES: The finished edge of a hooked rug must be planned before hooking is begun, or, if using a frame, before the foundation fabric is placed in the frame.

One method is to stitch 1¼″-wide rug binding at the edge of the rug design, on the front. The seam should be exactly on the edge of the rug, with the seam allowance of the binding and backing extending beyond. When hooking is completed, trim foundation to ½″, turn binding over edge of foundation, and slip-stitch to back of rug.

HOOKING: Hand hooking is a simple method of putting loops of narrow strips of fabric through meshes (between threads) of background fabric. If you have never hooked before, practice on a small area outside the rug design. Hold the hook above the foundation fabric in the right hand; hold the fabric strip underneath with the left. Push the hook through the fabric to draw a loop up through to the desired height; then reinsert the hook in the fabric close by and pull up another loop. Give hook a little clockwise twist as you pull the loops through. This makes a firmer and longer wearing pile. Care must be taken to have all loops the same height; height is determined by the fabric used and the width of strip. If loops are to be cut, they should be no longer than usual. For fine hooking, loops are pulled through the mesh about 3/16″; for coarser hooking, pull the loops approximately ¼″ high. You will gauge how far apart your stitches should be by the width or thickness of the strands and the height of the loops; they should be close enough together to stay in place, yet far enough apart so that the rug will not buckle. Continue inserting hook through burlap and pulling up loops. Do as much of one color as possible at one time. Pull ends through to top when starting and ending a strand; clip ends even with loops.

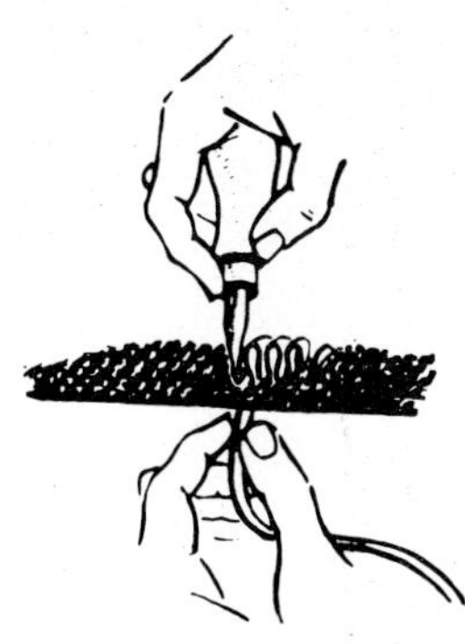

Hand Hooked

Usually, the design part of the rug is worked before the background, and the portion of design that appears in "front" or "on top" is worked first in order to keep the shapes from being lost. To obtain an interesting background texture, do not work in straight lines. Fill in background around the motifs, then continue to keep direction of lines irregular. If you are working the rug in a small frame, work all motifs and background around before rolling to new section.

Antique Floral Rug

This traditional, hand-hooked rug blends beautifully with any decorating scheme for a pleasing effect year after year.

SIZE: 30″ x 48″.

EQUIPMENT: Hand hook. Large needle. Scissors. Ruler. Soft pencil. Tracing paper. Rug frame (optional). Dressmaker's tracing (carbon) paper. Tracing wheel or dry ball-point pen.

MATERIALS: Foundation fabric 34″ x 52″. Wool fabrics in following colors and approximate amounts: deep red, 1 lb.; bright red, ½ lb.; deep yellow, ½ lb.; light blue-green, ¼ lb.; medium blue-green, ½ lb.; medium green, ¼ lb.; medium yellow-green, ½ lb.; olive green, 1 lb.; black, ½ lb.; beige, 3 lbs.; lavender, ¼ lb. Rug binding, 4½ yds. Carpet thread.

DIRECTIONS: Read General Directions on page 272. Enlarge patterns for center design, oval border, and corners on paper ruled in 1″ squares. Mark outline of rug, 30″ x 48″ on burlap. Fold burlap in half crosswise and lengthwise; mark center and middle of each side; open burlap. Place center design, evenly spaced, on burlap and transfer, using carbon paper. Mark an oval on burlap, pointed at each end, with sides of oval 4½″ from marked side of rug, and pointed ends 6½″ from edge of rug. Transfer oval border all around marked oval, repeating the two scrolls so they meet at ends as shown in illustration. Mark a line 1″ in from edge of rug all around. Transfer corner motif in all four corners.

Stitch binding to rug fabric following General Directions. Hook flowers, leaves, and scrolls, following color key and numbers on patterns. Shade flowers on dotted lines, if desired. Reverse the red and yellow flowers in opposite corners. Make all stems, petal separations, and leaf accents black unless otherwise marked on pattern. Hook outer straight border with three rows of olive. Fill in background with beige.

Finish binding according to General Directions.

Antique Floral Rug

Oval Border

Corner

Color Key

1 Deep Red
2 Light Red
3 Deep Yellow
4 Light Blue-Green
5 Medium Blue-Green
6 Medium Green
7 Medium Yellow-Green
8 Olive Green
9 Lavender
10 Black

Color Key

1 Deep Red
2 Light Red
3 Deep Yellow
4 Light Blue-Green
5 Medium Blue-Green
6 Medium Green
7 Medium Yellow-Green
8 Olive Green
9 Lavender
10 Black

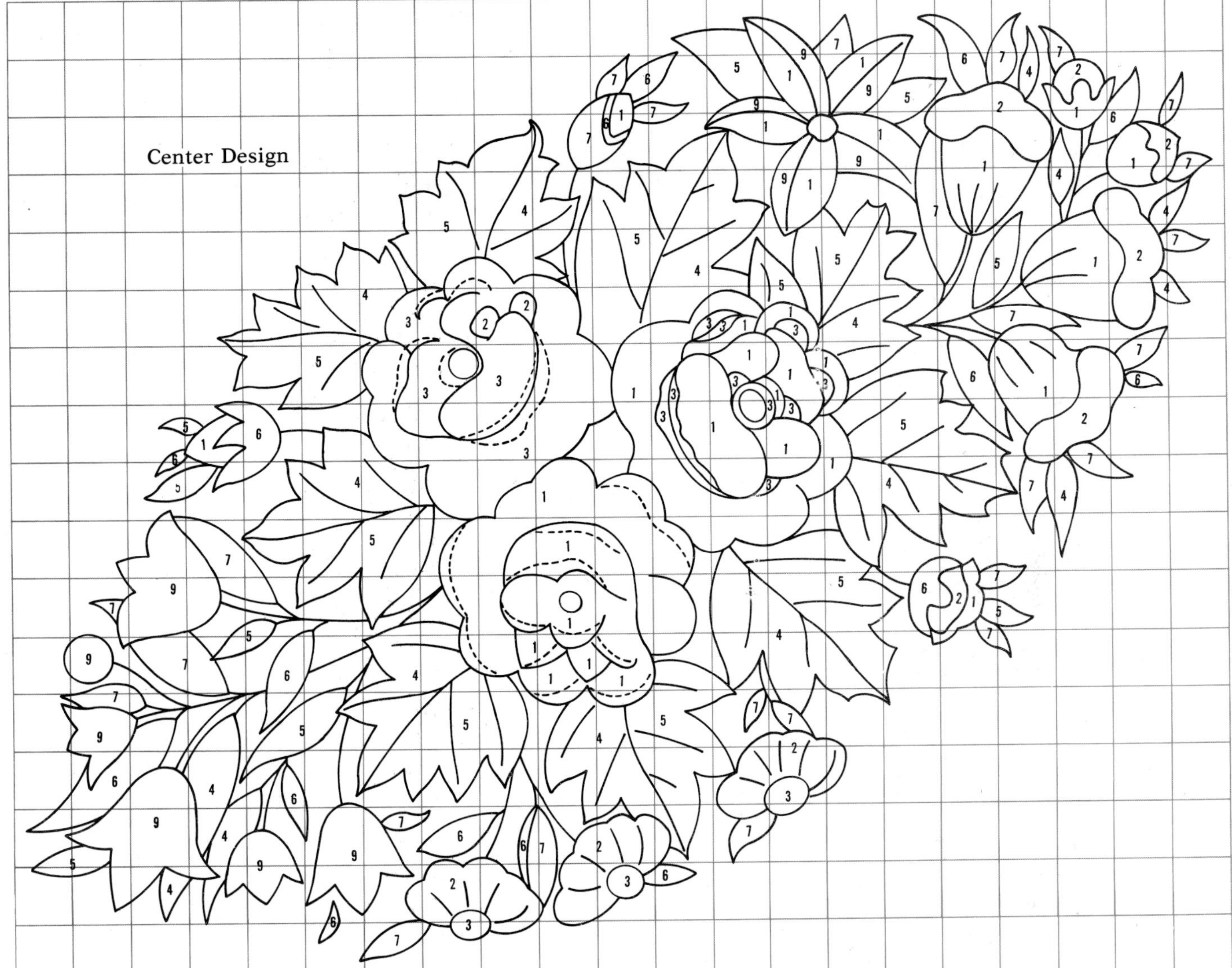

Damask Rose Rug

Damask roses in shaded pinks and reds, framed in deep-toned scrolls, are reminiscent of traditional hand-hooked rug designs. With the directions is a detailed explanation of dimensional color shading.

SIZE: About 30″ x 49″.

EQUIPMENT: Hand hook. Large needle. Scissors. Ruler. Soft pencil. Paper for pattern. Tracing paper. Rug frame (optional). Dressmaker's (carbon) tracing paper and dry ball-point pen or tracing wheel.

MATERIALS: Wool fabric in the following colors: small amounts of six blending shades through light, medium, and deep pink to medium, dark, and very dark red; five blended shades of blue-green from pale aqua to dark blue-green; five shades of yellow-green from light to dark; approximately 2 lbs. light beige and 2½ lbs. dark beige. Foundation fabric, 34″ x 53″. Rug binding, 4½ yds. Carpet thread.

DIRECTIONS: Read General Directions on page 272. Draw a rectangle 30″ x 49″ on foundation fabric (finished rug will be a little smaller); draw horizontal and vertical center lines as guide for design. Enlarge pattern by copying on paper ruled in 1″ squares; center lines of pattern are indicated by arrows.

Mark pattern on foundation fabric, using

Shading Diagrams for Damask Rose Rug

Center Leaves C

Scrolls E

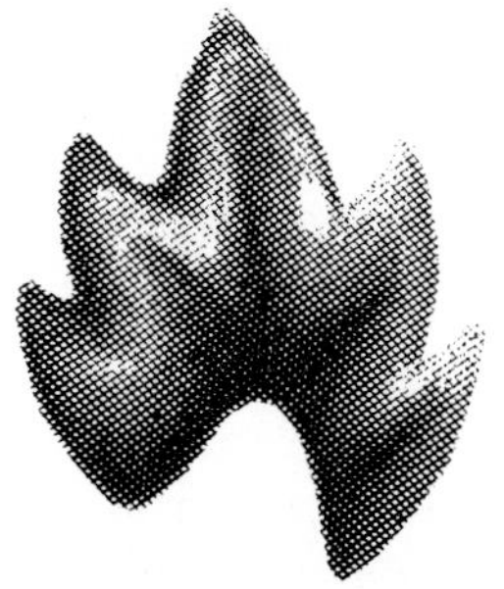

Leaves B

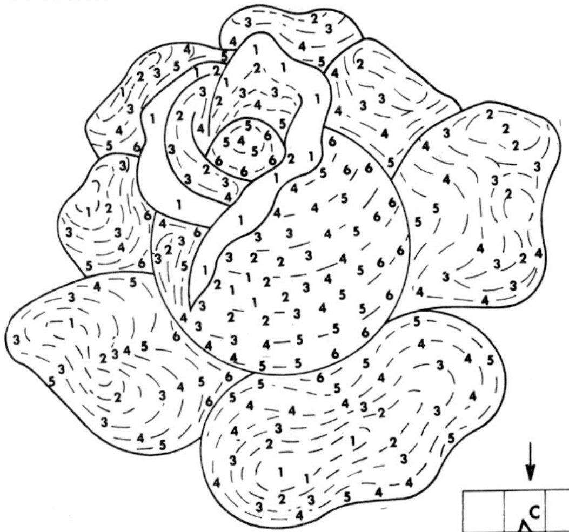

Roses A

Rosebuds D

Leaves G

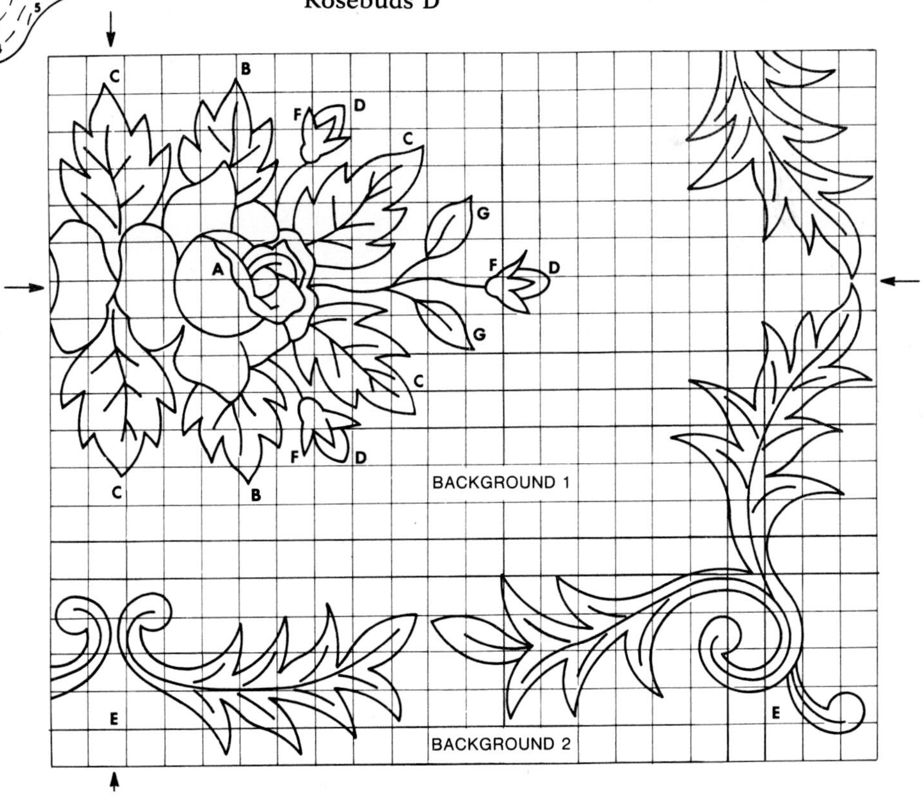

BACKGROUND 1

BACKGROUND 2

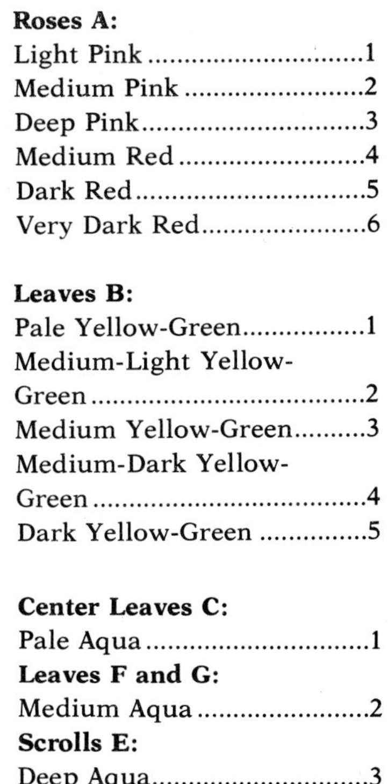

Roses A:
Light Pink 1
Medium Pink 2
Deep Pink..............................3
Medium Red 4
Dark Red...............................5
Very Dark Red.......................6

Leaves B:
Pale Yellow-Green.................1
Medium-Light Yellow-Green....................................2
Medium Yellow-Green..........3
Medium-Dark Yellow-Green 4
Dark Yellow-Green 5

Center Leaves C:
Pale Aqua 1
Leaves F and G:
Medium Aqua 2
Scrolls E:
Deep Aqua.............................3
Medium Blue-Green.............4
Dark Blue-Green 5

Rosebuds D:
Deep Pink..............................3
Medium Red 4
Dark Red...............................5

Background 1:
Light Beige
Background 2:
Dark Beige

dressmaker's carbon and tracing wheel or dry ball-point pen; match center lines on fabric with arrows on pattern. Mark complete scroll section shown between arrows in each corner of foundation. Mark right rose motif, plus center leaves and one petal of left rose, then reverse pattern and complete left rose motif. Stitch binding to fabric, following General Directions.

Work rug, following Shading Diagrams and working colors as indicated by numbers and shaded sketches. Numbers run 1, 2, 3, 4, 5, 6—from light to dark. Broken lines indicate direction for working stitches. Letters on pattern indicate placing of colors.

When working center rose A, in six shades from light pink (1) to very dark red (6), note how the gradations are planned to give the flower roundness and form. To keep each part of the flower clearly defined, always work first the shape that appears in front of the adjoining shapes. For example, the curled-over part of the petal appears in front of the rest of the petal. The bowl section is in front of the outer petals. These shapes should be outlined and filled in, shading as indicated. Outline each petal and fill in. Work other rose, leaves, buds, and scrolls. Work Background No. 1 in light beige and Background No. 2 in dark beige.

Finish binding rug.

GENERAL DIRECTIONS FOR LATCH HOOKING

MATERIALS AND EQUIPMENT: Wool rug yarn comes already cut into correct lengths for latch (also called lachet or latched) hooking, packaged according to color; or, yarn from a skein may be cut into approximately 2½" lengths by winding it around a piece of cardboard about 1¼" deep and cutting with scissors. For ease in working, put each color into a separate plastic bag; mark each bag with the symbol for that color given in the chart's color key.

Canvas in a large mesh, usually 3⅓- or 4-meshes-to-the-inch, is used with the latch (latchet) hook.

No frame is used in latch (latchet) hooking; the rug is worked in the lap or on a large table.

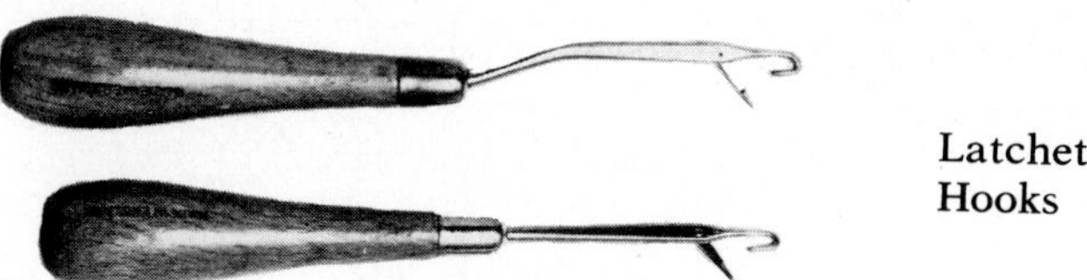

Latchet Hooks

LATCH (LATCHET) HOOKING: Lay the canvas on a table with the selvage edges at the sides and about 2" of the canvas extending off the table toward you; roll up the other end of canvas. Before starting to work knots, turn four or five rows of the extended edge of canvas to front; work through this doubled canvas to form a finished end. If the width of the canvas equals the intended width of the rug, work across canvas from selvage to selvage. A large rug may be worked in sections and the sections sewn together (see Joining Canvas, right). If canvas is wider than the rug, plan design from the center of canvas and work first row from center out to edges of design. Trim side edges of canvas to about 2" (see Finishing, right).

Patterns for latch (latchet) hooked rugs may be bought with the designs painted on the canvas. The designs given in this book are in chart form; each square on chart represents one mesh on canvas.

The drawings (Figures 1 through 4) illustrate how to make knots with a latch (latchet) hook. Fold yarn over shank of hook; hold ends with left hand (Fig.1). With hook in right hand, hold latch down with index finger; push hook down through mesh of canvas, under double horizontal threads, and up through mesh above (Fig. 2). Draw hook toward you, placing yarn ends inside hook. Be sure yarn is completely inside the hook when the latch closes, so that end of hook does not snag or split the yarn (Fig. 3). Pull hook back through the canvas, drawing ends of yarn through loop; tighten knot by pulling ends with fingers (Fig. 4).

Yarn must be knotted on the weft threads—those running across the canvas from selvage to selvage. For an evenly knotted rug, work completely across canvas before starting next row. Work from right to left or left to right, whichever is more convenient.

Work rug to within five rows of the end. Cut off excess canvas beyond ten rows, turn up five rows, and work last five rows through doubled canvas, as at the beginning.

FINISHING: Turn under side edges (leaving selvage edges on); slip-stitch firmly to back of rug with carpet thread. If there is excess canvas at the sides, fold to back of rug and baste in place. Sew rug binding to back over edges of canvas, stitching along both edges of binding with carpet thread.

JOINING CANVAS: It is not always convenient to work a large latch (latchet) hook or needlepoint rug on one piece of canvas. If working in sections, be sure to use canvas of the same mesh and weight for all pieces. Plan to work five rows over the joined sections; if using a chart, mark chart with parallel lines enclosing the five rows. Start work for each section 2″ from edge to be joined. (If working in needlepoint, block each piece separately after it has been worked.) To join, carefully cut away all but four rows of unworked mesh on one of the two edges to be joined. Lap cut edge over corresponding edge so that the four rows of meshes on top coincide with the four rows of meshes below. Be sure both sides of both pieces line up correctly, matching warp (vertical) and weft (horizontal) threads. Pin pieces together, with large needles or pins, through center of lapped edges. Following pattern, work five rows over double thickness of canvas.

If a canvas thread is weak or has been accidentally cut, it is advisable to patch the area. Cut a piece of matching canvas ½″ larger than the weak spot. Baste the patch to the wrong side of the canvas with matching wool, aligning the mesh of the two pieces. Continue working in pattern, stitching through both layers of canvas. Trim away ends of any canvas threads showing through.

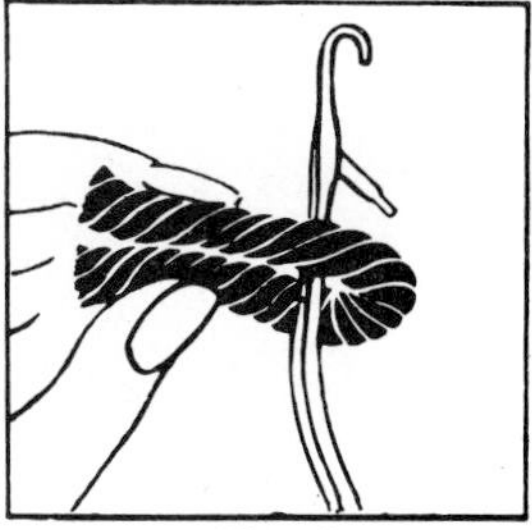
Fig. 1

Fig. 2

Fig. 3

Fig. 4

Victorian Fruits Rug

A branch of fruits provides a theme rich in nostalgia. Adapted from a Victorian original, this latch-hooked rug is worked with precut yarn on 3⅓-mesh-to-inch canvas.

SIZE: 30″ x 50″.

EQUIPMENT: Latch (latchet) hook. Scissors. Large-eyed sewing needle.

MATERIALS: Precut rug yarn: tobacco brown, 2 packs; jade green, 4 packs; watermelon red, 1½ packs; light yellow-green, 6½ packs; medium green, 5½ packs; tan, 31 packs; orange, 2 packs; purple, 2½ packs; golden brown, ½ pack. Rug canvas, 3⅓-mesh-to-the-inch, 30″ wide, 1½ yds. Rug binding, 4½ yds. Carpet thread.

DIRECTIONS: Read General Directions on

Victorian Fruits Rug

page 272. Starting at selvage, work across first row through double canvas, following first row at one end of chart below. Continue working rows across through double thickness. Work remainder of rug to opposite end through single canvas, up to last five rows of design on chart. Work end through double canvas.

Finish according to General Directions.

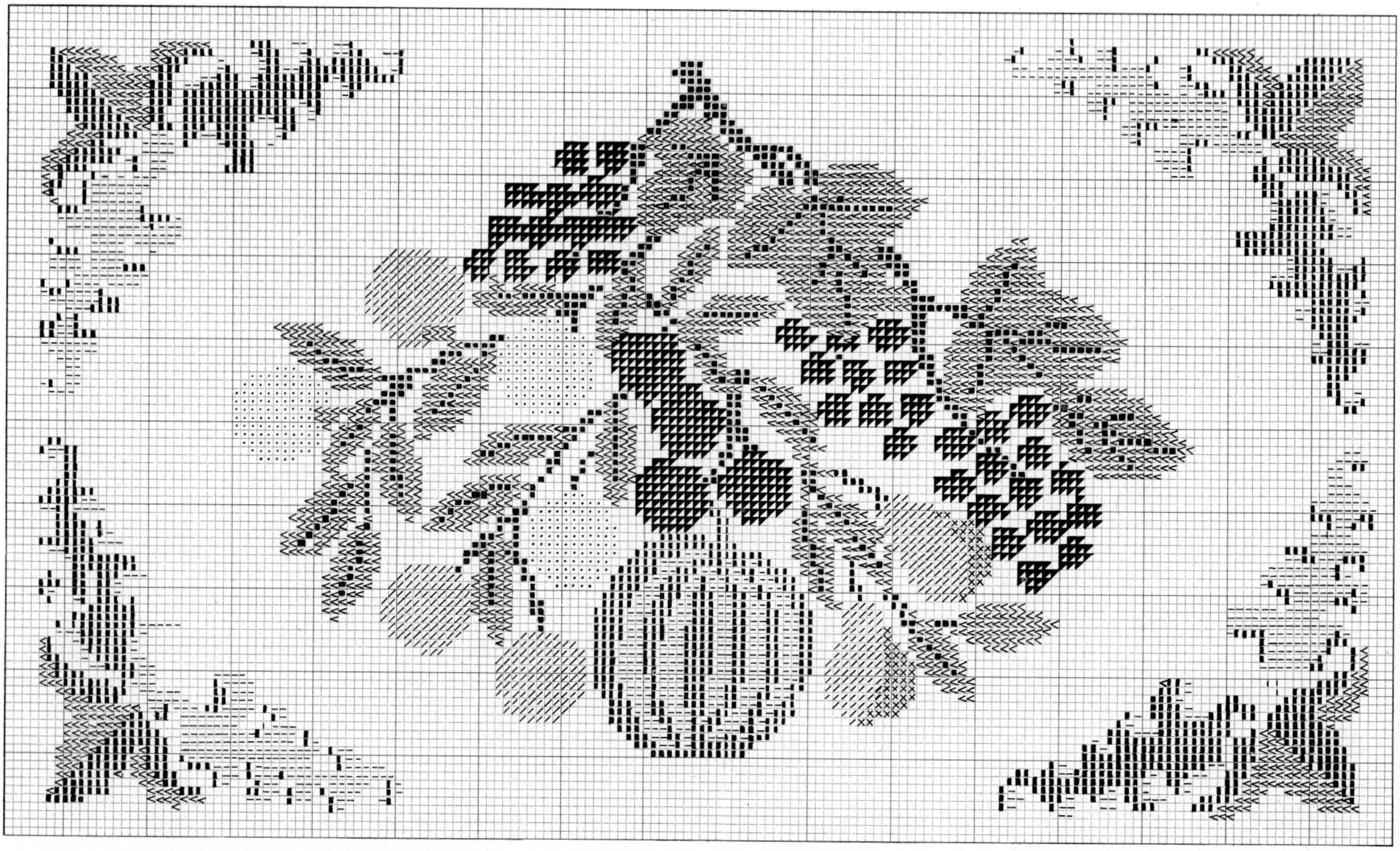

Color Key

- Medium Green
- Jade Green
- Light Yellow
- Watermelon
- Orange
- Purple
- Tobacco Brown
- Golden Brown
- Tan

Bowknot Rug

Double Bowknots, bold and handsome, pattern a latch-hook rug inspired by a hand-woven coverlet that was loomed in Ohio about 1867 and is now in the Smithsonian Institution, Washington, D.C.

SIZE: 45″ x 41½″.
EQUIPMENT: Pencil. Latch hook. Scissors.
MATERIALS: Rug canvas 45″ wide, 1½ yards (3⅓-mesh-to-the-inch). Precut rug wool, 30 packs scarlet; 24 packs each of beige and navy.
DIRECTIONS: Read General Directions on page 272. Rug chart, which is one-quarter of complete design, is 76 squares wide and 76

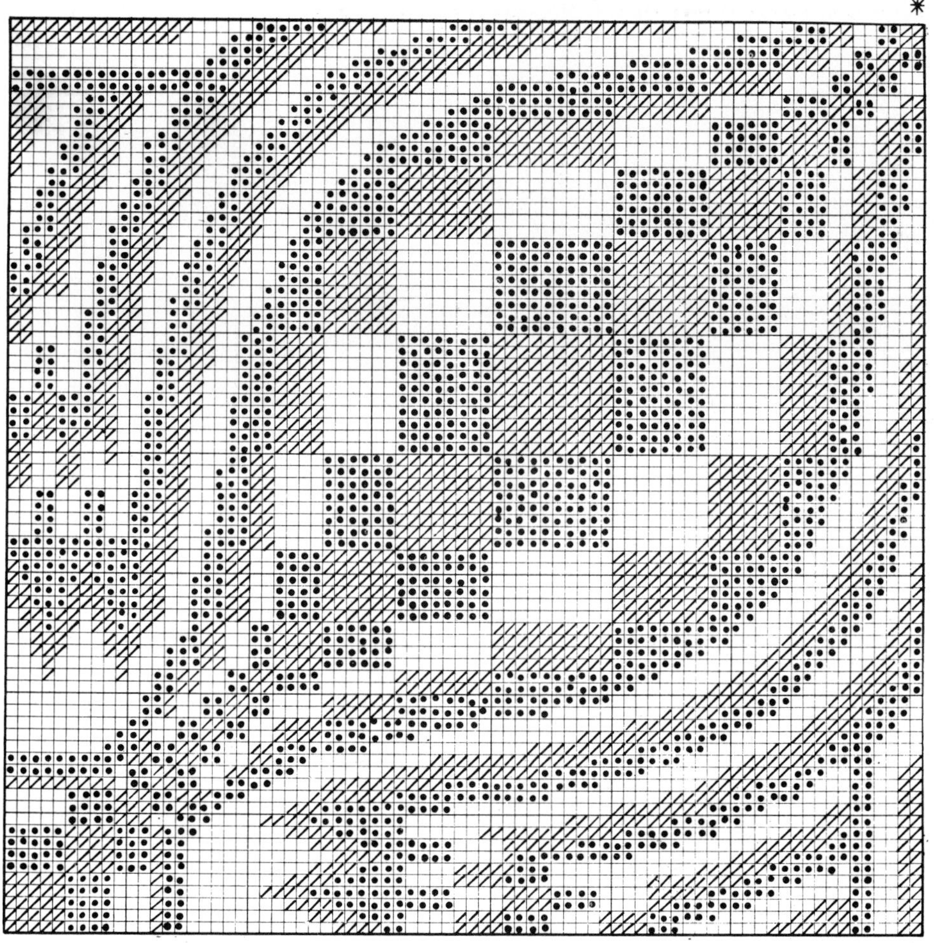

Color Key
- ▣ Scarlet
- ◪ Navy
- ☐ Beige

Each square on chart represents one knot.

squares long. On one cut edge of canvas, mark the center. Chart is to be worked twice across canvas (from selvage to selvage), and twice along length. The design area will not be quite square because the canvas is not perfectly square.

Turn under four rows of the extended edge of canvas; work through this doubled canvas to form a finished end. Work the first row of knots from center to left edge. Continue to work across in rows from right (center) to left edge until one-quarter is completed. For second quarter, repeat chart in reverse, omitting center starred vertical row. For second half of rug, repeat design in reverse omitting center starred horizontal row. Before reaching end, fold canvas under and work last four rows through doubled canvas as you did at the start. Trim off excess canvas on wrong side. Finish as instructed in General Directions.

Scarlet Tanager Rug

The bold Scarlet Tanager, framed in blossoms, is a delightful design taken from a hand-hooked rug of the Colonial period and reinterpreted here in the latch-hook technique.

SIZE: 32″ x 43″.

EQUIPMENT: Latch (latchet) hook. Large-eyed needle. Scissors. Soft pencil.

MATERIALS: Packs of cut wool rug yarn: 24 tan; 6 hunter green; 5 coral; 4 black; 3 geranium red; 3 watermelon red; 3 turkey red; 2 jade green; 2 autumn brown. Rug canvas, 3⅓″-mesh-to-the-inch: 1 yard 45″ wide. Rug binding, 4½ yards. Carpet thread.

DIRECTIONS: Read General Directions on page 272. There are 134 squares across width of chart (long side); each square represents one knot stitch. Mark off 134 meshes in center of canvas by drawing a pencil line down each side. As rug is illustrated, there are five knots in background color all around rug which are not shown on chart. Follow chart for design of rug, adding five rows of background color to beginning and end and five knots beyond each line at sides.

Finish according to General Directions.

Color Key

- ◪ Autumn Brown
- ■ Black
- ▨ Geranium Red
- ☐ Tan
- ⊡ Coral
- ⊟ Watermelon Red
- ⎕ Jade Green
- ⊙ Hunter Green
- ⊠ Turkey Red

Paisley Rug

A bold paisley pattern in a harmony of four reds makes a stunning accent for a traditional setting.

SIZE: 60″ x 90″.

EQUIPMENT: Latch (or latchet) hook. Scissors. Large-eyed sewing needle.

MATERIALS: Precut wool rug yarn: geranium red, 20 packs; blue, 40½ packs; watermelon red, 25 packs; grass green, 13 packs; coral, 8 packs;

Color Key

⊠ Geranium Red	◙ Watermelon Red	⊡ Coral
◪ Blue	◫ Grass Green	□ Turkey Red

turkey red, 46½ packs. Rug canvas, 3⅓-mesh-to-the-inch, 60″ wide, 2¾″ yds. Rug binding, 7 yds. Carpet thread.

DIRECTIONS: Read General Directions on page 272.

Place canvas on flat surface with selvages at sides. Rug is worked from half-chart above, bottom to top. Each square of chart is a knot and each symbol on chart represents a different color (see color key). Leaving a 3″ margin of canvas at bottom, knot first row of rug design in exact center of first row of meshes; be sure that there is an equal number of meshes on either side of first row (see Note below). Continue to work across in rows from right to left or left to right as desired, until center of rug is reached. Turn chart around and work from center to far end. Do not turn rug while working, so that knots will always be made in the same direction.

When rug is finished, trim away canvas margin all around to about 1¼″, tapering at center to edge of selvage. Turn margin to back of rug and sew securely in place with carpet thread. Finish as instructed in General Directions on page 272.

NOTE: At center of rug, design will cover entire width of canvas, selvage to selvage. It is thus extremely important that rug be started and remain in exact center of canvas throughout knotting; chart must be followed carefully. An alternate method of working: Fold canvas in half widthwise and crease to mark center. Work first half of rug from center to end nearest you, following chart. Turn chart around and work second half from center to far end.

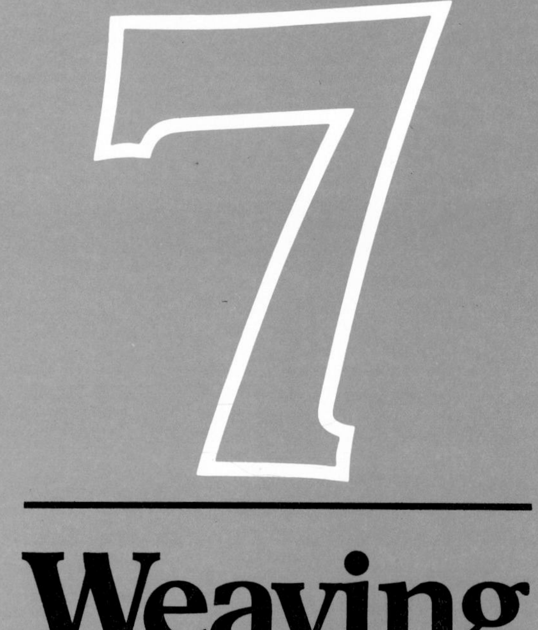

Weaving

Rib-Weave Pillow

This enticing lounging pillow is created with warm colors worked together in an easy pattern—making it a perfect project for beginners. The woven piece is worked on a table loom in rug yarn; separate 28" strands are woven across and beaten down so the warp threads are completely covered; then the ends are left free to form a thick fringe. The pillow is backed with felt.

SIZE: 12½" x 13", without fringe.

EQUIPMENT: Lilette small frame loom. Stiff, heavy cardboard. Scissors. Yardstick. Sewing machine. Sewing needle.

MATERIALS: Heavy rug yarn: rust, 6 oz.; chocolate, light brown, 4 oz. each; honey, 3 oz.; white, 1 oz. (or colors desired). For warp: mercerized crochet cotton or carpet warp. Felt, 14" x 13½" dark brown. Sewing thread in dark brown. For inner pillow: muslin, two pieces each 14½" x 13½". For stuffing: Dacron fiberfill.

DIRECTIONS: Following manufacturer's directions, warp loom with crochet cotton to width of 12½", making warp threads 30" long. Leave 1" unwoven; insert a 1"-wide strip of cardboard between the warp threads to beat against. Cut yarn in 28" lengths. Following chart and color key for number of rows and color sequence, weave in plain weave, using a length of yarn for each row. Leave an equal amount of yarn free at beginning and end of each row; free ends will be fringe. Weft is tightly beaten so no warp threads are visible.

When weaving is completed, remove from loom, knotting warp ends together in pairs to prevent raveling. Trim warp ends to ½". Staystitch across fringe ends.

To Make Pillow: With right sides facing, stitch one knotted end of weaving to the 13½"-long side of felt; stitch along weaving, 2 strands in and ½" from felt edge. Turn right side out, with weaving and felt together. Pin 14" sides together; topstitch together, ½" in from felt edges and over staystitching of weaving. Trim felt 1/4" from topstitching.

To make inner pillow, stitch two muslin pieces together all around, making ½" seams; leave 4" opening at center of one side. Turn other side out. Stuff firmly. Turn unstitched edges in ½"; slipstitch opening closed. Insert inner pillow in woven pillow. Turn in knotted side of weaving and unstitched felt side; slip-stitch opening closed. Trim fringe to 4".

Color Pattern

3 x B
W
3 x B
H
2 x B
W
2 x B
10 x {R, B}
2 x R
W
2 x R
B
2 x R
W
2 x R
10 x {C, R}
2 x C
W
2 x C
R
2 x C
W
2 x C
10 x {H, C}
2 x H
W
2 x H

C
2 x H
W
2 x H
10 x {R, H}
2 x R
W
2 x R
H
2 x R
W
2 x R
10 x {B, R}
2 x B
W
2 x B
R
2 x B
W
2 x B
10 x {C, B}
2 x C
W
2 x C
B
2 x C
W

2 x C
10 x {R, C}
2 x R
W
2 x R
C
2 x R
W
2 x R
10 x {H, R}
2 x H
W
2 x H
R
2 x H
W
2 x H
10 x {C, H}
2 x C
W
2 x C
R
2 x C
W
3 x C

Color Key

B—Light Brown
W—White
H—Honey
R—Rust
C—Chocolate

Navajo Mat

To weave on an authentic Navajo loom or a conventional tapestry or two-harness loom, this bold Navajo pattern fits in beautifully with contemporary decor. For a rug, sew three mats together!

SIZE: 18″ x 37″.

EQUIPMENT: Tapestry or 2-harness loom. Beater (such as a table fork). Shuttles or bobbins. Paper for pattern. Ruler. Pencil. Scissors.

MATERIALS: For warp: Rug warp, 8/4, 220 yards. For weft: Medium-weight, single-ply wool yarn of uniform size (sometimes called "fine" yarn by handspun yarn suppliers): white (or natural), orange, mixed brown-black, mixed brown-white, mixed orange-brown, 4 ozs. each; red, 1 oz. Scrap yarn. White, 2-ply heavy yarn for edgings, about 9 yds. (**Note:** This is an old piece that combines natural-color yarns with yarns colored with commercial dyes; it would be difficult to duplicate the colors exactly. For example, the orange-brown yarn was probably obtained by spinning brown fleece with white fleece into a brown-white yarn, then dipping the yarn into an orange commercial dye. You can, however, obtain similar interesting effects with many modern yarns, both handspun and commercial.)

DIRECTIONS: Warp loom according to the manufacturer's directions. Make warp about 55″ long (length of weaving plus 18″ for tying up and warp lost). There are 144 warp ends. For a 2-harness loom, thread in a straight draw (1, 2), one end per heddle. Draw ends through an 8-dent reed, 1 end per dent. Width of warp is 18″.

For cartoon, enlarge pattern, page 288 by copying on paper ruled in 2″ squares; complete quarter-pattern indicated by dash lines. Darken the outlines so they are visible when placed under warp. Weave about 1″ heading, using scrap yarn; this will be removed later. Place cartoon below warp, and pin bottom edge to heading. If desired, transfer the outlines to warp threads with waterproof ink. (**Note:** It may be necessary to cut up the cartoon into sections to fit behind warp when using a 2-harness loom.) Wind shuttles or bobbins of each color and follow color key for placement of colors.

Weaving: Cut two pieces of white 2-ply heavy yarn, each 2 yds. long, for edging. Tie ends together around left side of loom frame above heading, wrapping around frame several times. Twine pieces together with fingers (see detail) through warp; wrap ends around right frame of loom and tie securely. (If working on a harness loom, edging may have to be untied from sides of loom before completing piece; tie loose ends into a knot at each corner and let ends dangle.) Selvage cords also may be woven into each side of mat as illustrated. (These cords were used to add strength to Navajo rugs and saddle blankets and may be omitted if desired.) Cut two long strands of heavy 2-ply white yarn, each about 2½ yards long. Wrap one strand around bottom of loom frame at left of warp, wrapping center of strand twice around frame; bring ends up to top of loom frame, wrap around twice, and tie. One-half of cord will lie directly above other half. Repeat at right of warp with second long strand. Tension of selvage is snug but not as tight as warp. As you work, weave around top half of each cord, going around cord and outer warp end as if they were one end. Leave bottom half of cord free. After 12 rows (six weft turns on each side), untie each cord at top of loom, twist so that bottom half is now on top, and retie. Continue as before, untying, twisting, and retying after every 12 rows.

Mat is woven in plain weave. Weave the first stripe, beating down hard to cover the warp completely. Throw a shot of white, then weave the second stripe. To weave pattern, work all areas across simultaneously, using several bobbins of the same color where necessary; do not carry a color from one area over to another. Open shed; throw one shot of each required color within the outlined areas only. Beat down. Leave bobbins hanging in place. Change shed, and throw the next shot of each color in the opposite direction. Continue weaving back and forth within the outlined areas. Where colors meet on a diagonal, they lie next to each other between warp ends (see Straight Edge detail). Where colors meet to form a vertical line, they are "teethed," i.e., they lie next to each other between alternating warp ends (see Serrated Edge detail). Weave in ends as you go. (The Navajo method: Yarn is broken rather than cut, to leave tapered ends; to break, untwist against the spin and pull. Broken ends of one color are overlapped 1" in same shed; new colors are brought just to the pattern line; the heavy beat holds ends in place.)

When weaving is completed, twine an edging cord as at the beginning, using either the 2-ply white heavy yarn as before or the orange yarn, as illustrated. Untie selvage cords and edging cords from the loom and tie them together at corners. Remove heading. Knot warp ends close to weaving and trim close.

Rug: To make a rug 3 ft. x 4½ ft., make three mats as above, omitting the selvage cords from one mat and from one side of the other two mats. Sides of the three mats must be kept straight. Sew mats together as shown in diagram, tying the edging cords of adjacent mats together where they meet.

Three Mats Make a Rug.

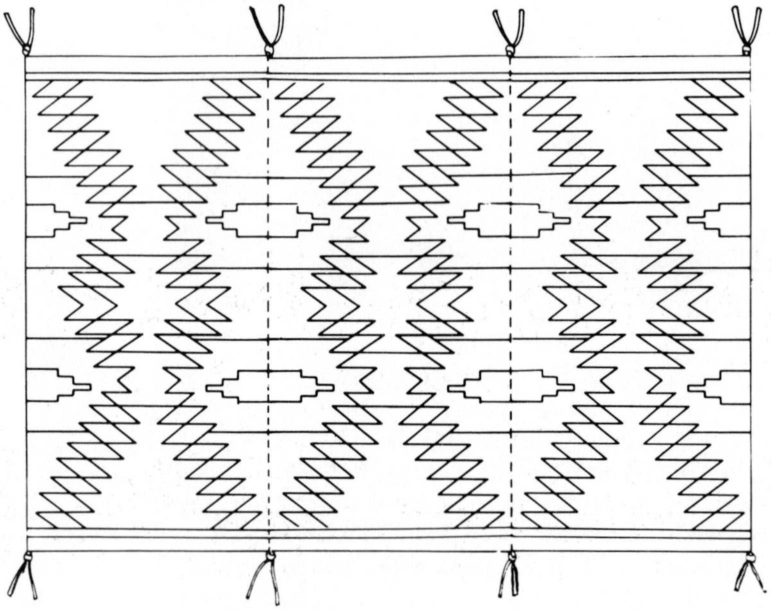

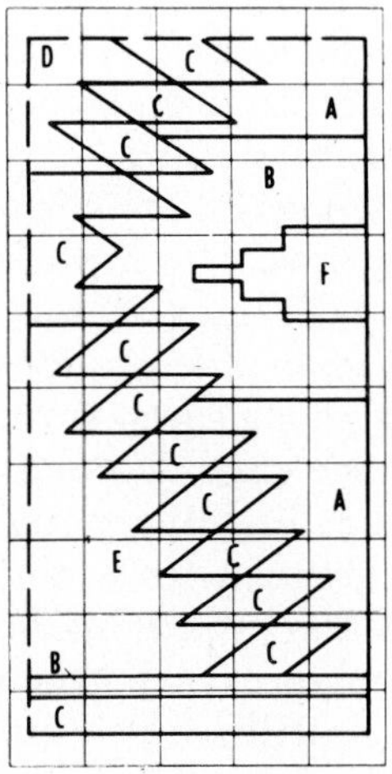

Quarter-Pattern for Mat

Color Key

A—White
B—Orange
C—Brown-Black
D—Brown-White
E—Orange-Brown
F—Red

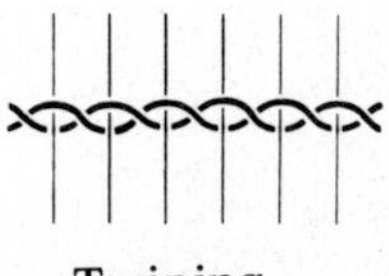

Twining

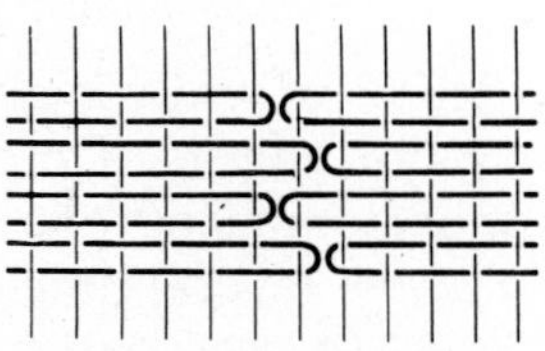

Serrated Edge

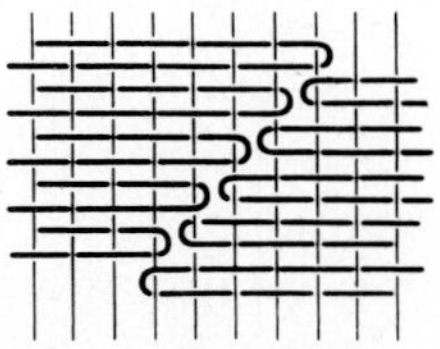

Straight Edge

Harvest Sun Rug

A half-sun sinks into reflecting bands of color to reappear on the other side. Each rib-weave band merges into the next by changing one color.

SIZE: 27" x 74" (plus fringe).

EQUIPMENT: Four-harness loom with weaving width of 27". Shuttles. Scissors. Ruler. Pencil. Paper for pattern.

MATERIALS: For warp: 3-ply cotton warp, about 720 yards. For weft: Single-ply heavy cow's hair yarn put up in 110-yard, 4-oz. skeins: 5 skeins each yellow and dark brown; 3 skeins each yellow-orange and orange; 2 skeins each yellow-gold, bright orange, and medium brown. Rug linen, 1 oz.

DIRECTIONS: Warp loom according to the manufacturer's directions. Warp is 96" long (length of rug plus 24" for tie-up and warp lost). There are 270 warp ends; draw them in a 10-dent reed, one end per dent. (See Threading and Tie-up drafts.)

Enlarge half-pattern for sun shape by copying on paper ruled in 3" squares; complete half-pattern indicated by dash lines. Darken outline so it is visible when placed behind warp. When indicated, place pattern under warp, and trace outline onto warp. Use yellow for sun, and wind an extra shuttle of dark brown for background. Follow weaving draft, using both colors. To avoid a slit in straight areas of sun shape, interlock adjacent wefts every few shots, as shown in diagram, page 290. The remainder of the weaving consists of horizontal stripes with interlocking vertical stripes. For each horizontal stripe, use two shuttles, one of each color indicated; throw one shot of first color, change shed, and throw a shot of second color. When changing colors for the next horizontal stripe, make sure that the color carried over from the previous stripe is woven in the same shed as before. Thus, a continuous vertical stripe of the color is formed through all the adjacent horizontal stripes in which it appears.

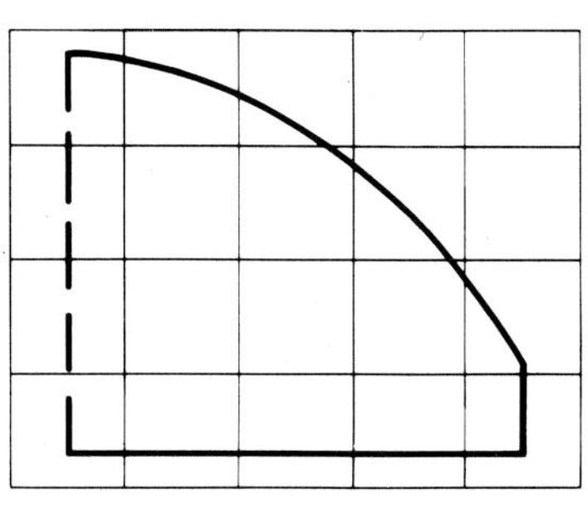

Half-Pattern for Sun

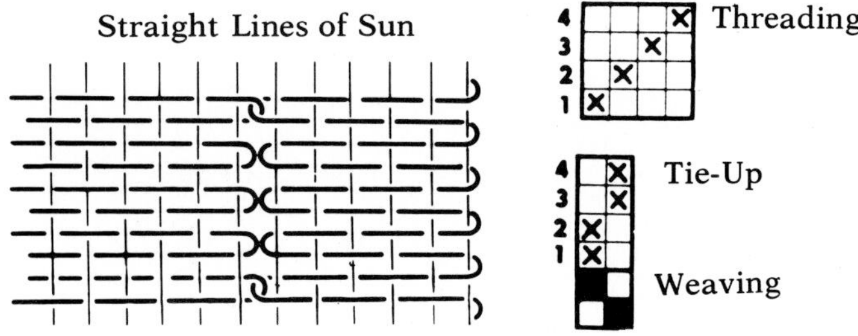

Weaving: Follow draft for weaving and beat tightly, so no warp shows. Weave 3″ heading with heavy scrap yarn.

*1″ linen

4¾″ dark brown (then trace sun outline on warp)

11½″ yellow for sun area, with brown background

3″ yellow/yellow-gold

3″ yellow-gold/yellow-orange

6″ yellow-orange/orange

3″ orange/bright orange

3″ bright orange/medium brown*

6″ medium brown/dark brown

Repeat from * to * in reverse to make symmetrical design.

Finishing: Remove weaving from loom; remove heading. Separate warp ends into groups of four. With each group, tie a single knot close to weaving. Trim ends to 3″.

Snowy Owl Wall Hanging

A rotund snowy owl perched on a branch is an unusual—but delightful—subject for a weaving that may be framed or not. It is woven on a frame loom. The warp and background weft are finer than the design threads, giving the background a sheer translucence when it is hung unframed. Design is woven using the laid-in method.

SIZE: 18″ x 24″ framed.

EQUIPMENT: Frame loom, or table or floor loom (use two harnesses). Scissors. Paper for cartoon, at least 13½″ x 19½″. Pencil. Yardstick. Sewing or tapestry needle. Heavy yarn for heading.

MATERIALS: For warp and background weft: Fine polished linen or cotton warp, 360 yards avocado green. For laid-in weft (design colors): Linen yarn in the following colors and amounts —black 22 yards; brown, 25 yards; white, 8 yards; orange ⅓ yard. Orange-painted aluminum ready-to-assemble strips to make classic metal frame, ¾″ deep and 5/16″ rim, one package 18″ and one package 24″ lengths (available at art supply stores). Matboard 18″ x 24″ with center opening 13″ x 18½″ (purchase when buying frame strips). Natural-color linen fabric, 20″ x 26″.

Masking tape or all-purpose glue. Several pieces of cardboard, 18″ x 24″.

DIRECTIONS: Amounts of yarn are approximate. Warp and background weft should be finer than the design threads; this results in a sheer background, with the design standing out clearly. The design colors should be all the same weight.

Following manufacturer's directions, warp loom, making warp 1 yard long and 15″ wide. There are 12 warp ends per inch; draw them in a 12-dent reed, one per dent (total of 180 ends). Thread in plain weave (1, 2, 1, 2).

Enlarge pattern for cartoon by copying on paper ruled in 1″ squares. Pattern is given in reverse, since this technique calls for weaving from the wrong side. Weave 2″ plain with heavy yarn for heading. Weave ½″ of background yarn (background is plain weave, 15 picks per inch, for entire weaving). Place enlarged cartoon under warp ends; tape in place if necessary. The shapes of the design are woven using the laid-in method. The design thread is laid in the same shed with a background thread. The design thread moves back and forth only within the area of the design, while the background thread runs from selvage to selvage. The background thread is always thrown across the warp first, then the design thread is laid on top of it (see Figure, page 291). Make butterfly bobbins for each design color (make by wrapping yarn around thumb and little finger, then wrapping around center to secure; pull yarn from center). Note that in some cases, there are several areas of the same color to be laid in the same shed. Therefore, you will need to make 4 brown bobbins, 2 black, 2 orange, 2 white. Follow the pattern for placement of colors: #1 is brown, #2 is black, #3 is white, and #4 is orange. Leave a 3″ end of design thread when beginning and ending a design area, and, when bobbin runs out, make sure end lies at the beginning or end of a row, rather than the middle. To avoid slits where design edges meet, interlock the weft threads of adjacent design shapes. Although the warp measures 15″ in the reed, you can expect the weaving process to result in about 1½″ shrinkage; minimize this as much as possible by laying the background weft threads in diagonally, and beating lightly.

When design is complete, weave ¾″ plain background. Cut weaving from loom. Weave in ends at back of work.

Center weaving on one piece of cardboard; secure with tape or glue around edges. Center matboard on linen; with pencil, mark outline of opening on linen. Mark 11″ x 16½″ rectangle in center of first. Cut out inner rectangle, and slash corners to outer rectangle. Replace matboard on top of linen; fold back inner and outer fabric margins and glue or tape to board. Place on top of mounted weaving. Following manufacturer's directions, assemble frame around mounted weaving and matboard; back with several pieces of cardboard as needed to fit mounted weaving snugly into frame.

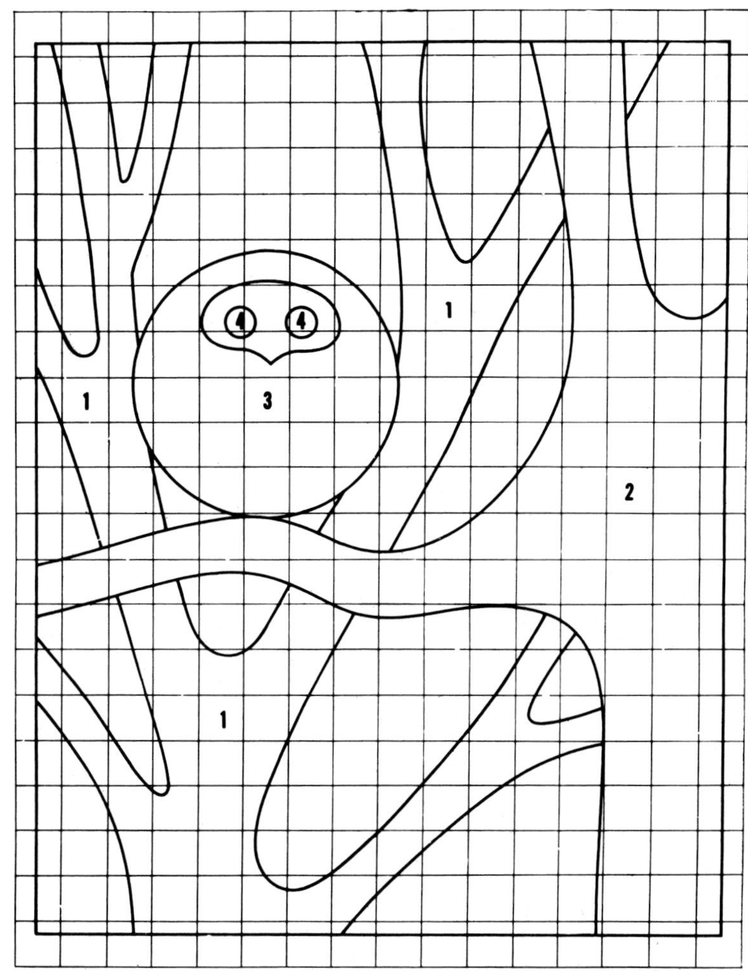

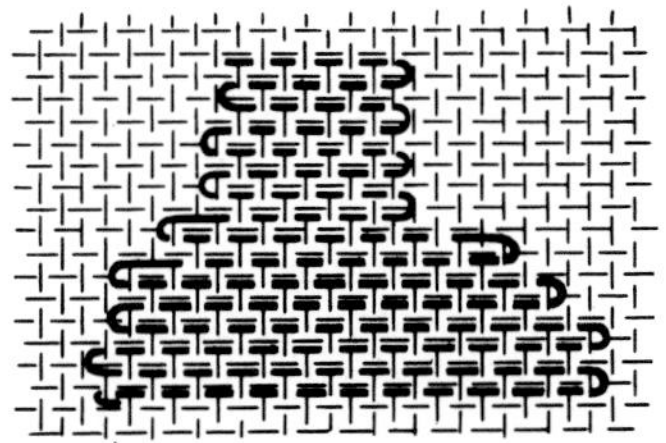

Laid-In Weaving Technique

Abstract Wall Hanging

This delicate wall hanging combines soft browns in a shadowy pattern both transparent and opaque. The piece is woven on a two-harness loom in plain weave to create a sheer background of lightweight, off-white weaving worsted. The laid-in design areas are worked in five yarns of contrasting colors, weights, and textures.

SIZE: 29″ x 52″.

EQUIPMENT: Loom: 2-harness or 4-harness (use only 2 harnesses). Scissors. Paper for cartoon, 29″ x 52″. Pencil. Yardstick. Sewing machine with zigzag attachment.

MATERIALS: For warp and background weft: light weaving worsted in off-white, ½ lb. For laid-in weft (design colors): five different natural colors in five different weights and textures, such as a thick and thin, heavy twist, bouclé, silk, yarn with a slub. Seam binding and sewing thread in off-white. Two ¼″ dowels, 29″wide.

DIRECTIONS: Following manufacturer's directions, warp loom, making warp threads 2½ yards long. There are 15 warp threads per inch: draw them in a 15-dent reed, one per dent, except for the selvages, where you draw three in each of the first and last three dents. When finished, it should measure 30″ in the reed; weaving process results in 1″ take-up (shrinkage) in width. Thread in plain weave (1, 2, 1, 2).

Plan design on paper following illustration or as desired. Weave 4″ plain weave with background yarn. Weave background in plain weave, 15 weft threads per inch, for entire weaving. Place design under warp threads; tape in place if necessary. Make several butterfly bobbins (make by wrapping yarn around thumb and little finger, then wrapping end around center to secure; pull yarn from center) of each of the five design colors, using 10-yard lengths of yarn for each. The shapes of the design are woven using the laid-in method (see figure below); use colors as desired, using one color for each shape. The pattern thread is laid in the same shed with a background thread. Leave a 3″ end of design thread at beginning and end of each butterfly. The pattern thread moves back and forth only within the area of design, while the background thread runs from selvage to selvage. The background threads are finer than the design threads and are beaten lightly, resulting in a sheer background with the design standing out clearly. Always throw the background thread across the warp first, and lay the pattern thread on top of it. To avoid slits where design edges meet, interlock the weft threads of the adjacent design shapes.

Weave 4″ plain weave with background thread only, when design is complete. Cut weaving from loom, and weave threads in work at back. Sew seam binding across each top and bottom edge (this must be done with a zigzag stitch, or it will not hold). Fold and stitch a 1″ hem to back, forming a casing for dowels. Insert dowel in casings.

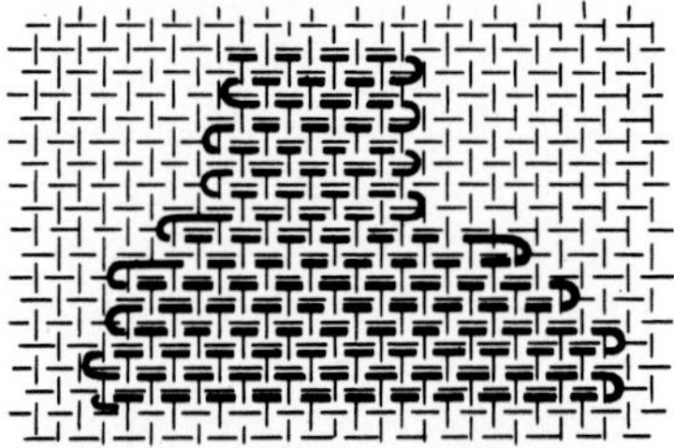

Laid-In Weaving Technique

Dolls and Miniatures

Antique Fashion Doll

Carved wooden dolls of the early nineteenth century were dressed and coiffed in the style of the day, as models of what the well-dressed lady wore. This antique doll is from about 1810. The replica, cut from sugar pine, then shaped and whittled, duplicates the original's proportions and 17″ height.

WOODEN DOLL

EQUIPMENT: Whittling knife (oil stone and machine oil to keep knife sharp). Jig or coping saw. Wood file, ½″ flat. Hand drill, ⅛″ and ½″ bits. Lathe (optional). Vise. Pliers. Rags. Fine wire. Paintbrushes: small flat for painting body; fine sable for features. Wooden mallet. Straight pin. Tracing paper.

MATERIALS: Sugar pine, 2″ x 2″ x 8¼″ for body. Two pieces sugar pine, 2″ x 2″ x 5¼″ for arms and legs. Two pieces ⅝″ dowel, 5½″ long for upper legs. Two pieces ½″ dowel, 3″ long for upper arms; one piece ½″ dowel, 2½″ long for shoulder piece. Dowel ⅛″ diameter for joints, about 8″. Flat white paint. Oil or poster paints: black, white, red, yellow, blue. Shellac.

DIRECTIONS: Actual-size patterns for carving doll are on pages 296–297. Trace all parts for body, arms, and legs (except dowel upper leg and upper arm pieces). Trace patterns onto 2″ x 2″ wood as shown on patterns. Saw arm and leg sections apart along dash lines. Body is shaped by turning on lathe, following pattern; solid black outline is turning guide. If you do not have a lathe, shape by sawing profile front and side and rounding with knife; use jig or coping saw to go around curves. Be sure to leave plenty of wood around pattern lines to prevent breaking while shaping parts. Whittle with knife going the way of grain. Sharpen knife frequently on oil stone. A dull knife may slip and ruin work. Knife should go down from high to low places (see Fig. 1). Sandpaper all pieces to smooth finish.

Fig. 2 shows a dowel piece with tenon (top) and mortise (bottom), which is a slot cut out to receive the tenon of another piece. The tenon and mortise on dowel pieces are cut at different angles to allow correct movement of limbs. Diagonal lines at top of upper leg and side leg patterns show angle to cut bottom of tenon; upper arm and side arm tenons are cut straight across. Circles on patterns are drilled holes; dash lines across pieces show direction of holes through ends. Use jig or coping saw to shape tenons, and file smoothly to ¼″ thickness. But do not drill hole until assembling. Round tops of tenons with knife. Mortises are 3/16″ x ⅞″ deep. When mortise is sawed out, file smooth; round ends with knife. Sand ends smooth.

Legs: When lower leg is well shaped, gradually shave foot down to its correct size. Right and left legs are exactly the same. Upper leg is ⅝″ dowel;

cut tenon and mortise as indicated on pattern. Join leg and upper leg. Perfect fit is necessary. When properly fitted, place legs in a vise so they will not move, and drill ⅛″ hole through both. Force-fit ⅛″ dowel into hole, tapping gently with wooden mallet; trim off ends. Leg is now joined at knee.

Arms: Reverse pattern for lower arm to make right and left hands. Upper arm is ½″ dowel. The mortise in upper arm must be cut at a slight angle from tenon to allow arms to bend up and in (see patterns and Fig. 2). Assemble arms as for legs.

Shoulder Piece: Cut ⅝″-deep mortise at each end of ½″ dowel; round ends. Fit tops of upper arms into mortises and drill ⅛″ holes, but do not assemble until body is carved.

Body: Shape according to Directions. Mark perpendicular center lines at top and bottom and down front, back, and sides for guidelines in whittling. Drill ½″ hole in body through center line, from side to side, to accommodate shoulder piece. Whittle away solid black areas of diagrams. Whittle away sides of waist under shoulders. Round chest and shoulders. Narrow neck under chin and ears; shape and flatten back of head, making neck at back straight. Saw off wood above head and in front of comb. Round head smoothly. Curve inside front of comb and shape back. As pencil lines are carved away, draw in the necessary ones again so that the carving does not get out of shape. To make ears seem raised, lower the sections behind, above, and below them. Do not make cuts straight down, but slant slightly outward. This gives the appearance of greater thickness to ears. Pare down cheeks from ears to make a pointed chin. Curve forehead and lower bridge of nose to bring nose out. Pare down section under nose and above chin. This will raise a hump, which looks unattractive for the moment, but will be necessary for carving the mouth later. Carefully carve two arches for eyes and bring them down to sides of nose. Under eyes, lower and round cheeks to side of nose, also under mouth to sides of chin. Keep looking from side to front to be sure fullness of cheeks is moving down in all directions. Carve a little slit for mouth and remove excess wood, curving it back at sides to meet cheeks. Doll's expression comes out in painting, so do not worry if you cannot get the expression you want with the knife.

Assembling: Sandpaper shoulder piece to ease it into the hole under shoulders. Set mortises vertically and adjust arms in place with dowel pieces

as for other joints. Adjust tenons of upper leg in mortises of body. Drill hole through mortises and leg tenons and insert dowel.

Earrings: Carve two tiny earrings following pattern. Bore holes in tips of ears and earrings with pin. Make four tiny wire loops, link two together, pinch ends together, insert in holes of earrings and ears.

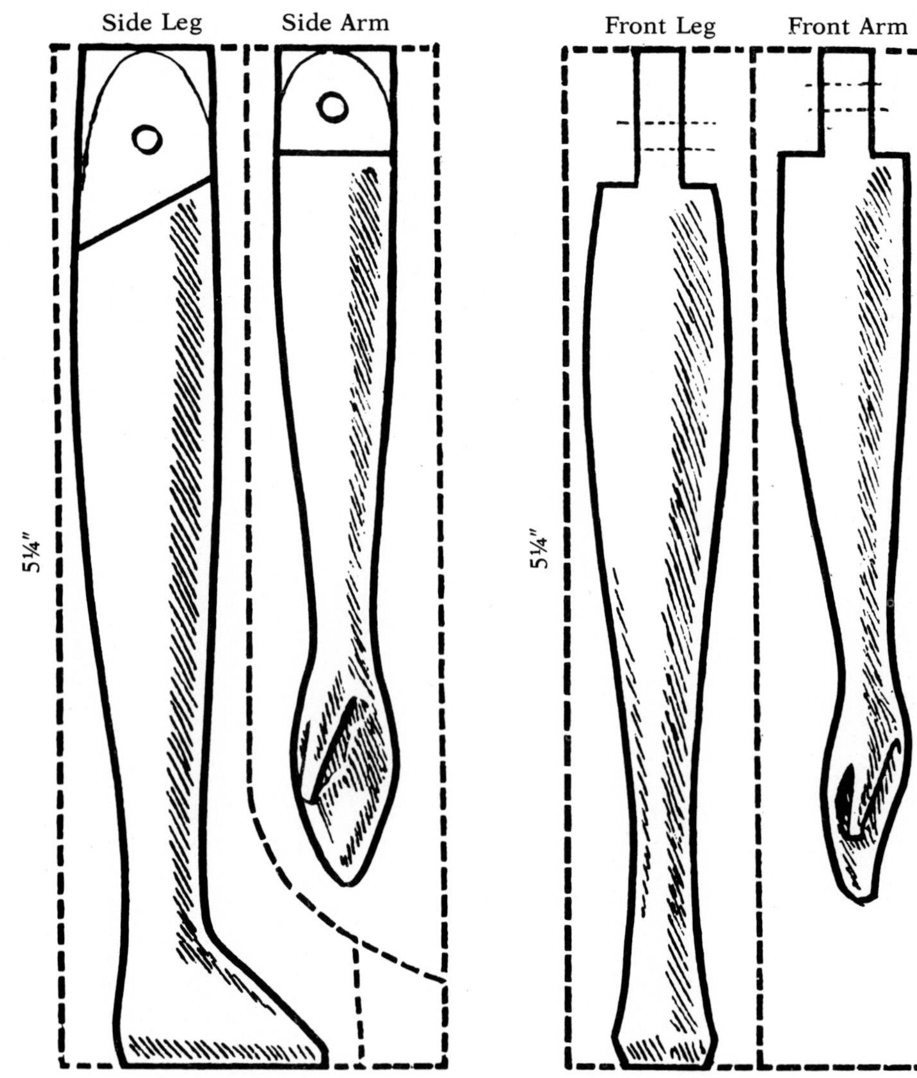

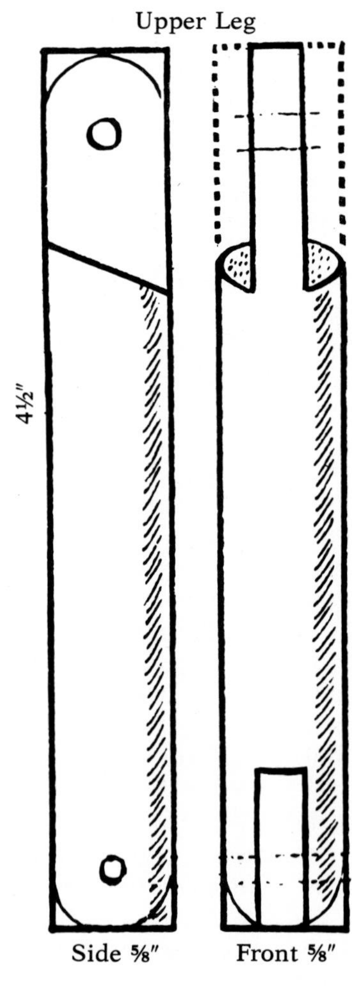

Painting: Sand all surfaces and wipe clean. If using oil-base paints, give entire doll a coat of shellac. If using water-base paint, do not shellac. Give head, shoulders, lower arms, and lower legs undercoating of flat white paint. When dry, cover with flesh tone (mix small amounts of red and yellow with white). Let dry. Paint in features as shown in drawing as follows: Place blue dots on lower edge of carved arches for eyes. Dot with black for pupils and add black lines for eyelashes above and below eyes. Fill in whites of eyes. Make black eyebrows as shown. With red, paint fine curved line in mouth slit, paint in lower and upper lips. Paint cheeks red, shading at edges or, if using water-base paints, use dry rouge on cheeks. With very thin black paint, make two bold, swift curving lines from forehead to ears. Fill in rest of hair solid black, curving back hairline from ear to ear. Paint front of comb yellow, back of comb black, earrings green (add blue to yellow). Paint shoes red. When dry, shellac.

To make doll's clothes, see page 298.

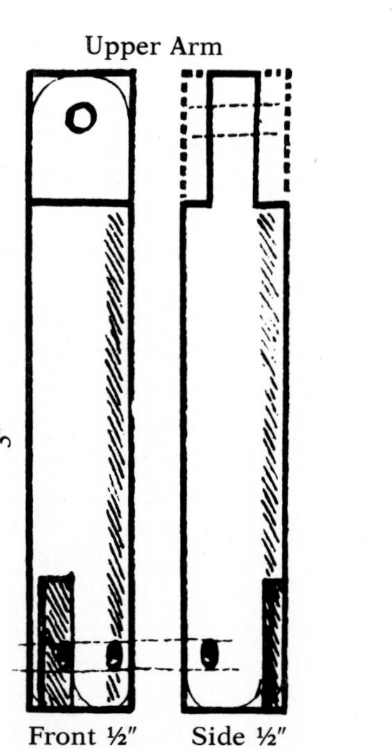

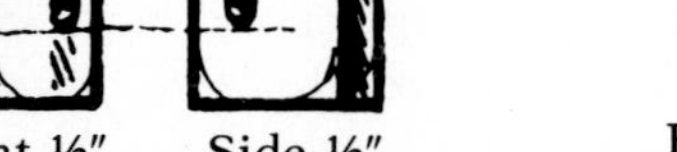

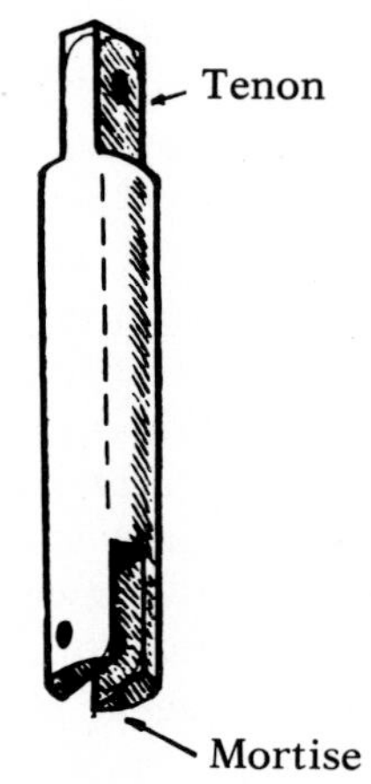

Fig. 2

Earrings

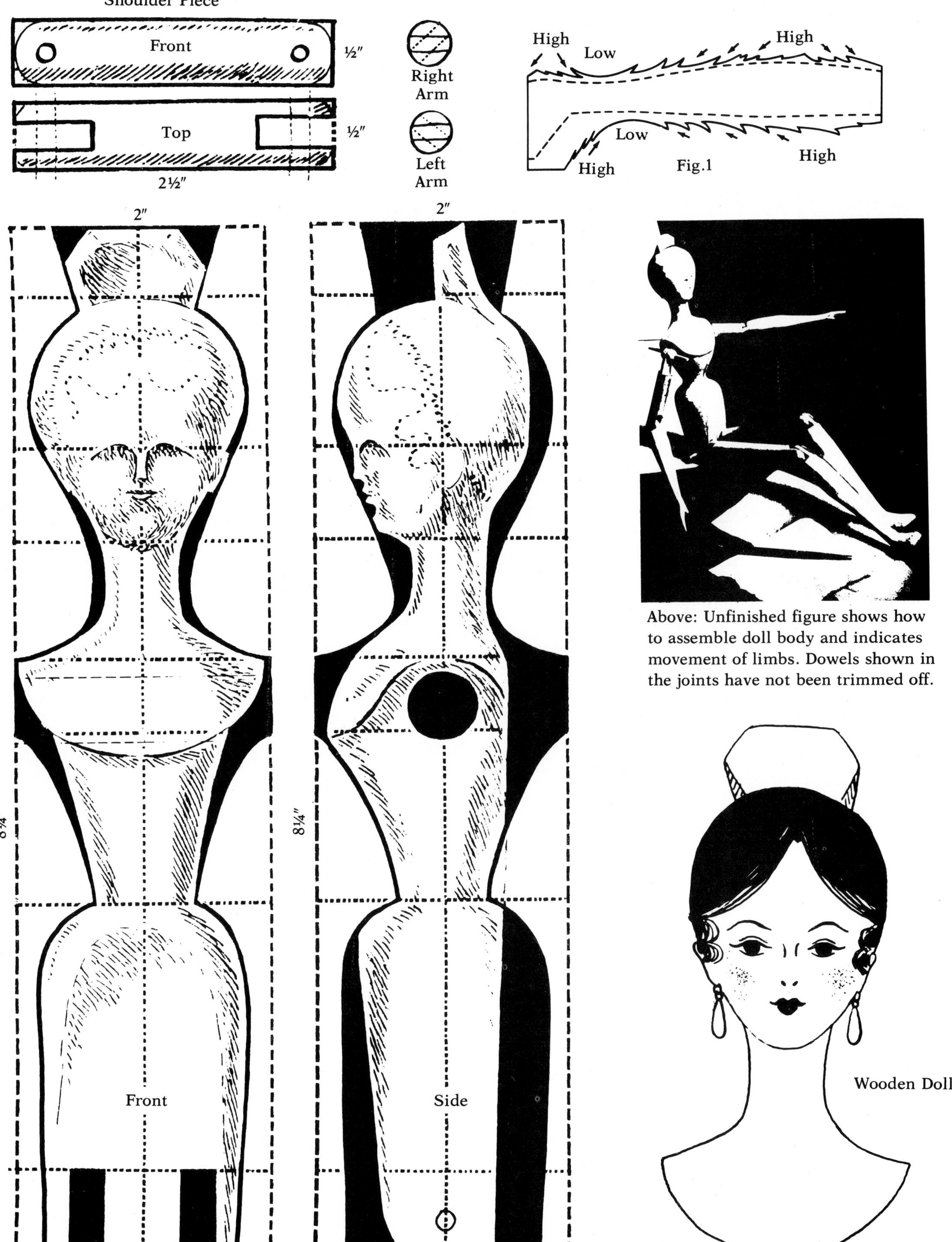

Above: Unfinished figure shows how to assemble doll body and indicates movement of limbs. Dowels shown in the joints have not been trimmed off.

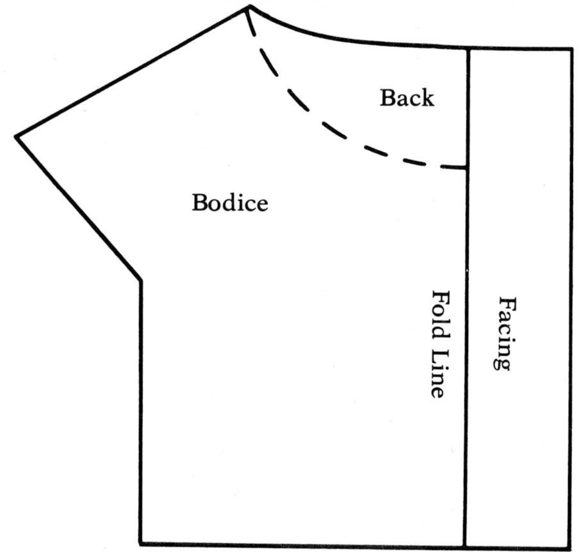

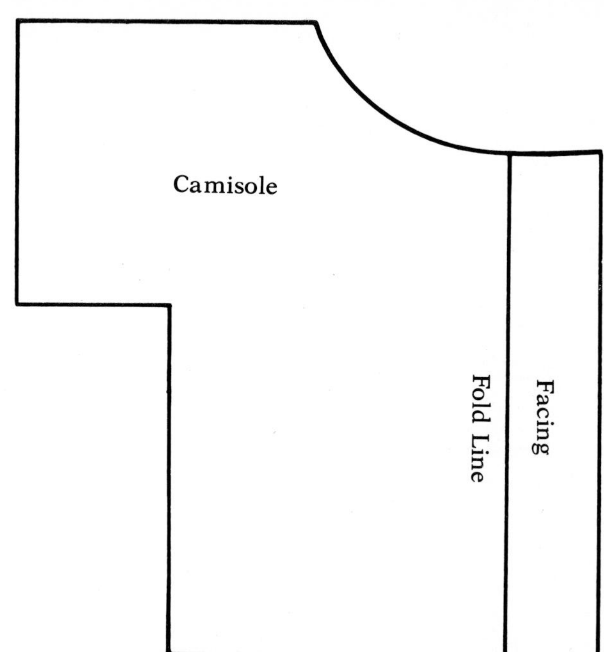

WOODEN DOLL'S CLOTHES

EQUIPMENT: Paper for pattern. Pencil. Scissors. Needle. Tape measure.

MATERIALS: For Undergarments: White percale, ½ yard 36″ wide. Very narrow ribbon for drawstring, 12″ long. Narrow lace, 1 yard. Lace 4″ wide, ¼ yard. Eyelet 1½″ wide, ½ yard. **For Dress:** Thin cotton print, ½ yard 36″ wide. Narrow cording, ¼ yard. Narrow lace, ¼ yard. Narrow ribbon, ¾ yard. Small snap fasteners.

Directions: Actual-size patterns are given above. Other garment pieces are straight pieces (see individual directions). All seam allowances are ¼″. Sew all seams with right sides of fabric together either by hand with small running stitches, or by machine.

Petticoat: Cut white fabric 9¼″ x 24″. Sew 9¼″ edges together for back seam, leaving 2″ open at top for placket. Turn in edges of placket opening and hem each side. Make ½″ hem along top for casing; insert narrow ribbon through casing for drawstring; gather to fit around waist. Sew narrow lace around bottom of petticoat.

Pantalets: Cut two pieces of white fabric 5″ x 10″. Cut two pieces of eyelet each 5″ long. Stitch eyelet to one 5″ edge of each piece of white fabric; add narrow lace along edge of eyelet. Fold each white fabric piece in half lengthwise and seam each together from bottom (lace edge) up to 4″ from top for legs. Stitch the open 4″ of legs together for front seam; leave back seam open. Hem back opening for placket. Cut a strip of white fabric 1″ x 5″ for waistband. Fold waistband in half lengthwise; turn in long edges and ends; press. Gather top of pantalets to fit doll's waist. Insert gathered edge in between halves of waistband and stitch together. Sew snap fastener to ends of waistband.

Camisole: Using pattern, cut front in one piece, placing fold line of pattern on fold of doubled white fabric. Cut two back pieces, including facing. Place backs and front together and sew shoulder, underarm, and side seams. Turn in back facings and hem. Make narrow hems around neck, sleeves, and bottom. Cut two pieces of wide lace 4¼″ long; sew ends of each together. Gather one edge of each to fit sleeves and sew to ends of sleeves. Sew three snap fasteners to back facings.

Dress: Cut a piece of print fabric 11″ long and 24″ wide for skirt. Seam the 11″ edges together, leaving 3½″ open at one end for top. Make 1¾″ hem around bottom.

Using pattern, cut front bodice in one piece, placing fold line of pattern on fold of doubled print fabric; cut neck on dash line. Cut two back pieces, including facings, and cut neck along solid line. Place backs and front together; sew shoulder and side seams. Turn in back facing and hem. Cut three strips of print fabric on the bias ½″ wide, long enough to fit around neck and armholes. Fold bias strip in half lengthwise and insert cording into fold. Stitch covered cording around neck and armhole edges for firmness, making seam line close to cording. Sew narrow lace around neck cording. For sleeves, cut two pieces of fabric on the bias, 3½″ wide and 4½″ long. Fold each in half crosswise and stitch 3½″ edges together for underarm seams. Cut two pieces of fabric for ruffles 1½″ wide and 8½″ long. Fold each in half crosswise and seam 1½″ ends. Hem one long edge of each and gather other long edge to fit sleeve. Sew ruffles to sleeve ends. Gather other end of sleeves to fit armhole; stitch sleeves in armholes.

Gather bodice slightly at waist; gather top of skirt to fit waist. Stitch skirt and bodice together. Sew three snap fasteners to back facings, placing one at waist, one at top and one in between.

Tie 22″ narrow ribbon around waist.

Three Sisters Dolls

A charming trio from the past—Amanda, Elspeth, and Lilly—are fabric dolls dressed in the style of the 1860s. Create their "printed" fabrics with tube embroidery paint in desired colors.

SIZE: About 16″ tall.

EQUIPMENT: Paper for patterns. Soft lead pencil. Dressmaker's carbon (tracing) paper. Ruler. Scissors. Sewing needle. Poster board, 20″ x 24″. Straight pins. Thumbtacks or masking tape. Crochet hook or small wooden dowel with rounded end.

MATERIALS: Beige or ecru wash-and-wear cotton fabric, 1 yard 40″ wide (for three dolls). Matching sewing thread. Tubes of ball-point embroidery paints in desired colors (we used black, white, red, brown, yellow, blue, green, and gold). Cotton for stuffing. Clear plastic spray.

DIRECTIONS: Enlarge front and back patterns for each doll on paper ruled in 1″ squares. To complete back pattern for dolls Amanda and Lilly, trace top back pattern; reverse tracing, match to top front, and copy bottom of front pattern, leaving out dolls' dolls. Cut fabric into four 18″ x 20″ rectangles. Each rectangle will make one complete doll.

For each doll, tack or tape fabric edges to poster board. Put board and fabric on flat working surface. Place pattern over fabric with carbon between. With soft pencil, go over pattern completely to transfer outline and designs to fabric. If you prefer, you may use basic outlines of pattern and make your own fabric design. Remove carbon and tracing; leave fabric attached to board. Make any marks necessary for designs in soft pencil directly on fabric.

Following directions that come with ball-point tube paints, go over all lines and outline with black paint, except for line between eyelid and eyebrow and lines within areas marked X on pattern. Lines in these areas should be done in white or pale color. Except for faces, necks, hands, and any other design area you wish to leave the color of fabric, fill in areas thickly, staying within black lines. Use brown or yellow for hair, blue or brown for eyes. Make irises, boots, and dolls' doll hair black. Put white highlight dot on colored part of eye. Make lips and line over eyelid red. Paint dolls' doll skin areas white or pink. Paint dresses in colors desired, following illustration and pattern lines. Add flowers, polka dots, stripes, buttons, ribbons, and jewelry as given or as desired. For jewelry, gold paint will appear deeper if painted over an area painted yellow first as a base. If desired, when painting is finished, sign name and date on back side of skirt. Spray fabric with clear plastic spray to keep fabric soil-proof and from stretching.

Lilly Back

Amanda Back

Lilly Front

Amanda Front

Cut out fabric around each outline, adding ¼″ all around for seam allowance. With right sides facing, pin fabric edges together. To make sure both pieces match exactly, hold them up together in front of a strong light. Sew completely around doll twice along black outline. Painted line will show through fabric for clear guide. Trim seams neatly and clip into seam allowance around curves. Holding front of doll away from back, cut a slit in center back of skirt as indicated by heavy line with crosslines at ends on back pattern. Turn doll right side out. Use crochet hook or small dowel to push out feet. Stuff feet with little pieces of cotton. Tamp with hook or dowel. Stuff skirt ends and head; fill shoulders tightly. Stuff skirt and middle last, keeping body tight but flat. Turn edges of opening in; pin, and then whip opening closed with tiny stitches. Press doll with hands to smooth stuffing. If edges need touching up, you can add paint at this time. Give doll final coat of plastic spray.

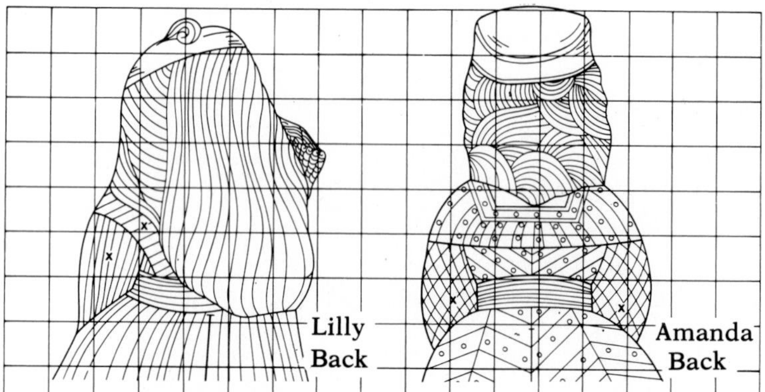

Early American Quartet

Right from the pages of American history, these delightful dolls can also double as pillows. Colorful marking pens "print" the designs, front view and back, on the muslin; a few simple embroidery stitches and buttons are added for accents.

SIZE: Approximately 18″ tall.

EQUIPMENT: Paper for patterns. Hard- and soft-lead pencils. Tracing paper. Ruler. Scissors. Dressmaker's tracing (carbon) paper. Straight pins. Sewing and embroidery needles.

MATERIALS: Unbleached muslin, 44″–45″ wide, approximately ⅜ yard for each doll. Medium- and fine-tipped permanent ink marking pens, black and colors shown or as desired. Dacron fiberfill. Off-white sewing thread. Small amounts of six-strand embroidery floss in colors desired. Round buttons, about ⅜″ diameter: six brown; twelve gold.

DIRECTIONS: To Cut Out Doll: Enlarge patterns by copying on paper ruled in 1″ squares; trace patterns for dolls. Place tracings on muslin with carbon between; pin in place. Go over entire outline of front and back of each and all details with hard pencil to transfer design to muslin. Following contour of doll design, cut front and back pieces ¼″ larger all around for seam allowance.

To "Paint" Doll: Using both fine and medium black pens, go over all detail lines of design (except outer contour), including finer lines; fill in shaded areas such as eyes, mouths, and bouquet with solid black. Color in areas with colored marking pens as desired or following illustrations for colors and shading.

To Embroider: Use six strands of floss for all embroidery. Refer to stitch details on page 15. For eyes, using green or brown, make several satin stitches either horizontally or vertically in center of each eye. For mouth, using red, make line across mouth in satin stitch. Embroider over ink lines where indicated by fine lines on patterns. Refer to individual directions for stitches.

To Assemble: With right sides facing, pin front and back pieces together. Stitch ¼″ in from edges all around (use contour outline as stitching line), leaving about a 4″ opening at one side. Clip into seam allowance at curves. Turn to right side. Push out corners and curves smoothly. Stuff doll fully but softly. Turn in edges of opening and slip-stitch closed.

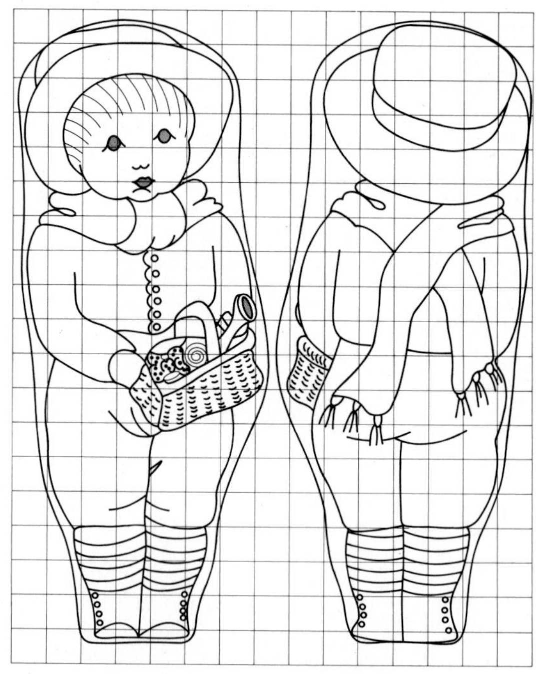

COLONIAL GIRL

Embroider lines over bangs in straight stitch; side curls in outline stitch. For bouquet, make a line of straight stitches just inside zigzag outline of bouquet; make dots in French knots; make circles in flower petals in outline stitch; make petals in lazy daisy stitches.

BOY WITH BASKET

Embroider lines of hair in outline stitch. In basket, make dots in French knots, circles in outline stitch and fill in some small areas with satin stitch.

Sew on six brown buttons down center of shirt following circles on pattern.

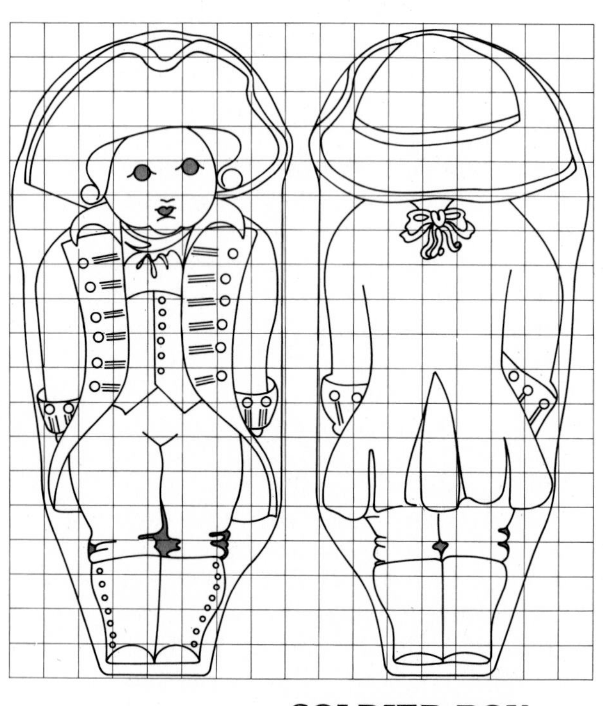

SOLDIER BOY

Embroider lines on coat front and sleeves in chain stitch.

Sew six gold buttons on each coat lapel at large circles on pattern.

GIRL WITH FLAG

Embroider doll as follows: Make lines on hair, sash, collar, dress hem, and sleeve cuff in straight stitch.

Cornhusk Dolls

Five dainty ladies, each about 8" tall, are fun to make from dried cornhusks, dyed and plain. Husks form head and body; the skirt, made of several layers, is all that the doll needs to stand. Hair, braided or flowing, is of cornsilk; features are drawn on.

EQUIPMENT: Ruler. Scissors. Glass-head pins. Sewing needle. Large porcelain pot for dyeing husks. Stick for stirring. Tissue paper. Fine, felt-tipped pens or ball-point pens in red and black. Newspapers.

MATERIALS: Cornhusks. Cornsilk. Fabric dyes (in colors given in individual directions, or as desired). Liquid dish detergent. Household string or fine cord. White pipe cleaners. Brown thread.

DIRECTIONS: Soak dried cornhusks in warm water for five minutes, or until pliable. Husks are always worked on while wet. For head, remove husk from water; cut off bottom; tear into strips ¼" wide and wrap tightly into a ball ¾" in diameter (No. 1); stick pin in end until ready to use. Do the same for the body but make ball 1" in diameter. For arms, place a pipe cleaner across length of 1"-wide strip of husk and roll up husk (No. 2); turn ends in and tie with small piece of husk ⅛" wide. Using the inner surface of husk for face, fit a strip over the front of the head; give three twists at top and bring down over the back of head, leaving an excess of 3½" at both ends (No. 3); tie in place with string. Wrap string around twice each time it is used to secure head, body and skirt. Put arms between husk ends of head; add body below and tie at bottom (No. 4); split husk ends as shown. Remove pins fron head and body. Make a skirt by placing narrow ends of husks around waist with bottom ends turning in; tie in place (No. 5). Add additional layers until desired fullness is obtained (or until doll can stand alone). Trim ends at waist, leaving excess of ½" above string. Measure 5½" below waist; cut off excess and trim evenly around skirt bottom. Pin skirt by lapping one husk over another (No. 6).

Method One for Blouse: Hold husk at narrow end and tear wide end about one-fourth of the way up. With solid portion at front, drape divided ends over shoulders and back; hold in place and tie a narrow strip of husk around waist (No. 7).

Method Two for Blouse: Slit lengthwise along center of husk; drape each half over a shoulder and cross them on front and back; tie around waist as for Method One. For hair, soak cornsilk in warm water for five minutes; wrap around head in desired hair style; sew to head with brown thread (see No. 7). Leaving pins in place, carefully slip some tissue paper under skirt. Let stand overnight in dry, but not too warm spot. Remove pins from skirt. Paint on features using black and red pens.

Assemble dolls as instructed in individual directions.

To Dye Husks: Heat 1½ gallons of water to boiling point; add ½ package of dye and two tablespoons of liquid dish detergent. Place cornhusks in boiling solution a few at a time (do not crowd) and simmer for 15 minutes, stirring occasionally. Pour off solution and run cold water over husks until excess dye is removed. Place husks on newspapers and let dry until ready to use.

To Braid: Tear husks into narrow strips; soak in water; tie three or more strips together and braid.

DOLL WITH BAG

Follow General Directions for making the doll. Arrange hair with a braid at each side of head. For head scarf, use half or less of husk torn lengthwise; tie at back of head. For blouse, dye husks blue; for skirt, brown. Make blouse by Method Two. For bag, use a piece of husk about 1½" wide; fold up one end as shown in No. 8; tie top of bag with string. Slit top ends of remainder of husk and fold down over one side of bag. Roll a strip of husk and tie around top of bag; tie ends together for handle. Bend arms in position; hang bag on arm.

DOLL WITH BROOM

Follow General Directions for making the doll. Make blouse by Method One. Arrange hair around top and sides of head; make one braid down the back; tie with piece of brown thread to secure. For head scarf, use a half or less of husk torn lengthwise; tie under chin. For broom, roll a pipe cleaner 6½" long in a strip of husk; turn top end in and tie; tie broom bristles around bottom end. Bend arms in position and sew on broom handle.

DOLL WITH HEADBAND

Follow General Directions for making the doll. Make blouse by Method Two, using two contrasting strips of husk, dark brown and blue, 2" wide. Hair is worn long and loose. For headband, make a braided strip of husk (in blouse colors) and tie in place. Scarf is dark blue. Make bag as instructed for "Doll with Bag."

DOLL WITH HAT

Follow General Directions for making the doll. Dye husks for blouse, hat and skirt dark red; bag, dark brown; belt, dark blue. Make blouse by Method Two. Wrap hair around head; sew in place. For hat, coil braided husk in a circle and sew edges of braids together; continue adding braids, shaping side crown. Add brim by sewing braided husk to bottom edge of side crown; encircle twice, sewing in place as you go. Stuff inside of hat with tissue paper to hold shape; pin brim flat on piece of cardboard until dry. Pin on head when dry. Make bag as instructed for "Doll with Bag". Bend arms in position and hang on arm.

DOLL WITH BABY

Follow General Directions for making the doll. For blouse, dye husks brown; for skirt, dark green. Make blouse by Method Two. Wrap hair around head; sew in place. For hat, coil braided husks in a circle and sew together at edges; add braided husks and with finger gently press at center of circle to shape hat to desired head size. Pin to head. Make belt of brown and natural braid.

BABY

Roll a very small ball of husk (about ¼" diameter) and cover as for the head of large doll. Arms are made as for the large doll, but use 1½" of pipe cleaner; place between ends of head husk and tie in place. Do not make a body ball. Lay doll on strip of husk; tie to husk around neck with string (No. 9). Fold top of husk down around sides and back over string. Wrap a piece of string around doll until dry; remove string when dry. Tear a strip of husk ¾" wide and center over head for bonnet; tie at neck; cut off excess husk. Using pens, draw two dots for eyes, small circle for mouth. Bend arms of large doll for baby.

Kachina Dolls

Kachina dolls, replicas of handmade dolls that represent the gods of the Pueblo Indians, are carved from balsa and painted with poster paints. Fur, feathers add splendor to costumes. No frame is illustrated.

EQUIPMENT: Tracing paper. Pencil. Ruler. Straight gouge chisel, ¾". Mat knife. Wood rasp. Fine sandpaper. Small flat and pointed paintbrushes. Scissors. Compass. Coping saw. Hammer. Awl or ice pick.

MATERIALS: Balsa wood, 36"-long pieces: two 1" x 3"; two 3" x 3". Contact cement. Acrylic paints: white, turquoise, black, yellow, orange,

Actual-size patterns for the dolls.

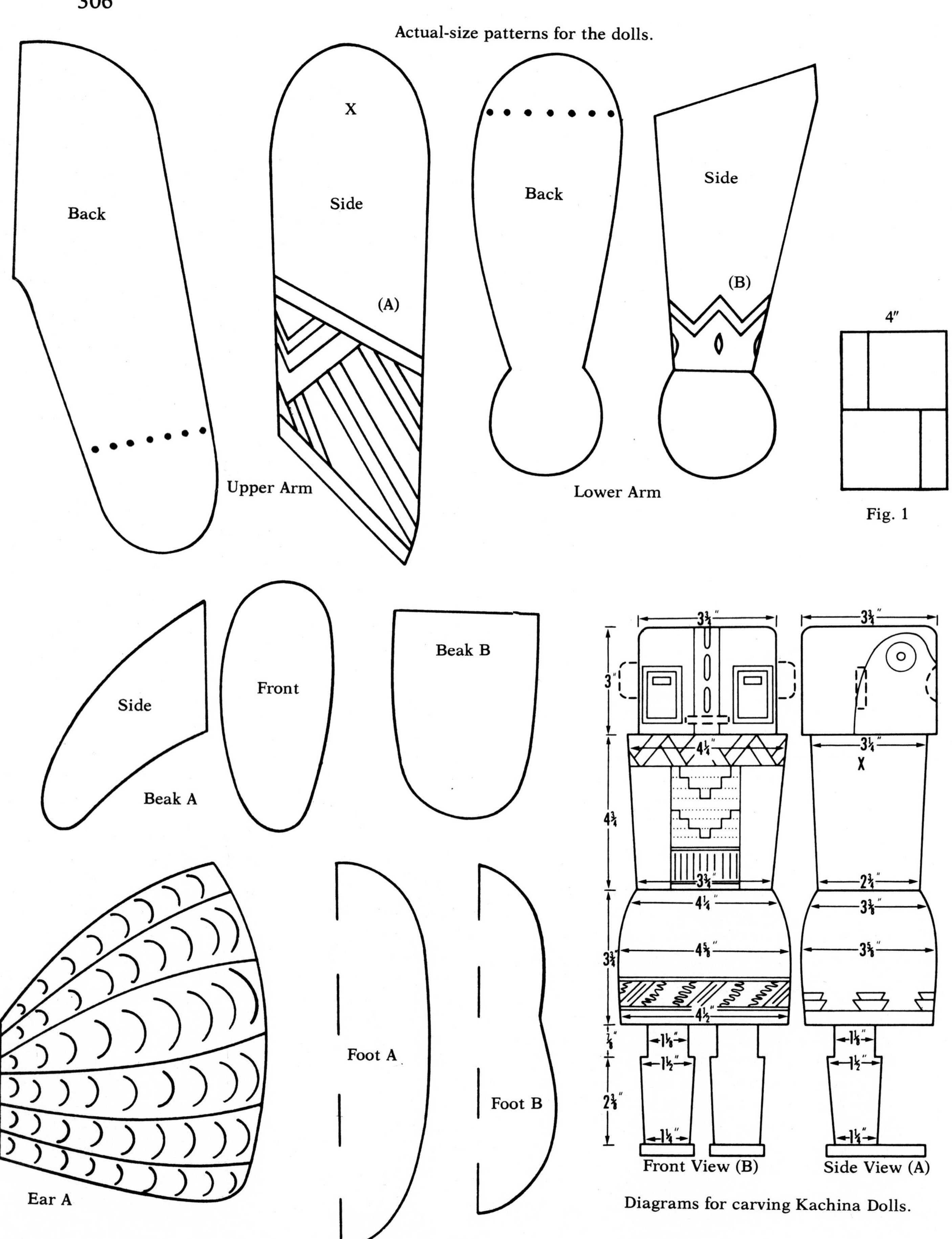

Diagrams for carving Kachina Dolls.

brick red, brown. Scraps of leather, suede, and chamois (or use felt): gray, brown, rust, beige. Brown shoe polish. Yellow-dyed feathers. Scraps of fur. Wooden oval bead about 1″ long. Wooden dowel ⅛″ diameter, 2″ long. Thin finishing nails about 2″ long. Clear acrylic spray.

DIRECTIONS: Trace actual-size patterns for upper and lower arms, ears, beaks, and feet for dolls A and B; complete half-patterns indicated by long dash lines.

For head, upper body, and lower body, you will need balsa blocks 4″ x 6″, the length of each part of body (see diagrams for measurements). Therefore, cut two pieces of 3″ x 3″ balsa and two pieces of 1″ x 3″ balsa, and glue together to form a 4″ x 6″ block, Fig. 1. Put contact cement on both surfaces to be joined and let dry, then press firmly together. Let blocks dry completely before carving.

For head, draw a circle 3¾″ in diameter centered on 4″ x 6″ surface of the 3″ block. For upper body piece, draw an oval shape 4¼″ x 3¼″ centered on top end of 4¾″ block. For lower body piece, draw an oval 4¾″ x 3¾″ centered on top end of 3¼″ block. To shape blocks, use chisel to make rough round or oval shape from top to bottom of block. Then use knife and rasp to smooth and taper blocks, following measurements on diagrams of front and side views. Round corners as shown on diagrams. Dolls may be made exactly the same size, or make one top body piece slightly shorter than other.

Legs and feet are separate pieces. For legs, use balsa 3″ square, 3¼″ long. For one doll, mark two circles 1½″ in diameter on top of block; cut block in half lengthwise for 2 legs; shape and notch outward as shown in front and side views. For other doll, make two legs 1¼″ in diameter at top, without notches, tapered to 1⅛″ in diameter at bottom. For feet, use patterns A and B, and cut feet from ⅜″-thick balsa; round top edges of feet and taper slightly to make thinner at toe end. Glue feet to bottoms of legs; glue legs to bottom of lower body, spaced as shown in front and side diagrams. Glue upper and lower body pieces together; glue head on as shown in front and side diagrams.

Cut two upper and two lower arms for each doll from 3″-square balsa, following back and side arm patterns. Shape arm pieces; taper bottom of upper arm from dotted line down to back and lower arm from dotted line up to back as shown in side view. Glue lower arms to bottom of upper arms. Attach arms to body sides at X's with nails if you want movable arms; or glue in position desired.

Cut two ears A from ⅜″-thick balsa; round corners and glue at sides of head as shown by short dash line on side view diagram. Cut 1″-diameter circles of ⅝″-thick balsa for ears B on other doll; round outer edges.

Cut beak A from 1″ balsa, following front and side patterns. Cut beak B from ¼″ balsa using pattern. Glue beaks and ears on heads as indicated by short dash lines on both front and side diagrams.

Paint dolls entirely white. Following designs on front and side diagrams A and B and in illustration, paint dolls in colors shown; repeat designs around each piece. When dry, coat with clear acrylic spray.

For garments of doll A, cut apron of chamois 3¼″ square and ⅛″ strip for ties 20″ long; dye brown with shoe polish. Punch a hole in each top corner of apron; lace tie through holes and tie around waist of doll. From gray leather, cut an isosceles triangular cape with 20″ base and 7″ high. Drape over one shoulder and bring under opposite arm. Slash through one end of triangle and pull other end through slash; pin one end to body under cape. Cut a strip of rust suede ¾″ wide, 16″ long; fringe both ends. Drape over bare shoulder and tuck under cape. For ornament, glue wooden bead (painted orange) on 2″ long dowel (painted white); tuck a bit of yellow feather in end of bead. Punch a hole in top of one hand and glue end of dowel into hole. Glue fur around each leg, to bottom of body. Punch five holes across center top of head; glue pieces of yellow feathers from 2½″ long to 3½″ long in holes.

For garments of doll B, cut triangular skirt of rust suede 13″ wide by 5″ deep; cut off point, rounding triangle to 4″ deep. Fringe diagonal sides and rounded edge; turn straight edge of triangle in ¼″ and wrap around waist, pinning ends to body at one side. Cut five ⅛″ strips of black and rust leather from 10″ to 16″ long; tie around one upper arm, alternating colors, and let ends hang down. Cut two 20″-long pieces of chamois ¼″ wide. Glue and pin center point of one at center back of each foot; lace around legs as shown and tie in front. Glue fur around neck. Punch two rows of six holes across center top of head. Glue pieces of yellow feathers from 2½″ to 5″ long in holes in head for the doll's headdress.

Apple-Head Grandma

An apple-head grandma is framed in her own shadow box. The art is simple—just carve an apple and let it dry. The body is a plastic bottle with pipe-cleaner arms.

EQUIPMENT: Paring knife. Scissors. Paper for pattern. Pencil. Ruler. Needle.

MATERIALS: For Grandma: Medium-size, hard, late fall apple, such as Winesap or Baldwin. Absorbent cotton. Two black seed beads. Two artificial seed pearls. Plastic liquid detergent bottle about 7" tall. Air-hardening clay. Two pipe cleaners 12" long. Green satin fabric ¼ yard, 36" wide. Fancy green and gold braid ¾" wide, about ½ yard. Bits of white lace. Piece of lace from white petticoat. Tiny artificial flowers. Tiny green jewels. Scrap of magenta ribbon. Green sewing thread. Masking tape. Narrow wooden dowel. Gold paint. **For Shadow Box:** Wooden picture frame 7¾" x 9½" rabbet size. Cardboard box 8" x 9¾", 2¼" deep. Brown paper. Scraps of wrapping paper, magenta colored, with tiny repeat pattern. Narrow gold paper edging. Small color illustration. Green velvet 2¼" x 8". Scrap of gold thread. Short glass jar (such as old perfume bottle). Toy plastic grandfather's clock 6" tall. Plastic pill bottle 3" tall. Artificial plastic plant. All-purpose glue.

DIRECTIONS: Grandma: For head, make a few apple heads, so you can choose the best (each apple dries differently, even though cut the same). Peel apple carefully. Decide which end of apple is best for bottom of head, then cut out core at bottom and insert a sharpened dowel stick into bottom (Fig. 1). Smooth apple with knife, taper narrower at bottom. Cut features deeply into apple (Fig. 2), cutting triangle shapes for eyes with slits above that will form lids. Carve out some of apple at sides of nose. Shave at sides for cheeks and cut small grooves under cheeks. Taper bottom at front for chin (Fig. 3), cut out small amount under chin. Cut curved grooves at sides for ears; cut bits of apple away under and in back of ears. Scrape apple smooth. For wrinkles, score with thumbnail across forehead, cheeks, and chin (Fig. 4). As apple dries, rescore if necessary.

Set apple on dowel stick in a jar and place on radiator or stove to dry for about three weeks. When the apple is really dry, it will keep for two or three years. Glue black seed beads in center of eyes. Glue cotton on head for hair. Glue seed pearls to ears for earrings. For body, insert dowel into plastic bottle; glue and tape head to neck of bottle. For arms, twist two pipe cleaners together. Glue and tape center portion across back "shoulder" of bottle, bend arms at each side to curve downward. For hands, shape small wads of clay and insert ends of arm pipe cleaners into clay; let dry.

Enlarge pattern for dress top by copying on paper ruled in 1" squares. Complete half-pattern indicated by dash line. Cut dress top from green satin. Fold in half across arms and slash down center back. Sew each side and arm seam. Cut skirt 5¼" x 23" of green satin. Sew 5¼" ends together and gather one long edge for waist. Sew gathered waist to bottom of dress top. Put dress on doll. Hem bottom edge of skirt a little longer than bottom edge of bottle. Taper and hem sleeves at wrists. Trim dress with lace around sleeves and at front of dress. Glue tiny jewels and magenta bow to lace on front. Sew braid around waist. Sew back opening closed. Glue lace from petticoat around bottle under dress so that lace shows at bottom. For cap, make a ruffle of lace and fit around top and sides of head; glue to hair. Glue flower to hat. Glue bouquet in her hand.

Shadow Box: Cover sides and back of inside of box with paper; glue smoothly. Cover bottom with green velvet; glue. Glue pill bottle and clock on top securely to back as shown. Glue gold paper edging around color illustration; glue to back as shown, with gold thread above as if picture were hanging from it. Glue jar (with neck painted gold) in corner as shown, with plant secured at top of it. Tape and glue box securely to back of picture frame. Glue brown paper around outside edges of box. Glue gold paper edging along inner edges of frame as shown. Glue Grandma in place.

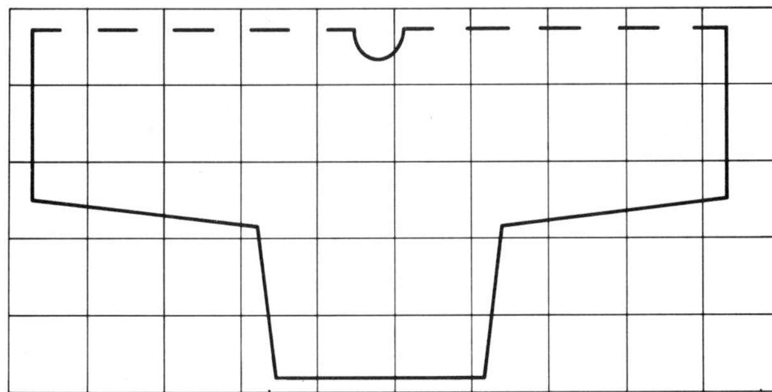

Half-Pattern to Make Dress Top

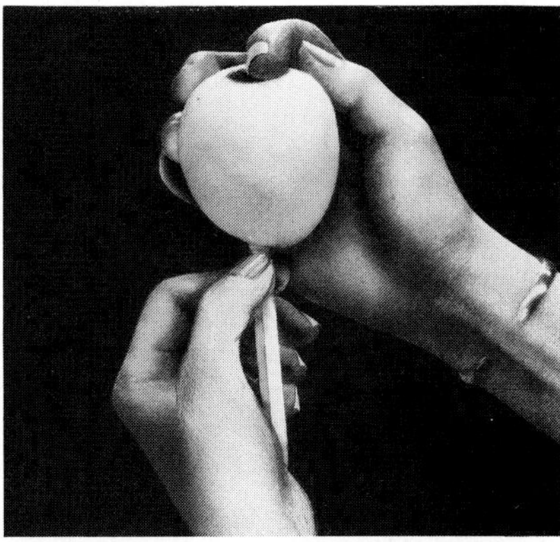

Fig. 1. Remove core from bottom of apple and insert dowel stick.

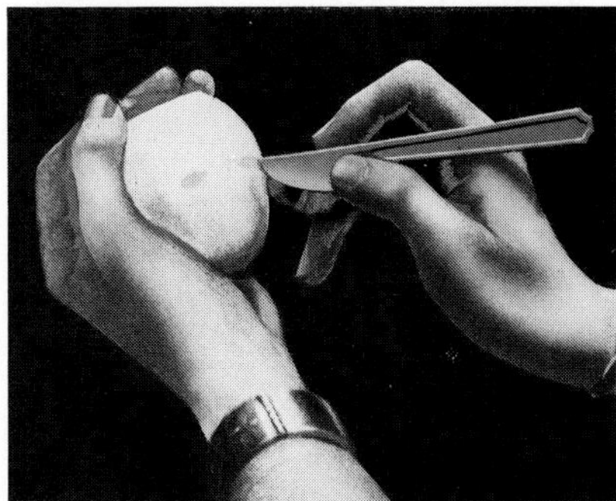

Fig. 2. Smooth and taper apple. Cut features deeply with a knife.

Fig. 3. Carve away parts of apple to shape nose, cheeks, and chin.

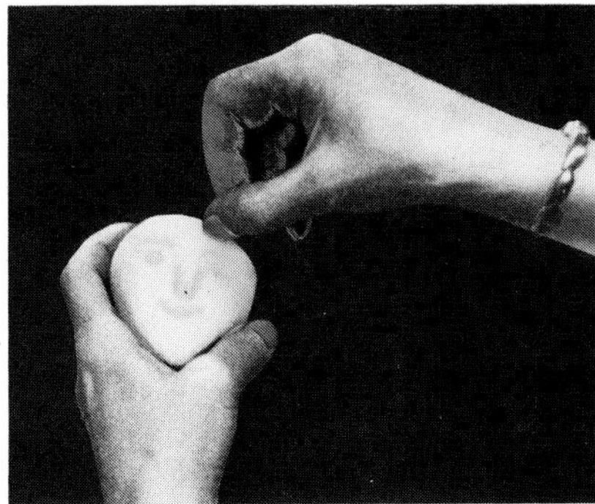

Fig. 4. For wrinkles, score with thumbnail on forehead and cheeks.

Colonial Dollhouse

Take a tour through a charming Early American home! On the first floor is a cozy keeping room and, on the second, a simple but cheerful bedroom. Constructed of plywood with balsa and pine detailing, the house measures 26½" high, 16¼" deep and 19" wide. The two fireplaces are built in; the ceiling has exposed "beams," and the walls have paneling and woodwork. An inside staircase joins the floors and there are windows to look into. A few simple tools and a lot of love are all you need to make the house and some of the basswood furniture; crockery, pewter and other accessories and furnishings are store-bought so you can finish decorating the home to your own taste.

HOUSE

EQUIPMENT: Pencil. Paper. Ruler. Yardstick. Square. Saber saw. Coping saw. Awl or other sharp pointed tool. Sandpaper. Steel wool. Paintbrushes, small and medium size. Turpentine. India ink pen. Mat knife and blades.

MATERIALS: Woods (see directions for measurements): Plywood, ¼" and ½" thick; balsa wood, 1/16", ⅛", ¼", and ⅜" thick; clear pine, 1" x 2" and 2" x 6"; dowel, ⅛" diameter; lap-spaced siding 3/32" thick, ⅜" lap and ½" lap. For fireplaces (optional): Basswood, ⅛" thick. All-purpose white glue. Brads. White paint. Small amount black paint. Small tube cadmium red oil paint. Black India ink. Acetate sheet. Polyurethane varnish. Wood stain. Plastic wood. Small wooden beads. Ball-point pen.

DIRECTIONS: Walls: Cut the following pieces: From ¼" plywood, front and back walls each 16" x 16¾"; fireplace wall 18½" x 25¾"; two ceilings each 16" x 18". From ½" plywood, one base piece 16" x 18".

Following Diagram 1A, cut triangular top of fireplace wall. Using Diagrams 1B and 1C, cut window and door openings as marked. Sand all edges. Lightly mark on inside of all three wall pieces the location of the first-floor ceiling, 8½" up from bottom edges; the second-floor ceiling, 16½" up from bottom edges. On fireplace wall, between bottom edge and 8½" mark, use the awl to score vertical lines 1" apart all across, for paneling. This is the fireplace wall of the Keeping Room. Sand lightly. Stain the scored Keeping Room wall. Paint the remaining area of the fireplace wall, applying two coats of white and sanding after first coat dries. Apply two coats ot white paint to the interiors of the front and back wall pieces including the cut edges of the window and door openings; also paint one side of one 16" x 18" ceiling piece. Apply coat of varnish to paneled wall of Keeping Room and allow to dry overnight; rub lightly with steel wool when dry. Lightly remark first-floor and second-floor ceiling lines.

Windows: Measure window openings. Using ⅛" x ¼" balsa wood strips and following Diagrams 2A-2C, cut enough strips to make *two* frames for each window, butting ends of strips. Sand and stain strips. Following Diagram 2A, glue strips together to make four frames 2" x 5" (for two windows); following Diagram 2B, glue together two frames 2" x 3"; following Diagram 2C, glue together four frames 2" x 2".

Cut one piece of acetate for each window, making it slightly smaller than the outer dimensions of the frames. Use India ink pen and ruler to delineate panes as shown in Diagram 2D. Attach each acetate window to one of its respective frames with small dots of glue. Weight it down

with a book or two until dry. Then glue the second frame to the other side. When dry, glue each window into openings, keeping frame flush with exterior surface of the walls.

Door: Cut and sand a piece of ¼" plywood to fit door opening. Score both sides vertically to resemble three or four random-width planks. Stain twice, sanding between applications.

Cut two ⅛" x ⅜" balsa wood strips, each to measure the width of the door. Sand and stain. Glue one strip across door ½" from top edge; the other, 1" up from bottom edge. Measure diagonally from lower right edge of top strip to upper left edge of bottom strip. Cut ⅛" x ⅜" balsa wood strip to fit, with ends cut at an angle. Sand, stain, then glue in place. Purchased strap hinges may be glued to one side of each horizontal strip. Purchase or make handles from small blocks of wood about 1" x ¼"; glue one to each side of door.

For door frame, measure and cut ⅛" x ⅜" balsa wood strips to fit around sides and top of the door opening, mitering the corners. Sand, stain and glue to interior wall around the door opening.

Base (Keeping Room Floor): From 1/16" x 3" balsa strips cut: Four pieces each 18"; two pieces each 5"; one piece 18" long, trimmed to ¾" width. Use awl to score flooring in random-width planks with imitation nail holes as in Diagram 3. Sand lightly, then apply two coats of stain, letting each dry thoroughly.

Trial-fit flooring onto ½" plywood base piece, leaving open area for hearth (Diagram 3): Place the two 5" strips along the 18" edge, leaving 8" space in center; next place ¾"-width strip across; then place the four 18" x 3" strips. If necessary, sand strips to fit. Glue flooring in place. When dry, apply coat of varnish, leaving it overnight to dry. Rub lightly with steel wool until smooth.

For hearth area, cut one piece of 1/16" balsa wood to fit uncovered area of floor. Use ball-point pen to score brick pattern as in Diagram 4. Mix small amount of stain and cadmium red oil paint to get a brick color; stain hearth. When dry, glue in place on base.

Attaching Walls: Using brads, glue and nail the front and back pieces to the base along the 16" sides, keeping lower edges of front and back pieces flush with lower edge of the base. Glue and nail fireplace wall to base and front and back, keeping all edges even.

Stairway: From 2" x 1" pine, cut these lengths: Four pieces each 5"; two pieces each 2"; one 3" piece; one 2½" piece; one 1¾" piece; two pieces each 1½" and two pieces each 1". Sand and stain all pieces. Stack and glue the four 5" blocks together for base. For the short stairs, stack and glue the 1" block onto the 1½" block onto the 2" block keeping edges even on three sides while the fourth side forms the steps. For the long stairs, stack and glue the remaining blocks in the same manner, placing each in ascending order of shortness.

Following Diagram 5A, glue stairs to base block. Then glue stairway into corner, placing it against walls as diagrammed.

Stairway Enclosure: From ⅛" balsa wood, cut two pieces (see Diagram 5B), one 2" x 8½", one 3" x 8½". For enclosure of short stairs, cut a piece of ⅛" balsa wood to fit as shown in Diagram 5C. Cut newel post 4" high from ¼"-square balsa strip. Sand all pieces, then apply two coats of white paint. Glue two main enclosure pieces to stairs as in Diagram 5B; glue slanted piece to side of short stairs as in Diagram 5C. Glue newel post in place.

From ⅛" x ⅜" balsa strips, cut horizontal trim to fit across each upper and lower edge of each stairway enclosure piece and lower edge of the slanted piece. Cut three vertical trim strips to fit between horizontal strips on both sides of the corner enclosure (Diagram 5B). Cut balsa wood strips to fit as trim along slanted edge and as railing between newel post and enclosure edge (Diagram 5C). Sand and stain all trim strips; glue in place.

Fireplace (Keeping Room): From ¼" balsa wood, cut two front pieces each 8" x 4" and two side pieces each 1½" x 8". Glue two front pieces together horizontally to measure 8" x 8" (tape or pin to hold until dry). Following Diagram 6A, cut out fireplace opening and oven door opening, rounding off oven door opening at the top edge as shown. Use cutout piece or cut a new piece for oven door; sand and stain. Cut, sand and stain a small piece of balsa wood for handle; glue onto oven door. Glue oven door into opening, gluing small piece of balsa across back of fireplace and door to hold it in place.

As directed for hearth floor area, score and stain fireplace front and two sides in brick pattern, being sure to make details around oven door as in Diagram 6B. When dry, glue sides at right angle to front piece. Measure width between sides at back; cut piece of ¼" balsa that width and 4½" high. Score and stain in brick pattern; glue between two side edges.

Measure from each edge of fireplace opening at

an angle to the back brick wall (see Diagram 6C). Cut two pieces to fit measurement, making each 4½" high for inner sides; edges must be cut at an angle. Score and stain in brick pattern. Glue in place. Smudge on black paint to give effect of soot.

For mantel, from ⅛" basswood (balsa may be used, but basswood is smoother), cut one piece 7¾" x ¾" and one piece 7¾" x ½". Sand and stain planks. Glue one lengthwise edge of ½"-wide plank onto the ¾"-wide plank (top) as in Diagram 7.

Measure corner between two mantel planks. Cut 2 support triangles to fit; sand and stain. Glue in place ¾" in from each end. Glue mantel one brick's width above fireplace opening, leaving equal margins on sides.

Ceiling (Keeping Room): Trial-fit 16" x 18" plywood ceiling board along 8½" ceiling marks on inner walls, being sure painted side is turned as ceiling side. Sand if necessary to fit. Measure, then cut opening for staircase; sand edges.

With pencil, mark placement for ceiling beams on painted side of board following Diagram 8. Using brads, nail and glue plywood board in place, with painted side as ceiling.

From ⅛" x ⅜" balsa strips, cut trim strips as follows: Horizontal strips to go around lower edges of three walls, excluding staircase enclosure, which has been trimmed, and fireplace; horizontal strips to go around upper edges of three walls including the fireplace but excluding the staircase enclosure; vertical and horizontal strips to go around both windows as in Diagram 9. Sand and stain all strips; glue in place.

For center beam, use 1" x 1" square balsa wood cut to measure from front edge of ceiling to fireplace. For smaller beams, cut ⅜" x ⅜" balsa strips to measure from center beam to walls. Use mat knife to carve three lengthwise corners of each beam piece to resemble hand-hewn beams. Sand lightly and stain. Glue center beam in place, then glue side beams in place along each marked ⅜" row.

Bedroom Floor: Follow directions for Keeping Room floor but measure for only a 5" x 3" hearth opening and allow for staircase. Score and stain in plank pattern as for Keeping Room floor; glue in place.

For hearth, measure and cut 1/16" balsa wood to fit 5" x 3" opening. Sand lightly. Divide in half lengthwise, marking with pencil. In one 1½"-width area, score and stain in brick motif as for other hearth floor. In the remaining area, score in various size rectangles to resemble slate. Mix black and white paints to make gray; paint to resemble slate. When dry, glue hearth floor in place.

Stair Rail: From ¼"-square balsa wood, cut two posts each 2¾" and two crosspieces each 5" long. Sand and stain. On both posts mark ⅜" in from each end. Glue one crosspiece between posts at lower marks; glue the other between posts at upper marks. Measure distance between the two crosspieces; from ⅛" dowel, cut seven pieces to fit. Stain. Glue dowels between crosspieces, spacing equally. If desired, glue a wooden bead on top of each end post. Glue railing to bedroom floor along stairway opening, attaching one end of railing to wall.

Fireplace (Bedroom): From ⅛" basswood (or balsa), cut two pieces (front and back) each 4" x 5" and two side pieces each 1½" x 4". To make the fireplace opening, cut out a 2½"-high and 2¼"-wide area from center of one 5" side of the piece for the front. Sand all pieces. If desired, ornamental molding may be used around fireplace opening edge. As for other fireplace, score and stain brick pattern on one surface of uncut 4" x 5" piece. Smudge slightly with black paint to give effect of soot. Glue two side pieces to each side of brick backing. Glue front piece to side pieces. Paint sides and front with two coats of white, sanding between coats.

Measure and cut mantelpiece 5¾" x 1⅞". Sand, then paint with two coats of white. When dry, glue to fireplace with ⅜" overhang at front and sides. Glue fireplace onto hearth floor and wall.

Ceiling (Bedroom): Trial-fit remaining 16" x 18" plywood board along 16½" ceiling marks on inner walls. Sand if necessary to fit. Paint one side with one coat of white paint.

From ¼" plywood, cut a gable as shown in Diagram 10. Using brads, nail and glue triangular piece to unpainted side of ceiling flush with the painted 18" edge, allowing ¼" overhang at each end. Countersink brads; fill in with plastic wood and sand smooth. Paint ceiling and edge again.

Measure, cut, stain, and glue balsa wood trim strips ⅛" x ⅜" to fit horizontally around the upper and lower edges of the bedroom walls and around the windows as for Keeping Room.

Put ceiling in place with triangular gable piece at the open side of the house. Glue and nail.

Exterior Trim: Using ⅛" x ¼" balsa wood strips, measure and cut strips for each window as shown in Diagram 11A. Sand, paint white, and glue in place.

For door frame, cut four pieces of ⅛" x ⅜" balsa wood to measure height of door opening; glue two together along ⅜" sides to make each side piece. Cut lintel piece of ⅜"-square wood to measure across top edge of door opening plus width of side trims. Sand; paint white. Glue two side strips vertically on exterior wall around door opening; glue lintel across top edge of opening.

For corner trims, use ⅛" x ⅜" wood strips: cut two vertical pieces for each of the four corners. Trim upper ends at angle following gable lines to accommodate roof. Sand; paint white. Glue a pair to both sides of each corner, butting edges of trim (Diagram 11B). Cut, sand and paint one ⅛" x ⅜" strip for horizontal facing trim across the bedroom floor piece. Cut, sand and paint one ⅛" x ½" strip for horizontal facing trim across the base floor piece. Glue facings in place.

Chimney: From 2" x 6" pine, 28" long, cut as in Diagram 12. On one 6" side and both 2" sides, score brick pattern and stain twice; on other 6" surface, score and stain only upper area which will be visible when attached to the house. Glue chimney (undecorated side) to exterior of fireplace wall with equal margins to each corner.

Siding: When chimney and trim are completely dry, measure for siding. Use 3/32"-thick, ⅜" lap-spaced siding (available from hobby shops). Cut and glue in place on three exterior walls, being sure not to cover the facings. Also glue in place on both gable areas. Paint with two coats of white.

Roof: From ¼" plywood, cut one piece 16¼" x 13¼" and one 16¼" x 13". Glue and nail smaller piece onto sides of triangular gable pieces keeping upper edge flush (Diagram 13). Glue and nail larger piece onto other side keeping upper edge flush with edge of smaller roof piece. Cut ⅛" x ¼" balsa strips to fit along side edges of roof pieces, mitering at the peak. Paint with two coats of white. Glue in place.

Use 3/32"-thick ½" lap-spaced siding for roof shingles; measure and cut to fit roof. Score in irregular shingle pattern as shown in Diagram 14. Sand edges lightly and stain. When dry, glue onto roof.

FURNITURE

EQUIPMENT: Pencil. Tracing paper. Scissors. Ruler. Tape measure. Coping saw. Small wire cutters or pliers with cutter. Drill with ⅛" wood bit. Mat knife and blades. Fine sandpaper. Steel wool. Cheesecloth. Small paintbrush.

MATERIALS: Basswood, 1/16", ⅛", and ¼" thick, as listed in individual directions. Dowel, ⅛" diameter. White glue. Polyurethane varnish. Wood stain in color desired.

GENERAL DIRECTIONS: Following individual directions for each piece of furniture, mark component pieces onto wood. Where necessary, for several furniture pieces, cut pattern as directed, then trace onto wood. Use coping saw to cut out pieces. For fine detailing of pieces, such as curved edges of bench legs, use mat knife. When all pieces are cut, sand edges and surfaces lightly. Stain each piece using brush to apply the stain and cheesecloth to wipe off excess. Let dry thoroughly.

According to individual directions and assembly diagrams, glue component pieces together. Let dry thoroughly. Sand seams smooth. If desired, restain and let dry. Use small paintbrush to apply coat of polyurethane varnish. Let dry overnight. Rub with steel wool until smooth. Make other finishing details according to individual directions.

BLANKET CHEST: Cut the following pieces: From ⅛" basswood, two ends each 1¼" x 1¾"; one bottom 1¼" x 2¾". From 1/16" basswood, two sides each 1¼" x 3"; top A 1½" x 3⅛"; top B 1¼" x 2¾".

Use a penny to mark and cut a half circle from one narrow edge of each end piece (see Diagram 15).

Following assembly Diagram 15, first glue bottom between end pieces ½" above lower edges. Glue one side piece at a time to end pieces and bottom. Center top B onto top A and glue together. Place top on chest without gluing.

TRESTLE TABLE: Cut the following pieces: From ⅛" basswood, one tabletop 5½" x 3"; two end pieces of tabletop each ¼" x 3"; two legs each ½" x 2". From ¼" basswood, two foot pieces each ¼" x 2½"; four braces each ¼" x 2"; one stretcher bar ¼" x 4".

Following Diagram 16A, glue end pieces to each narrow end of tabletop. Glue one brace to each end of tabletop, placing each one 1" in from ends and leaving equal margins to the sides. Round off top ends of each foot piece as in Diagram 16B. Glue a leg to each foot piece keeping it centered. Glue other end of each leg to center ot inside edge of each brace. Glue second brace to

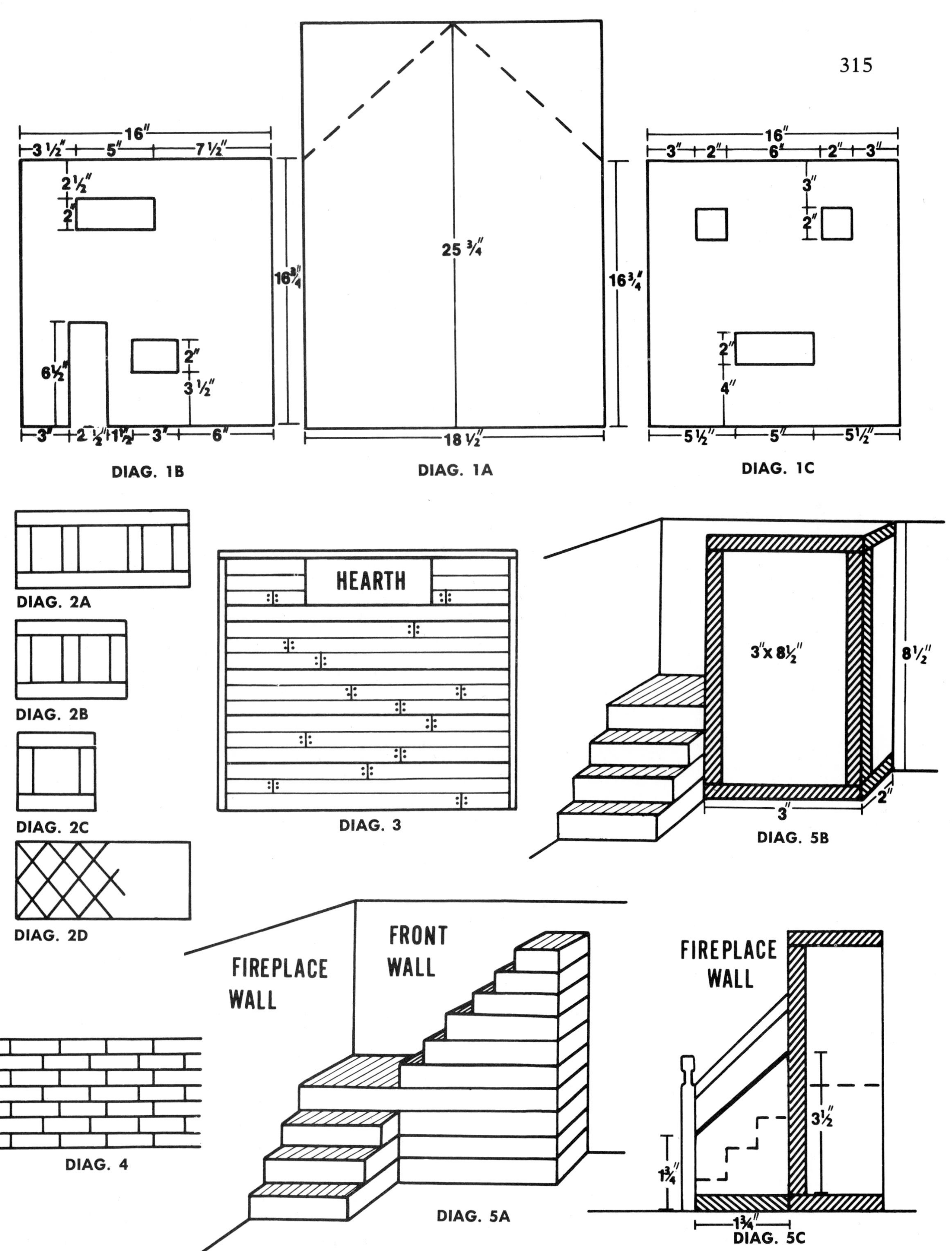

DIAG. 1B

DIAG. 1A

DIAG. 1C

DIAG. 2A

DIAG. 2B

DIAG. 2C

DIAG. 2D

DIAG. 3

DIAG. 5B

DIAG. 4

DIAG. 5A

DIAG. 5C

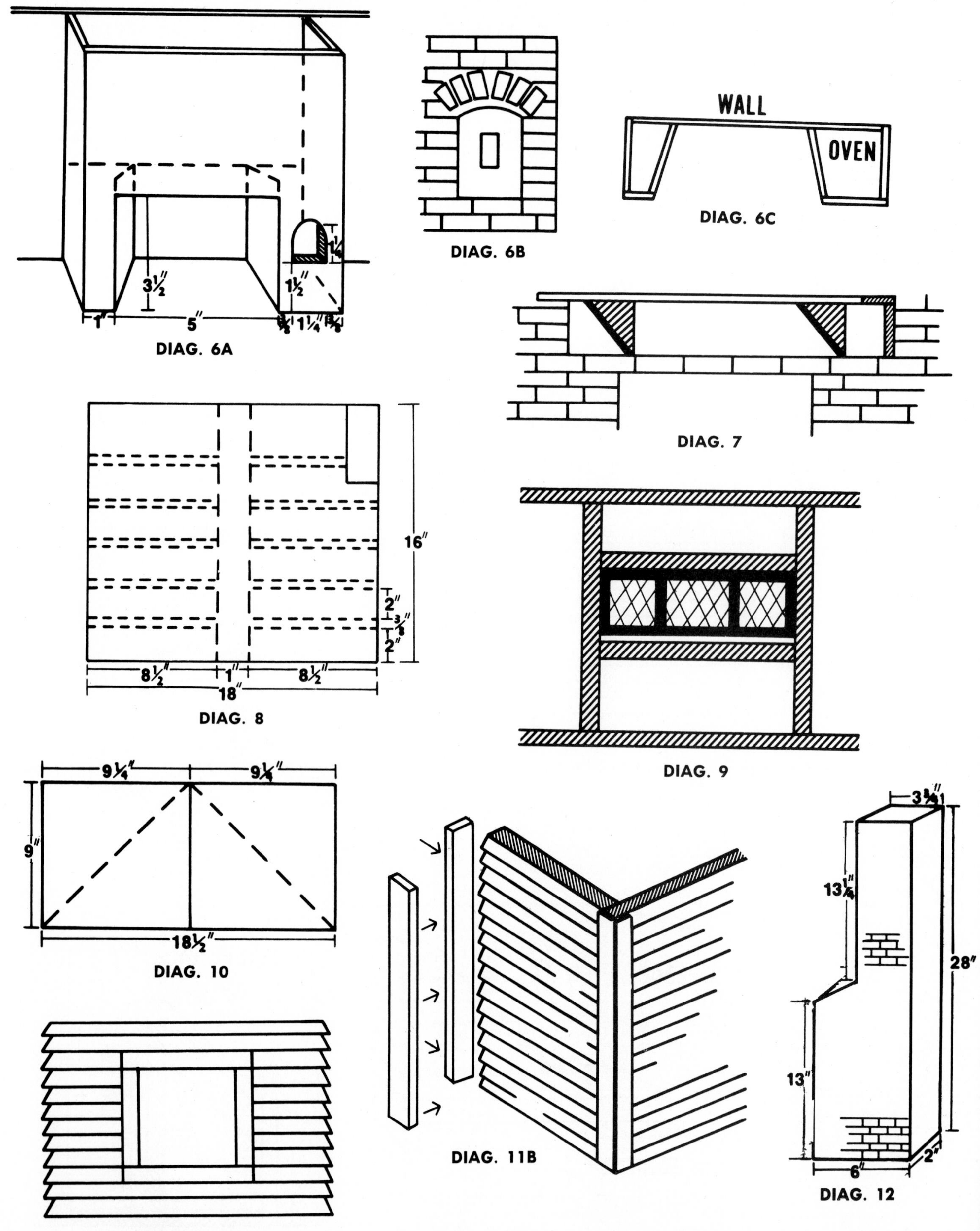

DIAG. 6A

DIAG. 6B

DIAG. 6C

DIAG. 7

DIAG. 8

DIAG. 9

DIAG. 10

DIAG. 11A

DIAG. 11B

DIAG. 12

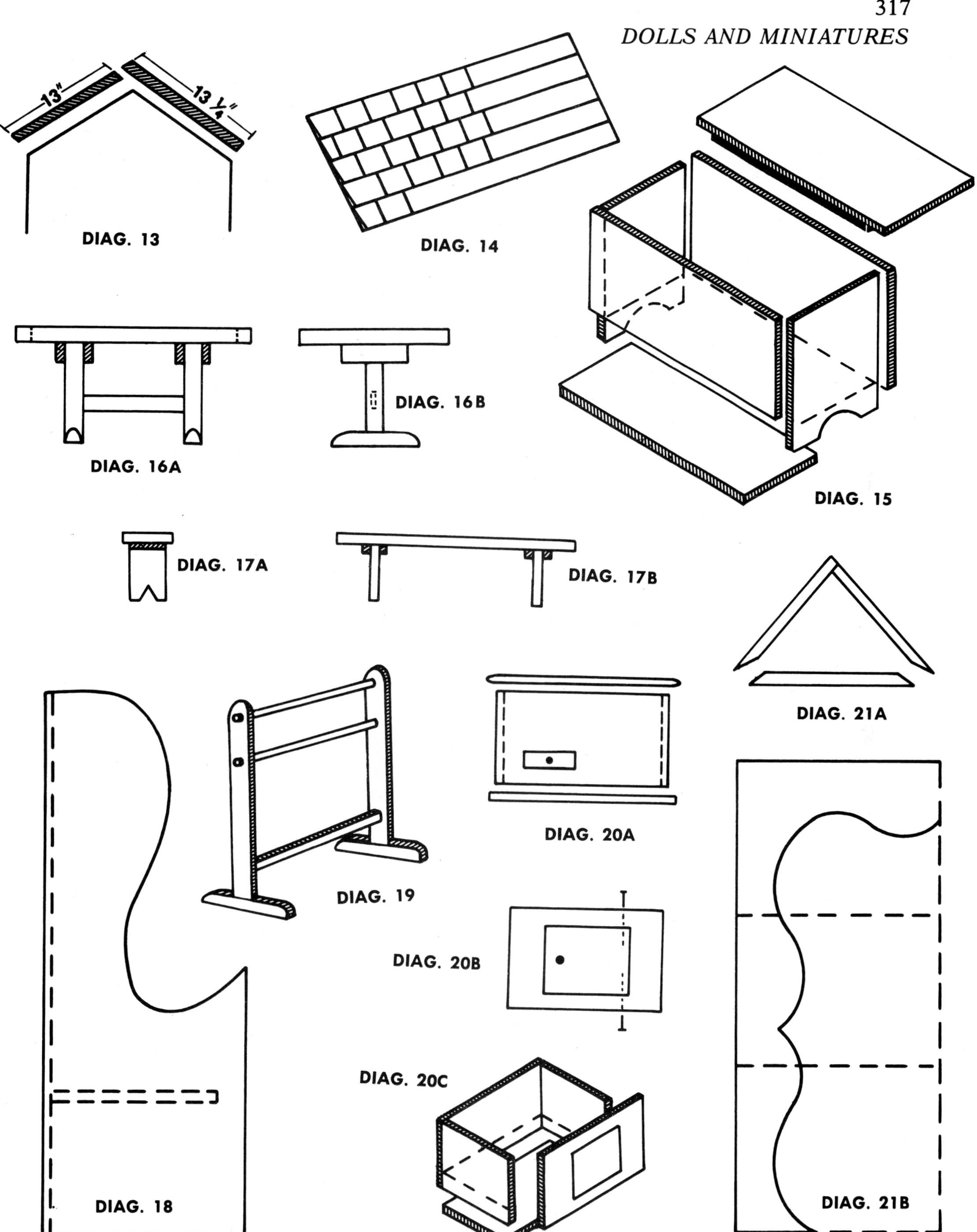
13″
13 1/4″
DIAG. 13
DIAG. 14
DIAG. 15
DIAG. 16A
DIAG. 16B
DIAG. 17A
DIAG. 17B
DIAG. 18
DIAG. 19
DIAG. 20A
DIAG. 20B
DIAG. 20C
DIAG. 21A
DIAG. 21B

the table on the inside of each leg. Measure exact distance between legs about 1″ below tabletop. Trim stretcher bar as needed to fit this distance; center and glue in place.

TRESTLE BENCH: Cut following pieces from ⅛″ basswood: One top ¾″ x 5½″; four braces each ⅛″ x ½″; two legs each 1¼″ x ½″.

On one narrow end of each leg piece, cut out a ⅜″-high triangle (see Diagram 17A). Following Diagram 17B, glue one brace to each end of bench top ½″ from the end with equal margins to each side. Glue uncut ends of each leg to inside of each brace. Glue second brace to bench on the inside of each leg.

SETTLE: Trace side pattern, Diagram 18; copy dotted lines which show placement of pieces. Cut out pattern. Cut following pieces from ⅛″ basswood: Two sides using the pattern; one back 4″ x 3″; one seat 3″ x 1¼″.

Glue back between the side pieces along the straight 4″ edges. Glue seat flush against back and between sides along dotted lines.

TOWEL RACK: Cut the following pieces: From ⅛″ basswood, two sides each ⅜″ x 2¾″; one stretcher ⅛″ x 2¼″. From ¼″ basswood, two foot pieces each 1¼″ x ¼″. From ⅛″-diameter dowel, two rods each 2¾″ long.

Round off top ends of foot pieces and both side pieces (see Diagram 19). Drill two ⅛″-diameter holes through center of each side piece: the first about ⅛″ below top; the second, about ½″ below the first. Glue straight ends of side pieces to tops of foot pieces, centering them. Glue stretcher between two side pieces ½″ above bottom edge. Glue dowels into holes, letting ends extend equally on both sides.

COMMODE: For the top half, cut the following pieces: From ⅛″ basswood, front and back pieces each 2¼″ x 1″; two end pieces each 1½″ x 1″; one lid 2½″ x 2″; one base piece 2½″ x 2″. From 1/16″ basswood, one fake drawer piece 1″ x ⅜″.

Glue two end pieces onto front piece; then glue back piece onto ends (see Diagram 20A). Glue this rectangle to the base keeping the back edges flush so the front edge of the base extends slightly. Bevel one long edge (front) and two side edges of the lid. Restain. For lid hinge, cut a piece of fabric ⅝″ x 2″. Glue one lengthwise half to top inside of back piece; glue other half to inside of back lid. Glue fake drawer as shown in Diagram 20A. Push white-headed straight pin through center of drawer for knob.

For bottom half, cut following pieces from ⅛″ basswood: Front and back pieces each 2″ x 1½″; two side pieces each 1¼″ x 1½″; one bottom piece 1¾″ x 1¼″.

From the front piece, cut out an opening 1″ square allowing ¼″ margins at top and bottom and ½″ margins at sides (see Diagram 20C). For door, use cutout 1″ square or cut another. Sand and restain door, door edges and opening in front piece. Lay front piece with door in place on flat surface. Push straight pin in through top of front piece into top edge of door (see Diagram 20B); snip off remainder of pin close to wood, pushing any protrusion into wood. Repeat for lower hinge of door. Insert white-headed pin as knob; clip off pinpoint.

Glue each side piece to the back piece. Glue bottom to back and sides about ¼″ above the lower edges as shown by dotted lines in Diagram 20C. Glue front onto sides and bottom. Glue bottom half to top half keeping back edges flush and centering it.

CORNER HUTCH: For the lower half, cut following pieces from ⅛″ basswood: Left side piece 2⅛″ x 2½″; right side piece 2″ x 2½″; front piece 3″ x 2½″; two triangular pieces to be cut later.

Following Diagram 21A, bevel one 2½″ side of each of the two side pieces, then glue the back edges together. Cut out a 2″-square opening from center of the front piece. For door, use cutout 2″ square or cut another. Bevel the two side edges of the front piece to fit the side pieces. Sand and restain door edges and opening. As directed for bottom half of Commode, attach knob and hinge the door using pins. Glue front piece onto side pieces. Measure and cut two triangular pieces to fit on top and bottom; glue in place.

For the top half, trace half-pattern for the top front (Diagram 21B); complete half-pattern; cut out. Cut following pieces from ⅛″ basswood: One side piece 2″ x 3½″; one side piece 2⅛″ x 3½″; one shaped front piece using pattern; two triangular shelves and a triangular top to be cut later.

Bevel and glue side pieces as for the lower half. Measure and cut out two triangular shelves which should be flush with beveled edges. Sand to fit exactly. Stain all pieces. Glue top shelf 1⅛″ down from top edge of sides; glue second shelf 1″ below the first one. Bevel the two side edges of the front piece to fit the side pieces; glue to sides. Cut triangular piece of wood to fit on top of the hutch; sand, stain and glue on top. Glue top half to bottom half keeping edges even.

9

Candlemaking

GENERAL DIRECTIONS

EQUIPMENT: Newspapers. Waxed paper. Double boiler or large and small cans and a large pan. Stick for stirring wax. Candy thermometer. Salt or baking soda (in case of fire, pour on slowly).

MATERIALS: Paraffin wax (see amounts in individual directions). Stearic acid. Wax color dyes; wax coloring cakes or wax crayons in desired colors. Spoon or spatula. Candlewicking.

DIRECTIONS: Note: Be sure you are working in well-ventilated area. Cover working area with newspapers and waxed paper to catch spilled wax.

Melt wax in top of double boiler or in can set in pan of water. Never melt wax over direct heat or leave unattended on a lighted stove. Keep salt or baking soda at hand. Add stearic acid (to harden wax; the ratio is 90% wax to 10% stearic acid) and wax color dyes.

To color wax, shave off pieces of color cakes and gradually add to melted wax until color is a shade or two darker than desired color; wax will lighten in color as it solidifies. Test color by letting small amount solidify on spoon. Do not attempt to mix batches of wax colored with different types of dyes; if dye bases are not the same type, the wax will not fuse. Stir wax to blend color. Use new can for each color.

To determine amount of wax needed, fill mold with water, then pour water into can or top of double boiler. Note level and add ⅛ more for amount of liquid wax needed (to allow for shrinkage). Melt wax, putting in one pound at a time. Temperature of wax should be about 160° F. before pouring into mold or dipping.

Insert wicks as indicated in directions.

Sprigged Candles

Pressed flowers and sprigs of fern combine for charming candle decor. Use mimosa, daisies and baby's breath, as shown, or select your favorites for unique designs. The flowers are pressed in a book, dipped in wax and then added to ready-made candles.

EQUIPMENT: See General Directions above. Heavy book for press. Tweezers.

MATERIALS: Purchased candles in size desired (the type which burns down center core rather than sides). Paraffin wax, about ¾ lb. Wild flowers, leaves, ferns.

DIRECTIONS: Read the General Directions above. To press flowers, etc., place them in a large, heavy book; leave them to dry for about two weeks.

When flowers are dry, melt wax. Holding dried flower, leaf, or fern carefully with tweezers, dip into wax: coat thoroughly. Immediately press in place on candle.

Pumpkin Candles

Glowing pumpkins grin on a frosty night to light up the goblins' way! The 2½" tall candle jack-o'-lanterns are easy to form by dipping water-filled balloons in melted orange wax. The hardened molds are filled with a yellow wax center, and the features are then carved in the outer surface.

EQUIPMENT: See General Directions on page 320. Round balloon. Drill or ice pick. Tracing paper. Pencil. Sharp knife.

MATERIALS: 3 lbs. paraffin wax for three candles. Orange and yellow wax dye. Candlewicking.

DIRECTIONS: Read General Directions on page 320. Melt one half of the wax in a 3"-diameter can to depth of 2½". Add stearic acid, then orange dye.

Stretch mouth of balloon around water faucet; fill balloon with cold water until it is desired size (candles shown are about 2½"-diameter). Remove balloon from faucet; hold securely at neck.

Heat wax to 160°F. Dip ball of balloon completely into wax, coating it to top. Still holding balloon, let wax coating cool; continue dipping balloon until wax layer is about ¼" thick. Dip coated balloon into cold water to give wax a gloss. Let water out of balloon; remove balloon from wax shell. Melt remaining wax in double boiler or in can. Add stearic acid, then yellow dye. Heat wax to 150° F. Carefully pour wax into orange shell, a bit at a time, allowing yellow wax in shell to cool between pourings. Continue pouring until shell is completely filled and a solid ball shape is formed. Let candle cool.

Before candle has completely hardened, use knife to flatten top and bottom surfaces. Trace actual-size patterns for features; cut out and place patterns on side of candle. With knife, mark around outlines of patterns; carefully carve features from orange layer of wax; remove orange layer so that yellow shows through.

To insert wick, make hole through center with electric or hand drill or with heated ice pick. Stiffen wick (length determined by height of candle plus ¾") by dipping into hot melted wax. Insert wick into hole. Carefully pour a small amount of melted wax into center top of candle to secure wick.

Imprinted Candles

Colored with crayons, these chunky candles are molded in soup cans and milk cartons cut to the desired height. The designs are "incised" by tapping ordinary hardware—nuts, screws, knobs and skewers—against the sides of the finished candles.

EQUIPMENT: See General Directions on page 320. Ruler. Darning needle. Spoon or spatula. Pencil. Ice pick. Nail. Soup can 2½" diameter, 3¾" high. Square milk cartons, one-quart size. Masking tape. Smooth-textured dish towel. Medium-weight hammer. Implements obtainable at hardware or dime stores, such as: Two hex nuts ⅜" and ¾" diameters. Phillips-head screw with ½" diameter head. Bolt ⅛" diameter. Two screw eyes ¾" and 1⅜" long. Skewer (or straight piece of wire coat hanger with one end bent into skewer-head shape ⅝" diameter) 6" long. Lamp switch knob ¼" diameter (or use hollow rivet).

MATERIALS: Blocks of paraffin wax, about five to seven bars for each candle, or half of 11-lb. slab for all (do not use store-bought candles as they have an extra-hard outer coating of wax that makes them unsuitable for imprinting). Wax coloring. Candlewicking.

DIRECTIONS: See General Directions on page 320. Have soup can and cartons clean and ready. Cut milk carton to desired height of candles. Hammer ice pick or nail in center bottom of each container to make a hole no larger than wicking. Cut wicking about 4" longer than needed to reach bottom of cartons or can. Dip the wick in melted wax (to melt, see below), thread it through a darning needle, and draw it through hole in bottom of cartons or can; tie knot at outside bottom end; tie top end to pencil; place it across container top to hold wicking taut.

Melt wax over low heat in top of double boiler and keep over hot, but not boiling water. Using separate container for each color, color wax as desired, following General Directions. Remove wax from heat. Let wax cool a little, then fill cartons and can with wax. As the candles cool, hollows may form around wicks. Fill depressions with more melted wax. When wax in cartons has cooled and hardened, remove candles by tearing away cartons. Candle in can may be removed by placing can in warm water for a few minutes. Let candles harden for at least a day before imprinting.

To Imprint Designs: Make a pad on which to lay candle by folding dish towel. Practice your design on old candles or slabs of unmelted wax. To make design, place designing implement in position; imprint by tapping it firmly with hammer. **Note:** When working design near corner edge of candle top, be careful not to crack corner of candle. Work design on one side at a time; then repeat design on remaining sides. Always have lines on one side meeting lines on adjacent sides.

Small Green Candle (2¾" x 4"): With skewer, imprint large X going from top corners to bottom corners of candle side. Make diagonal lines 1/2" apart across candle, forming diamond-shaped areas. Within these areas, make double-circle imprint with lamp switch knob, leaving partial diamond shapes at edges empty.

Pink Candle (2¾" x 3¾"): Lightly mark centers at outer edges of each side along top, bottom, and sides with nail. Lay skewer on candle, making first line at angle from center top to side center; repeat from side to bottom, bottom to side, and side to top. This leaves large diamond shape in center. Then make two more skewer lines ¼″ apart in each outer corner. Imprint Phillips-head screw design in center and around inner edges of diamond.

Orange Candle (2¾″ x 3″): Lightly mark center of side; make an imprint with lamp switch knob. Make seven imprints, using ⅜″ screw eye, around this circle. Then make 14 imprints, using lamp switch knob, evenly spaced around screw eyes.

Purple Candle (2¾″ x 5″): With skewer imprint head and line down center. Work two more skewer head-line designs on each side of first imprint; then two more designs between and ¼″ below the three. Finish each side with three slanted lines of varying lengths. Be sure these lines meet those on adjacent side for continuous design around candle. Imprint lamp switch knob design in center of skewer heads.

Large Red Candle (2¾″ x 6″): With skewer, make three vertical lines about ¾″ apart along length of candle, dividing it into four equal columns. Make horizontal line ¾″ from top and another ¾″ from bottom. In each top and bottom square, make imprint of round screw-eye head only. Then make three full imprints of screw eye in each of the four columns with heads up in first column; alternate position of head in remaining columns.

Large Green Candle (2¾″ x 6¼″): Center two columns of ¾″ hex nut imprints down length of candle, making six pairs. Then make lamp switch knob imprint in center of each hex nut imprint.

Round Small Red Candle (2½″ diameter, 3¾″ tall): Around top edge of candle, make small light markings, dividing it into six equal parts. Make two vertical skewer lines ¼″ apart down outside of candle on each side of six marked points to make six pairs of lines. Make a column of five ⅜″ hex nut imprints between each pair of lines. Imprint end (opposite head) of ⅛″ bolt inside each hex nut imprint.

Petaled Candles

Graceful petals of wax are molded on spoons in a simple technique adapted from an Ecuadorian folk art. Flower centers, framed by petals, are molded in a thimble.

EQUIPMENT: See General Directions on page 320. Corn oil. Electric soldering iron or large nail. Four spoons in graduated sizes: doll-size (or demitasse) teaspoon, tablespoon, large serving spoon. Thimble and scissors.

MATERIALS: One lb. paraffin wax, ⅓ lb. beeswax. Red, blue, yellow wax dye colors. Tapers: one green 15″ long, one blue 12″ long, one pink 10″ long. Narrow colored paper ribbons. Cellophane tape.

DIRECTIONS: Method: Read General Directions on page 320. Melt wax, following directions. For the flower candles shown, you will need the following colors: pale, medium, and deep blue; pink (use red dye moderately); orange (use red and yellow dyes); yellow; gold (yellow with small amount of red dye).

Candles are decorated with rows of petals formed in bowl of spoon; the size of petal is determined by the size of spoon used. To make petal, heat wax to approximately 180° F. Grease bowl of spoon lightly with corn oil. Using another spoon, pour a small amount of wax into oiled spoon bowl; rotate spoon to coat bowl evenly. Remove wax from spoon while wax is still warm by sliding it off with your thumb. Pinch petal at one end to complete shape of white petals; curl petals to form rose petal shapes.

To attach petals, use soldering iron or heated nail tip to melt vertical grooves for each row around taper and to soften the ends of petals. Insert one petal end into each groove. If petal does not adhere well, apply a small amount of wax at the joint. Let wax harden and attach next petal around.

Rows are made up of overlapping curved petals. On 15″ taper, start petals 6″ down from top. On 12″ taper, start 4½″ down from top. On 10″ taper, start 3½″ down from top. To attach petals, soften wax on taper and end of petal with soldering iron or heated nail; press petal to taper. Start with medium-size spoon; shape petal and attach to taper. Complete first row of petals around taper, overlapping them. Use larger spoon for second an third rows of petals. If petal has a ragged edge, trim with scissors while still warm.

To make a complete rose, grease the thimble with corn oil and dip outside of thimble into wax. Remove wax and use the thimble-formed shape as core of rose. Adhere graduated-size petals made on spoons around core using soldering iron or heated nail. Adhere the completed rose to taper below the rows of petals as follows: Melt the back of rose and taper with soldering iron or heated nail; press together. See illustration for ways to arrange roses.

To decorate, cut about ten long streamers of ribbon. Tape end of each around bottom of taper and 1″, 2″, and 3″ up from bottom. Curl the loose ends with scissor blade. Cut several more streamers; curl both ends. Tape at centers around taper bottom.

Column Candles and Sand Candles

Column Candles

Festive embossed columns have applied wax strips. The cube designs are molded on a trivet; the spiral ridging is achieved from a corrugated cardboard mold.

EQUIPMENT: Newspapers. Waxed paper. Double boiler or large coffee can. Large shallow pans. Stick for stirring. Lightweight cardboard. Pencil. Ruler. Sharp knife. Knitting needle. Spoon. Large trivet with cube-shaped indentations. Corrugated cardboard.

MATERIALS: Store-bought candles (slow-burning type), round and oval column. Candle, household, or paraffin wax. Candle dye, wax coloring cakes, or wax crayons.

DIRECTIONS: Read General Directions on page 320.

To make patterns for ends of candles, place candle on piece of lightweight cardboard; with pencil, mark around shape. Cut shape out of cardboard (one for each candle); mark placement of wick on cardboard pattern and make hole in cardboard.

Melt wax in cans; color as desired. Place waxed paper inside pans. Let wax cool slightly. Then pour wax from can into pan to form a thin slab. Leave a small amount of wax of same color in can to have ready supply of hot wax when needed. When wax is firm but still slightly warm, impress designs or cut out strips with sharp knife as instructed in individual directions below. Place cardboard pattern for end on wax slab; with sharp knife, cut out two end pieces for each candle. On only one end piece (for top end), poke hole through wax with knitting needle large enough to accommodate wick. Lift up pieces of wax. While still warm, apply wax pieces to candles so pieces will assume shape of candle. First secure ends, then design pieces. Apply hot wax the same color to back of each piece with spoon and press pieces in place to secure. Trim off any excess wax at edges. To insure adherence, when all pieces are in place on candle, turn on oven broiler and, when hot, expose candle to heat very briefly at 2" distance.

Striped Candle: Cut cardboard strip the height of candle and desired width; determine number of strips needed to go around candles and cut out of wax. You will need two colors of wax melted in separate cans and two pans for separate slabs.

Impressed Candles: Press trivet or corrugated cardboard into the warm wax slab. Lift up wax, wrap around candle; seal seam with hot wax of same color.

Sand Candles

Fluted, scalloped, star or plain round, the sand candles shown have an elegant pottery look. The colored wax and wick that fill the center cavity may be replaced with fresh wax when the candle has burned.

EQUIPMENT: Newspapers. Waxed paper. Double boiler or large can (coffee or juice). Various articles to be used as molds (jello molds, shallow and deep plastic and metal bowls). Cookie pan. Fine kitchen sieve. Measuring cup. Bottle caps. Silicone mold release (available at candle shops). Stick for stirring. Sharp knife. Hammer. Nail.

MATERIALS: Sand or garden earth. Paraffin wax or stubs of used candles. Candlewicking. Candle dye, wax coloring cakes, or wax crayons. Tin cans. Floral clay. Bits of colored glass.

NOTE: The candles are hollow bowl shapes made of hot wax mixed with sand or earth of various types and filled with wax and wick to create refillable candles. The texture of the sand determines how much melted wax should be used.

DIRECTIONS: Read General Directions on page 320. Strain earth if necessary.

Select mold; fill with sand 1⅓ times; empty sand onto cookie pan; spread evenly and heat in warm oven. Spray mold with silicone mold release following manufacturer's directions. Sand candles do not release from molds easily, especially if mold is convoluted, deep, or made of plastic. Shallow bowl shapes may be cast in metal bowls using cooking oil as a releasing agent.

Combine ⅓ of a cup of hot wax and 1 cup of sand in double boiler (or large can set in pot of water). With earth, a little more wax may be needed. Stir to consistency of wet sand, soft but not runny. When using earth, stir to consistency of soft mud, but not runny. Put several heaping tablespoons of hot sand-wax mixture into mold. On top of this, place a tin-can lid. The lid provides a base through which candle will not melt when burned. On top of the lid put several more spoonfuls of the mixture. Next form a cavity by placing a can or star-shaped dish (cavity mold), outside sprayed with mold release, in center of mold. Pack more of the sand-wax mixture in the perimeter of the mold. Let cool for five minutes. At this point designs can be pressed or scratched onto the surface of the sand-wax mixture with a clean hot tablespoon or teaspoon. Now place a sharp knife at a 60° angle against the inner surface of the mold, rotate the mold, removing a ⅜″ strip of the congealing mixture. Remove the cavity mold. If the wax has become too hard set and the cavity mold does not come out clean, fill it with hot water for a minute; then try again. Put mold in refrigerator for about an hour; invert and the sand-wax shape should come out easily.

For candle in center, melt the paraffin wax or candle stubs in top of double boiler or in large can set in a pan of water.

To color wax, gradually add pieces of color cakes, crayons, or candle dye to melted wax until color is a shade or two darker than desired color; wax will lighten in color as it solidifies. Stir wax to blend color. Mix yellow and red for orange; blue and yellow for green; use white crayon for toning.

Drive a hole through a soda bottle cap with a nail; thread 6″ of wick through the cap and tie a double knot on the serrated side. Put several tablespoons of the candle wax in the bottom of the cavity. Let set until congealed but not hard. Press the serrated side of bottle cap into this layer and let wax get cold. Fill cavity layer by layer, letting wax cool between each layer to get an even final surface.

To decorate, press a thin coil of floral clay around outside edge of wax candle and press bits of colored glass into clay.

After candle has been burned, old wax may be cut out, remelted, and the center filled with fresh wax and wick.

10

Stained Glass

GENERAL DIRECTIONS

EQUIPMENT: Paper. Pencil. Ruler. Oak tag or other heavy cardboard (not corrugated). Felt-tipped pen. Mat knife. Glass cutter with tapping ball. Glass pliers, 6″ size. Regular pliers. Adhesive tape. Masking tape. Small, stiff-bristle acid brush. Soldering iron with flat or pyramid tip, 40 to 100 watts. Newspaper and plywood board for working surface. Glass scraps for practice cutting. Rags. Eyeglasses or plastic goggles. Adhesive-backed plastic for mirror.

DIRECTIONS: Enlarge patterns by copying on paper ruled in 1″ squares; complete half- and quarter-patterns indicated by long dash lines; solid lines indicate cutting line. Using patterns and measurements in individual directions, cut each piece of each design from oak tag or cardboard for pattern.

Before working on actual glass pieces, practice glass cutting and soldering on scraps. Cover plywood board with newspaper to avoid spreading glass dust. Wear eyeglasses or plastic goggles for protection.

Place cardboard pattern on smooth side of glass. Mark outline with pen. To make straight cuts, place ruler along outline. For curved edges, use pattern edge pressed down on glass, or cut freehand. To score glass with cutter, draw cutter toward you in one continuous, firm motion. Do not go over score line; it dulls cutter and can make an uneven break. If cutter works stiffly, put a drop of any household oil on cutter. Break glass along score as follows: For straight edges, firmly grasp glass at each side of score; bend down and outward, pressing evenly. For curved edges, use ball end of cutter to tap once directly beneath score, ½″ from end; break away glass. Use glass pliers to trim away jagged edges that might remain. On small strips you may need to use regular pliers, with jaws covered with adhesive tape. If using mirror, cover entire back of piece with adhesive-backed plastic to prevent silver from coming off.

When you have cut all glass shapes needed for one design, arrange pieces over paper pattern to check fit. Wrap foil evenly around all edges of each piece. To wrap, place each glass edge in center of strip of copper foil tape, letting equal amounts extend over each side. Overlap foil ends about ¼″ where two ends meet; cut. Fold foil edges tightly over glass edges; use finger to flatten foil to glass.

Check fit again; leave design assembled, but separate pieces from each other. In well-ventilated area, brush flux over all copper foil surfaces with stiff-bristle brush. Continue brushing frequently during soldering process.

(Note: If soldering iron has never been used, the copper tip must be tinned as follows: heat iron; brush tip with flux; apply a small amount of solder.)

To solder, hold heated tip of soldering iron close to copper and apply end of solder wire to iron, letting solder flow down tip onto copper. First, spot solder at several points to hold pieces together; then solder pieces together by drawing iron along copper tape, spreading solder. Do not allow soldering iron to remain at any one point for more than an instant. Solder seams together on outside (or front); cool. Solder inside seams (or back); cool. Continue soldering until all copper is covered. For beaded seams, raise iron from surface a fraction of an inch; continue soldering until edges are rounded slightly at top.

When thoroughly cooled, sprinkle whiting powder on piece, wipe off with cloth to remove excess flux oil. Wash piece until solder is shiny and glass is clean; dry.

Candle Dazzlers

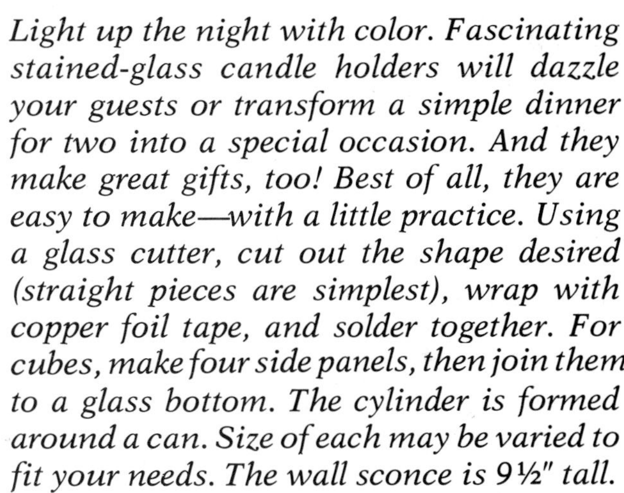

Light up the night with color. Fascinating stained-glass candle holders will dazzle your guests or transform a simple dinner for two into a special occasion. And they make great gifts, too! Best of all, they are easy to make—with a little practice. Using a glass cutter, cut out the shape desired (straight pieces are simplest), wrap with copper foil tape, and solder together. For cubes, make four side panels, then join them to a glass bottom. The cylinder is formed around a can. Size of each may be varied to fit your needs. The wall sconce is 9½" tall.

EQUIPMENT: See General Directions on page 328. Tin can, 3" diameter, for cylinder shaping.

MATERIALS: Opalescent glass in colors shown or as desired; see individual directions and patterns for measurements. Copper foil tape with adhesive backing, ¼" wide, 36-yd. rolls. Tube of liquid soldering acid called flux. Solid core wire solder 50/50, one-lb. spools. Copper sulfate powder. Spray wax polish. Free-standing candles, such as votive lights, 2" tall, for boxes; candle no larger than 1" diameter for sconce. **For Sconce:** Mirrored glass; see individual directions for amount. One thumbtack. One paper clip (optional).

DIRECTIONS: Read General Directions on page 328. To make boxes, place shape on base with bottom edges of sides on top of base piece; solder together, but do not solder underneath base piece (this keeps an even base). Let cool. Continue soldering right side until all copper is covered and seams are beaded—i.e., rounded slightly at top (about 1/32″ high); cool. For strength and appearance, wrap another layer of copper foil around boxes' perimeters; resolder.

When finished, wash piece thoroughly until solder is shiny and glass is clean; dry. For antiquing, add 4 oz. copper sulfate to quart of water; with rag, rub solution on solder until it appears dark and brassy; let dry. Wash, dry. Polish with spray wax.

STRIPED BOXES

All striped boxes have sides 3″ wide and a base 3¼″ square. All stripes are ⅜″ wide. Finished heights are 3¼″, 4⅜″, and 5⅜″. **Small Yellow Box:** Cut one light orange base, four yellow side pieces 2¼″ high, four stripes of purple, and four of light orange. Assemble with stripes at top edge as shown. Complete according to General Directions. **White and Blue Box:** Cut one purple base. Using Pattern A, cut one side of box from each panel of pattern using white for large areas, purple and blue-green for stripes. Assemble with diagonals on opposite sides of box and stripes meeting at all corners. Complete according to General Directions. **Orange Box:** Cut one blue-green base. Using Pattern B, cut one side of box from each panel of pattern, using light orange for large areas, purple and green for stripes. Assemble with stripes meeting at all corners. Complete according to General Directions.

SUNSET BOX

Cut one 3¼″ square of yellow for base. Using Pattern C, cut four panels using red for two half-suns, and alternating yellow, pink, and light orange segments for rays. Join panels together with half-suns at adjacent corners. Complete according to General Directions.

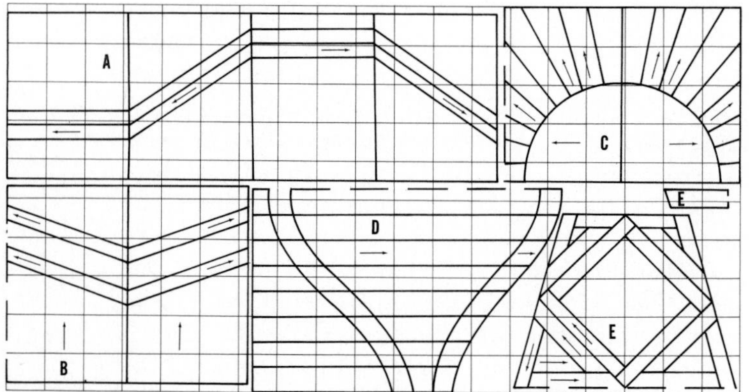

CYLINDER

Using compass, make 3″-diameter base pattern; cut one from light orange glass. Cut one strip pattern 8″ high and ½″ wide; using pattern, cut sixteen glass strips: eight of light orange; four green; four purple. Arrange in color sequence shown. To align curved edges, mark all strips at one time as follows: Place Pattern D on top of strips, lower edges even. Trace top curve onto glass strips; cut pattern down to second curve and mark on glass, keeping lower edges even. Repeat for two other curves. Cut each glass strip into its four pieces.

Wrap foil on all pieces; solder each vertical strip together. Using 3″-diameter tin can, place strips, in turn, around it and solder only at top of strips to hold sections together. Solder at bottom of strips. Let cool. Solder the length of each piece; cool. Solder according to General Directions.

SCONCE

Using Pattern E and referring to illustration, cut panel pieces from light orange, yellow, and green glass; cut center diamonds from mirrored glass (be careful cutting mirror so as not to chip backing). Assemble, wrap and solder panel completely, being careful not to apply direct heat to mirror backing, as it will burn off. Wrap copper foil and solder panel perimeter a second time.

Using small Pattern E, cut one front piece for base of sconce. Mark and cut four pieces each 1″ x 1⅛″ for bottom. Cut two pieces ⅜″ x 1⅞″ for sides of base. Solder four bottom pieces together into one 2″ x 2¼″ piece. Solder at right angle onto panel at bottom front. Solder sides onto base and panel; solder front onto base and sides. Solder thumbtack, point up, onto center of bottom of base to hold candle. If desired, sconce may have hook for hanging. Cut one end from paper clip and solder onto center of upper back edge of panel.

Four Window Plaques

Color-rich medallions gleam in the sunlight, glow softly in the rain. Multicolored crown and star, striped shield and royal fleur-de-lis are pieced together with bits of stained glass, then edged with copper foil and soldered together. Suspended from a window frame, they provide a fascinating color play.

EQUIPMENT: See General Directions on page 328.

MATERIALS: Cathedral stained glass in colors shown or as desired. One roll copper foil tape 3/16″ wide. Tube of liquid soldering acid called flux. Solid core wire solder. Copper sulfate powder. Stiff wire for hanging.

DIRECTIONS: Read General Directions page 328. When finished making window plaques, you may antique them, if desired, by adding 4 oz. copper sulfate powder to quart of water; rub solution onto all solder with rag until solder appears dark and brassy. Let dry. Wash and dry again.

Victorian Terrariums

Build a terrarium with a Victorian air. Window glass is combined with stained glass for a jewel-like effect. The glass is cut, wrapped with copper foil tape and soldered together. Blue-topped pagoda (left) is 18″ high.

EQUIPMENT: See General Directions for Stained Glass, page 328. Square. Masking tape.

MATERIALS: See General Directions and individual directions for additional materials.

DIRECTIONS: Read General Directions, page 328. Cut patterns from cardboard, following dimensions given in individual directions and diagrams. Cut glass pieces and solder together with beaded seams, following General Directions.

To plant terrariums, consult your local garden shop. Cover planted terrariums with glass covers.

PAGODA TERRARIUM

Additional Materials: Cathedral glass sheets ⅛″ thick, 6″ x 8″, four each of amber and blue. Clear plate glass; see directions for sizes of individual pieces (these pieces can be cut by a glazier).

Terrarium is an octagon, measuring approximately 18″ high and 12¼″ wide at base.

Patterns: Cut cardboard patterns as follows: Base: Mark 12¼″ square on cardboard. Divide square into halves, quarters, then eighths with a horizontal, a vertical, and two diagonal lines (see Diagram A). On each diagonal line, mark a point 2½″ in from corner. Connect points marked, with points where horizontal and vertical lines meet square, to make an octagon, with each side measuring 4 11/16″; see heavy lines on Diagram A. Cut out octagon shape for base pattern. Side Panel: Cut rectangle 4 11/16″ x 12″. Cover: See Diagram B, which shows one side of the octagonal cover. Cut rectangles B (2½″ x 2¾″), C (½″ x 2½″), and D (1″ x 3¼″). Cut trapezoid A by first drawing a rectangle 1½″ x 3¼″, then mark points on long sides ½″ from each corner. Draw lines from these points to corners on opposite sides as shown. Cut on lines for pattern A. Cut trapezoid E in same manner, first drawing a rectangle 2¼″ x 5¼″, then marking points on sides ¾″ from corners, as shown. To make pattern for top of cover, cut an octagonal piece in same manner as for base, starting with a 7″ square; mark points on diagonal lines 1¼″ from corners. See inner heavy lines on Diagram A for shape. Sides of piece should measure 2¾″.

Glass Pieces: From clear glass, cut one pagoda base, eight side panels, eight B pieces, and one top of cover. From blue glass, cut eight A pieces, sixteen C pieces, and eight D pieces. From amber glass, cut eight E pieces.

Assembling: Following General Directions, prepare each piece for soldering. Then, starting with lower part of terrarium, place each side panel perpendicular to and touching each of the eight sides of base, having bottom edges of panels flush with bottom edge of base; see illustration. Use masking tape to hold pieces together, both to check fit and to facilitate soldering. Solder panels to each other and to base, following General Directions.

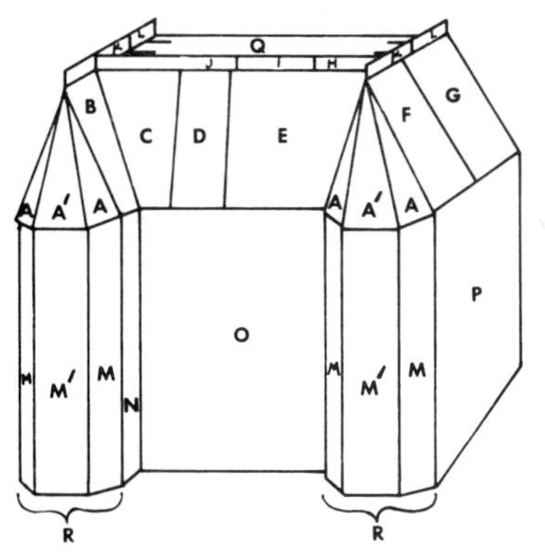

Diagram for
Green Terrarium

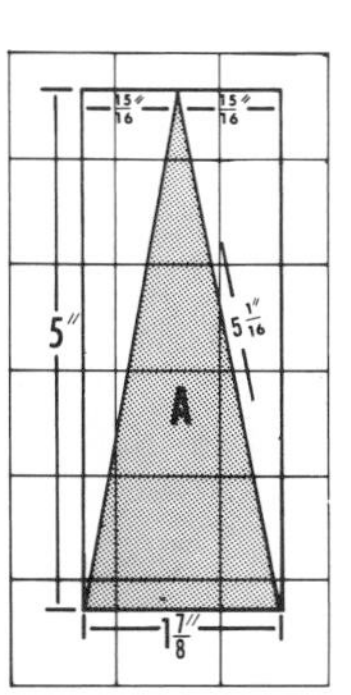

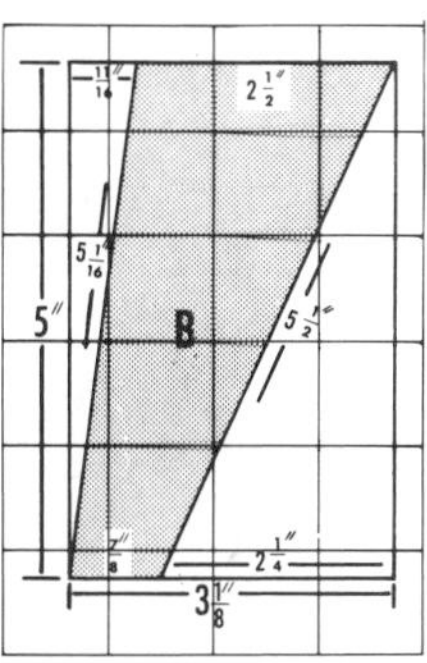

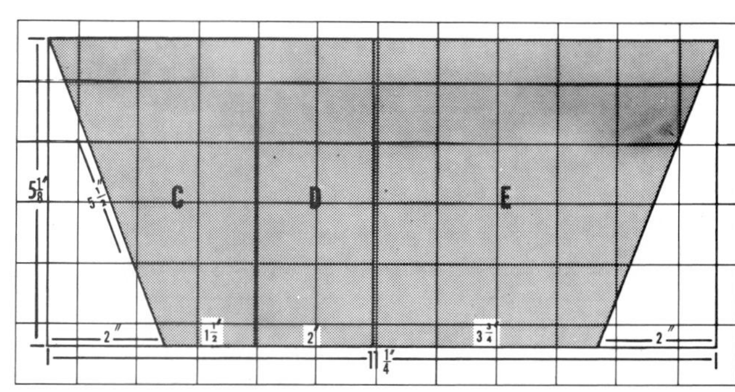

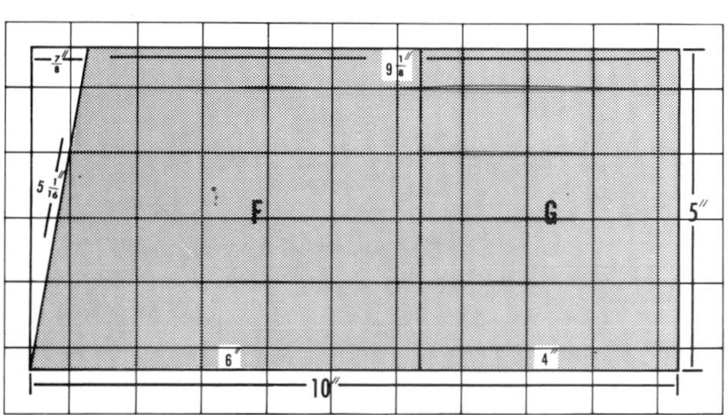

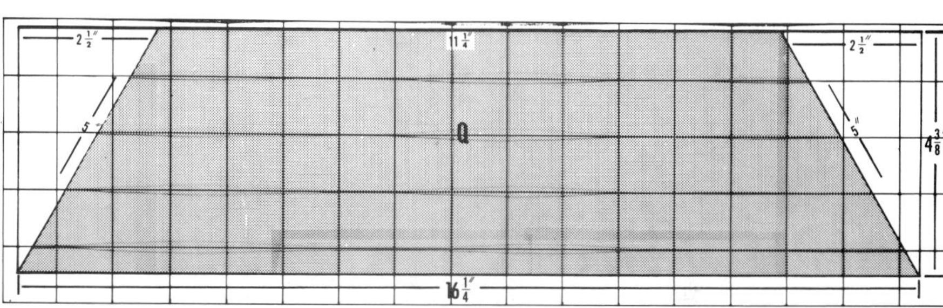

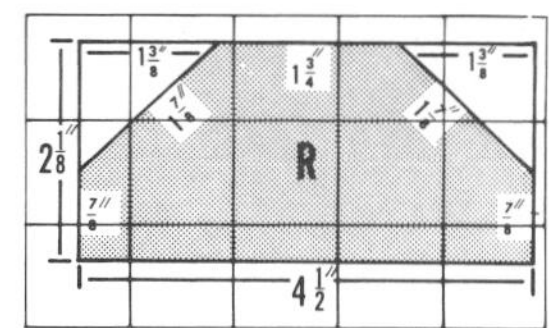

Green Terrarium

For cover, start by placing octagonal top on working surface. Tape the eight A pieces around top and to each other; the A pieces will slant outward; solder. Fit two C pieces and a D piece around each B piece as shown in Diagram B; solder. Solder B-C-D pieces made to A pieces. Fit and solder E pieces to D pieces and to each other. Place cover on planted lower part of terrarium for pagoda.

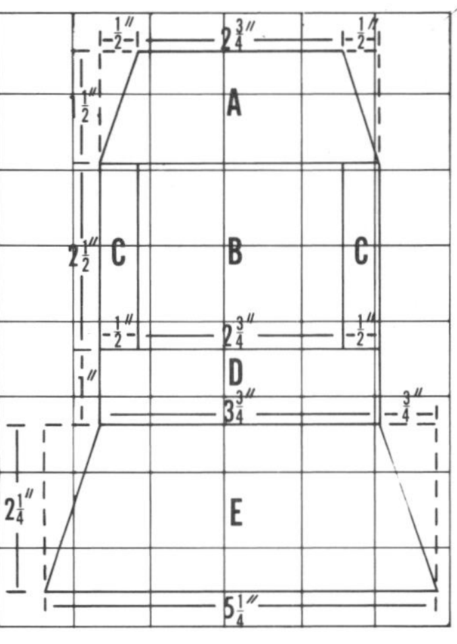

Diagram B
for Pagoda

GREEN TERRARIUM

Additional Materials: Cathedral glass ⅛″ thick, 6″ x 8″, one blue, seven green. Clear plate glass; see directions for sizes of individual pieces (these can be cut by a glazier). Mirror sheets; see directions. Rigid wire, four 3″ pieces.

Terrarium measures approximately 15½″ high, 16¼″ wide, and 11½″deep.

Patterns: Cut cardboard patterns, labeling each one. Make patterns A, B, C, D, E, F, G, Q (upper back), and R, as shown by shaded areas in diagrams. Make pattern A′ in same manner as pattern A, but using a rectangle 1¾″ x 5″. For patterns H, I, J, K, and L, cut five strips ½″ wide, in following lengths: H: 2¼″, I: 3″, J: 6″, K:6″, and L: 3⅛″. Pattern M: 1⅞″ x 10″. Pattern M′: 1¾″ x 10″. Pattern N: ⅞″ x 10″. Pattern O: 7¼″ x 10″. Pattern P: 10″ x 16¼″. For base, cut pattern 9⅛″ x 16¼″.

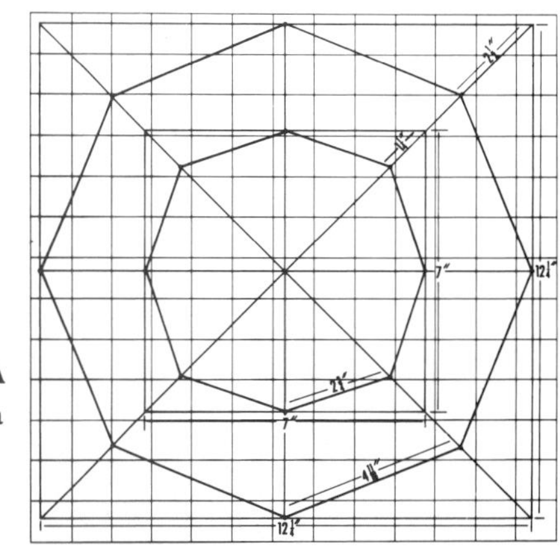

Diagram A
for Pagoda

Before cutting glass pieces, tape cardboard patterns together to check fit, cutting extra pattern pieces for this purpose; see Diagram for Green Terrarium.

Glass Pieces: From green glass, cut 4 of A, 2 of A′, 2 of B, 1 each of C, D, and E, 2 each of F and G. From blue glass, cut 1 each of H, I, and J, 2 each of K and L. From clear glass, cut 4 of M, 2 of M′, 2 of N, 1 of 0, 2 of P and R, and 1 base. (Reserve enough clear glass for cover.) From mirror, cut 1 of Q and 1 of lower back. Check fit again.

Assembling: Following General Directions, page 328, prepare all pieces for soldering. Referring to Diagram for Green Terrarium, solder pieces together. Start by attaching R pieces to one long side of base, to complete foundation. Solder P pieces to lower back and base, then solder M, N, and O pieces. Use masking tape to secure pieces as you work. Finish with roof pieces.

Solder two pieces of 3″ wire to inner bottom of K and L pieces on each side of roof; see Diagram for Green Terrarium. Cut piece of clear glass to fit snugly inside roof, resting on wires. Plant terrarium, then cover with the glass.

Wreath Mirror

The fairest mirror on the wall frames any face with delicate azure blooms and a wreath of green leaves. Stained-glass pieces are cut and then joined with solder for a "frame within a frame" that has a mirror base. The complete mirror is 14″ square.

EQUIPMENT: See General Directions on page 328.

MATERIALS: Cathedral stained glass in colors shown or as desired. Mirror 14″ square. Aluminum section frame strips, two packages, each 14″ size. One roll copper foil tape 3/16″ wide. Tube of liquid soldering acid called flux. Solid core wire solder. Copper sulfate powder.

DIRECTIONS: Read General Directions on page 328.

Cut a 14″-square template of oak tag and use to obtain correct size stained-glass frame. Following pattern, cut and arrange glass pieces on cardboard template. Copper-wrap and solder pieces together where they touch. Place glass frame on top of mirror. Frame both together with aluminum strip section frame.

Jeweled Cache

In hues of amethyst and twilight, this stained-glass "treasure" has a "clasp" of pretty beads on a copper wire strand. A mirror forms the bottom; the medallion in the lid is a Victorian portrait decal, seen through a vivid glass "jewel."

EQUIPMENT: See General Directions on page 328. Cotton swabs. Forty-watt soldering iron.

MATERIALS: See General Directions for Stained Glass on page 328. Two sheets purple cathedral glass, each 8″ x 12″. Small amount of opalescent glass in shades of purple. Small piece of blue opalescent glass. Mirror, about 4″ x 8″ for box bottom, scraps for lid. Black self-adhesive plastic (such as Con-Tact®). One blue translucent glass nugget, about 1½″ long. Paper decal or magazine illustration of Victorian face to fit under glass nugget. Clear epoxy cement. Barrel hinge, 3″ long. Brass wire for rod, 3½″ long. Thin, nickel-plated copper wire for clasp, 1½″ long. Fine chain, 4½″ long. Brass ball feet, ⅜″ diameter, six. Beads with small holes for clasp: two tiny pearls, two small round gold, one oval in shades of purple (Venetian-type bead or as desired). Copper sulfate antiquing solution. Clear nail polish.

DIRECTIONS: Read General Directions on page 328. From mirror, cut box bottom, four of pattern B, two of pattern K. Cut glass and adhere the Con-Tact®. From purple cathedral glass, cut four each of C, A, and F; cut two of H. From shades of purple opalescent glass, cut four each of G and I. From blue opalescent glass, cut two of J. Follow General Directions for preparation of all pieces.

Box Bottom: Solder one brass ball to back of mirror box bottom at each of the six points. Following General Directions, join each side section according to pattern and illustration (four side sections are the same; front and back sections are the same). Keeping bottom edges flush, join each section to the mirror and each section to the other to form six-sided box. Solder barrel hinge to back top of box.

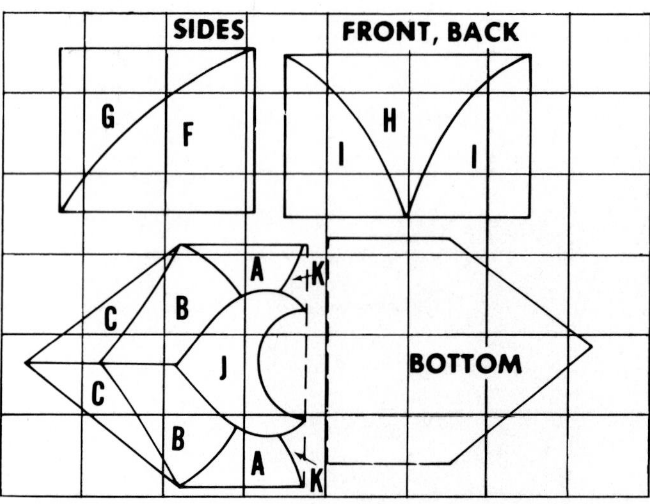

Lid: Using epoxy cement, affix decal face to flat side of nugget (so face shows through rounded surface of nugget). Solder pieces to each other as shown on pattern and in illustration. Position nugget, rounded side up, in center. Laminate decal to nugget with several coats of clear nail polish.

Bend in ¼″ at each end of brass rod; center and solder to back section of lid top with bent ends out.

For antiquing, apply copper sulfate solution to solder with a cotton swab; rub with cloth until solder appears dark or brassy. Let dry; wash with soapy water; rinse; dry again. Join lid to bottom by inserting bent ends of brass wire rod into hole at each end of barrel hinge.

For Clasp: Slip beads onto 1½″ wire as follows: pearl, small gold, oval Venetian, small gold, pearl. Shape each end of wire into a small decorative loop. Attach to center at top front of lid with a small wire ring through each decorative loop; solder to lid.

Solder one end of 4½″-long chain to right-hand side of inside of lid; solder other end to front point on box side, as illustrated.

11

Pottery

Molded Pottery Projects

Pretty pottery accents with old world charm are created from old-fashioned butter molds and cookie presses! To make a trinket jar or a tiny vase, form the clay in the bowl of mold. The design on the jar lid is impressed with the mold's motif. The size of the jar depends on the size of your mold. Special-occasion cookie presses make unusual paperweights and wall plaques. Here, too, the size of the finished object depends on the size of your mold. Most of the following are glazed, then fired.

NOTE: These directions are written for those who have had previous experience in making pottery. Instructions for preparing clay, drying, glazing and firing are not given here. For a description of these techniques, read the directions for the Herb Garden on page 341.

EQUIPMENT: Basic pottery studio equipment. Wooden butter molds with removable design heads; cookie presses.

MATERIAL: Ceramic clay: red, white or buff. Stoneware clay for tiles. Glazes, one-stroke ceramic colors, stains, cones as indicated in the individual instructions.

DIRECTIONS: Use well-wedged clay, free of air bubbles and pliable enough to bend without cracking. Clean wooden molds and presses thoroughly; they must be free of oil, wax and dust.

Pressing Designs: The size of wooden mold will determine the amount of clay needed. Roll clay to thickness indicated in individual instructions. Whenever possible, use the wooden mold as a pattern for cutting clay. Place mold or paper pattern on rolled clay and cut clay by holding knife in vertical position (cut more pieces than required for project to make allowance for defects; experiment with defects for decoration techniques of glazes and colors). Place the cut clay piece loosely over the carved cavity design side of wooden mold. To obtain clear impression of mold, press clay gently but firmly into mold cavity, starting at center and working to outer edges. Trim excess clay away from outer edges. Check thickness of clay and build up thin areas by moistening surface with a little water and adding small pieces of clay. Be sure to press the additional clay firmly into place without locking in air bubbles. Allow project to stand for about five minutes (if wooden press mold is a good antique, do not leave clay in too long as the dampness may cause mold to crack).

To release clay from mold, place hands in a cupped position around project; gently lift the edge on far side, then continue to release edge completely around mold. Slight tapping on the underside of mold will help release the clay, but too much agitation will cause the clay to become soft and will interfere with removal of clay from mold. Place a piece of plaster wall board or plaster bat on clay and reverse bat, clay and mold in one action. This will prevent the clay from twisting or bending, causing warping when fired. Place project on table and carefully lift the mold off. Study surface of clay for defects or desired corrections. If clay is slightly out of shape, square straight sides with guide sticks or rulers pressed against opposite sides, or smooth round pieces with damp fingers. If the background of design is too smooth, or you wish to create a wood-grained effect, it may be added at this time with a dull tool such as the handle of a fine paintbrush. Make slight, smooth grooves rather than cuts for the texture (cuts could cause air pockets under the glaze, creating pinholes or craters in the glaze during firing). Leave the clay on plaster board to dry slowly, covered lightly with a loose piece of plastic or cloth to prevent warping.

RECTANGULAR TILES

Stoneware clay was used. Clay was rolled to ¼″ thickness. Back of clay scored or roughened for proper gripping surface. No bisque firing. Glazed with two coats of white stoneware glaze (no glaze on sides or bottom). Decorated on unfired glaze with one coat of one-stroke ceramic colors; raised details of designs were colored in shades of yellow-green, blue-green, brown and pink. Tiles were fired once to cone 05.

ROUND PLAQUE

White clay was used, rolled to ¼″ thickness. Bisque fired to cone 05. Stained with ceramic unfired stain, polished, following manufacturer's directions. Opaque cantaloupe, transparent wood brown were used. No further firing.

PAPERWEIGHTS

Red clay was used, rolled ½″ thick. Mold was used as pattern and clay cut by holding knife at about 45° angle, to form an undercut, making the base smaller than the pattern top. While clay is still pressed in mold, press three equally spaced holes ¼″ deep, using pencil eraser, in bottom of clay to allow for proper drying and firing. Paperweight may be personalized on back while clay is leather-hard. Bisque fired to cone 05. Unglazed.

JARS WITH LIDS

Remove wooden design head from bowl of butter mold. Fill small hole in bowl with clay. Make paper patterns for sections of jar and lid (see Fig.1). Measurements for rectangular pattern piece A are obtained by measuring inside circum-

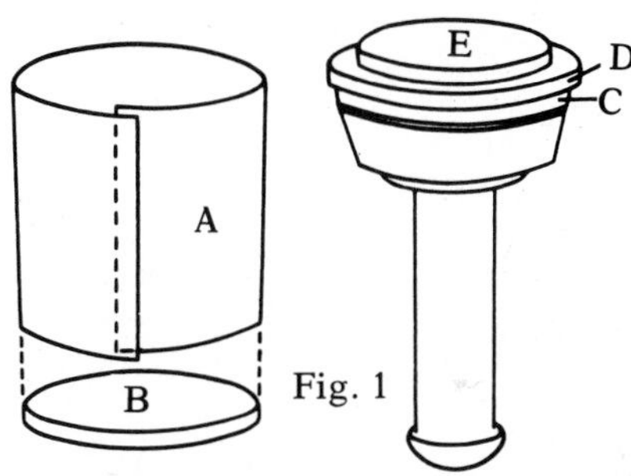

Fig. 1

ference and depth of butter mold bowl. Pattern for circular base piece B is diameter of A. Use wooden design head of mold for pattern C; pattern D for lid fits over top diameter of A. Pattern for inner lid piece E fits inside A. Jars are assembled in bowl of butter mold.

Use white or buff clay, rolled to 3/16″ thickness. Place patterns on rolled clay and cut around them with knife in vertical position. Place clay pieces on a bat.

To assemble jar, put paper pattern B for base in bottom of mold and clay disk B on top. Line sides of mold with paper pattern A. Bevel and score ends of clay piece A so that they overlap about ½″ and make even thickness. Place clay piece A inside; use slip to join overlapped ends together. Join B to bottom of A, scoring and reinforcing with clay coil. Trim excess clay from around lip of mold and set aside while assembling lid.

To assemble lid, press clay piece C in cavity of wooden design head. Press clay into mold as instructed in General Directions. Score plain side of

C and leave in mold. Score one side of disk D, join to C; score other side of D and one side of disk E and join as before. While assembled lid is still on design head, gently but firmly press it on plaster board. If design head has a deep cavity, clay lid will be quite thick at this point; press eraser of pencil gently ¼″ deep into thick clay to allow vent for proper drying and firing. Check fit of lid on jar; if inner lid is too big, trim to fit, allowing room for thickness of glaze. Remove lid from head of mold. Remove jar from mold. Place jar on plaster board with lid in place to dry slowly. Bisque fire to cone 08 with lid on jar.

For an antique effect on jars, brush brown stain on bisque ware and sponge it off. Glaze with two coats of clear or transparent matt glaze. The large jar was brushed with green stain and sponged off. Glaze with two coats of matt glazes in turquoise with touches of blossom pink on lid. When dry they were fired to cone 06-05.

Sculpted Flower "Vase"

Basically simple in shape, this girl's head is formed over a rubber ball, with holes poked through the crown for her magnificent flower headdress.

EQUIPMENT: Pottery kiln 9″ x 9″ x 9″, or larger, with firing temperature of 1900° F, or higher. Rolling pin. Oilcloth 12″ x 18″. Rubber balls, 4″ to 6″ diameter. Knife. Sponge. Modeler. Skewer. Ruler. Pencil. Paper. Brushes. Fine sandpaper.

MATERIALS: Clay, any desired color. Slip made by mixing clay and water to heavy cream consistency. Glazes and underglazes in colors desired. Salad oil.

NOTE: Prepare clay for use by kneading and wedging to free from air bubbles. See Directions for Herb Garden on page 341 for method.

DIRECTIONS: Lightly oil rubber ball with salad oil and wipe off excess. Using fairly moist clay, cover oiled ball with pellets of clay to cover entirely, about ½″ thick. Roll ball lightly with palm of hand on hard, smooth area to smooth out surface of clay. Let dry several hours until firm to touch, but not dry. Cut through clay to form two halves; gently remove clay from ball with twisting motion. With ball removed, place two halves of clay together with slip and wedge seam until smooth and invisible. If shape is distorted it can be regained by rolling clay ball gently again on smooth surface. For neck, roll coil of clay about 2½″ thick; cut to about 3″ length and taper slightly at one end; flatten other end on table. Overlap ends and wedge together. With modeler, hollow out coil slightly to aid in drying. Attach neck to ball firmly with slip and soft clay; shape smoothly and flare out bottom a little. The neck should be fairly heavy to balance larger head. With soft clay, model a simple nose on head. Using modeler, cut lines in head to resemble hair and mouth. With pointed pencil, gently poke through clay for eyes. Using skewer and working in concentric circles, push holes through clay on top of head (be sure holes are large enough to hold flower stems and allow for shrinkage in firing). Dry thoroughly; sand or sponge to remove rough edges formed by modeler; fire to maturing temperature of clay.

Herb Garden Clay Pots

Hang a garden in your window! These clay pots, made by the pinch method, have coils added at the top for decoration and for handles. Leather thongs, simple or braided, complement the natural color of the clay.

EQUIPMENT: Sturdy flat working surface. Oilcloth. Cutting wire. Plastic wrap. Ruler. Scissors. Sharp knife or large hat pin or large, sturdy needle. Flat wooden or rubber paddle, Japanese rice paddle, or large, flat wooden spoon. Bowl or receptacle with narrow opening to rest ceramic pot in. Sponge for smoothing and for color wash. Kiln with firing temperature for clay used.

MATERIALS: Stoneware clay, approximately 1 to 2 lbs. for each pot. Medium grog, ¼ cup for each lb. (this must be added to the clay for porousness). For colorant: 1 tsp. red iron oxide powder (in one cup water). Linen yarn or tan leather lacing for hangers (see directions for amounts).

NOTE: For those who are experienced in mixing clays and have the tools and equipment for making special formulas, the exact composition of the clay is as follows: 11 lbs. fire clay, 1½ lbs. ball clay, 1 lb. red art Cedar Heights clay, 6 lbs. grog, ½ lb. bentonite. Colorant: 1 tsp. bone ash or colmanite (in ½ cup water).

DIRECTIONS: Cover working surface with oilcloth, wrong side up. Mix the clay and grog together thoroughly (or prepare composition given). Wedge all the clay to be used at one time. To wedge the clay, use wire to cut the mass in half. Throw one half down, then throw the other half on top of first. Then press clay with both hands and knead it like dough, until smooth and free of air bubbles when cut in half again. (Clay must be free of air bubbles as they may cause pot to explode during firing or cause the clay to crack). From this point on, work with just enough clay needed at a time, keeping remaining clay moist in plastic wrap. Pots are made by the pinch method, with coils added at top of pots for decorative trims and for handles.

To make pinch pot, use hands to pat a 1- to 2-lb. ball of clay (the size of medium-size orange) as round as possible (Fig. 1). Holding ball in one hand and using thumb of other hand, press a hole into the center, going down to within ½″ of bottom of the ball (Fig. 2). With ball still in one hand, gradually turn ball and press or pinch gently with thumb and fingers of other hand, enlarging the hole and stretching and forming the clay into pot shape (Fig. 3). Eventually width of pot should be at least 4″ if intended for herbs. Smallest pot (on table) is 4½″ deep; largest is 5½″ deep. Work slowly; do not press too hard, and keep thickness of sides of pot as uniform as possible. Keep hands just slightly moist while shaping. Pull clay upward and outward, starting from the bottom and working up gradually. Rub your fingers over the top rim frequently to reinforce the top and to prevent splitting or cracking of the clay. Continue in this manner until the upper three-quarters of the pot is the thickness desired (ours are from ⅛″ to ¼″ thick). If the rim is uneven, straighten it by cutting with scissors; smooth the cut edge with your fingers. Wrap the bottom of the pot in plastic so that it remains soft while the pot is left to set until its top rim firms up and holds its shape.

When top rim is fairly firm, begin to press out the bottom thickness of the pot until it and walls are even throughout, and pot is the general shape desired. Turn pot upside down onto its rim. Gently paddle the pot into shape, rounding the bottom, or slanting it at an angle to the sides (see illustration). Paddling the clay also smooths it, erases fingermarks, and fortifies the structure in general. Leave pot in this position until bottom of pot is fairly firm.

To finish the rim without disturbing the bottom shape of pot, set pot in bowl or receptacle with narrow enough opening so that bottom does

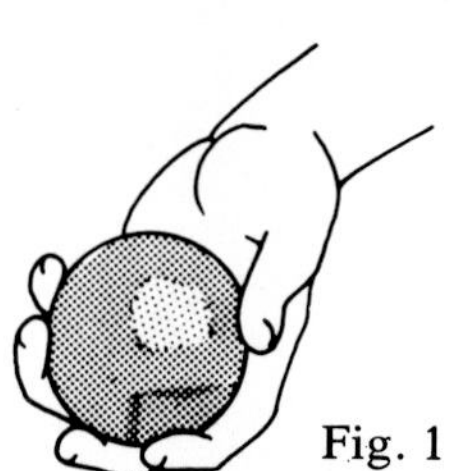
Fig. 1

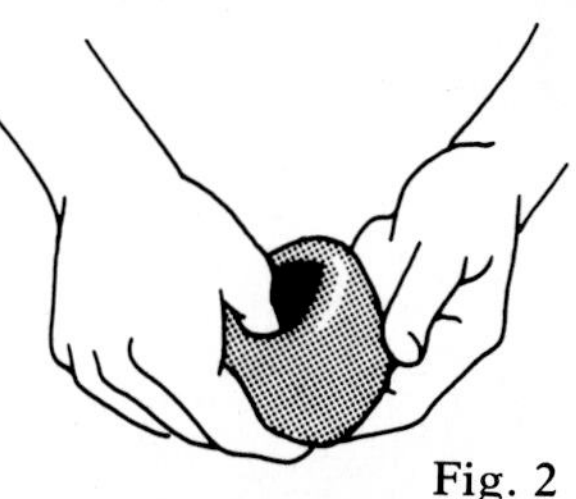
Fig. 2

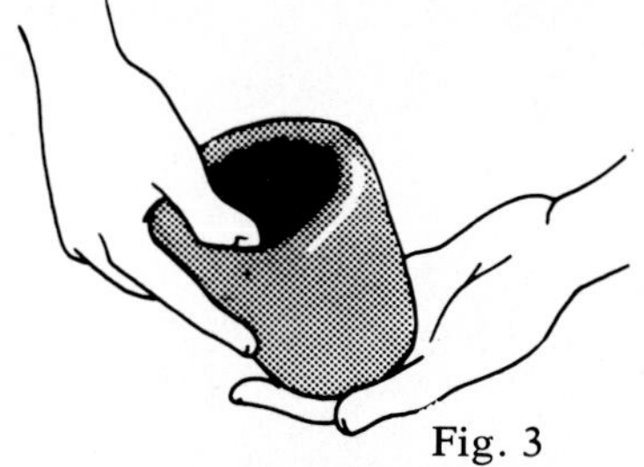
Fig. 3

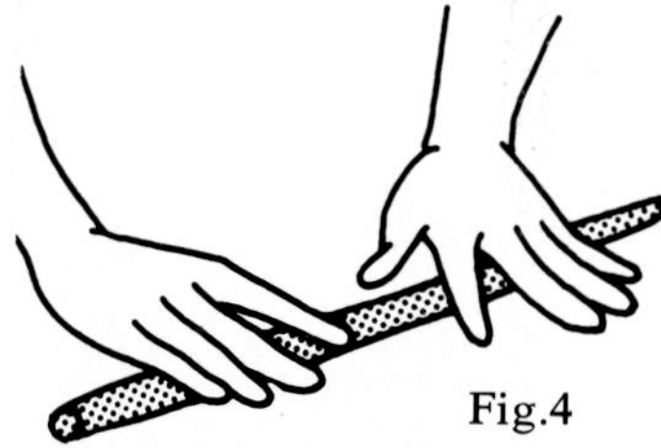
Fig.4

not touch. Rim can be smoothed with fingers and left plain, or coils can be added for decoration as shown in illustration.

To make coil, start with small ball of clay and roll ball evenly; move hands from center outward to keep coil uniform (Fig. 4). Work on a freshly dampened surface to keep clay moist and prevent breaking. Make coil the thickness of pot rim, or thicker if desired. To secure coil, use knife or needle to make crosshatch marks on rim of pot; then dampen with a bit of water on your finger. Apply the coil to the moistened rim; paddle it down gently. Erase the inside seamline by smoothing coil and pot together. Leave the seam of the coil on the outside for definition. Add as many coils as desired in same manner, crosshatching and moistening the coil already on pot each time you add another coil; smooth each seam of added coils on inside.

The handles of pot at center right of illustration were formed by placing coils around rim, then adding more coils in same fashion with three evenly spaced openings, creating a wavy-patterned edge.

Other handles shown were made by rolling thick or thin coils for handles, using them singly, or winding two together. Apply to rim after crosshatching and moistening area where handle is to be joined. Then press coil firmly to pot. Two, three, or four handles may be added on each pot, depending upon width and design of pot. Handles may be left round on the outside or they can be paddled to slightly flatten outer surface.

The two handles for the widest pot (center left) were made of a very thick coil, flattened with paddle, and then applied to pot.

Tassels on pot at upper right were formed by bunching a number of very small short coils together at one end and then joining them at this point to pot handles as shown, after crosshatching and moistening area at bottom center of handles.

Decoration of pot on table was made by taking a tiny ball of clay, rolling it slightly and pinching it at one side to form point. Each was secured to pot by crosshatching and moistening the pot at each point of joining.

Let pot dry in its bowl support, or set on table if bottom is flat enough. When pot becomes leather-hard, rub it with a damp sponge to smooth out any rough areas or irregularities.

When pot is completely dry, color wash may be sponged on. For stoneware, mix red iron oxide powder in one cup of water. Dip sponge into this wash and gently dab the sponge over the surface of the pot, inside and outside. Be careful not to make the sponge too wet with wash, as it may make the pot damp again.

If the special composition clay is used, mix 1 tsp. bone ash or colmanite in ½ cup water. Apply as for above. This wash will appear as a faint chalky coating which dries immediately. When fired, this will simply intensify the natural rusty color of the clay.

NOTE: The color of clay after firing will depend upon how evenly and thoroughly the wash has been applied, and, possibly, the position of the pot in the kiln. However, uneven coloring generally enhances the appearance of a handmade pot.

The pots are now ready for firing in the kiln. Follow firing directions as specified by the supplier of the clay. The pots made of the special composition clay can be bisque-fired and then fired again to 2300°, or they can be once-fired, directly to cone 9 or 10.

NOTE: These pots are not watertight if they have been only once-fired and/or if they are made with a clay which contains a lot of grog (as the special formula does). However, they only perspire slightly, which actually helps keep the plant soil healthy.

Hangers: Leather Lacing: Each hanger takes about 6 yds., folded in half. Insert the folded end through handle; draw ends of lacing through the loop formed and pull ends all the way through loop to tighten. Make one for each handle on pot; for the largest pot, make three hangers for each handle.

Linen Hangers: For each, cut eight 6-yd. strands; double. (Strands of different earth colors may be used for interesting effect). Secure hangers to pot loops as above; then braid, twist, or knot strands as desired.

To plant herbs, consult your local garden shop.

12

Decorative Painting

Chippendale Tray

This tray has a bouquet in the center, and scrolls and tiny flowers along the border. The designs are painted with oils, in two layers—the basic design is painted first, and then the details are added.

EQUIPMENT: One each of camel hair or sable brushes, Nos. 2, 4 and 6; 1" soft, flat brush for background; l" soft, flat brush for varnish (final finish). Palette knife. Small dish for mixture of Japan drier and turpentine. Small dish for mixture of bronzing powder and varnish. Soft, lintless rags for wiping brushes, etc. Newspapers. White and black carbon paper. Stylus or hard pencil; medium-soft pencil. Paper for patterns. Tracing paper. Masking tape. Dry ball-point pen. Powdered pumice stone (optional).

MATERIALS: Chippendale-style tray, approximately 20" x 25" (unfinished or painted black). Tube oil colors: large tube titanium or flake white; one small tube each of alizarin crimson, vermillion, cadmium yellow medium, lemon yellow, yellow ochre, viridian green, cobalt blue, raw umber, burnt sienna. Gold bronzing powder. Pint of turpentine. Tube of ivory drop black Japan color (for unpainted tray). Small amount of Japan drier. Small amount of spar varnish. Small amount of dull varnish (if antiquing is desired).

DIRECTIONS: Cover work table with newspapers to protect it. Before painting, be sure surface is dry and free from dust. Keep a quantity of clean, soft, lintless rags handy to use for keeping all materials clean. Wash brushes frequently in turpentine.

When painting, pick off immediately any loose hairs or bristles that may fall from your brush. Paint and varnish background in one direction only.

If redoing an old tray, remove all traces of oil, paint, rust, etc., with steel wool and No. 00 sandpaper; or use a reliable paint remover.

To Paint Tray Background: Wipe tray clean and dry. Put a quantity of ivory drop black Japan color into a small dish. Thin it with a small amount of turpentine to which has been added a few drops of Japan drier (paint should be consistency of thin cream). Paint front of tray. Let dry. Paint reverse side of tray. Let dry. Varnish back of tray with spar varnish. Allow to dry.

Preparing Paints: Mix paints on newspaper pad according to Chart for Mixing Colors, page 346. The newspaper absorbs excess oil from the oil colors so that colors will dry more quickly on the metal tray; it also makes them easier to apply.

After colors are mixed, lift your globs of color with palette knife onto a fresh newspaper pad. Allow about a 3" area between colors.

When applying, thin paints to a creamy, workable consistency by moistening with brush which has been dipped into a half-and-half mixture of Japan drier and turpentine.

Use Nos. 2 and 4 brushes for small areas and details. Use No. 6 brush for larger areas.

Painting: Enlarge patterns by copying on paper ruled in 1" squares. As you work, keep a piece of paper under your hand to prevent blurring of pattern. When painting, let the brush strokes show, poviding they follow the natural growth of petals, leaves, etc.; do not worry about getting the paint absolutely smooth. Thus each petal and leaf will be distinguishable even though some may touch and be of the same color.

Step 1: Place pattern for Center Motif on tray, using guidelines on pattern for accurate centering. Hold motif in place at top edge with a strip of masking tape. Insert white carbon, face down, beneath pattern. Go over pattern with stylus or dry ball-point pen to transfer motif to tray. Be sure to transfer guidelines also (used later in Step 5). Transfer Floral Corner Motif to four corners of tray by method given above (reverse pattern to transfer motifs to opposite sides).

Step 2: Refer to directions for method of mixing paints and applying. Mix color shades according to Chart for Mixing Colors. Paint all areas of Center Motif in solid colors; follow symbols for placing colors. Paint all areas of Floral Corner Motif in solid colors; follow color symbols. While painting Floral Corner Motif, hold tray in such a working position that the Corner Motif is nearest you, so your hand will not reach across the wet paint of Center Motif. Allow tray to dry at least 12 hours. Save leftover paint for shading (used in Step 6).

Step 3: If the tray has dried overnight, you should be ready, with careful handling, to transfer Border Motifs A and B. Follow transfer directions given above under Step 1. First transfer Motif A to beveled corners of tray, then transfer Motif B.

Step 4: In a small dish, mix about a thimbleful of bronzing powder with enough varnish to get the mixture to a creamy consistency. Mix more gold paint if needed. Paint Motif A; next paint Motif B. Allow to dry at least 12 hours.

Step 5: Center Motif has now dried at least 48 hours and is not tacky. Take tracing paper the same size as paper used for all of Center Motif. Mark guide lines of Center Motif on tracing paper. Place tracing paper over blue Floral Shading for Center Motif, matching guide lines. Trace. Place tracing on tray over Center Motif, matching guide lines. Using black carbon paper, transfer according to Step 1.

Step 6: Paint all areas of Floral Shading for Center Motif in solid colors. Follow symbols for

---

Overtone Shading for Center Motif

Lily: Paint fine dotted areas—W1
Paint heavy dotted areas—Y2
Paint solid blue areas—W4

Yellow Rose: Paint fine dotted areas—W1
Paint heavy dotted areas—Y2
Paint all solid blue areas—R3

Pink Rose: Paint fine dotted areas—W1
Paint heavy dotted areas—R1
Paint solid blue areas—R4

Leaves and Stems

Paint all unlettered white areas—G2
Paint all dotted areas—G3
Paint all black areas—G4

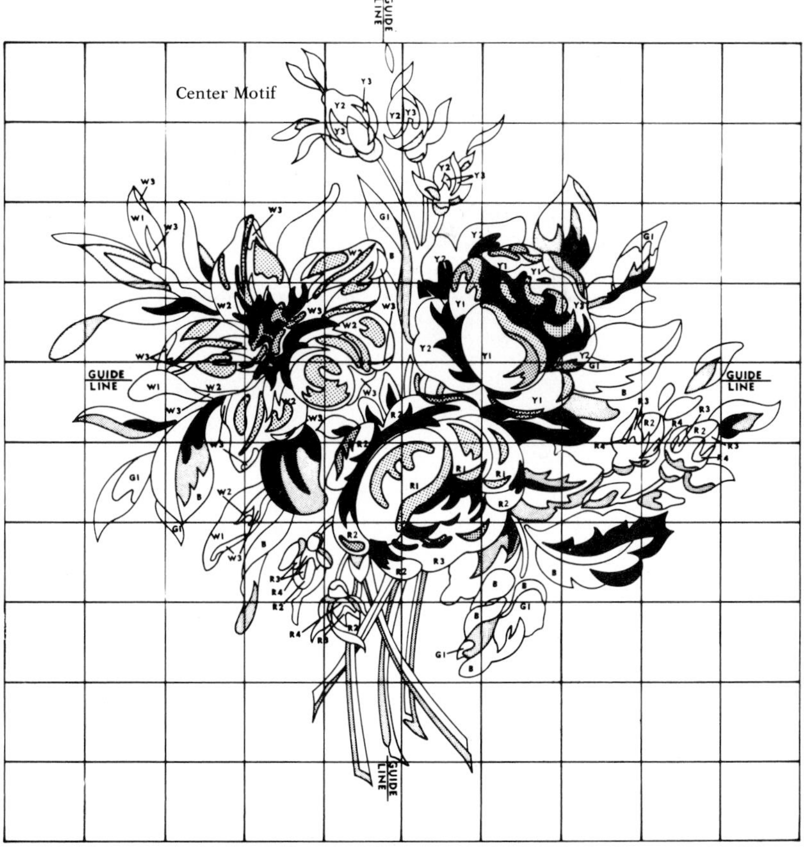

Paint unlettered white areas—G2
Paint dotted areas—G3
Paint black areas—R4

painting, using colors left over from Step 2. Allow to dry. Varnish with spar varnish. Dry thoroughly.

Step 7: If desired, tray may be antiqued by rubbing raw umber over design and border and wiping off with a clean, lintless rag. Finish with a dull varnish. To "satinize" tray, rub with powdered pumice stone.

Chart for Mixing Colors

Lily: W1—white (from tube). (White mixed with Japan drier gives an "off-white," slightly yellowish color.)

W2—pale gray (white, lemon yellow, yellow ochre, cobalt blue). Be sure to keep color light by using large amount of white.

W3—light medium gray (white, yellow ochre, cobalt blue, vermillion). Be sure not to make too dark; very little vermillion.

W4—dark gray (W3 with a little raw umber added).

Yellow Rose: W—white (from tube).

Y1—pale yellow (white, lemon yellow, cadmium medium, yellow ochre).

Y2—medium yellow (white, lemon yellow, more cadmium medium than Y1, yellow ochre).

Y3—orange yellow (white, a little lemon yellow, quite a bit of cadmium medium, yellow ochre, speck of vermillion).

Overtones—R3 shading under lower petals and center. Highlight in center is R1. Overtone on center petals is Y3. White accents.

Pink Rose: W—white (from tube).

R1—yellowish peach (white, a little lemon yellow, cadmium medium, yellow ochre, and speck of vermillion).

R2—rose peach (white, a little lemon yellow and cadmium medium, more yellow ochre and vermillion).

R3—medium rose (white, alizarin crimson, yellow ochre, speck of cobalt blue).

Overtones—R4 dark red (vermillion, alizarin crimson, yellow ochre, speck of cobalt blue); Y1 on center petals; R1 on edge of outer petals; white accents.

Leaves, etc.: G1—light yellow green (white, lemon yellow, viridian green, yellow ochre, speck of burnt sienna).

G2—pale lime green (white, lemon yellow, viridian green, yellow ochre, speck of burnt sienna and cadmium medium).

G3—medium green (white, viridian green, yellow ochre, a little cadmium medium, burnt sienna).

G4—dark green (viridian green, yellow ochre, burnt sienna).

B—light medium brown (very little white, lemon yellow, cobalt blue, burnt sienna).

Painted Tinware

Painted tinware, first made in Wales in the seventeenth century to replace lacquered wood, is a perfect complement to Early American decor. Here's an adaptation of a traditional tole motif used to decorate a desk set, a wall candelabrum, and an old-fashioned collar box—now a dried-flower holder! Items are purchased, then painted with artists' oil colors. The letter holder measures 4½" x 6" and stands 16" tall.

EQUIPMENT: Tracing paper. Masking tape. White dressmaker's tracing (carbon) paper. Brushes: 1″ wide good quality flat; red sable water-color brushes, round-tipped No. 6 and No. 2; 1½″-wide for varnish. Hard, sharp pencil. Clean cotton rags. Newspapers. Bottle caps. Fine steel wool. Sandpaper.

MATERIALS: Turpentine. Metal primer paint. Flat black enamel. Artists' oil paints in small tubes. American vermillion, yellow ochre, titanium white, chromium oxide green, alizarin crimson, raw umber. Rubbed-effect varnish. New, unpainted tinware or prepared old pieces.

DIRECTIONS: Cover working surface with newspapers; be sure surface is clean and free of dust. Have soft rags handy to keep materials clean. Clean brushes frequently in turpentine. If bristles come off brush while painting, pick them out immediately. If redoing old tinware, remove all traces of paint and rust with paint remover, steel wool and sandpaper. Wash new or old tinware with hot soapy water, rinse and dry thoroughly.

To Paint Background: Apply primer to both sides of pieces; let dry 24 hours. Sand lightly. Apply second coat and allow to dry thoroughly.

Thin the flat black enamel with turpentine to get an easy flowing consistency, and mix thoroughly. Paint tinware black; first coat may not cover completely, but do not go over work to touch up. Let dry 24 hours. Sand lightly to remove any ridges. Apply second coat and third coat, allowing to dry 24 hours and sanding between coats.

To Transfer Designs: Trace the design; complete half-pattern where necessary as indicated by dash line. For some of the border designs, you will need to trace the pattern several times to get the correct length for item. Place pencil tracing of the design in position on tinware item with dressmaker's carbon paper between tracing and tinware. Secure the tracing to the surface with several pieces of masking tape. Then go over lines of design completely with a hard pencil. Remove traced design and carbon paper.

Practice Painting: Trace the border design on an extra sheet of paper and use this for practicing. To make a palette for mixing colors, take a double sheet of newspaper and fold it into eighths. Newspaper is ideal for this because it absorbs the extra oil in the paint. Fill a bottle cap with varnish; this is used as a medium for all colors. Squeeze out a little color on the newspaper palette and, using a brush, mix it with a small amount of varnish, just enough to make it manageable but not too thin. Load the entire brush, not just the tip, and practice painting strokes on the border design. Lower the brush and apply a little pressure for a wide area; raise the brush gradually, and move it toward you to taper the stroke to a point. Practice this motion, working slowly until you feel you have control of the brush. Reload brush as necessary to keep it filled for each stroke. Position your work so that it is comfortable for you. Use No. 2 brush for small shading strokes, lines and dots. Use No. 6 brush for larger strokes and to fill in areas.

If paint begins to thicken, clean brush in turpentine. Squeeze out some fresh paint onto a clean area of the palette and thin with varnish.

To Paint Designs: Plan design for tinware pieces as shown, or to fit your particular pieces, and transfer designs to tinware.

Mix some colors, use others as they are, but mix varnish with all. Apply colors in the order listed below, following numbers on patterns. Allow each color to dry at least 24 hours before using next color. When you have mixed a color, paint all areas on all items requiring that color, since it is difficult to match the same mixture.

Chart for Mixing Colors

No. 1—Salmon Pink: Mix a little American vermillion and yellow ochre with white. Paint flower and bud areas numbered 1.

No. 2—Chromium Oxide Green: Use as it is. Paint leaf areas numbered 2 and parts of borders numbered 2.

No. 3—Dark Red: Mix alizarin crimson with just a touch of raw umber. Paint center areas of flowers numbered 3.

Desk Organizer
Corner Motif
Collar Box
Blotter Corners
Border Motif

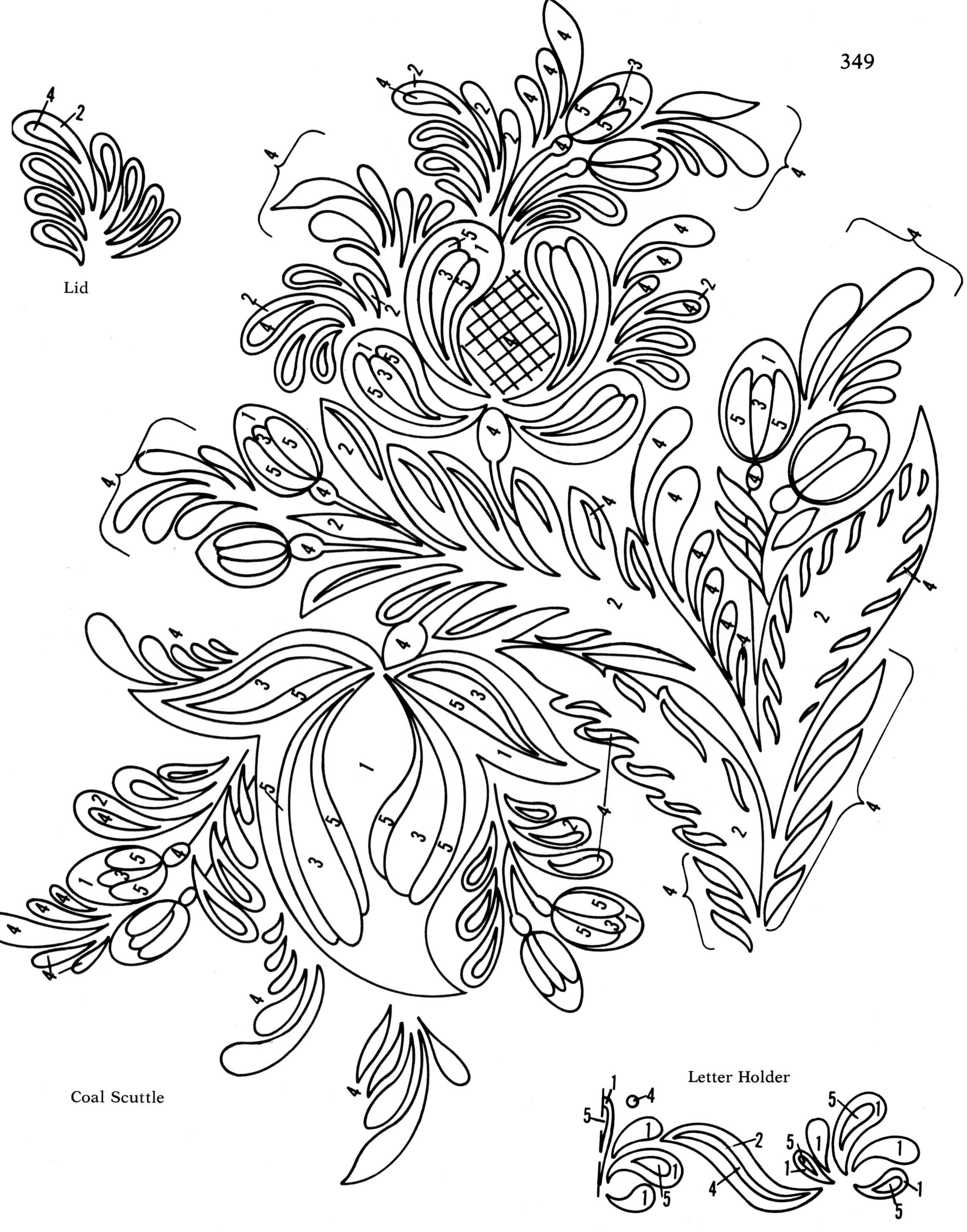

Lid

Coal Scuttle

Letter Holder

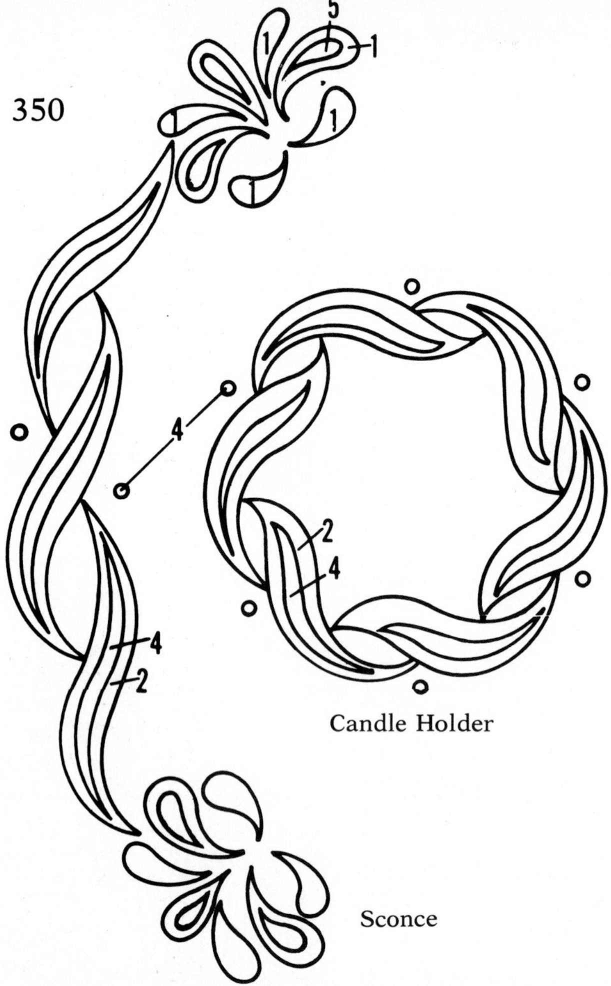

No. 4—Yellow Ochre: Use as it is. Paint leaves numbered 4, dots and shading on green leaves numbered 4. Paint parts of borders numbered 4. Paint lines of crosshatching on some flower centers at this time if it is possible without smudging other areas.

No. 5—Shaded White: Add a slight touch of American vermillion to a thin white mixture. Paint areas of flowers and buds numbered 5. Allow to dry 24 hours.

Varnishing: The varnish coat is a protective finishing process which also adds a smooth satin gloss to the tinware. Apply varnish only to a completely dry piece of tinware which has been dusted and is lint-free. The varnish and the tinware should be at a room temperature of about 70° F.

Place the pieces to be varnished on clean newspaper in an area where they can dry without being disturbed. Using a clean, dust-free 1½″-wide brush, apply a thin coat of varnish to the tinware in even brushstrokes, working quickly. Do only one surface at a time. If necessary pick up any air bubbles or loose hairs with the tip of the brush. Allow to dry 24 hours.

Continue the varnishing process by dusting off the items and applying a second coat of varnish. Let dry for 24 hours.

After the second coat has dried thoroughly, rub item on the diagonal with steel wool. Dust off, being careful to remove all of the pieces of steel wool. Apply the third and final coat of varnish and allow to dry for 2 days.

Antiqued Bucket

Genuine Early American motifs, painted in the popular Pennsylvania Dutch style, decorate this traditional wooden bucket. The design is painted in flat tones; overtones are applied later.

EQUIPMENT: Tracing paper. Hard and soft pencils. Masking tape. Paintbrushes: fine-pointed, square-tipped quill, and 1″ flat. Flat plate for palette. Small jar or glass. Clean rags. Fine sandpaper.

MATERIALS: Wooden bucket about 10″ diameter, 10″ high. Artists' tube oil paints: chrome yellow medium, cadmium vermillion, Prussian blue, black, titanium white, yellow

Color Key

R—Red
B—Blue
Y—Yellow
W—White
F—Flesh
Bl—Black
G—Green

Border Designs

Brushstrokes used in freehand painting. Use a square-tipped quill brush. Practice the strokes, pressing down a corner of brush, rolling brush, and lifting it at the end of stroke.

ochre, raw umber. Turpentine. Shellac. Satin-finish varnish.

DIRECTIONS: Sand bucket until smooth. Apply one coat of shellac and let dry.

Trace horse design and two borders; complete wide border for one repeat design. Go over lines on back of tracings with soft pencil. Tape horse design to top of bucket lid. Go over lines with sharp hard pencil to transfer design to lid. Transfer narrow border around sides of lid in same manner, adjusting pattern to make ends of border meet. On bucket, transfer wide border motif three times around middle, making space between repeats of design equal.

Have small containers of turpentine and varnish handy. Mix a small amount of paint in colors indicated on page 351 on flat plate or palette, using varnish to thin the paint to a smooth texture.

Entire design is first painted in flat tones, following letters on pattern and color key. When dry, overtones are applied. Mix a lot of varnish with white paint for overtones, making it slightly transparent. On leaves, tulips, and flowers on lid, overtones are white. On wide border, overtones are red brushstrokes on tulips. Overtones on narrow border are white.

Solid black areas on pattern are painted with a mixture of black paint and varnish. When design is completely painted, let dry 48 hours. Add details of black on leaves of lid and borders, working with a thin brushstroke between white and green, or along one edge. Let dry thoroughly.

Mix a small amount of raw umber paint in varnish and give bucket and lid one coat. Let dry 24 hours and sand lightly; give another coat of varnish. Let dry.

To Mix Colors: Red for coat and flowers—cadmium vermillion with a speck of white and yellow ochre.

Blue for flowers—Prussian blue mixed with white for a light blue; add a little yellow ochre and a speck of raw umber for antique effect.

Yellow for saddle, flowers, dots, etc.—chrome yellow medium with a speck of raw umber.

Green for leaves and border—chrome yellow medium, with Prussian blue and a speck of raw umber.

White—Add a speck of raw umber to titanium white.

Flesh color for face and hands—white with a small amount of yellow ochre and a speck of cadmium vermillion.

Hitchcock Chair

Here is a Hitchcock chair stenciled with the classic fruit bowl design, accented with rich bands of gold. The stenciling is done with bronzing powders, using the actual-size patterns provided here.

EQUIPMENT: Work table. Newspapers. Medium and 6/0 sandpaper. Brushes: flat brushes 1½" wide for painting and varnishing; striping brush 1½" long; fine pointed sable brush; show card brush No. 6. Steel wool No. 4/0. **For Stencils:** Tracing paper. Pencil. Architect's tracing linen ½ yard. Piece of velour 8" x 12". Tightly woven velveteen in 3" square scraps, one for each color bronzing powder. Fine, sharp-pointed scissors. Black India ink. Fine drawing pen. Waxed paper. Cleaning fluid for cleaning stencils and brushes. Lint-free cloth. White pencil. Bottle caps for mixing

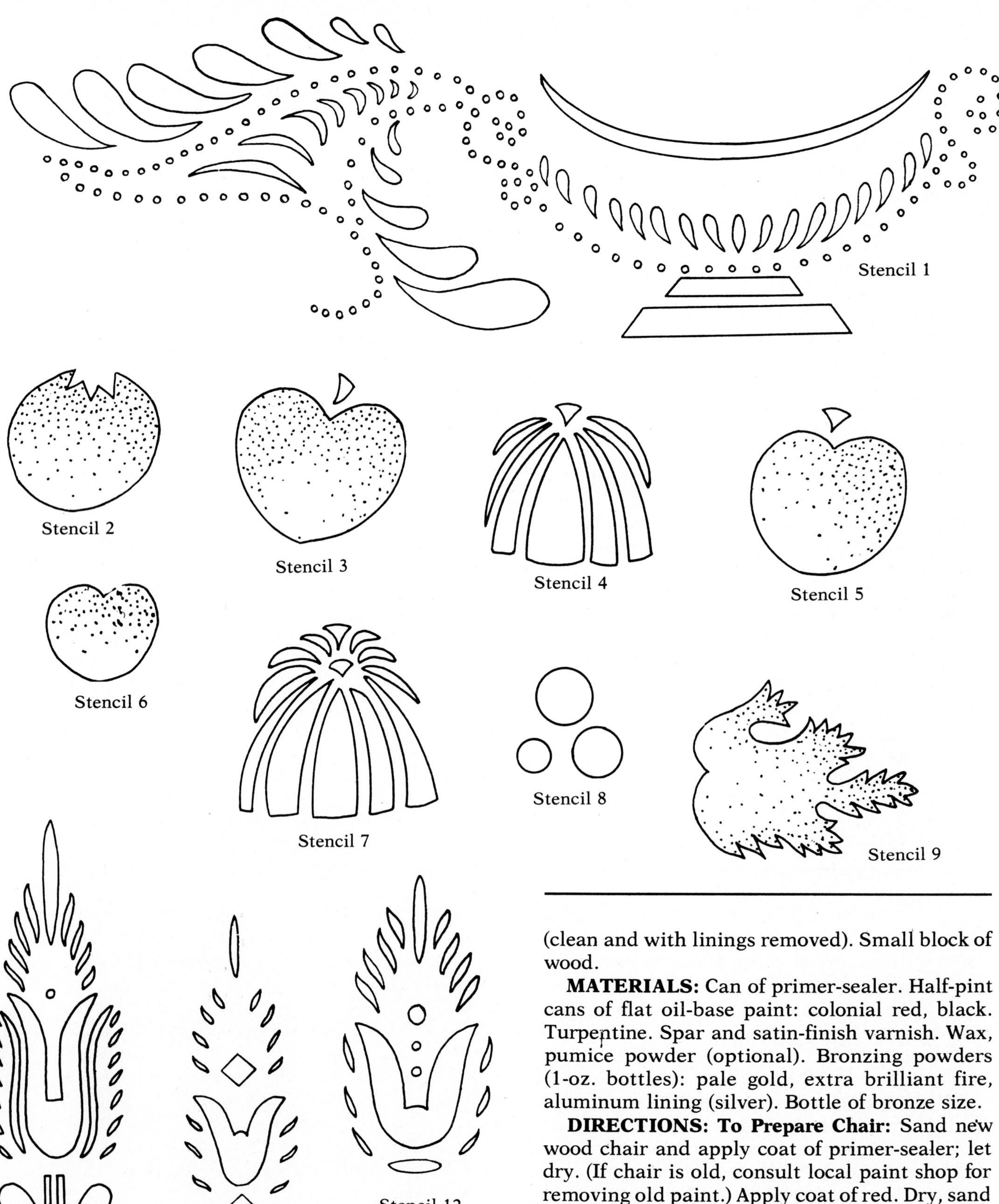

(clean and with linings removed). Small block of wood.

MATERIALS: Can of primer-sealer. Half-pint cans of flat oil-base paint: colonial red, black. Turpentine. Spar and satin-finish varnish. Wax, pumice powder (optional). Bronzing powders (1-oz. bottles): pale gold, extra brilliant fire, aluminum lining (silver). Bottle of bronze size.

DIRECTIONS: To Prepare Chair: Sand new wood chair and apply coat of primer-sealer; let dry. (If chair is old, consult local paint shop for removing old paint.) Apply coat of red. Dry, sand smooth; apply second coat; dry and sand lightly.

To Make Stencils: Trace actual-size stencil patterns; complete half-patterns indicated by dash lines. Dotted areas denote shading. Using pen and ink, trace units of separate designs on linen, placing shiny side of linen down over stencil units. Allow 2″ of linen around each unit. Keep even, clean edges when cutting stencils. Always cut small inside details first, large areas last. In cutting small circles, barely insert point of scissors in center; turn stencil as you make tiny snips. Smooth edge on shiny side of stencil with 6/0 sandpaper. Place stencils in waxed paper envelopes, marking each with design and unit number.

Clean stencils with cleaning fluid and lint-free cloth immediately after use.

To Prepare for Bronzing: For bronze palette, hem 8″ x 12″ piece of velour. Place small amounts of bronze powders 3″ apart in center. Fold lengthwise, roll up and fasten with rubber band, leaving powders ready for use when palette is opened.

For applying bronzes, make pounce for index finger by hemming two opposite sides of 3″ velveteen square, then whipping together other two sides. Make one for each color; keep under rubber band of palette.

Cover work table with newspapers. Place chair, back down, on table. Lay out working materials and stencils. Make sure work area is free of dust or anything that will stick to varnish. Paint flat black on areas to be stenciled. Apply two coats, letting dry after each coat. Apply spar varnish to black areas. When varnish is tacky (at point when a slight click is heard as finger is withdrawn from varnish; coating is still dull and no varnish sticks to finger) immediately stencil chair.

Bronzing: Hold stencil unit down firmly with one hand on tacky varnish; leave other hand free for work. Always apply shiny side of stencil to varnish area except when reversing stencil. Before bronzing, run finger over all edges of stencil to fasten them to the varnish to prevent bronzes from slipping under unit. Apply bronze with pounce wrapped tightly over index finger. Touch pounce to powder, then pat it out on clean area of palette, thus distributing deposit of powder on pounce and removing surplus. Only a little should remain on pounce.

Apply powder with circular rubbing motion through open sections. Work from stencil edges unless otherwise directed. Gradually work away from heavily bronzed parts, shading to no deposit at all. This requires patience for smooth work. The secret of even, smooth shading is a light, even distribution of powder on the pounce and many applications.

Before picking up stencil from work, rub pounce over stencil, picking up loose particles as you progress. Complete bronzing at one time, if possible.

Make any necessary corrections, such as fuzzy edges on stenciling, misplaced bronze, etc. Clean edges are needed for good effects. Use fine brush and some flat black paint to correct outlines freehand.

To Decorate Chair: Varnish center back slat. When tacky, apply center slat stencils 1-9 as follows. Make tiny dot with white pencil at center top and bottom of slat (under edge) where it is not varnished. Dot is guide for center bowl stencil and is removed after stenciling is dry. Center dot should be placed on bowl stencil also. When stenciling, sections of a group that appear to be on top are stenciled first. Unless specially indicated, other motifs shade in behind the top one. Although stencil is cut for entire unit, bronze is usually applied at top only. Place stencil 1 (bowl) on slat, matching center dots. Press down edges of stencil into varnish. Holding pounce lightly, pass touch of silver bronze powder over bowl in circular motion; do top rim and bottom of bowl, side handle dots, and loops and dots of cornucopia for left of bowl. Repeat loops and dots of cornucopia for right side of bowl. Next, rub over cornucopia centers and lower part of bowl with pale gold and a little fire mixed to make pink. Remove stencil; clean. Smudge in pink between top rim and bottom of bowl (smudging is freehand shading without stencil; wipe bronze lightly with pounce across area, blending into varnish like a brush stroke).

Center stencil 2 (fruit) on rim of bowl. With fire, bronze upper left side, touch right side, then blend with tiny touch of silver at lower right edge; shade off before reaching bowl rim. Note that lower half of fruit disappears into bowl; do not touch rim. Place stencil 3 (fruit) behind stencil 2; rub edges with a touch of silver toward center. For pink, touch with fire at center and top. Place stencil 4 at left of stencil 2; rub in silver and add pink to edges. Place stencil 5 at right of stencil 2; rub center and top in silver; blend into shadow behind other fruit. Place stencil 6 above stencil 5 and rub in silver and pink, blend into black, not touching top of other fruit. Repeat this stencil above in silver. Again repeat stencil 6 on left side of bowl, above 4, rubbing in silver and pink and silver for last piece of fruit. Use stencil 7 for melon in cornucopia; rub in silver; touch a little pink on sides. Repeat stencil 7 for other melon in the cornucopia on the other side. At outside of melon, use stencil 6: rub in silver and pink. Place stencil 8 (grapes) at outside edge of cornucopia: use large size for top grape in silver, rub silver and pink alternately on small grapes. Place stencil 9 (leaves) around fruit in bowl and cornucopia; rub faint pink and pale gold over top edges. Dry.

Varnish top of chair, small center slat, top sides. When tacky, use stencil 10 for center top and stencil 11 for center slat and top sides, using touch of pale gold with silver. Dry.

Varnish black areas on front of seat. When tacky, place stencil 11 at center front of chair; rub in gold and silver. Clean and reverse stencil to complete motif. Use stencil 12 for sides and front. Rub in silver and gold. Dry.

To Stripe Chair: Mix pale gold bronze powder in bottle cap with half varnish, half bronze size; add a little silver and mix to creamy consistency. Mark stripe lines with white pencil (see illustration). Fill striping brush with paint; make one or two brush strokes on waxed paper to assure an even flow of paint. Lay brush lightly on beginning of line to be striped, and pull along, guiding hand with little finger placed against edge of side of chair. Lines must stay same width. Rings on legs and rungs of chair are to be painted with same mixture, to which more gold is added for a slightly deeper tone. Use fine sable brush for this freehand painting, being careful to follow turning of rings. For black striping, mix equal parts of varnish and flat black paint at bottom of can after top of paint has been poured off.

To Finish Chair: Apply coat of varnish over entire chair after work has dried. For antique finish, add small amount of raw umber to varnish. Two or three more coats may be applied. Sand off blemishes after second coat of varnish with steel wool. Apply satin-finish varnish for a fourth coat or hand finish after third coat of varnish by rubbing with wax and pumice powder, using small block of wood. Wax gives a final soft patina. Do not rub stenciled areas.

Lone Star Floor

This is a stencil adaptation of a familiar quilt pattern. The design is stenciled with sponges and a stippling technique; the fast-drying acrylics wear well under a coat of varnish.

MOTIF SIZE: Approximately 6′10″ diameter.

EQUIPMENT: 45° metal or plastic triangle. Soft pencil to contrast to floor color. Long straight ruler. Masking tape. Mat knife. For stippling: Synthetic sponges with large holes, 3 pieces 2½″ x 2½″; three saucers. Brush to paint floor (optional). Cleaning fluid. Mixing sticks. Brush for varnish. Soft cloth.

MATERIALS: Oil-base enamel paint to cover entire floor area; we used navy blue. Design may be stippled on painted or stained wooden floor. For stippling: Small amounts of acrylic paints: red (R), gold (G), white (W). Clear varnish.

DIRECTIONS: Paint or clean entire floor thoroughly before planning motif area. Determine area for star motif, with a diameter of approximately 7 ft. Find exact center of area and, with triangle, rule off an exact right angle, as indicated by heavy lines in Diag. 1. Using angle lines, divide area into quarters, extending all lines from center about 3½ ft., as indicated by dotted lines in Diag. 1. Then use angle to divide area into eighths, extending lines in same manner (short dash lines, Diag. 1).

To draw diamonds, make four marks 6″ apart along lines of right angles and along lines dividing quarters of area into eighths. First mark will be 6″ from center. Begin ruling diamonds in upper left quarter of star (see Diag. 2); position 45° angle at marks on lines and rule diamonds as shown in Diag. 2. Each of four sides of each diamond is 6″. Continue lines with long ruler to complete star points. Mark diamonds in same manner in each quarter of star.

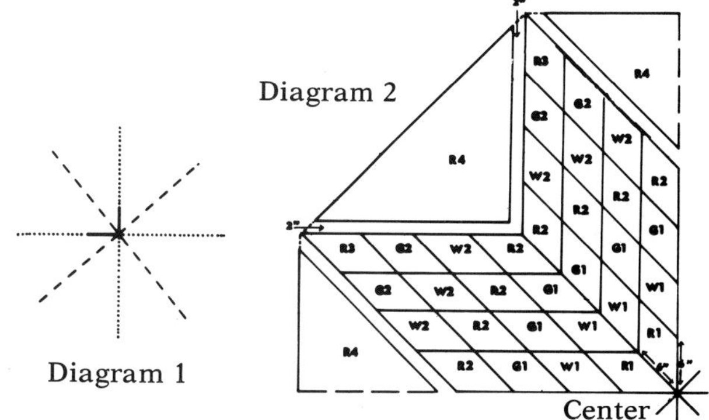

When star is completely drawn, rule large outer triangles 2″ from star (see Diag. 2 and illustration). To complete outer line of triangles, rule a line from star point to point, beginning and ending 2″ from star.

To Stipple: For each color used, mix paint well and pour small amount in saucer. Dampen sponge with water. Dab sponge in paint in saucer, but do not saturate sponge with paint. Lightly dab area so floor color is still visible. Stipple.

To Stencil: Referring to diagram and illustration, begin by masking off every other round of diamonds, starting at center—e.g., all diamonds marked R1, G1, W2 and R3 in Diag. 2. Carefully place tape around each diamond outside of marked lines; do not mask between adjacent diamonds of same letter and number. With mat knife, carefully trim any ends of tape from edges of areas to be painted. Stipple each diamond with color indicated by letter; let dry thoroughly, referring to drying time on paint container. Remove tape and mask off diamonds W1, R2, G2, and R4 triangles. Stipple in same way. Let entire motif dry thoroughly. Varnish.

Knots-and-Tassels Floorcloth

The design for this floorcloth is stenciled on canvas—a technique first developed in eighteenth-century America to take the place of Oriental rugs. The acrylics are applied with a stencil brush and wear well under a final clear acrylic coating.

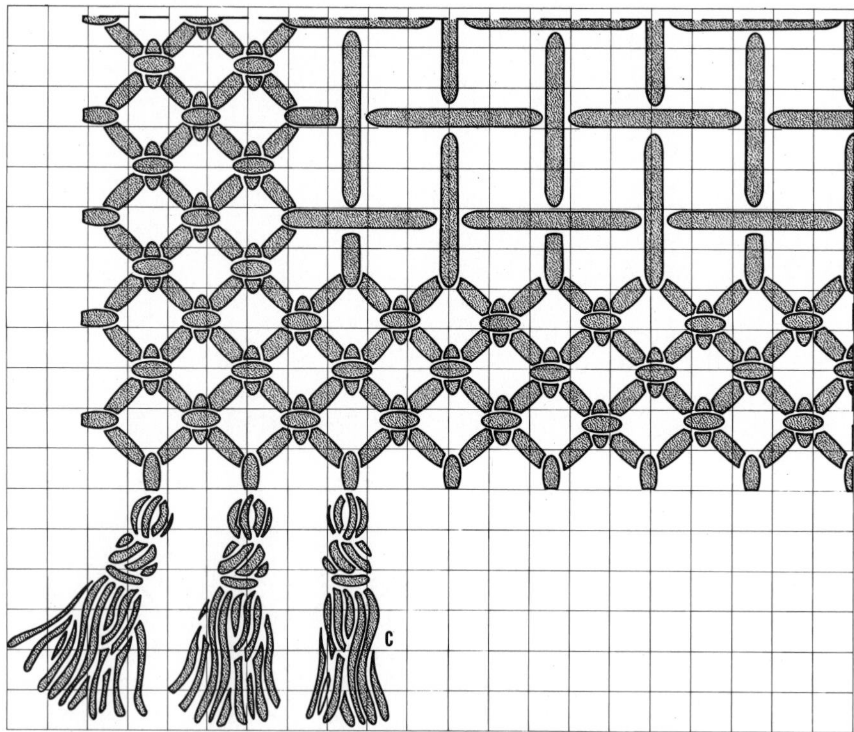

SIZE: 37″ x 52″.

EQUIPMENT: Paper for pattern. Pencil. Ruler. Tracing paper. Stencil paper (or sheet of tracing cloth, which is more durable than paper) at least 18″ x 21″. Rubber cement. Masking tape. Scissors. Glass or other hard surface for cutting stencil. Mat knife with #11 blade. Cardboard or stencil paper scraps for palette. Stencil brushes. Soft rag. Newspapers. Sewing machine.

MATERIALS: Heavy cotton canvas or duck, 44″/45″ wide, 1½ yards beige. Acrylic tube paints: titanium white; yellow medium, azo; burnt sienna. Beige heavy-duty sewing thread. Iron-on rug binding, 5 yards. Crystal clear acrylic spray-on coating.

DIRECTIONS: To Make Pattern: Enlarge pattern by copying on paper ruled in 1″ squares. Trace pattern; do not complete quarter-pattern.

To Cut Stencil: Cement tracing at corners and edges onto stencil paper. Place stencil paper on glass surface. With knife, cut out design areas indicated by shading on pattern. Hold knife at slight angle, pointing toward cut-out area to make slightly beveled edge. Cut all the way through in one stroke so edges will be clean. Turn stencil paper so that you always cut toward you. When design is completely cut out, remove tracing. Cut a second stencil of tassel marked C, which will be repeated several times.

To Prepare Paints: Use acrylic paints full strength. Mix small amounts of burnt sienna with yellow until you obtain the gold color illustrated or desired.

To Paint Design: Cut canvas fabric 40″ x 54″. Tape fabric to flat working surface covered with newspapers; make sure fabric is taut. Lightly mark lengthwise and crosswise center of fabric. Tape stencil to fabric, matching dash lines on pattern to center lines on fabric. Since paints are very concentrated, use only a small amount on brush at a time. Dip brush into paint and rub off on paper until almost dry. Hold brush upright and work paint into fabric with a dabbing or stippling motion. Go over area with additional coats of paint if area is not dark enough. When working on one area of stencil, protect areas of fabric you are not stenciling at the moment by covering with pieces of scrap paper. Acrylic paint dries very quickly and makes stenciling fairly easy.

Following illustration, paint center area gold; paint border area white and gold; paint tassels white with bands of gold. After you have worked one-quarter of the design as given, remove stencil and wipe clean with wet rag; dry. Reverse stencil and paint second quarter of design. Repeat for third and fourth quarters. To complete tassel border, use tassel marked C, wiping and reversing stencil for every other tassel. When finished stenciling, wash brush in water, and wipe stencils clean with wet rag.

To Finish Rug: Fold corners diagonally about 2″ to wrong side, then fold all edges to wrong side about 1½″. Stitch all around by machine ¼″ from fold. Iron strips of rug binding over raw edges along each side on back.

Place rug out flat. Spray entire top surface of rug with acrylic coating; let dry. Spray two more times, allowing spray to dry thoroughly between coats.

Bouquet on Velvet

This bouquet and vase, on a background of tiny diamond shapes, are painted on velveteen using a stencil and acrylic colors. The picture measures 14" x 18".

EQUIPMENT: Paper for pattern. Tracing paper. Ruler. Pencil. Rubber cement. Stencil paper. Glass or other hard surface for cutting stencil. Mat knife with #11 blade. Masking tape. Stencil brushes. Soft rags. Newspapers.

MATERIALS: Light brown (or desired color) cotton velveteen, 36" wide, ½ yard. Acrylic tube paints, in colors shown or as desired. All-purpose glue. Cardboard, 18" x 14".

DIRECTIONS: To Make Pattern: Enlarge pattern for stencil design by copying on paper ruled in 1" squares. Trace design. Cement tracing at corners and edges onto stencil paper 18" x 14".

To Cut Stencil: Place stencil paper on glass surface. With knife, cut out design areas indicated by shading on pattern. Hold knife at slight angle, pointing toward cut-out area to make slightly beveled edge. Cut all the way through in one stroke so edge will be clean. Turn paper so that you always cut toward you. When design is completely cut out, remove pattern.

To Prepare Paints: Use acrylic paints full strength. Use small amounts of paints when experimenting in mixing colors. Use scraps of stencil paper for palette.

To Paint Design: Tape fabric to flat working surface covered with newspapers; make sure fabric is taut. Center and tape stencil to fabric. Since paints are very concentrated, use only a small amount on brush at a time. Dip brush into paint and rub off on piece of paper until almost dry. Hold brush upright and work paint into fabric with a dabbing or stippling motion. For larger areas, begin at edge and work toward center of design. To darken or shade a section, go over area with additional coats of paint. When coloring one

area of stencil, protect areas of design you are not stenciling at the moment by covering with pieces of stencil paper. Paint as desired or follow illustration.

When all areas are stenciled, remove stencil carefully and let paint dry thoroughly.

To Clean Brushes and Stencil: Wash brushes in water. Gently wipe stencil with a wet rag.

To Mount: Center velveteen on one surface of cardboard; turn over and tape 2″ margins to back of cardboard making sure fabric is taut. Frame as desired.

Tinsel Flowers

These brilliant flowers, painted in translucent tones on glass, are backed with crumpled foil for a silvery glow—the Victorians used tea paper; we use aluminum.

UNFRAMED SIZES: Small: 6½″ x 8¼″. Large: 14½″ x 13½″.

EQUIPMENT: Paper for pattern. Pencil. Ruler. Tracing paper. Masking tape. Pen with fine point. Fine-pointed paintbrushes. Rags. Scissors.

MATERIALS: Clear window glass: 6½″ x 8¼″ for small picture; 14½″ x 13½″ for large picture. Black India ink. Artists' oil paints: Mars black, cerulean blue, yellow ochre, chrome yellow, lemon yellow, emerald green, alizarin crimson, titanium white. Artists' turpentine. Aluminum foil.

For Framing: Wooden frames, 1″ and ¾″ wide to fit glass. Stiff cardboard, same size as glass. Small nails.

DIRECTIONS: To Transfer Design to Glass: Pattern for small picture is given actual size. Enlarge other pattern by copying on paper ruled in 1″ squares. Trace designs. Clean glass thoroughly; dry. Center and tape traced pattern, wrong side up, on glass. Turn glass over. Mark over all lines of design on top of glass with pen and ink. Remove pattern; let glass dry.

To Paint: Paint glass on the same surface as inking. Paint the background first, following directions below, all around design and in unmarked areas between flowers and leaves. Be careful to keep paint from spreading over the design lines. Mistakes may be carefully wiped off with clean rags and turpentine. By painting the background first, you will not have to be as careful in painting the design areas, since small mistakes will not show through the opaque background.

For the first coat of background, thin the paint slightly with turpentine so it spreads easily and smoothly. To avoid dividing lines, brush in two directions to blend on large areas. Let dry at least one day. Make second coat quite thick for opaque quality. Let dry at least 3 days.

To paint flowers, leaves, stems, and basket, thin all oil paints with turpentine to a thin wash Aluminum foil will show through these areas.

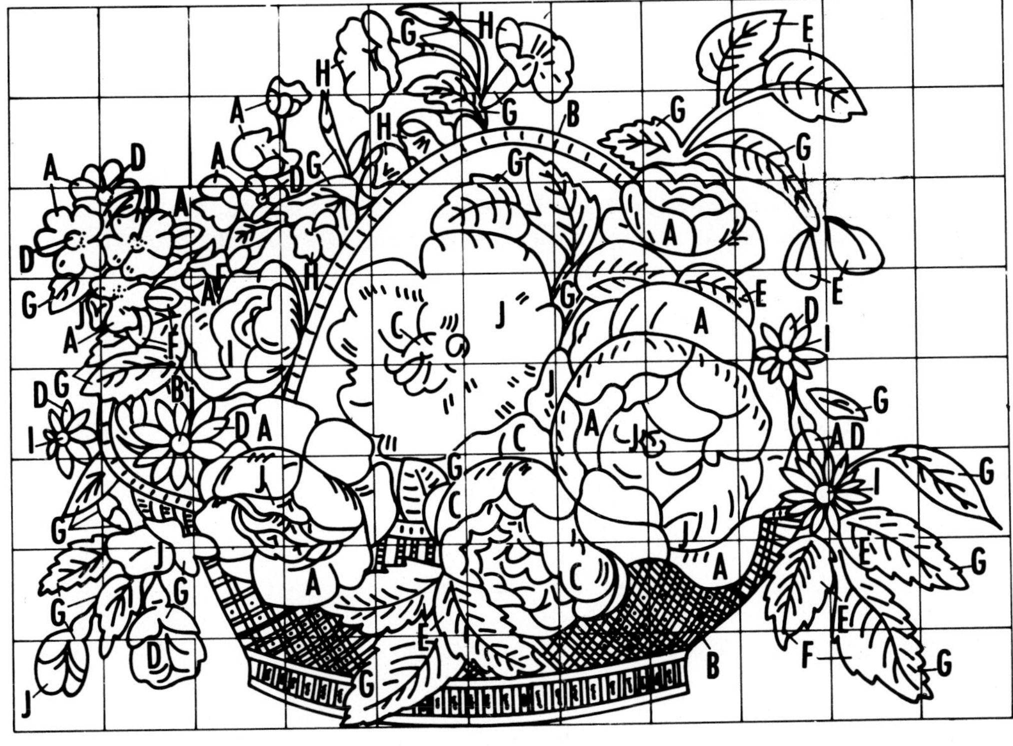

Paint both backgrounds Mars black.

A—White (Titanium)
B—Yellow Ochre
C—Yellow Ochre + Lemon Yellow + White
D—Lemon Yellow + Chrome Yellow + White
E—Emerald Green
F—Emerald Green + White
G—Lemon Yellow + Emerald Green
H—Cerulean Blue
I—Alizarin Crimson
J—Alizarin Crimson + White

Following letters on pattern, mix one or two colors, as indicated on color key, with turpentine, making paint very thin. Paint flowers with one thin coat. Let dry. To obtain shading, use two or more coats as necessary to get the depth of color desired, without losing transparency (see illustration for shading). To keep from smudging paint, you may find it a help to place the frame over the glass to use as a hand rest. Let set for about two days until thoroughly dry.

To Tinsel: The painted side is back of picture. Try to use aluminum foil in one piece to cover a whole area. Gently crush foil, then straighten it out, leaving the creases. Tape foil to glass under flower and leaf areas. The crushed foil will show through these areas and reflect light.

To Frame: Place painted glass in frame with cardboard in back. Fasten in frame with small nails hammered into inside edges of frame.

A—Emerald Green + White
B—Lemon Yellow + Emerald Green
C—Yellow Ochre + Emerald Green + White
D—Alizarin Crimson
E—Alizarin Crimson + White
F—White
G—Burnt Sienna

GENERAL DIRECTIONS FOR GOLD LEAFING

It is important that all surfaces be thoroughly prepared before decoration is applied. Directions given below are for natural wood or metal in good condition.

Preparing Metal Surfaces for Undercoat: Even new metal surfaces rust quickly and should be painted immediately after all rust has been removed with fine steel wool. For extra-fine work, it is advisable to go over the metal with a rust-inhibiting solution; but for ordinary work, paint with a metal sanding primer. (Ask your dealer for advice regarding the products he or she carries.) Use a fine, soft chiseled brush for painting groundcoats on metal, such as an ox-hair "signwriter's" brush. Allow to dry thoroughly and sand. To avoid breaking through, be careful not to rub too vigorously, especially over irregular surfaces of metal.

Preparing Wood Surfaces for Undercoat: Sand the surface thoroughly with 00 sandpaper, 4/0 silicon carbide or fine garnet finishing paper. Dust well with old lintless cloth. Cover all surfaces with shellac (be sure shellac is fresh, otherwise it is likely to be gummy). Use a mixture of three parts shellac to one part alcohol. Apply with a clean, dry brush. When shellac is thoroughly dry (about an hour later) sand again, using sandpaper and 000 steel wool. Wipe clean. Coat again with shellac as described above. When dry, finish with 000 steel wool.

Undercoat and Groundcoat: Two or more coats of paint are applied to article before it is ready for decorating. The first coats are called the undercoats, and the final coat is called the groundcoat.

The undercoats are used for body-building and perfecting after the surface is primed. Undercoats are the same color as the groundcoat.

To Transfer Designs: Trace design. Using dressmaker's carbon and dry ball-point pen, transfer design onto prepared surface; hold pattern in place with masking tape. Then, transfer same design, reversing side, onto the white backing of the gold leaf. Cut out pieces of design, using embroidery scissors.

To Adhere Gold to Article: Make sure your surface is clean and well prepared before starting. Woods such as balsam or poplar should be shellacked, as they are porous and absorb the moisture from the glue on back of gold.

Use shallow pan with few inches of water at room temperature. Soak each piece of the cut-out gold design in the water for 30 seconds. Carefully *slide* (do not peel) the gold film from the white backing. (There is a special adherent left on gold film when you slide it off the white backing.) Immediately place gold film where indicated on design. The gold film can be moved slightly in order to get it in correct position but must be handled gently. Smooth with your fingers and blot with cleansing tissue; press any "bubbles" out. If you do get a "bubble" that will not come out, puncture it with a sharp pin. If you should tear a piece of your design, it can be easily pushed into place. Should you find some pieces not sticking well, add a good vegetable glue. Always use the same gold sheet for a single project; cut so that pieces fit one against the other, following the grain of the gold. Allow to dry for 24 hours.

To avoid confusion in placing the various pieces of the design, adhere each piece to the article being decorated before cutting out another.

Gold-Leafed Dragon Box and Bird Tray

The handsome Chinese Dragon Box and Bird Tray are reminiscent of the treasures brought home on the old clipper ships. The designs, applied in pure gold, are high-style objects of real beauty and lasting value.

DRAGON BOX

EQUIPMENT: 00 sandpaper, 4/0 silicon carbide, or fine garnet finishing paper. Lintless cloth. Flat brush, 1½" wide. Saucer for palette Palette knife. Tracing paper. Pencil. Dressmaker's (carbon) tracing paper. Dry ball-point pen. Masking tape. Shallow pan. Embroidery or nail scissors.

MATERIALS: Unfinished wooden box about 5½" x 10½" x 3½". One sheet of gold leaf. White shellac. Denatured alcohol. Tempera paint: one tube each red, white, and chrome yellow. Japan drier. Spar varnish.

DIRECTIONS: Read General Directions on page 362. Prepare box for undercoat as directed. To mix paint, squeeze about 2" of red, 1" of white, and 1" of yellow into a saucer. Add two drops of Japan drier and three drops spar varnish. Mix well with palette knife. Apply to shellacked box with clean brush, using long, smooth strokes. Dry at least four hours. Apply second coat. Dry.

Trace actual-size patterns for side, front, and top of box. Using dressmaker's carbon and dry ball-point pen, transfer designs to painted box, being careful to draw lines just inside edges of design.

Transfer patterns to backing of gold leaf in numerical order and cut out, following directions. Adhere gold pieces to box. After 24 hours, add a coat of spar varnish. Let dry thoroughly.

BIRD TRAY

EQUIPMENT: Orange stick. Soft camel's hair or sable brush, No. 3. Dressmaker's carbon (tracing) paper. Dry ball-point pen. Pencil. Tracing paper. Masking tape. Embroidery scissors. (If using unfinished tray: Fine steel wool. Sandpaper.)

MATERIALS: Round metal tray, 19" in diameter, black or unfinished. Two sheets gold leaf. One tube red tempera. Spar varnish. (If using unfinished tray: Black flat paint. Turpentine. Metal sanding primer or rust-inhibiting solution.)

DIRECTIONS: Read General Directions on page 362. If using an unpainted tray, prepare tray and paint black as directed.

Trace actual-size patterns for center and border motifs. Using dressmaker's carbon and dry ball-point pen, transfer center motif to black tray, being careful to draw lines just inside edge of design; transfer only solid outlines and key numbers. Transfer center motif to backing of gold leaf, transferring solid lines and key numbers only. Cut out pieces and adhere to tray in numerical order. When center motif is in place on tray, apply border motif in same manner. Dry 24 hours.

Place tracing of center motif over gold leafing on tray. With hard pencil or dry ball-point pen, go over all dash lines. Remove tracing. If necessary, deepen lines made with an orange stick. With No. 3 soft brush dipped in India ink, go over etched lines. With same brush, make stippled areas as shown on pattern. Always direct brush strokes to follow the growth and direction of feathers and contours of the body. Do not paint these areas solid. Where the ink seems to draw away from the gold, let it. Paint solid black areas of pattern red. Let dry 24 hours. Varnish with spar varnish. Dry thoroughly.

Center Motif for Tray

Design for
Side of Box

Border Motif for Tray

Design for Top of Box

Design for Front of Box

13

Nature Crafts

Seaside Bouquets

Fabulous flowers are yours to create with shells collected on your summer vacation. Just choose shell "petals" of uniform size and color, then build your flowers in a glue-soaked cotton pad. The stems are florist's wire. Select your shells with care; the right color and the right shape are all-important–the arrangement is up to you.

EQUIPMENT: For work sheet, plastic sheet, large plastic lid, or coated paper plate. Needle-nosed pliers. Small wire cutters. Knife. Manicure scissors. Drill with small bit. Towels.

MATERIALS: Shells: All types of bivalves for flower petals including cup shells, pearly clams, small cockleshells, small yellow and purple clamshells, blue mussels, coquinas (butterfly shells); slipper shells, fluted conches, large and small whelks, keyhole limpets, barnacles, snails, etc. Large fish scales for leaves. Green vegetable dye. For flower centers, black and yellow seeds, peppercorns, cloves. Plastic or cloth-coated florist's wire, size 18, 20, and 21. Green florist's tape. All-purpose glue. Absorbent cotton. Small blocks of styrofoam or florist's clay. Spray lacquer.

DIRECTIONS: All flowers are made of shells. We suggest you study pictures of flowers or actual flowers before starting this project. Decide which flowers you wish to make before selecting shells. For petals, choose shells of uniform size and color or vary shades, using smaller shells of deeper shades in centers of flowers and lighter, larger shells around outer edges.

Clean all shells before using. Wash in warm soapy water using a soft brush or cloth to remove all particles and dirt. Rinse in clear water.

For the best bonding of flowers, use a ball of cotton soaked in glue (except for sprays and clusters). Place cotton ball on work sheet; place the shell petals around with ends imbedded in cotton ball (either hinge edge up or down depending upon flower) one layer at a time. The cotton will eventually dry to a china-like hardness, forming the center core of flower. When dry, lift up flower from plastic work sheet with knife. Trim away any excess glue with scissors.

When flowers are completely dry, add coiled stem. Cut length of heavier gauge wire and bend into coil shape using pliers (Fig. 1). Length of wire depends upon length of stem required for height of planned arrangement. Place some cotton with glue over the face of coil to cover. Place center of flower on top of cotton-covered coil. Insert stem into styrofoam temporarily until ready to assemble arrangement. Use styrofoam blocks or clay to secure arrangement in vase or other container.

Leaves: Use large fish scales. Prepare the green dye and let it cool; immerse scales; when scales begin to turn dark green, remove from dye bath and dry with towel. Place between dry towels and weight down to flatten. Before using, spray with lacquer or other fixative to seal in the dye. With pliers, bend a wire (Fig. 2); glue on scale leaves (Fig. 3).

Roses and Other Double Flowers: Set the glue-soaked cotton down and arrange three shell petals (hinges up for roses) in the center (Detail 1). Then place one or two rows of shells around them, slanting each row out a little more to open flower (Detail 2). You can make this closed petal center or, for other flowers, make it slightly open and glue a cluster of seeds or tiny shells for center. Glue to coiled stem.

Daisies, Dogwood and Other Single Flowers: Make a single row as for roses, slanting the petals outward (hinges out), almost flat. Add center of one small snail shell or black seeds.

Small Flowers for Sprays and Clusters: Instead of using cotton ball, squeeze a ¼″ to ½″ globule of glue on work sheet. Place four or five small shells in it, overlapping them slightly as you go around. Drop several seeds in the glue at center. When glue is dry, lift up the flower and use as follows: For cluster, use seven or eight 5″ lengths of thinner gauge wire. With pliers, twist a small coil in end of each. Glue a small flower on each coil, then gather the flowers into a cluster and wrap the stems together with florist's tape. Secure to a longer, heavier gauge wire as you wrap.

For sprays, bend loops along a 21-gauge wire stem and glue small finished flowers on the loops. Use at least seven flowers for each spray. See Detail 3.

Water Lily: Use large heavy shells. Drill two holes in one side of each shell. Insert a length of 21-gauge wire through each hole to midpoint of wire; bend the wire ends together. Make five of these petals separately and cup them together around a center made of a conch, whelk, or other bud-shaped shell which has been drilled and secured to a wire. Then add another row of large

wired petals; bunch all the wires and wrap together with tape.

For leaves and lily pads, use green-dyed (see "Leaves") scallop shells; drill holes, and wire as for above. Bring wires of these and two wired buds all together with those of the large petals; wrap with tape.

Flower Spikes: Use coquina (butterfly) shells. First bend a long loop at one end of wire stem, using 18-gauge wire and form a spike of glue-soaked cotton over it. Start at top and begin lapping the little coquina shells around in layers (see Detail 4). Finish the flower end by wrapping green tape around it.

Buds: Use single conches, whelks or other bud-like shells (or three closely cupped shells). For the univalve shell, sand or grind a hole at the closed end of shell and secure a wire stem in hole with a bit of cotton soaked in glue. Finish the lower part by wrapping green tape around it, continuing down the stem.

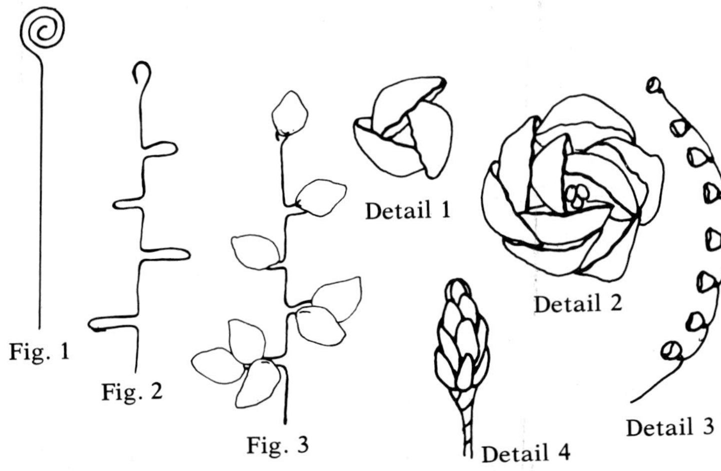

Seashell Frame

Frame a reflection in a treasury from Neptune's garden. The mirror center is framed, then "matted" with a rich incrustation of shells. Finish with your choice of a frame.

EQUIPMENT: Ruler. Mat knife or single-edged razor blade. Metal straight edge.

MATERIALS: Outer frame (ours is 15" x 16½" with rabbet size 13" x 14½"). Inner framed mirror (ours is 6" x 8" with rabbet size 5" x 7"). Heavy cardboard or mounting board. Masking tape. An abundant variety of seashells and coral (see illustration). White glue.

DIRECTIONS: Measure and then cut out, with knife and metal straight edge, a piece of cardboard to fit in outer frame. In same manner, cut out center for opening the exact size of inner frame. Place mirror frame in opening in cardboard and tape securely in place with masking tape on back. Secure cardboard in outer frame.

Arrange shells between inner and outer frame, overlapping each other as illustrated. Arrange small shells over inner frame to cover. When pleased with arrangement, glue each shell carefully and securely in place, one layer at a time.

Shell Flower Plaque

A delicate bouquet of exotic flowers, some real. some imaginary, is mounted on burlap-covered cardboard. Many small shells make a hyacinth and a mum; only a few make a lily of the valley and other simple flowers; pipe cleaners of florist's wire become the flower stems.

EQUIPMENT: Hand drill. Pliers. Wire cutters. Scissors. Ruler. Compass.

MATERIALS: Shells in various sizes and shapes. Heavy and fine florist's wire (covered with green tape) for stems. Plain fine wire. White cotton piping with cord removed. Green pipe cleaners or chenille stems for hyacinths. Thin white cardboard for mum and round petal flowers. Small amount absorbent cotton. Straight pins. Stiff, heavy cardboard 11½" x 16½". Green burlap 15" x 20". White felt 1½" x 18". All-purpose glue.

DIRECTIONS: Use heavy wire for all stems except lilies of the valley. Assemble flowers as directed below, then coat stem thinly with glue and insert into piping.

For hyacinth, use about 90 conical shells all approximately the same size. Cut a 1" length of pipe cleaner or chenille stem for each shell; glue end into each shell cavity; let glue dry. With plain fine wire bind pipe cleaner ends together to length of heavy wire, covering top section of stem with mass of shells.

For mum, use pointed, elongated shells in three sizes. Cut 3"-diameter circle of cardboard and of felt. Glue felt to cardboard. Make two holes in center of circle about ¼" apart. Glue largest shells with points outward around outer edge. Continue gluing shells in circles to fill area, but leave holes uncovered. When dry, thread one end of heavy wire through center holes (in one and out the other), extending other end for stem; with pliers, twist end behind flower. Glue small white snail-like shell to center of flower covering holes and wire. Crush small shells; spread glue on back of cardboard disk and sprinkle with crushed shells.

For lily of the valley, use tiny white snail-like shells with small points. Glue small wads of cotton into shell openings. Dip fine florist's wire 6½" long in glue and insert into cotton. When dry, group several together and twist one wire around other wires to hold all in place.

For round petal flowers, use bivalve shells in varied sizes and conical shells. Cut circles of cardboard and felt slightly smaller than group of selected shells. Glue felt to cardboard. Make two holes in center of circle about ¼" apart. Glue shells to felt side in a variety of ways: Some of the large shells can be placed face down, with areas between shells and center filled with smaller, conical shells; large shells can be placed face up, overlapped around edges, with tiny bivalve shells overlapping and filling in center area. Before centers are filled, thread end of heavy wire through center holes (in one and out the other), extending other end for stem. With pliers, twist wire end in place behind flower. Crush some small shells; brush glue on back of disk and sprinkle with crushed shells.

For simple flower, use two bivalve shells, one larger than the other, and one dark snail-like shell. Drill two holes in base of larger shell. Thread one end of length of heavy wire through holes (in one and out the other), twist together with pliers at back of shell to hold in place. Glue smaller shell inside larger. Glue snail-like shell in place for flower center.

For background, cover one side of large cardboard with burlap; bring edges to back, making sure front is smooth; glue edges to back securely. Carefully pin and glue flowers in arrangement on burlap-covered cardboard. Tie strip of white felt into neat bow; trim ends as shown. Pin and glue bow over stems.

GENERAL DIRECTIONS FOR DRIED FLOWERS

Pick materials in perfect condition; a small hole in petal will be a large hole when dried. Pick flowers on a dry day at peak of bloom; if too mature they will shatter or lose their color in drying. Be sure there is no moisture in the flower heads; if there should be any, allow stems to stand in 2" or 3" of warm water until flower heads are completely free of moisture. Cut off or wipe wet part of stems before processing. Strip all leaves from flower stems. Be sure there is no insect in the flower heads. Handle all plant material carefully.

To press, cover a page in a large magazine or telephone directory with paper towel: lay out the flowers, leaves, and petals, being sure they do not touch. Cover completely with paper towel. This procedure may be repeated every few pages until all materials are between pages. Weight down with several large books and place in a dark, dry area. The dryness is essential, since materials will mildew if they are left in an area that is even slightly damp.

Leave materials undisturbed until thoroughly dry; the time varies with materials, but generally two to three weeks are enough.

If you wish to develop special lines or curves, gently shape them by hand before processing.

Flowers shrink in drying, and you need a good selection when making arrangements, so dry at least twice as many as you think you may need.

NOTE: When picking wildflowers, be sure of what you are handling. The results of carrying home the attractive foliage of poison ivy or poison sumac can be disastrous. It is also wise to check your state conservation list of plants that cannot be picked if growing wild.

Dried Flower Meadow Scene

Delicate flowers, ferns and grasses create a meadow scene that brings the charm of nature indoors. The flowers and foliage are pressed to dry, then mounted with tree bark "ground." Collect the materials from outdoors, around your home.

SIZE: 22¾" x 27", framed.

EQUIPMENT: Large quantity of newspapers. Suit boxes or similar objects for light weight. **For Framing:** Backsaw and miter box. Small flat paintbrush. Hammer. Nail set. Clean rags. Straight pins.

MATERIALS: Delicate wild flowers and garden flowers, such as Queen Anne's lace, black-eyed Susans, poppies, bachelor buttons, petunias; wild grasses, ferns and other foliage; small pieces of flat bark. White fabric such as monk's cloth, 24" x 28". Cotton batting, 20" x 24". Plywood, ¼" thick, 20" x 24". Pine stripping, ¼" thick, 1½" wide, 8 feet. Flat picture molding, ¾" thick, 1½" wide, 9 feet. Simulated bamboo molding, ⅝" wide, 9 feet. Wood putty. Flat white paint. Flat cream-color paint. Brown oil stain. Finishing nails. Carpet tacks. All-purpose glue.

DIRECTIONS: Read General Directions on page 371, and dry flowers accordingly.

Making Arrangement: Place one layer of cotton batting over plywood background; tack in place. Stretch monk's cloth over padding, using pins to hold fabric on edges while stretching and straightening; be sure threads of fabric are straight. Turn excess fabric to back of board, glue; hold with pins until dry.

Arrange dried flowers, stems, and foliage on fabric background, keeping it light and airy. Use small ferns at bottom of arrangement. Adhere flowers, stems, and foliage to fabric with little dabs of glue. Glue small pieces of bark over ends of stems and ferns at bottom.

Framing: Cut pine stripping to fit around plywood picture with butt joints. Paint strips white on all sides. When dry, nail around picture with one ¼" surface even with back of plywood; stripping extends 1¼" on front for shadow-box effect. Cut picture molding with mitered corners to fit over pine stripping. Glue and nail molding together; let dry. Cut bamboo molding with mitered corners, ¼" shorter than picture molding pieces. Place on top of picture frame, matching miters and glue in place; let dry. Countersink all nails; fill holes with wood putty. Paint frame cream color. When dry, antique by brushing on stain and wiping off excess; let dry. Brush bamboo "joints" lightly with white paint. Dry. Glue frame on shadow box.

All-Year Bouquets

Capture the delights of spring with lovely pressed-flower pictures. The drying process is simple. To begin your arrangement, use whole flowers or create your own with separate petals. Then add a vase or a basket (a photo or a bit of real wicker), glue in place, and frame. The possibilities are limitless—you can even "build" a still life apple or pear!

EQUIPMENT: Large magazines or telephone directory. Heavy books for weighting. Paper toweling. Tweezers. Metal edge and sharp knife. Cotton swab or absorbent cotton and toothpick. Cup for glue mixture.

MATERIALS: Grasses, leaves, and flowers such as phlox, delphiniums, baby's breath, pansies, daisies, geraniums, roses, marigolds, chrysanthemums, coleus, ferns, salvia, spirea, poppies, dogwood, wisteria, Queen Anne's lace. Illustrations of vases and bowls from magazines. Pieces of flat basket materials. **For Background:**

Fabric, gift-wrap paper, or tissue paper. Heavy mounting board or cardboard. Mat board. All-purpose glue. Doublefaced masking tape. Standard-size lucite box frames.

DIRECTIONS: Read General Directions on page 371. Generally, whole, thick flowers do not press well and are not suitable for pictures; however, thick flower petals can be pressed separately and used successfully. For the pictures shown, you will need both whole flowers and petals (see individual directions).

Select desired frame size, then plan your arrangement to fit it. See individual directions for the exact sizes used. Select background color and mat board color. Cut cardboard or mounting board to fit frame. Cut background fabric or paper 1" larger all around than cardboard; center and glue background over one surface of cardboard, turning excess to back. If using mat, cut mat board to fit frame, then cut out center opening, using a metal edge and sharp knife. Put double-faced tape around opening and outer edges on wrong side of mat, then center on background (covered cardboard).

Plan flower design on paper first, then, using tweezers if necessary, arrange pieces on background as desired. If magazine illustration is being used for container, glue it into position first, so that flowers may be "arranged" in bowl. Mix a solution of two-thirds glue and one-third water. Dip cotton swab into glue mixture. Apply small amounts of glue mixture to dried materials to hold them in place, being careful not to spot background. Do not saturate flowers or petals; frame top will hold flowers in place. If straw mat scrap is used for basket, glue in place. Add a few blossoms over straw if desired. Let glue dry thoroughly. Assemble frame.

Following are the sizes and components of the pictures as they are shown on page 373:

Basket of Pansies: 8" x 10". Use whole pansies, leaves on stems, and scrap of straw mat.

Pitcher of Flowers: 12" x 16", mat size. Use rose petals, carnation petals, geraniums, phlox (each floret dried separately), pansies, bachelor's buttons, baby's breath, purple strawflowers, grasses, leaves, and ferns, Use magazine pitcher illustration.

Pear: 5" x 7", mat size (mat is white and very narrow). Use carnation petals for pear, bit of bark for stem. Use decorative paper for background.

Bowl of Flowers: 8" x 10". Use rose petals and ferns. Use magazine illustration of bowl.

Basket of Flowers: 12" x 16", mat size. Use daisies, poppies, bachelor's button petals, rose petals, phlox (each floret dried separately), leaves, ferns and stems. For basket, use scrap of basket material.

Apple: 5" x 7", mat size (mat is white and very narrow). Use rose petals, apple leaf, bit of bark gift paper for background.

Rooster and Hen Plaques

This barnyard family boasts a colorful display of plumage. The hen and rooster have feathers of sunflower seeds, rice, split peas and beans; combs and wattles are red-dyed rice, and feet and legs are corn kernels. The chicks have split-pea "down." Cut the hen and chicks from a 15"-square piece of plywood, the rooster from a 19" square.

EQUIPMENT: Coping saw. Sandpaper. Small paintbrush. A few toothpicks. Carbon Paper. Pencil. Paper for patterns. Bowl. Paper towels. Waxed paper. Slotted spoon.

MATERIALS: Plywood ⅜" thick; 19" square for Rooster; 15" square for Hen and Chicks. One package each of the following, or less as indicated: dried green split peas; dried pink beans (pinkish color); sunflower seeds; white rice; yellow popping corn; half package yellow split peas; a few whole black peppercorns; six black beans. All-purpose glue. Flat white paint. Clear spray lacquer. Red and yellow food coloring. Picture wire and small screw eyes for hanging.

DIRECTIONS: Enlarge patterns by copying on paper ruled in 1" squares. With carbon paper, trace outline of each onto plywood; Hen and four Chicks can be placed on 15" square; reverse chick pattern for remaining three chicks as shown. Cut out each with coping saw. Cut out area between legs, or leave solid and mark inner leg lines. Sand all edges and surfaces smooth. Give pieces two coats of white paint.

Mix a little red food coloring with some water in a bowl. Drop white rice into red dye, small amounts at a time. The rice will quickly reach a bright red shade. Remove from dye with slotted spoon, and spread on paper towels to blot; then place on waxed paper to dry. Color a small amount of rice yellow in same manner, for Hen's beak.

Using carbon paper, transfer all section lines of Rooster, Hen and Chicks onto painted pieces. Following color key and letters on patterns, fill in each section with designated material. To fill sections evenly and neatly, first outline section with one row, then fill in successive rows to center. For small sections, spread glue generously over complete section and press peas, beans, or seeds in

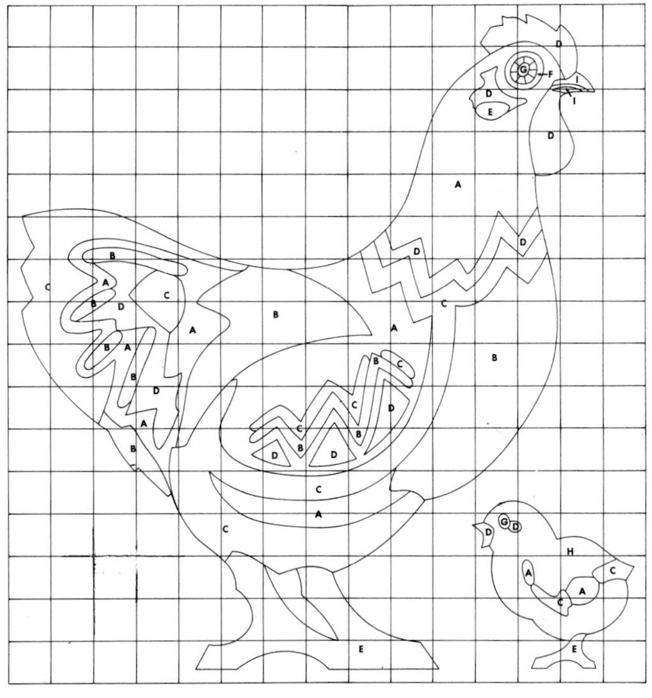

Color Key
A—Green Split Peas
B—Pink Beans
C—Sunflower Seeds
D—Red Rice
E—Corn
F—Whole Pepper
G—Black Bean
H—Yellow Split Peas
I—Yellow Rice

place; for large areas, spread glue on only part of section at a time. In handling rice, use a toothpick with a tiny dab of glue on point to pick up rice kernels; spread glue on area to be filled with rice and set kernels in place end to end. To fill sunflower-seed areas, overlap ends of seeds slightly when setting in place. In filling green split-pea areas, a few yellow peas may be intermixed with the green ones. For Hen and Rooster eye, outline first with whole peppercorns; then glue a red rice kernel on each radiating line; glue black bean in center. For Chick eye, use a black bean and a few kernels of red rice below, as shown in illustration.

When glue is thoroughly dry, give plaques three coats of spray lacquer, letting lacquer dry after each coat.

To hang Hen and Rooster, attach suspending wire or cord across body back with center below back curve. For Chicks, form wire into a loop below point where head and back meet. The seed plaques may be glued and nailed to a painted board in a permanent formation as shown in the illustration, if desired.

14

Basketry

Twined Baskets

Five beautiful baskets are made in a twining technique that involves the weaving of two or more weft pieces around the warp ends. The baskets—in twine, jute, rope and linen—range from the 2"-tall basket with worked-in handles to the 6"-high basket with a fringed and flared "collar."

EQUIPMENT: Scissors. Tapestry needle size 18. Tape measure.

MATERIALS: Cord, rope, twine and waxed linen, available from cordage companies, hardware and marine supply stores. (Refer to individual directions for materials used in specific baskets.)

VOCABULARY: Twining technique in basketry includes the weaving of two or more weft pieces around spokes or warp. Warp ends—spokes; weft—twining weavers.

DIRECTIONS: Read Directions through completely and then refer to individual directions before beginning work. The base on all baskets is made by weaving two sections, which are then joined; this creates a strong, double-layer base.

To make the base: Cut appropriate number of lengths of material for warp ends and one length of weaving material (weaver) for weft. Fold length of weaver in half so that the free ends of weaver are to the left. With warp ends numbered 1 and 2 lying side by side, and beginning in approximately the center of the warp ends, cross weavers by bringing one weaver end from back to front and one end from front to back (see Fig. 1). To the left of the cross of weaver, lay warp ends 3 and 4 parallel to those already held by weavers. Repeat twining cross. Continue working toward left by adding pairs of warp ends and crossing between pairs until there are four pairs (see Fig. 1). While working, hold materials firmly in right hand and use left hand to add warp ends and manipulate weavers. During the first rows of twining, warp ends tend to flop about and will feel awkward, but will be held more firmly as rows of twining build. When the first row is completed (4 pairs of warp ends with one twining cross between each pair), make a twining cross at the end. *This cross is very important.* Turn whole unit around in hand so that work again moves from right to left, and each new row of twining builds up from previous ones. Continue twining between pairs until left side is again reached. Make cross and turn unit in hand as before. Continue the technique until a square area of the warp ends is covered by the weavers. Push rows gently together so that a solid twined surface is created in the center of the warp ends. **NOTE:** Add in new lengths of weaver when about one inch of original piece remains. Lay new piece next to old side by side and, as if they were one, twine around two or three warp ends. Leave short piece at back to be trimmed later. Continue on with new weaver. Count number of rows required to make the square and set this section of work aside.

Cut another set of warp ends and another weaver and repeat operations as above. When the same number of rows of twining have been completed as in the first section, compare the two to be sure an equal area of warp in each section is completely covered by the twining.

To Build the Sides: On lap or tabletop, lay one square section across the second square section with warp ends of each section at right angles, and all four weavers coming from the same corner (see Fig.2). Keeping everything in this position and being sure the final cross of the weavers is maintained in each section, take the back weaver from the bottom section and the back weaver from the top section and use as one. In same manner take the front weaver from the bottom section and the front weaver from top section and use as one. Continue with the same twining technique as before, working from right to left around all the warp ends. When the top section is secured to the bottom (usually one row is sufficient), drop one strand from each pair of weavers and continue twining with the one front and one back remaining. The discontinued pieces may be left at the back of the work and trimmed later. After only one or two rows the twined area will change from a square to a circle. For a small basket, the sides will automatically begin to curve upwards. To prevent premature curving and to create a larger, flat base for larger baskets, begin twining crosses between each warp end instead of between pairs of warp ends. Continue twining in this manner until the sides gradually curve up from the flat base. Increasing tension on the weavers will have a direct effect on the shape of the curve. *Control of tension is very important in proper shaping and may require a little practice.*

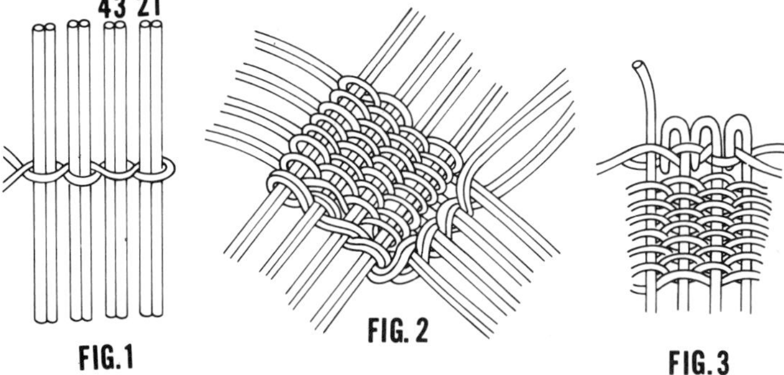

FIG.1 FIG. 2 FIG. 3

Finishing the Basket: When the sides of the basket reach the desired height, trim weavers to approximately 2″ in length and thread each separately on tapestry needle. Insert needle, point down, in back of and parallel to one warp end, until it emerges three rows below the top row of twining. Trim off weaver flush, and firmly push twined rows next to one another to cover inserted weaver. Do the same to any pieces of weaver left at back when new pieces were added. Finish edge of basket according to individual directions for specific baskets.

Read all instructions through before beginning to work.

SQUAT BASKET

SIZE: 3″ tall.

MATERIALS: For warp and weft: Approximately 140 feet 2-ply sisal twine, ⅛″ diameter.

Cut sixteen 12″ lengths of sisal for warp and one 60″ length for first weaver; use eight warp ends for each base section. Follow Directions for base sections. Continue the base with three rows of twining over pairs of warp ends and five rows over single warp ends. Be careful not to apply too much tension at first on weavers or sides will come up abruptly. Sides are about 19 rows with tension gradually increased to curve inward.

Avoid adding new weavers in last three or four rows as it detracts from finished edge. When desired height is reached, cut warp ends to 1½″. Edge is completed by tucking top of each warp end next to warp at left (see Fig.3). Final row of twining will go around both as if they were one. Tails of warp ends are on inside of basket shown, but could be brought to outside to form a decorative fringe. When row of edging is completed, sew weavers into basket as described in "Finishing the Basket" in the Directions.

ROPE BASKET

SIZE: 5″ tall.

MATERIALS: For warp and edge: Approximately 26 feet 3-ply sisal rope, about ¼″ diameter. For weft: Approximately 200 feet 2-ply sisal twine, ⅛″ diameter. White thread. Glue.

Cut eight 24″ lengths of sisal rope for warp ends and one 90″ length of 2-ply sisal twine for first weaver (use an especially long weft when warp is large diameter). Follow Directions, but use only four warp ends for each section and twine from the start over four single warp ends rather than pairs for each base section. Continue base with four rows of twining. Be careful not to bring up the sides yet. Cut eight 11″ lengths of sisal rope for additional warp ends. On each of the eight pieces, untwist ply for about 1″ on one end and cut off at an angle. This will minimize bulk when you add in the additional warp ends. With 5″ pieces of thread, tie each new warp end to an original one. Use a little glue to hold new warp ends in place. In order to make the joined warp ends secure, continue twining four more rows, twining over new warp end and warp end to which it is attached as if they were a pair. Then twine, making crosses between new and old warp ends. Add the eight new warp ends evenly spaced around base. At this point you should be twining around 24 warp ends. Proceed with sides, making about 33 rows.

To make overcast rim, measure circumference of basket at last row of twining and cut length of 3-ply sisal rope 1″ longer. Trim each end on an angle and glue ends together to form a circle. Be sure one weaver is at least 60″ long before beginning to overcast rim. Cut other weaver to 2″; thread on needle and finish according to Directions. The longer weaver is then used to lash the circle of rope onto the basket as a rim. Place rope circle around outside of basket. If circumference is correct, rope circle should rest just on top row of twining. If size is incorrect, adjust by adding or subtracting rows of twining. Thread long remaining weaver on a needle. Bring needle from inside of basket to outside between last two rows of twining. Pass over rope trim to inside, across warp to the left and pass over last row of twining; bring needle to the outside again between last two rows. Repeat process until entire circle is overcast in place, then finish by sewing weaver into basket as described in Directions. Trim and fringe warp ends evenly to finish.

BASKET WITH HANDLE

SIZE: 2″ tall.

MATERIALS: For warp: Approximately 21 feet 4-ply polished jute, ⅛″ diameter. For weft and wrapping handle: About 30 yards dark 4-ply waxed linen.

Cut fifteen 15″ pieces of 4-ply polished jute for warp ends; and one 33″ piece for warp end and handle. Cut one 60″ piece of waxed linen for the first weaver. Warp piece measuring 33″ will be used as warp end #5 on one base section and will extend longer than the other warp ends to eventually become the two-part handle after basket sides are completed. Following Directions, twine over four pairs of warp ends for each base section, then continue for three rows to complete base. Twine over single warp ends for sides which are about 32 rows. After finishing according to Directions, trim remaining two long warp ends of warp #5 to 7″ and short ones to ¼″ above woven basket. Tightly wrap each one of the two long warp ends with a 90″ piece of dark linen; leave ½″ of each end of warp uncovered and 5″ of wrapping linen dangling. Twist long warp ends around each other so that free ends meet the opposite sides of basket. Cut free end of each warp end on an angle. Use free 5″ dangling end of linen to wrap warp ends together. Thread linen on needle and stitch into basket as described in "Finishing the Basket" under Directions. Finish each handle in the same manner. Glue joinings.

SMALL FRINGED BASKET

SIZE: 4″ tall with fringe.

MATERIALS: For warp: 16 feet 6-ply jute, 5/32″ diameter. For weft: Approximately 60 feet cotton express twine.

Cut sixteen 12″ warp ends of 6-ply jute and one 60″ length of express twine for first weaver. Follow Directions for base sections. Continue with 5 rows of twining over pairs of warp ends. The 2″ sides are formed by 9 rows of twining over single warp ends and then reverting to a final four rows of twining over pairs of warp ends for a slightly tapered neck. Finish by sewing weavers into basket as described in Directions. Trim warp ends to 2″ and use a needle to unravel plies and open fibers into a brushlike fringe.

FLARED-TOP BASKET

SIZE: 6″ tall with fringe.

MATERIALS: For warp: 32 feet 4-ply polished

jute, ⅛" diameter. For weft: Approximately 180 feet 2-ply polished jute.

Cut sixteen 24" warp ends of 4-ply jute and a 5 foot length of 2-ply jute for first weaver. Follow Directions for base sections. Continue with five rows of twining over pairs of warp ends. The 5" sides (36 rows) are formed by twining over single warp ends with increased tension on weavers, causing gradual sloping of sides. Resume twining over pairs of warp ends for 4 rows, to bring in neck further. Next row of twining will be over single warp ends, but work it ½" above last row. The space created will be used later in forming the collar. A 1" band (6 rows) of twining, as you decrease tension, forms the flared top. Trim weavers, then finish by sewing weavers into basket as described in Directions. Trim spokes to 1½" above woven area. Use needle to unravel cord for fringed effect. Fold flare top down at ½" space, so that flare forms a collar on the basket.

Coiled Indian Baskets

Rounds of pliant sisal are fascinating to shape and bind with strands of jute in natural or vibrant colors. The larger basket is 17" in diameter with worked-in handles.

EQUIPMENT: Mat knife. Scissors. Ruler. Glue. Yarn needle.

MATERIALS: Off-white sewing thread. White plastic 1" ring, one for each basket. Sisal twine, ⅛" diameter, a 2-ft. length for each basket. **For Natural Basket:** Sisal rope, 3-ply ½" diameter, 100 ft. Natural jute, 2- or 3-ply ⅛" diameter, 8 oz. **For Red and Gold Basket:** Sisal rope, 3-ply ¼" diameter, 100 ft. Jute, 2- or 3-ply ⅛" diam., 4 oz. gold, 8 oz. red.

NATURAL BASKET

DIRECTIONS: Using needle threaded with the 2 ft. of sisal twine, work buttonhole stitch as shown on page 15 around ring; work closely to cover ring. Cut off excess; tie end of sisal twine to one end of sisal rope with sewing thread to prevent raveling. Using needle threaded with natural jute in a comfortable working length, draw jute through one loop of buttonhole stitch from back to front, leaving 4" end underneath. With left hand, hold sisal rope next to ring with end of rope at right, so rope can be coiled around ring counterclockwise. Side facing up is outside; hide end of rope on underside. Wrap jute around rope and through buttonhole stitch from back to front. Continue coiling rope around ring counterclockwise, wrapping jute over rope into each adjacent buttonhole stitch. Catch 4" end of jute under stitches; trim end. To start second round, hold piece with unworked rope at top and jute coming out on front. Coil counterclockwise around piece, wrapping jute around second round of rope to back and down over first round. Insert needle between first rope round and buttonhole stitches, to left of first stitch; bring needle out to front to right of same stitch. Continue second round in this manner, always inserting needle at back to left of next stitch and coming out on front to right of same stitch. Keep rope snug, but do not pull jute too tightly, or it will be difficult to work next round. Work third round in same manner, wrapping jute around new coil to back, and down over second round, through first stitch. As you continue making rounds, stitches will become wider apart. On front, jute will make pattern of curved spokes; on back, a mesh-like pattern. Coil and stitch four rounds, forming flat disk. When working length of jute gets short, bring to underside and catch around next stitch twice; catch end of new length under a few stitches and continue in last stitch worked. Work fifth round in same manner, but increase jute stitches after every stitch by wrapping between stitches around new coil and fourth round. Work rounds 6 through 9 without increases.

At tenth round, increase jute stitches again while beginning to curve basket upward. To curve, place rope beside ninth round, slightly to underside, so edge will begin curving away from you. Underside will be inside of basket. Shape basket sides, curving each coil outward for five more rounds. At round 15, start to even sides by placing coil directly on top of previous coil; repeat through round 22. At round 23, make one handle by pulling out a 10″-long loop of rope between two jute stitches. Halfway around basket, pull out 2nd handle. Work round 24 as for 15.

To finish, make lip of basket by wrapping round 25 on outside of round 24. Coil round 26 on top and between rounds 24 and 25. Instead of wrapping jute over rope, stitch through coil, catching only one ply of rope every 2″. Cut off excess rope; glue end; stitch to basket with jute.

RED AND GOLD BASKET

DIRECTIONS: Following directions for Natural Basket, cover ring. Start basket using gold jute over ¼″-diameter sisal rope. Use same technique as for Natural Basket; however, for each stitch, wrap jute twice around rope.

Coil and stitch basket for nine rounds, then increase stitches as for Natural Basket. Continue flat disk for eighteen rounds, ending gold jute and beginning red jute at round 15. At the same time, begin to build sides of basket by coiling round 16 on top of round 15. Continue shaping basket for rounds 17 through 20. Then make bulge of basket by allowing more rope in coils, placing each coil slightly to outside edge of coil beneath. Basket should have largest diameter in rounds 26–27; then begin narrowing basket. At round 28, change from red to gold jute for six more rounds. For rounds 35–37, change back to red jute and form lip by wrapping last round on outside edge of previous round. Finish top edge with same stitches. Cut and glue rope end; attach with several stitches of jute.

To make lid, begin by making a ring of two rounds of rope. Using red jute, overcast around ring approximately 20 times. Work lid in same manner as basket, but catch jute in overcast stitches rather than buttonhole stitches. Make disk same size as basket bottom, including increase; do not change colors. When disk will fit basket, place next round of rope at underside of last round worked to make sides of lid. Finish with one more round.

Crocheted Bottle Covers

Unique "slips" cover a trio of tinted wine bottles. The designs are worked in the round in easy crochet stitches and adapted to fit each shape—the base and neck are in single crochet; the cover in double crochet, wrong side out. Top with a cork to cover.

SIZE: Quart, half-gallon and gallon sizes.

MATERIALS: No. 21 seine twine, 8 ozs. for quart size, 16 ozs. for half-gallon size, 24 ozs. for gallon size. For cork trim, small amount of lighter weight cord. Aluminum crochet hook size H. Steel crochet hook No. 00.

GAUGE: 2 sts = 1".

COVERS: For quart size: With size H hook, ch 5. Sl st in first ch to form ring.

Rnd 1: Ch 1, 8 sc in ring. Do not join rnds.

Rnd 2: 2 sc in each sc around—16 sc.

Rnd 3: *.Sc in next sc, 2 sc in next sc, repeat from * around—24 sc.

Rnd 4: * 2 sc in next sc, sc in each of next 2 sc, repeat from * around—32 sc.

Rnd 5: * Hdc in each of next 2 sc, 2 hdc in next sc, repeat from * around, hdc in each of last 2 sc—42 hdc.

Rnd 6: Ch 4 (counts as 1 tr), * sk 1 hdc, tr in next hdc, repeat from * around—21 tr. Sl st in top of ch 4.

Rnd 7: Ch 4, tr in each tr around. Sl st in top of ch 4. Try piece on bottle. Work tighter or looser as needed.

Rnds 8-11: Repeat rnd 7.

Rnd 12: Place cover on bottle, wrong side out (or right side out, if crocheting is too difficult). Ch 4, tr in next tr, * sk 1 tr, tr in next tr, repeat from * around—11 tr. Sl st in top of ch 4.

Rnd 13: Ch 4, tr in next tr, * sk 1 tr, tr in next tr, repeat from * around—6 tr. Sl st in top of ch 4.

Rnd 14: Ch 1, sc in same tr as sl st (2 sc in next tr, sc in next tr) twice, 2 sc in last tr—9 sc. Do not join.

Work even in sc until cover reaches top of bottle. Sl st in next sc. End off.

For Half-Gallon Size (oval bottom)**:** With size H hook, ch 9.

Rnd 1: Sc in 2nd ch from hook and in each of next 6 ch, 3 sc in last ch. Working back on opposite side of ch, sc in each of next 6 ch, 2 sc in ch with first sc of rnd—18 sc.

Rnds 2-4: Sc in each sc around, inc 3 sc evenly around each end—36 sc.

Rnd 5: Work sc in each st around ends and dc in each st on sides—36 sts. Sl st in first st.

Rnd 6: Ch 3 (counts as 1 dc), dc in each st around. Sl st in top of ch 3.

Rnds 7-12: Ch 3, dc in next dc and in each dc around. Sl st in top of ch 3. While working, try cover on bottle. Work tighter or looser as needed.

Rnd 13: Working with cover on bottle, work in dc, sk 6 sts evenly spaced around—30 dc.

Rnds 14 and 15: Working in dc, sk 5 sts evenly spaced around—20 dc.

Rnd 16: Working in dc, sk 6 sts around —14 dc.

Rnd 17: Working in dc, sk 2 sts in rnd—12 dc.

Rnd 18: Sc in each dc around. Work even in sc for 9 rnds or until cover reaches top of bottle. Sl st in next st. End off.

Trim cork with a coil of twine, glued on.

For Gallon Size: With size H hook, ch 5. Sl st in first ch to form ring.

Rnd 1: Ch 3 (counts as 1 dc), 9 dc in ring— 10 dc. Sl st in top of ch 3.

Rnd 2: Ch 3, dc in same st as sl st, 2 dc in each st around—20 dc. Sl st in top of ch 3.

Rnd 3: Repeat rnd 2—40 dc.

Rnd 4: Ch 3, dc in same st as sl st, * dc in next dc, 2 dc in next dc, repeat from * around, end dc in last dc—60 dc.

Rnd 5: Work in dc, inc 4 dc evenly spaced around—64 dc.

Rnds 6-14: Work even in dc. While working, try cover on bottle. Work tighter or looser as needed.

Rnd 15: Work in dc, sk 8 sts evenly spaced around—56 dc. Place cover on bottle, wrong side out (or right side out, if crocheting is too difficult).

Rnds 16-18: Work in dc, sk 8 sts evenly spaced around—32 dc.

Rnd 19: Ch 3, dc in next dc, (sk next dc, dc in next dc) 7 times, dc in each of next 2 dc, (sk next dc, dc in next dc) 7 times—18dc.

Rnd 20: Sc in each dc around—18 sc. Work even in sc for 8 rnds or until cover reaches top of bottle. Sl st in next st. End off.

Cork Trim: With lighter weight cord, and No. 00 hook, ch 6, sl st in first ch to form ring. Ch 3, work 15 dc in ring. Sl st in top of ch 3. End off.

For knob, leaving end for sewing, ch 4, sl st in first ch to form ring. Ch 1, 6 sc in ring. End off; leave end for sewing. Bring ends through hole in center of trim, sew ends to trim. Glue trim in place on top of cork.

Dried-Flower Basket

Rows of openwork encircle a sturdy basket (shown at left on page 382) crocheted in basic stitches with a double strand of twine for a perfect holder for dried flowers.

SIZE: 10" high, 9" diameter.

MATERIALS: 4 8-oz. balls No. 24 seine twine. Crochet hook size J.

GAUGE: 2 sc = 1" (double strand).

Note 1: Do not join each rnd with sl st, but mark beg of each rnd.

Note 2: Work with 2 strands of twine held tog throughout.

BASKET: Beg at bottom, ch 4, sl st in first ch to form ring.

Rnd 1 (right side)**:** Ch 3 (counts as 1 dc), work 9 dc in ring—10 dc.

Rnd 2: 2 sc in each st around—20 sc.

Rnds 3-7: Working in sc, inc 8 sc evenly spaced each rnd—60 sc. Turn work so that wrong side is facing you.

Rnd 8: Working in back lp only, sc in each sc around.

Rnd 9: Working in both lps, sc in each sc around.

Rnds 10-13: Repeat rnd 9.

Rnd 14: Sl st in first sc, ch 3, * sk next sc, hdc in next sc, ch 1, repeat from * around, end ch 1, sk last sc, sl st in 2nd ch of ch 3.

Rnd 15: Ch 1, sc in same place as sl st, sc in each ch and hdc around—60 sts.

Rnds 16-18: Sc in each sc around.

Rnds 19-23: Repeat rnds 14-18.

Rnds 24-28: Repeat rnds 14-18.

Rnd 29: Sc in each sc around.

Rnd 30: Sl st in each sc around. End off.

Crocheted Vegetable Storer

A distinguished lidded basket (shown at right on page 382), complete with handles, makes an unusual vegetable storer. The design is worked in a half double crochet pattern with natural jute twine.

SIZE: 5" high, 10" diameter.

MATERIALS: About 3 lbs. of natural stiff jute twine. Crochet hook size J. Rug needle.

GAUGE: 2 sc = 1".

BASKET: Beg at center, ch 6, sl st in first ch to form ring.

Rnd 1: Ch 1, 12 sc in ring. Sl st in first sc.

Rnd 2: Ch 2 (counts as first hdc), hdc in same place as sl st, * 2 hdc in next sc, repeat from * around —24 hdc. Sl st in top of ch 2.

Rnd 3: Ch 2, 2 hdc in same place as sl st * sk next hdc, 3 hdc in next hdc, repeat from * around, sl st in top of ch 2—36 hdc.

Rnd 4: Ch 2, * 3 hdc in next hdc, sk 1 st, hdc in next st, repeat from * around, end 3 hdc in next to last st, sl st in top of ch 2—48 hdc.

Rnd 5: Ch 2, 2 hdc in same place as sl st, * sc in each of next 2 sts, sk 1 st, 3 hdc in next st, repeat from * around, end sc in next 2 sts, sl st in top of ch 2—60 sts.

Rnd 6: * Sc in each of next 2 sts, sk 1 st, 3 hdc in next st, sk 1 st, repeat from * around, end sl st in first sc—60 sts.

Rnds 7-13: Ch 1, sc in each st around. Sl st in first sc. End off at end of rnd 13.

HANDLES (make 2)**:** Make a ch 10" long; leave end for sewing. Sl st in 2nd sc from hook and in each ch across. Sl st in each ch along opposite side of ch. End off; leave end for sewing. Sew a handle to each side of basket along top edge.

COVER: Beg at center, ch 4. Sl st in first ch to form ring.

Rnd 1: Ch 3, 9 dc in ring, sl st in top of ch 3—10 dc.

Rnd 2: Ch 3, dc in same place as sl st, * 2 dc in next dc, repeat from * around, sl st in top of ch 3 —20 dc.

Rnd 3: Ch 1, 2 sc in each dc around, sl st in first sc—40 sc.

Rnd 4: Ch 1, sc around, inc 10 sc evenly spaced around, sl st in first sc—50 sc.

Rnd 5: Repeat rnd 4—60 sc.

Rnds 6-8: Work even in sc.

Rnd 9: Sl st in each sc around. End off.

Knob: Ch 3; sc in 2nd ch from hook and in last ch. Sew knob to cover. Sew cover to basket through 1 st on side edge.

15

Macrame

GENERAL DIRECTIONS

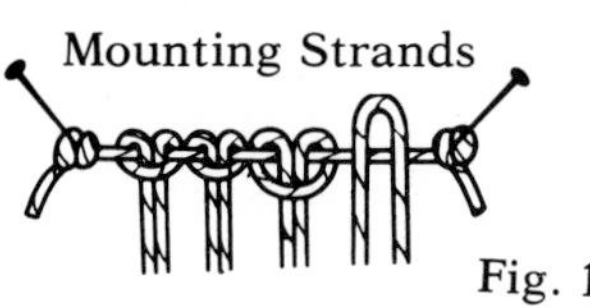
Mounting Strands
Fig. 1

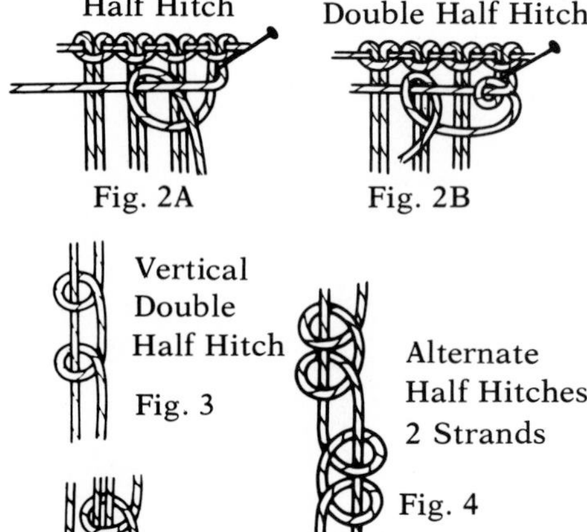

Fig. 2A Fig. 2B Fig. 3 Fig. 4 Fig. 5

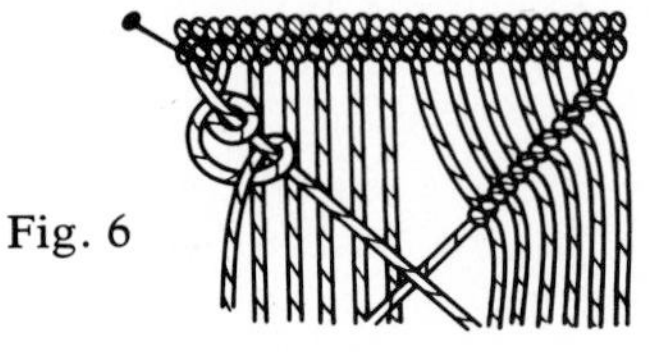
Diagonal Bar—Left and Right
Fig. 6

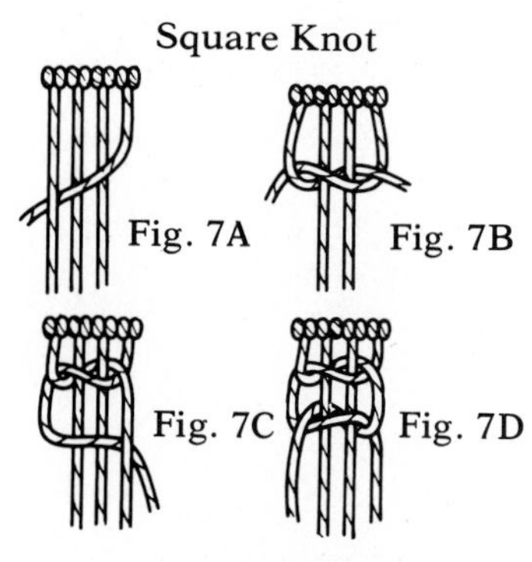

Fig. 7A Fig. 7B Fig. 7C Fig. 7D Fig. 8

EQUIPMENT: Glass-headed pins. Scissors. Working surface such as a plastic foam pillow form. Rubber bands. Tape measure. Crochet hook size 1 or 0. Needle and thread.

MATERIALS: Heavy- or medium-weight tightly twisted yarn or cord is most suitable. See Materials in individual directions.

Knotting Techniques: Practice making the knots on a sample first to become familiar with the technique. The working surface, such as a plastic foam pillow form or pad, may be placed on a table or held in the lap. Some pieces may be easier to work if suspended from a hook.

Mounting: A mounting cord to start the macrame piece is pinned horizontally across working surface. To do this, cut a strand of the yarn being used, about 6" longer than the width of planned macrame piece. Knot both ends with an overhand knot (Fig. 8) and pin knots to working surface to hold strand taut; place pins along length of cord if necessary. The working strands of yarn are tied onto the mounting cord, and the macrame knots are tied with these strands to form the design. To figure the length to cut required working strands, allow about 8 times the length of the finished macrame piece for each strand. Fold each strand in half and tie doubled strand on mounting cord as shown in Fig. 1. Hold doubled strand in front of mounting cord, fold over to back and pull ends through loop, tightening knot (Fig. 1). Mount required working strands close together.

To make working with long strands easier, wind each strand up, leaving about 15" free below work; fasten each strand with a rubber band. As work progresses, unfasten rubber band and release more yarn.

Knots: The macrame designs are formed using two knots—the half hitch and the square knot—in various ways.

Half-Hitch Bars: The half hitch is used to make bars as in Fig. 2A and Fig. 2B. Bars are made over an end working strand, called a knot bearer. Always keep the knot bearer taut, and form the knot with another working strand over the knot bearer. Use pins to hold knot bearer in place whenever necessary (see Fig. 2A). With each working strand, make a half hitch as shown in Fig. 2A, then repeat, making a double half hitch as shown in Fig. 2B. Work bars from right to left or from left to right. Work second bar close to first.

Diagonal Bars: These are made in same manner as horizontal bars with double half hitches, but the knot bearer is held diagonally downward to either right or left (Fig. 6). For double diagonal bars, use two end strands as knot bearers. Work double half hitches over outside strand for each bar, making second bar directly below first diagonal bar.

Vertical Double Half Hitch: Use one working strand, held vertically, as knot bearer. Work double half hitches over vertical knot bearer as shown in Fig. 3. Knot is made the same as for horizontal bar.

Alternate Half Hitches: Work first double half hitch as for Fig. 3. Then, using second strand as knot bearer, make another double half hitch with first strand, Fig 4. Four strands may also be used, Fig. 5. Work a double half hitch first with fourth strand over two center strands, then with first strand, again over the two center strands.

Square Knot: This knot is made with four strands. Keeping the two center strands straight, tie knot with the two outer strands as shown in Figs. 7A, 7B, 7C, and 7D. Always hold center strands taut and tighten knot by pulling the two outer strands up into place. A simple square knot may also be made with just two strands, eliminating the center strands.

Overhand Knot: A small knot is sometimes used to bring strands together (Fig. 8). Mounting cord is also knotted at both ends with an overhand knot.

Sinnets: Long lines called sinnets can be made by repeating the first half of the square knot on four strands, which will twist the line as it grows. By repeating the complete square knot on four strands, you will get a flat sinnet. Sinnets can also be made with half-hitch knots.

Long-Fringed Evening Bag

Reminiscent of the old-fashioned reticule, this dainty evening bag is an easy beginner's project. A rectangular macrame piece is knotted with a fine cord in diagonal bars as well as square-knot sinnets, twisted and flat. The macrame piece, 8″ deep without the fringe, is attached to the front of a velvet bag.

EQUIPMENT: See General Directions on page 386.

MATERIALS: Light brown fine macrame cord, 182 ft. Matching thread. Glass beads, approximately 5/16″ diameter, with hole large enough to accommodate two strands: 28 clear; 26 amber. Dark brown velvet, approximately 20″ x 7″.

DIRECTIONS: Refer to General Directions on page 386. Cut one 6-ft.-long cord; fold in half and pin to working surface. Make sure this mounting cord is centered, as it will be the strap of the bag. Cut 24 7-ft.-long strands; fold in half and mount on double mounting cord (Fig. 1). Separate strands into twelve groups of four. Using first group of strands at left of work, make a twisted sinnet by repeating first half of square knot (Figs. 7A and 7B) fifteen times. Sinnet will be approximately 1¼″ long. Make 11 more sinnets across work.

Using two center strands as knot bearers, make a diagonal bar of double half hitches (Fig. 6) on each half of work. Begin at center, directly below last knot of sinnet, and work out and down toward sides. Last knot of bar should measure 2½″ from bottom of outside sinnet. Be sure to leave strands between sinnets and bars loose enough to keep work flat. Make two more diagonal bars on each side directly below first, using center strands each time as knot bearers.

Anchor last knot bearer at end of left diagonal bar; slip this strand under remaining strands on left side diagonally downward; pull taut and pin again at center of work 4½″ below last diagonal bar. This strand will act as a guide in the working of the next section. Separate strands on left side of work into one group of seven strands (first seven strands from left) and four groups of four strands. Working from center of work toward left side, make a twisted sinnet with first group of four strands, beginning directly below last diagonal bar and ending when guide strand is reached. Using next group of strands, make a flat sinnet of square knots (Figs. 7A, 7B, 7C, 7D) reaching from last diagonal bar to guide strand. Using next group, make a twisted sinnet; with next group, make a flat sinnet as before. Leave last seven strands free. Repeat on right side of work, in reverse.

Slip all strands under guide strands. Using guide strands as knot bearers, make a diagonal bar of double half hitches on each side, beginning at outside of work and working toward center. Repeat diagonal bar eight times on each side, always using outermost strand as knot bearer. Join the two center cords with two overhand knots (Fig. 8).

Thread each pair of strands with first an amber bead and then a clear bead; push beads up. Tie an overhand knot 10″ below last diagonal bar. Push beads down to knots. Trim all strands ½″ from knots. Thread each end of strap with first a clear bead, then an amber bead, then clear again. Push beads all the way to sides of work; tie overhand knots close to beads. Join all four strands with an overhand knot 7″ from first two; tie another overhand knot 2″ from last, another 4″ from last. Tie an overhand knot ½″ from end of two cut strands.

To Make Bag: Measure macrame piece, excluding fringe. Double the length and add two more inches; add one inch to the width. Cut the velvet to this size. Fold in half with right sides together. Stitch ½″ seam at each side. Turn in 1″ around top edge and slip-stitch. Turn right side out. Place macrame on top of bag with fringe extending below. Whipstitch to bag along edge, along sides at diagonal bars, and at bottom where two center strands were joined.

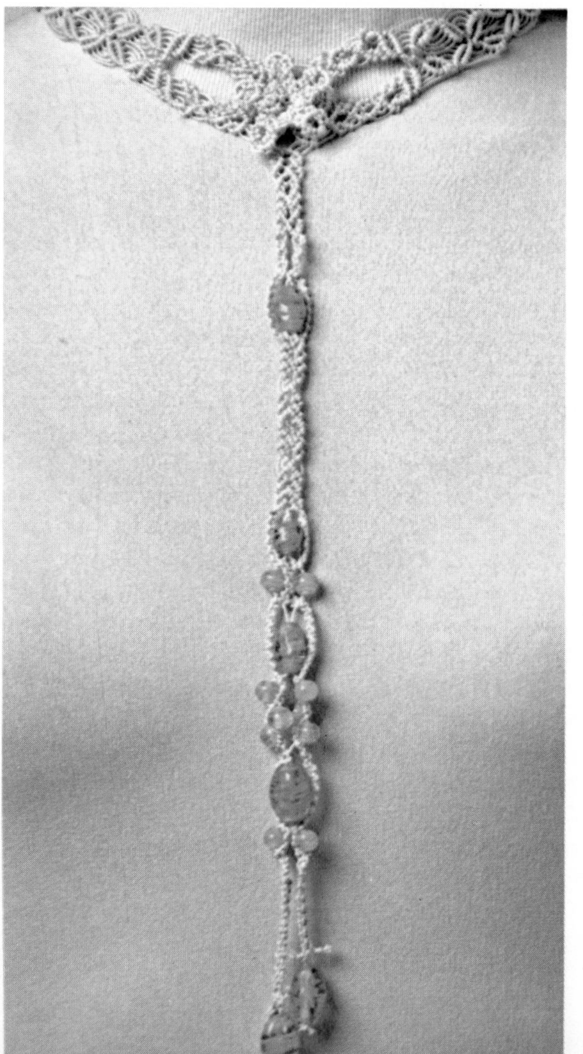

Jeweled Pendant

This beautiful and delicate pendant is a real test for the expert! Made with a fine thread (fishing line or bedspread cotton), the pendant incorporates baroque beads in various sizes and a few seed beads. The flower motif, shown in detail, is actual size.

EQUIPMENT: See General Directions on page 386.

MATERIALS: 4-lb. test linen fishing line or ecru bedspread cotton, 90 ft. Oval baroque green beads: ¾″ long, 3; ⅝″ long, 2; ½″ long, 2. Round green beads ¼″ diameter, 10. Large seed beads, 18.

DIRECTIONS: Refer to General Directions on page 386. Cut fifteen 6-ft.-long strands. Separate strands into five groups of three strands each. Each group will make an eyelet petal. Work on one group at a time throughout, unless otherwise stated. Center strands and knot bearers are joined with a pair of alternate half hitches (two center knots of Fig. 4).

Holding two strands together, mount third strand on center of the two as in Fig. 1. Pin group of strands to working surface at knot with strands used to tie mounting knot separated at top (two groups of three strands on each side of knot).

With left group, using any strand (except strand used to tie mounting knot) as knot bearer, tie a diagonal bar of double half hitches (Fig. 6) from knot down to left, with remaining two strands; use strand used to tie mounting knot as last working strand. Using strand at right as knot bearer, tie a double half hitch with next strand. Using original knot bearer (of first diagonal bar) as knot bearer, tie a diagonal bar from left side toward center with remaining two strands. Left half of petal shape is completed.

With right group, repeat directions for left group in reverse. Join last two knot bearers at center. Using outside strands as knot bearers, tie a diagonal bar on each side of eyelet directly under last bar. Join knot bearers. Work four more eyelet petals in same manner with remaining groups.

Join Eyelets: Place any two eyelets side by side and join with pairs of alternate half hitches, using outer strands.

Divide six strands from each petal into two groups of three each. Using two groups of three strands between petals, tie a bar of vertical double half hitches with each group (Fig. 3), using center strands as knot bearers. Join knot bearers, forming a tiny leaf. Repeat with other petals until all are joined in a circle. Pull all strands through center opening to back of work.

Maintain each group of six strands in proper position below petals. Using two center strands of each group as knot bearers, tie vertical double half hitches with two remaining strands of each group (two bars in each group). Tie a diagonal bar with each half of each group from sides toward center. Join knot bearers at center of each group. Tie two more diagonal bars in same manner, joining knot bearers at center as before.

There are now five eyelet petal shapes in a circle underneath original eyelet petals. Pin these last five eyelets to working surface so they lie flat. Join eyelets with pairs of alternate half hitches, using uppermost strands (first working strands of last diagonal bar). Make sure strands are loose enough so petals remain flat. Regroup strands into groups of six, with the two strands used to join eyelets at center. Work with one group at a time. Using two center strands as knot bearers, tie a diagonal bar with each half of group, starting at center and working out toward sides. Tie a second diagonal bar on each half using center strands as knot bearers. Join two center strands and, using these as first knot bearers, work an eyelet; join last knot bearers at center. Repeat with remaining four groups.

Neckband: Each half is worked with two of the five groups of six strands (total of 12). Remaining group of six will form pendant. Directions are for one half only; complete one half first, then go on to second half. Keep strands in two groups of six strands. Using two center strands of each group as knot bearers each time, tie two diagonal bars, starting at center of each group and working toward sides.

Leaf Pattern: Pattern is composed of four leaves, each leaf worked with six strands and joined at center.

With strands separated into two groups of six, work first group of strands on left: Using first strand on left as knot bearer, tie a diagonal bar with remaining five strands, from left down toward center. Tie a second diagonal bar below first, using outer left strand as knot bearer; curve center down slightly to form leaf. Repeat leaf bars with group on right in reverse. String seed bead on each of last two knot bearers; push beads up close to bars. Join knot bearers close to beads. String another bead on each knot bearer; push beads close to joining knot. Working first with group of strands on left, tie another leaf of two diagonal bars from center down to left side. Repeat leaf bars with group of strands on right in reverse. Repeat leaf pattern four times, omitting beads at center.

Now treat the strands as one group of twelve strands. Using first strand at right as knot bearer, tie a diagonal bar with next six strands, from right side toward center. Using first strand from left as knot bearer, tie a diagonal bar with next six strands, from left toward center, ending below first bar. This necessitates using knot bearer and last working strand of first bar as working strands in second bar and results in interlocking of bars. Tie four more interlocking bars in same manner. Both halves of neckband are worked alike up to this point.

Neckband Ending: Right End: Separate strands into two groups of six strands each. Starting with first (outside) strand of group on right, tie half hitch (second knot of Fig. 4) on second strand from right. Using same second strand, tie a half hitch (third knot of Fig. 4) on first strand. Using second strand again, tie half hitch (second knot of Fig. 4) on next strand to left (third strand). Using third strand, tie a half hitch (third knot of Fig. 4) on second strand. Continue in this manner across group of strands. Repeat row of alternating half hitches with left group of strands in reverse. Join two center strands. Tie five more rows with all strands of each group. Tie four more rows with each group, leaving one outside strand free per row. There are five free strands on each side. Tie an overhand knot (Fig. 8) with each free strand, close to half hitches; trim ends close to knots. Join two center strands. String one ½" bead on one of remaining strands; secure with an overhand knot close to bead. Tie four overhand knots at ⅛" intervals with other remaining strand. Join strands below bead with alternate half hitches. Tie overhand knot with each strand close to joining knot; trim off ends.

Left End: Separate strands into six pairs. Tie a 1½"-long sinnet of alternate half hitches with each pair. Using adjacent strands, join sinnets in a row with pairs of alternate half hitches. String seed bead on each of four outer strands. Push beads up close to joining knots; tie two overhand knots with each strand close to edge; trim off all ends close to knots.

Pendant: Divide remaining group of six strands below eyelet into two groups of three strands each. Tie two diagonal bars toward center with each group, using outside strands as knot bearers each time. Join last two knot bearers. Work two sinnets of alternate half hitches as follows: Work first with right group of strands, always using strand at right to tie first half hitch. Tie a pair of alternate half hitches with two strands on right. Using same two strands, tie a second pair of alternate half hitches. Using center strand and left strand of group, tie a pair of alternate half hitches. Tie a pair of alternate half hitches with two right strands. Tie six more pairs of alternate half hitches in same manner. Repeat sinnet with group of strands on left, in reverse, and always using left strand to tie first half hitch.

Join two center strands with a pair of alternate half hitches. *String a ⅝" bead on two center strands; secure with a pair of alternate half hitches close to bead. There are two pairs of strands, one on each side of bead. Tie a sinnet of alternate half hitches with each pair, loosely encircling bead. Using adjacent strands, join each sinnet to one center strand with alternate half hitches*. Join two center strands.

Separate strands into two groups of three strands each. Tie four diagonal bars with each group from sides toward center, using outside strands as knot bearers each time and joining knot bearers at center after second and fourth pairs of bars. Tie two diagonal bars with each group from center toward sides, using center strands as knot bearers each time. Join two strands at center. Using center strands as knot bearers, tie a diagonal bar with each group of strands from center toward sides. String a seed bead on each of the two center strands. Using outer strands as knot bearers, tie a diagonal bar with each group of strands from sides toward center, forming diamond shape. Join two knot bearers at center. Tie two diagonal bars with each group of strands from sides toward center, directly below last bar of diamond, and using outside strands as knot bearers each time. Join last two knot bearers at center. Tie four diagonal bars with each group from center toward sides, joining two center strands after second and fourth pairs of bars. Repeat from * to *, using a ½" bead, and omitting alternate half hitches directly under bead.

For remainder of pendant, string on beads and make sinnets of alternate half hitches with pairs of strands as follows: Add ¼" bead to outer strand on each side; make a sinnet around inner side of each bead; join three strands below each bead. String on a ⅝" oval bead on two center strands; make a loose sinnet on each side of bead. Join bead strand with two outer strands on each side. String on a ¼" bead on each outer strand and make a sinnet around inner side of each bead. String on a ¼" bead on each of two center strands and make a sinnet around outer side of each. String on a ¼" bead on each outer strand and make a sinnet around inner side of beads. Join two center strands and string on a ¾" oval bead at center. Make a loose sinnet around outer sides of oval bead. Join a center strand with two outer strands on each side and string a ¼" bead on each outer strand; make a sinnet around inner side of each bead. Join the three strands below each bead.

Make a sinnet below each bead by tying alternating half hitches with three strands each as before; make one sinnet 2" long, the other 1".

String ¾" oval bead on center strand of each sinnet; secure with several overhand knots close to bead; trim ends off close to bead. Tie an overhand knot on each remaining strand close to work and trim off ends.

Flowerpot Holders

Earth-toned patterns look like Indian weavings, but they are actually done in macrame. The large holder, designed to fit an 8″-high flowerpot, is suspended from thick knotted cords. The smaller cover hangs from strands of yarn.

SIZE: Small: 4″ diameter; 4½″ deep. Large: 7″ diameter; 8″ deep.

EQUIPMENT: See General Directions on page 386.

MATERIALS: Small: Heavy rayon-cotton rug yarn, one skein each rust and black, or colors desired. One ball of 24-ply parcel-post twine. **Large:** Heavy rayon-cotton rug yarn, one skein each of brown, burnt orange, and rust (one skein will do both). One ball of 24-ply parcel-post twine (one ball will do both). Plastic "bone" rings, ¾″ diameter.

SMALL BASKET

DIRECTIONS: Refer to General Directions on page 386. From parcel-post string, cut one 60″ mounting cord and eighteen 40″ working strands. Near one end of mounting cord, tie a loop about 1″ in diameter. Wind up long end, leaving about 15″ free and secure with rubber band to facilitate working; this end will be used as the knot bearer; short end should be worked in as you go along.

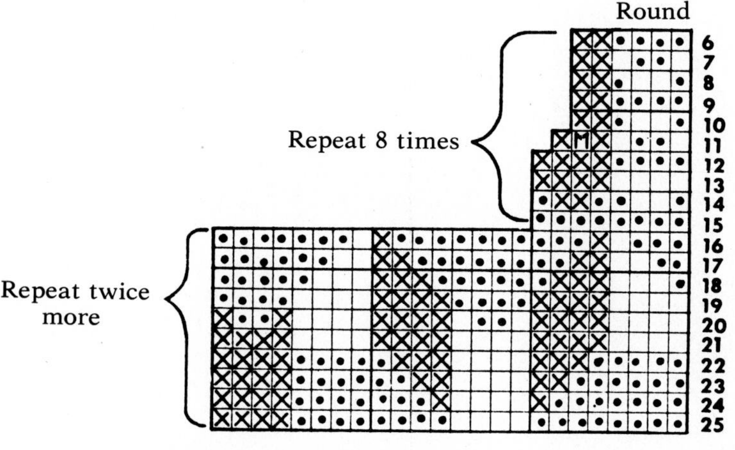

Color Key
☐ White
☒ Rust
⊡ Black
M Mount (see Directions)

Fold each 40″ cord in half and mount on 1″ loop as in Fig. 1. Wind up all ends and secure each with rubber band.

With T-pins, mount loop onto board. Working clockwise over the knot bearer, make a double half hitch (Figs. 2A and 2B) with each working strand in turn until you have completed one round (36 half hitches). Keep knot bearer taut and make all knots close to one another. Work two more rounds of double half hitches.

From rust yarn, cut nine 40″ cords. Mount one rust cord on knot bearer at beginning of Round 4; continue making half hitches as before, adding a rust cord after every fourth double half hitch.

For Round 5, make a double half hitch with all cords, stopping just before last rust cords. Here change knot bearer from string to black yarn: Cut 11-yd. length of black yarn; wind up all but 15″ and hold with rubber band. Cut off string knot bearer to about 3″. Holding end of string and black yarn together, make an overhand knot (Fig. 8) next to last double half hitches. Make double half hitches with rust cords, being sure they cover overhand knot (Round 5 is not a complete round).

The remaining rounds are worked from the color chart, which reads from right to left. According to color of knot (see color key), work horizontal or vertical double half hitch (Fig. 3) with each cord in turn. If the chart calls for black, work one vertical double half hitch, using string as knot bearer; work all rust and white knots horizontally over black knot bearer. For Rounds 6-15, repeat each line of chart eight times to complete each round. In Round 11, where M is indicated, mount (Fig. 1) a 40″ doubled cord of rust yarn onto the black knot bearer. For Rounds 16-25, repeat each line of chart two more times to complete each round.

After finishing all rounds, cut ends of string only to ½″; fringe. With each group of four strands of rust, tie alternate half hitches (Fig. 5) to a length of 1½″. Roll down to outside of basket and pull ends through center of lower edge of alternating half hitches. Glue or stitch on wrong side; trim ends. Trim black yarn end.

From rust yarn, cut three 40″ lengths. Fold each in half and mount one onto basket through center of every third rust loop at same place alternating half hitches were ended. About 5″ up on each pair of cords, tie an overhand knot; repeat about 9″ from first knots. Tie all cord ends into one overhand knot; trim ends.

LARGE BASKET

Cut the following lengths: From rust yarn, twelve 90″; from burnt orange yarn, eight 108″; and from string, twenty-four 108″. Mount four rust cords and four string cords alternately on bone ring according to General Directions and Fig. 1 (page 386).

With T-pins, mount ring onto working surface. From string, cut knot bearer about 2 yds. long. To add a new knot bearer, hold end of old knot bearer and beginning of new one together; work several knots over these cords. (If you add a new one while working vertical knots, you can only work one knot over new end.) Push ends to inside of cover and do not trim. To begin, hold working surface vertically in your lap. Hold knot bearer cord next to ring and allow 2″ end at beginning. Working clockwise over the knot bearer around the outside of the ring, make double half hitch (Figs. 2A and 2B, page 386) with each working strand in turn as follows: one cord of string, first cord of rust, second cord of rust, one cord string, mount two doubled cords of burnt orange onto knot bearer; repeat three times to complete Round 1. Keep knot bearer taut and make all knots firm and close to one another.

Round 2: Work double half hitches with each string and rust cord in turn; do not use orange cords yet.

Round 3: Work double half hitches as Round 2, but mount a new doubled string cord between each pair of string cords and a new doubled rust cord between each pair of rust cords.

Round 4: Work double half hitches with all string and rust cords, but not burnt orange cords.

Round 5: Work double half hitches with all cords but orange cords. With each group of orange cords, work a sennit of ten half square knots (Figs. 6A and 6B).

Round 6: Work horizontal double half hitch with first string cord. Then use string knot bearer to work vertical double half hitches (Fig. 3, page 386) over four rust cords. Work horizontal double half hitches with next two cords of string, then with each cord of orange from the sennit, and then with the next cord of string. * Repeat pattern from * to * three more times to complete the round.

Round 7 and 8: Repeat Round 6.

Round 9: * Work horizontal double half hitch with string cord. Work horizontal double half hitches with next four rust cords, mounting doubled rust cord in center of four knots. Work horizontal double half hitches with next two string cords, mounting doubled string cord in center of two knots. Work horizontal double half hitches with four orange cords in turn and then next string cord. Mount doubled string cord. * Repeat pattern from * to * three more times to complete the round.

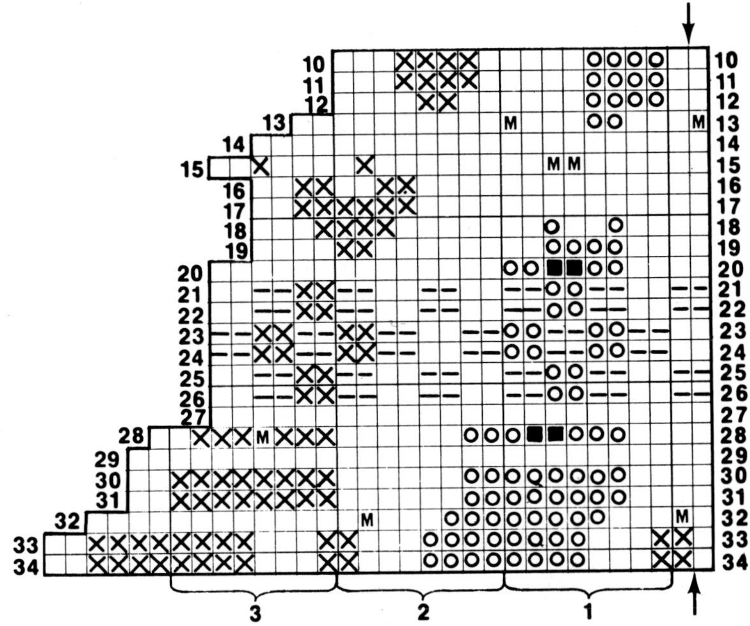

Color Key
White
Orange
Rust
Brown
Mount (see Directions)
See Directions

Rounds 10-34: Follow chart which reads from right to left. According to color of knot (see Color Key), work horizontal or vertical double half hitches with each cord in turn. All rust and orange double half hitches are horizontal. Until Round 20, all string knots (the blank on the chart) are vertical. To complete each round repeat each line of chart three more times, working each line on chart four times in all. Count across chart line for each round; do not compare one chart line to another. Any additional Round directions such as mounting new cords (M on chart) are given below.

Round 13: Mount new string cords.

Round 15: Mount orange cords each 80″ long. With each group of four orange cords, work a sennit 2″ long of vertical alternating half hitches using four cords (Fig. 5, page 386); leave sennits free until Round 20.

Round 20: For first solid block on chart, use first outer cord of sennit to work horizontal double half hitch; for second solid block, use second outer cord for next horizontal double half hitch. Use the two center cords of the sennit to tie vertical alternating half hitches using two cords (Fig. 4, page 386) for 2″. At end of round, you have four orange sennits to be used later. At end of Round 20 and beginning of next, replace string knot bearer with brown knot bearer. From Round 21 on, all string knots are horizontal.

Round 26: At the end of this round and beginning of next replace brown knot bearer with string knot bearer.

Round 27: From this round on, all string knots worked over string will be horizontal; if worked over yarn, vertical.

Round 28: For each solid block on chart, use cord from the sennit to work horizontal double half hitch. For M, mount new rust cord 60″ long.

Round 32: Mount new rust cord 60″ long.

Round 34: This round completes sides of basket.

To finish off ends, work individually with groups of eight cords as indicated by brackets under Round 34 of chart. With first group in bracket #1, use rust cord from right side to work vertical double half hitches over each of the three string cords; then work horizontal double half hitches with next four orange cords to complete row 1. Turn work upside down so you will always be working from right to left. For second row, reverse and repeat row 1. Continue turning work and knotting until you have four rows.

With group in bracket #2, to begin, turn basket so you will be working right to left. Using rust cord form left side of bracket, work four rows as for bracket #1.

For bracket #3, use rust cord on right side to work three vertical double half hitches; then with each rust cord, work four horizontal double half hitches to complete row 1. Rotate work to always knot from right to left; then for second row reverse and repeat row 1. Rotate and repeat until you have four rows.

For fourth group (not designated by bracket on chart), use next eight cords of basket to work four rows as for bracket #3, using rust cord from left side.

Repeat above procedure three more times to complete the edging.

Finishing: For groups with rows of all rust knots, separate string and rust ends. For string ends, work vertical alternate half hitches over one string and rust knot bearer using other two string ends; make about 1½″ long. Cut all ends even and glue. For rust ends, use inner rust cord to make half hitches over all other rust cords; work about 1½″. Cut ends and glue. Repeat on all rust groups with all rust knots. Turn to inside of basket along edge of Round 34; glue to inside.

For groups with orange and rust knots, separate the two color cords. For orange ends, work half hitches as directed above for rust. For string ends, work alternate half hitches over one string cord and the rust knot bearer using other two string ends. Work 1½″, then cut off rust cord; continue knotting string to 10″ length. Repeat on all groups with orange and rust knots. Gather all 10″ string sennit ends together; knot them tightly with small piece of string; ravel all string ends. Fold orange sennits to inside of basket along last row of orange knots and tack with glue.

16

One-of-a-Kind Crafts

Waxen Flowers from Yesteryear

Delicate wax flowers, extremely popular in the past, were first featured in McCall's Needlework and Crafts *in 1925. Each pretty blossom is created by cutting crepe paper petals, forming them into a bloom and dipping them into wax.*

EQUIPMENT: Tracing paper. Pencil. Ruler. Wire cutter or old scissors. Sharp scissors. Pinking shears. Small pointed paintbrush. Old double boiler. Newspapers to cover working surface.

MATERIALS: Crepe paper in flower colors and leaf greens. Green cotton covered wire No. 7; green covered spool wire. All-purpose glue. Old white candle stubs or paraffin. Spray colors and tints (colors given in individual directions) optional. For Nosegay, white paper lace doily 6″ in diameter. For Anemone, black seed beads. Yellow flower stamens.

DIRECTIONS: Trace petal and leaf patterns. Complete half-patterns, indicated by long dash lines. Dash lines on bachelor's button and carnation patterns indicate repeat of shape.

Following directions for individual flowers, cut centers, petals, calyx, and leaves from crepe paper (in colors shown here). Always cut petals and leaves with grain of paper running along length. To cup petals, hold both sides of petal with forefinger and thumb of both hands and stretch middle portion into a cup shape. To flute petals, hold top edge between forefinger and thumb of both hands and stretch gently, twisting a little. To curl petals, hold scissors blade against petal with thumb on top; draw blade up to top of petal.

Cut No. 7 wire desired length for stem. Form and attach flower center to end of stem; glue petals around center, then wire in place, using spool wire. Glue calyx around bottom of petals. Cut crepe paper leaves. Cut spool wire about 1″ longer than leaf; brush glue along one side of wire and press on leaf lengthwise along center; let glue dry. Cut ⅜″-wide strips of paper across grain of paper for wrapping the stems.

For more realism, flowers may be sprayed

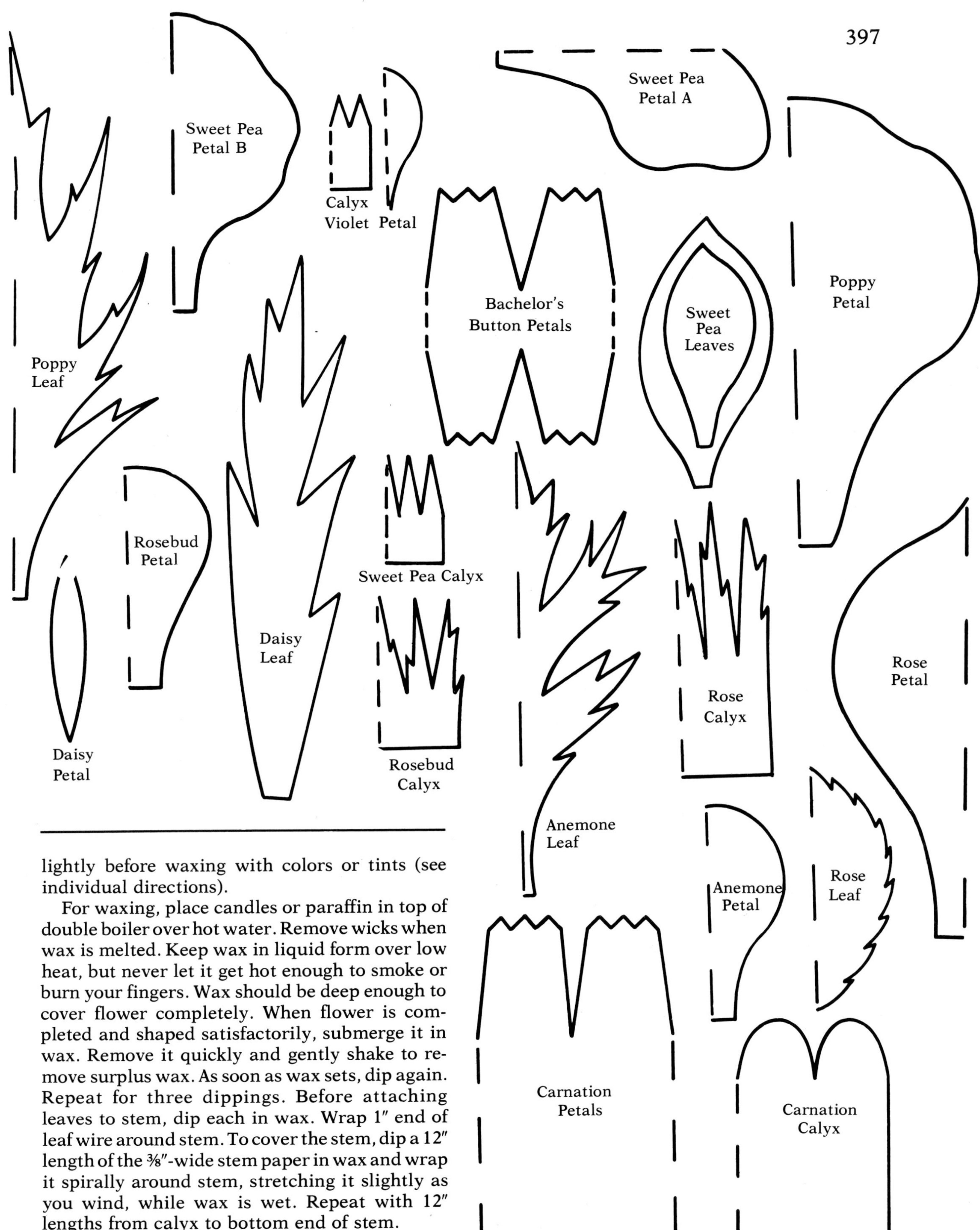

lightly before waxing with colors or tints (see individual directions).

For waxing, place candles or paraffin in top of double boiler over hot water. Remove wicks when wax is melted. Keep wax in liquid form over low heat, but never let it get hot enough to smoke or burn your fingers. Wax should be deep enough to cover flower completely. When flower is completed and shaped satisfactorily, submerge it in wax. Remove it quickly and gently shake to remove surplus wax. As soon as wax sets, dip again. Repeat for three dippings. Before attaching leaves to stem, dip each in wax. Wrap 1″ end of leaf wire around stem. To cover the stem, dip a 12″ length of the ⅜″-wide stem paper in wax and wrap it spirally around stem, stretching it slightly as you wind, while wax is wet. Repeat with 12″ lengths from calyx to bottom end of stem.

Carnation: Cut crepe paper 45″ long across the grain, 2½″ wide for petals. Cut one long edge with pinking shears. Following pattern, cut slits into pinked edge for petals. For leaves, cut three strips of crepe paper with the grain, 4″ long, ¼″ wide; taper ends to points.

Wrap petal strip tightly around end of wire stem, wrapping each successive row slightly lower than previous row so that flower fans out; glue and wire in place. Following Directions, glue on calyx and finish flower. Pink carnation was made of pink crepe paper sprayed lightly with red tint and true pink color before dipping in wax. Red and white carnation was made of white crepe paper and sprayed with red tint, covering about ½″ at pinked edge of petals, before flower was assembled.

Rose: Cut five large rose petals, group 1, and cup deeply near the top; cut five petals, group 2, curl top edge and cup in middle; cut five petals, group 3, curl deeply at top and cup at base. Roll one petal from group 1 tightly around stem to form center. Arrange other four petals around center, overlapping each halfway. Continue arranging petals of group 2 and then group 3 around previous petals. Wire in place. Glue calyx around base of petals; curl points down. Make two leaf sprays of three leaves each. For each spray, cut three pieces of spool wire and glue a leaf to end of each; twist the three wires together, leaving leaves spread. Finish flower, following Directions. Make rosebuds in same manner with only first five petals. The talisman rose is buttercup yellow paper sprayed lightly with true pink color and peach blush tint; pink rose is pink paper sprayed with true pink color and peach blush tint.

Poppy: For center, cut three 2″ squares of bright green crepe paper. Crumble two together into a tight ball; place the other over ball and stretch around ball smoothly. Glue center over end of stem. Cut four 1/16″ x 1″ pieces of black crepe paper; glue in a double cross over top of center. Cut a strip 25″ long across grain of black crepe paper, 1½″ wide; cut slits 1″ deep, ⅛″ apart along one edge to fringe. Roll fringes between fingers to make each finer. Wrap fringe around center; glue. Cut four petals of bright orange crepe paper; flute each several times at top; cup each in middle deeply. Glue petals around center overlapping one third. Make leaves and finish as directed in Directions. Spray petals with red tint.

Anemone: Make center same as Poppy center, of black paper, and make a black fringe of 1″ x 8″ strip. Glue a black seed bead to end of each fringe. Glue fringe around center. Cut 10 petals. Cut three leaves; finish as directed in Directions, with the leaves near the top of the flower stem.

Daisy: From buttercup yellow crepe paper, cut a strip 24″ long across the grain with pinking shears, and ½″ wide. Cut 20 white petals. Glue end of strip to top of stem and wind strip tightly around, with pinked edge up. Finish as directed in Directions with four or five leaves spaced along stem.

Bachelor's Button: From midnight blue crepe paper, make a fringe with a ½″ x 5″ strip as for Poppy. Wrap fringe tightly around end of stem. From orchid crepe paper, cut a strip 18″ long across the grain, 1½″ wide. Following pattern, cut into strip for petals, and pink edges. Fold strip in half lengthwise and gather on a piece of spool wire placed into the fold; wrap around fringe center. For leaves, cut three or four strips of crepe paper 8″ long with the grain, ½″ wide; taper ends to points. Finish flower following Directions. Spray unevenly with royal blue color; tip fringe with white.

Sweet Pea: From primrose yellow or white crepe paper, cut one inside petal A and one outside petal B for each blossom. Cut a 2″ square for center; fold in half diagonally and bring points together. Glue center to end of a spool wire stem. Cup inside petal and curl sides forward; glue around center. Cup outside petal and curl sides back; glue in place. Cut calyx, small and large leaves. Glue calyx around base of petals. Make several blossoms for each spray. Twist stems together, spacing flowers at uneven distances. Wrap stem, adding unwired leaves at intervals and a few pieces of coiled wire for tendrils.

Nosegay: Using rosebud pattern, make sweetheart rose in same manner as large rose, with about 16 petals; curl all petals out. Make 16 rosebuds in same manner with six petals. Do not wrap stems.

For violets, cut five petals of orchid crepe paper; curl petals back. Bend ½″ at top of stem at right angle; glue a yellow stamen to this end. Glue petals around stamen so they curl away from it. Spray with royal blue color. Glue calyx around petals. Do not cover stems.

Cut a ¾″-diameter hole in center of a white 6″ paper doily. Insert stems of flowers in doily hole, with sweetheart rose at center, violets surrounding it, and rosebuds around outside. Bend stems as needed to hold flowers in place. Cut off stems to 3½″ below doily. Wrap stems together as for covering individual stem.

Four Seasons Paperwork Plaques

Charming visual poems are created in four pictures that represent the seasons. The delicate designs are cut from white paper, cemented to background paper in muted shades and mounted on cardboard. A plywood backing and narrow frame finish off the projects to perfection.

EQUIPMENT: Regular and embroidery scissors. Ruler. Soft pencil. Ball-point pen. Tracing paper. Single-edge razor blade. Soft brush. **For Framing:** Handsaw. Square. Hammer. Small paintbrush. Miter box and backsaw.

MATERIALS: White bond paper. Heavy cardboard 6¼" square for each. Construction paper for background, different color for each. Rubber cement. **For Frame:** Plywood ½" thick, 8¼" square. Pine stripping ¾" wide, 3'. Small brads. White, black flat paint. All-purpose glue.

DIRECTIONS: To Make Plaques: Use one piece of cardboard 6¼" square. Cut piece of construction paper 7¾" square. Lay cardboard down in center of paper. Clip corners of paper diagonally to corners of cardboard. Fold edges of paper over edges of cardboard so that paper edges overlap. Spread cement around edges of cardboard and press paper down smoothly. Cut second piece of construction paper 5½" square; cement to back of cardboard plaque, covering edges of first piece of construction paper.

To Make Designs: Trace half-patterns indicated by dash lines, using soft pencil. Turn tracing paper over and lay it down on white paper that has been folded in half; align dash lines of traced pattern with fold line of white paper. Retrace design carefully with ball-point pen, pressing down so that the pencil impression will transfer to the white paper. Try not to tear tracing paper. Sharpen details on transferred design with pencil, if necessary. Cut out design very carefully with embroidery scissors, cutting through both layers of folded paper. Use razor blade to cut very delicate areas if necessary. Some parts connected with very thin stems may be cut separately and then cemented in position on plaque. Other parts are separate pieces. For Spring, cut four eggs for

center of design the same size as one in pattern. Unfold cutout design carefully.

With small, soft brush, apply a thin layer of cement to penciled side of cutout design; be careful not to use too much cement, as it will smear onto front of paper and on plaque. Press cemented side of design and separate pieces neatly onto center of plaque; smooth in place.

To Frame: Cut an 8¼″ square of plywood; paint white. Using backsaw and miter box, measure and cut four pieces of pine stripping to fit side of plywood. Paint strips black. Glue and nail strips to plywood with small brads; touch nail heads with black paint. Center paper plaque on plywood. Attach by hammering a small brad through each corner into plywood.

Paper Bouquet

Paper cutouts, gently curved and glued in place, make a lacy bouquet of three-dimensional flowers. To make the flowers identical, cut two of each at the same time. The two-color flowers are made from double layers of paper.

SIZE: 28″ x 22″ unframed.

EQUIPMENT: Paper for patterns. Pencil. Ruler. Tracing paper. Carbon paper. Mat knife or single-edged razor blade. Metal straight edge. Square. Small flat paintbrush. Masking tape. Newspaper for padding.

MATERIALS: Paper in colors shown or desired. White illustration cardboard for background 30″ x 40″. All-purpose glue. Shadow box frame 22″ x 28″ with aluminum edging. Glass to fit frame. Small pieces of wood lath, or styrofoam. Apple green enamel paint.

DIRECTIONS: If possible, have half-pattern enlarged to 11″ wide by photostat process (such service is available in most cities); or enlarge by copying on paper ruled in 1″ squares. Complete half-pattern indicated by long dash line. Trace each motif and transfer to colored paper with carbon. Using straight edge and square, mark and cut background cardboard 22″ x 28″. Work on flat surface covered with thick padding of newspaper and cut with knife or razor blade. Cut the individual motifs out of paper; cut away areas in motifs where second colors appear; see illustration. Two matching motifs may be cut at once by taping two pieces of paper together. Arrange pieces on white mounting cardboard. Wherever you have cut-out areas on flowers, you can place another color paper underneath for contrast. For varied effect, glue some pieces down flat, and, for other pieces (especially the flowers and ferns), glue small pieces of wood about ⅛″ x ⅜″ in different lengths from ½″ to 1½″ underneath to lift motifs up from rest of picture. Work with motifs until satisfied with arrangement; see illustration. Make sure pieces are glued to background securely.

Frame: Mask the aluminum edges of frame to keep paint-free. Paint outside green. Turn frame wrong side up; set glass into ridge of frame with glue. Measure and cut a strip of cardboard to fit inside sides, top, and bottom of frame behind glass. Glue strips to frame, thus securing glass in place. Fit background piece to back of frame; tape in place securely.

Wooden Sunburst Plaque

Built entirely of packing crate lumber, this dramatic sunburst has sunrays nailed to a stained background; face and features are then added to give a four-level dimension to the plaque.

SIZE: 44″ in diameter.

EQUIPMENT: Paper for pattern. Thin cardboard. Pencil. Ruler. Scissors. Thin nail, string, and pencil for compass. Saw. Hammer. Flat paintbrushes. Nail set. Coarse sandpaper.

MATERIALS: Wood: packing crate lumber, 63 feet of 6″ boards (read through directions before purchasing wood to determine total number and lengths of boards): 1″ x 2″ pieces of lumber—one 40″ long, two 32″, one 20″, and two 18″ long. Poster

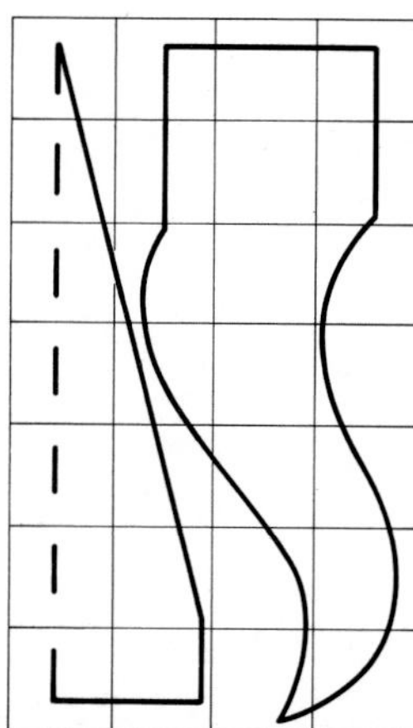

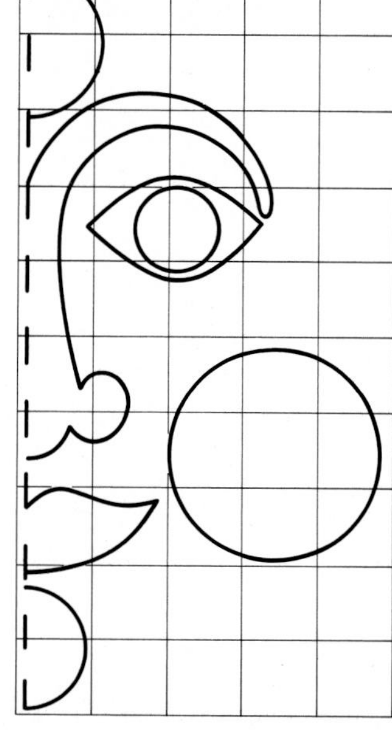

paint: blue, yellow, and orange. Finishing nails. Plastic wood.

DIRECTIONS: Enlarge patterns for face and rays by copying on paper ruled in 2″ squares; complete half-patterns indicated by long dash lines. Mark face pieces and each ray on thin cardboard and cut out for patterns.

Lay eight 46″-long boards together vertically. For braces, nail 40″ strip of wood across center and back, two 32″ strips above and below and equidistant from center. To mark circle on boards, hammer a nail at center of boards, tie string to nail and tie a sharp pencil to string 22″ away from nail. Using this as a compass, swing a circle 44″ in diameter. With saw, cut off boards to form circle. To form head, lay four 24″-long boards together vertically; for braces, nail 20″ strip across center back and two 18″ above and below equidistant from center. Mark a circle on boards in same manner as above, tying pencil 11″ from nail. With saw, round off boards to form circle.

Place cardboard face pieces and rays on pieces of 6″ board; go around outline with pencil to mark on wood. Repeat each ray shape eight times. Cut out all pieces with saw. Sand all edges.

Thin poster paint with water so that it will only stain the wood and the grain will show through. Paint 44″ background circle blue; 22″ head circle, triangular rays, and pupils yellow; paint wavy rays, nose-brow pieces, outer eyes, mouth, cheeks and chin and forehead circles orange; let dry.

To assemble, mark eight equidistant points around outer edge of blue circle. Nail a triangular ray on front of blue circle with point outward and at edge of circle as shown; repeat around at each marked point. Place wavy rays, all going in same direction, overlapping and between triangular rays as shown; nail in place. Nail features in place on head circle. Center head circle on background circle over rays and nail. Countersink all nails which show on front; fill holes with plastic wood; sand flat and touch up with thinned paint.

Beaded Strawberry Basket

As sparkling as morning dew, a basket of berries and buds to center your breakfast table. The beads are strung on wire, bent into shape; the flowers and foliage are arranged in a small ceramic basket.

EQUIPMENT: Jeweler's pliers. Wire cutter. Ruler. Scissors. Thumbtack.

MATERIALS: Green floral tape, one roll. Green-covered stem wires, 16-gauge, one package, 12″ long (42 in pack). Silver-colored beading wire, 28-gauge, one 69-gram spool. Round beads, size 11/0 bunches, in following colors: One bunch (consisting of twelve 20″ strands) each of opaque white, yellow, light red; two bunches each of transparent chartreuse and medium green. Small amount of floral clay or green styrofoam, and artificial floral moss. Small, white ceramic basket.

Note: Basket as shown is made up of approximately 36 leaves, eight strawberries, four flowers, and two buds.

DIRECTIONS: Beaded flowers are made by stringing beads onto wire and shaping wire into petals, centers, leaves, etc. Unwind about one yard of 28-gauge wire; wrap once at that point around thumbtack pushed into one end of wire spool (this keeps remaining wire neatly on spool). Carefully pull one strand of beads from bunch; knot thread at one end. At other end of strand, insert end of wire through five to six beads at a time and carefully pull thread out. Continue until wire is filled with appropriate color and number of beads (see individual directions below): knot or crimp wire at threading end. Do not cut beaded wire from spool; flower shaping is done directly from spool. If you should run out of beads before you finish a flower, unwind enough wire to finish flower plus 6″ extra; cut from spool and thread beads on at cut end. Be sure to keep beadwork close and tight.

The following are basic techniques for shaping flowers from wire threaded with required number of beads. Refer to individual directions for number and color of beads needed to make the specific pieces shown in color illustration.

Single Loop Petals: Slide desired number of beads up to within three inches of knotted end of wire; shape beaded wire into loop; cross bare wires and twist together twice. Continue making number of loops needed, twisting wires between each loop. Leave 4″ bare wire and cut from spool.

Double Loop Petals: Make first loop as for Single Loop Petals. Slide up twice as many beads as for first loop. Encircle first loop with larger loop of beaded wire; twist wire around base of petal. Continue making number of double loop petals needed as above.

Crossed 3-Row Petals: Make a single loop as for Single Loop Petals. Push up half as many beads as for first loop. Bring beaded wire up face of loop and between top two beads of loop; carry bare wire down back of loop. Flatten petal so bare wire does not show. Twist wire around base of petal.

Pointed Leaf: Slide five or six beads up to within 3″ of knot end. Below beads, make bare wire loop of about 6″ and twist wire several times. Slide up to loop the same number of beads as in first row plus four or two additional beads, for wider or narrower leaf respectively. Curve this row up and around one side of first row and loop wire onto bare wire just above beads. Slide up number of beads in second row plus two or four additional beads. Bend down on other side of first row and twist around original twist. Continue to make rows, adding two or four beads to each and bending to alternate sides; finish at loop end, which will be stem. Cut wire from spool 4″ from beading; cut knot end of wire ½″ from beads and bend down to back. Flatten and shape leaf. Using basic techniques, follow individual directions below for specific flowers:

YELLOW AND WHITE FLOWERS: Stamen: Use yellow opaque beads. For each flower, cut four pieces of beading wire, each approximately 1″ long. Twist one end of each wire into a small loop to prevent beads from falling off. Thread four beads into each piece; twist together the four bottom bare sections of wire partially forming the stem.

Petals: Use white opaque beads. For each flower, make four continuous petals, using double loop technique. Each inner loop is made of 11 beads; outer loop is made of 24 beads.

Twist wire ends together, forming partial stem; cut from spool. Place twisted wire ends of stamen in center of four white petals; twist both sets of wire together, forming partial stem.

WHITE BUDS WITH GREEN PETALS: Buds: Use white opaque beads. For each bud, make four continuous petals using technique for Crossed 3-Row Petals. Use 15 beads for loop; use 5 beads for crossed row of petal.

Twist wire ends together, forming partial stem; cut from spool.

Petals: Use transparent chartreuse beads. For each bud, make a set of four continuous loops for petals, using technique for Single Loop Petals. Use 12 beads for each loop.

Twist wire ends together, forming partial stem; cut from spool. Place one white bud in center of each set of chartreuse loops. Twist bottom wires together to form partial stem.

Leaves: Use chartreuse and medium green beads and technique for Pointed Leaf. Make three different size leaves by working varying numbers of rows.

STRAWBERRIES AND PETALS: Strawberries: Use red opaque beads and Pointed Leaf technique. Use three beads for inside center of strawberry and 7 beads around each side. Add another row, using approximately 10 beads on each side. Continue making rows, adding two beads to each row for about seven rows to form a cone shape.

Twist wire ends together, forming partial stem; cut from spool.

Petals: Use medium green beads. For each strawberry, make a set of four continuous loops for petals, using technique for Single Loop Petals; use 18 beads for each loop.

Twist wire ends together, forming partial stem; cut from spool. Insert one strawberry into center of each set of loops. Twist bottom wires to form partial stem.

To Assemble: Cut stem wire to length desired. Hold flower, bud, berry, or larger leaf to end of stem; cut off bead wires at slightly varying lengths to make smooth stem joining. Wrap smoothly and thinly with floral tape; add smaller leaves to stem as desired while continuing wrapping to bottom of stem.

Fill small, white ceramic basket with floral clay or styrofoam; cover with artificial moss. Arrange flowers, buds, leaves, and strawberries as pictured.

Indian Beadwork Bags

Indian beadwork adds charm to these attractive and easy-to-make chamois skin bags, which first appeared in the 1919 edition of McCall's Embroidery Book. *A fun accessory for today, the small bag shown here is approximately 6½" x 7¾"; the larger one is 7¼" x 9".*

EQUIPMENT: Paper for patterns. Tracing paper. Pencil. Scissors. Ruler. Beading needle. Sewing needle. Artgum eraser.

MATERIALS: Chamois, about 18" x 23" for each bag. Indian seed beads: for large bag, 5 bottles red, 6 bottles blue, 3 bottles green, 7 bottles white; for small bag, 6 bottles white, 6 bottles blue, 2 bottles red, 2 bottles green. Spool white beadcraft thread. Rubber cement.

DIRECTIONS: Enlarge half-patterns by copying on paper ruled in 1" squares; finish top portion of large bag pattern. Using tracing paper, trace over enlarged pattern. Turn tracing over and go over lines with pencil on wrong side. Mark the size of bag front on chamois; for small bag, mark and cut chamois 6½" x 7¾"; for large bag, mark and cut chamois 7¼" x 9". Handle chamois carefully, as it soils very easily.

Place border pattern ⅜" in from edges of chamois for front, at one bottom corner and trace side and half of bottom border onto chamois. Complete borders along bottom and opposite side by flopping pattern and retracing. Place center half-pattern on front and trace pattern to transfer design. Flop pattern over, match dash line and trace again to complete circle.

Dots on patterns indicate the number of beads in row and direction of rows across areas. Follow outlines of patterns and color illustration for bead colors.

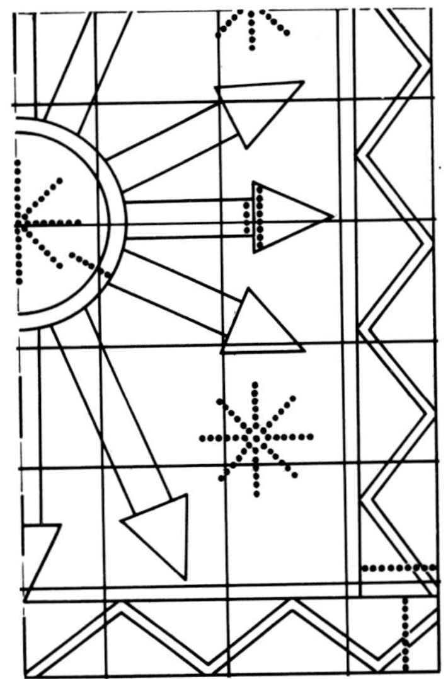

To bead, knot thread and bring needle up to front of chamois on first line of beading. String on number of beads indicated to fill line; insert needle to back at opposite end of line. Do not pull thread too tight, or string of beads will buckle. Make a small couching stitch over thread between each bead. Be careful to keep spacing of beads even, and strings of beads straight. This can be accomplished in the couching. The white beads are sometimes slightly larger than the other colors, so some adjustments may be necessary in the spacing or number of the other-color beads. It is best to practice the beading of rows in diamond shapes before starting on the project. Fasten the thread on back after every two or three rows. Bead center design first. Then work borders, making rows of beads as indicated by dotted lines on patterns.

Cut another piece of chamois for back, the same size as front. To line bag, cut two pieces of chamois ¼″ smaller all around than outside pieces. Apply rubber cement to wrong side of one lining piece and wrong side of bag front; let cement dry. Carefully press the cemented sides of pieces together. Repeat with other lining piece on bag back. With wrong sides of front and back together, sew sides and bottom edges together with close buttonhole stitches ⅛″ long, leaving about 1½″ at top of each side open. Turn in ⅛″ of front around top and side openings, pressing cemented sides together.

Sew beads in loops over side and bottom seams and around both sides of top opening edges. To make loops, attach thread at one side of seam, string on five beads for small bag and seven beads for large bag loops; take a stitch diagonally over seam so beads form a loop; bring needle out opposite the end of the loop, on other side of seam. Continue in this manner, making loops, using two or three colors of beads for each loop. Make loop edge the same over top edges of the purse.

For fringe at bottom, attach thread at one corner, string on about ⅞″ of each of three colors of beads. Push strung beads up to bottom of bag; thread on another bead, then run needle back up through all beads and secure thread inside at bottom of bag. String bead fringe in this manner across bottom, making the beaded strands as close together as possible.

To make drawstring, cut four strips of chamois each ⅝″ x 23″ long; it will be necessary to seam two strips together for each drawstring; make overlapping seams as smooth as possible and sew with small stitches. Cut six vertical slits in top portion of bag, starting 1″ from open side edges and spacing them 1″ apart, on both front and back. Run one drawstring in and out of slits from one side edge, around bag, and end at same side. Even up strings and tie ends together. Run other string through slits from opposite side.

To clean bag, work over chamois surface with Artgum eraser and soft clean brush.

Flower Basket Picture in Cardboard

Cardboard cutouts in simple shapes are mounted on canvas for a lovely still life. Strips of cardboard are woven and glued for the basket shape; flowers and leaves are textured with modeling paste and cloth.

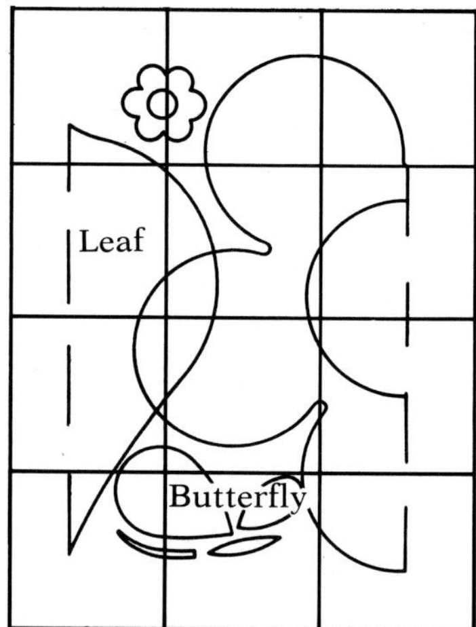

EQUIPMENT: Paper for patterns. Pencil. Ruler. Scissors. One small pointed paintbrush for paint. One large flat paintbrush for gesso and lacquer. Rags.

MATERIALS: Stretched 9″ x 12″ canvas. Liquid gesso. Thin cardboard. Acrylic or poster paints. Clear lacquer. Cheesecloth. All-purpose white glue. Frame, 9″ x 12″, rabbet size.

DIRECTIONS: Buy canvas already stretched, or stretch canvas yourself. Canvas board may also be used.

To make basket, cut eleven 5″ x ¼″ strips of cardboard; weave strips together with eight strips going in a horizontal direction and three vertically. Glue strips together. When dry, cut into basket shape measuring 5″ at top and 3″ at bottom. Glue onto canvas, referring to illustration.

To make flowers, enlarge patterns by copying on paper ruled in 1″ squares; complete half-patterns indicated by long dash lines. Cut pieces out of cardboard. Texture large flowers by gluing a layer of cheesecloth on petals. Glue cardboard circle at center. Texture small flowers and leaves with glue, allowing several layers to build up. Glue flowers, leaves and butterfly to canvas, following illustration, or arranging as desired. Allow glue to dry completely.

Paint entire piece with gesso, getting it into all crevices. When dry, paint with acrylic paints as illustrated or as desired; let dry. Lacquer piece and let dry. Antique piece with equal parts of brown and black paint mixed with water, brushing it on and wiping off excess with clean rag. When dry, lacquer again. Frame as shown in illustration or as desired.

Decoupage Treasures

Antique and elegant, the craft of decoupage has renewed popularity today. Tiny cutouts, applied to a surface, are covered with many coats of varnish and gently sanded until they blend into the surface and have a softly mellowed patina. Branches of berries, flowers, and Oriental prints decorate our collection of decoupage, but the possibilities for finding interesting cutouts are endless—flower and bird prints, museum and art store reproductions, even children's books! The only requirement is that the paper quality be good. The thin paper of magazines should not be used, because, when you start to varnish, the print from the other side may bleed through. But once you have found your cutouts, the how-to's are simple—you add the creativity when you plan your design!

EQUIPMENT: Scissors: small, straight-bladed and curved cuticle. Mat knife or single-edged razor blade. Sponge, cut into small squares. Tack cloth. Brayer. Ruler. Soft cloths. Brushes: small, soft for gluing; small, flat for paint and varnish. Containers for glue, water, and varnish; coffee can with plastic top for solvent to clean brushes. Sandpaper and steel wool, see directions.

MATERIALS: Objects for decoupage. Paper prints for designs. Gold paper or other trims desired. Oil- or water-based colored pencils, watercolors, or acrylic paints (see directions). Sealer such as clear acrylic spray. Decoupage paste or all-purpose white glue. Denatured alcohol. Paint or stain to cover object. Solvent. Matte and/or semi-gloss varnish for interior woods. Small amount detergent. Pumice powder. Small amount lemon or linseed oil. Fine furniture wax. Rubber cement.

DIRECTIONS: The beginning step of decoupage is selection of the object to be decorated. Although almost any surface may be used, we will mention only wood and metal. The surface may be raw, painted, or varnished, old or new, as long as it is properly prepared before decorating. For a beginning project, a simple shape is recommended—a plaque, a rectangular box, a light switch plate, a tray, or a planter.

Selecting Prints: Keeping your object in mind, select decorations for it. Collect many so you can then select exactly what you want. Any extras can be used for future decoupage projects. Paper prints—color for modern decoupage or black and white for traditional—are recommended and thin paper is best to use. Sources include books, especially old ones; new and old prints; greeting cards; magazines; calendars; pictures from fine coloring books; catalogs; and many others. It is best to avoid wallpaper, postcards, photographs, fabrics, printed embossed wrapping paper, and any prints that bleed. As in any craft, do not waste your time using cheap materials that only make all your work very temporary. You may use pictures that have printing on both sides, but be sure to seal the wrong side (see directions below) so it won't show through. For your own original decoupage design, combine elements, taking one or more parts from several prints. Do not be afraid to mix nursery rhyme characters with botanical prints if the need arises. Above all, choose what is suitable for the space of the object at hand.

Coloring Prints: If your prints are black on white, as is traditional for classic decoupage, you must first color your prints. Use oil- or water-based colored pencils, watercolors, or thinly applied acrylic paints, each for its own effect. Do not use opaque colors as they obliterate the outlines of the prints. For applying flat planes of color, use color evenly within the shape. For modeling areas, begin coloring with the lightest value (for a pencil, the lightest pressure). Do not try to use all colors on one design; limit your palette to make your job easier. Keep paints very thin to avoid leaving any texture. Use your finger to smooth out pencil marks in areas colored with pencils.

Sealing Prints: To prevent damage to your print during the gluing operation, it must be sealed. Sealing strengthens the paper and prevents discoloration. The easiest sealer to use is a clear acrylic spray readily available in hobby, photography, and art supply stores. Spray each side of your print two or three times, allowing each coat to dry before the next. Or you can use one or two coats of shellac.

Cutting: When the print is thoroughly dry, you are ready for cutting, the most important step in the process. Take all the time you need and use the best scissors. Using small, straight-bladed scissors, such as embroidery scissors, cut away the excess paper around the design area. Then use curved cuticle scissors to cut out the design. Scissors are held in relaxed manner by the thumb and middle finger with the curved blade resting on the index finger and pointing away from the edge to be cut. Feed the print into the scissors, keeping the scissors moving in a steady rhythm with small cuts. It is usually best to first cut away interior space in the design. Holding the scissors underneath the design, punch a tiny hole to insert the scissor's blade, then trim. Finally, cut around the contour of the shape.

Preparing the Object: Now you must prepare the surface of the object to be decorated. If the object is hinged or decorated with other hardware, remove it if possible. Prepare the surface as outlined below.

Raw Wood: Sand first with #100 garnet paper. Sink any nailheads and fill any cracks with wood or vinyl filler. Sand with #220 garnet paper. Dust with tack cloth. If wood is to be stained, see below.

Painted Wood: For a badly painted piece, remove the previous paint, using paint remover and putty knife. When finished, wash with denatured alcohol; let dry, and treat as for raw wood. For a well-painted piece, remove grease by washing the object with turpentine or mineral spirits. Lightly sand surface. If filler is needed, fill and sand down, but shellac this area to seal it.

Varnished Wood: Wash with denatured alcohol; sand to provide surface texture; however, there is no need to get to bare wood.

New Metal: Clean with denatured alcohol, then use oil-based primer to prevent rust and provide painting base. Allow to dry overnight; use second coat if necessary. You can treat your hardware in this manner.

New Painted Metal: If paint is in good condition, do not remove; wash with denatured alcohol; sand if surface is glossy.

Old Painted Metal: Use wire scraper, steel wool, emery cloth and/or rust remover to eliminate rust. Wash with denatured alcohol; apply one coat metal primer. Let dry overnight; sand lightly.

When the object is prepared, it is ready to be finished. If it is wood and you want it stained only, use a water-soluble alcohol-based stain or water-diluted acrylic paint. Sponge or brush on in direction of wood grain. Let dry completely. When dry, seal with two coats of shellac diluted half with denatured alcohol or seal with acrylic polymer medium; let each coat dry before applying the second.

If the object is metal or wood and is to be painted, use flat enamel paints, mixing to get the color desired. If paint is too thick, dilute with solvent so paint will level out flat when applied. Depending on the surface, the object will probably require three or four coats of paint. Do not use same brush used for shellac. Let each coat dry before the next, sanding each coat smoothly before applying the next. When painted surface is smooth and richly covered, enough coats have been applied. Clean paintbrush in solvent, then wipe with solvent-dipped rag; finally wash with warm water and soap. Shape bristles flat and smooth, and allow to dry.

Gluing Design: Arrange placement of your design on the object. Use a drop of rubber cement to hold pieces in place. Arrange, add, eliminate but make the most of your design for all this work. Try not to overlap designs as this adds thickness. When you have decided on the arrangement, use paste or white glue to permanently affix the design, beginning with the largest elements; fine trims are last. Decoupage paste is easier to use in that it is water soluble when dried so excess may be wiped off after drying (excess of white glue must be wiped off before drying). Apply glue sparingly, thinning with water if necessary; use camel hair brush or fingers to spread it thinly on the reverse side of the design, or on the immediate area of the object itself, whichever is easier. With clean fingers, put design in place, smoothing it from the center out to the edges, being careful to leave no air bubbles; you can roll over it with brayer, the end of a round paint brush or even a cylindrical water glass. After design has set a few minutes, use small pieces of damp sponge to remove all of excess glue. If a spot needs a bit more glue, use a toothpick to add it. If there is an air bubble, slice into it carefully with razor blade, insert glue on toothpick, then smooth down firmly. Be sure every edge of every piece is glued firmly. Let all glue dry thoroughly. If design pieces overlap where box opens, slit around opening with razor blade.

Finishing: Now you are ready to varnish. Select a good brush of the appropriate size for the object (½″-2″), tack cloth, a glass jar for the varnish, a coffee can to hold the brush, and supports to suspend the object evenly at all times. Use either matte or semi-gloss varnish depending upon finish desired. Varnish has a short shelf life and once the can is open, varnish tends to form a layer of skin on the top surface, therefore it is best to use small-size cans. Transfer the varnish to a jar, then turn the jar upside down to keep the layer formed on the bottom of the varnish. The addition of a thin layer of solvent on top of the varnish is an excellent way to prevent varnish from hardening.

Use a razor to cut small X in plastic top of coffee can. Suspend brush in solvent up to the ferrule. As for any brush, do not let bristles rest on the bottom of the can. Every once in a while, clean brush thoroughly as you did for the other brushes.

Dip the brush halfway into the varnish, pressing brush against the sides of the can or jar to remove excess without allowing air bubbles to form (do not scrape brush across the top as this makes more bubbles). Apply the varnish in long, slow strokes all in the same direction. Use ample varnish to cover but not enough to run or sag. If a bristle gets caught, pick it up with your brush held almost horizontally. Check for drips and brush them out or use solvent-dampened cloth; check the bottom edges especially. The most important task is keeping air bubbles out, for once dried in, they are permanent. If you seem to be having trouble, thin the varnish with solvent, one part solvent to eight parts varnish. As this stiffens the varnish, you must brush it on harder in one direction; then, holding the brush vertically, lightly (with just the tip) brush in the other direction. After each coat of varnish is applied, allow 24 hours to dry regardless of directions for the varnish itself.

Before each successive coat, dust with tack cloth. After about ten coats, begin sanding process. Use #400 wet or dry sandpaper and a bit of detergent. Wet the sandpaper and the object, then sand along the grain of wood, adding detergent to help eliminate small scratches. Sand well, but not down to the design or through the paint at the edges of the box. Clean object with damp sponge; let dry. Then apply six to ten more varnish coats before sanding again. Sanding is to lower the level over the design, but not around it; to imbed it, cover with successive varnish coats. If necessary, sand after every 5-6 coats of varnish and continue until smooth; it is unlikely you can apply too many coats of varnish. For the final sandings use #0000 steel wool. The final varnishing is two coats (24 hours apart) of matte varnish. Then rub with steel wool to smooth the surface. (Note: Traditional decoupage is not antiqued. If subtle antique coloring is desired, use antique glaze before applying last two varnish coats.)

To eliminate faint scratches made by steel wool, mix light paste of pumice (or rottenstone) powder with lemon or linseed oil. Rub on with soft cloth. Finally, polish with fine furniture wax. Do not put anything on top of the object for a month afterward, as it still needs maturing time.

If your object is a box, varnish the inside with several coats. Paint the inside or line the box with fabric, wallpaper, marbleized paper, etc. Remount hardware.

Dressing Old Prints

Prints of ladies' long-ago fashions are easy to dress! Cut dresses from old fabric and lace scraps, using the print for patterns. Back the fabric with buckram, then gather and drape it into shape and glue to the print. Deep frames create a shadow-box effect. The print shown is taken from Godey's Lady's Book; *other old prints can be found in antique and second-hand shops.*

EQUIPMENT: Scissors. Single-edged razor blade. Tracing paper. Pencil. Needle. Thick cardboard at least as large as prints. Straight pins. Small flat paintbrush. Tack hammer. Sandpaper. Small paint roller. Triangle. Steel-edged ruler.

MATERIALS: For Picture: Godey or other fashion prints about 8" x 10" for two-figure prints; 12" x 13½" for five-figure prints. Scraps of fabrics such as satin, velvet, taffeta, silk, embroidered eyelet, organdy, etc., in various colors. Bits of lace, ribbon, braid, buttons, beads, and small artificial flowers. Buckram or crinoline. Thread to match fabrics and trims. All-purpose glue.

For Frame: Illustration board or matting board. Flat oil base paint, pale pink or desired color. Casein or flat water base paint, off-white and white. Wooden frames, one deep and one narrow for each picture: 9" x 12" rabbet size for two-figure prints; 14" x 16" rabbet size for five-figure prints. White velvet ribbon ½" wide, enough to go around rabbet. Small brads ½" long. Glass to fit rabbet of frame. All-purpose glue.

PICTURES: Trace outline of gowns from figures in prints, marking bodice, sleeves, and skirt separately. Cut buckram or crinoline for each part, using traced patterns. Cover buckram pieces with suitable fabrics, similar to those shown in print; leave extra fabric all around buckram; drape and gather fabric to form style shown in print, tacking fabric to buckram. When one gown overlaps another, leave a little extra fabric for folding over softly. Sew on cuffs, lace ruffles, braid trims, etc., as indicated on print; sew ruffled lace under skirt for petticoat. Turn extra fabric to wrong side of buckram, fitting snugly on bodice piece and turning loosely and draping on other pieces for softness. Baste fabric to wrong side of buckram.

Place print on a piece of cardboard. With razor, carefully cut around hands and part of arm if it overlaps any part of gown; lift arm carefully. Place skirt on print, holding in place with pins pushed through fabric and into cardboard; pin bodice and sleeve in place, carefully lifting arm and placing it over gowns. Sew gown to print with running stitches taken at sides so they do not show on front. When pieces are sewn in place, remove print from cardboard. Glue lace, ribbons, and flowers onto print to trim hair or hats.

FRAMES: For mat, use illustration or matting board (illustration board is easier to cut). Using right-angle triangle for marking and steel-edged ruler and razor for cutting, cut mat 10" x 13" for small prints, 15" x 17" for large prints. Measure size of picture area to be utilized (length and width) and deduct these measurements from size of mat. Divide the remainder of width to get equal margins at sides; top margin is the same as sides; bottom margin is usually wider to give pleasing balance. Mark this area on mat, using triangle, and cut out with razor and steel-edged ruler. Using oil base paint and roller, paint mat. When dry, place mat over print, lifting any part of gown that will extend over mat. Glue mat to print.

Sand both frames smooth with medium, then fine sandpaper. Give both frames a coat of off-white paint; let dry. Turn deep frame back to front (this is the way it will be used to create a shadow-box effect). Glue lace around deep frame at top outside edge (use a bold-patterned lace so the design will show up and look like carving when painted). When dry, apply another coat of off-white paint, making it rather thick over lace, but not thick enough to clog holes; let dry. Now paint irregularly over both frames with white paint; let dry 12 hours. Rub down with steel wool or very fine sandpaper to bring the undercoat up through the white. Do not overdo the rubbing; let some areas remain untouched.

Glue white velvet ribbon along rabbet of deep frame, folding it in half lengthwise to fit in groove of rabbet and on both sides.

Attach glass to narrow frame inside the rabbet, holding in place with two small brads on each side. Glue narrow frame to top of deep frame.

Fit matted print to back of deep frame. Cover back of print with white paper. Seal to frame with strips of masking tape.

Battenberg Lace

Battenberg lace (sometimes called Renaissance lace) was a popular form of lacemaking in the years around 1900. Using a variety of tapes or braids manufactured for the purpose, the enthusiastic amateur could imitate some of the traditional laces made entirely by hand; tape was laid along the lines of a pattern and the spaces then filled in with lace stitches. We have revived the technique by enlarging and simplifying the design of an old Battenberg-lace doily, shown in black and white. As the delicate Battenberg braids are no longer generally available, we used guimpe braid and worked the stitches in pearl cotton. Our 15" design was appliquéd to a velvet pillow.

EQUIPMENT: Paper for pattern. Tracing paper. Soft pencil. Ruler. India ink. Fine-pointed drawing pen. Straight pins. Embroidery scissors. Crisp-finish lining material, piece about 23" square, in color contrasting to braid. Basting thread, pastel color. Sewing needle. Blunt-pointed needle. Compass.

MATERIALS: Guimpe braid ½"wide, white, 8 yds. Pearl cotton #3, white, 4 skeins. White sewing thread. Clear colorless nail polish or all-purpose glue. Round pillow form, 16", with 2" boxing. Blue velvet, 36" wide, ⅔ yd. Blue sewing thread.

DIRECTIONS: Lace Appliqué: Enlarge quarter-pattern by copying on paper ruled in 1" squares. Draw a cross in center of tracing paper and trace quarter-pattern four times around intersection to complete pattern. Pin lining material to paper pattern and trace onto fabric with India ink and fine-pointed drawing pen. Unpin and discard paper pattern. Cut pieces of braid, indicated by number on pattern: No. 1—8 pieces, each 7" long; No. 2—4 pieces, 7¾" long; No. 3—4 pieces, 10" long; No. 4—4 pieces, 20¾" long; No. 5—1 piece, 64" long. Seal ends with colorless nail polish or all-purpose glue; blot off excess. Starting with outer edge of design, pin braid pieces to fabric pattern—No. 1 pieces first, then No. 2 and No. 3 pieces, then No. 4 pieces, overlapping ends as you go (the ends of No. 1 pieces will just touch outer edge of No. 4 pieces). Pin on No. 5 piece last, in one continuous piece for center cross, folding braid over at four points of design.

Baste braid to fabric pattern with a zigzag stitch, so that both inner and outer edges are firmly anchored. Using blunt-pointed needle, run white sewing thread through all inside-curving edges, passing needle through spaces between loops at edge of braid; do not go through fabric pattern. Every inch or so, hold braid down with finger and tug gently at thread so that braid conforms to curves of pattern and lies flat. Sew together, touching and overlapping edges of braid.

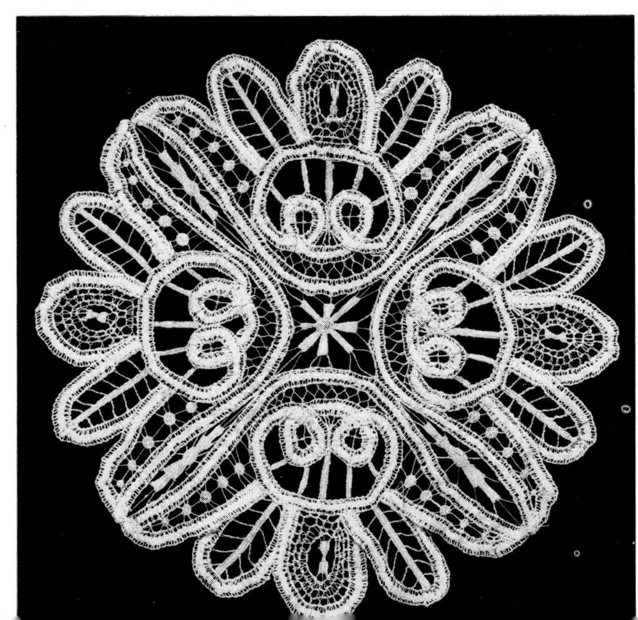

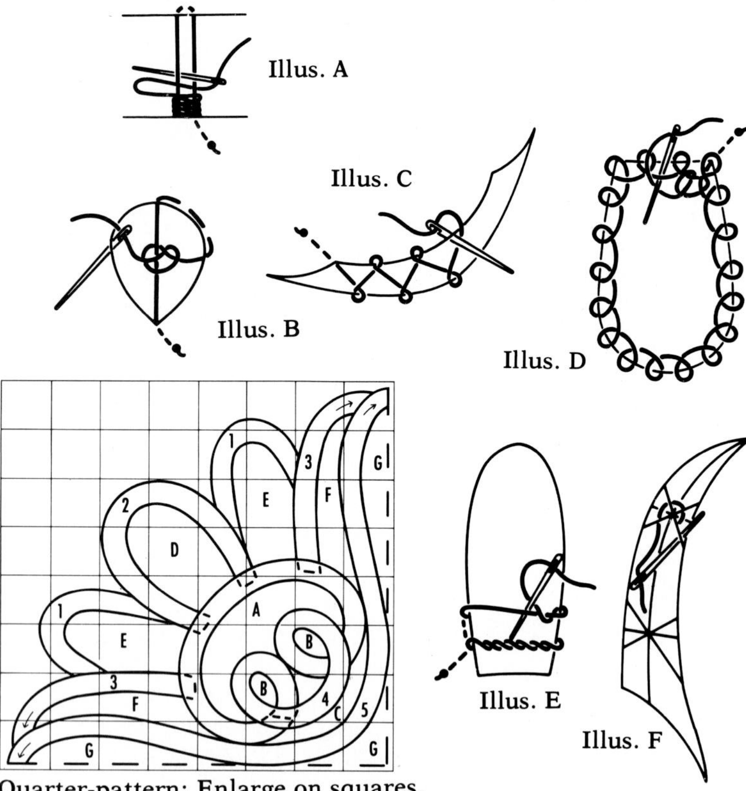

Quarter-pattern: Enlarge on squares.

Make lace stitches (see details above) with white pearl cotton and blunt-pointed needle. Pass needle through loops at edge of braid; do not go through pattern. Knot end of each new thread and weave through braid before starting stitch; end thread by weaving back and forth through braid (unless otherwise indicated). For lace designs in each braid area, see letters on quarter-pattern and corresponding stitch details. Follow illustration for placement of lace designs. Practice each lace design first before working actual piece. When all stitches are completed, carefully snip basting thread from underneath pattern and lift off lace appliqué.

Pillow: From blue velvet, cut two circles 17″ in diameter; cut two strips 3″ x 26½″ for boxing. Sew ends of strips together with ½″ seams. Sew boxing strip to one circle (top) with ½″ seams. Notch seam allowances every ½″. Center lace appliqué on top and tack down carefully. Sew other circle to boxing strip two-thirds way around; notch seam allowances. Insert pillow form; with tiny stitches, blind-stitch remainder of pillow cover.

BATTENBERG STITCHES: A—Darning Stitch: Place two tacking threads close together. Weave over and under threads alternately, back and forth, pressing down on each new stitch with finger to flatten and keep stitches close.

B—Knots: Make a cross, knotting second leg of cross around first leg where they intersect in the center.

C—Herringbone Stitch: Pass needle from under upper braid through top of lower braid, then back through top of upper braid, crossing over first stitch. Continue in this manner. Leave one loop of braid between each upper stitch and place lower stitch exactly opposite this loop.

D—Tulle Stitch and Darning Stitch: Make a row of loops around opening, crossing threads as for Herringbone Stitch (see C). At end of row, wrap thread around first loop and make a second row of loops, working in opposite direction; make loops smaller and skip over corner loops of first row. When second row is completed, run thread through all inside loops and pull up slightly, pressing down on work.

Place three tacking threads across open space lengthwise, crossing the two outer ones at center. Weave a triangle in Darning Stitch (see A) to intersection of tacking threads; wrap thread around twice at center; weave second triangle.

E—Overcast Bars and Darning Stitch: Stretch tacking thread from one side of braid to opposite side. Return to starting side by wrapping thread four or five times around tacking thread, holding stitch down with finger as you go. Make six Overcast Bars at even intervals across space.

Place two tacking threads close together down center of space lengthwise, weaving in and out of Overcast Bars. Starting from top, weave over threads in Darning Stitch.

F—Wheels: Place seven tacking threads as shown. To begin each wheel, knot end of a new thread and anchor at intersection by splitting one tacking thread. For top wheel, weave in and out for one round. For bottom wheel, make two rounds, passing thread over or under two adjacent spokes at once when beginning second round. To end off, pass thread back through wheel.

G—Wheels and Darning Stitch: Place tacking threads as shown in illustration on page 411, starting with two long threads that intersect at center of design, then go through the braid and extend to four points of cross design. At each of four point areas, place three short tacking threads, all crossing at center over long thread. At center of design, place four short tacking threads, all crossing at center of design. At each intersection of threads, work a 3-row wheel (see F); do not end thread; continue design by weaving triangular section beyond wheel. Carefully pass thread through stitches made and work another triangular section—four sections at center of cross design, two sections at each point.

Soap Staffordshire Dogs

Staffordshire dogs, favorite Victorian ornaments, were used to grace mantlepieces and end tables. This appealing pair reproduces the original ceramic antiques—but they are carved from soap! The snowy white dogs are an example of the once-popular art of soap carving. Patterns are traced on large bars of soap and then carefully carved with a knife. Breakage can be easily remedied with a tiny bit of melted soap. The curly "hair" on each dog is made by pushing on the finished sculpture with the rounded end of a desk pen; color accents—brown eyes, bright ties, yellow name tags—are painted on.

EQUIPMENT: Pencil. Tracing paper. Felt-tipped ink marker. For modeling: 2 orangewood sticks with pointed ends; 1 knife with medium-length blade; 1 case or pocket knife, or any other tool with a small, thin pointed blade. Object with blunt, well-rounded point, such as the tip of a desk pen. Lid from shallow box or tray for work area. Fine-pointed paintbrush. Small bowl for melting soap.

MATERIALS: For two dogs, 3 large cakes of white soap (3" x 4½"). Watercolor paints.

DIRECTIONS: Trace patterns on page 414. Because entire bar of soap is needed for sculpture, it is necessary to fill all indentations of soap. Shave pieces from extra bar of soap into bowl of hot water. When shavings soften, press into soap bar so that no markings are visible. Let dry overnight. Holding patterns against soap, outline dog with pointed orangewood stick; press hard so that outline will show. When dog is completely outlined, use felt-tipped marking pen to accent lines on soap.

With knife, cut away the soap up to the dotted line indicated on patterns. Do the same with front and back. The result should be a rough silhouette of the dog.

Using smaller tools, work carefully down to the actual form of the pattern. Cut off only a little soap at a time; turn your sculpture often, comparing each side with its corresponding pattern.

NOTE: If a piece breaks off, it may be mended with a small part of a toothpick or a sliver of wood as follows: First, scoop out a small opening in both the dog and the broken part. Then insert the wood in the dog, leaving a small end projecting. Next, soften shavings of soap as indicated above. Take a small amount on the point of a knife and fill the small, scooped-out openings. Press broken parts together and allow the sculpture to harden for a few hours. Test piece gently to be sure that pieces are adhered thoroughly.

When dog is complete, let stand for a day or two to set before putting on markings. For markings, use blunt, rounded object (desk pen tip). Press slight but firm indentations over head, body and tail to represent the curly hair of dog. With watercolors paint eyes brown, lashes black; outline nose and mouth in black; make dots for whiskers in black. Paint ribbon around neck in your favorite color; name tag is yellow; base on which dogs sits is black.

When soap carvings become soiled, clean by wiping carefully with damp cloth. Do not put in water.

Actual-size patterns for front, back, top, and sides of dogs.

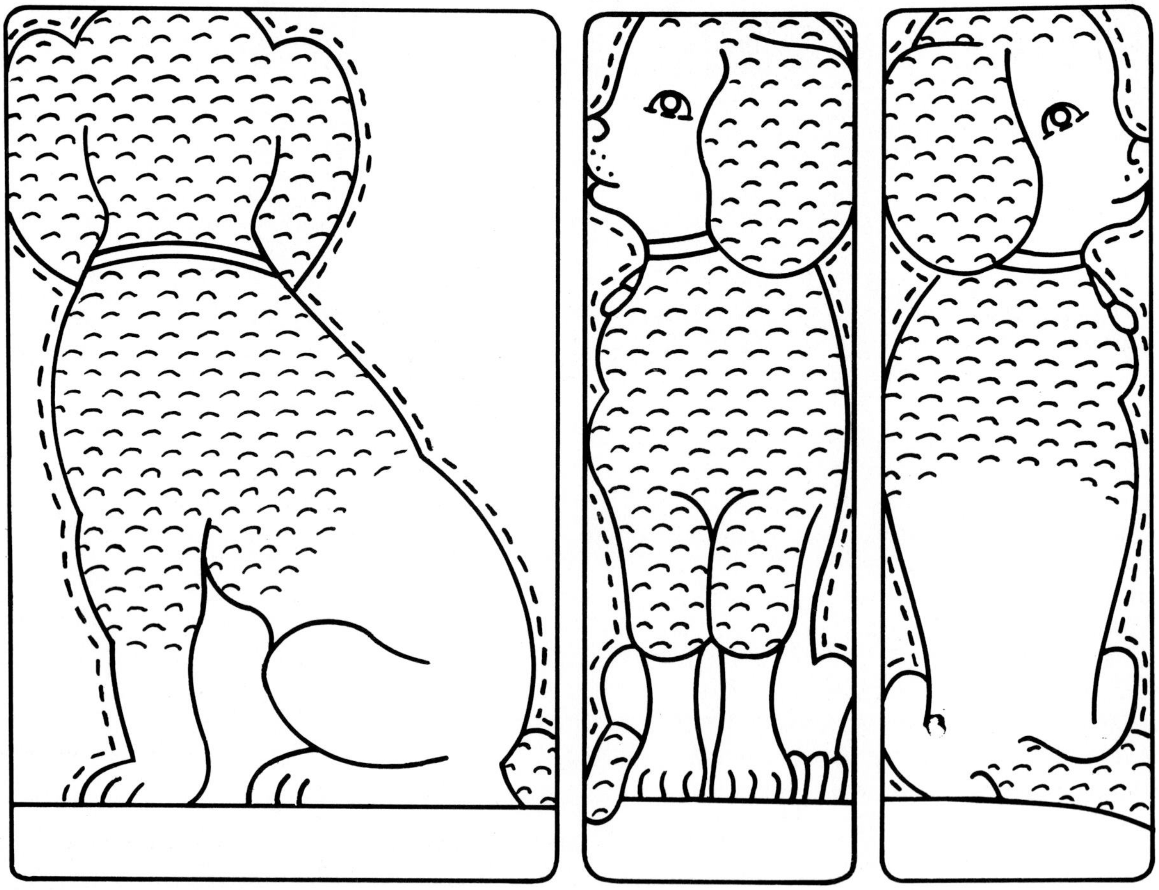

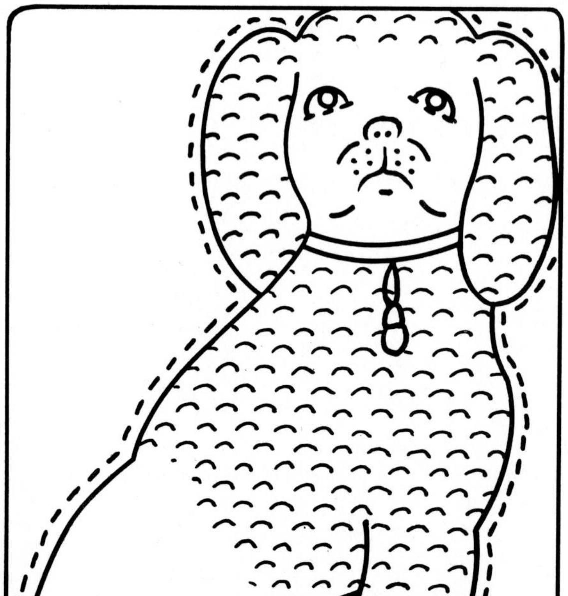

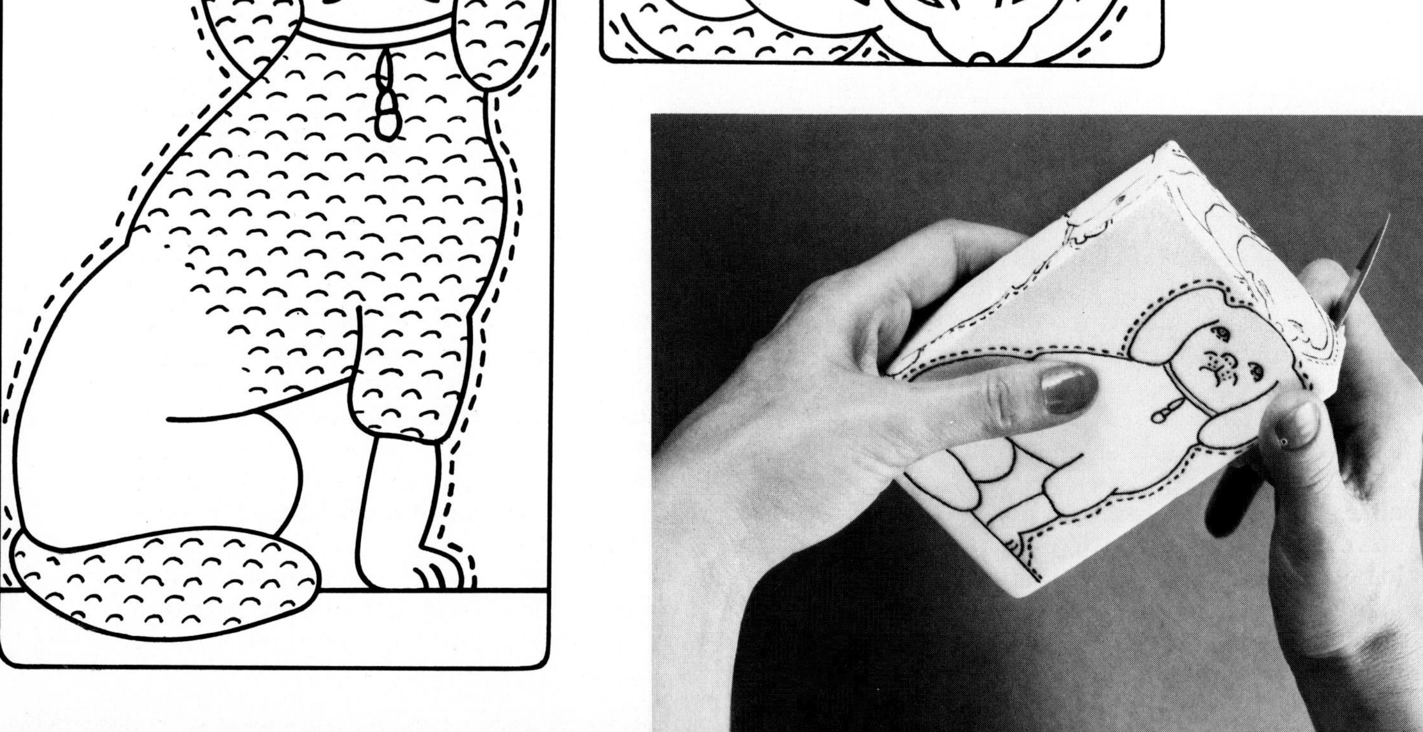

Additional How-To's

TO ENLARGE AND REDUCE DESIGNS

There are various ways of enlarging or reducing designs so that all parts remain in proportion. The most commonly used are the "square" method, No. 1, and the diagonal method, No. 2. (Designs can also be enlarged or reduced by photostat, wherever such services are available.)

Method 1: If design is not already marked off in squares, make a tracing of original design. Mark off tracing with squares, ⅛″ for small designs and ¼″, ½″, or 1″ for proportionately larger designs. On paper, mark the same number of squares, similarly placed, in the space to be occupied by the enlarged design. For instance, if you want to make the original design twice as high and twice as wide, make the squares twice as large. Copy design from smaller squares. Reverse procedure for reducing design to size needed.

Method 2: Make a tracing of original design. Draw a rectangle to fit around it. Draw a second rectangle of same proportions to fit desired size of design. Draw diagonals from corner to corner of each rectangle, as illustrated. In each rectangle, the point where diagonals meet is the center. Draw horizontal and vertical lines to divide each rectangle equally. Copy design from smaller divisions in corresponding larger divisions.

Method 3: To enlarge or reduce a magazine illustration easily and quickly, halve and quarter the original picture as indicated in figure. Mark the dimensions for actual-size design on plain paper. On illustration to be copied, draw vertical and horizontal lines 1-1 to halve and quarter picture. Draw lines 2-2 to divide picture into 16 equal parts. Draw lines 3-3 vertically and horizontally to divide picture into 64 equal sections. Continue dividing the sections down to the size needed to accurately copy details of the original illustration. Divide actual-size area into the same number of sections. Copy design from each section of original in corresponding section on actual-size pattern. Same method may be used for reducing pictures to size wanted.

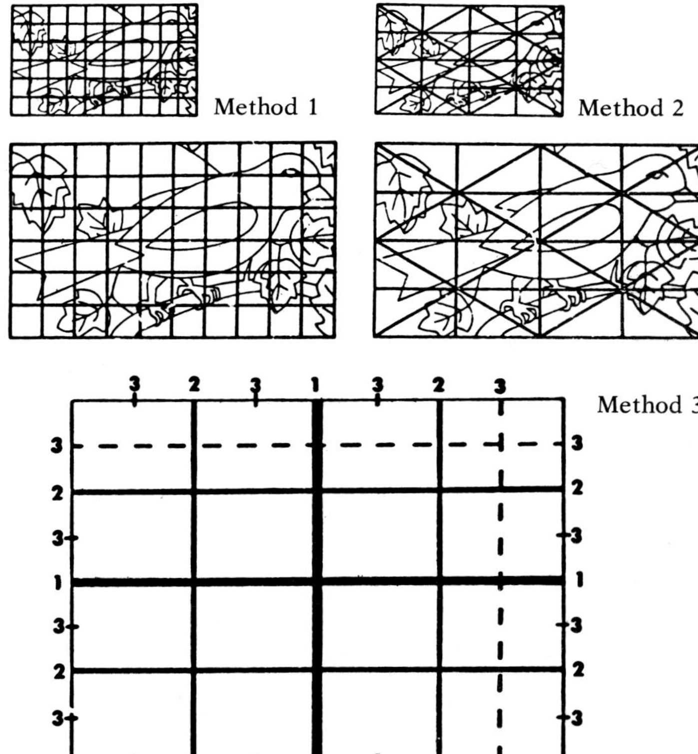

TO MAKE A TASSEL

Wind yarn around cardboard cut to size of tassel desired, winding it 20 or more times around, depending on plumpness of tassel required. Tie strands tightly together around top as shown, leaving at least 3″ ends on ties; clip other end of strands. Wrap piece of yarn tightly around strands a few times, about ½″ or 1″ below tie and knot. Trim ends of tassel evenly.

TO MAKE A POMPON

Cut two cardboard disks desired size of pompon; cut out hole in center of both. Thread needle with two strands of yarn. Place disks together; cover with yarn, working through holes. Slip scissors between disks. Cut all strands at outside edge. Draw strand of yarn between disks and wind several times very tightly around yarn; knot, leaving ends for attaching pompon. Remove disks; fluff out yarn into a pompon.

TO DRAW AN OVAL

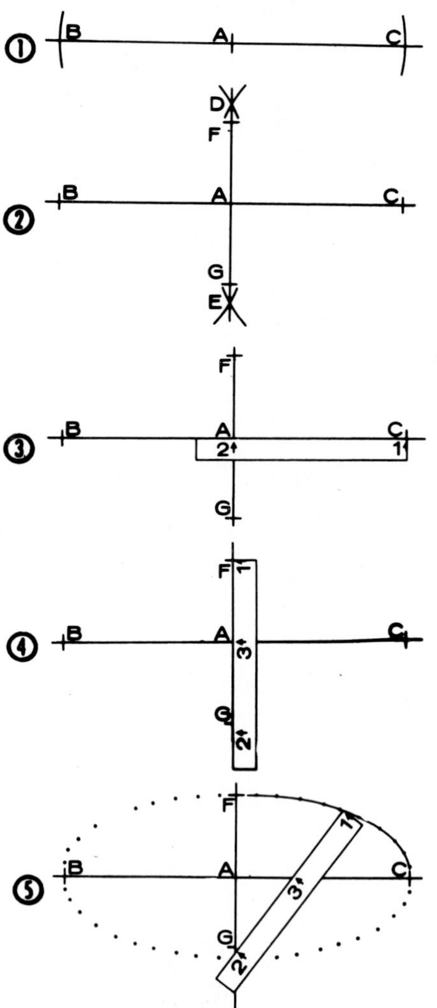

Fig. 1: Draw a straight line longer than desired length of oval. At center of line, establish point A. With compass, swing arcs to points B and C, oval length.

Fig. 2: From B and C, swing arcs above and below line BC. Connect their intersections with line DE. On this line, mark points F and G equal distances from A to establish width of oval.

Fig. 3: Mark points 1 and 2 to match A and C on a straight, firm strip of paper.

Fig. 4: Turn this measuring paper vertically along line FG so that point 1 is at F. Mark point 3 at A.

Fig. 5.: Rotate the measuring paper clockwise, moving point 3 along line AC and point 2 along AG. Make dots opposite point 1. Connect these dots with a line which completes first quarter of oval. Repeat procedure in other three parts to complete oval (or make tracing and transfer curve).

TO MAKE A TWISTED CORD

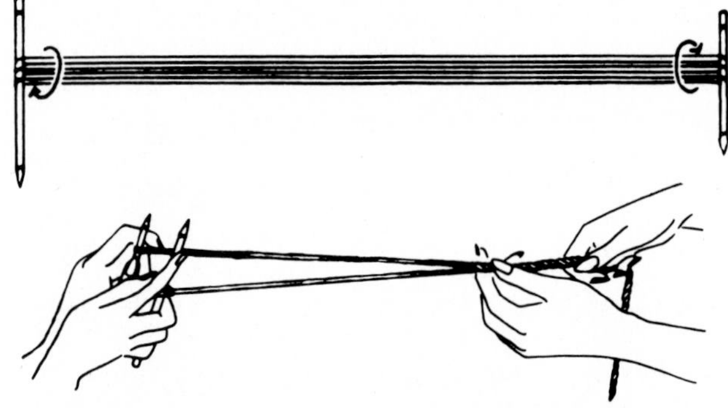

Method requires two people. Tie one end of yarn around pencil. Loop yarn over center of second pencil, back to and around first, and back to second, making as many strands between pencils as needed for thickness of cord; knot end to pencil. Length of yarn between pencils should be three times length of cord desired. Each person holds yarn just below pencil with one hand and twists pencil with other hand, keeping yarn taut. When yarn begins to kink, catch center over doorknob or hook. Bring pencils together for one person to hold, while other grasps center of yarn, sliding hand down at short intervals and letting yarn twist.

Seams may be covered with a twisted cord made of same yarn as needlepoint. Leave about ½″ of cord free at one corner of a square pillow or least conspicuous place on a round pillow; sew cord over seam with a matching thread, taking small blind stitches close together through cord and edges of needlepoint; pin cord in place for a few inches ahead of sewing, being careful not to pull cord. At center where cords meet, trim off other end to ½″. Open seam of needlepoint about ½″; overlap cord ends and insert into open seam. Sew seam closed.